THE
HARVEST READER

THE
HARVEST READER

William A. Heffernan

Saddleback College

Harcourt Brace Jovanovich, Publishers
San Diego   New York   Chicago   Washington, D.C.   Atlanta
London   Sydney   Toronto

ISBN: 0-15-535250-4

Library of Congress Catalog Card Number: 83–82441

Printed in the United States of America

Copyrights and Acknowledgments:

PUERTO VALLARTA, MEXICO   Excerpted selection from *The Diary of Anaïs Nin*, Volume Seven, © 1980 by Rupert Pole as trustee under the Last Will and Testament of Anaïs Nin. Reprinted by permission of Harcourt Brace Jovanovich, Inc.

NOTEBOOKS, 1962/63   From "Rose and Percy B" in *Johnny Panic and the Bible of Dreams* by Sylvia Plath. Copyright © 1961, 1962 by Sylvia Plath. Reprinted by permission of Harper & Row, Publishers, Inc.

THE GOSPEL ACCORDING TO THE HARVARD BUSINESS SCHOOL   Excerpts from *The Gospel According to the Harvard Business School* by Peter Cohen. Copyright © 1973 by Peter Cohen. Reprinted by permission of Doubleday & Company, Inc.

JULIA   From *Pentimento* by Lillian Hellman. Copyright © 1973 by Lillian Hellman. By permission of Little, Brown and Company.

FIRST COMMUNION   From *Family Installments* by Edward Rivera. Copyright © 1982 by Edward Rivera. By permission of William Morrow & Company.

CONFESSIONS OF A BLUE-CHIP BLACK   From *A Man's Life* by Roger Wilkins. Copyright © 1982 by Roger Wilkins. Reprinted by permission of Simon & Schuster, a Division of Gulf & Western Corporation. This article first appeared in *Harper's*, April 1982.

Credits and acknowledgments continue on pages 569–72, which constitute a continuation of the copyright page.

For my children, and my grandson, Christopher Ryan

To the Student

There was nothing very noteworthy about the fact that my Scots grandfather was a master carpenter by profession, or that he had single-handedly built the house where I grew up. But, in our family at least, two of his accomplishments gave him notoriety. He played the fiddle—and he read books.

Grandfather had no formal musical training. He had taught himself. And on sleet-gray winter afternoons when it seemed the New York streetlights winked on an hour before either God or the Consolidated Edison Company had intended, my grandfather would play the fiddle. We could hear him in the dormered attic of his private quarters, scraping his bow, singing some old Scots song no one else had troubled to remember, while three stories below the dining room chandelier danced to the rhythm of his foot tapping out the beat of the tune.

Grandfather's reading was even more remarkable. In Scotland his formal education had ended with the third grade. Yet his rooms in our New York house were filled with musty books no one else in my family had ever heard of, much less read. To me their odor, the brownish yellow of their pages was as dangerous and tempting as a jackknife or a book of matches. Later, I got as far as reading the spines: Macaulay's *History*, Thoreau's *Walden*, Hughes' *Tom Brown's Schooldays*, Collins' *The Moonstone* (which held a strange fascination for me, though I wasn't sure why, or even what it meant).

Grandfather aside, reading was viewed with great suspicion by other members of my family—probably because it seemed less an activity than a pastime. Grandfather's appetite for books was, from the family's point of view, not merely unproductive—it was downright subversive. Sunday dinners always seemed to erupt in heated arguments between my grandfather and my father. Usually these disagreements involved politics or government, but any topic— even toilet paper once—would do. Always my parents left me with the impression that Grandfather's ideas were "strange." Certainly his opinions were far different from what I heard from my friends or their parents or what I learned at parochial school. Above all, I was left with the impression—the insinuation, really—that Grandfather's "strange" notions were the effects of his unconventional reading. It took me years—years stretching all the way to college— to find confirmation of what he said. Unfortunately, Grandfather died before discovering that I too had begun to read, before finding that someone much younger than he had been listening attentively to that strange music from upstairs.

The point of this reminiscence is that my grandfather did not earn his living from reading, yet he read without pause decade after decade until his death. Why? Each year, I'm reminded of my grandfather when a new student asks, "Why should I read this? I'm going to be a computer programmer (or an accountant, or a chemist)." I never asked my grandfather why he read, but now I think I know the reason. I believe he would have said, "How else can a poor fellow from the slums of Glasgow find out about things?" By "things," I think he would have meant more than facts; he would have meant some of those "subversive" ideas, different ways of looking at the world, that neither his environment (Scotland of the 1880s) nor mine (New York of the 1950s) would ever have provided had we not been interested in reading.

So, one reason for reading a book is to free yourself from the limitations of your surroundings, not only in the sense of escaping (there is nothing wrong with reading for entertainment and escape), but in the sense of finding yourself, growing through exposure to new ideas, different ways of considering old ideas or seeing their renewed importance. A philosopher once observed that if at the end of your college years you hold exactly the ideas you began with, "You've been indoctrinated; you've not been educated."

I didn't know my grandfather as a carpenter; I knew him best as a human being who had eccentric ideas and who, when he wasn't living at home, lived on a small farm in upstate New York. While there he wrote long, amusing letters that sometimes overflowed onto the margins of the paper when he was carried away with a description of one of the trials of his self-sufficient life. Grandfather's letters were lively and conversational—very much like the way he talked. And his letters too were full of interesting and controversial information—just as though he were standing there trying and testing his ideas against the prejudices and suppositions of his readers.

Although writing is harder (and slower) than reading—after all, carrying on an intelligent conversation is more taxing than merely listening and being entertained by it—there is great pleasure to be had in the play of words and in the crafting of ideas to express what you mean. Sometimes I wonder if Grandfather got as much pleasure writing those letters as he did building the house that sheltered his family for over half a century. Then I recall Grandfather during one of those clamorous Sunday dinners, or I remember his letters, and I'm inclined to believe he got at least as much pleasure from reading and writing as from his carpentry. At 75, still proud of his carpentry, he put another dormer in the attic. Today, none of his family lives in that house; yet, his annotated copy of *Walden* survives. So does the memory of his ideas and letters.

To the Instructor

The organization of *The Harvest Reader* resembles the order in which writing is actually done. The book begins with diaries and journals that illustrate the search for ideas in an associative context—a free flow of thoughts, uninhibited by rules of usage or problems of organization. Professional writers record their experiences for later use in diaries and journals. Because beginning writers, too, may use diaries and journals as a continuing source of ideas, I urge students to keep a journal as a source-book for writing assignments. Selections from diaries, journals, and autobiographies reveal, furthermore, that personal experience is the starting point for most writing; unless the topic flows from the actual experience of the writer, the result is likely to be a dismal forced effort—rewarding neither to writer nor to reader.

Narrative and descriptive writing are presented next, because they, too, often grow out of personal experience, and because the problems of organization and concreteness are easier to solve here than in other types of writing. Writing description and narration is generally easier than writing exposition or persuasion because the subjects fall within the range of the writer's direct experience. Somewhat more sophisticated are the abstractions of exposition and the complex problems of organization inherent in the need to explain something or to explore an idea. Finally, and most sophisticated of all, is the ability to persuade, to discover the means of convincing an audience.

In many other texts, the framework of the text exercises primary sway over the selections; in this book, pieces were chosen first because of their intrinsic excellence, and second because of their appropriateness to the pattern of the text. Although a few selections appear in other anthologies, I have avoided pieces that are routinely reprinted in freshman anthologies. All selections are contemporary, since the book aims to provide recent models of style and thought. A number of selections deal with themes or issues raised by other selections. These echoes and reverberations are intended to stimulate critical thought on important issues that will, in turn, generate thoughtful student writing. Another significant feature of the book is that several authors are represented more than once. Several selections by the same author allow the beginning writer to examine how technique is purposely altered from one essay to another. The assumption underlying this reader is that students learn much about writing from reading and through imitation. Successful imitation requires a sufficient sampling of works by an author for observation and analysis.

In the exposition section of this book, the selections are organized according to the traditional patterns of expository prose (definition, example, cause–effect, and so on), not because writers begin with an empty pattern of organization and then fill in the form, but because these patterns are useful descendants of Aristotelian topics, mental categories that help the writer think about the subject. It is an artificial exercise to ask someone to write a definition essay (a pure example seldom exists), but the exercise does help illustrate the organic nature of writing. A single sentence explaining the cause of something can grow into a whole paragraph of development. For writers who struggle to find words and sentences to say what they know, sometimes it is a blessing to be given a ready-made form, even an artificial one. The antidote to this over-simplification is a closer scrutiny of the essays classified under a single rubric, or the deliberate inclusion of essays which amply demonstrate mixed modes. Both antidotes are here.

The questions and writing assignments that follow each selection are closely tied to the text of the essays. The questions expose underlying techniques of development, style, and organization. The sole focus of inquiry and commentary is writing, not intellectual discussion, however significant some of the issues might be. A composition course that focuses on issues without helping students to become better writers fails in an important way, but so does one that presents technique without showing students how to express ideas about issues that affect them and their fellow citizens.

Every book is a collaborative effort. While I accept responsibility for any shortcomings of this book, I would like to acknowledge the valuable contributions made by friends and colleagues whose names do not appear on the cover. I especially thank the members of the rhetoric and composition seminar at the University of Nebraska, Lincoln—particularly Dudley Bailey, its director—and the National Endowment for the Humanities, which sponsored the seminar. For their research assistance, I am grateful to E. Ann Hagerty, Tom Weisrock, and the librarians at the University of Nebraska and Saddleback College. I also appreciate the editorial teamwork of the Harcourt Brace Jovanovich staff: Jack W. Thomas, my manuscript editor, without whose good taste and assistance much of what is valuable would not be here, and Paul H. Nockleby, my acquisitions editor, who guided the book through a maze of changes, and whose encouragement, good advice, and suggestions rescued me from several cul de sacs. Finally, I thank my wife, Debbie, who listened and read through bitter Nebraska blizzards and hot California simooms: "Pacience is an heigh virtu, certeyn."

William A. Heffernan
Saddleback College

Table of Contents

Thematic Table of Contents

Introduction

Whether you plan to become an accountant or a chemist, a machinist or a zoologist, you need to know how to write. Writing skills—not just the pragmatic variety necessary for letter or memo writing, but the finer kinds that involve organizing complex ideas or convincing an audience outside your chosen specialty—are demanded in virtually every profession. A college course in writing can help you master both kinds.

This book, *The Harvest Reader,* can help you become a better writer in several ways. First, the book can be used as a collection of model essays to analyze and imitate. Second, *The Harvest Reader* can be used as a rhetoric, a book of advice—with illustrations—about the composing process from the blank sheet to the finished paper: how writers get ideas (invention), how they organize their materials (disposition), and the sort of expression they choose (elocution or style).

Imitation is one of the oldest ways to learn a skill (which is, after all, what you are learning in a composition class—the skill of writing); there is no specific body of knowledge, as in history or science, on which you will be tested. Like other kinds of skills—hitting a tennis ball accurately, performing effective surgery—you will be judged on how well you perform. One way of learning how to perform well is to watch a master of the skill in the act, and try to imitate what is successful about the performance. This book offers you a collection of successful performances, with commentary on why they are successful so you can more easily see what is worth imitating. In order to give you a second, or even a third look at a successful performance—a kind of replay—there are occasionally two selections by the same author so you can see what techniques are carried over from situation to situation, and what techniques are adapted to new conditions. For example, George Orwell, engaged in a controversy about the kind of science education that should take place in the public schools, writes one way for a daily paper, but quite another way when he narrates witnessing a public execution in a piece against capital punishment intended for book publication. You can also examine how different writers perform when handling the same subject. For example, how do E. B. White and Gay Talese view the crowding and excitement of New York? What do Margaret Mead and Joan Didion think of women's struggles to achieve parity in employment? What do Marie Winn and Sally Helgesen think of the way mass media influences our attitudes? In other words, the way a writer handles a subject is as personal and unique as the performance of a skilled athlete.

Along with imitating the models, you can benefit from advice concerning the procedures used by skillful writers. Each section of the book begins with a brief introductory discussion concerning the particular techniques required to produce a paper of the sort exemplified by the selections. The characteristics of the form—narration, description, exposition, persuasion—are explained and illustrated, first within the introduction, then with a short example, and finally with several selections. Following each selection are questions intended to help you analyze the organization, content, and technique. (Successful imitation and analysis of what makes a successful performance are inseparable.) After you have mastered several types of writing, you will find it advantageous to combine the techniques of one form with those of another. Several sections of this book lead you toward that goal.

Finally, the book is organized to lead you logically from easier to more difficult types of writing. You will undoubtedly find writing about personal experiences and concrete tangible things easier to follow and interpret than writing about abstractions or social, political, and ethical issues. In general, personal interest is the starting point for most successful writing. The book, like successful writing, begins with the concrete and personal—diaries and journals, autobiographies, narrations, descriptions—and ends with the abstract and intellectual—exposition and persuasion.

Skillful writing is a cumulative process. The beginner naturally feels self-conscious and awkward in taking the first faltering steps toward mastering the skill. It's easy to be awed, perhaps even frightened, by someone else's mastery of a skill. Everyone is afraid of looking foolish in comparison with demonstrated mastery. But, like learning other skills, learning one part of the skill of writing makes mastery of the next part of the skill a bit easier; one success leads to other successes, which in turn lead to the loss of self conscious- ness that comes with the fear of looking foolish. The models in this book, and the advice that accompanies them, are intended to increase your cumulative skill in writing so that you can not only admire the mastery of others without self-conscious fear of comparison, but you may also, at times, demonstrate some of that mastery yourself.

THE
HARVEST READER

PART 1
Journals and Diaries: Writing for Self-Expression

Where does writing begin? Does it begin with the thoughts that immediately precede your putting pen to paper, or your touching the keys of your typewriter? Or does it begin further back in the past with something you heard or read that has lain dormant until you began to write? Rhetoric, the art of finding ideas that will persuade people, has been relatively silent about where these ideas come from—that is, how we invent—except to say that in persuasive writing we should take into account the knowledge and prejudices of our audience; we need to list those ideas that the audience will accept. But on the actual source of ideas—the starting point of writing—there are few practical hints.

Several decades ago, Donald Loyd, an internationally-known linguist, wrote that Americans—who as a nation are especially glib—freeze up, become tongue-tied if you hand them a pen and ask them to transcribe their thoughts. He blamed our "terror of the blank page" on what he called "our national mania for correctness." But if you have ever stared out the window, chewed the nub of your pencil, and felt precious minutes fade away as the time approached when the paper must be handed in, you probably thought, "I simply have nothing to say." Both analyses are correct; if you are not adequately prepared or if the already difficult task is further complicated by difficulties with clear word choice, conventional grammar, and logical organization (which most writing classes require), you can't say—or write—anything.

The dilemma posed by the question *Where does writing begin?* is not as unresolvable as it might at first seem. When you mull over what you're going to say, you may be closer to the demands of real

1

writing than is the more facile student who can immediately meet the formal classroom demands of the writing assignment. Free-writing—writing done without regard for the conventions of grammar or rhetoric, or the niceties of phrase or word choice—is the sort usually found in unedited notebooks, journals, and diaries. When you were stuck for something to say, inhibited by the usual requirements of formal organization and grammatical correctness, you would have experienced less of the writer's block associated with writing on demand if you had your own journal at hand, especially if the instructor had carefully correlated the assignments with journal-keeping.

The answer to the question *Where does writing begin?* can be found in the practice of professional writers whose unedited notes, journals, workbooks, diaries, and outlines reveal the gestation or birth of their ideas. This shower of ideas sometimes goes through several stages—more for some writers than for others. Some people can hold several conflicting ideas in their minds simultaneously prior to working out their exact relationships, whereas others need to commit each idea to paper and work out the relationships visually, as it were, before them. For all the variations in the final product—whether a poem, a play, a work of fiction, an essay, or a piece of technical writing—the stages of the process are essentially the same: Some notion begins to interest us; we collect information both consciously and unconsciously over a period of time; broad categories* and a "shape" begin to suggest themselves; we start to sort and discard bits of information, all the while extending, restricting, and adjusting our categories. Even the drafting process involves further gathering in and throwing away.

Because all of this miscellany of activity occurs prior to finally sitting down to begin the first draft of a piece of writing, it is sometimes called pre-writing, or brainstorming, sometimes merely note-taking or observing. Listen to John McPhee, a staff writer for *The New Yorker*, describe with fascination the working methods of Henry David Thoreau—methods which, interestingly, McPhee himself almost exactly duplicates in composing his own work.

---

*What Donald M. Murray calls the "magnet theory"; bits of information begin to stick to the writer, like metal filings to a magnet. I am indebted to Murray's essay "Write Before Writing," *College Composition and Communication*, 29 (December, 1978), 337–81, for several ideas in this introduction.

He had in his pack some pencils and an oilskin pouch full of scratch paper—actually letters that customers had written to his family's business, ordering plumbago and other printing supplies. On the backs of these discarded letters he made condensed, fragmentary, scarcely legible notes, and weeks later, when he had returned home to Concord, he composed his journal of the trip, slyly using the diary form, and writing at times in the present tense, to gain immediacy, to create the illusion of paragraphs written—as it is generally supposed they were written—virtually in the moments described. With the advantage of retrospect, he constructed the story to reveal a kind of significance that the notes do not reveal. Something new in journalism. With the journals as his principal source, he later crafted still another manuscript, in which he further shaped and rearranged the story, all the while adhering to a structure built on calendar dates. The result, published posthumously in hardcover form, was the book he called *The Maine Woods*. [*The Survival of the Bark Canoe* (Farrar, Straus, and Giroux, 1975), 36.]

As the passage suggests, there is a formal, as well as a functional distinction between a notebook, a journal, and a diary. To begin with the last, as everyone knows, diaries are meant to be daily records of the events of a day. They may include observations, judgments, impressions of events, people, places, but they generally summarize, if kept with constancy, the important events of a single day. Notes, on the other hand, are much more random, and are taken on the spur of the moment, or when that is not practical (as in the case of Thoreau in a canoe), soon afterward. Of the three, journals tend to be the most retrospective; in them, the writer looks back, at not too great a distance in time, and sifts through many impressions for those that seem most important or that form themselves into the most significant patterns. The aim of keeping a journal is not to write a masterpiece, but to record facts, impressions, patterns: to have a place where transitory events, random observations, or careful research might safely be stored for possible use when the actual writing begins.

Here is part of a diary kept by a writer who spent a winter in a small isolated town in the Cascade Mountains of central Washington State:

December 21   Snow is almost three feet deep and still falling. The mail boat has made one of its thrice-weekly winter visits, and most of the village's 40 year-round residents met it—including me.
January 27   We've had a cold spell, with the thermometer shivering around zero. I have to wake up every two hours during the night to

stoke the fire in my wood stove to keep the inside water pipes from freezing. Staying warm is almost a full-time job. . .[Pat Hutson, "Where Solitude Is in Season," *National Geographic* (April 1974,), 572–74.]

In their most basic form, notebooks, journals, and diaries can be used as a sort of rehearsal, a preliminary or practice for the real thing. They can also be used to overcome the inertia of facing a blank page—as a practical means to get the act of writing going, the "juices flowing." In addition to stimulating the physical momentum of the act of writing, the notebook–journal–diary serves four important purposes:

1. It serves as a *storehouse* from which your observations, descriptions, facts—the whole range of raw material for actual writing—can be retrieved for later use. It takes time not only to think out what you will say—after you have observed, noted, listened, read—but also to allow the facts come together or jell in your mind. It is here that you can go back to the notebook–journal–diary to read and reread, to see what you can make of the otherwise fleeting impressions. The notebook–journal–diary, then, is a highly tentative exploration of "facts" that strike you as important at the time they are recorded. It is a good idea to keep a notebook in which you can jot down notes and impressions for any paper you are required to write.

2. It has the effect of *stopping time*, of giving you a chance to study and contemplate what might otherwise be lost or distorted in the welter of events. A notebook–journal–diary places the actions and ideas of the past in perspective. From a train window, nearby objects pass too swiftly to allow either recognition or appreciation, but the rapid movement of the train does not hinder contemplation of more distant objects. The notebook–journal–diary allows you that same kind of distancing—the alchemy of time often renders a clearer meaning to many events. Even though this time gap might not be more than a few days in a writing class, nevertheless, some perspective is gained between note-taking time and drafting time. In an essay entitled "On Keeping a Notebook," Joan Didion talks about rereading earlier entries to recapture the emotional and mental makeup of the person she used to be, a process called "journal feedback" by Ira Progoff [*At a Journal Workshop* (Dialogue House Library, 1976)].

It all comes back. Perhaps it is difficult to see the value in having one's self back in that kind of mood, but I do see it; I think we are well advised to keep on nodding terms with the people we used to be, whether we find them attractive company or not. Otherwise they turn up unannounced and surprise us, coming hammering on the mind's door at 4 a.m. of a bad night and demand to know who deserted them, who betrayed them, who is going to make amends. We forget all too soon the things we thought we could never forget. We forget the loves and the betrayals alike, forget what we whispered and what we screamed, forget who we were . . . It is a good idea, then, to keep in touch, and I suppose that keeping in touch is what notebooks are all about. [*Slouching Toward Bethlehem* (Farrar, Straus, and Giroux, 1968), 139–40.]

3. It *selects* certain events, impressions, and facts out of the mass of details available, thereby investing them with an importance they lack as part of the whole. Suppose you wish to describe the Arizona desert. Will you tell the truth about the desert if you write down as many facts about it as the pages of a book will hold? Or will you begin by selecting just those facts that will best tell the uninformed what the desert is like? Edward Abbey goes one step further; while insisting he is drawing from the facts recorded in his journals ("journals I kept and filled through the undivided, seamless days of those marvellous summers"), he is equally insistent that the facts are not merely true to the surface of things, but provoke meanings beyond themselves.

In recording these impressions of the natural scene I have striven above all for accuracy, since I believe that there is a kind of poetry, even a kind of truth, in simple fact. But the desert is a vast world, an oceanic world, as deep in its way and complex and various as the sea. Language makes a mightly loose net with which to go fishing for simple facts, when facts are infinite. . . What I have tried to do then is something a bit different. . . . Since you cannot get the desert into a book any more than a fisherman can haul up the sea with his nets, I have tried to create a world of words into which the desert figures more as a medium than as material. Not imitation but evocation has been the goal. [*Desert Solitaire* (McGraw-Hill, 1968), xii.]

Annie Dillard also claims to be setting down more than mere facts, even though most of the time nature seems to present simply more of the same. Receptivity, staying awake to those moments when nature's selection is particularly worth recording, seems to be Dillard's method of sifting through the facts. In *Pilgrim at Tinker Creek*, she writes "I propose to keep here what Thoreau called 'a meterological journal of the mind,' telling some tales and describing some of the sights of this rather tamed valley, and exploring in fear and trembling, some of the unmapped dim reaches and holy fastnesses to which those tales and sights so dizzyingly lead."

4. It reveals the *patterns* formed by (2) the arresting of time, and (3) the selection of facts. By going over and over your notes, invariably some kind of order emerges, whether in the form of labelled file folders with subtopic headings, as it does for John McPhee, a seemingly random memo with an underlying less obvious pattern, as it does for Tom Wolfe in "The Kandy-Kolored-Tangerine Flake Stream-line Baby," or the very human demand to know *What does it mean?* as it does for Joan Didion in "The White Album":

> We look for the sermon in the suicide, for the social or moral lesson in the murder of five. We interpret what we see, select the most workable of the multiple choices. We live entirely, especially if we are writers, by the imposition of a narrative line upon disparate images, by the "ideas" with which we have learned to freeze the shifting phantasmagoria which is our actual experience. [*The White Album* (Simon and Schuster, 1979), 11.]

The aim of this chapter, then, is to present the notebook–journal–diary as an aid to your writing, not as an end in itself—as a tool rather than as a finished piece, as a sourcebook rather than as the completed work. Consequently, the four points outlined here have concentrated on the uses of a journal, not the specific techniques of how to keep one. Some sourcebooks by gifted writers have indeed been published works; in some cases, Anais Nin's *Diary* for example, the published version has previously been edited from manuscript. But even these more polished professional examples can teach you more of the uses of recording your observations than any set of programmatic instructions. The best advice about keeping a journal is simply this: Put down whatever seems important, whatever seems of possible use now or later. The entries can be facts or quotations culled from research done for a specific paper or random observations that may be of some future use.

What you can learn from the journal and diary entries that follow is an appreciation for practiced observation—seeing not just shape and color, but transparency and depth; hearing not just sound, but nuance and harmony; feeling texture as well as firmness; tasting sour or tart as well as sweet or bitter; smelling and remembering the smell—in short, the records of minds that can harmoniously blend all these faculties to reveal the normally unobserved connections between objects, ideas, and actions. No formal set of principles can unerringly guide you toward that full sense of perception in which these faculties of body and mind coalese in written form. But watching it happen, and then imitating what is pleasing, may bring you closer to it.

SHORT EXAMPLE

LEWIS MUMFORD
Random Notes

Lewis Mumford (born 1895) attended but never graduated from Columbia and New York Universities, City College of New York, and the New School for Social Research. All of his degrees are honorary. He has taught at numerous major universities and published dozens of books on architecture, city planning, art criticism, history, philosophy, and biography. *Among them are* Sticks and Stones: A Study of American Architecture and Civilization *(1924),* The City in History *(1961), and the two-volume* The Myth of the Machine *(1967, 1970). In the following excerpt from his journal,* Findings and Keepings *(1975), we see the young Mumford determinedly setting out to record his ideas and feelings before he loses them to time.*

I have begun these notes, partly in imitation of Samuel Butler,* and partly because I stand aghast at the fund of gristy material I have wasted in the past. At best one's most vivid memories are only memories; they are flighty, unaccountable, and never around when you are really in need of them. And then, they are ever so much more pallid than the real materials of sense that you wish to recover. I would give anything for a ten reel moving picture of my life during the last four years, with copious inserts to register the ever-changing succession of mental states, philosophies, dreams, desires, plans, aspirations, and what not. It might grieve me, of course, to learn how pitifully foolish a young man can be; but it would give my present self a more solid foundation. On the other hand, I am not

*Nineteenth-century novelist, essayist, and satirist.

sure whether too great a degree of self-consciousness might not overbalance the worth of such a record. To be neither completely self-conscious, nor completely unconscious is the trick. My last three years have been wasted if I have not acquired it.

DISCUSSION

This random note from Lewis Mumford's journal echoes Joan Didion's remark that keeping a notebook is a way of keeping in touch with ourselves, of uncovering "bits of the mind's string too short to use." Mumford begins his entry by reminding himself that memories have a way of fading and becoming pallid when compared with the real thing. It's not merely what you did and saw that's worth recording before it fades from memory, but your own mental states— dreams, desires, plans, aspirations—that are worth preserving. Socrates' famous dictum, "The unexamined life not worth living," is paralleled by Mumford's dichotomy between being self-conscious and unconscious. The best journals are written by those writers who remain conscious of the life around them and their own mental states, without becoming self-conscious poseurs. This entry is good advice to the prospective journal keeper, but it is also a good example of the short, rambling entries that, taken together, form "ten reel moving pictures" of your life.

ANAÏS NIN
Puerto Vallarta, Mexico

Anaïs Nin (1903–1977) was born in Paris, emigrated to New York as a child, and later returned to Paris, where she joined the bohemian circle of novelist Henry Miller. She became interested in psychoanalysis, and studied with Freud's student, Otto Rank. Much of her early fiction was commercially unsuccessful. With the publication of her diaries in the mid-60s, she finally found the audience that had eluded her. Their literary merit and their applicability to the women's movement of the seventies have made Nin's diaries classics. The following selection reveals Nin's zest for the exotic as well as her preoccupation with the dream as a tool for examining the psyche.

First of all the warm, caressing air. It dissolves you into a flower 1
or foliage. It humidifies the sun-opened pores. The body emerges
from its swaddling of clothes. Rebirth. Then the colors, the infinite
variations of greens, deep, dark or golden. The banana tree the
darkest foliage of all, wide, dense, heavy. The fringes and interlac-
ings of palms. Then the birds, vivid, loud, vigorous, talkative, whistles, cries, gossip, clarinets and flutes. Trills, tremolos, vibratos,
arabesques.

Then the flavor of margaritas, ice cold, with salt on the rim of 2
the glass.

Rented a jeep and excursions began, to Los Tres Arcos, three 3
huge rocks with caves and tunnels, delight of snorklers from which
they return with descriptions of fish which rival descriptions of
fashion shows. Blue stripes and gold tails. Three fan tails of bright
red on a silver-gray body, small transparent fish like Lucite. We hike
up the mountain, past a little village, along the river, to find a pool.
Marianne Greenwood had made a map of what we should see.

Nightmares: My mother and I are cleaning up the kitchen, a 4
terribly messy one. We are in our slips. Drudges. My father is coming. Anxiety at what he will think of us, he with his mania for
aesthetics and beauty.

But the body is healed by the Mexican life. There is a stillness in 5
my head. I am content with warm little pleasures, because of the
warm cuddling by the air, the feeling of nervelessness. Passive
drinking in of color, the cafés, the shops, people; and the thrill of
looking into open homes, open windows, open doors. An old lady
in a rocking chair. Photographs on the walls. Palm leaves from last
year's ritual Easter. One room reminded me of Barcelona. The
whitewashed house. The room painted sky blue. I have known
such a room, with potted palms, lace doiles on the table. Pictures
of Christ, of course, artificial flowers and bric-a-brac.

I do not understand the nightmares. Again last night I was clean- 6
ing the rim of an incredibly dirty bathtub, picking up dirty glasses.
My mother was having a sewing party. I went in to consult with
her. Why should my spirit be so heavy when my body is at home
in Mexico?

Returning on the boat and looking at the lush tropical vegetation, 7
my eyes filled with tears. I do not want to die. I love this earth, the
earth of Mexico, the sun.

I sit now on a small beach, facing a huge rock. The snorklers   8
swam through caves, saw bats and darkness. I am surrounded by
butterflies, black with gold stripes and pearls at the tip of their
wings.

I answer a letter or two a day.   9

This morning I saw the most beautiful fern in a wild field, feath-   10
ery, lacy and of a green so light it seemed touched with gold.

I have been reading Arthur Clarke. He envisages a future where   11
our minds are influenced by machines, programmed. People can
erase others' memories. Memory banks can distort history. Some
practice telepathy. But all this has happened already. TV is the machine
which brainwashes us. We do erase others' memories. Our minds
are constantly tampered with (distorted, lying history and lying
media). We influence each other more than we are aware.

My purple postcards have given stimulus to so many. I drop ten   12
or twenty cards in the letter box each day. I can't answer in many
words, but I respond. What they write me is usually gray. It is
usually negative. Respond, respond. Turn gray into red, respond,
transform gray into gold.

The women washing their laundry in the river. Some have planted   13
umbrellas. They choose a smooth rock. They rub sheets, table-
cloths, shirts and underwear. They rinse and fill baskets with clean
clothes. The children play at the edge of the river.

The market. Stuffed animals, snakes, iguanas, raccoons. Arma-   14
dillos, coatamundis, squirrels. Orange, purple, white shawls. The
dress I found has the tones of Balinese batik, all brown and gold,
with designs of birds and impalas.

* * *

I am still trying to reach the sun, to immerse myself in the sun,   15
but for several days we have had thunderstorms at night. Drops of
rain fell on the diary yesterday while I sat at the beach. Count them.

Snorklers describe a three-foot sea snake, a fish that is blue,   16
purple, with three light blue electric dots which shine like lights.
A fish with a gray body and a bright yellow stripe running along
its body, and a magenta tail. Another was all black and white, with
three fan tails. Another pure yellow, small, with two black tails.
Another was exactly divided into two colors, front half gray, back
jet black.

River scenes. All the women at work. As the clothes are laid out   17
to dry on the rocks, they form an abstract pattern of red, yellow,
blue, orange, white. Later the women go home with basins filled
with clothes balanced on their heads. One was climbing a hill with
her load. A merry scene because of the children playing around
them, naked, splashing, swimming, teasing each other.

Here comes the sun.   18

In the sun the pelicans sit rigid on the rocks watching for fish.   19
The black-and-red butterflies mate on the sand just barely out of
the reach of the waves. The birds sing with a lust unknown to
Northern birds.

In Los Angeles I became enslaved by my correspondence, such   20
touching, moving, poetic letters. They must be answered. I felt
enmeshed by own responsiveness.

It rains every afternoon, every night. I don't go dancing because   21
the electronic music is too loud. What a difference between the Latin
orchestras of Acapulco, so soft and seductive, and this shrieking
ugly rock and roll. It was too loud on the boat too, ruined the
sailing, but I loved watching the dancing. The boat trip took us to
a beach. From there we hiked up a mountain to a pool and a waterfall.

Warm rain. Real steamy jungle. Overloaded mango trees, gliding   22
frigate birds. We sit in a café by the seaside and drink beer.

CONTENT

1. Judging from this portion of her *Diary*, what kinds of observations interest Nin the most?
2. From the details presented, do you have a clear picture of what
   Puerto Vallarta is like? Or are the details too personal?
3. Why does Nin include her nightmares in the *Diary?* Why does
   she think of scenes from her childhood? Why does she think
   of death the next day?
4. What do you think of her comments about TV? About machines?

ORGANIZATION

5. Diaries and journals use chronological organization. Instead of
   a formal logical pattern, the writer puts down impressions as
   they occur. Are there any subconscious connections among the
   impressions that Nin records?

6. This portion of the *Diary* moves back and forth between personal thoughts and objective descriptions. Can you find examples of this pattern?

TOPICS FOR WRITING

7. Keep a journal of your impressions on a trip you are about to take. Describe people you see, the place itself, and your reactions to them.

8. Keep a daily record of the dreams you have. Write them down as soon as you awake, before they begin to fade from your memory. When you can, also record what seem to you to be the sources of the things you have dreamed.

SYLVIA PLATH

Notebooks, 1962/63

Sylvia Plath (1932–1963) was born in Boston and graduated from Smith College in 1955. Her autobiographical novel, The Bell Jar *(1963), is about a student editor who attempts suicide (Plath attempted suicide at age 19); it was published several months before her successful suicide attempt at age 30. Her works include* The Colossus *(1960), and the posthumous* Crossing the Water *(1971) and* Johnny Panic and the Bible of Dreams *(1978). The following selection reveals Plath's fascination with the details of death. Her biographer, A. Alvarez, contends that with the poems in* Ariel *(1966) she made "poetry and death inseparable. The one could not exist without the other."*

June 7

Well, Percy B is dying. That is the verdict. Poor old Perce, says   1
everybody. Rose comes up almost every day. "Te-ed," she calls in her
hysterical, throbbing voice. And Ted comes, from the study, the
tennis court, the orchard, wherever, to lift the dying man from his
armchair to his bed. He is very quiet afterward. He is a bag of bones,
says Ted. I saw him in one "turn" or "do," lying back on the bed,
toothless, all beakiness of nose and chin, eyes sunken as if they
were not, shuddering and blinking in a fearful way. And all about
the world is gold and green, dripping with laburnum and buttercups and the sweet stench of June. In the cottage the fire is on and

it is dark twilight. The midwife said Percy would go into a coma this weekend and then "anything could happen." The sleeping pills the doctor gives him don't work, says Rose. He is calling all night: Rose, Rose, Rose. It has happened so quickly. First Rose stopped the doctor in January when I had the baby for a look at Percy's running eye and a check on his weight loss. Then he was in hospital for lung X rays. Then in again for a big surgery for "something in his lung." Did they find him so far gone with cancer they sewed him up again? Then home, walking, improving, but oddly quenched in his brightness and his songs. I found a wrinkled white paper bag of dusty jelly babies in the car yesterday from Rose. Then his five strokes. Now his diminishing.

Everybody has so easily given him up. Rose looks younger and younger. Mary G set her hair yesterday. She felt creepy about it, left baby Joyce with me and came over in between rinses in her frilly apron, dark-haired, white-skinned, with her high, sweet child-voice. Percy looked terrible since she had seen him last, she said. She thought cancer went wild if it was exposed to the air. The general sentiment of townsfolk: doctors just experiment on you in hospital. Once you're in, if you're old, you're a goner.

June 9

Met the rector coming out of house-building site across the road. He turned up the lane to the house with me. I could feel his professional gravity coming over him. He read the notice on Rose's door as I went on up, then went round back. "Sylvia!" I heard Rose hiss behind me, and turned. She was pantomiming the rector's arrival and making lemon moues and rejecting motions with one hand, very chipper.

July 2

Percy B is dead. He died just at midnight, Monday, June 25th, and was buried Friday, June 29th, at 2:30. I find this difficult to believe. It all began with his eye watering, and Rose calling in the doctor, just after the birth of Nicholas. I have written a long poem, "Berck-Plage," about it. Very moved. Several terrible glimpses.

Ted had for some days stopped lifting Percy in and out of bed.

He could not take his sleeping pills, or swallow. The doctor was starting to give him injections. Morphia? He was in pain when he was conscious. The nurse counted forty-five seconds between one breath and another. I decided to see him, I must see him, so went with Ted and Frieda. Rose and the smiling Catholic woman were lying on deck chairs in the yard. Rose's white face crimpled the minute she tried to speak. "The nurse told us to sit out. There's no more we can do. Isn't it awful to see him like this?" See him if you like, she told me. I went in through the quiet kitchen with Ted. The living room was full, still, hot with awful translation taking place. Percy lay back on a heap of white pillows in his striped pajamas, his face already passed from humanity, the nose a spiraling, flesh-less beak in thin air, the chin fallen in a point from it, like an opposite pole, and the mouth like an inverted black heart stamped into the yellow flesh between, a great raucous breath coming and going there with great effort like an awful bird, caught, but about to depart. His eyes showed through partly open lids like dissolved soaps or a clotted pus. I was very sick at this and had a bad migraine over my left eye for the rest of the day. The end, even of so marginal a man, a horror.

When Ted and I drove out to Exeter to catch the London train the following morning, the stone house was still, dewy and peaceful, the curtains stirring in the dawn air. He is dead, I said. Or he will be dead when we get back. He had died that night, Mother said over the phone, when I called her up the following evening. 6

Went down after his death, the next day, the 27th. Ted had been down in the morning, said Percy was still on the bed, very yellow, his jaw bound and a book, a big brown book, propping it till it stiffened properly. When I went down they had just brought the coffin and put him in. The living room where he had lain was in an upheaval—bed rolled from the wall, mattresses on the lawn, sheets and pillows washed and airing. He lay in the sewing room, or parlor, in a long coffin of orangey soap-colored oak with silver handles, the lid propped against the wall at his head with a silver scroll: Percy B, Died June 25th, 1962. The raw date a shock. A sheet covered the coffin. Rose lifted it. A pale white, beaked face, as of paper, rose under the veil that covered the hole cut in the glued white cloth cover. The mouth looked glued, the face powdered. She quickly put down the sheet. I hugged her. She kissed me and burst into tears. The dark, rotund sister from London with purple eye circles deplored: They have no hearse, they have only a cart. Friday, 7 the day of the funeral, hot and blue, with theatrical white clouds passing. Ted and I, dressed in hot blacks, passed the church, saw the bowler-hatted men coming out of the gate with a high spider-wheeled black cart. They are going to call for the corpse, we said; we left a grocery order. The awful feeling of great grins coming onto the face, unstoppable. A relief; this is the hostage for death, we are safe for the time being. We strolled round the church in the bright heat, the pollarded green limes like green balls, the far hills red, just plowed, and one stooked with newly glittering wheat. Debated whether to wait out, or go in. Elsie, with her stump foot, was going in. Then Grace, Jim's wife. We went in. Heard priest meeting corpse at gate, incanting, coming close. Hair-raising. We stood. The flowery casket, nodding and flirting its petals, led up the aisle. The handsome mourners in black down to gloves and handbag, Rose, three daughters including the marble-beautiful model, one husband, Mrs. G and the Catholic, smiling, only not smiling, the smile in abeyance, suspended. I hardly heard a word of the service, Mr. Lane for once quenched the grandeur of ceremony, a vessel, as it should be.

Then we followed the funeral party after the casket out the side door to the street going up the hill to the cemetery. Behind the high black cart, which had started up, with the priest swaying in black and white, at a decorous pace, the funeral cars—one car, a taxi, then Herbert G, looking green and scared, in his big new red car. We got in with him. "Well, old Perce always wanted to be buried in Devon." You could see he felt he was next. I felt tears come. Ted motioned me to look at the slow, uplifted faces of children in the primary school yard, all seated on rest rugs, utterly without grief, only bland curiosity, turning after us. We got out at the cemetery gate, the day blazing. Followed the black backs of the women. Six bowler hats of the bearers left at the first yew bushes in the grass. The coffin on boards, words said, ashes to ashes—that is what remained, not glory, not heaven. The amazingly narrow coffin lowered into the narrow red earth opening, left. The women led round, in a kind of goodbye circle, Rose rapt and beautiful and frozen, the Catholic dropping a handful of earth, which clattered. A great impulse welled in me to cast earth also, but it seemed as if it might be indecent, hurrying Percy into oblivion. We left the open grave. An unfinished feeling. Is he to be left up there uncovered, all alone? Walked home over the back hill, gathering immense stalks of fuchsia foxgloves and swinging our jackets in the heat.

8

CONTENT

1. Why is there so much emphasis on the flowers and the heat of early summer? What bearing does it seem to have on Plath's reactions to Percy's death?

2. When she visits the dying man, why does Plath say "some awful translation" (paragraph 5) was taking place? How do subsequent details in the description of the dying man elaborate on this observation?

3. In what way is Percy's death a relief for everyone? Why does Plath make what seems an irreverent observation on the day of the funeral: "The awful feeling of great grins coming onto the face, unstoppable" (paragraph 7)? What's funny about death? Why is the Catholic woman always smiling?

4. Is there a contradiction in Plath saying she was very moved by Percy's death, later calling it "a horror," and her final action after the funeral, picking flowers and nonchalantly swinging her jacket "in the heat"?

ORGANIZATION

5. Plath's *Notebooks* are arranged in diary fashion, although she doesn't write an entry every day. She skips several weeks before the July 2 entry during which time Percy B. died. How does the bald statement which begins the entry, "Percy B. is dead" (paragraph 4), dictate the order and importance of the details which follow?

6. Certain observations reoccur in different entries in this passage. For example, Rose growing younger and more beautiful, the bird-like appearance of Percy, the combination of indifference and great sorrow. Locate these in the passage and explain their cumulative effect.

7. How is the observation in paragraph 8 about the primary school children appropriate? If it were left out, what would be lost from the final paragraph?

TOPICS FOR WRITING

8. Write an account of the death or funeral of someone. Include both your own recollection of your feelings as well as your observation of others.

9. Percy B. died at home. Write an essay arguing for or against patients' rights to die at home rather than in a hospital.

10. Concentrate in a section of your journal or notebook on some of the incongruities which you observe in people as a result of their inability to express their true feelings, either because of social conventions or because their feelings conflict with their duties.

PETER COHEN
The Gospel According to the Harvard Business School

Peter Cohen, born in Switzerland in 1939, received his bachelor's degree from Princeton University in 1963, and entered the Harvard Business School in 1968. After graduating at the top third of his class, he published The Gospel According to the Harvard Business School *(1973), a record of his two years in the MBA program. At present, he heads his own company in Switzerland. The selection from Cohen's diary records the early adjustments to the HBS and the intense competition which causes some students to leave.*

The first floor of Aldrich Hall, together with its carbon copies, the second and the basement floors, is a moving tribute to so total a lack of imagination as to make the entire building stand out, even among the dull and faceless newer buildings at the Business School as an achievement of monumental non-distinction. On every floor, the same drafty alcoves, the same hallway wrapped around the same classrooms. (Except that on the second floor the Coke machines are at the opposite end.) 1

Section B's classroom—Aldrich 108—is on the first floor, just off the hallway which, in exact intervals, is decorated with life-size photographs of bald professors, staring out into the slow waters of the Charles. As the second of the two heavy doors swings shut behind you, there opens up a windowless realm of everlasting neon light where only the silent electric clock above the door tells of the changing light outside. Rising up against the bare, faint beige walls, forming a half circle which opens toward the blackboards, are the benches and wooden swivel chairs of Section B. An uninviting, strictly functional arena where, if what we've heard is true, the play 2 goes on in the stands and the lonely spectator, the professor, sits down front, in the middle of the stage.

Tomorrow we'll know. The first day of classes.   3

September 12: The welcoming ceremony began at 8:30 A.M., in   4
Carey Cage, which is an old Harvard Gym. Squeezed in, on bench, amid bench after jammed bench of spiffed-up, shivering guys, you endure all kinds of threats in the guise of good advice and a terrible draft that makes your teeth chatter.

* * *

Then, in the third and final class, we meet Duncan McKay. He   5
stands with one foot on the teacher's table, tall, even bent as he is, his massive face resting on the pointing stick he has planted on the table. Looking at nobody in particular, he says that he doesn't want us to love him. That he doesn't care if we hate him. That if we are lucky, some of us are going to be leaders and that we shouldn't bother to come to his class without a coat and tie.

That said, he takes his foot off the table, announces tomorrow's   6
case, and piles into the classroom door so that its wings scream in their hinges for some time after he has left. The class is too stunned to even breathe.

* * *

September 19: The case method is to the Harvard Business School   7
what the crooked tower is to Pisa. The Harvard Business School invented the method; the Harvard Business School succeeded with it; the Harvard Business School swears by it, and we have to put up with it, every grinding minute of every grinding day. There are no lectures, no labs, few textbooks even. Only cases, cases, and more cases.

In its outward appearance, a case is a bundle of mimeographed   8
pages—some thirty to forty on the average—written in a heavy-handed, lumbering prose that creaks from an overload of nouns. It describes a real event (although the names may be disguised) that happened in the course of some real business campaign, at times giving a general's grand view, at times a corporal's blurred impressions; it reports on the conditions in the trenches and bunkers of the business front; on the progress of the armies of salesmen march-

ing against each other, of supply convoys steaming down channels of distribution. It is a factual listing of men, money, and materials risked; of brilliant victory, of losses beyond imagination.

It often begins with grandiose flourishes: "For J. Hamilton Pea- 9 cock, chairman of the board of the First Haverhill National Bank, planning was not a luxury. . ." Invariably it ends with a question that is beginning to haunt us in our sleep: "What would you do?"

These aren't the "case histories" people get in law or medical 10 school. You know, and here is what the judge said. Or here is what the doctor ordered. Our cases have no ending. They just kind of dump the whole mess into your lap—tables, columns, exhibits, and all—and you can't run away from it because tomorrow ninety-four people—the entire Section—will be waiting for your decision. You may not be the guy the professor calls on "to lay out the case," but then again you may, which makes for a lot of motivation.

Three cases a day; sixty, maybe a hundred, maybe more than a 11 hundred pages a night. You almost read yourself to death, just to find out what the problem is. And then, of course, you need a solution.

Here you are, a strapping production manager, or financial vice- 12 president, or marketing executive, alone in a jungle of unfamiliar terms and technology, with no lecture notes, no fundamentals, or formulas to go by; with, perhaps, a reading list and a textbook and an equally confused, dry-mouthed roommate. And if you haven't done so already, you do a lot of growing up in a hurry, because you've got a problem. And no time. And little help. And something like your life depending on your finding a solution.

* * *

October 2: The name of the game is to make a point. Both, the 13 kind that proves something and the kind that can be added up to give a grade. McKay has announced that he will grade every sound we make in class. Although the others haven't told us so, we know that they are doing more or less the same.

The trouble is that with ninety-four players and the time per 14 game limited to ninety minutes, it's difficult to score. It often isn't so much a matter of knowing the stuff but knowing how to let the professor know that you know it. To overcome these difficulties, we are developing a number of special techniques. Like the "preventive attack" in which you start the class by "laying out the case," showing what, according to you, is the problem and what should be done, which gives you some five to ten uninterrupted minutes.

If, as is normal, you find yourself playing someone else's game, there are a number of "defensive" techniques. Of these, the most effective is the "questioning of premises." While the guy who is laying out the case is building the second and third levels of his argument, you demolish the foundations. If those foundations should prove too well made, try "pseudo participation" or "the single point technique." The latter is useful when you don't know what the case is all about. You relax and let yourself be inspired by what other people are saying. Sooner or later you will be led to some (usually minor) point, some dot on the "i" that the main speakers have overlooked.

Pseudo participation is more demanding. It is the opposite of the single point for it applies where you are well prepared, where you have a point to make, but not the discussion in which to make it. You cannot blatantly change the topic. So the trick is to start your "contribution" with a smoke screen and then with a quick "however" to turn the whole thing around to suit your purpose. As a kind of last resort, you can always fall back on sheer "trifling." You may not score, but at least you show that you are there.

Whatever happens, jump at the argument as if it were a loose ball. Develop a unique pattern of waving your hand. And most of all, be unscrupulous. Try to corner the argument, get it into a little nook all of your own, and hammer away at it there until the angry mob catches up with you.

Yet, lest all of the above give you a false sense of security, it is never easy—even with all this preparation and technique—to join the action. More often than not, you will find yourself sitting there, well prepared and eager, with the public argument dancing in front of your eyes, like a piece of paper torn out of your hand by the wind, almost within reach, yet again and again eluding your grasp.

* * *

McKay can flex his ego the way a weight lifter does his biceps, casting a huge, defiant shadow on our ambitions. A challenge far more intense even than the fear he inspires. So we're beginning to fight in his class, as we do in no other. Fight one another hard and relentlessly as if trying to prove to the somber, taciturn man up front that we are every inch as tough as he is.

Duncan McKay is playing a dangerous game because sooner or later somebody is going to look beyond his shadow to his real size. 20

October 10: On its way through Cambridge the river Charles is a smelly, unpleasant fellow, rolling its waters back and forth through numerous bends like a Sunday sleeper, unwilling to get out of bed. In fact, because of its many bends, the Charles seems like the only river in the world that you can cross and end up on the same shore. 21

Following the border between the townships of Brookline and Cambridge, it gently bends around the Business School, cutting it off from the rest of the Harvard campus—if you can call it a campus. Sure, across from the Business School, there is Harvard Yard, guarded by a heavy, wrought-iron fence, dotted with undergraduate dorms and class buildings. But the Yard measures no more than about five walking minutes in breadth and length. All the rest of the university is tucked away in the maze of narrow Cambridge streets, amid businesses and barbershops, boutiques and boardinghouses. 22

Aside from the Yard, the Business School is the only part of Harvard that you could really call a campus. Built on the riverbank opposite the rest of the school, it sits at the edge of a small plain, worn into the landscape by the Charles. Surrounded by athletic fields, a huge parking lot, and farther to the rear, by storage houses, car dealers, and gas stations. An elegant front for a sprawling commercial area that is crisscrossed by multiple lane highways and throughways. 23

Still, for all the complicated local geography, "across the river" isn't a place, it's a state of mind. 24

From the Business School, as we are beginning to find out, across the river means the hippies, the "kids"—the emotional people, the shouters. Those who discuss problems instead of solving them. 25

From the Business School, "across the river" is a threat. Something stirring up fears that the crowds from over there—the daydreamers, the self-righteous idealists, the critics blinded by their own enthusiasm, the fools who mistake a flash of insight for the light of truth—might try to smash the whole intricate apparatus of which we very much want to be a part. 26

But across the river also is where the girls are, the coffee houses, the subway trains to Boston, and an ice-cream cone with jimmies in one of the greasy spoons around Harvard Square. 27

And, although they never admit it, across the river for many of us is the slightly bitter taste of a dream only partly come true. Of an undergraduate education spent at a small, obscure place where the work was just as hard but the prestige infinitely smaller. The view of the Harvard Yard. The realization that we, as graduate students—and especially as graduate students of business—are kind of stepsons of this prestigious family.

"Abolish the B School," someone has written on a wall, over in the Yard. That's what across the river seems to mean to them over there: a subsidiary of IBM. A farm club for the CIA. A machine spewing out briefcase-carrying tin soldiers—mercenaries in the battle for higher profits; little shmucks who are willing to sell their left hand for the right to build a new Coca-Cola factory in outer Swaziland.

And so, when somebody says, "across the river," it isn't which but whose side he is on. Though there are two convenient bridges, each side has neither the time nor the interest to cross over for anything other than football, sex, or ice-cream cones.

October 11: When he finally spoke everybody turned around and looked. Just like McKay had said: "The longer you wait to speak up, the more difficult it will be."

The voice was Blotner's who sits in the last row, all the way over to the door. He isn't a big guy, Blotner, of middle height and at twenty-two he looks very much his age. The force of the seesawing argument kneads the soft mold of his face, making the mouth twitch nervously as he rocks his chair, his hands fiddling with a heavy golden class ring. You could hear in his voice the urgent desire to speak up, to claim his place in the Section. But you could also hear the terror of being rebuked, contradicted, or worse—ignored. His gesticulating hands, rather than adding emphasis, told of a vain attempt to grab hold of himself. But already his voice stuttered and stalled, his argument broke before anybody got a chance to jump on it.

* * *

October 16: Today, McKay brought a big fish to class. He had wrapped it into a newpaper and the newspaper into two layers of plastic foil.

He carefully pulled it out, down at the table, and laid it on the   34
newspaper for everybody to see. The fish had a reddish head and
a yellow, almost golden belly.

"Here's what happens," McKay said, pointing to the dead fish,   35
"to those who open their mouth at the wrong time."

CONTENT

1. Cohen's diary records the struggle to survive in Harvard's Business School. How realistic does the portrayal seem? What details of the educational process seem to create tension among the students?

2. Does the case method seem an effective way to teach business practices? Why do you think it is preferred? Does it have shortcomings?

3. Why do you think Cohen included material in his diary about the reputation of the Business School in the Harvard community? Do the details of daily life in the Business School bear out its reputation?

ORGANIZATION

4. The organization of a diary is easy because it is merely a record of daily impressions. Yet, because this is meant to be read by outsiders, Cohen has to make sure that the characters who appear in several entries are explained to the reader. Does he do this successfully? How?

5. Occasionally, Cohen pulls away from the particularities of Section B to draw some general conclusions about the teachers, the methodology, or the school itself. Show where several of these general remarks occur. Is there any pattern to the way Cohen introduces them?

TOPICS FOR WRITING

6. Keep a daily record, like Cohen's, of one of your classes. Include in it portraits of students and the teacher, and recount any memorable incidents.

7. Record your daily progress in learning any skill by keeping a diary.

PART 2
Autobiography: Writing from Personal Experience

Except for the free-form writing of diaries and journals, you are likely to experience the least difficulty writing autobiography. Autobiography is a form of self-expression, of recalled personal experiences. Although it may seem egocentric, the aim of autobiographies is to share those experiences which make us human. In an age which Tom Wolfe has labelled "The Me-Generation," autobiography appears on the best-seller lists more often than any other type of non-fiction, indicating that there is some need to write and read about important moments in our lives. But are popular autobiographies more often embroidery than fact? Is a given autobiography more akin to the "lies" of fiction than to the "facts" as they actually happened? As a writer of autobiographical essays, you should know to what degree artistic license permits you to transform literal facts into an interesting tale, as opposed to a mere documentary recounting which, while literally true and correct, may be dull and lie flat on the page.

A fruitful way to come to grips with autobiography (how truthful it is and what its elements are) is to examine a sampling of passages from classic autobiographies. Although the following passages are only fragments, these keyhole glimpses nevertheless reveal several features characteristic of the autobiographer's art.

> All men of whatsoever quality they be, who have done anything of excellence, ought, if they are persons of truth and honesty, to describe their life with their own hand. . . Many untoward things can I remember, such as happen to all who live upon our earth. . . I can also bring to mind some pleasant goods and some inestimable evils, which, when I turn my thoughts backward, strike terror in me, and astonishment that I should have reached this age of fifty-eight, wherein, thanks be to God, I am still travelling prosperously forward.
>
> —*The Autobiography of Benvenuto Cellini*

25

Dear Son: I have ever had pleasure in obtaining any little anecdotes of my ancestors. . . . Imagining it may be equally agreeable to you to know the circumstances of my life, many of which you are yet unacquainted with, and expecting the joy of a week's uninterrupted leisure in my present country retirement, I sit down to write them to you. To which I have besides some other inducements. Having emerged from the poverty and obscurity in which I was born and bred, to a state of affluence and some degree of reputation in the world, . . .the conducting means I made use of, which with the blessing of God so well succeeded, my posterity may like to know, as they may find some of them suitable to their own situations, and therefore fit to be imitated. . . . I should have no objection to a repetition of the same life [but] since such a repetition is not to be expected, the next thing most like living one's life over again seems to be a recollection of that life, and to make that recollection as durable as possible by putting it down in writing.

Hereby, too, I shall indulge the inclination so natural in old men, to be talking of themselves and their own past actions; and I shall indulge it without being tiresome to others, who, through respect to me, might conceive themselves obliged to give me a hearing, since this may be read or not as anyone pleases. And, lastly (I may as well confess it, since my denial of it will be believed by nobody), perhaps I shall a good deal gratify my own *vanity*.

—*The Autobiography of Benjamin Franklin*

I am commencing an undertaking, hitherto without precedent, and which will never find an imitator. I desire to set before my fellows the likeness of a man in all the truth of nature, and that man myself.

Myself alone! I know the feelings of the heart, and I know men. I am not made like any of those I have seen; I venture to believe that I am not made like any of those who are in existence. If I am not better, at least I am different. Whether nature has acted rightly or wrongly in destroying the mould in which she cast me, can only be decided after I have been read. . . . I have told the good and the bad with equal frankness. I have neither omitted anything bad, nor interpolated anything good. . . . I have shown myself as I was: mean and contemptible, good, high-minded and sublime, according as I was one or the other. . . . Gather round me the countless host of my fellowmen; let them hear my confessions, lament for my unworthiness, and blush for my imperfections.

—*The Confessions of Jean Jacques Rousseau*

Even a quick study of this sampling shows us some obvious similarities in technique and substance. Notice that writers usually tell their personal history in the *first person*, "I". Using the first person produces a *tone of familiarity*, of intimacy, ease, and informality—as if the reader and writer were in some comfortable room, talking not just about the bare facts of the writer's life, but about those more private thoughts that reveal the inner person. For instance, Franklin's epistolary style (the *Autobiography* was begun as a letter to his son and continued for his grandson) is a written equivalent of the familiar heart-to-heart father-son talk. Franklin, the father, is giving advice based on years of experience to his son; the familiar tone and informal style are typical of most autobiographies.

All the writers claim to be *telling the truth*, the whole truth, and nothing but the truth. However, this characteristic claim of auto-biographies is not as verifiable as it might at first seem. The issue of veracity is complicated by ontological questions (What is reality, and therefore truth?), as well as psychological (How well do we remember?) and artistic questions (Does this detail fit the pattern of the scene I am creating, and if not should I alter or delete it?). Consequently, although the autobiographer may claim to be telling the truth, we must determine which truth and whose version of it is being told before we can judge whether or not an autobiography is an accurate reflection of the facts.

In a lecture published in book form as *Aspects of Biography,* Andre Maurois expressed doubts about the possibility of autobiography accurately representing the truth. "Autobiographical narrative is inaccurate or false," he contended, because we forget; we deliberately falsify on aesthetic grounds; we expurgate the disagreeable; our sense of shame alters things; we rationalize events afterwards; and we wish to protect our friends. Maurois concluded, "It is impossible, then, to retrieve the past; it is impossible not to change it unconsciously, and, further, it is impossible not to change it consciously."

The greatest critic of autobiography, Samuel Johnson, was as aware of the possibility of falsehood as Maurois, but he rejected the notion that it was impossible to tell the truth.

> The writer of his own life has at least the first qualification of an His-torian, the knowledge of the truth; and though it may be plausibly objected that his temptations to disguise it are equal to his opportunities of knowing it, yet I cannot but think that impartiality may be expected with equal confidence from him that relates the passages of his own life, as from him that delivers the transactions of another. Certainty of knowledge not only excludes mistakes but fortifies veracity. [*Idler,* Nov. 24, 1759.]

However, *all autobiography is retrospective*—that is, all autobiogra-phers are reviewing past events—and time does affect the way writers perceive events. This is one reason why many of the most accurate and vivid autobiographies have been drawn from diaries and journals. Anaïs Nin, we have already seen, began to keep her *Diary* to counteract the distorting power of time.

Each of the three autobiographers justifies writing his life story with *some motive, some purpose either personal or societal.* Cellini, for example, feels a duty to tell his story as a man who has accomplished something of "excellence," in his case his sculpture. Franklin, while admitting his primary purpose to be the instruction of his descendants, candidly admits the vanity and the personal pleasure of reliving events and leaving a memorial. Rousseau assumes that by telling his own unique story, others will somehow profit from the lesson.

Two additional important characteristics of autobiography are suggested in the quoted passages. First, unlike any other kind of writers, *in pure autobiography the author exhibits a curious duality: He or she is both the observer and the subject.* We have already touched on this duality in our discussion of the use of the first person and the nature of truth. If, as many critics believe, all prose is to some extent autobiographical, then the line between factual writing and fictional writing begins to blur. *Time is the other universal subject in autobiography*—both chronological time (from childhood to adulthood, or wherever the autobiography begins and ends) and time in a more ultimate sense, a continuing autobiographical present in which, as Franklin suggested, the autobiographer has a sort of second chance, an opportunity to play the game over again. When you write an autobiographical piece, you relive the experience, this time with greater perception gained from hindsight.

A reconstruction of events, dialogues, and travels, a remembrance of the people, places, dangers, and pleasures of our experience—in short, the panorama of a man's or a woman's life—has such cumulative intensity that it can make the past part of the present. Without the past there can be no future. Anthropologist Margaret Mead expressed it this way:

> If I were twenty-one today, I would elect to join the communicating network of those young people, the world over, who recognize the urgency of life—supporting change—as an anthropologist. But even so, I speak out of the experience of my own lifetime of seeing past and future as aspects of the present. Knowledge joined to action—knowledge about what man has been and is—can protect the future. There is

hope, I believe, in seeing the human adventure as a whole and in this shared trust that knowledge about mankind, sought in reverence for life, can bring life. [*Blackberry Winter: My Earlier Years* (William Morrow & Co., 1972), 296.]

Autobiographical writing, then, is rewarding in many senses. Although you will probably not have occasion to recount your entire life story in a book-length autobiography, in writing even a short autobiographical essay several benefits are in store for you: the discovery that you have something to say that is interesting and unique, the pleasure of sharing a closely felt event or personal thought with a responsive audience, and the confidence that, at least in this area, you are an expert—no one knows more about the subject, which is, after all, *you*.

SHORT EXAMPLE

TRUMAN CAPOTE
A Voice from a Cloud

Truman Capote's first novel, Other Voices, Other Rooms *(1948) met with critical acclaim before he was twenty-five years old. Since then the controversial, outspoken author has produced novels, short stories, musical plays, television scripts, screenplays, and non-fiction works. The most famous of these may be* Breakfast at Tiffany's *(1958) and* In Cold Blood *(1966), both of which were later adapted as films. His childhood friend, Harper Lee, used her memories of Capote as a child to create the character of Dill in* To Kill a Mockingbird. *In the following autobiographical excerpt from* The Dogs Bark *(1973) Capote describes his early education.*

I was born in New Orleans, an only child; my parents were divorced when I was four years old. It was a complicated divorce with much bitterness on either side, which is the main reason why I spent most of my childhood wandering among the homes of relatives in Louisiana, Mississippi and rural Alabama (off and on, I attended schools in New York City and Connecticut). The reading I did on my own was of greater importance than my official education, which was a waste and ended when I was seventeen, the age at which I applied for and received a job at *The New Yorker* magazine. Not a very grand job, for all it really involved was sorting cartoons and clipping newspapers. Still, I was fortunate to have it, especially since I was determined never to set a studious foot inside a college classroom. I felt that either one was or wasn't a writer, and no combination of professors could influence the outcome. I still think I was correct, at least in my own case; however, I now realize that most young writers have more to gain than not by attending college, if only because their teachers and classroom comrades provide a captive audience for their work; nothing is lonelier than to be an aspiring artist without some semblance of a sounding board.

DISCUSSION

Capote's brief summary of his early life rests on his aspirations as a writer and the role of school in furthering those aspirations. He correctly points out that most writers need school if only to provide an audience for their work. However, from the outset, Capote's childhood was nonconforming due to the divorce of his parents and his sporadic education. Notice how self-direction characterizes the life he describes, and how even in his job at *The New Yorker*, he succeeds in culling the best out of limited opportunities. Capote's brief sketch has at least two characteristics of longer autobiographies: First, the focus is on the self, the discovery for the reader, of those unique qualities that define the writer's personality. Count how many times the personal pronoun "I" is used by Capote. Second, Capote's sketch allows him to revise his earlier judgment about the value of a college education and, with the greater insight of years, to see that what may have worked for him may not work for others.

LILLIAN HELLMAN
Julia

For the half-century since the initial performance of The Children's Hour *(1934), Lillian Hellman has been a major American playwright. She has been twice a recipient of the New York Drama Critics Circle Award—for* The Watch on the Rhine *(1941) and* Toys in the Attic *(1960). In addition,* The Little Foxes *(1939), and her libretto for Leonard Bernstein's opera* Candide *(1956) are regarded as major events in the modern American theater. Her memoirs—An* Unfinished Woman *(1969),* Pentimento *(1973),* Scoundrel Time *(1976), and* Maybe *(1980)—reveal the private friendships and publicized issues that helped shape her life. In this passage from* Pentimento, *Hellman observes that although the details of her childhood might fade, their importance to her development remains vivid in her mind.*

Childhood is less clear to me than to many people: when it ended   1
I turned my face away from it for no reason that I know about,
certainly without the usual reason of unhappy memories. For many
years that worried me, but then I discovered that the tales of former
children are seldom to be trusted. Some people supply too many
past victories or pleasures with which to comfort themselves, and
other people cling to pains, real and imagined, to excuse what they
have become.

I think I have always known about my memory: I know when it   2
is to be trusted and when some dream or fantasy entered on the
life, and the dream, the need of dream, led to distortion of what
happened. And so I knew early that the rampage angers of an only
child were distorted nightmares of reality. But I trust absolutely
what I remember about Julia.

Now, so many years later, I could climb the steps without a light,   3
move in the night through the crowded rooms of her grandparents'
great Fifth Avenue house with the endless chic-shabby rooms, their
walls covered with pictures, their tables crowded with objects whose
value I didn't know. True, I cannot remember anything said or done
in that house except for the first night I was allowed to sleep there.
Julia and I were both twelve years old that New Year's Eve night,
sitting at a late dinner, with courses of fish and meats, and sherbets
in between to change the tastes, "clear the palate" is what her
grandmother said, with watered wine for us, and red and white
wine and champagne for the two old people. (Were they old? I don't

know: they were her grandparents.) I cannot remember any talk at the table, but after dinner we were allowed to go with them to the music room. A servant had already set the phonograph for "So Sheep May Safely Graze," and all four of us listened until Julia rose, kissed the hand of her grandmother, the brow of her grandfather, and left the room, motioning for me to follow. It was an odd ritual, the whole thing, I thought, the life of the very rich, and beyond my understanding.

Each New Year's Eve of my life has brought back the memory of 4 that night. Julia and I lay in twin beds and she recited odds and ends of poetry—every once in a while she would stop and ask me to recite, but I didn't know anything—Dante in Italian, Heine in German, and even though I could not understand either language, the sounds were so lovely that I felt a sweet sadness as if much was ahead in the world, much that was going to be fine and fulfilling if I could ever find my way. I did recite Mother Goose and she did Donne's "Julia," and laughed with pleasure "at his tribute to me." I was ashamed to ask if it was a joke.

Very late she turned her head away for sleep, but I said, "More, 5 Julia, please. Do you know more?" And she turned on the light again and recited from Ovid and Catullus, names to me without countries.

I don't know when I stopped listening to look at the lovely face 6 propped against the pillow—the lamp throwing fine lights on the thick dark hair. I cannot say now that I knew or had ever used the words gentle or delicate or strong, but I did think that night that it was the most beautiful face I had ever seen. In later years I never thought about how she looked, although when we were grown other people often said she a "strange beauty," she "looked like nobody else," and one show-off said a "Burne-Jones face" when, of course, her face had nothing to do with Burne-Jones or fake spirituality.

* * *

A few years after that childhood New Year's Eve, I was moved 7 to a public school. (My father was having a bad time and couldn't afford to pay for me anymore.) But Julia and I saw each other almost every day and every Saturday night I still slept in her grandparents' house. But, in time, our lives did change: Julia began to travel all

summer and in winter holidays, and when she returned all my
questions about the beauties of Europe would be shrugged off with
badly photographed snapshots of things that interested her: two
blind children in Cairo—she explained that the filth carried by flies
caused the blindness; people drinking from sewers in Teheran; no
St. Mark's but the miserable hovel of a gondolier in Venice; no news
of the glories of Vatican art but stories about the poverty of Tras-
tevere.

Once she returned with a framed photograph of a beautiful woman   8
who was her mother and an Englishman who was her mother's
husband. I asked her what she felt about seeing her mother—in all
the years I had never heard her mention her mother—and she
stared at me and said that her mother owned a "very fancy castle"
and the new husband poured drinks for all the titles who liked the
free stuff, but there was also mention of Evelyn Waugh and H.G.
Wells and Nancy Cunard, and when I wanted news of them she
said she didn't know anything about them, they'd said hello to her
and that she had only wanted to get out of the way and go to her
room.

"But I didn't have a *room*," she said. "Everybody has a suite,   9
and there are fourteen servants somewhere below the earth, and
only some of them have a window in the cell my mother calls their
room, and there's only one stinking bath for all of them. My mother
learns fast, wherever she is. She does not offend the host country."

Once, when we were about sixteen, we went with her grand-   10
parents at Easter time to their Adirondacks lodge, as large and
shabby as was every place they lived in. Both old people drank a
good deal—I think they always had, but I had only begun to notice
it—and napped after every meal. But they stayed awake late into
the night doing intricate picture puzzles imported from France, on
two tables, and gave each other large checks for the one who finished first.

I don't remember that Julia asked their permission for our camp-   11
ing trips—several times we stayed away for weekends—on or near
Lake Champlain. It wasn't proper camping, although we carried
blankets and clean socks and dry shoes and canned food. We walked
a great deal, often I fished for trout, and once, climbing a high hill,
Julia threw a net over a rabbit, running with a grace and speed I
had never before seen in a girl, and she showed me how to skin
the rabbit. We cooked it that night wrapped in bacon and it is still

among the best things I ever ate, maybe because *Robinson Crusoe* is one of the best books I ever read. Even now, seeing any island, I am busy with that rabbit and fantasies of how I would make do alone, without shelter or tools.

When we walked or fished we seldom did it side by side: that   12
was her choice and I admired it because I believed she was thinking stuff I couldn't understand and mustn't interfere with, and maybe because I knew even then she didn't want to be side by side with anybody.

At night, wrapped in our blankets, the fire between us, we would   13
talk. More accurately, I would ask questions and she would talk: she was one of the few people I have ever met who could give informaton without giving a lecture. How young it sounds now that although I had heard the name of Freud, I never knew exactly what he wrote until she told me; that Karl Marx and Engels became men with theories, instead of that one sentence in my school book which mentioned the Manifesto. But we also talked like all young people, of possible beaux and husbands and babies, and heredity versus environment, and can romantic love last, mixing stuff like that in speeches made only for the pleasure of girls on the edge of growing up.

One night, when we had been silent for a long time because she   14
was leaning on an elbow, close to the fire, reading a German grammar, I laughed at the sounds coming from her mouth as she repeated the sentences.

She said, "No, you don't understand. People are either teachers   15
or students. You are a student."

"Am I a good one?"   16

"When you find what you want, you will be very good."   17

I reached out and touched her hand. "I love you, Julia." She   18
stared at me and took my hand to her face.

CONTENT

1. Why does Hellman begin her autobiographical recollection with a statement about the unreliability of childhood memories? What does she imply is the reason hers is to be trusted regarding Julia?

2. In paragraph 15, Julia says, "People are either teachers or students. You are a student." How does this define part of their relationship?
3. What does Julia's interest in the subjects of her photographs from her travels (paragraph 7) tell us about the sort of person she is growing up to be? Why is Julia more interested in the servants and their living conditions than in her mother's famous friends?

ORGANIZATION

4. The whole of "Julia," from which this excerpt was taken, uses a series of flashbacks in time, of which this childhood recollection is merely one. Show how the juxtaposition of details, some suggesting young girls' interests and activities, others suggesting the two adults these girls are to become, is like the juxtaposed time segments of the whole work.
5. How do paragraphs 3 and 10, describing the grandparents, underscore and perhaps explain Julia's difference? What would be the effect of omitting these paragraphs?

TOPICS FOR WRITING

6. Select a childhood friend who had an influence on you as you grew up. Describe that friend and the interests that affected you.
7. The following passage is taken from the opening page of *Pentimento*, the book in which "Julia" appeared. In it Hellman explains why she went back to sketch those whom she remembered from her past.

Old paint on canvas, as it ages, sometimes becomes transparent. When that happens it is possible, in some pictures, to see the original lines: a tree will show through a woman's dress, a child makes way for a dog, a large boat is no longer on an open sea. That is called pentimento because the painter "repented," changed his mind. Perhaps it would be as well to say that the old conception, replaced by a later choice, is a way of seeing and then seeing again.

That is all I mean about the people in this book. The paint has aged now and I wanted to see what was there for me once, what is there for me now.

Write a portrait of someone whom you knew in the past, and still know, to show what differences (or similarities) have emerged in his or her personality from then until now.

8. Julia clearly was different from her parents and grandparents. Describe such a person.

EDWARD RIVERA
First Communion

Edward Rivera was born in Orocovia, Puerto Rico, but educated in the public and parochial schools of New York's Spanish Harlem. In the following excerpt from his first book, Family Installments: Memories of Growing Up Hispanic *(1982), Rivera gives us a taste of what parochial school is like for a young student about to make his first communion. His alter ego, Santo Malánguez, is acutely aware of the nun's condescension toward him, the other students, and other Spanish-speaking members of a "foreign culture."*

There was something both cold-hearted and generous about our nuns that gave at least some of us reason to be grateful our parents had signed us up at Saint Miseria's. Sister Mary Felicia, for example. Third grade. The nicest thing Sister Felicia did for me was buy me an unused First Communion outfit in the Marqueta on Park Avenue when she found out I was a Welfare case. She didn't have to do that, because Papi somehow always found a way to scrounge up the funds for whatever we needed. I think he had credit everywhere, though he wasn't one to abuse it. But Sister didn't bother consulting him or Mami about their resources. Maybe my plain, Third Avenue clothes and my apologetic look gave her the impression we were in such bad shape at home that Papi couldn't put out the money for a cheap Communion outfit: a white shirt without a label inside the collar, a pair of Thom McAn shoes (blisters guaranteed) that expanded like John's Bargain Store sponges as soon as it rained, and an even-cheaper Howard Clothes suit with a vest and a big label over the jacket's wallet pocket, so that whenever a man opened up that jacket and reached inside for his wallet, others could see he was moving up in this world. No more Third Avenue cheap stuff for this *elemento*. Unless he had somehow stolen that label and had his wife the seamstress sew it into the wallet pocket just to impress the kind of people who kept an eye on labels. If Sister Felicia was one of those types, she kept it to herself. All she wanted was for every boy and girl in her class to show up at First Communion ceremonies in a prescribed, presentable outfit: the girls in white, the boys in black, with an oversized red ribbon around the elbow.

"Making your First Communion," Mami told me in private one [2] day when she was in a joking mood, "is almost as important as making your first *caca* all by yourself."

"So why do I have to wear this uniform, then?" I said, confused. [3]

"Because it's a ceremony. The most important of your life so far. [4] Except for Baptism. It's like when you get married for the first time." Meaning what, I didn't know or ask. And what was this about people getting married more than once? Another joke? Sometimes she went over my head and didn't explain the point. Some things I should find out for myself, I guessed. You can't always be depending on your mother to fill you in. She wouldn't even tell me how she felt about Sister Felicia's generosity.

At the time it may have been a nice favor on Sister's part—and [5] on Sister's Principal's, because she was the one who dispensed their funds—putting out all that money for a kid on ADC.* For one thing, they were Irish, all of them, so why should they give a damn for people like me? But they did sometimes. More confusion on my side. And a long time later, when I thought back on it, I was still confused.

One afternoon, after the last class bell, Sister told me and a cou- [6] ple of other classmates not to leave the room because she wanted to talk to us about something important. Right away I figured she was going to bleed our knuckles with her twelve-incher for something, some sin we had committed unawares. Unawares was no excuse. Happened all the time in St. Miseria's. I started going over all the things I'd said and done that day in public, and then in private, and I couldn't come up with a single sin. Which didn't mean a thing. The nuns knew a lot better than you did what sin was and wasn't; they had technical training in those things, and they didn't miss a thing. Almost every day somebody got extra homework for daydreaming in class, or the knuckles job for laughing at something

*Aid to Dependent Children.

serious somebody had said, or for picking his or her nose in public. That's what Marta Cuevas had done the week before I got my outfit. She was good-looking, too. She was short and hefty, she had a good profile, and she sat in the first row, right up there where every move you made was seen by everyone else, especially by Sister, who used to pace back and forth, with an opened book in one hand, and the twelve-inch ruler in the other, from the exit (closed) to the window (opened just a crack for fresh oxygen). And she, Marta, nervous because Sister was going to call on her next, forgot the rule about picking your nose and committed that infraction right under Sister's own nose. She must have thought she was back home or something; in a dark movie, where nobody noticed what you were doing with your hands.

Sister shut her mouth in the middle of a question, placed her   7
book face down on her desk—her hands were shaking—and put a difficult question to Marta: Where had she learned such repulsive manners? Certainly not in school, hinting that in Marta's home personal habits were still primitive. One could imagine, if one had that kind of stomach, what their table manners must be like, and what kind of "meals" they sat down to, if they bothered to sit at all. They probably all ate standing, or squatting right there on the kitchen floor, like their ancestors the Caribs, cannibalistic Indians from the jungles of South America (we had read about them already during the history hour; they ate their enemies raw). The only fire they knew anything about came from Huracán, their thunder god. She went on to tell us that the Caribs hadn't even discovered friction, that's how primitive they were. It was the Europeans, the Spaniards, who had brought them friction, the True Faith, and other forms of Christian civilization.

"The word friction comes from the Latin *fricare*, children," she   8
said. "And when you rub two dry sticks or stones or bodies of certain things together, if you do it long enough and briskly enough, you produce fire. And fire is necessary for cooking and warmth."

She went on to demonstrate friction by rubbing her index fingers   9
together. Briskly. I had seen a magician do the same thing in a movie, and it had worked. His fingers—all ten of them—went up in flames. I had tried it myself, and it hadn't worked. I knew I was no magician. I'd have to stick to matches. And now Sister Felicia was trying it herself, and it wasn't working, either. No flames. Not even sparks. So she stopped rubbing, looked around at no one,

embarrassed for a few seconds, and said, "It doesn't always work, boys and girls. My hands are cold this morning." She began slapping her cold hands, as if to wipe off the failure of her friction magic. "No fire this time," she said, smiling. Then she became serious again. "Now open up your catechisms"—the Baltimore edition— "to page forty-three. Briskly, briskly." I felt letdown and confused. And she never mentioned friction again in class.

But there was another kind of friction going on in our class all 10 the time, and Marta Cuevas, who had no answer to Sister's tough question on her repulsive nose-picking, was demonstrating it. All she could do just then was stare up at Sister—I had a good view of her attractive cannibal profile—with a paralyzed, agonized look.

"Stand up, Marta Cuevas!" Sister commanded—boomed. She 11 could have scared the loincloth off Huracán himself.

Marta stood up as if stone-faced José Bosquez, sitting right behind 12 her, had given her the biggest goose of her life so far—and it wasn't likely she'd be getting another one like it soon—and before Sister asked her to, she put out her hand, the right one (she knew which one was going to get it), and made a tight fist, with her thumb curled outward and wagging away like the classy-looking stump of a fancy dog's former tail. Her fingernails needed trimming, too. This kid descended from pagans had a lot to learn. With her free hand she had to hold the other hand by the wrist, because it kept shaking so much, this hand that got it, that Sister swung and missed the first and third times she took a cut at it with her ruler. Marta didn't scream, thank God. And when it was all over she just sat back down, her jaw clenched as tight as she could make it, and dropped a few tears on her opened book, a reader about a group of boys and girls, Jean and Paul, Monique and Simone, who lived in a place called Timber Town up in French Canada. From time to time Marta sneaked her right hand up to her mouth, unclenched her jaw, and blew on her knuckles. Sister pretended not to notice. She didn't even call on her the rest of the day. So in a way Marta got herself off the hook, because I don't think she had studied too much the night before. Probably spent her homework hours reading comic books. *The Living Hulk, Wonder Woman, Heart Throb*— enough to corrupt "an idle brain," as Sister said.

So as far as I could tell, when Sister asked a handful of us to stay 13 behind after class let out that day, we had violated some rule and were going to get it, a mass purge, or "purgation," a word the sisters liked to throw around, the way Father Rooney back in church liked to throw around Latin things like *Dominus vobiscum* and *Hoc est* my body and blood, before the Pope said you had to use English in church and spoiled the whole mystery. "Gave the whole game away, Gino," I heard one of the ushers say to another usher in church one Sunday.

But I was wrong about Sister's intentions. "We're going to purchase your First Communion outfits, boys and girls," Sister Felicia told us. Now she was smiling. A fine smile, too. They took good care of their teeth in that order. And all we could do was look at each other in wonder. First they hit you and make certain embarrassing hints about your family habits and your man-eating ancestors, and then they treat you to a free purchase of clothes. The whole bunch of us had a lot to learn about these women, and a lot to be grateful for as well. Not that we had much choice, but still . . .

Six boys and girls and two nuns. One of the girls was Marta Cuevas, who wasn't crying anymore or bringing her fingers anywhere near her nose, no sign on her face that she'd been "purgated" that very morning in front of the public. We split up as soon as we hit the first Marqueta stall on 110th and Park, where a pandemonium of merchants sold a mixed bag of merchandise: tropical products (mostly starchy tubers), religious articles (plastic and plaster statuettes and badly reproduced prints of wonder-working saints), "botanical" herbs with healing properties (Mami had a few back home, but they never healed anything from what I could tell; they just smelled up the house), voodoo pamphlets and recipes, evil-looking effigies with stringy hair, and charms for secret rituals of one kind or another. But that was only a fraction of the merchandise you could buy in those stalls. There was an immense assortment of private wear, too, most of it for women and girls: girdles, brassieres, skirts, blouses, panties; nylon stockings in every possible shade; slippers, plain or with bright-colored pompons over the toes; bathing suits, one-piece outfits for girls of all ages, or for women who would still fit into a girl's size and didn't mind looking like a case of arrested development; teenage girls' "jumpers"; widows' black shawls, chintzy mantillas for that special Spanish look, happily married women's polka-dot neckerchiefs, headkerchiefs of all kinds and colors; and a lot of other stuff, including smoked, boiled, and uncooked pork.

One of the stands we passed was displaying the close-shaved 16
head of a pig with bent ears that had lost their pink—maybe it was
embalmed to retard spoilage. It was wearing a sailor's cap on a slant,
a pair of smoked glasses, and a red bow tie, and in its mouth the
owner had stuck a half-smoked cigar, the long, thin panatela type.
On the cap the embalmer had pinned a message in red: "Eat Me,
Im' Delishious." Moses would have passed out.

"That man can't spell," said Sister Felicia, and turned her head 17
away. The rest of her train, three boys, followed her timidly, no
smiles. I was feeling a little snobbish about that man's lousy spelling. Here was a grown man, probably the father of half a dozen or
more, and he didn't know where to put his apostrophe. This was
the kind of father who handed down his ignorance to his children,
and then they would pass it on to theirs and and drive women like
Sister Felicia out of their minds. She was looking mad, too, but
under control, tolerant, long-suffering. And she was leading us
through the mobs of shoppers at a fast clip. A lot of them, mostly
mothers and their kids, made way for us when they saw her coming
toward them with that long-suffering, angry look on her face. Their
own surprised faces would turn serious all of a sudden, and they'd
step out of our way and follow us with frightened eyes. Nobody
was going to mess with us as long as we stuck close to her, this
woman who was going to spend money on us even though the
Sisters of Misericordia were always on a tight budget.

They carried all their funds for the day in a little black purse 18
made of leather, or something that looked just like leather, with a
silver-looking snap at the top; they kept it inside their plackets, the
mysterious innards of their long plain gowns, and they always cast
a cautious scan around them whenever they reached inside the
placket for the purse. You could never tell who was a thief. One of
the boys in my class had sneaked back inside the classroom once
during lunch hour and stolen a red-and-white magnet she had con-
fiscated from another student, who had been applying it to the head
of the girl sitting in front of him. His excuse, when sister caught
him, was that he had been looking for lice in that girl's hair. He
found a few, too, he said, but that didn't get him off the hook. And
the other one, the one who sneaked upstairs and stole the magnet,
was caught by Sister Mary Monitor, as we called whichever nun
was guarding the stairs that day. They made him bring in his parents

next day for a good dressing-down—all three of them were dressed down—and if the parents hadn't apologized with all their might, their son would have been expelled, exiled to public school, which as we saw it was as close as you could come to perdition before actually dying with all your sins unconfessed. "Let that be a lesson," Sister Felicia had told the rest of us, just in case we had missed the point. We hadn't.

Now she was smiling away as everyone in the Marqueta made   19 way for us. She was a fast walker, almost as if she were running to catch the New York Central, which was rumbling right over our heads: The market stalls were inside the arcade beneath the elevated railroad tracks, and I was always afraid one of those trains, crammed with well-dressed passengers headed for their homes in the country, would come crashing down through the ceiling of those stalls and destroy everyone in the place. A good headline for *El Diario*,* worse than the Lisbon earthquake we had read about already.

With that peril rumbling overhead, I couldn't understand why   20 Sister was all smiles all of a sudden, as if she were actually enjoying the sight of all that Marqueta merchandise. "It's all chit, man," one of the two boys I was with said. "Right?"

"That's *your* opinion, Almendras," I said. (During school hours   21 we were all on a last-name basis, and as far as I was concerned, we were still in school just then.)

"So what's wrong with *your* opinion?" Almendras said.   22

"My mother shops here," I said. "Every Saturday."   23

"And you come with her, right?"   24

"Yeah, so what?"   25

"Nothing."   26

I knew what he was getting at, but with Sister right there I couldn't   27 start anything. She wasn't speaking to anyone until we got to the stall she wanted.

"I want," she told Don Jorge Mercado, who specialized in cere-   28 monial outfits, "three white shirts for these three boys, three red ties, three red armbands, the First Communion kind, three pairs of white socks, and three tie clasps with a cross, if you have them. If you don't have them with a cross, please tell me who does. We're in a hurry." Just like that. Brisk, no nonsense, always in character.

*New York City's Spanish newspaper.

"Absolutelymente, Sister," said Don Jorge. What kind of answer 29
was that? I thought He was avoiding her question about the three
crucifixion clasps. I knew that at least one other merchant had them:
Doña Dolores Flores of the Flores Botánica establishment on Park
Avenue, a short walk away. Doña Flores, a widow without dependents, sold odds and ends on the side, almost like contraband; but
Don Jorge wasn't about to put in a good word for one of his competitors, not even for the benefit of a nun. He had an extended
family to feed.

He squatted behind his high counter for a few seconds, disap- 30
peared completely, and then reappeared with a big grin and a nine-
by-twelve box full of those First Communion tie clasps. It was like
looking at a large collection of dead grasshoppers. He sifted through
the collection and picked three out in a showy, meticulous way as
if only the very best dried grasshoppers would do for Sister Felicia
and her three timid charges. Then, like a master magician, still
grinning away, he held them up for inspection and approval.

She nodded, unsmiling, as if she could expect no better from a 31
swindler of his sort. "We'll take them."

"They all come out of the same mother hopper, Malánguez," 32
Almendras whispered in my ear. "Spooky." I gave him a little kick
on the ankle to shut him up. His sarcasm might end up getting us
in trouble with Sister.

". . . shirts," she was telling Don Jorge. 33

"What's your neck size, boys?" Don Jorge asked us. 34

Almendras and our other companion had no trouble telling him, 35
and he pulled the same vanishing act behind the counter and came
up with two identical-looking First Communion shirts and three
red ties with a clasp at the back and a ready-made knot.

"Those came out of the same mother too," Almendras whispered 36
to me. This time I ignored him. His type eventually got into trouble
with the law and all kinds of authorities, because he couldn't take
anything serious seriously.

"And what's your neck size, young man?" Sister asked me. I 37
knew she would. I didn't know my neck size. Mami always took
care of that. She had it written down somewhere in the house, along
with my shoe size, my waist, the number and kind of vaccinations
I'd already had, and when, what other vaccinations I still had coming to me, and other vital statistics and records. And now, because

I hadn't bothered to check any of that out, I was about to get into trouble with Sister, and to suffer a humiliation in front of my two classmates and Don Jorge the First Communion magician. And if all those shoppers around us got wind of my ignorance, I'd just have to live with the humiliation. I turned red while she and Don Jorge and the other two charges waited for my answer. This was turning into a test of my intelligence.

"Well, Mr. Malánguezzz?" she hissed, losing patience. She had things to do back at the nunnery.

"I am not sure, Seester," I said, finally.

She couldn't believe it. "Do you mean to tell me, Ssantosss Malánguezzz, that you still don't know you own neck size?" Don Jorge and the other two charges chuckled. The merchant in the next stall was grinning.

"I think it is a fifteen and a half, Seester," I said. That was Papi's neck size. He kept it and other sizes written down in a little memo notebook inside our dining-room closet. I'd peeked into it. I knew his sizes better than mine.

"Fifteen and a half?" Sister said. "That's impossible. I'm almost tempted to suspect you of lying, young man. Just look at your neck." I tried but I couldn't. "You're not a fifteen and a half. You're more like a five and a half. Isn't that what you meant?" She was trying to save face for me in front of Don Jorge and the others; so I nodded. Don Jorge was still smiling; so was the other merchant, and Almendras, and the other charge, someone named Macario something. I couldn't remember his last name just then. I didn't want to.

"That is okay, Sister," Don Jorge cut in. "I take care of it no trouble. I know from the experience long the sizes right." He disappeared behind the counter again and came up with a tape measure. It was long and yellow, a huge tapeworm that looked to be coming apart from years of use; so maybe I wasn't the only ignorant customer Don Jorge had ever had. "Here, Sister," he said, "you take the size from the neck of my friend Malánguez over here, and I will pull out for him the shirt. I will bet to you that it is a six, no?"

"I don't gamble, Mr. Mercado," she said, frowning at his familiarity, and took the tape measure from him with a look of disgust.

"Anyway, Sister," he went on, "if Jorge Mercado is wrong, he will give to you a free cruficixion claps. And if you are the one who is all wrong, I don't charge extra."

"It's *cruci-fix*, Mr. Mercado," she corrected. "And *clasp*. *Claps* is a   46
verb, sir. Third person singular."

"That is what I say, Sister," he said, winking at the rest of us. I   47
didn't like people pulling our nuns' legs, and pretended not to
understand his prank.

She ringed the tapeworm around my neck and stooped to squint   48
at the answer. For a second there I thought she might decide to
choke me with that thing, and just then I couldn't blame her. "It's
more than five and a half and less than six," she told Don Jorge,
changing her mind about choking me.

"What kind of size that is?" Almendras asked Macario Some-   49
thing. His own neck was fat, too much starch in his diet. Rice and
beans for breakfast, lunch, and dinner. He was one of those who
went home for lunch and missed out on the peanut butter sandwiches, cold macaroni and cheese, and green apples the rest of us
were treated to most of the time.

"I don't split the hairs," Don Jorge was telling Sister. "I will give   50
to you one free crufixion for the tie."

"As you wish," she told him, unsmiling. But I think she was   51
pleased by his generosity; and he for his part was ensuring himself
of more First Communion business from her and the other nuns.
A shrewd merchant.

The other items Sister bought us—the red-ribbon armband, the   52
white socks, the belts with the cardboard lining—were no problem.
The socks were the nylon stretch-hose type, the armbands, like the
knotted ties, were all the same size, and the tape measure took care
of our waists. We measured those ourselves.

The complete purchase must have come to over fifteen dollars,   53
a lot of money to be spending on us. She pulled her purse out of
her placket and pulled two fives and a ten out of the purse and
handed them to Don Jorge, who gave her her change back, while
Almendras, Macario, and I looked at each other in amazement: all
that money changing hands for our benefit.

"Come back again fast, Seester," Don Jorge said, handing her   54
three boxes, each box neatly tied with blue string.

She thanked him, he thanked her back and said any time, and   55
then she told him she'd see him next day at the same time. "I have
six other boys just like these three,"she said, making us sound like
her sons, and probably thinking of us as sons of a sort.

She handed each of us his gift box. My hands were shaking and I dropped mine, right there on the dirty Marqueta floor, among crushed vegetables and all kinds of garbage. She didn't say any - thing; nobody did. She just stood over me, looking down at me, while I stooped and quickly picked up the box. I was afraid to look her in the eye, and didn't. The ground was the only place fit for my stare just then. And she didn't say a thing to me, to any of us, on our way to the exit, or out on the street; nor did we say anything to her or to each other—a very solemn exit—until we got to the corner of 107th and Park, where I was going to make a right turn toward my block.

"Get your correct suit size and shoe size from your mother, Santos Malánguez," she told me.

"Yes, Seester," I said. Another surprise coming. I was afraid to ask her why, but I could guess.

"You too, Almendras," she said. "And you, Macario Iglesias." So that was his last name. Macario "Churches," in translation. A future priest, it turned out.

Almendras couldn't control himself. "For why, Sister?"

"You mean *what for,* young man." A stickler for correctness. "Because we're not finished shopping for your outfits. This was only the first stage of our purchase. Next week we shop for suits and shoes." No comment, only looks of additional amazement exchanged by Almendras, Iglesias, and Malánguez.

"Well, Malánguez," she said, "take good care of that outfit. You'll look fine in it, I'm sure. Don't dawdle on the way home." They actually used words like that. Sometimes they even said "tarry." "And don't be tardy for Mass tomorrow morning."

Of course not. When had I ever been? She knew I knew what was good for me. I told her I wouldn't be, and thanked her for Part One of the outfit.

"You're welcome. And don't forget to ask your mother for those *sizes.*" Now she was rubbing it in about my neck again. I said I wouldn't, and made a quick turn toward my block, forgetting to say goodbye to Almedras and Iglesias, who would be walking with her for a couple more blocks. Her bodyguards, though she didn't need any protection. Nobody started trouble with our nuns, at least not before the drug pushers and their customers entered our neighborhood like the great Medieval plague she had told us about during our history period.

CONTENT

1. How does the opening line of "First Communion" prepare us for the two incidents which Rivera narrates? How is the mixed attitude of the nun, Sister Felicia, revealed in the clothes-buying episode? Cite examples.
2. Why does Rivera mention that the nuns were Irish? Why is the usher called Gino? Why is the nun correcting their English, as well as the English of the merchant who sells them the communion outfits? What is the attitude of the older residents of New York City toward the newly arrived Puerto Ricans?
3. Explain the irony in the names Rivera chooses: Saint Miseria, Sister Felicia, Sister Mary Monitor, Jorge Mercado.
4. What is Malánguez' economic status? What kinds of incidents force on him an awareness of his poverty? How do the cheap clothes illustrate the frustration of the poor over never being able to get ahead?

ORGANIZATION

5. Why does Rivera interrupt a narrative about shopping for communion clothes with a separate story involving Marta Cuevas? How does it help reinforce his point?
6. Within the Marta Cuevas episode, why does Rivera use a flashback to another incident about friction? How does this other incident establish the nun's attitude toward the members of the class?

TOPICS FOR WRITING

7. Recreate an embarrassing incident from your early school days which involves either you, or someone else in your class. Show how the teacher's handling of the incident revealed his or her real attitude toward you or the other student.
8. Tell about an incident from your past which you feared would have an unpleasant outcome, but instead were surprised to find had a pleasant conclusion.

ROGER WILKINS
Confessions of a Blue-Chip Black

Roger Wilkins received his doctorate in law from Central Michigan University in 1974. In Washington, he worked as a special assistant administrator to AID, assistant U.S. Attorney General, program director for the Ford Foundation, and staff writer for the Washington Post. *He was a columnist for* The New York Times *from 1977 to 1979. In this selection, adapted from his autobiography* A Man's Life *(1982), Wilkins explains the disadvantages of being a black raised in white surroundings.*

Early in the spring of 1932—six months after Earl's brother, Roy, 1 left Kansas City to go to New York to join the national staff of the National Association for the Advancement of Colored People, and eight months before Franklin Roosevelt was elected president for the first time—Earl and Helen Wilkins had the first and only child to be born of their union. I was born in a little segregated hospital in Kansas City called Phillis Wheatley. The first time my mother saw me, she cried. My head was too long and my color, she thought, was blue.

My parents never talked about slavery or my ancestors. Images 2 of Africa were images of backwardness and savagery. Once, when I was a little boy, I said to my mother after a friend of my parents left the house: "Mr. Bledsoe is black, isn't he, mama."

"Oh," she exclaimed. "Never say anybody is black. That's a ter- 3 rible thing to say."

Next time Mr. Bledsoe came to the house, I commented, "Mama, 4 Mr. Bledsoe is navy blue."

When I was two years old and my father was in the tuberculosis 5 sanitarium, he wrote me a letter, which I obviously couldn't read, but which tells a lot about how he planned to raise his Negro son.

Friday, March 22, 1934

Dear Roger—

Let me congratulate you upon having reached your second birthday. Your 6 *infancy is now past and it is now that you should begin to turn your thoughts upon those achievements which are expected of a brilliant young gentleman well on his way to manhood.*

During the next year, you should learn the alphabet; you should learn 7 *certain French and English idioms which are a part of every cultivated person's vocabulary: you should gain complete control of those natural functions which, uncontrolled, are a source of worry and embarrassment to even the best of grandmothers: you should learn how to handle table silver so that you will be able to eat gracefully and conventionally: and you should learn the fundamental rules of social living—politeness, courtesy, consideration for others, and the rest.*

This should not be difficult for you. You have the best and most patient of mothers in your sterling grandmother and your excellent mother. Great things are expected of you. Never, never forget that.   8

Love,
Your Father

We lived in a neat little stucco house on a hill in a small Negro   9
section called Roundtop. I had no sense of being poor or of any anxiety about money. At our house, not only was there food and furniture and all the rest, there was even a baby grand piano that my mother would play sometimes. And there was a cleaning lady, Mrs. Turner, who came every week.

When it was time for me to go to school, the board of education   10
provided us with a big yellow bus, which carried us past four or five perfectly fine schools down to the middle of the large Negro community, to a very old school called Crispus Attucks. I have no memories of those bus rides except for my resentment of the self-ishness of the whites who wouldn't let us share those newer-look-ing schools near to home.

My father came home when I was four and died when I was   11
almost nine. He exuded authority. He thought the women hadn't been sufficiently firm with me, so he instituted a spanking program with that same hard hairbrush that my grandmother had used so much to try to insure that I didn't have "nigger-looking" hair.

After my father's death, the family moved to New York. Our   12
apartment was in that legendary uptown area called Sugar Hill, where blacks who had it made were said to live the sweet life. I lived with my mother, my grandmother, and my mother's younger sister, Zelma. My Uncle Roy and his wife, Minnie, a New York social worker, lived on the same floor. My Aunt Marvel and her husband, Cecil, lived one floor down.

As life in New York settled into a routine, my life came to be   13
dominated by four women: my mother, her sisters, and her mother. Nobody else had any children, so everybody concentrated on me.

* * *

Sometime early in 1943 my mother's work with the YMCA took her to Grand Rapids, Michigan, where she made a speech and met a forty-four-year-old bachelor doctor who looked like a white man. He had light skin, green eyes, and "good hair"—that is, hair that was as straight and as flat as white people's hair. He looked so like a white person that he could have passed for white. There was much talk about people who had passed. They were generally deemed to be bad people, for they were not simply selfish, but also cruel to those whom they left behind. On the other hand, people who could pass, but did not, were respected.

My mother remarried in October 1943, and soon I was once more on a train with my grandmother, heading toward Grand Rapids and my new home. This train also took me, at the age of twelve, beyond the last point in my life when I would feel totally at peace with my blackness.

My new home was in the north end of Grand Rapids, a completely white neighborhood. This would be the place I would henceforth think of as home. And it would be the place where I would become more Midwesterner than Harlemite, more American than black, and more complex than was comfortable or necessary for the middle-class conformity that my mother had in mind for me.

Grand Rapids was pretty single-family houses and green spaces. The houses looked like those in *Look* magazine or in *Life*. You could believe, and I did, that there was happiness inside. To me, back then, the people seemed to belong to the houses as the houses belonged to the land, and all of it had to do with being white. They moved and walked and talked as if the place, the country, and the houses were theirs, and I envied them.

I spent the first few weeks exploring Grand Rapids on a new bike my stepfather had bought for me. The people I passed would look back at me with intense and sometimes puzzled looks on their faces as I pedaled by. Nobody waved or even smiled. They just stopped what they were doing to stand and look. As soon as I saw them looking, I would look forward and keep on riding.

One day I rode for miles, down and up and down again. I was past Grand Rapids' squatty little downtown, and farther south until I began to see some Negro people. There were black men and women and some girls, but it was the boys I was looking for. Then I saw a group: four of them. They were about my age, and they were dark. Though their clothes were not as sharp as the boys' in the Harlem Valley, they were old, and I took the look of poverty and the deep darkness of their faces to mean that they were like the hard boys of Harlem.

One of them spotted me riding toward them and pointed. "Hey, lookit that bigole skinny bike," he said. Then they all looked at my bike and at me. I couldn't see expressions on their faces; only the blackness and the coarseness of their clothes. Before any of the rest of them had a chance to say anything, I stood up on the pedals and wheeled the bike in a U-turn and headed back on up toward the north end of town. It took miles for the terror to finally subside.   20

Farther on toward home, there was a large athletic field. As I neared the field, I could see some large boys in shorts moving determinedly around a football. When I got to the top of the hill that overlooked the field, I stopped and stood, one foot on the ground and one leg hanging over the crossbar, staring down at them. All the boys were white and big and old—sixteen to eighteen. I had never seen a football workout before, and I was fascinated. I completely forgot everything about color, theirs or mine.   21

Then one of them saw me. He pointed and said, "Look, there's the little coon watchin us."   22

I wanted to be invisible. I was horrified. My heart pounded, and my arms and my legs shook, but I managed to get back on my bike and ride home.   23

The first white friend I made was named Jerry Schild. On the second day of our acquaintance, he took me to his house, above a store run by his parents. I met his three younger siblings, including a very little one toddling around in bare feet and a soiled diaper.   24

While Jerry changed the baby, I looked around the place. It was cheap, all chintz and linoleum. The two soft pieces of furniture, a couch and an overstuffed chair, had gaping holes and were hemorrhaging their fillings. And there were an awful lot of empty brown beer bottles sitting around, both in the kitchen and out on the back porch. While the place was not dirty, it made me very sad. Jerry and his family were poor in a way I had never seen people be poor before, in Kansas City or even in Harlem.   25

Jerry's father wasn't there that day and Jerry didn't mention him. But later in the week, when I went to call for Jerry, I saw him. I   26 yelled for Jerry from downstairs in the back and his father came to the railing of the porch on the second floor. He was a skinny man in overalls with the bib hanging down crookedly because it was fastened only on the shoulder. His face was narrow and wrinkled and his eyes were set deep in dark hollows. He had a beer bottle in his hand and he looked down at me. "Jerry ain't here," he said. He turned away and went back inside.

One day our front doorbell rang and I could hear my mother's troubled exclamation, "Jerry! What's wrong?" Jerry was crying so hard he could hardly talk. "My father says I can't play with you anymore because you're not good enough for us."

Creston High School, which served all the children from the north end of Grand Rapids, was all white and middle-class. Nobody talked to me that first day, but I was noticed. When I left school at the end of the day I found my bike leaning up against the fence where I had left it, with a huge glob of slimy spit on my shaggy saddle cover. People passed by on their way home and looked at me and spit. I felt a hollowness behind my eyes, but I didn't cry. I just got on the bike, stood up on the pedals, and rode it home without sitting down. And it went that way for about the first two weeks. After the third day, I got rid of the saddle cover because the plain leather was a lot easier to clean.

But the glacier began to thaw. One day in class, the freckle-faced kid with the crewcut sitting next to me was asking everybody for a pencil. And then he looked at me and said, "Maybe you can lend me one." Those were the best words I had heard since I first met Jerry. This kid had included me in the human race in front of everybody. His name was Jack Waltz.

And after a while when the spitters had subsided and I could ride home sitting down, I began to notice that little kids my size were playing pickup games in the end zones of the football field. It looked interesting, but I didn't know anybody and didn't know how they would respond to me. So I just rode on by for a couple of weeks, slowing down each day, trying to screw up my courage to go in.

But then one day, I saw Jack Waltz there. I stood around the edges of the group watching. It seemed that they played forever without even noticing me, but finally someone had to go home and the sides were unbalanced. Somebody said, "Let's ask him."

As we lined up for our first huddle, I heard somebody on the   32
other side say, "I hope he doesn't have a knife." One of the guys on
my side asked me, "Can you run the ball?" I said yes, so they gave
me the ball and I ran three quarters of the length of the field for a
touchdown. And I made other touchdowns and other long runs
before the game was over. When I thought about it later that night,
I became certain that part of my success was due to the imaginary
knife that was running interference for me. But no matter. By the
end of the game, I had a group of friends. Boys named Andy and
Don and Bill and Gene and Rich. We left the field together and
some of them waved and yelled, "See ya tomorra, Rog."

And Don De Young, a peasant round-faced boy, even lived quite   33
near me. So, after parting from everybody else, he and I went on
together down to the corner of Coit and Knapp. As we parted, he
suggested that we meet to go to school together the next day. I had
longed for that but I hadn't suggested it for fear of a rebuff for
overstepping the limits of my race. I had already leaned one of the
great tenets of Negro survival in America: to live the reactive life.
It was like the old Negro comedian who once said, "When the man
asks how the weather is, I know nuff to look keerful at his face 'fore
even I look out the window." So, I waited for him to suggest it, and
my patience was rewarded. I was overjoyed and grateful.

I didn't spend all my time in the north end. Soon after I moved   34
to Grand Rapids, Pop introduced me to some patients he had with
a son my age. The boy's name was Lloyd Brown, and his father was
a bellman downtown at the Pantlind Hotel. Lloyd and I often rode
bikes and played basketball in his backyard. After a while, my mother
asked me why I never had Lloyd come out to visit me. It was a
question I dreaded, but she pressed on. "After all," she said, "you've
had a lot of meals at his house and it's rude not to invite him back."
I knew she was right and I also hated the whole idea of it.

With my friends in the north, race was never mentioned. Ever.   35
I carried my race around with me like an open basket of rotten eggs.
I knew I could drop one at any moment and it would explode with
a stench over everything. This was in the days when the movies
either had no blacks at all or featured rank stereotypes like Stepin
Fetchit, and the popular magazines like *Life, Look,* the *Saturday Evening Post,* and *Colliers* carried no stories about Negroes, had no ads
depicting Negroes, and generally gave the impression that we did

not exist in this society. I knew that my white friends, being well brought up, were just too polite to mention this disability that I had. And I was grateful to them, but terrified, just the same, that maybe someday one of them would have the bad taste to notice what I was.

It seemed to me that my tenuous purchase in this larger white world depended on the maintenance between me and my friends in the north end of our unspoken bargain to ignore my difference, my shame, and their embarrassment. If none of us had to deal with it, I thought, we could all handle it. My white friends behaved as if they perceived the bargain exactly as I did. It was a delicate equation, and I was terrified that Lloyd's presence in the North End would rip apart the balance.

I am so ashamed of that shame now that I cringe when I write it. But I understand that boy now as he could not understand himself then. I was an American boy, though I did not fully comprehend that either. I was fully shaped and formed by America, where white people had all the power in sight, and they owned everything in sight except our house. Their beauty was the real beauty; there wasn't any other beauty. A real human being had straight hair, a white face, and thin lips. Other people, who looked different, were lesser beings.

No wonder, then, that most black men desired the forbidden fruit of white loins. No wonder, too, that we thought that the most beautiful and worthy Negro people were those who looked most white. We blacks used to have a saying: "If you're white, you're all right. If you're brown, stick around. If you're black, stand back." I was brown.

It was not that we in my family were direct victims of racism. On the contrary, my stepfather clearly had a higher income than the parents of most students in my high school. Unlike those of most my contemporaries, black and white, my parents had college degrees. Within Grand Rapids' tiny Negro community, they were among the elite. The others were the lawyer, the dentist, the undertaker, and the other doctor.

But that is what made race such exquisite agony. I did have a sense that it was unfair for poor Negroes to be relegated to bad jobs—if they had jobs at all—and to bad or miserable housing, but I didn't feel any great sense of identity with them. After all, the poor blacks in New York had also been the hard ones: the ones who tried to take my money, to beat me up, and to keep me perpetually intimidated. Besides, I had heard it intimated around my house that their behavior, sexual or otherwise, left a good deal to be desired.

So I thought that maybe they just weren't ready for this society, but that I was. And it was dreadfully unfair for white people to just look at my face and lips and hair and decide that I was inferior. By being a model student and leader, I thought I was demonstrating how well Negroes could perform if only the handicaps were removed and they were given a chance. But deep down I guess I was also trying to demonstrate that I was not like those other people; that I was different. My message was quite clear: I was *not nigger.* But the world didn't seem quite ready to make such fine distinctions, and it was precisely that fact—though at the time I could scarcely even have admitted it to myself—that was the nub of the race issue for me.

I would sometimes lie on my back and stare up at passing clouds and wonder why God had played a dirty trick by making me a Negro. It all seemed so random. So unfair to me. To *me!* But in school I was gaining more friends, and the teachers respected me. It got so that I could go for days not thinking very much about being Negro, until something made the problem unavoidable.

One day in history class, for instance, the teacher asked each of us to stand and tell in turn where our families had originated. Many of the kids in the class were Dutch with names like Vander Jagt, De Young, and Ripstra. My pal Andy was Scots-Irish. When it came my turn, I stood up and burned with shame and when I would speak, I lied. And then I was even more ashamed because I exposed a deeper shame. "Some of my family was English," I said—Wilkins is an English name—"and the rest of it came from . . . Egypt." Egypt!

One Saturday evening after one of our sandlot games, I went over to Lloyd's. Hearing my stories, Lloyd said mildly that he'd like to come up and play some Saturday. I kept on talking, but all the time my mind was repeating: "Lloyd wants to play. He wants to come up to the North End on Saturday. Next Saturday. Next Saturday." I was trapped.

So, after the final story about the final lunge, when I couldn't put it off any longer, I said, "Sure. Why not?" But, later in the evening, after I had had some time to think, I got Lloyd alone. "Say, look," I said. "Those teams are kinda close, ya know. I mean, we don't switch around. From team to team. Or new guys, ya know?"

Lloyd nodded, but he was getting a funny look on his face . . .   4ɛ
part unbelieving and part hurt. So I quickly interjected before he
could say anything, "Naw, man. Naw. Not like you shouldn't come
and play. Just that we gotta have some good reason for you to play
on our team, you dig?"

"Yeah," Lloyd said, his face still puzzled, but no longer hurt.   47

"Hey, I know," I said. "I got it. We'll say you're my cousin. If   48
you're my cousin, see, then you gotta play. Nobody can say you
can't be on my team, because you're family, right?"

"Oh, right. Okay," Lloyd said, his face brightening. "Sure, we'll   49
say we're cousins. Solid."

I felt relieved as well. I could have a Negro cousin. It wasn't   50
voluntary. It wouldn't be as if I had gone out and made a Negro
friend deliberately. A person couldn't help who his cousins were.

There began to be a cultural difference between me and other   51
blacks my age too. Black street language had evolved since my
Harlem days, and I had not kept pace. Customs, attitudes, and the
other common social currencies of everyday black life had evolved
away from me. I didn't know how to talk, to banter, to move my
body. If I was tentative and responsive in the North End, where I
lived, I was tense, stiff, and awkward when I was with my black
contemporaries. One day I was standing outside the church trying,
probably at my mother's urging, to make contact. Conversational
sallies flew around me while I stood there stiff and mute, unable
to participate. Because the language was so foreign to me, I understood little of what was being said, but I did know that the word
used for a white was *paddy*. Then a boy named Nickerson, the one
whom my mother particularly wanted me to be friends with, inclined
his head slightly toward me and said, to whoops of laughter, "technicolor paddy." My feet felt rooted in stone, and my head was aflame.
I never forgot that phrase.

I have rarely felt so alone as I did that day riding home from   52
church. Already partly excluded by my white friends, I was now
almost completely alienated from my own people as well. But I felt
less uncomfortable and less vulnerable in the white part of town.
It was familiar enough to enable me to ward off most unpleasantness.

And then there was the problem of girls. They were everywhere,   53
the girls. They all had budding bosoms, they all smelled pink, they
all brushed against the boys in the hall, they were all white, and,
in 1947–49, they were all inaccessible.

There were some things you knew without ever knowing how 54
you knew them. You knew that Mississippi was evil and dangerous,
that New York was east, and the Pacific ocean was west. And in the
same way you knew that white women were the most desirable and
dangerous objects in the world. Blacks were lynched in Mississippi
and such places sometimes just for looking with the wrong expression at white women. Blacks of a very young age knew that white
women of any quality went with the power and style that went
with the governance of America—though, God knows, we had so
much self-hate that when a white woman went with a Negro man,
we promptly decided she was trash, and we also figured that if she
would go with him she would go with any Negro.

Nevertheless, as my groin throbbed at fifteen and sixteen and 55
seventeen, *they* were often the only ones there. One of them would
be in the hallway opening her locker next to mine. Her blue sweater
sleeve would be pushed up to just below the elbow, and as she
would reach high on a shelf to stash away a book, I would see the
tender dark hair against the white skin of her forearm. And I would
ache and want to touch that arm and follow that body hair to its
source.

Some of my friends, of course, did touch some of those girls. 56
My friends and I would talk about athletics and school and their
loves. But they wouldn't say a word about the dances and the hay-
rides they went to.

I perceived they liked me and accepted me as long as I moved 57
aside when life's currents took them to where I wasn't supposed to
be. I fit into their ways when they talked about girls, even their
personal girls. And, indeed, I fit into the girls' lives when they were
talking about boys, most particularly their own personal boys.
Because I was a boy, I had insight. But I was also Negro, and therefore a neuter. So a girl who was alive and sensuous night after night
in my fantasies would come to me earnestly in the day and talk
about Rich or Gene or Andy. She would ask what he thought about
her, whether he liked to dance, whether, if she invited him to her
house for a party, he would come. She would tell me her fears and
her yearnings, never dreaming for an instant that I had yearnings
too and that she was their object.

There may be few more powerful obsessions than a teenage boy's 58
fixation on a love object. In my case it came down to a thin brunette
named Marge McDowell. She was half a grade behind me, and she

lived in a small house on a hill. I found excuses to drive by it all the time. I knew her schedule at school, so I could manage to be in most of the hallways she had to use going from class to class. We knew each other, and she had once confided a strong but fleeting yearning for my friend Rich Kippen. I thought about her constantly.

Finally, late one afternoon after school, I came upon her alone in a hallway. "Marge," I blurted, "can I ask you something?" 59

She stopped and smiled and said, "Sure, Roger, what?" 60

"Well I was wondering," I said. "I mean. Well, would you go to 61 the hayride next week with me."

Her jaw dropped and her eyes got huge. Then she uttered a small 62 shriek and turned, hugging her books to her bosom the way girls do, and fled. I writhed with mortification in my bed that night and for many nights after.

In my senior year, I was elected president of the Creston High 63 School student council. It was a breakthrough of sorts.

CONTENT

1. Why does Wilkins mention the different moves his family made? How do varied neighborhoods affect his consciousness of his race?

2. Look up the name of the first school Wilkins attended. Who is the school named after? Is there an irony in the cultural identification of the school?

3. Why does Wilkins' stepfather introduce him to the son of a black friend? How does this friendship prove awkward?

4. What is Wilkins' position with his white classmates? Does he want to belong or is he indifferent to their attitudes? What sexual problems arise from the taboo about interracial relations?

ORGANIZATION

5. As in most autobiographies the presentation of the chief facts of Wilkins' life are in chronological order. Why does Wilkins skip large time frames to concentrate chiefly on his relationship with his contemporaries?

6. Each narrative portion seems to have a conclusion of its own. Point out where the separate portions of Wilkins' narrative occur, and what point he draws from each of them. Is there a clear progression from each narrative portion of the autobiography?

TOPICS FOR WRITING

7. Read Eldridge Cleaver's "The Allegory of the Black Eunuchs" in *Soul on Ice* and compare the account of Wilkins' sexual frustration with the analysis of miscegenation presented by Cleaver.
8. Write an account of an attempt to fit into a group that rejected you for reasons you did not understand.

EDWARD HOAGLAND
City Rat

Born in New York City in 1932, Edward Hoagland was educated at Harvard. Hoagland's essays have been collected in several volumes, among them The Courage of Turtles *(1971),* Red Wolves and Black Bears *(1976), and* The Tugman's Passage *(1982). Taken from* Walking the Dead Diamond River *(1973), "City Rat" describes the survival instincts that keep native New Yorkers walking just a half step faster than most people.*

Delightedly, I used to cross Park Avenue wearing an undershirt 1 on my way to digs far to the south and east. I could remember waiting, as a boy of eight, on almost the same street corner for the St. Bernard's school bus in a proper tweed blazer, striped tie and shiny shoes, and so this gulf between costumes seemed sweet. Sweaty, bare-shouldered, strolling the summer streets, I felt my class or creed unidentifiable, which very much pleased me. Physically I was in my prime, I liked to jog, and, long and loose like a runner, though still smooth-faced, I felt as if I were a thousand miles and a whole world away from that small boy. I'd sit around on door stoops after a walk of eighty blocks or so, up from the Battery or down from Yankee Stadium, and watch the world go by. If I'd been an out-of-towner, awed by the city, these walks would have been ideal for adjusting. Wherever I ran out of steam, I'd sit, keeping an eye peeled, and try to pretend that this was now my territory and I must figure it out quickly. It should be remembered that fifteen years ago violence in New York City was fairly well contained within a framework of teenage gangs attacking other gangs, not wayfarers; Negro bitterness bore down mainly on other Negroes, and though sometimes the Mafia in Brooklyn dumped a body on Avenue D, the Lower East Side itself and other such areas were quite peaceful.

I was in the theater district once, sitting on a stoop, enjoying the stream of life, when a brisk, well-preserved man with custom-fitted pants, a cane and good coloring halted in front of me. "Young man," he said abruptly, "are you trying to break into the theater?" Aware that it was a funny question, he raised his eyebrows while he waited, as if I'd been the one who'd asked. I was holding my knees and looking up at him. He tapped my feet with the point of his cane as though he were buying me and I was supposed to stand.

I was too nervous to answer. Superciliously he stared at me. "You'd better come along. There are a great many young men trying to get into the theater. I'm in the theater." He tapped me again. I still didn't trust myself to speak, and he glanced at my Army boots, laughed and said, "Are you a paratrooper? Come now, last chance, young man. Fame and fortune. There are a great many of you and one of me. What's going to set you apart?"

My embarrassed silence made him uncomfortable, as well as the possibility that somebody might recognize him standing there in this peculiar conversation. As he left, he called back, "Good luck, little friend, whoever you are." But I grinned more confidently at him as he got farther off, because a couple of months before I'd had my picture in *Time* as a blazing new author; perhaps he never had. That was the second fillip to wandering in my undershirt along Fifth or Park Avenue: the fact that on other days I'd be wearing a snaky gray flannel suit, slipping through the crowds in the sky-scraper district, and shooting up high in a building for a swank lunch. I wasn't really masquerading as a carpenter; on the contrary, I'd made no choices yet—I was enjoying being free.

Banging around on a motor scooter down the length of Manhattan by way of the waterfront, I'd unwind in the evening after writing all day. New York was compartmentalized; Harlem was in Harlem, and on Delancey Street there were live ducks for sale, and in a shop with big windows, shoemakers cutting soles for shoes. I looked at coming attractions under the various movie marquees and watched the traffic on the stairs to a second-floor whorehouse (sailors coming down and a cop going up). Since I was both bashful and lonely, I would leave notes on the bulletin boards of some of the coffeehouses—"Typist wanted "—then wait by the telephone.

The girls were under no illusions about what I was up to when they called, except that they usually did want some work out of the arrangement as well, and, unfairly enough, that's what I was reluctant to give. I kept my manuscripts in the refrigerator as a precaution against fire and was a nut about safeguarding them. Inevitably, then, the sort of girl who'd phone me blind and invite me over for a screw on the strength of a note I'd left in a coffeehouse was not a girl I'd trust my typing to.

One girl had a beachboy crouching naked on the floor painting her bathtub red when I arrived; the rest of the apartment was a deep black. Another, on Houston Street, immediately embraced me with her head swathed in bandages from the blows that her husband had bestowed the night before. Pulling the bookcases over, he'd strewn the books around, broken all the china and announced he was leaving. Nothing had been picked up since. The baby, only a year old, cried desperately in the playpen, and though his mother naturally hoped I would be able to step right into the father's role and comfort him, I wasn't that skillful. A window was broken, so it was cold. She took me to the bedroom, moaning, "Hit me! Hit me!" When things there didn't work out she led me downstairs to a kind of commune, introduced me around and announced to the members that I was impotent.

Still, I was busy, once sleeping with three different women in as many days, and covering the city better than most news reporters, it seemed to me, recognizing innumerable street nooks and faces which epitomized New York for me. Perhaps the air was rather sooty, but it didn't cause headaches or give people bleeding throats. Now I sometimes spit blood in the morning and feel raw sulfur in my gullet from breathing the air; in midtown or around Canal Street I breathe through my teeth like a survivalist who specializes in outlasting Black Lung. This morning when I went out to buy milk for breakfast I saw a clump of police cars and a yellow car which had slid out of the traffic and come to rest against the curb, empty except for a gray-looking dead man in his thirties slumped sideways against the wheel. I stood rubbernecking next to the delicatessen owner. One night last year I'd stood in a crowd and watched most of the building that houses his store burn to a shell, all of us—he wasn't there—as silent and spellbound as if we were witnessing public copulation. Though he is not a friendly man, I like his Greek bluntness and at the time I'd felt guilty to be watching as a mere spectacle what was a catastrophe for him. But here he was, rubbernecking at this fellow's death just like me, only less solemnly; he chuckled, shaking his head. I kept a straight face and felt a pang, but while I crossed the street with the groceries and rode up in the elevator the incident entirely slipped my mind; I didn't even mention it when I got home.

Such imperviousness is a result of changes in the city as well as   8
in me. If I have lost my bloom, so has the city, more drastically. Among the beggars who approach me, almost weekly I see a mugger who is clearly screwing up his nerve to do more than just *ask* for money. I have the New Yorker's quick-hunch posture for broken-field maneuvering, and he swerves away. A minute later, with pounding feet, there he goes, clutching a purse, with a young woman in forlorn pursuit. Recently, riding in a bus, I saw a policeman with his gun drawn and his free hand stretched out tiptoe hastily after a suspect through a crowd and make the nab as the bus pulled away. It's not any single event, it's the cumulative number of them—shouted arguments, funerals, playground contretemps, drivers leaning on their horns, adults in tears, bums falling down and hitting their heads, young men in triumph over a business deal—that one sees in the course of a midday walk which veneers one with callousness.

We each work out a system of living in the city. With music, for   9
instance, I put trumpet voluntaries on the phonograph in the morning, organ fugues after supper, and whale songs or wolf howls in the silence at night. I go to a Village bar which is like a club, with the same faces in it day after day, although as a hangout it does acquire a tannic-acid taste if you go too often because most of the people are divorced or on that road. The newspapermen see it as belonging to them; hungry poets and movie novelists view it as a literary saloon; the seamen, photographers, carpenters, folk singers, young real-estate impresarios, political lawyers, old union organizers and Lincoln Brigade veterans all individually believe it's theirs.

I'm tired of Washington Square, Tompkins Square Park, Abing-   10
don Square, even Central Park (I lived next to it for several years and found it to be ground as overused as the banks of the Ganges are). And the last time my wife and I picnicked in Van Cortlandt Park, which is more countrified, we needed to cut at top speed through the woods to escape two men who were stalking us. Space

is important to me, and each of these public resting spots has its own character and defines a particular period for me. In the early sixties I was in Washington Square, watching among other things, the early stirrings of Negro belligerence, still indirect. It seemed to take the form of their ballplaying, sometimes one man alone, throwing a rubber ball as high as he could and catching it on the second or third bounce. They were lanky, like men just out of the army or prison, and when they played catch they loped all over the park, taking possession everywhere. Already they had secret handshakes and contemptuous expressions, and this gobbling up the whole park with their legs and lofting a rubber ball into the stratosphere bespoke the blocked energy, the screened anger that would soon explode. The explosion is past; new developments are brewing in these parks, but I am fatigued with watching.

The Chinese laundryman we go to is mean of heart and keeps   11
his children home from school to iron for him while he loafs. The two girls next to us are sleeping with the super, and sit in triumph while their apartment is painted, as a consequence. Perhaps he sleeps well, but I'm almost sleepless from fighting with my wife. And there are explosions going off nightly down in the street. I have no idea what they are; years ago I would have thought just firecrackers. New York is a city of the old and young, and looking out the window, I sometimes see old people fall. One has cancer of the mouth. When he feels well he sits outside the barber shop or in the park, not looking up, withdrawn into his memories, but seeming tranquil there; certainly nobody enjoys the sunshine more. But the next day when you walk past he is sitting quietly hemorrhaging into his handkerchief, looking at it fearfully, then boosting himself off the bench to go back to the nursing home.

In the apartment on the other side of us are two young men who   12
entertain a lot, and one day somebody leaned out their window with a rifle equipped with a spotting scope, searching the courtyard and the street. I assumed it was a toy, but in any case I simply pulled down the blinds; one can't react to everything. We'd had a stink in the corridor the week before that gradually grew stronger. It was a really hideous smell, subterraneanly terrifying, and we and some of the neighbors began to wonder whether somebody might not have died. It was pervasive, hard to isolate, and we were all city procrastinators—with so many emergencies, so many lonely people, why get involved? At last, however, where our consciences

had failed, our noses got the better of us and we called the cops. It turned out to be a decomposing chicken which someone had defrosted before a trip and forgotten about. A month or so later the same putrid smell invaded our floor all over again. Holding our noses, we complained left and right, trying to ignore it. Even so, again the police had to be called. This time they found a young woman dead of an overdose of heroin, with her headband wrapped around her arm as a tourniquet and her cat still alive, having managed to subsist on her body fluids.

Year round, I keep my air conditioner on, its steady hum submerging the street sounds. But one of the neighbors upstairs, finding this noise, too, unnerving, has lent me a white-sound machine, an instrument which, like a sort of aural sun lamp, manufactures a sense of neutrality and well-being. Right now neutrality seems to be the first condition of peace; these devices have become commonplace. People are seeking to disengage, get out of town, or at least stay indoors and regale themselves with surfy sounds. The question everybody is asking is, Where does one live? New York is the action scene; one won't feel the kinesis of the 1970s in a Sicilian fishing village, and very few people are really quite ready to write all that off. Maybe the best of both worlds is to be a New Yorker outside New York. Anyway, I'm at my best as a traveler, and looking back when I am elderly, I may be fondest of some of my memories of hauling a suitcase along, grinning, questioning strangers, breathing the smoke of their wood fires, supported, although I was far from home, by the knowledge of where I'd come from. Arriving in Alaska, straight from New York, one feels tough as a badger, quick as a wolf. We New Yorkers see more death and violence than most soldiers do, grow a thick chitin on our backs, grimace like a rat and learn to do a disappearing act. Long ago we outgrew the need to be blow-hards about our masculinity; we leave that to the Alaskans and Texans, who have more time for it. We think and talk faster, we've seen and know more, and when my friends in Vermont (who are much wiser folk than Alaskans) kid me every fall because I clear out before the first heavy snow, I smile and don't tell them that they no longer know what being tough is.

Setting out from home for the landmark of the Empire State building, I arrive underneath it as a countryman might reach a nearby bluff, and push on to the lions at the public library, and St. Patrick's, and the fountain in front of the Plaza. Or in fifteen minutes I can take my two-year-old daughter to the Museum of Natural History, where, after waving good-by to the subway train, she strides inside, taking possession of the stuffed gorillas, antelopes, spiny anteaters, modeled Indian villages and birds and fish— the pre-twentieth-century world cooked down to some of its essentials. Six or seven puppet shows and several children's plays are being presented in the city this afternoon, and there are ships to watch, four full-scale zoos, and until recently goats, monkeys, chickens and ten horses were quartered on an eccentric half-acre a few blocks from our building. Just the city's lighted skyscrapers and bridges alone will be with my daughter forever if her first memories are like mine—she lies on her back looking upward out the window when we ride uptown in a taxi at night, with the lights opals and moons.

But is it worth the blood in the throat? Even when we go out on   15
a pier to watch the big ships, what comes blowing in is smudgy smoke instead of a clean whiff of the sea. For me it's as disquieting as if we had to drink right out of the Hudson; our lungs must be as calloused as the soles of our feet. Is it worth seeing a dead man before breakfast and forgetting him by the time one sits down to one's orange juice? Sometimes when I'm changing records at night I hear shrieks from the street, sounds that the phonograph ordinarily drowns out. My old boyhood dreams of playing counterspy have declined in real life to washing perfume off my face once in a blue moon when, meeting an old girlfriend in a bar, I get smooched, but I still have a trotting bounce to my walk, like a middle-aged coyote who lopes along avoiding the cougars and hedgehogs, though still feeling quite capable of snapping up rabbits and fawns. Lightness and strength in the legs is important to me; like the closed face, it's almost a must for the city. There's not a week when I don't think of leaving for good, living in a *house*, living in the West, perhaps, or a smaller town. I will never lose my New Yorker's grimace, New Yorker's squint and New Yorker's speed, but can't I live with them somewhere else?

CONTENT

1. Why does Hoagland call his essay "City Rat"? Does the conclusion of the essay support or contradict his choice of title?
2. New Yorkers are said to have a love–hate relationship with their city. Does this describe Hoagland's attitude toward New York?

How do Hoagland's attitudes compare with those of Gay Talese (page 226) and E. B. White (page 352)?

3. In spite of the negative examples of life in New York City, what does Hoagland find holds him there? Why does he still find life in the City exciting?

ORGANIZATION

4. Hoagland begins his autobiographical essay with a series of short narrative recollections. What do these recollections have in common?

5. Hoagland shifts tense from past to present several pages into the essay. Can you find the place where the shift takes place? What is the point of the change? Does this structuring device have an effect on the content of the essay?

TOPICS FOR WRITING

6. Read William Saroyan's "Places and People" (page 527) and write a comparison of his views on the influence of place on a person with those of Hoagland.

7. Write an autobiographical account of a place where you have lived. Include in it an event which gives a positive impression of the place and one event which gives a negative impression. Draw a conclusion in the account about your personal preference.

THOMAS McGUANE
Me and My Bike and Why

Thomas McGuane (born 1939) has written four novels, The Sporting Club *(1969),* The Bushwacked Piano *(1973), and* Panama *(1978). McGuane has been a special contributor to* Sports Illustrated *and his sports writing has been collected in the volume,* An Outside Chance: Essays on Sport *(1980). "Me and My Bike and Why" will strike a familiar chord in anyone who has (or who has wanted to) feel the speed and freedom of driving a motorcycle.*

Like many who buy a motorcycle, there had been for me the   1
problem of getting over the rather harrowing insurance statistics

as to just what it is that is liable to happen to you. Two years in California—a familiar prelude to acts of excess—had made me an active motorcycle spectator. I watched and identified, finally resorting to bikers' magazines; and evolved a series of foundationless prejudices.

Following the war, motorcycling left a peculiar image in the national 2 consciousness: porcine individuals wearing a sort of yachting cap with a white vinyl bill, the decorative braid pulled up over the hat, their motorcycles plated monsters, white rubber mud flaps studded with ruby stars hung from both fenders. Where are those machines now? Surely Andy Warhol can't have bought them all. Not every one of them is a decorative planter in a Michigan truck garden. But wherever they are, it is certain that the ghosts of cretinism collect close around the strenuously baroque plumbing of those inefficient engines and speak to us of an America that has gone.

It was easy for me initially to deplore the big road bikes, the 3 motorcycles of the police and Hell's Angels. But finally even these "hogs" and show bikes had their appeal, and sometimes I had dark fantasies of myself on El Camino Real, hands hung overhead from the big chopper bars, feet in front on weirdly automotive pedals, making all the decent people say: "There goes one."

I did it myself. Heading into San Francisco with my wife, our 4 Land Rover blaring wide open at 52 miles per, holding up a quarter mile of good people behind us, people who didn't see why anybody needed four-wheel drive on the Bayshore Freeway, we ourselves would from time to time see a lonesome Angel or Coffin Cheater or Satan's Slave or Gypsy Joker on his big chopper and say (either my wife or myself, together sometimes): "There goes one."

Anyway, it was somewhere along in here that I saw I was not 5 that type, and began to think of sporting machines, even racing machines, big ones, because I had no interest in starting small and working my way up as I had been urged to do. I remember that I told the writer Wallace Stegner what I intended, and he asked, "Why do you people do this when you come to California?"

"It's like skiing," I said, purely on speculation. 6

"Oh, yeah? What about the noise?" 7

But no one could stop me. 8

There was the dire question of money that ruled out many I saw. 9 The English-build Triumph Metisse road racer was out of the question, for example. Some of the classics I found and admired—Ariel

Square Fours, Vincent Black Shadows, BSA Gold Stars, Velocette Venoms or Phantom Clubmen, Norton Manxes—had to be eliminated on grounds of cost or outlandish maintenance problems.

Some of the stranger Japanese machinery, two-cycle, rotary-valved   10 engines, I dismissed because they sounded funny. The Kawasaki Samurai actually seemed refined, but I refused to consider it. I had a corrupt Western ideal of a bike's exhaust rap, and the tuned megaphone exhausts of the Japanese motorcycles sounded like something out of the next century, weird loon cries of Oriental speed tuning.

There is a blurred moment in my head, a scenario of compulsion.   11 I am in a motorcycle shop that is going out of business. I am writing a check that challenges the contents of my bank account. I am given ownership papers substantiated by the state of California, a crash helmet, and five gallons of fuel. Some minutes later I am standing beside my new motorcycle, sick all over. The man who sold it to me stares palely through the Thermopane window covered with the decals of the noble marques of "performance." He wonders why I have not moved.

I have not moved because I do not know what to do. I wish to   12 advance upon the machine with authority but cannot. He would not believe I could have bought a motorcycle of this power without knowing so much as how to start its engine. Presently he loses interest and looks for another tormented creature in need of a motorcycle.

Unwatched, I can really examine the bike. Since I have no notion   13 of how to operate it, it is purely an *objet*. I think of a friend with a road racer on a simple mahogany block in front of his fireplace, except that he rides his very well.

The bike was rather beautiful. I suppose it still is. The designa-   14 tion, which now seems too cryptic for my taste, was "Matchless 500," and it was the motorcycle I believed I had thought up myself. It is a trifle hard to describe the thing to the uninitiated, but, briefly, it had a 500-cc., one-cylinder engine—a "big single" in the patois of bike freaks—and an eloquently simple maroon teardrop-shaped tank that is as much the identifying mark on a Matchless, often otherwise unrecognizable through modification, as the chevron of a redwing blackbird. The front wheel, delicate as a bicycle's, carried a Dunlop K70 tire (said to "cling") and had no fender; a single cable led to the pale machined brake drum. Over the knobby rear wheel curved an extremely brief magnesium fender with, instead of the lush buddy-seat of the fat motorcycles, a minute pillion of leather. The impression was of performance and of complete disregard for comfort. The equivalent in automobiles would be, perhaps, the Morgan, in sailboats the Finn.

I saw all these things at once (remember the magazines I had been reading, the Floyd Clymer books I had checked out of the library), and in that sense my apprehension of the motorcycle was perfectly literary. I still didn't know how to start it. Suddenly it looked big and mean and vicious and no fun at all.   15

I didn't want to experiment on El Camino Real, and moreover, it had begun to rain heavily. I had made up my mind to wheel it home, and there to peruse the operation manual, whose infuriating British locutions the Land Rover manual had prepared me for.   16

I was surprised at the sheer inertial weight of the thing; it leaned toward me and pressed against my hip insistently all the way to the house. I was disturbed that a machine whose place in history seemed so familiar should look utterly foreign at close range. The fact that the last number on the speedometer was 140 seemed irresponsible.   17

It was dark by the time I got home. I wheeled it through the back gate and down the sidewalk through a yard turned largely to mud. About halfway to the kitchen door, I somehow got the thing tilted away from myself, and it slowly but quite determinedly toppled over in the mud, with me, gnashing, on top of it.   18

My wife came to the door and peered into the darkness. "Tom?" I refused to vouchsafe an answer. I lay there in the mud, no longer struggling, as the spring rains of the San Francisco peninsula singled me out for special treatment. I was already composing the ad in the *Chronicle* that motorcycle people dream of finding: "Big savings on Matchless 500. Never started by present owner. A real cream puff." My wife threw on the porch light and perceived my discomfiture.   19

The contretemps had the effect of quickly getting us over the surprise that I had bought the motorcycle, questions of authorization, and so on. I headed for the showers. Scraped and muddy, I had excited a certain amount of pity. "I'll be all right."   20

No one told me to retard the spark. True enough, it was in the manual, but I had been unable to read that attentively. It had no plot, no characters. So my punishment was this: when I jumped   21 on the kick starter, it backfired and more or less threw me off the bike. I was limping all through the first week from vicious blow-backs. I later learned it was a classic way to get a spiral fracture. I tried jumping lightly on the kick starter and, unfairly, it would blast back as viciously as with a sharp kick. Eventually it started, and sitting on it, I felt the torque tilt the bike under me. I was afraid to take my hands off the handlebars. My wife lowered the helmet onto my head; I compared it to the barber's basin Don Quixote had worn into battle, the Helmet of Mambrino.

I slipped my toe up under the gearshift lever, lifted it into first, released the clutch, and magically glided away and made all my shifts through fourth, at which time I was on Sand Hill Road and going 50, my shirt in a soft air bubble at my back, my Levi's wrapped tight to my shins, my knuckles whitening under the giddy surge of pure undetained motion as I climbed gently into the foothills toward Los Altos. The road got more and more winding as I ascended, briskly but conservatively. Nothing in the air was lost on me as I passed through zones of smell and temperature as palpable transitions, running through sudden warm spots on the road where a single redwood 100 feet away had fallen and let in a shaft of sunlight. The road seemed tremendously spacious. The sound was behind me, so that when I came spiraling down out of the mountains and saw some farm boy had walked out to the side of the road to watch me go by, I realized he had heard me coming for a long time. And I wondered a little about the racket.

These rides became habitual and presumably more competent. I often rode up past La Honda for a view of the sea at the far edge of a declining cascade of manzanita-covered hills, empty and foggy. The smell of ocean was so perfectly evocative in a landscape divided among ranches and truck gardens whose pumpkins in the foggy air seemed to have an uncanny brilliance. A Japanese nursery stood along the road in clouds of tended vines on silver redwood lattice. I went past it to the sea and before riding home took a long walk on the ribbed, immense beach.

A fascinating aspect of the pursuit, not in the least bucolic, was the bike shop where one went for mechanical service, and which was a meeting place for the bike people, whose machines were poised out front in carefully conceived rest positions. At first, of course, no one would talk to me, but my motorcycle ideas were theirs; I was not riding one of the silly mechanisms that purred down the highways in a parody of the equipment these people lived for.

One day an admired racing mechanic—"a good wrench"—came out front and gave my admittedly well-cared-for Matchless the once-over. He announced that it was "very sanitary." I was relieved. The fear, of course, is that he will tell you, "The bike is wrong."

"Thank you," I said modestly. He professed himself an admirer of the "Matchbox," saying it was "fairly rapid" and had enough torque to "pull stumps." Ultimately, I was taken in, treated kindly, and given the opportunity to ride some of the machinery that so excited me: the "truly potent' Triumph Metisse, an almost uncontrollable supercharged Norton Atlas from New Mexico, and a couple of road-racing machines with foot pegs way back by the rear sprocket and stubby six-inch handlebars—so that you lay out on the bike and divide a sea of wind with the point of your chin.

One day I "got off on the pavement," that is, crashed. It was not much of a crash. I went into a turn too fast and ran off the shoulder and got a little "road burn" requiring symbolic bandages at knees and elbows. I took the usual needling from the crew at the bike shop, and with secret pleasure accepted the temporary appellation, "Crash Cargo." I began taking dawn trips over the mountains to Santa Cruz, sometimes with others, sometimes alone, wearing a wool hunting shirt against the chill and often carrying binoculars and Audubon field guide.

Then one day I was riding in my own neighborhood when a man made a U-turn in front of me and stopped, blocking the road. It was too late to brake and I had to put the bike down, riding it like a sled as it screeched across the pavement. It ran into the side of the car and I slid halfway under, the seat and knees torn out of my pants, scraped and bruised but without serious injury. I had heard the sharp clicking of my helmet against the pavement and later saw the depressions that might have been in my skull.

The man got out, accusing me of going 100 miles an hour, accusing me of laying for a chance to create an accident, accusing me of being a Hell's Angel, and finally admitting he had been daydreaming and had not looked up the street before making his illegal maneuver. The motorcycle was a mess. He pleaded with me not to have physical injuries. He said he had very little insurance. And a family. "Have a heart."

"You ask this of a Hell's Angel?"

At the motorcycle shop I was urged to develop nonspecific spinal
trouble. A special doctor was named. But I had the motorcycle
minimally repaired and sent the man the bill. When the settlement
came, his name was at the top of the stationery. He was the owner
of the insurance company.

Perhaps it was the point-blank view from below of rocker panels
and shock absorbers and the specious concern of the insurance man
for my health that gave my mortality its little twinge. I suddenly
did not want to get off on the pavement anymore or bring my road
burn to the shop under secret bandages. I no longer cared if my
bike was rapid and sanitary. I wanted to sell it, and I wanted to get
out of California.

I did both those things, and in that order. But sometimes, in the
midst of more tasteful activities, I miss the mournful howl of that
big single engine as it came up on the cam, dropped revs, and
started over on a new ratio; the long banking turns with the foot
pegs sparking against the pavement and the great crocodile's tears
the wind caused to trickle out from under my flying glasses. I'm
behind a sensible windshield now, and the soaring curve of accel-
eration does not come up through the seat of my pants. I have an
FM radio, and the car doesn't get bad mileage.

CONTENT

1. Why does McGuane begin his autobiographical essay with a
   series of "foundationless prejudices"? What details does he
   include in the body of the essay to disprove these prejudices?
2. Is any explanation offered for why McGuane buys a motorcycle? When he decides to sell the motorcycle, how much does
   the accident have to do with his decision? Why does he add,
   "I wanted to get out of California"?
3. As did Hoagland, McGuane exhibits a bittersweet attitude toward
   his subject. What do the mixed feelings McGuane has toward
   motorcycles tell you about him as a person? Has he changed at
   the end of the essay? Why does he add the last comment, ". . . and the car doesn't get bad mileage"?

ORGANIZATION

4. Like the title of the essay, the organization is in three parts—
   the motivation for buying the bike, the growing competence in

handling the bike, the disillusionment following the accident. How does this narrative organization make for more interesting reading than a more direct causal analysis of why McGuane bought a motorcycle?

5. The narrative section that relates how McGuane became a competent rider is, itself, divided into two sections: buying the bike and experiencing the pleasure of the first rides. How does the contrast between these two sections help to capture the essential ambivalence toward biking which pervades the whole essay?

TOPICS FOR WRITING

6. Write an autobiographical account about buying something for which you had mixed feelings.

7. Write an autobiographical narrative that shows how the possession of something entitled you to belong to a certain group, and to claim eventual kinship with that group.

PART 3
Narration: Writing to Recreate Events

Narration is often one of the easiest kinds of writing for students to do. It's easy for them chiefly because, first, narration involves telling a story—something that comes naturally to most people; second, narration is easier because the problem of organization is often already solved if the story follows a straight-forward chronological pattern; third, because the material frequently draws from personal experience; and last, because the problem of "person" is solved, if the story is told in the first person, ("I") by the writer. Sometimes essays written to explain something or to persuade someone will incorporate a narrative segment to help clarify a point. Such essays differ from pure narration in that their primary purpose is explanation rather than entertainment. A good way to begin appreciating the nature of narrative writing and the techniques involved in writing it, is to study the elements of narration.

Narrative and Plot   The best place to begin considering what goes into writing narration is with a time-honored distinction between "narrative," (this happened and then this happened) and "plot" (this happened because this happened). Novelist E. M. Forster illustrates the distinction clearly and succinctly:

> Let us define plot. We have defined a story as a narrative of events arranged in their time sequence. A plot is also a narrative of events, the emphasis falling on causality. "The king died and then the queen died," is a story. "The king died, and then the queen died of grief" is a plot. The time-sequence is preserved, but the sense of causality overshadows it. [*Aspects of The Novel* (Harcourt, Brace & Co., 1927), 130]

So, narration focuses on events in their time relationship, which is more often sequential–chronological—that is, events are narrated in the order in which they occurred, whereas, a plot adds to this sequence the important element of cause and effect. In plot, events

75

don't merely follow one another like links in a chain, they *cause* one another. Narration merely appeals to the curiosity of the audience— "*What* happens?"—whereas, plot appeals to the intelligence of the audience as well—"*Why* did it happen?" In other words, in some ways plot construction is a more complicated, more difficult order of activity than constructing a chronological narrative. Fortunately, most assignments in narration require only that you build clear chronological connections between the parts of your narrative; that you have some overriding purpose or thesis, either as an explicit statement at the beginning (acting as a framework for the events narrated); or that your narrative move toward a climax or culminating event (in which the meaning of the narrative is implied.)

An assignment in chronological narration, however, should not prevent you from attempting to construct a plot in which each event is causatively connected in such a way that the meaning of the piece emerges in stages from each section of the plot, rather than as a preface or epilogue, as it does in chronological narration. George Orwell's classic essay, "A Hanging," has many of the elements of what Forster describes as a plot—that is, one event seems inextricably bound to the next. Similarly, James Thurber's satiric fable, "The Rabbits Who Caused All the Trouble," makes clear from its opening paragraph the predictability of the rabbits' destruction by the wolves since Thurber creates the conditions for that destruction: "The wolves announced that they did not like the way the rabbits were living." There is a buildup toward the climax, with each incident increasing the likelihood that the wolves will eat the rabbits. Thurber intensifies this causal connection with repeated pseudo-self-evident truths: "it is well known that . . . rabbits cause earthquakes . . . it is well known that lettuce-eaters cause lightning . . ." until the climax is reached: "The wolves descended on the rabbits for their own good." S. J. Perelman's travelogue, like Thurber's fable, is a humorous story, but in Perelman's narrative each incident follows the next rather than causing it. This is the essential difference between a narrative and a plot. In Perelman, the humor of each incident has a similar basis—bureaucratic inefficiency; there are even some connecting links between the incidents—the knives Perelman's wife purchases, the inconvenience of having the dog on the trip—but there is not a causal connection between the incidents as there is in Thurber and Orwell. In your own writing, although you may not do it consciously, you must decide whether you are constructing a plot or a narrative; then you must decide whether you wish the story to have a chronological sequence with an overall purpose, as in Perelman, or a causal connection out of which the purpose emerges, as in Thurber and Orwell.

Character, or the People of the Story   Notice how Orwell creates a distinct narrator (perhaps himself) to tell the story, then includes the narrator among the other spectators, "We," but he is not a distinct person until the ninth paragraph—that is, until the story is almost half over. The point seems to be that the narrator, a sensitive individual and an accurate observer, is aware that his reactions to the hanging are shared by the others, but that the others are too embarrassed to admit it and too ashamed to closely observe one another. In addition to the narrator, there is Francis, the head jailer, somewhat more calloused by his experience of hangings than the others. The superintendent, who tries to maintain his British source of authority and his nerve, uses anger to hide his own fear and revulsion. Finally, there is the prisoner, who changes from being an object, a source of inconvenience ("The man ought to have been dead by this time"), to a human being ("When I saw the prisoner step aside to avoid the puddle, I saw the mystery, the unspeakable wrongness, of cutting a life short when it is in full tide"), and back again to an object ("The superintendent reached out with his stick and poked the bare body; it oscillated, slightly.") In his book, Forster divides characters into two types: *flat characters*, whose behavior is predictable and typical of the social or occupational category in which the author has placed them, and *round characters* who develop, change, and show qualities unique to them as individuals. The superintendent is, therefore, flat—a typical colonial administrator. The narrator, a colonial functionary, identifies with the prisoner's humanity, and is stunned by the ease and finality with which the line between life and death is crossed; he is clearly a round character.

Setting   Remember, in a good piece of narrative writing all the parts fit tightly together. The physical world within which the action and dialogue of the narrative takes place is no exception. To select the most obvious example from Orwell's narrative, notice how the opening description of the climatic setting of Burma, as well as the immediate setting of the jail, convey a mood of hopelessness in which humanity seems to have been reduced to its lowest animal common-denominators. Like all good settings, Orwell's description of Burma helps define the characters themselves:

> It was in Burma, a sodden morning of the rains. A sickly light, like yellow tinfoil, was slanting over the high walls into the jail yard. We were waiting outside the condemned cells, a row of sheds fronted with double bars, like small animal cages. Each cell measured about ten feet by ten and was quite bare within except for a plank bed and a pot of drinking water.

Note that Orwell's setting is a description, and that narrative writing without some description is rare. The primary aim and the primary content of any piece of writing will tell you whether it should properly be called narration or description. Orwell's setting is effective largely because he uses concrete details that appeal to the senses. Figures of speech (comparisons) also aid the reader in recreating the experience ("like yellow tinfoil," "like small animal cages"). We will discuss the mixing of description and narration in a later section.

Theme   The meaning, significance, or purpose of the narrative is distinct from the moral. Much narrative writing suffers because some explicit moral "tag line" has been attached to an otherwise entertaining story. (The exception to this rule is a type of narrative writing known as a "fable" in which the "Moral" is one of the conventions. Thurber follows this convention which dates back to Aesop.) Notice how Orwell resists the temptation to turn his narrative into an explicit sermon against capital punishment. Although his ultimate purpose is to show his revulsion for the practice, Orwell lets the details speak for themselves—the incongruous laughter while the Burmese and English share a bottle is juxtaposed with the serious fact that "The dead man was a hundred yards away." Subtle implications should convey the theme; if it is likely that the audience may miss the point, an explicit prologue should contain the meaning and act as a measure of relevance for the incidents which make up the narrative. Often narrative writing is used in other kinds of essays—particularly expository and persuasive essays—to support or develop the writer's main idea. In these cases, narrative writing is used to illustrate a point or provide a dramatic example, and the narrative portion may be only a paragraph or two enclosed within a larger essay. This use of narrative writing will be discussed more fully in a later section.

Point of View The method by which the story is narrated—that is, who tells the story—determines the point of view. To oversimplify a vastly complex subject, the possibilities are primarily two: Either you tell the story yourself in the first person, "I" (essentially what Orwell has done) or you have one of the characters tell the story. For example, Ken Kesey divides his novel *Sometimes a Great Notion* into several different sections, each assigned to a distinctly different character, to show that a different perspective of the same scene can reveal a different reality.

Conflict A clash between two forces lies at the heart of a good narrative. The audience's interest lies not so much in the passage of time, but in the obstacles encountered in getting from one point to another. Out of this tension between two forces—which can be two people, a person and his environment, two conflicting sets of values within a person—an interesting narrative is built. In Orwell's narrative, for instance, the clash implied between the narrator's professional duty to witness the execution of the prisoner and his humane impulse to identify with the condemned man radiates outward to explain the "strange" behavior of the other characters and, for example, their irritation at the presence of the stray dog.

In a well-constructed narrative, conflict runs through the several parts that make up the *structure of narration*. These parts are: 1) *exposition*, in which the background information necessary to understand the nature of the conflict is given; 2) *complications*, or those incidents that actualize and initiate the potential conflict in the exposition; 3) *climax*, or turning point, at which the resolution of the conflict becomes inevitable—that is, from this point forward, although it may not be immediately evident to the reader, one of the forces in the conflict is beginning to emerge as dominant, while the other is being dominated; 4) *resolution*, where the dominant value, person, or force clearly emerges as a result of other incidents; and 5) *denouement*, literally the untying or unravelling, in which the nature of the conflict is explained.

As has been observed, modern tastes incline toward a more subtle approach, allowing the resolution of the conflict to make the statement of significance implicitly rather than through an explicit "unravelling." The plot triangle, as it is sometimes called, is graphically depicted as follows:

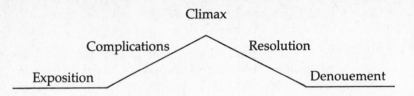

This adaptation of Aristotle's outline of dramatic action from the *Poetics* should be used with caution both as a tool for analysis and as a suggested structure; many narratives do not follow it rigidly or even include all the parts. For example, instead of following a strictly chronological order, many narratives begin with a later event and then, using *reverse chronology*, go back in time to account for it. Faulkner's classic short story "A Rose for Emily" opens with Miss Emily Grierson's funeral, the next to last event of the story, then goes back to the beginning of the sequence to account for the town's attitude toward her. Almost exactly like this is the device of *flashback*, familiar from the movies, in which a straightforward chronological sequence is interrupted to fill in explanations from earlier events, by going back in time, before the narrative flow into the present is resumed. When using either of these devices, in order not to confuse the reader, it is necessary to clarify the verb tenses of your narration to signal changes between the remote past and the simple past. If you choose to narrate in the present tense for vividness, when shifting to the past tense for a flashback, you may make the common mistake of shifting to the present before you have gotten to where you can resume your present tense narration. Even a straightforward narrative needs transitions to keep the sequence of events clear. Notice that Orwell keeps his narrative verbs all in the past tense and uses spatial reference points on the way to the gallows ("forty yards . . . five yards"), but also gives us a time frame ("Eight o'clock struck. . . ," " 'Eight minutes past eight. Well, that's all for this morning, thank God' ").

Too much analysis of the many ways in which a narrative can go wrong may be a negative way to end a discussion of narrative discourse. If we return to where we began, we may have a more fruitful way to approach narrative writing. If you are like most students, you will find it enjoyable, relatively easy—story-telling seems to come naturally to most people—and creative, because you can draw largely on your own direct experience or that of others.

SHORT EXAMPLE

JAMES THURBER
The Rabbits Who Caused All the Trouble

James Thurber (1894–1961) is still regarded over two decades after his death as America's greatest humorist. His many books of humor and drawings include Is Sex Necessary? *(1929), written with E.B. White,* The Owl in the Attic *(1931),* Let Your Mind Alone *(1937),* Alarms and Diversions *(1957), and* Lanterns and Lances *(1961). A collection of Thurber's work,* The Thurber Carnival *(1945), was made into a play and had a successful run on Broadway.* Fables for Our Time *(1940) contains some of Thurber's most memorable pieces. "The Rabbits Who Caused All the Trouble" transcends the historical metaphor that underlies the animal fable to reveal some unpleasant truths about human greed and the cowardice of the uninvolved.*

Within the memory of the youngest child there was a family of   1
rabbits who lived near a pack of wolves. The wolves announced that they did not like the way the rabbits were living. (The wolves were crazy about the way they themselves were living, because it was the only way to live.) One night several wolves were killed in an earthquake and this was blamed on the rabbits, for it is well known that rabbits pound on the ground with their hind legs and cause earthquakes. On another night one of the wolves was killed by a bolt of lightning and this was also blamed on the rabbits, for it is well known that lettuce-eaters cause lightning. The wolves threatened to civilize the rabbits if they didn't behave, and the rabbits decided to run away to a desert island. But the other animals, who lived at a great distance, shamed them, saying, "You must stay where you are and be brave. This is no world for escapists. If the wolves attack you, we will come to your aid, in all probability." So the rabbits continued to live near the wolves and one day there was a terrible flood which drowned a great many wolves. This was blamed on the rabbits, for it is well known that carrot-nibblers with long ears cause floods. The wolves descended on the rabbits, for their own good, and imprisoned them in a dark cave, for their own protection.

When nothing was heard about the rabbits for some weeks, the   2
other animals demanded to know what had happened to them.

The wolves replied that the rabbits had been eaten and since they had been eaten the affair was a purely internal matter. But the other animals warned that they might possibly unite against the wolves unless some reason was given for the destruction of rabbits. So the wolves gave them one. "They were trying to escape," said the wolves, "and, as you know, this is no world for escapists."

Moral: Run, don't walk, to the nearest desert island.   3

DISCUSSION

In "The Rabbits Who Caused All the Trouble," James Thurber uses one of the earliest forms of narration, the beast fable. In Thurber's beast fable, the animal characters play the roles assigned them— the wolves are rapacious and the rabbits are the timid victims. All the parts of a narrative are here as well, from the opening exposition, which tells about the proximity of the rabbits and wolves, to the denouement, which announces one of the meanings of the fable. What gives Thurber's piece its ironic humor, however, is language—language used in such a way as to reveal what George Orwell called in *1984* "doublethink." When the wolves descend on the rabbits and kill them, the wolves justify what they have done by turning the other animals' words back on them. The wolves explain that the rabbits were trying to escape from the dark cave where they were imprisoned "for their own good," so they had to be destroyed for "as you know, this is no world for escapists." Thurber has in mind the genocide of World War II justified by Nazis with racial and ethnic stereotyping. The rabbits are blamed for all sorts of natural calamities, and the other animals, "who lived at a great distance," offer empty promises ("we will come to your aid, in all probability"), and finally are partly responsible for the destruction of the rabbits. Thurber's fable is not merely about history's worst example of oppression. It is about rapacity justifying itself. It is about victims naively believing in the selfless help of others. And it is about the futility of moral rectitude without action. Like Aesop's beast fables, it is about the sad way we humans sometimes behave toward one another.

S. J. PERELMAN
Misty Behind the Curtain

*S. J. (Sidney Joseph) Perelman (1904–1979) is universally regarded as one of America's greatest humorists. He is best known as the author of Marx Brothers comedies—*Monkey Business *(1931) and* Horsefeathers *(1932)—and for the Oscar-winning script of* Around the World in Eighty Days *(1956). Perelman once called Hollywood, "a dreary industrial town controlled by hoodlums of enormous wealth." Perelman's style combines the erudite with the surprising and the absurd. "Misty Behind the Curtain" is from* Chicken Inspector No. 23. *(1966). All the Perelman elements are here: an absurd situation, responses that don't quite fit, bizarre twists of logic, and elegance which barely holds its own against anarchy.*

Late of a sweltering July afternoon this past summer, the hundred-odd occupants of a streetcar clanging along the waterfront of Trieste were handed a delicious, unexpected treat—the spectacle of an American tourist, ever a favorite target for derision, making a bloody ass of himself. A balding presbyopic individual with a ragged handlebar mustache and a complexion the color of beetroot, about to embark on a tour of Yugoslavia honeycombed with such hazard and tribulation as to dwarf the *Anabasis* of Xenophon, he was vainly attempting to wedge three dozen tins of dog food into an already overburdened compact. Nearby, and cucumber-cool in her simple but expensive cottons, stood a statuesque *signora* resembling Jetta Goudal* in her prime, holding the leash of another thoroughbred, a magnificent silver standard poodle, and proffering the kind of wifely advice that induces apoplexy. As the dog food tumbled out of the car windows, bounced off the pavement, and rolled helter-skelter across the tramway lines, a veritable paroxysm of joy shook the passengers; they guffawed, bellowed, cackled and pounded each other's scapulae in sheer pleasure. At last the overwrought American—who, by a breathtaking coincidence, bore the same passport and social security number as myself—could endure no more. Uttering a plaintive bleat like the paschal lamb, I sank down onto the curb and, burying my face in my hands, dissolved into sobs.

---

*A tall, imposing brunette who played exotic leads in many silent movies.

"I wish I were dead," I wailed. "I wish I was in Dixie, in Bali, in   2
Fiji—anywhere but this godforsaken hole. Why didn't we leave well
enough alone? I was so happy in Provence—*foie gras* at every meal,
three bottles of Burgundy a day—"

"There, there," my wife comforted me. "Once we get to the Dal-   3
matian coast, everything'll be peaches and cream. Don't you
remember those lovely posters we saw in London—the sparkling
blue Adriatic, the immaculate ships, the cheery, colorful peasants
thronging to sell their handicrafts for a few dinars?"

Whether it was the catharsis of tears or the contact of her cool   4
finger tips, my mood suddenly underwent a magical change. Ener-
getically bundling her and Misty, the poodle, into the car, I presented the onlookers with a small token of Italo-American amity—
to wit, the evil eye—and, springing behind the wheel ere they could
reciprocate, made for the pier where the S.S. *Pascudnik*, our carrier
to Dubrovnik, lay berthed. Word had apparently been flashed ahead
from Interpol that a couple of society jewel thieves disguised as
Judge Harold Medina* and Jetta Goudal were Yugoslavia-bound, for
a whole phalanx of customs officials collared us at dockside. After
a microscopic scrutiny of our visas, *triptyque*, driving licenses, credit
cards, and the poodle's ears, they discovered we lacked the most
vital of all documents, a tourist gasoline permit—without which,
they gloated, no motorist could quit the country. Luckily I had some
fluency in the Italian vernacular, having at one time composed dialogue for Chico Marx,** and finally convinced them that since we
were half-wits who might become a public charge, we should be
expelled posthaste. The ship's bosun, who had been dancing about
in a fever of impatience meanwhile, thereupon signaled his crew
to load the car. They flung nets over it at random, neatly entangling
the dog and several spectators, and with a volcanic jerk hoisted the
seine aloft, where it instantly fouled in the hawsers. I was strongly
tempted to box the winchman's ears and show the dunderheads
how the thing should be handled, but on looking around discovered that my wife had pinioned my arms. Ultimately the pandemonium simmered down to chaos; the car was snugly stowed on
deck and the sun roof left open as a receptacle for orange peel,

*Presided over a famous trial in 1949 of eleven Communists charged with conspiracy.
**One of the Marx Brothers who spoke with a very heavy comic Italian accent.

cigarette butts and trash, and amid a turmoil of whistles, bells and hysteria that outdid the annual fair at Nizhni Novgorod, the *Pascudnik* cast off.

As a climax to his celebrated escape act in vaudeville about 1921, the late Harry Houdini used to have himself entombed, upside down and lavishly manacled, in a forty-quart milk can—an exploit billed, for some reason, as the Chinese Water Torture. Compared to our situation aboard the *Pascudnik*, Houdini was in clover. Our cabin, approximately the size of Dr. Wilhelm Reich's renowned orgone box,* faced the engine room, a location that guaranteed an unfailing supply of steam. It contained two grimy bunks, a sink encrusted with verdigris, and a strip of matting just broad enough for a band of roaches in Indian file. To further insure claustrophobia, someone had painstakingly screwed down the porthole and painted it fast. During the three nights we spent in this pressure cooker, the mercury never dipped below ninety-five. A devastating blanket of heat lay over the *Pascudnik* as it inched its way along the coast; stupefied from lack of sleep, leaden-footed and eyes red-rimmed, we tottered about like somnambulists. If we expected any stimulus from our fellow-passengers, we were soon disabused. Of the fifteen assorted *Mitteleuropans* glowering at us in the lounge, none spoke any recognizable tongue, nor were they disposed to fraternize. At the sight of the poodle, they gibbered with terror and crossed themselves as if exorcising a werewolf. The most harrowing feature of the journey, however, was the food. Even a goat would have rebelled at the unending parade of greasy soup, Wiener schnitzels tougher than blowout patches, and malodorous cabbage that issued from the galley. In desperation, we finally fell back on a box of dog biscuits exhumed from our luggage which, when steeped in hot water, gave us the illusion of nourishment. I hated to deprive Misty, but it was a case of *sauve qui peut*.

The three ports the *Pascudnik* called at en route—Rijeka, Zadar and Split—afforded some surcease, minor though it was, from our misery. In Rijeka, the onetime city of Fiume where that fiery *littérateur* Gabriele D'Annunzio had found an outlet for his military genius, I found two bars of mildewed chocolate and some stale Fig

---

*Austrian psychiatrist famous for his theory that cosmic energy—orgone energy—fills the atmosphere and can be captured in a box called an "orgone accumulator."

Newtons that partly allayed our hunger. Otherwise, it was a dispiriting spot reminiscent of Fall River, Massachusetts,* made no more endearing by those ubiquitous portraits of Big Brother.† Zadar was somewhat cheerier; here, at least, there was a seaside café whose slivovitz was potable and whose clientele had drunk enough of it to temper their scowls. Split was good value for the first time—a vital, turbulent community centered inside the magnificent palace Diocletian had built for his declining years. Thanks to a knowledgeable guide who took pains to communicate his enthusiasm, we whiled away a carefree hour among the antiquities and stored up sufficient moxie to face the remainder of the voyage.

To those unquenchable romantics on whom a walled city acts like   7
adrenalin, who long to scale towers and sniff the mold of dungeons, I can unhesitatingly recommend Dubrovnik. It abounds in drawbridges, portcullises, casemates, barbicans, *chevaux-de-frise*, and similar remnants of the days when knighthood was in flower. It was my misfortune in youth, however, to be dragged through *Ivanhoe* and the Arthurian cycle by a singularly repulsive teacher, and in the process I contracted a lifelong allergy toward chivalry. Within a quarter of an hour I began sneezing so violently and broke out in such hives that my wife had to bathe my temples with Courvoisier and rush me back to the hotel.

The Venezuela–Riviera, as it was majestically named, was a pre-   8
tentious fleabag of stucco and red tile on a promontory outside the town. During our tour of the sights, some nonpareil fathead had dumped a mountain of timber against the shed wherein our car was parked. Inasmuch as we were slated to take off at daybreak, this naturally set my foot tapping, but the manager smoothly assured us that we would be sprung. We were, in every sense. At ten that evening, a couple of Torquemadas†† in leather jerkins arrived with a gasoline-fed chain saw and, stationing it directly beneath our window, fell to work. The screech of the blade ripping through the green lumber must have been audible in Thessalonica. It exploded our eardrums, shook the plaster out of the walls and set Misty howling in anguish. For seven mortal hours the obscene rasp of the

---

* Site of the Lizzie Borden murders of 1892.
† The despotic leader of Oceania in Orwell's 1984.
†† An infamous Dominican monk, who as first grand inquisitor during the Spanish Inquisition, was responsible for 2,000 burnings at the stake.

saw dominated the night, and when, at last, we shook the sawdust of Dubrovnik from our feet, I was so addled that I drove thirteen miles with the hand brake on before recovering my wits.

There are doubtless worse roads in the world than those in Montenegro, the constituent republic of Yugoslavia we were traversing, but if so, nobody thus far has bothered to map them. As we rocked along in low gear, skidding in and out of craters, crawling perilously over tree stumps and boulders, the trek southward became a nightmare out of *Pilgrim's Progress*. Time and again we lost our way and floundered into immense valleys of scree where the road dwindled into a mule track; for hours on end we crept across bottomless gorges, our wheels spinning on the edge of eternity. At Cetinje, in an outdoor *Stube* filled with desperadoes clearly plotting to waylay us, we snatched a morsel of sustenance, some Turkish coffee and a flavorful sausage embodying the flesh of a mastodon, and pressed on. Ultimately, and through what I can only believe was divine intercession, our plucky little vehicle found its way back to the coast, and, bone-weary, filthy and with catastrophic headaches, we fetched up at that highly publicized watering place, Sveti Stefan.

Though faintly reminiscent of a copywriter's dream or one of James Fitzpatrick's ineffable travelogues, this fishing village converted by governmental fiat into a sanctuary for rich divorcées and their *cicisbei* nevertheless furnished some surcease from our tribulations. All too soon, however, an incident that had occurred prior to our embarkation at Trieste began to effloresce. As I was transferring a handful of maps to the boot of the car at an AGIP station outside Venice, I had noticed among our impedimenta a mysterious brown parcel about twelve inches long, from the wrapping of which protruded the blade of a knife.

"What's the matter?" my wife queried as I resumed my seat and reached for the ignition key. "Is anything wrong with the car?"

"There's a bundle in the back I never noticed before," I said, frowning. "It's got a knife or something sticking our of it."

"Oh, *that*," she said, with the silvery chuckle her sex always employs to conceal underlying guilt. "Goodness, from your expression I thought Lord knows what had happened. Your face looked like Maurice Schwartz* in the last act of *King Lear.*"

*Actor who starred in the Yiddish Art Theatre in New York, and played character parts in Hollywood.

"Never mind the character study," I said impatiently. "You bought   14
something you shouldn't have and now you're trying to squirm out
of it."

"All right then, so I did," she admitted. "It's only a few little steak   15
knives I picked up the morning I went shopping in Milan. You're
forever complaining how dull ours are, and these were such a bargain that I couldn't resist."

"Honeybunch . . . sugarplum," I groaned. "What are we, in   16
heaven's name—a vaudeville act? It's a wonder you didn't buy a
bullwhip while you were at it, so we could flick cigarettes out of
each other's mouths."

"I wouldn't trust myself," she retorted. "I might be tempted to   17
give you a lesson your parents should have taught you seventy
years ago."

Had it not been for a couple of beefy Teutons alongside us in a   18
Mercedes who were monitoring the exchange, I would have boxed
the creature's ears, but, sensing that it might tarnish the American
image, I had contained myself and driven on. I clean forgot the
episode until an hour after our arrival at Sveti Stefan, when another
fragment of the past revived it.

Staying at the hotel was a former show-biz acquaintance of mine,   19
a Paramount starlet of the vintage of Toby Wing.* Folly Lou Zuck-
erman, as she was now known, had just crossed Turkey and Greece
in a white convertible, accompanied by a Pekinese and a miniature
schnauzer. The three of us and the three dogs shared a meal that
made welkins ring throughout Montenegro, and Folly Lou retired
early, pleading that she had to start for Zagreb at daybreak. At dawn
the next morning, the hotel was awakened by lamentations and
tohubohu louder than that attending the destruction of the Portland
vase. Folly Lou's entire wardrobe, furs, and jewelry, which she had
packed in her car the night before, had vanished into thin air. In
due course, a pair of sullen, unshaven Yugoslav detectives materialized. As they were pottering around the convertible and dusting
it for fingerprints, I opened the rear of our compact, parked nearby,
to ascertain whether our belongings were intact. All of a sudden,
one of the gumshoes appeared beside me and peered intently into
the boot.

*Silent film actress.

"What's eating you, Charlie?" I demanded. (I believe in being 20 forthright with shamuses, Communist or not.) "You don't think *I* had anything to do with this heist, do you?"

He mumbled some evasive reply in Serbo-Croatian and, plucking 21 the bundle of steak knives from the interior, went into a whispered huddle with his colleague. Then, summoning the desk clerk to translate, the two subjected me to a catechism that left me sweating with fear. Not only did I lack a permit to import cutlery but our admitted destination was Belgrade, the government seat, and my enthusiasm for Marshal Tito so tepid as to stamp me a potential assassin. At this critical juncture, Fate mercifully interceded to save our skins. A begrimed militiaman roared up on a motorcycle, bearing news that three Bosnians in a jeep had been apprehended in Ulcinj with the ex-starlet's effects. Instantly, the fog of suspicion enveloping us dissipated; the detectives, wreathed in smiles, returned the knives with abject apologies, everybody trooped off to the neighboring café to pledge one another's health in slivovitz, and the last we saw of Folly Lou she and the militiaman, blind drunk, were headed for Ulcinj at sixty miles per hour in the white convertible.

After another three days, thoroughly parboiled and rendered 22 queasy by the twitter of the loose-wristed fraternity around the hotel, we mutually agreed it was imperative to vamoose, and pushed off. The route we chose northward to Belgrade, via Titograd, wound across the great coastal range that parallels the sea and, while we were blessedly unaware of it, includes some of the most difficult terrain in eastern Europe. Armed with no more than a packet of sandwiches and a tankful of *benzina*, we set off one hot morning at eight, fatuously convinced that we could drive the four hundred and sixty kilometers to the capital by nightfall.

It must have been about dusk that day, as we were emerging 23 from the ninth in a series of unlit mountain tunnels between two pinpricks on the map named Bijelo Polje and Prijepolje, that our self-confidence began to wilt. Misty, who hitherto had lain curled in a ball on the floor, suddenly stood up and emitted a long, melancholy yowl.

"What's eating that beast of yours?" I snapped, swerving to avoid 24 a rock.

"Maybe she senses something," my wife ventured timidly. "We've 25 had a couple of vultures circling over us the past half hour."

The words had hardly escaped her lips when we got proof incontestable that the animal was clairvoyant. Slithering around the next bend, we came face to face with a steamroller abandoned by its crew in the middle of the road. With a chasm on one side and a cliff on the other, I had no choice but to stamp convulsively on the brakes and, *mirabile dictu,* stopped short a bare inch from the juggernaut. Our sole alternative now was to try to back through the tunnel until we found some point wide enough to turn. Forty-five minutes later, thoroughly dehydrated and my hair snow-white, we started retracing our way to Bijelo Polje in pitch-darkness. This tiny contretemps, it developed, was merely a curtain raiser for the trials in store—the crevasses spanned by rickety wooden bridges, the rock slides, the dizzying hairpins and switchbacks, and the interminable detours that punctuated our serpentine route. Aeons passed without signs of another vehicle, let alone a habitation of any sort, and whenever an onrushing truck or jeep did appear, the encounter became a lunatic joust on the edge of kingdom come. By slow, agonizing stages we struggled at length into a hamlet called Nadir, whose food and sanitation were everything its name implied, and where we made an electrifying discovery: the luggage boot containing all our possessions was hopelessly jammed. Under circumstances it was too arduous to attempt Belgrade, and we decided to break the trip at Titovo Užice, a provincial outpost hailed in the guidebook as a center of culture and rest. So asphyxiating was the stench of germicide in our room there, though, and so dubious the bed linen, that within three hours we were again in the saddle. Late that afternoon, grimy as chimney sweeps and nursing savage heartburn from the omnipresent Turkish coffee we rolled under the porte-cochère of the Athénée–Popinjay, Belgrade's foremost hotel.

About five minutes afterward, as we rolled back out into the Bulevar Revolucije, I recovered the power of speech that had temporarily deserted me in the lobby. "What do they mean, they don't take dogs?" I shouted at my wife. "I'll show 'em, I'll show the bastards! I'll call the American Embassy—no, I'll call my lawyers, Rough & Trumball—no, I'll call Tito personally—"

"For God's sake, control yourself," the woman implored me. "You look like a pregnant Concord grape. Ask that swineherd over there, or whatever he is, if there's any hotel that does accept pets."

Helped by a score of bystanders who swarmed around, I managed to translate our problem into Serbo-Croatian, and inside the

hour we were installed at the Villa Bedraglia, a ramshackle establishment harboring so many silverfish, earwigs and gnats that one
more animal passed unnoticed. Our first requisite, obviously, was
to undo the luggage boot, a task that defied the staff and the two
locksmiths they produced. The real virtuoso in such matters, they
confessed shortly, was one of the bellhops at the Athénée-Popinjay,
and cringing with humiliation, I had to creep back there to enlist
his aid. He fashioned an impromptu jimmy from a coat hanger and,
with dexterity born of long practice in rifling foreigners' baggage,
maneuvered open the catch. Perhaps, as my wife contended, the
twenty-five-cent piece I tipped him was niggardly, but since he
glommed my wrist watch while we were exchanging handshakes,
I felt the incident promoted a closer rapport between our two
ideologies.

I daresay that when nostalgia overtakes a Yugoslav songwriter, 30
he yearns to be carried back to old Belgrade, but whatever the
charm of that metropolis may be, it utterly eluded us. The gloomy
Parisian-style tenements and the offices sheltering the bureaucracy,
the myriad noisy streetcars and the shops filled with shoddy merchandise, cast a pall on spirits already sorely laden. As for the
vaunted artifacts—the embroidered blouses, the basketwork and
ceramics, and the icons—the preponderance was purest *schlock* off
the Atlantic City boardwalk. I reached the saturation point—and I
regard myself as a patient man—the fifth evening of our stay, just
as a gypsy violinist resembling Jan Peerce* was fiddling airs from
Countess Maritza into my wife's ear. Midway through his recital I
swept Serbian salad to the floor and arose.

"O.K., that tears it," I said decisively. "We can get this, without 31
dysentery, at Moskowitz and Lupowitz, on Second Avenue. We're
heading for the Rumanian frontier first thing tomorrow morning."

"Rumania?" my wife exclaimed, aghast. "Are you crazy? There's 32
nothing there but a lot of Seltzer drinkers and chicken thieves!"

"I know it," I said, "but it's the quickest way out of here. Bring 33
us a check, comrade waiter."

Eighty kilometers onward and nineteen hours later, we chugged 34
up to the frontier checkpoint at Vršac, a hut of stuccoed cement
amid illimitable wheat fields, presided over by a lady commissar
who, while she bore a striking resemblance to Mildred Natwick, †

*An American tenor and opera star.
†An actress known for her character roles.

possessed none of the latter's charm. As she scanned our passports, unable to detect any irregularity, her features puckered as though she had bitten into a quince. They brightened appreciably when one of her subordinates, emitting a series of clicks like a mechanical doll, stalked in and dropped our package of knives on her desk with a clatter.

"Aha!" she burst out. "Contraband goods—a clear violation."

"Of what?" I said, bristling.

"The law of March 27, 1953, protecting the public welfare," she snapped. "It is expressly forbidden, under pain of imprisonment, to introduce any weapons into the Rumanian People's Republic. Confiscate them," she barked at her aide. "And as for you, my dear sir—"

"Hold on there a moment," I interposed. "Is this your vaunted Socialist democracy? By what right do you have to deprive a person of his livelihood?"

It took her a moment to comprehend the sense of my words. "You mean you employ knives in your business?"

"We most certainly do," I said. "Madame here is a professional freak—a sword swallower. She engulfs the blades while I dance on my hands and our dog plays the harmonica. Would you like us to give you a demonstration?"

"No, no," she said hastily. "We never interfere with strolling players. Here, take your—ah—tools, and a prosperous engagement to the three of you in Rumania."

The Novy Moscovy, the hotel in Bucharest where we finally managed to wheedle a room after a fruitless circuit of the capital, was a dinghy edifice on the main thoroughfare, all red plush and peeling gilt. Our second-floor windows commanded an unobstructed view of three rows of trolley tracks, and the noise was cataclysmic, but, even so, it was preferable to the rear, which overlooked a swimming pool with an artificial-wave machine and a gypsy orchestra that performed until dawn. Within twenty-four hours, the illusion instilled in us by folk like Eric Ambler[*] and Sacheverell Sitwell[†] that Bucharest was the Paris of the Balkans went glimmering. The cuisine, the omnipresent Wiener schnitzel washed down by draughts of red wine adulterated with Seltzer, was disheartening, the populace either cowed or downright insolent, and the architecture third-rate

---

[*]Author of suspense novels and screenplays which involve foreign intrigue.
[†]Younger brother of poet Edith Sitwell, and author of numerous travel books.

Second Empire gone hopelessly to seed. To add to our disenchantment, I shortly began to be oppressed by a conviction that we were under surveillance. Whenever I took the dog out, there was invariably some faceless character in a grubby trench coat dawdling about the lobby, pretending to be absorbed in a newspaper, and twice when we unexpectedly cut short a day's sightseeing the concierge stalled us on the flimsiest of pretexts, obviously warning off someone engaged in searching our room. An episode I ordinarily would have dismissed as trifling confirmed my suspicions. We were seated at dinner one evening in a mosquito-ridden open-air restaurant, doggedly chewing our schnitzels and wincing at an accordion rendition of Liszt's "Fourth Hungarian Rhapsody" throbbing from a microphone apparently concealed in our dish of pickles. One of the waiters, brushing past with a heavily loaded tray, twitched the tablecloth and sent my knife spinning into the gravel. As I automatically craned to see where it had gone, a chap at the next table tapped me on the arm. "Permit me, sir," he said, graciously extending a knife. "Please use this—although," he hazarded, with an unmistakable wink, "I'm sure you would prefer your own, *n'est-ce pas?*"

My immediate impulse, of course, was to demand what the devil   43
he implied, but in the same instant I clearly perceived his design. The man was an *agent provocateur* trying to unnerve me, to elicit where I had secreted the steak knives, to goad me into an admission that we had sneaked them into Rumania for political mayhem. I threw him a glacial smile that told him I was not to be drawn, and turned my back.

Knowing that the occurrence was bound to agitate my wife, I   44
glossed it over, but the following morning I lost no time getting to the garage and checking the contents of the compact. My premonition was correct; the boot was visibly disordered, though the knives, surprisingly, were still there. Careful to insure that I was unobserved, I whisked them under my jacket and sped back to the hotel.

"Now, listen, dear," I said to my wife, having established to my   45
satisfaction that nobody was crouched at the keyhole. "Don't get hysterical or anything, but we're in a peck of trouble. I've got every reason to believe that the Securitate's been messing around in our machine. It's all topsy-turvy."

"Stuff and nonsense," she said, calmly buffing her nails. "That's   46
the way you left it, and you've got the only key. How would anyone else get into it?"

I repressed a sigh of exasperation. "You talk like a sausage," I   47
said. "Why, the Rumanians practically invented espionage—they're
past masters at it. We've been tailed ever since that dame at the
frontier spotted these knives. But never mind that now—where
can we hide them until we take off?"

While her attitude plainly betrayed that she thought me stiff with   48
paranoia, the woman could not dodge responsibility for causing
our dilemma, and she reluctantly stashed the package in a handbag—one of several she kept in a suitcase for dress wear. The next
couple of days were relatively free of care; as far as I could tell, our
luggage was unmolested, and the operative in the trench coat seemed
to have disappeared from the lobby. Then, the afternoon preceding
our scheduled departure, an untoward incident awakened all my
trepidation. Several days prior, we had attended a cocktail party
given by some embassy personnel, at which, made espansive by
the local plum brandy, I expressed a longing to visit the castle in
Transylvania associated with Count Dracula. At once, the whole
complex mechanism of diplomacy started whirring. Calls flew out
to the Foreign Office, ponderous formalities were exchanged, and
an appointment was set up for us to confer with the commissar for
Folklore, a Mr. Bulgic. It was on the afternoon in question, as we
were trudging into the Folklore Institute with laggard feet, that my
wife made a disconcerting revelation. "Oh, my God!" she exclaimed,
her jaw dropping. "You know what I've gone and done? I took along
the wrong pocketbook—the one that we hid the knives in."

"Well, of all the bonehead—" I sputtered, and quickly checked   49
myself. "Look, we haven't the time to go back to the hotel, and we
daren't leave 'em in the car. Just dummy up, and whatever happens,
don't let that bag out of your hands—do you hear?"

Mr. Bulgic was a squat, bullnecked individual with the pale, cold   50
eyes of a Malemute, and the icy flipper he held out plainly indicated
that we were impinging on his studies. Behind him stood a trio of
assistants summoned to furnish moral support—a fattish young
woman whose Tartar features sported a thick coat of rice powder;
a cadaverous youth with a fixed, supercilious smile; and a dwarflike
spinster on the order of Edna May Oliver.* The oval table around
which we grouped ourselves was dimly lit by a suspended lamp of

---

*Eccentric character actress best known for her role as Aunt Betsy Trotwood in the film
version of *David Copperfield*.

Tiffany glass, and, from the shadowy walls beyond, steel engravings of Lenin, Gorki, Tolstoi, and a number of other Russian notables eyed us accusingly. Excusing himself and his colleagues in rapid, heavily accented French for their inability to speak our language, Mr. Bulgic crisply inquired what service the Institute could render.

"Well, to tell you the truth, Mr. Bulgic," I confessed awkwardly,   51
"I'm afraid our quest is really a minor one. Would you by any chance happen to know where Dracula's castle is located?"

"Dracula?" he repeated blankly. "Who in the world is that? Some   52
mythical figure in one of your Western fairy tales?"

"No, no—the vampire," I said. "You know, the infamous noble-   53
man in Bram Stoker's novel, who ran around Transylvania drinking people's blood. Surely"—my voice seemed to acquire a shrill, piping quality in the half-darkened room—"surely you must have heard of *him?*"

Mr. Bulgic shrugged and, turning to his assistants, shot a ques-   54
tion in Rumanian at each of them. They all shook their heads. Perhaps, he suggested, I could give some inkling of the story—in fact, a précis of the plot. A rivulet of perspiratioin began coursing down my spine; it was forty years since I had read the book, and at least thirty since Bela Lugosi had held me spellbound with the movie version. Suddenly, as I sat there tongue-tied under the unwinking gaze of the quartet, I was overcome by the vast iniquity of my position. Why should I have been tricked into this predicament, compelled to undergo an oral exam like a quivering schoolboy, just because some busybody at a cocktail party had misconstrued a casual remark of mine? It was outrageous, insupportable. I sprang to my feet. "O.K., knock it off," I said roughly. "If that's how you feel, you can keep your old castle, and I hope a turret falls on you. Come on, honey."

I reached around, without looking, for my wife's arm, and then   55
it happened—the disclosure most shameful, the humiliation supreme. The strap of her handbag entwined itself around my wrist, and as I shook it off I projected a package of knives outward onto the middle of the table. There was no mistaking its contents; the sleazy paper had parted, and every blade, gleaming wickedly, lay exposed. The four Rumanians leaned forward as one man, their eyes distended in horror, and for all I know are seated there yet, turned to stone. We didn't tarry for their conclusion. We flew straight back to

the Novy Moscovy, collected the poodle, and drove like the wind through the Carpathians to the border. I suppose we passed Count Dracula's lair somewhere en route, but it never occurred to us to stop. Pretty tame stuff. After all, when you've tasted the Balkan intrigue we have, you don't frighten as easy as you used to.

CONTENT

1. Perelman's narrative consists chiefly of a series of complications that lead him behind, and out from behind, the Iron Curtain. What does each complication add to the humor of the situation?
2. How are the devices of the dog, Misty, and the knives, illegally purchased by his wife, used to create on-going humorous complications? How does Perelman employ stereotypes of East European officialdom, of tourist inconvenience and discomfort, and specifically of Romanian and Yugoslavian stereotypes to create comic situations?

ORGANIZATION

3. Does Perelman's comic narrative follow the traditional plot configuration of exposition, complications, climax, resolution, and denouement? What is the purpose of the opening paragraph describing Perelman's embarrassment before the passengers of a tram?
4. As in the Marx Brothers' movies for which Perelman wrote scripts, the comic situation is resolved through escalation of the absurdity of the dilemma. Give examples of several incidents in the narrative in which a temporary resolution comes after a series of wildly comic improbabilities.

TOPICS FOR WRITING

5. Write a narrative of a trip you took which turned out to be quite different from your expectations.
6. Comedy is based on surprise following reversed expectations. Write a comic narrative in which the reader's expectations are reversed with a comic outcome.

E. B. WHITE
The Geese

E. B. (Elwyn Brooks) White is best known to the public as the author of several children's books, among them Charlotte's Web *(1952) and* Stuart Little *(1945). Born in 1899 in Mount Vernon, New York, he joined the staff of* The New Yorker, *with which his name is now virtually synonymous. The simple direct style of his personal essays transforms the minutia of daily living into details of much greater significance. In "The Geese," White recounts a simple barnyard tale, but makes it speak to the essential facts of the human condition: birth, growth, aging, and death.*

To give a clear account of what took place in the barnyard early in the morning on that last Sunday in June, I will have to go back more than a year in time, but a year is nothing to me these days. Besides, I intend to be quick about it, and not dawdle.

I have had a pair of elderly gray geese—a goose and a gander— living on this place for a number of years, and they have been my friends. "Companions" would be a better word; geese are friends with no one, they badmouth everybody and everything. But they are companionable once you get used to their ingratitude and their false accusations. Early in the spring, a year ago, as soon as the ice went out of the pond, my goose started to lay. She laid three eggs in about a week's time and then died. I found her halfway down the lane that connects the barnyard with the pasture. There were no marks on her—she lay with wings partly outspread, and with her neck forward in the grass, pointing downhill. Geese are rarely sick, and I think this goose's time had come and she had simply died of old age. I had noticed that her step had slowed on her trips back from the pond to the barn where her nest was. I had never known her age, and so had nothing else to go on. We buried her in our private graveyard, and I felt sad at losing an acquaintance of such long standing—long standing and loud shouting.

Her legacy, of course, was the three eggs. I knew they were good eggs and did not like to pitch them out. It seemed to me that the least I could do for my departed companion was to see that the eggs she had left in my care were hatched. I checked my hen pen to find out whether we had a broody, but there was none. During the next few days, I scoured the neighborhood for a broody hen, with no success. Years ago, if you needed a broody hen, almost any barn or henhouse would yield one. But today broodiness is considered unacceptable in a hen; the modern hen is an egg-laying machine, and her natural tendency to sit on eggs in springtime had been bred out of her. Besides, not many people keep hens anymore—when they want a dozen eggs, they don't go to the barn, they go to the First National.*

Days went by. My gander, the widower, lived a solitary life— 4 nobody to swap gossip with, nobody to protect. He seemed dazed. The three eggs were not getting any younger, and I myself felt dazed—restless and unfulfilled, I had stored the eggs down cellar in the arch where it is cool, and every time I went down there for something they seemed silently to reproach me. My plight had become known around town, and one day a friend phoned and said he would lend me an incubator designed for hatching the eggs of waterfowl. I brought the thing home, cleaned it up, plugged it in, and sat down to read the directions. After studying them, I realized that if I were to tend eggs in that incubator, I would have to withdraw from the world for thirty days—give up everything, just as a broody goose does. Obsessed though I was with the notion of bringing life into the three eggs, I wasn't quite prepared to pay the price.

Instead, I abandoned the idea of incubation and decided to settle 5 the matter by acquiring three ready-made goslings, as a memorial to the goose and a gift for the lonely gander. I drove up the road about five miles and dropped in on Irving Closson. I knew Irving had geese; he has everything—even a sawmill. I found him shoeing a very old horse in the doorway of his barn, and I stood and watched for a while. Hens and geese wandered about the yard, and a turkey tom circled me, wings adroop, strutting. The horse, with one forefoot between the man's knees, seemed to have difficulty balancing himself on three legs but was quiet and sober, almost asleep. When I asked Irving if he planned to put shoes on the horse's hind feet, too, he said, "No, it's hard work for me, and he doesn't use those hind legs much anyway." Then I brought up the question of goslings, and he took me into the barn and showed me a sitting goose. He said he thought she was covering more than twenty eggs and

*A supermarket chain.

should bring off her goslings in a couple of weeks and I could buy a few if I wanted. I said I would like three.

I took to calling at Irving's every few days—it is about the pleas- 6
antest place to visit anywhere around. At last, I was rewarded: I pulled into the driveway one morning and saw a goose surrounded by green goslings. She had been staked out, like a cow. Irving had simply tied a piece of string to one leg and fastened the other end to a peg in the ground. She was a pretty goose—not as large as my old one had been, and with a more slender neck. She appeared to be a cross-bred bird, two-toned gray, with white markings—a sort of parti-colored goose. The goslings had the cheerful, bright, and innocent look that all baby geese have. We scooped up three and tossed them into a box, and I paid Irving and carried them home.

My next concern was how to introduce these small creatures to 7
their foster father, my old gander. I thought about this all the way home. I've had enough experience with domesticated animals and birds to know that they are a bundle of eccentricities and crotchets, and I was not at all sure what sort of reception three strange young-sters would get from a gander who was full of sorrows and sus-picions. (I once saw a gander, taken by surprise, seize a newly hatched gosling and hurl it the length of the barn floor.) I had an uneasy feeling that my three little charges might be dead within the hour, victims of a grief-crazed old fool. I decided to go slow. I fixed the make-shift pen for the goslings in the barn, arranged so that they would be separated from the gander but visible to him, and he would be visible to them. The old fellow, when he heard youthful voices, hustled right in to find out what was going on. He studied the scene in silence and with the greatest attention. I could not tell whether the look in his eye was one of malice or affection—a goose's eye is a small round enigma. After observing this intro-ductory scene for a while, I left and went into the house.

Half an hour later, I heard a commotion in the barnyard: the 8
gander was in full cry. I hustled out. The goslings, impatient with life indoors, had escaped from their hastily constructed enclosure in the barn and had joined their foster father in the barnyard. The cries I had heard were screams of welcome—the old bird was delighted with the turn that events had taken. His period of mourn-ing was over, he now had interesting and useful work to do, and he threw himself into the role of father with immense satisfaction

and zeal, hissing at me with renewed malevolence, shepherding the three children here and there, and running interference against real and imaginary enemies. My fears were laid to rest. In the rush of emotion that seized him at finding himself the head of a family, his thoughts turned immediately to the pond, and I watched admiringly as he guided the goslings down the long, tortuous course through the weedy land and on down across the rough pasture between blueberry knolls and granite boulders. It was a sight to see him hold the heifers at bay so the procession could pass safely. Summer was upon us, the pond was alive again. I brought the three eggs up from the cellar and dispatched them to the town dump.

At first, I did not know the sex of my three goslings. But nothing 9 on two legs grows any faster than a young goose, and by early fall it was obvious that I had drawn one male and two females. You tell sex of a goose by its demeanor and its stance—the way it holds itself, its general approach to life. A gander carries his head high and affects a threatening attitude. Females go about with necks in a graceful arch and are less aggressive. My two young females looked like their mother, parti-colored. The young male was quite different. He feathered out white all over except for his wings, which were a very light, pearly gray. Afloat on the pond, he looked almost like a swan, with his tall, thin white neck and his cooked-up white tail—a real dandy, full of pompous thoughts and surly gestures.

Winter is a time of waiting, for man and goose. Last winter was 10 a long wait, the pasture deep in drifts, the lane barricaded, the pond inaccessible and frozen. Life centered in the barn and the barnyard. When the time for mating came, conditions were unfavorable, and this was upsetting to the old gander. Geese like a body of water for their coupling; it doesn't have to be a large body of water—just any wet place in which a goose can become partly submerged. My old gander, studying the calendar, inflamed by passion, unable to get to the pond, showed signs of desperation. On several occasions, he tried to manage with a ten-quart pail of water that stood in the barnyard. He would chivvy one of his young foster daughters over to the pail, seize her by the nape of the neck, and hold her head under water while he made his attempt. It was never a success and usually ended up looking more like a comedy tumbling act than like coitus. One got the feeling during the water-pail routine that the gander had been consulting one of the modern sex manuals describing peculiar positions. Anyway, I noticed two things: the old fellow confined his attentions to one of the two young geese and let the other alone, and he never allowed his foster son to approach either of the girls—he was very strict about that, and the handsome young male lived all spring in a state of ostracism.

Eventually, the pond opened up, the happy band wended its way down across the melting snows, and the breeding season was officially opened. My pond is visible from the house, but it is at quite a distance. I am not a voyeur and do not spend my time watching the sex antics of geese or anything else. But I try to keep reasonably well posted on all the creatures around the place, and it was apparent that the young gander was not allowed by his foster father to enjoy the privileges of the pond and that the old gander's attentions continued to be directed to just one of the young geese. I shall call her Liz to make this tale easier to tell.

Both geese were soon laying. Liz made her nest in the barn cellar; her sister, Apathy, made hers in the tie-up on the main floor of the barn. It was the end of April or the beginning of May. Still awfully cold—a reluctant spring.

Apathy laid three eggs, then quit. I marked them with a pencil and left them for the time being in the nest she had constructed. I made a mental note that they were infertile. Liz, unlike her sister, went right on laying, and became a laying fool. She dallied each morning at the pond with her foster father, and she laid and laid, like a commercial hen. I dutifully marked the eggs as they arrived—1, 2, 3, and so on. When she had accumulated a clutch of fifteen, I decided she had all she could cover. From then on, I took to removing the oldest egg from the nest each time a new egg was deposited. I also removed Apathy's three eggs from *her* nest, discarded them, and began substituting the purloined eggs from the barn cellar—the ones that rightfully belonged to Liz. Thus I gradually contrived to assemble a nest of fertile eggs for each bird, all of them laid by the fanatical Liz.

During the last week in May, Apathy, having produced three eggs of her own but having acquired ten through the kind offices of her sister and me, became broody and began to sit. Liz, with a tally of twenty-five eggs, ten of them stolen, showed not the slightest desire to sit. Laying was her thing. She laid and laid, while the other goose sat and sat. The old gander, marvelling at what he had wrought, showed a great deal of interest in both nests. The young gander was impressed but subdued. I continued to remove the early eggs from Liz's nest, holding her to a clutch of fifteen and discarding the extras. In late June, having produced forty-one eggs, ten of which were under Apathy, she at last sat down.

I had marked Apathy's hatching date on my desk calendar. On 15 the night before the goslings were due to arrive, when I made my rounds before going to bed, I looked in on her. She hissed, as usual, and ran her neck out. When I shone my light at her, two tiny green heads were visible, thrusting their way through her feathers. The goslings were here—a few hours ahead of schedule. My heart leapt up. Outside, in the barnyard, both ganders stood vigil. They knew very well what was up: ganders take an enormous interest in family affairs and are deeply impressed by the miracle of the egg-that-becomes-goose. I shut the door against them and went to bed.

Next morning, Sunday, I rose early and went straight to the barn 16 to see what the night had brought. Apathy was sitting quietly while five goslings teetered about on the slopes of the nest. One of them, as I watched, strayed from the others, and, not being able to find his way back, began sending out cries for help. They were the kind of distress signal any anxious father would instantly respond to. Suddenly, I heard sounds of a rumble outside in the barnyard where the ganders were—loud sounds of scuffling. I ran out. A fierce fight was in progress—it was no mere skirmish, it was the real thing. The young gander had grabbed the old one by the stern, his white head buried in feathers right where it would hurt the most, and was running him around the yard, punishing him at every turn—thrusting him on ahead and beating him unmercifully with his wings. It was an awesome sight, these two great male birds locked in combat, slugging it out—not for the favors of a female but for the dubious privilege of assuming the responsibilities of parent-hood. The young male had suffered all spring the indignities of a restricted life at the pond; now he had turned, at last, against the old one, as though to get even. Round and round, over rocks and through weeds, they raced, struggling and tripping, the old one in full retreat and in apparent pain. It was a beautiful late-June morn-ing, with fair-weather clouds and a light wind going, the grasses long in the orchard—the kind of morning that always carries for me overtones of summer sadness, I don't know why. Overhead, three swallows circled at low altitude, pursuing one white feather, the coveted trophy of nesting time. They were like three tiny fighter planes giving air support to the battle that raged below. For a moment, I thought of climbing the fence and trying to separate the combatants, but instead I just watched. The engagement was soon over. Plunging desperately down the lane, the old gander sank to the ground. The young one let go, turned, and walked back, screaming in triumph, to the door behind which his newly won family were waiting: a strange family indeed—the sister who was not even the mother of the babies, and the babies who were not even his own get.

When I was sure the fight was over, I climbed the fence and closed the barnyard gate, effectively separating victor from vanquished. The old gander had risen to his feet. He was in almost the same spot in the lane where his first wife had died mysteriously more than a year ago. I watched as he threaded his way slowly down the narrow path between clumps of thistles and daisies. His head was barely visible above the grasses, but his broken spirit was plain to any eye. When he reached the pasture bars, he hesitated, then painfully squatted and eased himself under the bottom bar and into the pasture, where he sat down on the cropped sward in the bright sun. I felt very deeply his sorry and his defeat. As things go in the animal kingdom, he is about my age, and when he lowered himself to creep under the bar, I could feel in my own bones his pain at bending down so far. Two hours later, he was still sitting there, the sun by this time quite hot. I had seen his likes often enough on the benches of the treeless main street of a Florida city—spent old males, motionless in the glare of the day.

Toward the end of the morning, he walked back up the lane as far as the gate, and there he stood all afternoon, his head and orange bill looking like the head of a great snake. The goose and her goslings had emerged into the barnyard. Through the space between the boards of the gate, the old fellow watched the enchanting scene; the goslings taking their frequent drinks of water, climbing in and out of the shallow pan for their first swim, closely guarded by the handsome young gander, shepherded by the pretty young goose.

After supper, I went into the tie-ups and pulled the five remaining, unhatched eggs—the unlucky ones, the ones that lacked what it takes to break out of an egg into the light of a fine June morning. I put the eggs in a basket and set the basket with some other miscellany consigned to the dump. I don't know anything sadder than a summer's day.

CONTENT

1. What are the two rival ganders meant to represent? Which one does White sympathize with? Why? After the older gander's vanquishment by the young gander, why does White say, "I have seen his likes often enough on the benches of the treeless main street of a Florida city—spent old males, motionless in the glare of the day"?

2. After describing Irving Closson's farm, White begins paragraph 6 with the observation, "it is about the pleasantest place to visit anywhere around." What does this tell us about White and his values?

3. White mentions in paragraph 2 that geese make good companions and are very much like humans. What evidence is there for this in the essay? In paragraph 8, White describes the path the gander led the goslings down as "the long, tortuous course between blueberry knolls and granite boulders." What is White implying about the role of the gander in this scene?

4. Why does White conclude this narrative with the sentence, "I don't know anything sadder than a summer's day"? What have the geese to do with the seasons? What have the seasons to do with White?

ORGANIZATION

5. In paragraph 3, White includes what seems a digression about the difficulty of getting a broody hen to hatch the eggs of the deceased goose. Why does White add these remarks to the tale of the gander?

6. Paragraph 5 includes a description of an old sleeping horse being shod by a neighboring farmer. Does this have anything to do with the purpose behind White's narrative?

7. Notice the order in which White presents the narrative of the old gander. His roles are arranged in the reverse order in which they would normally occur during his life's span; that is, first, he is a widower, then a parent, and finally a lover. How does

this make his replacement by the younger gander a matter of inevitability?

TOPICS FOR WRITING

8. Narrate a situation in which the age of the characters determines their outcome.
9. Write a narrative about an incident which reveals that something valuable from the past has been lost with changing times.
10. Write a narrative demonstrating conflicting viewpoints about the responsibilities two people are willing to assume as parents.

GEORGE ORWELL
A Hanging

George Orwell (1903–1950) was the pseudonym of Eric Blair. Orwell hated all forms of oppression, including communist totalitarianism. The Civil War in Spain found Orwell fighting against the Fascists (Homage to Catalonia, 1938), and continuing to warn Europe about its spread (The Road to Wigan Pier, 1937). He is best known for his satiric beast fable Animal Farm (1945), and his futuristic look at the anti-utopian world of Big Brother in 1984 (1949). In "A Hanging" we see Orwell as a police officer witnessing a public execution, but the man inside the uniform is shocked at his participation in both the hanging and the ceremony afterward.

It was Burma, a sodden morning of rains. A sickly light, like   1
yellow tinfoil, was slanting over the walls into the jail yard. We were waiting outside the condemned cells, a row of sheds fronted with double bars, like small animal cages. Each cell measured about ten feet by ten and was quite bare within except for a plank bed and a pot for drinking water. In some of them brown silent men were squatting at the inner bars, with their blankets draped round them. These were the condemned men, due to be hanged within the next week or two.

One prisoner had been brought out of his cell. He was a Hindu,   2
a puny wisp of a man, with a shaven head and vague liquid eyes. He had a thick, sprouting moustache, absurdly too big for his body, rather like the moustache of a comic man on the films. Six tall Indian

warders were guarding him and getting him ready for the gallows. Two of them stood by with rifles and fixed bayonets, while the others handcuffed him, passed a chain through his handcuffs and fixed it to their belts, and lashed his arms tight to his sides. They crowded very close about him, with their hands always on him in a careful caressing grip, as though all the while feeling him to make sure he was there. It was like men handling a fish which is still alive and may jump back into the water. But he stood quite unresisting, yielding his arms limply to the ropes, as though he hardly noticed what was happening.

Eight o'clock struck and a bugle call, desolately thin in the wet air, floated from the distant barracks. The superintendent of the jail, who was standing apart from the rest of us, moodily prodding the gravel with his stick, raised his head at the sound. He was an army doctor, with a grey toothbrush moustache and a gruff voice. "For God's sake hurry up, Francis," he said irritably. "The man ought to have been dead by this time. Aren't you ready yet?" 3

Francis, the head jailer, a fat Dravidian in a white drill suit and gold spectacles, waved his black hand. "Yes sir, yes sir," he bubbled. "All iss satisfactorily prepared. The hangman iss waiting. We shall proceed." 4

"Well, quick march, then. The prisoners can't get their breakfast till this job's over." 5

We set out for the gallows. Two warders marched on either side of the prisoner, with their rifles at the slope; two others marched close against him, gripping him by arm and shoulder, as though at once pushing and supporting him. The rest of us, magistrates and the like, followed behind. Suddenly, when we had gone ten yards, the procession stopped short without any order or warning. A dreadful thing had happened—a dog, come goodness knows whence, had appeared in the yard. It came bounding among us with a loud volley of barks, and leapt round us wagging its whole body, wild with glee at finding so many human beings together. It was a large woolly dog, half Airedale, half pariah. For a moment it pranced round us, and then, before anyone could stop, it had made a dash for the prisoner and, jumping up, tried to lick his face. Everyone stood aghast, too taken aback even to grab at the dog. 6

"Who let that bloody brute in here?" said the superintendent angrily. "Catch it, someone!" 7

A warder, detached from the escort, charged clumsily after the   8
dog, but it danced and gambolled just out of his reach, taking everything as part of the game. A young Eurasian jailer picked up a
handful of gravel and tried to stone the dog away, but it dodged
the stones and came after us again. Its yaps echoed from the jail
walls. The prisoner, in the grasp of the two warders, looked on
incuriously, as though this was another formality of the hanging.
It was several minutes before someone managed to catch the dog.
Then we put my handkerchief through its collar and moved off
once more, with the dog still straining and whimpering.

It was about forty yards to the gallows. I watched the bare brown   9
back of the prisoner marching in front of me. He walked clumsily
with his bound arms, but quite steadily, with that bobbing gait of
the Indian who never straightens his knees. At each step his mus-
cles slid neatly into place, the lock of hair on his scalp danced up
and down, his feet printed themselves on the wet gravel. And once,
in spite of the men who gripped him by each shoulder, he stepped
slightly aside to avoid a puddle on the path.

It is curious, but till that moment I had never realized what it   10
means to destroy a healthy, conscious man. When I saw the prisoner step aside to avoid the puddle I saw the mystery, the unspeakable wrongness, of cutting a life short when it is in full tide. This
man was not dying, he was alive just as we are alive. All the organs
of his body were working—bowels digesting food, skin renewing
itself, nails growing, tissue forming—all toiling away in solemn
foolery. His nails would still be growing when he stood on the drop,
when he was falling through the air with a tenth-of-a-second to
live. His eyes saw the yellow gravel and the grey walls, and his
brain still remembered, foresaw, reasoned—reasoned even about
puddles. He and we were a party of men walking together, seeing,
hearing, feeling, understanding the same world; and in two minutes, with a sudden snap, one of us would be gone—one mind
less, one world less.

The gallows stood in a small yard, separate from the main grounds   11
of the prison, and overgrown with tall prickly weeds. It was a brick
erection like three sides of a shed, with planking on top, and above
that two beams and a crossbar with the rope dangling. The hangman, a grey-haired convict in the white uniform of the prison, was
waiting beside his machine. He greeted us with a servile crouch as

we entered. At a word from Francis the two warders, gripping the prisoner more closely than ever, half led half pushed him to the gallows and helped him clumsily up the ladder. Then the hangman climbed up and fixed the rope round the prisoner's neck.

We stood waiting, five yards away. The warders had formed in a rough circle round the gallows. And then, when the noose was fixed, the prisoner began crying out to his god. It was a high, reiterated cry of "Ram! Ram! Ram! Ram!" not urgent and fearful like a prayer or cry for help, but steady, rhythmical, almost like the tolling of a bell. The dog answered the sound with a whine. The hangman, still standing on the gallows, produced a small cotton bag like a flour bag and drew it down over the prisoner's face. But the sound, muffled by the cloth, still persisted, over and over again: "Ram! Ram! Ram! Ram! Ram!" 12

The hangman climbed down and stood ready, holding the lever. Minutes seemed to pass. The steady, muffled crying from the prisoner went on and on. "Ram! Ram! Ram!" never faltering for an instant. The superintendent, his head on his chest, was slowly poking the ground with his stick; perhaps he was counting the cries, allowing the prisoner a fixed number—fifty, perhaps, or a hundred. Everyone had changed color. The Indians had gone grey like bad coffee, and one or two of the bayonets were wavering. We looked at the lashed, hooded man on the drop, and listened to his cries—each cry another second of life; the same thought was in all our minds: oh, kill him quickly, get it over, stop that abominable noise! 13

Suddenly the superintendent made up his mind. Throwing up his head he made a swift motion with his stick. "Chalo!" he shouted almost fiercely. 14

There was a clanking noise, and then dead silence. The prisoner had vanished, and the rope was twisting on itself. I let go of the dog, and it galloped immediately to the back of the gallows; but when it got there it stopped short, barked, and then retreated into a corner of the yard, where it stood among the weeds, looking timorously out at us. We went around the gallows to inspect the prisoner's body. He was dangling with his toes pointed straight downwards, very slowly revolving, as dead as a stone. 15

The superintendent reached out with his stick and poked the bare brown body; it oscillated slightly. "*He's* all right," said the superintendent. He backed out from under the gallows, and blew out a deep breath. The moody look had gone out of his face quite suddenly. He glanced at his wrist-watch. "Eight minutes past eight. Well, that's all for this morning, thank God."

The warders unfixed bayonets and marched away. The dog, sobered and conscious of having misbehaved itself, slipped after them. We walked out of the gallows yard, past the condemned cells with their waiting prisoners, into the big central yard of the prison. The convicts, under the command of warders armed with lathis, were already receiving their breakfast. They squatted in long rows, each man holding a pannikin, while two warders with buckets marched round ladling out rice; it seemed quite a homely, jolly scene, after the hanging. An enormous relief had come upon us now that the job was done. One felt an impulse to sink, to break into a run, to snigger. All at once every one began chattering gaily. [17]

The Eurasian boy walking beside me nodded towards the way we had come, with a knowing smile: "Do you know, sir, our friend (he meant the dead man) when he heard his appeal had been dismissed, he pissed on the floor of his cell. From fright. Kindly take one of my cigarettes, sir. Do you not admire my new silver case, sir? From the boxwalah, two rupees eight annas. Classy European style." [18]

Several people laughed—at what, nobody seemed certain. [19]

Francis was walking by the superintendent, talking garrulously: "Well, sir, all hass passed off with the utmost satisfactoriness. It was all finished—flick! like that. It iss not always so—oah, no! I have known cases where the doctor wass obliged to go beneath the gallows and pull the prissoner's legs to ensure decease. Most disagreeable!" [20]

"Wriggling about, eh? That's bad," said the superintendent. [21]

"Ach, sir, it iss worse when they become refractory! One man, I recall, clung to the bars of hiss cage when we went to take him out. You will scarcely credit, sir, that it took six warders to dislodge him, three pulling each leg. We reasoned with him. 'My dear fellow,' we said, 'think of all the pain and trouble you are causing to us! But no, he would not listen! Ach, he wass very troublesome!" [22]

I found that I was laughing quite loudly. Everyone was laughing. Even the superintendent grinned in a tolerant way. "You'd better all come out and have a drink," he said quite genially. "I've got a bottle of whiskey in the car. We could do with it." [23]

We went through the big double gates of the prison into the road.   2
"Pulling at his legs!" exclaimed a Burmese magistrate suddenly; and
burst into a loud chuckling. We all began laughing again. At that
moment Francis' anecdote seemed extraordinarily funny. We all had
a drink together, native and European alike, quite amicably. The
dead man was a hundred yards away.

CONTENT

1. What is the function of each character in the essay? Which ones
   are stereotypes, and which ones seem more real? Why is the
   superintendent in a hurry? Why does everyone laugh at the
   head jailer's story about the doctor's having to pull on the legs
   of the deceased man?

2. What is the conflict in the narrative? On which character or
   characters does the conflict center? Does the narrator remain
   aloof from the others, or does he share their fear and guilt over
   the death of the prisoner?

3. What is the theme of "A Hanging"? How does the setting function to support the conflict and the theme? What atmosphere
   do the comparisons of the first paragraph create? How does
   the final scene contrast with this? Why? Why does Orwell include
   the final line about the dead man being a hundred yards away?

ORGANIZATION

4. Does Orwell's narrative follow the classic plot structure? Where
   does Orwell place the climax?

5. What is the function of the opening paragraph describing the
   setting? How is it tied to the purpose of the essay?

6. Orwell brackets the hanging scene itself with references to a
   stray dog. How is this both an organizing device, and another
   way of calling attention to the narrative's meaning?

TOPICS FOR WRITING

7. Write a narrative of a significant incident witnessed by several
   people; include the different ways in which these spectators
   reacted to it.

8. Select an incident that reveals some kind of social injustice (for
   example, racial or religious prejudice, callous reactions to pov-

erty, or the aged), narrate it, and include your own observations about what you witnessed.

9. Write a narrative account of an incident that reveals the existence of a previously unnoticed "pecking order."

PART 4
Description: Writing to Recreate Persons and Places

When you describe, you are recreating in words the physical characteristics of a person, place, or object, usually in the absence of the thing itself, and for an audience that may be totally or relatively unfamiliar with the thing. For example, New Yorker John McPhee describes the appearance and the workings of a farmers' produce market. Although the description is intended for a non-New York audience, even those who have visited that particular market, will find new insights through McPhee's powers of observation:

> There is a rhythm in the movement of the crowd, in the stopping, the selecting, the moving on—the time, unconsciously budgeted to assess one farm against another, to convict a tomato, to choose a peach. The seller comes to feel the rate of flow, and—for all the small remarks, the meeting of eyes—to feel as well the seclusion of anonymity that comes with the money aprons and the hanging scales. Rich Hodgson—handing them their blue free plums. They don't know he skis in Utah. Melissa Mousseau—changing a twenty for a bag of pears. They don't know that she goes, too. Hemmingway and Thueson, the athletes, have heard more encouraging sounds from other crowds. "If you charge for three pounds, give me three full pounds and not two pounds and fifteen ounces, boy." [*Giving Good Weight* (Farrar, Straus, Giroux, 1979), 67–68.]

A description must not merely reproduce reality as accurately as possible, but must involve your unique perspective as a writer, and your awareness of how much your audience does or does not know. Description frequently includes the physical characteristics of the thing described, but not all description is limited to the physical. Can you conjure up the essential characteristics or features of a person or a place without reference to outward appearances? Aren't invisible characteristics also part of the essence of a thing? To answer these questions let's examine a pair of descriptions, first John McPhee's physical description of Frank Boyden, the headmaster of Deerfield Academy in Massachusetts, then, Adam Smith's description of Baba Ram Daas (Richard Alpert), psychologist and convert to Eastern mysticism.

> His hair is not white but slate-gray, and his demeanor, which hasn't changed in forty years, still suggests a small, grumpy Labrador. He sometimes dresses in gray trousers, a dark-blue jacket, and brown cordovan shoes—choices that are somewhat collegiate and could be taken as a mild sign of age, because for decades he wore dark-blue worsted suits and maroon ties almost exclusively, winter and summer, hanging on to each successive suit until it fell off him in threads. One of his jacket pockets today has a four-inch rip that has been bound with black thread. He doesn't care. . . [*The Headmaster* (Farrar, Strauss, and Giroux, 1966), 10.]

* * *

> . . . this gentleman is balding, with graying beard and long hair in the back, and the one-stringed instruments have ceased their sound and he just sits there and smiles. And after the longest time, he says, "Well, here we are." And his voice is so warm and he is so relaxed and he smiles and gradually everybody starts to smile, "Here we are," he says again, and here we are, not just in this room but all together on the surface of the planet—"Here we are, and we'll just talk a little, I'll talk some, and then we can get up and walk around and maybe have some cider, and you can talk, or ask questions, and we'll all just hang out for a while." [*Powers of Mind* (Random House, 1975), 315.]

Few would quarrel with the notion that both of these are descriptions, but how different they are. Both start with the physical appearance of the person, but McPhee stays on that track except for two brief judgments (". . . could be taken as a mild sign of age," and "He doesn't care") piling up the physical details; Smith, on the other hand, after relating three brief physical details (balding, graying beard, long hair) shifts to dialogue and narrative except for two later physical characteristics ("his voice is so warm and he is so relaxed"). What should be evident is that McPhee concentrates on the external appearance of his subject, whereas Smith is more interested in the aura, the internal characteristics that create the charisma of Baba Ram Dass. Both selections try to capture the distinctive features of their subjects, but the features that account for the individuality of a thing, for its uniqueness, may not all be physical. The defining quality of all descriptions, then, is their ability to *indivi-*

duate, to distinguish this thing from all other things which may be like it. In the process, the writer may use expository modes—such as definition, classification, or contrast—or narrative modes, as Smith does in setting a scene and carrying the narrative along with action and dialogue. Because the primary purpose is to reveal the individuating quality of the subject, such a piece would be a description. In Peter Matthiessen's description of Delano, California, which follows this introduction, notice that not only are we given the appearance of the place, but the history of how it got to be that way, and the attitudes of its residents toward each other.

Descriptions, then, may be of several kinds. To select the broadest base, they could be distinguished as:

1. *Objective Realistic,* primarily a documentary approach concentrating mostly on externals, but verifying as carefully as possible, everything that is not purely external. A purely objective description is more of an ideal than a reality because the camera eye of the writer cannot turn to everything, and therefore must select some things to be included, others to be left out, still others to be given special prominence. We have already discussed some problems of selectivity in the introduction to journals. Yet, some highly selective descriptions give the impression of being purely objective. Here is John McPhee's objective description of the Indian Point No. 2 nuclear power plant:

> The containment structure looks vaguely like the Jefferson Memorial—a simple, stunning cylinder under a hemispheric dome, all in white reinforced concrete. Its diameter is a hundred and thirty-five feet. The dome and the side walls are from three and a half to four and a half feet thick and are lined with steel. *The Curve of Binding Energy* (Farrar, Straus, & Giroux, 1973), 99.]

2. *Subjective Impressionistic,* essentially a personal view of the reality being created. Like an impressionistic painting, it may not tell the literal truth, but will capture the essential quality of an object in a spot of time, in a certain light. In the sense in which Picasso meant his dictum, "Art is a lie which tells the truth," impressionistic descriptions attempt to capture the essential nature of the thing frequently missed by the more documentary realistic approach. Virginia Woolf's impressionistic description of dusk reflects not only the external scene, its feeling and texture, but also the mind of the

viewer. Notice that it recreates not the sights as the light fades, but the diminishing sounds:

> And now as if the cleaning and the scrubbing and the scything and the mowing had drowned it there rose that half-heard melody, that intermittent music which the ear catches but lets fall; a bark, a bleat; irregular, intermittent, yet somehow related; the hum of an insect, the tremor of cut grass, dissevered yet somehow belonging; the jar of a dorbeetle, the squeak of a wheel, loud, low, but mysteriously related; which the ear strains to bring together and is always on the verge of harmonising, but they are never quite heard, never fully harmonised, and at last, in the evening, one after another the sounds die out, and the harmony falters, and silence falls. . .With the sunset sharpness was lost, and like mist rising, quiet rose, quiet spread, the wind settled; loosely the world shook it self down to sleep, darkly here without a light to it, save what came green suffused through leaves, or pale on the white flowers in the bed by the window. [*To the Lighthouse* (Harcourt, Brace and World, 1927) 212–13.]

Another characteristic common to both types of descriptions as opposed to narrative writing, in which the subject is changing through time—is that the subject is regarded as static. In this sense, description is similar to painting or photography which, with a few exceptions, tries to freeze time and capture its subject at rest, or in a segment of action that does not, itself, change. Even Matthiessen's description of Delano, which goes back in time to California's Central Valley before today's large agricultural operations, is primarily interested in the area *now*; it merely uses the historical material to help explain the way Delano became what it is today. Narrative can be combined with description, as in the Baba Ram Dass description, but the real subject remains Baba Ram Dass *now*, at the moment in time Smith is describing him.

With a clearer understanding of what description is, we can now ask a related question: What are some of the elements of successful description?

Details   A successful description includes essential details that effectively recreate the subject, making it *perceptible, clear,* and *consistent for the reader.*

If a description is to be *perceptible*, it must be anchored in one or more sense perceptions. Thomas Wolfe uses such sense perceptions in the following description in which he recreates the main character's childhood memories by evoking a series of smells:

. . . the exciting smell of chalk and varnished desks; the smell of heavy bread-sandwiches of cold fried meat and butter; the smell of new leather in a saddler's shop, or of a warm leather chair, of honey and of unground coffee; of barrelled sweet-pickles and cheese and all the fragrant compost of the grocer's; the smell of stored apples in the cellar, and of orchard apple smells, of pressed-cider pulp; of pears ripening on a sunny shelf, and of ripe cherries stewing with sugar on hot stoves before preserving; the smell of whittled wood, of all young lumber, of sawdust and shavings; of peaches stuck with cloves and pickled in brandy; of pine sap, and green pine needles; of a horse's pared hoof; of chestnuts roasting, of bowls of nuts and raisins; of hot cracklin, and of young roast pork; of butter and cinnamon melting on hot candied yams. [*Look Homeward, Angel* (Scribners, 1929), 69.]

This torrent of sense perceptions is fairly unstructured, but that is precisely the point here: It is an accurate description of the way memory presents experience. Wolfe's description is successful because of the accumulated details.

The description of a subjective impression should be anchored in some tangible, sensually *perceptible* phenomenon. This is another way of saying that although abstractions, generalizations, and summary statements may occur in descriptions, they should be supported by something the reader can see, taste, smell, hear, or touch. Suppose you wished to describe a highly personal emotion—say, despair; you would need to relate it to something external to communicate the emotion to the reader. Emily Dickinson solved the problem by finding a series of tangible objects (what T. S. Eliot called objective correlatives), each of which ties the emotion to a different sense:

There's a certain Slant of light,
Winter Afternoons—
That oppresses like the Heft
Of Cathedral Tunes—

The visual image of light, the tactile feel of "heft" and the auditory word "tunes"—all provide a sensible basis for a description of the more abstract emotion "despair."

There must be some rationale for the selection of details presented to the reader. Often this will follow automatically from the writer's initial conception of the subject; at other times, in order to achieve *clarity* and *consistency*, it is necessary to create a dominant impression, a single overriding and controlling view of the subject. For example, anthropologist Loren Eiseley has described how, awakening just before dawn on the twentieth floor of a midtown hotel in New York, he looked down on the rooftops and saw a strange sight, a bit of wilderness in the city, a reminder of "the downright miraculous nature of the planet."

> I found I was looking down from that great height into a series of curious cupolas or lofts that I could just barely make out in the darkness. As I looked, the outlines of these lofts become more distinct because the light was being reflected from the wings of pigeons who, in utter silence, were beginning to float outward upon the city. In and out through open slits in the cupolas passed the white-winged birds on their mysterious errands. At this hour the city was theirs, and quietly, without the brush of a single wing tip against stone in that high, eerie place, they were taking over the spires of Manhattan. They were pouring upward in a light that was not yet perceptible to human eyes, while far down in the black darkness of the alleys it was still midnight.
>
> As I crouched half asleep across the sill, I had a moment's illusion that the world had changed in the night, as in some immense snowfall, and that if I were to leave, it would have to be as these other inhabitants were doing, by the window. . . To and fro went the wings, to and fro. There were no sounds from any of them. They knew man was asleep and this light for a while was theirs. . .
>
> Around and around went the wings. It needed only a little courage, only a little shove from the window ledge to enter that city of light. ["The Judgment of the Birds," *The Immense Journey* (Random House, 1957), 165–66.]

The dominant impression of the scene—whiteness—is repeated seven times in one form or another ("white," "light," "snowfall"); furthermore, the impression is intensified by the contrasting impression of darkness ("dark," "night," "midnight"), and the complementary impression of silence ("no sound," "quietly," "silence.") Eiseley has created an impression of the miraculous in the midst of the ordinary by showing us this whitened scene from "an inverted angle," not just the upside-down view of pigeons seen from above, but something unusual, a coincidence of timing and insight, of man and animal—what Eiseley calls "the border of two worlds." The strange scene is effectively recreated because Eiseley has focused his description on a dominant impression, and has effectively screened out any details which do not contribute to that impression.

Concrete Diction   As has already been stated, the details of a successful description must be conveyed in language that is concrete and particular. Often students are led to believe that a good description must have long strings of modifiers if it is to be successful. The following sentence from an article by Burton Bernstein was written for humorous effect: "They were a tightly knit, neighborly, backbiting, feuding, forgiving, gracious, vulgar, devout, banal, parochial, charitable, fearful, stalwart community. . ." ["The Bernstein Family—Part II," *The New Yorker* (March 29, 1982), 68.] Using concrete diction does not mean piling up a series of adjectives before every noun.

The first half of Jonathan Swift's definition of style, "the proper words in the proper place," provides a better clue to writing effective descriptions—namely finding the right word, not only the word with the exact connotations or associations, but the more concrete word, the word closest to what S. I. Hayakawa calls extensional reality. Hayakawa's concept of the ladder of abstraction is a graphic way of looking at the idea of various synonyms being available to describe a subject. The words at the bottom of the ladder are closest to the "real" object, the most particularized, and therefore the most exclusive; those at the top of the ladder, in contrast, are the least concrete, the least particular, and therefore the most inclusive. As one goes up the ladder, the terms become increasingly abstract, refer more to mental concepts, and less to tangible things. Using the central figure from Peter Matthiessen's description, and placing him on the ladder, the synonyms available might look like this:

ABSTRACT

spokesman

labor leader

President of the United Farm Workers

Caesar Chavez

CONCRETE

The point is not to avoid using synonyms altogether, but to recognize that in descriptive writing, barring other considerations such as monotonous repetition of the same word, it is preferable to choose the more concrete word:

In the following description from Ernest Hemingway's "Big Two-Hearted River: Part I," notice that the words are all simple and concrete, that the author doesn't shy away from repeating key words for their cumulative effect, that adjectives are used sparingly, but precisely, and that the entire description is written in short crisp sentences appropriate to the subject.

There was no underbrush in the island pine trees. The trunks of the trees went straight up or slanted toward each other. The trunks were straight and brown without branches. The branches were high above. Some interlocked to make a solid shadow on the brown forest floor. Around the grove of trees was a bare space. It was brown and soft underfoot as Nick walked on it. This was the overlapping of the pine needle floor, extending out beyond the width of the high branches. The trees had grown tall and the branches moved high, leaving in the sun this bare space they had once covered with shadow. Sharp at the edge of this extension of the forest floor commenced the sweet fern. [*The First Forty-Nine Stories* (Jonathan Cape, 1944), 168–69]

Choosing the right word also involves being aware of the connotations of words—that is, all of the suggestions and associations embedded in a word or phrase. Because English offers us so many synonyms, the difference between one word and another is often merely the connotations of these words. For example, a small vacation home might be described as a bungalow, a cottage, a cabin, a camp, or a shack. So, using precise, accurate diction is a matter of choosing both the degree of concreteness and the desired connotations of the various synonyms which mean not the same thing, but only *approximately* the same thing.

Figures of Speech   Comparisons or figures of speech help to extend the range of our sensory experience by connecting something being described with something within the reader's experience. Suppose in a paper on Central America you described Panama as "an isthmus between the Atlantic and Pacific Oceans." You would have used literal language, that is, language which is denotative and points directly to the thing for which it stands. If, however, you said, Panama was "like a four-way bridge between North and South America, the Atlantic and the Pacific" you would have used a *simile* (a limited comparison using "like" or "as"), or figurative language. We can draw a distinction between literal language which is purely denotative and points to the thing for which it stands, and figurative language. Figures of speech—similes, metaphors and symbols—extend the bounds of language by using the connotations or suggestive power of words. They draw together, as in the above comparison between Panama and a bridge, things not normally associated. In this way a writer forces us to see things in a new light, in a way we have never quite viewed them before. The Chilean poet Pablo Neruda called Panama "the delicate waist of the Americas," employing *a metaphor* or direct comparison. A metaphor establishes a temporary equality between the two halves of the comparison. Metaphors also allow you to explore the possibilities of the comparison, in this case the fragility of the link between the two continents. You can extend the comparison by asking, "How many ways is Panama like 'a delicate waist'?" Metaphors are somewhat like *analogies* (see page 350), comparisons used to clarify the unfamiliar with the familiar since both can extend the similarities. If you were to say that any United States overseas possession could become another Panama, you would be using Panama as a symbol—something that stands in place of something else—and would have extended your subject to cover an even broader range of implications. Like metaphors, symbols radiate meaning outward; but unlike similes and metaphors, symbols belong to the same conceptual order as the thing symbolized: territories and possessions, not bridges and waists. All three figures of speech make bland abstract descriptions more concrete, more vital and closer to the reader's experience.

Clear and Consistent Organization　The details of a description, even if written in concrete and accurate language, still must be arranged in a coherent fashion. This calls for some kind of pattern of organization which will present the material in a clear, consistent, and orderly way. With physical objects, descriptions present fewer problems if a writer follows an appropriate and consistent pattern of *spatial organization*. This means that a place could be described, for example, from top to bottom, from left to right, from near to far, or the reverse of any of these; a person, from head to toe, or the reverse, from prominent features to those less prominent, from clothes or manners to physiological features, or the reverse. A more subjective description would combine spatial organization with some inner judgments; for example, a description could move from important, spatially arranged details to secondary details that fill in the outline, or from outer to inner characteristics, or from first impressions to more lasting ones. The patterns are too numerous to illustrate, but it is important to be consistent in following the pattern chosen.

Climactic order is a pattern which proceeds from the unimportant—often, deliberately, even the trivial—to the important, ending on the most significant detail of the description. Notice how this pattern is adhered to in Flannery O'Connor's chilling description of a family's encounter with three escaped convicts who find the family's car has overturned in a ditch on a lonely country road. The leader, a killer named the Misfit, is described as the family sees him from the bottom of the ditch:

> The driver got out of the car and stood by the side of it, looking down at them. He was an older man than the other two. His hair was just beginning to gray and he wore silver-rimmed spectacles that gave him a scholarly look. He had a long creased face and didn't have on any shirt or undershirt. He had on blue jeans that were too tight for him and was holding a black hat and a gun. The two boys also had guns. ["A Good Man Is Hard To Find," *Complete Stories* (Farrar, Straus and Giroux, 1979), 126.]

The description ends on the most important detail, the gun, and it builds to it by including successively more important details such as the ill-fitting jeans of the escaped convict. The clothes (or lack of them) and the gun are a surprise following the opening descriptive details which focus on age and the scholarly look the spectacles lend the killer. The *angle of vision*, from the bottom of the ditch, is consistently maintained throughout with the inclusion of subsequent details one might notice looking up from a ditch: "He had on tan and white shoes and no socks, and his ankles were red and thin." Not only, then, is it important to be consistent in your choice of pattern or organization, but it is equally important to locate yourself with respect to the object being described, and to remain consistent in your *angle of vision*.

A description which effectively captures the uniqueness of a thing—its tangibility or its ineffability—begins when a writer makes a series of strategic choices after answering several questions: What kind of description is this? What details will support the dominant impression? How shall I organize the details? What words and what sentences best express the subject? If the writer is lucky, has answered the questions correctly and chosen the right strategies, then he or she will have created a memorable portrait of the subject and left an eloquent testimony to the recreative power of words.

SHORT EXAMPLE—DESCRIPTION OF A PERSON

GORE VIDAL
President John F. Kennedy

Gore Vidal wrote his first novel, Williwaw *(1946), when he was only nineteen. Since then his writing has included novels—*The City and the Pillar *(1949),* Julian *(1964),* Myra Breckinridge *(1968), and* Burr *(1973); plays—*Visit to a Small Planet *(1957) and* The Best Man *(1968); and essays—*Homage to Daniel Shays *(1972) and* Matters of Fact and Fiction *(1977). Always controversial, Vidal has run several times for national office—once for Congress from upstate New York and once for the Senate from California.*

Close to, Kennedy looks older than his photographs. The outline is slender and youthful, but the face is heavily lined for his age. On the upper lip are those tiny vertical lines characteristic of a more advanced age. He is usually tanned from the sun, while his hair is what lady novelists call "chestnut," beginning to go gray. His eyes are very odd. They are, I think a murky, opaque blue, "interested," as Gertrude Stein once said of Hemingway's eyes, "not interesting"; they give an impression of flatness, while long blond eyelashes screen expression at will. His stubby boy fingers tend to drum nervously on tables, on cups and glasses. He is immaculately dressed; although, disconcertingly, occasional white chest hairs curl over his collar.

DISCUSSION

This short close-up portrait of President Kennedy (Vidal was a relative by marriage of the Kennedys) is a departure from the usual idealized descriptions of the vigorous young president, but instead includes his "warts and blemishes." The first sentence announces Vidal's approach; he will focus on the details that make Kennedy look old "for his age." When viewed from afar, the impression is one of youth, of elegant outlines; but up close, disconcerting aging details contradict the first superficial impressions. Even when Vidal seems to be paying a compliment ("he is immaculately dressed"), the writer cannot resist leaving us with the dominant impression of hidden age reasserting itself ("occasional white chest hairs curl over his collar.") The youthful details of the traditional portraits are here, but are given an ironic twist. His mane of chestnut hair is "beginning to go gray"; his famous sparkling blue eyes are "odd," not so much sparkling as "murky, opaque blue"; and the much photographed fingers, touching a contemplative forehead in the classic view of the President during the Cuban Missile Crisis, are now "stubby boy fingers" drumming nervously. You may disagree with the accuracy of Gore Vidal's portrait, but it is certainly not stereotypic, nor is it inconsistent in its use of a dominant impression, or in the way Vidal marshalls details to support that impression.

TRUMAN CAPOTE
Marlon Brando

In 1954, when he wrote the screenplay for John Huston's cult classic Beat the Devil, *Truman Capote's reputation as a remarkable stylist with a deep affinity for eccentric characters, both fictional and real, had been well established. By 1980, with the publication of his non-fiction work* Music for Chameleons, *the controversial author had become as recognizable as the "beautiful people" who were often his subjects. The following descriptive portrait, adapted from* The Dogs Bark *(1973), contrasts Marlon Brando as he appeared in 1956 with the youthful actor Capote had met ten years earlier.*

Watching him now, with his eyes closed, his un-lined face white under an overhead light, I felt as if the moment of my initial encounter with him were being re-created. The year of that meeting was 1947; it was a winter afternoon in New York, when I had occasion to attend a rehearsal of Tennessee Williams' *A Streetcar Named Desire*, in which Brando was to play the role of Stanley Kowalski. It was this role that first brought him general recognition, although among the New York theatre's cognoscenti he had already attracted attention, through his student work with the drama coach Stella Adler and a few Broadway appearances—one in a play by Maxwell Anderson, *Truckline Café*, and another as Marchbanks opposite Katharine Cornell's *Candida*, in which he showed an ability that had been much praised and discussed. Elia Kazan, the director of *A Streetcar Named Desire*, said at that time, and has recently repeated, "Marlon is just the best actor in the world." But ten years ago, on

the remembered afternoon, he was still relatively unknown; at least,
I hadn't a clue to who he might be when, arriving too early at the
Streetcar rehearsal, I found the auditorium deserted and a brawny
young man stretched out atop a table on the stage under the gloomy
glare of work lights, solidly asleep. Because he was wearing a white
T shirt and denim trousers, because of his squat gymnasium physique—the weightlifter's arms, the Charles Atlas chest (though an
opened *Basic Writings of Sigmund Freud* was resting on it)—I took
him for a stagehand. Or did until I looked closely at his face. It was
as if a stranger's head had been attached to the brawny body, as in
certain counterfeit photographs. For this face was so very untough,
superimposing, as it did, an almost angelic refinement and gentleness upon hard-jawed good looks: taut skin, a broad, high forehead, wide-apart eyes, an aquiline nose, full lips with a relaxed,
sensual expression. Not the least suggestion of Williams' unpoetic
Kowalski. It was therefore rather an experience to observe, later
that afternoon, with what chameleon ease Brando acquired the
character's cruel and gaudy colors, how superbly, like a guileful
salamander, he slithered into the part, how his own persona evap-
orated—just as, in this Kyoto hotel room nine years afterward, my
1947 memory of Brando receded, disappeared into his 1956 self.
And the present Brando, the one lounging there on the *tatami* and
lazily puffing filtered cigarettes as he talked and talked, was, of
course, a different person—bound to be. His body was thicker; his
forehead higher, for his hair was thinner; he was richer (from the
producers of *Sayonara* he could expect a salary of three hundred
thousand dollars, plus a percentage of the picture's earnings); and
he'd become, as one journalist put it, "the Valentino of the bop
generation"—turned into such a world celebrity that when he went
out in public here in Japan, he deemed it wise to hide his face not
only by wearing dark glasses but by donning a surgeon's gauze
mask as well. (The latter bit of disguise is not so *outré* in Japan as
it may sound, since numerous Asians wear such masks, on the
theory that they prevent the spreading of germs.) Those were some
of the alterations a decade had made. There were others. His eyes
had changed. Although their *caffé-espresso* color was the same, the
shyness, any traces of real vulnerability that they had formerly held,
had left them; now he looked at people with assurance, and with
what can only be called a pitying expression, as though he dwelt
in spheres of enlightenment where they, to his regret, did not. (The

reactions of the people subjected to this gaze of constant commiseration range from that of a young actress who avowed that "Marlon is really a very *spiritual* person, wise and very sincere; you can see it in his eyes" to that of a Brando acquaintance who said, "The way he looks at you, like he was so damn sorry for you—doesn't it make you want to cut your throat?") Nevertheless, the subtly tender character of his face had been preserved. Or almost. For in the years between he'd had an accident that gave his face a more conventionally masculine aspect. It was just that his nose had been broken. And maneuvering a word in edge-wise, I asked, "How did you break your nose?"

". . . by which I don't mean that I'm *always* unhappy. I remember   2 one April I was in Sicily. A hot day, and flowers everywhere. I like flowers, the ones that smell. Gardenias. Anyway, it was April and I was in Sicily, and I went off by myself. Lay down in this field of flowers. Went to sleep. That made me happy. I was happy *then*. What? You say something?"

"I was wondering how you broke your nose."   3

He rubbed his nose and grinned, as though remembering an   4 experience as happy as the Sicilian nap. "That was a long time ago. I did it boxing. It was when I was in *Streetcar*. We—some of the guys backstage and me—we used to go down to the boiler room in the theatre and horse around, mix it up. One night I was mixing it up with this guy and—crack! So I put on my coat and walked around to the nearest hospital—it was off Broadway somewhere. My nose was really busted. They had to give me an anesthetic to set it, and put me to bed. Not that I was sorry. *Streetcar* had been running about a year and I was sick of it. But my nose healed pretty quick, and I guess I would've been back in the show practically right away if I hadn't done what I did to Irene Selznick." His grin broadened as he mentioned Mrs. Selznick, who had been the producer of the Williams play. "There is one shrewd lady, Irene Selznick. When she wants something, she wants it. And she wanted me back in the play. But when I heard she was coming to the hospital, I went to work with bandages and iodine and mercurochrome, and—Christ!—when she walked in the door, I looked like my head had been cut off. At the least. And *sounded* as though I were dying. 'Oh, Marlon,' she said, 'you poor, *poor* boy! And I said, 'Don't you worry about anything, Irene. I'll be back in the show tonight!' And she said, 'Don't you dare! We can manage without you for—for—well, a *few* days more.' 'No, no,' I said. 'I'm okay. I want to work. Tell them I'll be back tonight.' So she said, 'You're in no condition, you poor darling. I *forbid* you to come to the theatre.' So I stayed in the hospital and had myself a ball." (Mrs. Selznick, recalling the incident recently, said, "They didn't set his nose properly at all. Suddenly his face was quite different. Kind of tough. For months afterward I kept telling him, 'But they've *ruined* your face. You must have your nose broken again and reset.' Luckily for him, he didn't listen to me. Because I honestly think that broken nose made his fortune as far as the movies go. It gave him sex appeal. He was too beautiful before.")

CONTENT

1. Capote's portrait of Brando concentrates on the most prominent feature, the dominant impression—namely the sharp contrast between what Capote calls Brando's "gymnasium physique" and his "angelic" face. What does Truman Capote do to develop this impression?
2. Why does Capote include the story about Brando's breaking his nose? Does this contrast between his almost perfect good looks and his more rugged aspect increase the mystery of Brando? Is it why some observers think him sensitive, whereas others see him as looking down on people?

ORGANIZATION

3. Capote's description is almost completely enclosed within a flashback narrative. What advantages for effects does this arrangement give Capote?
4. Capote's description contrasts the youthful Brando with Brando nine years later. How do the descriptions differ? Does placing the narrative of the broken-nose incident after the contrasting descriptions of Brando help to emphasize the contrast or does it take our attention away from the physical appearance of Brando?

TOPICS FOR WRITING

5. Write a description of someone as they were ten or more years ago and as they are now. If your memory fails you, use an old photograph for the comparison.

6. Describe someone whom you know well; concentrate on a dominant feature, and build your description around the dominant impression.

TOM WOLFE
John Glenn, Astronaut

Tom Wolfe, known as the creator and spokesman for the New Journalism, developed his idiosyncratic style as a means of getting the reader's attention. The titles of his meticulously researched books reflect that flamboyancy: The Kandy-Kolored Tangerine-Flake Streamline Baby *(1965),* The Electric Kool-Aid Acid Test *(1968),* Radical Chic and Mau-Mauing the Flak Catchers *(1970), and* From Bauhause to Our House *(1981). Wolfe's comments about American society are incisive, witty, and irreverent, but few critics will quarrel with his ability to recreate accurately the essentials of a scene. In the following portrait of John Glenn from* The Right Stuff *(1977), Wolfe sees the astronauts both as national heroes and as ordinary men.*

From the very beginning this "astronaut" business was just an unbelievable good deal. It was such a good deal that it seemed like tempting fate for an astronaut to call himself an astronaut, even though that was the official job description. You didn't even refer to the others as astronauts. You'd never say something such as "I'll take that up with the other astronauts." You'd say, "I'll take that up with the other fellows" or "the other pilots." Somehow calling yourself an "astronaut" was like a combat ace going around describing his occupation as "combat ace." This thing was such an unbelievable good deal, it was as if "astronaut" were an honorific, like "champion" or "superstar," as if the word itself were one of the infinite variety of *goodies* that Project Mercury was bringing your way.

And not just *goodies* in the crass sense, either. It had *all* the things that made you feel good, including the things that were good for the soul. For long stretches you'd bury yourself in training, in blissful isolation, good rugged bare-boned isolation, in Low Rent surroundings, in settings that even resembled hallowed Edwards in the old X-1 days, and with that same pioneer spirit, which money cannot buy, and with everybody pitching in and working endless hours, so that rank meant nothing, and people didn't even have the inclination, much less the time, to sit around and make the usual complaints about government work.

And then, just about the time you were entering a good healthy state of exhaustion from the work, they would take you out of your isolation and lead you up to that balcony that all fighter jocks secretly dreamed of, the one where you walked out before the multitudes like the Pope, and . . . it actually happened! The people of America cheered their brains out for thirty minutes or so, and then you went back into your noble isolation for more work . . . or for a few proficiency runs at nailing down the holy coordinates of the fighter jock's life, which were, of course, Flying & Drinking and Drinking & Driving and the rest of it. These things you could plot on the great graph of Project Mercury in the most spectacular way, with the exception of the first: Flying. The lack of flying time was troubling, but the other items existed in such extraordinary dimensions that it was hard to concentrate on it at first. Any man who wasn't above a little regrouping now and then, to keep the highly trained mechanism from being wound up too tight, to "maintain an even strain," in the Schirra parlance, found himself in absolute Fighter Jock Heaven. But even the rare pilot who was aloof from such cheap thrills, such as the deacon, John Glenn, found plenty of *goodies* to even out the strain of hard work and mass adoration.

Each of them had an eye on Glenn, all right. Glenn's own personal conduct was a constant reminder of what the game was really all about. To all but Scott Carpenter, and perhaps one other, the way Glenn was going about this thing was irritating.

The seven of them were stationed at Langley Air Force Base in the Tidewater section of Virginia on the James River, about 150 miles due south of Washington. Langley had been the experimental facility of the old National Advisory Committee for Aeronautics and was now the headquarters of NASA's Space Task Group for Project Mercury. Every morning they could count on seeing John Glenn up early, out on the grounds, in the middle of everything, where nobody could miss him, doing his roadwork. He'd be out there in full view, on the circular driveway of the Bachelor Officers Quarters, togged out in his sweatsuit, his great freckled face flaming red and shining with sweat, going around and around, running a mile, two miles, three miles, there was no end to it, in front of everybody. It was irritating, because it was so unnecessary. There had been a vague medical directive to the effect that each of them would engage in at least four hours of "unsupervised exercise" per week, but that was the last that was heard of. The medical staff assigned to Project Mercury were mainly young military doctors, a bit dazzled by the mission, some of them, and they were not about to call an astronaut on the carpet and demand an accounting of his four hours. Fighter jocks, as a breed, put physical exercise very low on the list of things that made up the right stuff. They enjoyed the rude animal health of youth. They put their bodies through dreadful abuses, often in the form of drinking bouts followed by lack of sleep and mortal hangovers, and they still performed like champions. ("I don't advise it, you understand, but it *can* be done"—provided you have the right stuff, you miserable pudknocker.) Most agreed with Wally Schirra, who felt that any form of exercise that wasn't fun, such as waterskiing or handball, was bad for your nervous system. But here was Glenn, pounding through everybody's field of vision with his morning roadwork, as if he were preparing for the championship fight.

The good Marine didn't just do his roadwork and leave it at that, either. Oh, no. The rest of them had their families installed at Langley Air Force Base or at least in the Langley vicinity. Gordon Cooper and Scott Carpenter and their families were packed into apartments on the base, the usual sort of worn-out base housing that junior officers rated. Wally Schirra, Gus Grissom, and Deke Slayton lived in a rather sad-looking housing development on the other side of the Newport News airport. Around the development was a stucco wall of the color known as glum ocher. Alan Shepard and his family lived a little farther away in Virginia Beach, where they happened to be living when he was chosen for Project Mercury. But Glenn . . . Glenn has his family housed 120 miles away in Arlington, Virginia, outside of Washington, and at Langley he stays in the Bachelor Officers Quarters, the BOQ, and does his running out front in the driveway. If this had been some devilishly clever scheme for him to get away from home and hearth and indulge in Drinking & Driving & so forth, that would have been one thing. But he wasn't the type. He was living in a bare room with nothing but a narrow bed and an upholstered chair and a little desk and a lamp and a lineup of books on astronomy, physics, and engineering, plus a Bible. On the weekends he would faithfully make his way home to his wife, Annie, and the children in an ancient Prinz, a real beat-up junker that was about four feet long and had perhaps forty horsepower, the sorriest-looking and most underpowered automobile still legally registered to any fighter pilot in America. A jock with any natural instincts at all, with any true devotion to the holy coordinates, either possessed or was eating his heart out for the sort of car that Alan Shepard had, which was a Corvette, or that Wally Schirra had, which was a Triumph, i.e., a sports car, or some kind of hot car, anyway, something that would enable you to hang your hide out over the edge with a little class when you reached the Driving juncture on the coordinates several times a week, as was inevitable for everyone but someone like John Glenn. This guy was putting on an incredible show! He was praying in public. He was presenting himself in their very midst as the flying monk or whatever the Presbyterian version of a monk was. A saint, maybe; or an ascetic; or maybe just the village scone crusher.

Being a good Presbyterian, John Glenn knew that praying in public was no violation of faith. The faith even encouraged it; it set a salubrious example for the public. Nor did John Glenn feel the slightest discomfort because now, in post-World War II America, virtue was out of style. Sometimes he seemed to enjoy shocking people with his clean living. Even when he was no more than nine years old, he had been the kind of boy who would halt a football game to read the riot act to some other nine-year-old who said "Goddamn it" or "Aw shit" when a play didn't go right. This was an unusual gesture even where he grew up, which was New Concord, Ohio, but not so extraordinary as it might have been a lot of other places. New Concord was a sort of town, once common in America, whose peculiar origins have tended to disappear in the collective amnesia as *tout le monde* strives to be urbane. Which is to say, it began as a religious community. A hundred years ago any man in New Concord with ambitions that reached as high as feedstore proprietor or better joined the Presbyterian Church, and some of the awesome voltage of live Presbyterianism still existed when Glenn was growing up in the 1920's and 1930's. His father was a fireman for the B&O Railroad and a good churchgoing man and his mother was a hard-working churchgoing woman, and Glenn went to Sunday school and church and sat through hundreds of interminable Presbyterian prayers, and the church and the faith and the clean living served him well. There was no contradiction whatsoever between the Presbyterian faith and ambition, even

soaring ambition, even ambition grand enough to suit the invisible
ego of the fighter jock. A good Presbyterian demonstrated his *election* by the Lord and the heavenly hosts through his success in this
life. In a way, Presbyterianism was tailor-made for people who
intended to make it in this world, as well as on the Plains of Heaven;
which was a good thing, because John Glenn, with his sunny round
freckled country-boy face, was as ambitious as any pilot who had
ever hauled his happy burden of self-esteem up the pyramid.

So Glenn went pounding around the driveway of the BOQ of
Langley Air Force Base in his sweatsuit, doing his roadwork, and
he frankly didn't care if most of the others didn't like it. The running
was good for him on several levels. At thirty-seven he was the
oldest of the fellows, and there was a little more pressure on him
to demonstrate that he was in good condition. Besides that, he had
a tendency to put on weight. From the waist up he was of only
average size and musculature and, in fact, had surprisingly small
hands. But his legs were huge, real kegs, muscular and fleshy at
the same time, and he tended to pack on weight in the thighs. He
was pushing 185 when he was selected for this thing, and he could
well afford to get down to 170 or even less. As for living in the BOQ
. . . why not? He and his wife, Annie, had bought their house in
Arlington because the children would be in excellent public schools
there. Why transplant them again when he would be on the road
half the time and probably wouldn't see them except on weekends,
anyway?

If it looked to the others as if he were living a monastic life . . .
that wouldn't hurt too much . . . Competition was competition, and
there was no use pretending it didn't exist. He already had an
advantage over the other six because of his Marine flying record
and the way he tended to dominate the publicity. He was ready to
give a 110 percent on all fronts. If they wanted four hours of unsupervised exercise per week—well, give them eight or twelve. Other
people could think what they wanted; he happened to be completely sincere in the way he was going about this thing.

The goal in Project Mercury, as in every important new flight
project, was to be the pilot assigned to make the first flight. In flight
test that meant your superiors looked upon you as *the* man who
had the right stuff to challenge the unknowns. In Project Mercury
the first flight would also be the most historic flight. They had been

told that the first flight would be suborbital. There might be as many as ten or eleven suborbital flights, going to an altitude of about one hundred miles, fifty miles above the commonly accepted boundary line between the earth's atmosphere and space. These flights would not go into orbit, because the rocket they would be using, the Redstone, could not generate enough power to take a capsule to orbital speed, which would be about 18,000 miles per hour. The capsule would go up and come down in a big arc, like an artillery shell's. As it came over the top of the arc, the astronaut would experience about five minutes of weightlessness. These suborbital flights were scheduled to begin in mid-1960, and all seven pilots would get a crack at them.

Other men would no doubt go farther into space, into earth orbit   11 and beyond. But they, in turn, would be chosen from the first men to fly suborbitally; so the first astronaut would be the one the world remembered. When a man realized something like that, there was no use being shy about the opportunity he had. Glenn had not gotten this far in his career by standing still in a saintly fashion and waiting for his halo to be noticed. When he reached Korea, flying strafing and bombing missions in support of Marine ground troops, he realized that the biggest accolade was being assigned to Air Force fighter squadrons, on loan (like Schirra), for air-to-air combat up at the Yalu River. So he had gone after that assignment and had gotten it and had shot down three MiGs during the last few days of the war. As soon as the war ended, he realized that flight test was the hot new arena and had gone straight to his superiors and asked to be assigned to the Navy's Patuxent River Test Pilot School, and they sent him there. He had been in flight test barely three years when he dreamed up the F8U transcontinental run. He dreamed it up himself, as a major in the Marines! Although everyone knew it was possible, no one had ever made a sustained coast-to-coast flight at an average speed of greater than Mach 1. Glenn developed the whole scheme, the aerial rendezvous with three different AJ1 refueling tankers, the way he would dive down to 22,000 feet to meet them, the whole thing. He pulled it off on July 16, 1957, flying from Los Angeles to Floyd Bennett Field in New York, in three hours and twenty-three minutes. The word was that there were some test pilots who were put out because he got the assignment. They seemed to think they had done the major test work on the

F8U, and so forth and so on. But it was his idea! He got it launched! If he hadn't put himself forward, it wouldn't have happened at all. Last year, 1958, it was obvious to him that all the services were working on the problems of manned space flight. There was no Project Mercury yet, and no one knew who would be running the show when a manned program began. All he knew was that it was not likely to be the Marines but he wanted to play a part in it. So he had himself assigned to the Navy Bureau of Aeronautics. He volunteered for runs on the Navy's human centrifuge machine at Johnsville, Pennsylvania, exploring the high g-forces associated with rocket flight. By March of this year, 1959, just a month before the seven of them were selected as astronauts, he had been at the McDonnell Aircraft plant in St. Louis as a representative of the Bureau of Aeronautics on a NASA Mockup Review Board, reviewing progress of the manufacture of the Mercury capsule. He didn't know just how the seven of them were selected . . . but obviously all that hadn't hurt his chances.

And now the ante had been raised once more, and he was after nothing short of being the first man to go into space. NASA would have to beat the Russians to it, of course, for him or any other American to be first. But that was one of the things that made it exhilarating, exhilarating enough even to endure this sweaty pounding over a salty pine-tag circular driveway in Tidewater, Virginia. There was the same sort of *esprit*—usually called patriotism but better described as *joie de combat*—that had existed during the Second World War and, among pilots (and practically no one else), during the Korean War. Project Mercury was officially a civilian undertaking. But it struck Glenn as being like a new branch of the armed services. All seven of them were still in the military, drawing military pay, even though they wore civilian clothes. There was a warlike urgency and priority about the whole enterprise. And in this new branch of the military *no one outranked you*. It was almost too good to be true.

On the organization chart the seven of them had superiors. They reported to Robert Gilruth, the head of the new Space Task Group, who was a subordinate of Hugh Dryden, the deputy administrator of NASA. Gilruth was a superb engineer and a fine man; he had literally *written the book* on the handling characteristics of aircraft, the first scientific treatise on the subject, "Requirements for Satisfactory Flying Qualities of Airplanes," NACA Report No. 755, 1937, which had become a classic. He was a big, bald, shy man with a reedy voice. Most recently he had been head of the NACA Pilotless Aircraft Research Division, which had experimented with unmanned rockets. Gilruth was not used to marching the troops and certainly not a group of ambitious pilots. He was no Vince Lombardi. He was a genius among engineers, but he was not the type to take seven colossal stars who were suddenly the most famous pilots in America and mold them into Bob Gilruth's Astroteam.

They were so famous, so revered, so lavishly fussed and worried   14
over at all times that they were without peers in this new branch of the military. Everywhere they went in their travels people stopped what they were doing and gave them a certain look of awe and sympathy. Sympathy . . . because *our rockets all blow up.* It was a nice, friendly, warm look, all right, and yet it was strange. It was a sort of glistening smile with tears of joy suffusing it; both tears and joy. In fact, it was an ancient look, from the primordial past, never seen in America before. It was the smile of homage and astonishment—at such bravery!—that had been given to single-combat warriors, in advance, on account, before the fact, since time was.

Well . . . Glenn was ready; he was ready for *election;* he was ready   15
to be the first to go into the heavens when that debt of homage and honor and glistening faces came due.

One of the people who beamed that look at them with a sincere   16
devotion was a Washington lawyer named Leo DeOrsey. Walter Bonney, the NASA public affairs officer who had run the press conference, had seen the frenzy of publicity building up around the seven men and concluded that they needed some expert help in their new role as celebrities. He approached DeOrsey. DeOrsey was a tax lawyer. Harry Truman had once considered making him head of the Internal Revenue Service. He had represented many show-business celebrities, including President Eisenhower's friend Arthur Godfrey. So the seven of them wound up having dinner with DeOrsey in a private room at the Columbia Country Club outside of Washington. DeOrsey was an affable gentleman with a little round pot belly. He had terrific clothes. He put on a long face and related how he had been approached by Bonney. He said he was willing to represent them.

"I insist on only two conditions," he said.   17

Glenn thought to himself, "Well, here it comes."

"One," said DeOrsey, "I will accept no fee. Two, I will not be reimbursed for expenses."

He kept the grave look on his face for a moment. And then he smiled. There were no catches or angles. He was obviously sincere. He thought they were terrific and felt tickled pink to be involved with them at all. He couldn't do enough for them. And that was the way it went with Leo DeOrsey from that evening onward. He couldn't have been straighter or more generous.

DeOrsey proposed that the book and magazine rights to their personal stories be put up for sale to the highest bidder. Bonney was sure the President and NASA would allow it, because several military men had made such an arrangement since the Second World War, most notably Eisenhower himself. The selling point for NASA would be that if the seven of them sold exclusive rights to one organization, then they would have a natural shield against the endless requests and intrusions by the rest of the press and would be better able to concentrate on their training.

Sure enough, NASA approved the idea, the White House approved it, and DeOrsey started getting in touch with magazines, setting $500,000 as the floor for bids. The one solid offer—$500,000— came from *Life*, and DeOrsey closed the deal. *Life* had an excellent precedent for the decision. Few people remembered, but *The New York Times* had bought the rights to Charles Lindbergh's personal story before his famous transatlantic flight in 1927. It worked out splendidly for both parties. Having bought an exclusive, the *Times* devoted its first five pages to Lindbergh the day after his flight and the first *sixteen* the day after he returned from Paris, and all other major newspapers tried their best to keep up. In return for *Life's* exclusive rights to their personal stories and their wives', the astronauts would share the $500,000 evenly; the sum amounted to just under $24,000 a year for each man over the three years Project Mercury was scheduled to run, about $70,000 in all.

For junior officers with wives and children, used to struggling along on $5,500 to $8,000 a year in base pay, plus another $2,000 in housing and subsistence allowances and perhaps $1,750 in extra flight pay, the sum was barely even imaginable at first. It wasn't real. They wouldn't see any of it for months, in any case . . . Nevertheless, the *goodies* were the *goodies*. A career military officer denied himself and his family many things . . . with the understanding that when the *goodies* came along, they would be accepted and shared. It was part of the unwritten contract. The *Life* deal even provided them with foolproof protection against the possibility that their personal stories might become all-too-personal. Although written by *Life*, the stories would appear in the first person under their own by-lines . . . "by Gus Grissom" . . . "by Betty Grissom" . . . and they would have the right to eliminate any material they objected to. NASA, moreover, would have the same right. So there was nothing to keep the boys from continuing to come across as what they had looked like at the first press conference: seven patriotic God-fearing small-town Protestant family men with excellent backing on the home front.

Here in the summer of 1959 that was fine with *Life* and with the rest of the press, for that matter. Americans seemed to be deriving profound satisfaction from the fact that the astronauts turned the conventional notions of Glamour upside down. It was assumed— and the Genteel Beast kept underlining the point—that the seven astronauts were the greatest pilots and bravest men in America *precisely because of* the wholesome circumstances of their backgrounds: small towns, Protestant values, strong families, the simple life. Henry Luce, *Life's* founder and boss of bosses, had not played a major role, other than parting with the money, in making the astronaut deal, but eventually he came to look upon them as *his boys*. Luce was a great Presbyterian, and the Mercury astronauts looked like seven incarnations of Presbyterianism. This was no rural-American miracle, however. It was John Glenn who had set the moral tone of the Astronaut at the first press conference. The others had diplomatically kept their mouths shut ever since. From the Luces and Restons on down, the Press, that ever-seemly Victorian Gent, saw the astronauts as seven slices of the same pie, and it was mom's pie, John Glenn's mom's pie, from the sturdy villages of the American heartland. The Gent thought he was looking at seven John Glenns.

24

CONTENT

1. Tom Wolfe's description of John Glenn focuses on the dominant impression of Glenn, namely that he is a "slice of mom's pie." How does Wolfe create the impression that Glenn is an All-American Boy? What details support this impression?

2. Why does Wolfe emphasize Glenn's Presbyterianism in paragraph 7? What in his religious background explains his intense sense of competition?
3. On which details of Glenn's physical appearance does Wolfe concentrate? Why?

ORGANIZATION

4. In paragraph 4, Tom Wolfe writes: "Glenn's own personal conduct was a constant reminder of what the game was really all about." How are the subsequent details of the portrait organized to support this impression?
5. Wolfe does not follow a straight-forward chronological pattern in recreating Glenn's background. Why does Wolfe move back and forth between the present and the past?

TOPICS FOR WRITING

6. Describe a celebrity. Include both the actual physical appearance as well as the public image of the celebrity.
7. Describe someone you know well, using Wolfe's pattern of relating physical details of a person's appearance in alteration with narrative details from their biography.

JOHN UPDIKE
My Grandmother's Thimble

Many critics consider John Updike (born 1932) the most important contemporary voice in American fiction. Updike's work includes poems, short stories, essays, and book reviews. Among his novels are Rabbit Run *(1960),* The Centaur *(1963),* Couples *(1968),* Rabbit Redux *(1971), and* Rabbit Is Rich *(1981). The decay of relationships and the effects of time on people and places are recurrent themes in much of his work. "My Grandmother's Thimble" is adapted from* Pigeon Feathers *(1962); like much of his early fiction, it concerns the painful memories of growing up and the almost religious awe with which he now regards the influence of his grandmother.*

The other night I stumbled downstairs in the dark and kicked my wife's sewing basket from the halfway landing. Needles, spools, buttons, and patches scattered. In gathering the things up, I came upon my grandmother's thimble. For a second I did not know what it was; a stemless chalice of silver weighing a fraction of an ounce had come into my fingers. Then I knew, and the valves of time parted, and after an interval of years my grandmother was upon me again, and it seemed incumbent upon me, necessary and holy, to tell how once there had been a woman who now was no more, how she had been born and lived in a world that had ceased to exist, though its momentos were all about us; how her thimble had been fashioned as if in a magical grotto in the black mountain of time, by workmen dwarfed by remoteness, in a vanished workshop now no larger than the thimble itself and like it soon doomed, as if by geological pressures, to be crushed out of shape. O Lord, bless these poor paragraphs, that would do in their vile ignorance Your work of resurrection.

The thimble was her wedding present to me and my wife. I was her only grandchild. At the time I was married, she was in her late seventies, crippled and enfeebled. She had fought a long battle with Parkinson's disease; in my earliest memories of her she is touched with it. Her fingers and back are bent; there is a tremble about her as she moves about through the dark, odd-shaped rooms of our house in the town where I was born. Crouched in the hall outside my grandparents' room—which I never entered—I can hear her voice, in a whispering mutter that pierces the wall with little snapping stabs, irritably answer a question that my grandfather had asked inaudibly. It is strange; out of their room, he speaks loudest. When she bends over me, I smell a mixture of must, something like cough medicine, and old cloth permeated with dried sunlight. In my childhood she was strong, endowed with possessions and resources. By the time I married, she had become so weak only her piercing will carried her up and down the stairs of the little country house to which we had moved—the very house where she had lived as a bride. She spoke with great difficulty; she would hang impaled in the middle of a sentence, at a loss for the word, her watery eyes and wild white hair transfixed. She had no possessions. Except for her clothes and her bed, the elegant silver thimble—a gift from her father, inscribed with her maiden initials—was her last property, and she gave it to us.

* * *

When we were all still alive, the five of us in that kerosene-lit   3
house, on Friday and Saturday nights, at an hour when in the
spring and summer there was still abundant light in the air, I would
set out in my father's car for town, where my friends lived. I had,
by moving ten miles away, at last acquired friends: an illustration
of that strange law whereby, like Orpheus leading Eurydice, we
achieve our desire by turning our back on it. I had even gained a
girl, so that the vibrations were as sexual as social that made me
jangle with anticipation as I clowned in front of the mirror in our
kitchen, shaving from a basin of stove-heated water, combing my
hair with a dripping comb, adjusting my reflection in the mirror
until I had achieved just that electric angle from which my face
seemed beautiful and everlastingly, by the very volumes of air and
sky and grass that lay mutely banked about our home, beloved. My
grandmother would hover near me, watching fearfully, as she had
when I was a child, afraid that I would fall from a tree. Delirious,
humming, I would swoop and lift her, lift her like a child, crooking
one arm under her knees and cupping the other behind her back.
Exultant in my height, my strength, I would lift that frail brittle
body weighing perhaps a hundred pounds and twirl with it in my
arms while the rest of the family watched with startled smiles of
alarm. Had I stumbled, or dropped her, I might have broken her
back, but my joy always proved a secure cradle. And whatever irony
was in the impulse, whatever implicit contrast between this ancient
husk, scarcely female, and the pliant, warm girl I would embrace
before the evening was done, direct delight flooded away: I was
carrying her who had carried me, I was giving my past a dance, I
had lifted the anxious caretaker of my childhood from the floor, I
was bringing her with my boldness to the edge of danger, from
which she had always sought to guard me.

There is a photograph of my grandmother and me at the side of   4
the first house. There is snow on the ground. The brick walk has
been cleared. I am in a snowsuit, and its bulk makes my walking
doubly clumsy. We are both of us dark against the snow and the
white brick wall of the house. I am unsteady; my grandmother's
black shape bends over me with a predatory solicitude, holding one
of my hands in a hand that has already become, under the meta-
morphosis of her disease, a little clawlike. She was worried that I
would fall, that I would not eat enough, that the bigger boys of the
neighborhood would harm me, that a cold would strangle me; and

her fears were not foolish. There *was* danger in that kind house. Tigers of temper lurked beneath the furniture, and shadows of despair followed my father to the door and flattened themselves against the windows as he walked down the shaded street alone.

* * *

I believe her first language was Pennsylvania German. As some 5 parents speak secrets in French in front of the children, my grandparents used this dialect on my mother. Only two words have descended to me—*ferhuttled* and *dopich*, meaning "confused" and "lethargic." They were frequent words with my grandmother; it is the way other people must have looked to her. Shaped like a sickle, her life whipped through grasses of confusion and lethargy that in a summer month grew up again as tall as before.

* * *

I should here provide a catalogue of her existence; her marriage 6 to a man ten years older, the torment of her one childbirth, the eddies of fortune that contained her constant labor. The fields, the hired men, the horses, the stones of the barn and the fireplace, the three-mile inns on the road to market. The birth of my mother: the lamplight, the simmering water, the buggy clattering for the jesting doctor, fear like a transparent paste on the ceiling, the hours of pain piled higher and higher—my grandmother was a little woman, and the baby was large. Her size at the outset my mother felt as an insult ineradicably delivered to the woman who bore her, the first of a thousand painful awkwardnesses. But to me, from my remote perspective, in which fable, memory, and blood blend, the point of the story is the survival. Both survived the ordeal. And in the end all my impressions of my grandmother's life turn on the thin point of her piercing survival.

* * *

Of course, I came upon her late, with a child's unknowing way 7 of seeing. No doubt the innocence of my vision of her is my own innocence, her ignorance mine. I am told that in her day she was sophisticated and formidable. She liked fine clothes, good food, nice things. She was one of the first women in the region to drive a car. This automobile, an Overland, spinning down the orange dirt roads of rural valleys now filled with ranch houses and Philadelphia commuters, recedes into a landscape, a woman whom I must imagine, a woman who is not my grandmother at all.

The initials were K.Z.K. Picking up that thimble, with its crown 8 of stipples like a miniature honeycomb, and its decorative rim of five-petalled flowers tapped into the silver, I felt at my back that night a steep wave about to break over the world and bury us and all our trinkets of survival fathoms down. For I feel that the world is ending, that the mounting mass of people will soon make a blackness in which the glint of this silver will be obliterated; it is this imminent catastrophe that makes it imperative for me to cry now, in the last second when the cry will have meaning, that once there was a woman whom one of the continents in one of its square miles caused to exist. That the land which cast her up was harsher, more sparsely exploited, more fertile than it is now. That she was unique; that she came toward the end of the time when uniqueness was possible. Already identical faces throng the street. She was projected onto my own days by her willed survival; I lived with her and she loved me and I did not understand her, I did not care to. She is gone now because we deserted her; the thimble seems a keepsake pressed into my hand by a forsaken woman as in the company of others I launched out from an island into a wilderness.

CONTENT

1. Updike sums up his description of his grandmother by saying, "in the end all my impressions of my grandmother's life turn on the thin point of her piercing survival" (paragraph 6). What details of the portrait support this conclusion? Why are religious terms employed in the description?

2. In paragraph 8, Updike observes, "she was unique . . . she came toward the end of the time when uniqueness was possible." What do you think he means by "unique"? What examples do we have of her uniqueness in the portrait? What is the thimble a symbol of?

ORGANIZATION

3. The description of Updike's grandmother begins with an outline of what he is about to describe, the importance of his

grandmother to him. Is this an effective way to begin? Why, or why not? Why is the thimble so prominent in the first page?

4. Why does Updike flashback to earlier recollections of his grandmother before she became enfeebled with Parkinson's disease? How do these earlier details help support the dominant impression of her being a survivor from an earlier era?

TOPICS FOR WRITING

5. Describe one of your grandparents, focusing on the dominant impression which you feel defines their character and emphasizing details that support the dominant impression.

6. Write a descriptive portrait of a relative as they are now and as you remember them several years ago. Emphasize the changes that have taken place.

7. Describe someone in your family with whom you associate a particular object. Be sure to explain why you associate the person with the object.

SHORT EXAMPLE—DESCRIPTION OF A PLACE

MARY McCARTHY
Lisbon, Portugal

Mary McCarthy, one of America's most important novelists, was born in Seattle, Washington in 1921, and received her A.B. from Vassar in 1933. Her many books include The Company She Keeps *(1942),* The Groves of Academe *(1952),* Memories of a Catholic Girlhood *(1957),* The Group *(1963),* Vietnam *(1967),* The Writing on the Wall *(1970), and* The Birds of America *(1971). "Lisbon, Portugal," a charming description of Lisbon, is from* On the Contrary *(1961).*

The cleanness of Lisbon *is* dazzling. In January, the steep stone streets are washed several times daily by sudden tropical showers, and Nature is assisted by street-cleaners with brooms made of twigs. The Portuguese have a green thumb. Lisbon, in winter, is brilliant with orange calendulas, blooming everywhere, together with geraniums and succulents; oranges and lemons dangle from trees in

the walled gardens like bright Christmas balls, the oranges match-
ing the orange sails of the little fishing boats on the blue Tagus. The
seasons at this time of year are all awry. Autumn is present in the
calendulas and oranges; spring in the first wicker baskets of camel-
lias that come down from the nearby mountains to the florist shops;
summer lingers in a few exhausted petunias; winter—last January,
at least—came for a day in a fall of snow, which brought the population, marveling, out into the streets to touch it. As the new year
gets under way, everything is growing, all at once; even the old tile
roofs have windfall crops of grass and yellow mustard, which, if
you look down from a window, over the rooftops to the Tagus,
make the whole city seem fertile—a sort of semitropical paradise
that combines the exuberance of the south, with the huge palms in
the public squares, the oranges and the monumental statuary, and
the neatness and precision of the north, seen in the absence of dirt
and litter, the perfectly kept public gardens and belvederes, the
black-and-white mosaic patterns (ships and ropes and anchors) of
the sidewalks, and the bright tiles of so many house fronts, painted
in green-and-white diamonds or pink roses or solid Dutch blues
and yellows. Lisbon is a city built on hills, like San Francisco, and
it is full of beautiful prospects, of which every advantage has been
taken. It is designed, so to speak, for a strolling tourist, at sunset,
to ensconce himself in a belvedere and gaze out over the Tagus,
down to the pink-and-white dome of the Basilica of Estrela, or
across a ravine of buff and pink and gold buildings to the old fortress of São Jorge.

DISCUSSION

What impresses McCarthy most about Lisbon, and what her
description emphasizes, is the city's combination of tropical fertility
with "the neatness and precision of the north." She describes the
cleanliness of the streets, the geometric walks and gardens, and
the perfectly laid out prospects of a city rebuilt in an orderly northern manner after it had been leveled by an earthquake in the eighteenth century. But the dazzling color of the foliage, which stands
out in the sparkling light, seems to dominate the description.
Oranges, blues, greens, whites and pinks are splashed about in her
description like the colors of a Monet painting. She makes the reader
experience the paradox of Lisbon's fortunate geographic situation

by telling the little anecdote about the unaccustomed snowfall which brings home her observation about the jumble of Lisbon's seasons. By centering on the paradox of Lisbon's combining southern and northern characteristics, McCarthy combines a variety of details into one unified portrait.

JAMES AGEE
Shady Grove, Alabama, July 1936

James Agee (1909–1955) was a journalist, novelist, playwright, screenwriter, film critic, and poet. After taking his bachelor's degree at Harvard University, he wrote for Fortune *Magazine; one assignment took him with photographer Walker Evans to Alabama to research the lives of sharecroppers. The result is the beautifully lyrical story of those families,* Let Us Now Praise Famous Men *(1941). Tragically, Agee died of a heart attack at age 45. His posthumously published novel,* A Death in the Family *(1957) won the Pulitzer Prize. Agee's ability to project himself into the feelings of other people, and his power to capture the evanescence of life are both present in this delicately lyric description of a graveyard which concludes* Let Us Now Praise Famous Men.

1   Just beside it there is a large square white-painted church, which we got into. Bare benches of heavy pine, a lot of windows, partition-curtains of white sheeting run on wires, organ, chairs, and lectern.

2   The graveyard is about fifty by a hundred yards inside a wire fence. There are almost no trees in it: a lemon verbena and a small magnolia; it is all red clay and very few weeds.

3   Out at the front of it across the road there is a cornfield and then a field of cotton and then trees.

4   Most of the headboards are pine, and at the far end of the yard from the church the graves are thinned out and there are many slender and low pine stumps about the height of the headboards. The shadows are all struck sharp lengthwise of the graves, toward the cornfield, by the afternoon sun. There is no one anywhere in sight. It is heavily silent and fragrant and all the leaves are breathing slowly without touching each other.

5   Some of the graves have real headstones, a few of them so large they must be the graves of landowners. One is a thick limestone

log erected by the Woodmen of the World. One or two of the others, besides a headpiece, have a flat of stone as large as the whole grave.

On one of these there is a china dish on whose cover delicate hands lie crossed, cuffs at their wrists, and the nails distinct.

On another a large fluted vase stands full of dead flowers, with an inch of rusty water at the bottom.

On others of these stones, as many as a dozen of them, there is something I have never seen before: by some kind of porcelain reproduction, a photograph of the person who is buried there; the last or the best likeness that had been made, in a small-town studio, or at home with a snapshot camera. I remember one well of a fifteen-year-old boy in sunday pants and a plaid pullover sweater, his hair combed, his cap in his hand, sitting against a piece of farm machinery and grinning. His eyes are squinted against the light and his nose makes a deep shadow down one side of his chin. Somebody's arm, with the sleeve rolled up, is against him; somebody who is almost certainly still alive: they could not cut him entirely out of the picture. Another is a studio portrait, close up, in artificial lighting, of a young woman. She is leaned a little forward, smiling vivaciously, one hand at her cheek. She is not very pretty, but she believed she was; her face is free from strain or fear. She is wearing an evidently new dress, with a mail-order look about it; patterns of beads are sewn over it and have caught the light. Her face is soft with powder and at the wings of her nose lines have been deleted. Her dark blonde hair is newly washed and professionally done up in puffs at the ears which in that time, shortly after the first great war of her century, were called cootie garages. This image of her face is split across and the split has begun to turn brown at its edges.

I think these would be graves of small farmers.

There are others about which there can be no mistake: they are the graves of the poorest of the farmers and of the tenants. Mainly they are the graves with the pine headboards; or without them.

When the grave is still young, it is very sharply distinct, and of a peculiar form. The clay is raised in a long and narrow oval with a sharp ridge, the shape exactly of an inverted boat. A fairly broad board is driven at the head; a narrower one, sometimes only a stob, at the feet. A good many of the headboards have been sawed into the flat simulacrum of an hourglass; in some of these, the top has been roughly rounded off, so that the resemblance is more nearly that of a head and shoulders sunken or risen to the waist in the dirt. On some of these boards names and dates have been written or printed in hesitant letterings, in pencil or in crayon, but most of them appear never to have been touched in this way. The board at some of the graves have fallen slantwise or down; many graves seem never to have been marked except in their own carefully made shape. These graves are of all sizes between those of giants and of newborn children; and there are a great many, so many they seem shoals of minnows, two feet long and less, lying near one another; and of these smallest graves, very few are marked with any wood at all, and many are already so drawn into the earth that they are scarcely distinguishable. Some of the largest, on the other hand, are of heroic size, seven and eight feet long, and of these more are marked, a few, even, with the smallest and plainest blocks of limestone, and initials, once or twice a full name; but many more of them have never been marked, and many, too, are sunken half down and more and almost entirely into the earth. A great many of these graves, perhaps half to two thirds of those which are still distinct, have been decorated, not only with shrunken flowers in their cracked vases and with bent targets of blasted flowers, but otherwise as well. Some have a line of white clamshells planted along their ridge; of others, the rim as well is garlanded with these shells. On one large grave, which is otherwise completely plain, a blown-out electric bulb is screwed into the clay at the exact center. On another, on the slope of clay just in front of the headboard, its feet next the board, is a horseshoe; and at its center a blown bulb is stood upright. On two or three others there are insulators of blue-green glass. On several graves, which I presume to be those of women, there is at the center the prettiest or the oldest and most valued piece of china: on one, a blue glass butter dish whose cover is a setting hen; on another, an intricate milk-colored glass basket; on others, ten-cent-store candy dishes and iridescent vases; on one, a pattern of white and colored buttons. On other graves there are small and thick white butter dishes of the sort which are used in lunch-rooms, and by the action of rain these stand free of the grave on slender turrets of clay. On still another grave, laid carefully next the headboard, is a corncob pipe. On the graves of children there are still these pretty pieces of glass and china, but they begin to diminish in size and they verge into the forms of animals and into homuncular symbols of growth; and there are toys: small autos, locomotives and fire engines of red and blue metal; tea sets for dolls, and tin kettles the size of thimbles: little effigies in rubber and glass and china, of cows, lions, bulldogs, squeaking mice, and the characters of comic strips; and of these I knew, when Louise told me how precious her china dogs were to her and her glass lace dish, where they would go if she were soon drawn down, and of many other things in that home, to whom they would likely be consigned; and of the tea set we gave Clair Bell, I knew in the buying in what daintiness it will a little while adorn her remembrance when the heaviness has sufficiently grown upon her and she has done the last of her dancing: for it will only be by a fortune which cannot be even hoped that she will live much longer; and only by great chance that they can do for her what two parents have done here for their little daughter: not only a tea set, and a cocacola bottle, and a milk bottle, ranged on her short grave, but a stone at the head and a stone at the foot, and in the headstone her six month image as she lies sleeping dead in her white dress, the head sunken delicately forward, deeply and delicately gone, the eyes seamed, as that of a dead bird, and on the rear face of this stone the words:

> We can't have all things to please us, Our little Daughter, Joe An, has gone to Jesus.

It is not likely for her; it is not likely for any of you, my beloved, whose poor lives I have already so betrayed, and should you see these things so astounded, so destroyed, I dread to dare that I shall ever look into your dear eyes again: and soon, quite soon now, in two years, in five, in forty, it will all be over, and one by one we shall all be drawn into the planet beside one another; let us then hope better of our children, and of our children's children; let us know, let us *know* there is cure, there is to be an end to it, whose beginnings are long begun, and in slow agonies and all deceptions clearing; and in the teeth of all hope of cure which shall pretend its denial and hope of good use to men, let us most quietly and in most reverent fierceness say, not by its captive but by its utmost meanings:

Our father, who art in heaven, hallowed be thy name: thy kingdom come: thy will be done on earth as it is in heaven: give us this day our daily bread: and forgive us our trespasses as we forgive those who trespass against us: and lead us not into temptation: but deliver us from evil: for thine is the kingdom: and the power: and the glory: for ever and ever: amen.

CONTENT

1. On which details in the photographs on the headstones of small farmers does Agee focus? Why?
2. The graves of poor farmers and tenants are adorned with their prized possessions. What is particularly touching about the examples Agee chooses?

ORGANIZATION

3. The description of the graveyard begins with the church outside the graveyard and moves inward to the graveyard itself. Why has Agee chosen to include these outside details?
4. Agee's description of the graveyard is divided into sections, each of which focuses on a different social class. What different details characterize each section of the graveyard? Why does the description of the poorest section of the graveyard end with the graves of the children?

TOPICS FOR WRITING

5. Write a description of a place which begins with a view of the place from a distance, then moves closer to focus on a smaller confined area.
6. Describe a place (such as a stadium) in which sections are divided by price or social class (for example, an opera house or theater).

PETER MATTHIESSEN
Delano, California

Peter Matthiessen is one of America's most renowned nature writers. After graduating from Yale in 1950, he worked as a commercial fisherman, then began a career travelling and writing. His writing, which has taken him from the ocean's depths to the world's highest mountains, includes Wildlife in America *(1959),* The Cloud Forest *(1961), the acclaimed novel* At Play in the Fields of the Lord *(1965),* Blue Meridian *(1971),* The Snow Leopard *(1978), and* In the Spirit of Crazy Horse *(1983). The following description of Delano, California is from* Sal Si Puedes *(1970); it sets the scene for the conflict between the fruit and vegetable growers and the farm workers' union, headed by Caesar Chavez.*

Of all California's blighted regions, the one that man has altered most is this great Central Valley, which extends north and south for almost four hundred miles. The Sacramento Valley, in the northern half, was once a sea of grass parted by rivers; the San Joaquin Valley, in the south was a region of shallow lakes and tule marshes. Both parts of what is commonly known as the Valley supported innumerable animals and birds, among which the waterfowl, antelope and tule elk were only the most dominant; there were also wolves, grizzlies, cougar, deer and beaver. To the Spanish, centered in the great mission holdings along the south-central coast, the grasslands of the interior were scarcely known, and their destruction was accomplished almost entirely by the wave of Americans that followed hard upon the Gold Rush. Game slaughter became an industry, and the carnivores were poisoned; by 1875 the myriad elk and antelope were almost gone. Meanwhile, unrestricted grazing by huge livestock herds destroyed the perennial grasses. Oat grass, June grass and wild rye gave way to tarweed, cheat grass and thistle, which in turn were crowded by rank annual weeds escaped from imported food crops of the settlers. In landscape after landscape, the poppies, lupines, larkspurs and mariposa lilies were no more.

From the start, California land monopolies were so enormous that the big "farms" were not farms at all, but industrial plantations. (To this day, the Kern County Land Company owns 350,000 acres in Kern County alone.) In the latter part of the nineteenth century, the huge corporate ranches were challenged for the dying range by huge corporate farms; the first big factory crop was wheat, the second sugar beets. One by one the tule marshes were burned over and drained; by the end of the century, the lakes and creeks, like the wild creatures, had subsided without a trace. As the whole Valley dried, the water table that once had lain just below the surface sank away; in places, the competitive search for water made it necessary to resort to oil-drilling equipment, tapping Ice Age aquifers hundreds of feet down. To replace the once plentiful water, the rivers were dammed and rechanneled in the Bureau of Reclamation's Central Valley Project, begun in the thirties: Shasta Dam destroyed the Sacramento, and Friant Dam choked off the San Joaquin. Today there are no wild rivers in the Valley, and very few in all of California; the streams of the Coast Range and the Sierra Nevada have been turned to irrigation, seeping across the Valley floor in concrete ditches.

Hard-edged and monotonous as parking lots, the green fields ₃ are without life. The road we walked across the Valley floor was straight and rigid as a gun barrel, without rise or curve. Passing cars buffeted with hot wind the cornflowers that had gained a foothold between the asphalt and the dull man-poisoned crop, and pressed toads as dry as leaves gave evidence in death that a few wild things still clung to life in this realm of organophosphates and chlorinated hydrocarbons.

As the sun rose the sky turned white; the white merged with ₄ the atmospheric dust. The dry heat is tolerable, yet the soul shrivels: this world without horizons is surreal. Out here on the flat Valley floor there is nothing left of nature; even the mountains have retreated, east and west. On all sides looms the wilderness of wires and weird towers of man's progress, including a skeletal installation of the Voice of America, speeding glad news of democracy and freedom to brown peoples all over the world.

Chavez crossed the highway to greet his doctor, Jerome Lackner ₅ of San Jose, who contributes many Sundays to the farm workers; Dr. Lackner was being chauffeured by Marcia Sanchez, one of a number of Anglo volunteers who has married a farm worker and stayed on in Delano. The next car blared a loud greeting on its horn, and a child's voice—"Hi, Mr. Chavez!"—was whirled upward and away in the eddy of hot dusty wind in the car's wake. Soon another Sunday car, already bulging, offered a list, and when Chavez refused it, its occupants shouted in surprise. The car swayed on. A woman's warm laughter drifted back to us—". . . su penitencia?"*—and Chavez grinned shyly. "Sí, sí," he murmured. "Mi penitencia." We walked on.

From the crossroads at Albany and Garces, a mile ahead, a big ₆ black car came toward us; still at a distance, it eased to a halt along the roadside. Three men got out, and leaning against the car, watched our approach. As we came abreast, two of them crossed the highway to await us while the third turned the big car around and brought it up behind.

Chavez, greeting the two men, made no attempt to introduce ₇ me; I took this as a sign that I was not to join the conversation and dropped behind. In shining shoes and bright white shirts of Sunday dress, the men flanked Chavez as he walked along; they towered over him. Over the car engine, idling behind me, I could hear no voices, and Chavez, looking straight ahead, did not seem to be

*". . . your penance?"

speaking. There were only the two water-slicked bent heads, and the starched white arms waving excitedly against the whitening sky.

At the corner of Albany the men left us. They were "submarines"—Union men who cross the picket lines at a struck vineyard and work from within by organizing slowdowns and walkouts. Submarine operations, often spontaneous, are not openly encouraged by the Union, but they are not discouraged, either. Chavez does not seem comfortable with subversive tactics, even those traditional in the labor movement; he talks tough at times, but his inspiration comes from elsewhere, and such methods are at variance with his own codes. "Certain things are all right—sloppy picking and packing, slowdowns. Or marking the boxes wrong, which fouls up the record keeping and gets people upset because they're not paid the right amount. But it doesn't stop there, that's the bad part of it. The transition to violence is rarely sudden. One man slashes a tire, then two or three do it. One thing leads to another, and another and another. Then you have real destruction and real violence."

Some of Chavez's lieutenants, respecting his personal ambivalence, omit telling him about tactics that he could only permit at the risk of insincerity in his public statements. But of course he knows that the incidents don't happen by themselves, and so, in his own conscience, he must walk a narrow line. Apparently he walks it without qualms. It is useless to speculate whether Chavez is a gentle mystic or tough labor leader single-minded to the point of ruthlessness; he is both.

We neared the town. From the outlying fields on the west end, Delano has little character: the one-story workers' houses are often painted green, and the few trees are low, so that the town seems a mere hardening, a gall, in the soft sea of dusty foliage. The dominant structures in Delano are the billboards, which are mounted high above the buildings, like huge lifeless kites.

A farm truck came by, and the face of a blond boy stared back at us. I wondered if the occupants had recognized Chavez. "Some of the growers still get pretty nasty," Chavez remarked after a moment, " but the worst are some of these young Anglo kids. They come by and give you the finger, and you wave back at them. You don't wave back to make fun of them, you just wave back."

As he spoke Chavez stopped to pat a mangy dog, which flinched 12
away from him; he retraced his steps a little ways to squat and talk
to it. He liked dogs very much, he said, but had never owned one;
he petted the dog for a long time.

" *'Hay más tiempo que vida'*—that's one of our *dichos.* 'There is more 13
time than life.' We don't worry about time, because time and history
are on our side."

Children and a woman called to him from the shady yard near 14
the corner, and he called back, "Hi! *¡Poquito!* Hello! *¿Cómo está?*"
Still walking, he asked the woman whether her husband was still
working *en la uva* ("in the grape"). Cheerily she said yes. The woman's house was adjacent to the old Union office, now the hiring hall
at the corner of Asti Street which supplies workers to Union ranches
in the Delano area. The present Union offices, in the Pink Building,
are next door. This is the southwest corner of Delano, and across
the street, to the south and west, small patches of vineyard stretch
away. The hiring hall, originally a grocery, is in poor repair due to
old age and cheap construction, as well as several hit-and-run assaults
by local residents. "One truck backed right into it," Chavez said,
bending to show me the large crack in the wall. "Practically knocked
down the whole thing. See?" He straightened. "They broke all these
windows. One time they threw a soaked gasoline rag through the
window—that just about did it. But someone saw them throw the
fire rag and called the fire department, and they put it on the radio,
and my brother Richard was listening and took off and got over
here quick; he had it out before the fire department got here." Chavez
shook his head. "One second more and the whole thing would
have gone." He laughed suddenly. "Man, they used to come here
and shoot *fire* arrows into the roof with bows and arrows! We had
to keep a ladder and a hose on hand for a long time."

In the late afternoon, outside the motel where I was staying, I 15
ran into the blond boy I had seen that morning staring at Chavez
from the pickup truck. He turned out to be a nephew of a local
grower, and was working in the vineyards for the summer before
going to college. He had stared at Chavez because one of the fore-
men in the truck had said that those Mexicans on Albany Street
were probably some of Chavez's men, and now he was surprised

*Sayings.

to learn that he had actually seen Chavez himself: as I had already discovered, most of the growers had never laid eyes on this dangerous figure and probably would not recognize him if they did.

The nephew was handsome, pleasant and polite; he called me 1 "sir." He said that although his generation felt less violently than their fathers, and that some sort of farm workers union seemed inevitable, the Delano growers would let their grapes rot in the fields before signing a union contract with Chavez. I asked if this was because Chavez was a Mexican. No, he said, it was because Chavez was out for himself and had no real support; even that three-day fast last winter had been nothing but a publicity stunt. When I questioned this, he did not defend his views but merely shrugged; like a seedless California fruit, bred for appearances, this boy lacked flavor.

He asked, "Do you like California?" Rightly bored by his own 1 question, he gazed at the glaring blue-and-orange panels of the motel façade. "I think Delano is supposed to be the flower capital of the world," he said.

At dark I went to the Guadalajara restaurant, overlooking U.S. 1 99, where I had good beer and tortillas, and listened to such jukebox songs as "Penas a la corazón" and "Tributo a Roberto F. Kennedy." Seeking directions to this place, which is a farm workers restaurant, I earned the suspicion of the motel manager. "Guadalajara? That's a Mexican restaurant, ain't it?" In this small town of 12,000, he did not know where it was. Standing there behind his fake-plywood Formica desk, in the hard light and hum of air conditioning, he stared after me. "Good luck," he said in a sniping voice as I went through the glass door, which swung to on the conditioned air with a soft exhaling.

In the San Joaquin Valley summer night, far out beyond the neon 1 lights, crickets jittered and a dog barked in the wash of silence between passing cars. Alone in his office, the manager still stood there, hands on his barren desk, with as much vindictiveness in his face as a man can afford who believes that the customer is always right. Under the motel sign, the light read VACANCY.

CONTENT

1. How does the opening description of the Central Valley as it was hundreds of years ago fit into the story of the farm workers union?

2. Portraits of Chavez, the young nephew of a grower, and the motel owner sum up the different sides on the issue of the farm workers union. How does each portrait summarize the conflict?

ORGANIZATION

3. Why does Matthiessen interrupt his description of Delano and its environs with several portraits of people?
4. How does Matthiessen organize his description of the physical appearance and atmosphere of Delano?

TOPICS FOR WRITING

5. Describe a place by first showing what it looked like in the past, then what it looks like today.
6. Organize a description of a place in which you give an overview of the whole place, then focus on one segment of it.

PART 5
Mixed Narration and Description

Many forms of writing overlap. What distinguishes an autobiographical essay like Edward Hoagland's "City Rat" from George Orwell's narrative "A Hanging" may be just a matter of emphasis. If the primary purpose is to reveal your own personality, the resulting essay is autobiographical; but if your purpose is to tell an interesting story, then the result is a narrative essay. Sometimes the rigidity of forms dissolves, as in Truman Capote's descriptive portrait of Marlon Brando in which a narrative form joins a descriptive form.

In your own writing, and in many of the examples in this book, pure forms rarely exist. In fact, in writing an essay, you are likely to join together many forms to fulfill a primarily narrative, descriptive, expository, or persuasive aim. How this happens can best be illustrated by following the evolution of one student's paper.

When her English instructor assigned the class's third essay—"For next Thursday, describe a place out of your past which you later came to appreciate"—Jane Morrison at first had no idea what she would do. But after considering the arrangement for a while, she had an idea. The instructor was always saying you should write about what you knew best. Jane, who had grown up in Scotland, thought, "Why not write about the tenements in the center of Glasgow? Some of those buildings date back to the 1850s. Surely no one will write on this subject, so at least it will be different." Still, she had some doubts. For one thing, the assignment seemed vague. Did the instructor intend it to be a descriptive essay—he had said "describe"—or was it to be a narrative essay—he had also said "a place out of your past"? When the class questioned him about this, he was evasive. Jane got the impression he wanted the class to figure out the solution for themselves. She also began to grow annoyed at the lack of definiteness in this writing class. At least in a math class you knew whether you got the problems right or wrong. But here in the writing class there didn't seem to be any right or wrong.

Jane finally decided to plunge right into the description. The instructor had, after all, said "describe," and if he later thought otherwise, she could always cite his original instructions to justify her approach to the problem. After several false starts, Jane wrote the following descriptive paragraph:

TENEMENTS

The garden of the red sandstone tenement where my Granny lived had grass and some trees along the back fend to hide the alley and the "midden." The close and all the stairs to the top flats were whitewashed every week by an artist called Maggi who was the "stairwoman," and who had her own special style of swirls and sweeps, of patterns which came to an end with a dead straight line about three inches up the wall. The walls, themselves, always seemed to be painted in a dark color, like donkey brown, and at eye level there was a row of six-by-six cream-colored ceramic tiles with snowflake patterns of green and yellow. In this tenement, the whitewash above the tiles seemed blue-white like powdered starch. Streaks of light from the sparkling stained glass window on each landing bounced around the stairwell, glinted on the polished brass door knobs and letter boxes, and illuminated the nameplates on the heavy storm doors. My Grandmother's front door was glass with a stag engraved on it, and the floor of the porch, between the two doors, was mosaic (I think they called it terrazo-paving because my Aunt Jean's boyfriend used to sit on his hunkers all the time, and he said it was because he worked at terrazo-paving.)

This was a good beginning to a descriptive essay, but as soon as it was finished, Jane became aware of several problems. It seemed too heavy-handed without some kind of lead-in. And what would be the point of such a description? She couldn't count on the people in the class finding it interesting unless somehow the description meant something to them. "Maybe it needs to be connected to something the class already knows about. Well, best to think positively, and not be overwhelmed by these problems," she thought. At least she had already made a good start in describing the tenements.

After reading this portion of her description to other students in the class, Jane decided to consult with her instructor to see how she might "lead into" the description to give it some additional significance. Together they decided to add a narrative frame around the description. The result was the following narrative lead-in which establishes Jane's description as a flashback (see narrative writing), a recollection from her childhood:

> The sunlight darts and dances along the silver wings as the plane touches down at Prestwick Airport in Western Scotland. I close my eyes and take some deep breaths to calm myself; then, collecting the clutter of my long journey home from California, I join the bustle of passengers, and bump and bang my way along the aisle to the open doorway.
> Standing at the top of the gangway, I look out across the rolling hills of Ayrshire. Everything is so green; everything is so "wee". . . . A tiny farmhouse nestles in a stand of miniature Douglas Firs that sits amidst the fields of oats and clover, the tiny green fields like patches in a quilt all sewed together with low stone walls. I'm home. . . . I take one more deep breath, and this one, heavy with the scent of sodden peat, tells me that, despite the sunshine, the rain is not too far away. The airport bus rumbles along the thirty-odd miles to Glasgow, taking me ever closer to my "ain folk."
> As the first heavy raindrops spatter against the window, the bus squeals to a stop at some traffic lights in Kilmarnock; I turn my head to the left and am surprised to find that I am close enough to a butcher's shop window to be able to count the rows of lamb chops and the black-puddings strung like garlands around the window.
> The bus rumbles on, and my mind races back some thirty years to another butcher's shop, my father's. Every Saturday I earned my pocket money delivering orders to customers who lived in the tenements close by the shop. With four or five orders all neatly wrapped in shiny brown paper, and tied up with string, I'd set off up Garscube Road. (Jane Morrision, "Tenements," English 1A, Saddleback College)

Jane's final complete draft of this essay (of which these paragraphs are only a portion) contains a book-end narrative conclusion which brings the reader back into the present after the flashback description of the tenement: "'Buchanan Street Station,' cries the bus driver, and I awake with a start. As the bus pulls into the Glasgow depot, I stretch and smile. I am not the least bit sorry to be home."

Jane's assignment and its solution contain a valuable lesson for writers. Each writing assignment is a challenge in problem solving. Each writing task is unique, its uniqueness progressively multiplied by the number of people trying to solve the problem. In other words, unlike math problems which typically have one solution, writing problems have as many solutions as there are writers attempting to solve them. Jane's problem in descriptive–narrative writing was solved in a variety of ways by different students. Some chose a "before-and-after" approach, describing a place as it once was and as it is now. These essays were primarily narrative, emphasizing the changes that time had wrought on the appearance or atmosphere of a place. Others had taken a nostalgic approach: They had written an essay that started in the present, then flashed back to how the place once looked. Both approaches had emphasized time in the description; both had emphasized changes in the place itself. Jane had solved the problem in a different way. She had decided to show *herself* as changing, and had therefore decided to use a narrative frame, emphasizing her own transformation in relation to static description of a place set permanently in the unchanging past.

Even though each form of writing has its own unique characteristics and organization, common sense will tell you that these forms are rarely found in isolation from each other. It is virtually impossible to tell an effective story without describing something; conversely, it is nearly impossible to describe a person or place without including some of its narrative history. Because almost everything we write about has elements of both time and space, to effectively tell about it requires both narrative and descriptive skills. How you organize a piece of writing will not depend so much on any preconceived pattern, but on the nature of the subject. To put it simply, whether you organize a piece of writing chronologically or spatially, whether you view it as primarily narrative or descriptive, will depend on your interpretation of the subject. The word "organic" describes how the outward appearance of something grows out of its characteristics; for example, architecture is organic when its form follows its function or purpose. Writing is organic when it is organized in a way that reveals its primary function. The essay on tenements was written to reveal as much about the writer as the tenement. Given this purpose, the narrative frame grew organically from the intention; its form reflects its function. The lesson to be learned here is to adapt each form to the purposes of the assignment. What you say will dictate the appropriate way to say it.

SHORT EXAMPLE

MARK KRAMER

The Ruination of the Tomato

Mark Kramer has been a newspaper columnist for Boston's Real Paper *and an instructor of agricultural history and politics at the University of Massachusetts. He lives on a small New England farm where he wrote* Three Farms: Making Milk, Meat and Money from the American Soil *(1980), from which the following selection is taken.*

Sagebrush and lizards rattle and whisper behind me. I stand in   1
the moonlight, the hot desert at my back. It's tomato harvest time,
3 A.M. The moon is almost full and near to setting. Before me stretches
the first lush tomato field to be taken this morning.

* * *

Three large tractors steam up the road toward me, headlights   2
glaring, towing three thin-latticed towers which support flood-
lights. The tractors drag the towers into place around an assembly
field, then hydraulic arms raise them to vertical. They illuminate a
large, sandy work yard where equipment is gathering—fuel trucks,
repair trucks, concession trucks, harvesters, tractor-trailers towing
big open hoppers. Now small crews of Mexicans, their sunburns
tinted light blue in the glare of the three searchlights, climb aboard
the harvesters; shadowy drivers mount tractors and trucks. The
night fills with the scent of diesel fumes and with the sound of large
engines running evenly.

The six harvesting machines drift across the gray-green tomato-   3
leaf sea. After a time, the distant ones come to look like steamboats
afloat across a wide bay. The engine sounds are dispersed. A company foreman dashes past, tally sheets in hand. He stops nearby
only long enough to deliver a one-liner. "We're knocking them out
like Johnny-be-good," he says, punching the air slowly with his
right fist. Then he runs off, laughing.

The nearest harvester draws steadily closer, moving in at about   4
the speed of a slow amble, roaring as it comes. Up close, it looks
like the aftermath of a collision between a grandstand and a San

Francisco tram car. It's two stories high, rolls on wheels that don't seem large enough, astraddle a wide row of jumbled and unstaked tomato vines. It is not streamlined. Gangways, catwalks, gates, conveyors, roofs, and ladders are fastened all over the lumbering rig. As it closes in, its front end snuffles up whole tomato plants as surely as a hungry pig loose in a farmer's garden. Its hind end excretes a steady stream of stems and rejects. Between the ingestion and the elimination, fourteen laborers face each other on long benches. They sit on either side of a conveyor that moves the new harvest rapidly past them. Their hands dart out and back as they sort through the red stream in front of them.

DISCUSSION

Mark Kramer's account of a tomato harvest has everything a combined narrative–descriptive essay should have: a steady stream of action and enough descriptive details to recreate the scene. The first paragraph tells us what is going to happen; the second and third paragraphs show us the machines and people who are going to harvest the tomatoes; and finally, the fourth paragraph lets us watch, near at hand, while the machine and the workers harvest the tomatoes. The narrative form structures the paragraphs: The essay begins with a description of the inert field waiting to be harvested, then moves through the excitement of anticipation as equipment and crews arrive. It ends with a description of the giant harvester gobbling up tomato plants like "a hungry pig loose in a farmer's garden." Along the way, Kramer fills in his narrative with descriptive details calculated to enliven this experience with appeals to the eye, ear, and even the nose. The quiet "rattle and whisper" of lizards, the bright flood lights tinting blue the sunburns of the Mexican workers, the roar of the approaching harvesters, the excited shout of the company foreman, the smell of the diesel fumes: All these sensations are woven into the description which makes the narrative an experience, not merely a recitation of events. Kramer's particular talent is to find the apt simile which makes the unusual real and vivid. The distant harvesting machines are "like steamboats afloat across a wide bay"; viewed up close, one of the same harvesters "looks like the aftermath of a collision between a grandstand and a San Francisco tram car." Changing the comparison, the pig of a harvester's "hind end excretes a steady stream of stems and rejects." This excerpt illustrates how two kinds of writing—narration and description—complement each other and serve the mutual end of recreating experiences whether of events, people, or places.

GRETEL EHRLICH
Wyoming: The Solace of Open Spaces

Gretel Ehrlich (born 1946) was educated at Bennington College and UCLA. She has published several volumes of poetry: Geode/Rock Body *(1970),* To Touch the Water *(1980), and essays in* Atlantic, New York Times, Quest, Country Journal, *and* Reader's Digest. *She lives on a cattle ranch in North Central Wyoming. "The Solace of Open Spaces," which originally appeared in* Atlantic, *traces the connection between the direct simplicity of Wyoming's residents and the vast landscape.*

It's May, and I've just awakened from a nap, curled against sage- 1
brush the way my dog taught me to sleep—sheltered from wind. A front is pulling the huge sky over me, and from the dark a hailstone has hit me on the head. I'm trailing a band of 2000 sheep across a stretch of Wyoming badland, a fifty-mile trip that takes five days because sheep shade up in hot sun and won't budge until it cools. Bunched together now, and excited into a run by the storm, they drift across dry land, tumbling into draws like water and surging out again onto the rugged, choppy plateaus that are the building blocks of this state.

The name Wyoming comes from an Indian word meaning "at 2
the great plains, " but the plains are really valleys, great arid valleys, 1600 square miles, with the horizon bending up on all sides into mountain ranges. This gives the vastness a sheltering look.

Winter lasts six months here. Prevailing winds spill snowdrifts 3
to the east, and new storms from the northwest replenish them. This white bulk is sometimes dizzying, even nauseating, to look at. At twenty, thirty, and forty degrees below zero, not only does your car not work but neither do your mind and body. The landscape hardens into a dungeon of space. During the winter, while I was riding to find a new calf, my legs froze to the saddle, and in the

silence that such cold creates I felt like the first person on earth, or the last.

Today the sun is out—only a few clouds billowing. In the east, where the sheep have started off without me, the benchland tilts up in a series of red-earthed, eroded mesas, planed flat on top by a million years of water; behind them, a bold line of muscular scarps rears up 10,000 feet to become the Big Horn Mountains. A tidal pattern is engraved into the ground, as if left by the sea that once covered this state. Canyons curve down like galaxies to meet the oncoming rush of flat land.

To live and work in this kind of open country, with its hundred-mile views, is to lose the distinction between background and foreground. When I asked an older ranch hand to describe Wyoming's openness, he said, "It's all a bunch of nothing—wind and rattle-snakes—and so much of it you can't tell where you're going or where you've been and it don't make much difference." John, a sheepman I know, is tall and handsome and has an explosive temperament. He has a perfect intuition about people and sheep. They call him "Highpockets," because he's so long-legged; his graceful stride matches the distances he has to cover. He says, "Open space hasn't affected me at all. It's all the people moving in on it." The huge ranch he was born on takes up much of one county and spreads into another state; to put 100,000 miles on his pickup in three years and never leave home is not unusual. A friend of mine has an aunt who ranched on Powder River and didn't go off her place for eleven years. When her husband died, she quickly moved to town, bought a car, and drove around the States to see what she'd been missing.

Most people tell me they've simply driven through Wyoming, as if there were nothing to stop for. Or else they've skied in Jackson Hole, a place Wyomingites acknowledge uncomfortably, because its green beauty and chic affluence are mismatched with the rest of the state. Most of Wyoming has a "lean-to" look. Instead of big, roomy barns and Victorian houses, there are dugouts, low sheds, log cabins, sheep camps, and fence lines that look like driftwood blown haphazardly into place. People here still feel pride because they live in such a harsh place, part of the glamorous cowboy past, and they are determined not to be the victims of a mining-domi-nated future.

Most characteristic of the state's landscape is what a developer euphemistically describes as "indigenous growth right up to your front door"—a reference to waterless stands of salt sage, snakes, jackrabbits, deerflies, red dust, a brief respite of wildflowers, dry washes, and no trees. In the Great Plains, the vistas look like music, like kyries of grass, but Wyoming seems to be the doing of a mad architect—tumbled and twisted, ribboned with faded, deathbed colors, thrust up and pulled down as if the place had been startled out of a deep sleep and thrown into a pure light.

I came here four years ago. I had not planned to stay, but I 8 couldn't make myself leave. John, the sheepman, put me to work immediately. It was spring, and shearing time. For fourteen days of fourteen hours each, we moved thousands of sheep through sorting corrals to be sheared, branded, and deloused. I suspect that my original motive for coming here was to "lose myself" in new and unpopulated territory. Instead of producing the numbness I thought I wanted, life on the sheep ranch woke me up. The vitality of the people I was working with flushed out what had become a hallucinatory rawness inside me. I threw away my clothes and bought new ones; I cut my hair. The arid country was a clean slate. Its absolute indifference steadied me.

Sagebrush covers 58,000 square miles of Wyoming. The biggest 9 city has a population of 50,000, and there are only five settlements that could be called cities in the whole state. The rest are towns, scattered across the expanse with as much as sixty miles between them, their populations 2000, fifty, or ten. They are fugitive-looking, perched on a barren, windblown bench, or tagged onto a river or a railroad, or laid out straight in a farming valley with implement stores and a block-long Mormon church. In the eastern part of the state, which slides down into the Great Plains, the new mining settlements are boomtowns, trailer cities, metal knots on flat land.

Despite the desolate look, there's a coziness to living in this state. 10 There are so few people (only 470,000) that ranchers who buy and sell cattle know each other statewide; the kids who choose to go to college usually go to the state's one university, in Laramie; hired hands work their way around Wyoming in a lifetime of hirings and firings. And, despite the physical separation, people stay in touch, often driving two or three hours to another ranch for dinner.

Seventy-five years ago, when travel was by buckboard or horse- 11 back, cowboys who were temporarily out of work rode the grub line—drifting from ranch to ranch, mending fences or milking cows, and receiving in exchange a bed and meals. Gossip and messages traveled this slow circuit with them, creating an intimacy between ranchers who were three and four weeks' ride apart. One old-time couple I know, whose turn-of-the-century homestead was used by an outlaw gang as a relay station for stolen horses, recall that if you were traveling, desperado or not, any lighted ranch house was a welcome sign. Even now, for someone who lives in a remote spot, arriving at a ranch or coming to town for supplies is cause for celebration. To emerge from isolation can be disorienting. Everything looks bright, new, vivid. After I had been herding sheep for only three days, the sound of the camp-tender's pickup flustered me. Longing for human company, I felt a foolish grin take over my face, yet I had to resist an urgent temptation to run and hide.

Things happen suddenly in Wyoming: the change of seasons and   12 weather; for people, the violent swings in and out of isolation. But goodnaturedness is concomitant with severity. Friendliness is a tradition. Strangers passing on the road wave hello. A common sight is two pickups stopped side by side far out on a range, on a dirt track winding through the sage. The drivers will share a cigarette, uncap their thermos bottles, and pass a battered cup, steaming with coffee, between windows. These meetings summon up the details of several generations, because in Wyoming, private histories are largely public knowledge.

Because ranch work is a physical and, these days, economic strain,   13 being "at home on the range" is a matter of vigor, self-reliance, and common sense. A person's life is not a series of dramatic events for which he or she is applauded or exiled but a slow accumulation of days, seasons, years, fleshed out by the generational weight of one's family and anchored by a land-bound sense of place.

In most parts of Wyoming the human population is visibly out-   14 numbered by the animal. Not far from my town of fifty, I rode into a narrow valley and startled a herd of 200 elk. Eagles look like small people as they eat car-killed deer by the road. Antelope, moving in small, graceful bands, travel at 60 miles an hour, their mouths open as if drinking in the space.

The solitude in which westerners live makes them quiet. They   15 telegraph thoughts and feelings by the way they tilt their heads and listen; pulling their Stetsons into a steep dive over their eyes, or pigeon-toeing one boot over the other, they lean against a fence with a fat wedge of snoose beneath their lower lips and take the whole scene in. These detached looks of quiet amusement are sometimes cynical, but they can also come from a dry-eyed humility as lucid as the air is clear.

Conversation goes on in what sounds like a private code: a few phrases imply a complex of meanings. Asking directions, you get a curious list of details. While trailing sheep, I was told to "ride up to that kinda upturned rock, follow the pink wash, turn left at the dump, and then you'll see the waterhole." One friend told his wife on roundup to "turn at the salt lick and the dead cow," which turned out to be a scattering of bones and no salt lick at all.

Sentence structure is shortened to the skin and bones of a thought. Descriptive words are dropped, even verbs; a cowboy looking over a corral full of horses will say to a wrangler, "Which one needs rode?" People hold back their thoughts in what seems to be a dumbfounded silence, then erupt with an excoriating, perceptive remark. Language, so compressed, becomes metaphorical. A rancher ended a relationship with one remark: "You're a bad check," meaning bouncing in and out was intolerable, and even coming back would be no good.

What's behind this laconic style is shyness. There is no vocabulary for the subject of feelings. It's not a hangdog shyness, or anything coy—always there's a robust spirit in evidence behind the restraint, as if the earthdredging wind that pulls across Wyoming had carried its people's voices away but everything else in them had shouldered confidently into the breeze.

I've spent hours riding to sheep camp at dawn in a pickup when nothing was said; eaten meals in the cookhouse when the only words spoken were a mumbled "Thank you, ma'am" at the end of dinner. The silence is profound. Instead of talking, we seem to share one eye. Keenly observed, the world is transformed. The landscape is engorged with detail, every movement on it chillingly sharp. The air between people is charged. Days unfold, bathed in their own music. Nights become hallucinatory; dreams, prescient.

Spring weather is capricious and mean. It snows, then blisters with heat. There have been tornadoes. They lay their elephant trunks out in the sage until they find houses, then slurp everything up and leave. I've noticed that melting snowbanks hiss and rot, viperous, then drip into calm pools where ducklings hatch and livestock, being trailed to summer range, drink. With the ice cover gone, rivers churn a milkshake brown, taking culverts and small bridges with them. Water in such an arid place (the average annual rainfall

16

17

18

19

20

where I live is less than eight inches) is like blood. It festoons drab land with green veins: a line of cottonwoods following a stream; a strip of alfalfa; and on ditchbanks, wild asparagus growing.

I've moved to a small cattle ranch owned by friends. It's at the foot of the Big Horn Mountains. A few weeks ago, I helped them deliver a calf who was stuck halfway out of his mother's body. By the time he was freed, we could see a heartbeat, but he was straining against a swollen tongue for air. Mary and I held him upside down by his back feet, while Stan, on his hands and knees in the blood, gave the calf mouth-to-mouth resuscitation. I have a vague memory of being pneumonia-choked as a child, my mother giving me her air, which may account for my romance with this windswept state.

If anything is endemic to Wyoming, it is wind. This big room of space is swept out daily, leaving a boneyard of fossils, agates, and carcasses in every state of decay. Though it was water that initially shaped the state, wind is the meticulous gardener, raising dust and pruning the sage.

I try to imagine a world of uncharted land, in which one could look over an uncompleted map and ride a horse past where all the lines have stopped. There is no wilderness left; wildness, yes, but true wilderness has been gone on this continent since the time of Lewis and Clark's overland journey.

Two hundred years ago, the Crow, Shoshone, Arapaho, Cheyenne, and Sioux roamed the intermountain West, orchestrating their movements according to hunger, season, and warfare. Once they acquired horses, they traversed the spines of all the big Wyoming ranges—the Absarokas, the Wind Rivers, the Tetons, the Big Horns—and wintered on the unprotected plains that fan out from them. Space was life. The world was their home.

What was life-giving to native Americans was often nightmarish to sodbusters who arrived encumbered with families and ethnic pasts to be transplanted in nearly uninhabitable land. The great distances, the shortage of water and trees, and the loneliness created unexpected hardships for them. In her book *O Pioneers!*, Willa Cather gives a settler's version of the bleak landscape:

> The little town behind them had vanished as if it had never been, had fallen behind the swell of the prairie, and the stern frozen country received them into its bosom. The homesteads were few and far apart;

here and there a windmill gaunt against the sky, a sod house crouching in a hollow.

The emptiness of the West was for others a geography of pos-   26
sibility. Men and women who amassed great chunks of land and struggled to preserve unfenced empires were, despite their self-serving motives, unwitting geographers. They understood the lay of the land. But by the 1850s, the Oregon and Mormon trails sported bumper-to-bumper traffic. Wealthy landowners, many of them aristocratic absentee landlords, known as remittance men because they were paid to come West and get out of their families' hair, over-stocked the range with more than a million head of cattle. By 1885, the feed and water were desperately short, and the winter of 1886 laid out the gaunt bodies of dead animals so closely together that when the thaw came, one rancher from Kaycee claimed to have walked on cowhide all the way to Crazy Woman Creek, twenty miles away.

Territorial Wyoming was a boy's world. The land was generous   27
with everything but water. At first there was room enough, food enough, for everyone. And, as with all beginnings, an expansive mood set in. The young cowboys, drifters, shopkeepers, school-teachers, were heroic, lawless, generous, rowdy, and tenacious. The individualism and optimism generated during those times have endured.

John Tisdale rode north with the trail herds from Texas. He was   28
a college-educated man with enough money to buy a small outfit near the Powder River. While driving home from the town of Buf-falo with a buckboard full of Christmas toys for his family and a winter's supply of food, he was shot in the back by an agent of the cattle barons who resented the encroachment of small-time stock-men like him. The wealthy cattlemen tried to control all the public grazing land by restricting membership in the Wyoming Stock Growers Association, as if it were a country club. They ostracized from roundups and brandings cowboys and ranchers who were not members, then denounced them as rustlers. Tisdale's death, the second such cold-blooded murder, kicked off the Johnson County cattle war, which was no simple good-guy-bad-guy shoot-out but a complicated class struggle between landed gentry and less afflu-ent settlers—a shocking reminder that the West was not an egali-tarian sanctuary after all.

Fencing ultimately enforced boundaries, but barbed wire abrogated space. It was stretched across the beautiful valleys, into the mountains, over desert badlands, through buffalo grass. The "anything is possible" fever—the lure of any new place—was constricted. The integrity of the land as a geographical body, and the freedom to ride anywhere on it, was lost.

I punched cows with a young man named Martin, who is the great-grandson of John Tisdale. His inheritance is not the open land that Tisdale knew and prematurely lost but a rage against restraint.

Wyoming tips down as you head northeast; the highest ground— the Laramie Plains—is on the Colorado border. Up where I live, the Big Horn River leaks into difficult, arid terrain. In the basin where it's dammed, sandhill cranes gather and, with delicate legwork, slice through the stilled water. I was driving by with a rancher one morning when he commented that cranes are "old-fashioned." When I asked why, he said, "Because they mate for life." Then he looked at me with a twinkle in his eyes, as if to say he really did believe in such things but also understood why we break our own rules.

In all this open space, values crystallize quickly. People are strong on scruples but tenderhearted about quirky behavior. A friend and I found one ranch hand, who's "not quite right in the head," sitting in front of the badly decayed carcass of a cow, shaking his finger and saying, "Now, I don't want you to do this ever again!" When I asked what was wrong with him, I was told, "He's goofier than hell, just like the rest of us." Perhaps because the West is historically new, conventional morality is still felt to be less important than rock-bottom truths. Though there's always a lot of teasing and sparring around, people are blunt with each other, sometimes even cruel, believing honesty is stronger medicine than sympathy, which may console but often conceals.

The formality that goes hand in hand with the rowdiness is known as "the Western Code." It's a list of practical dos and don'ts, faithfully observed. A friend, Cliff, who runs a trapline in the winter, cut off half his foot while axing a hole in the ice. Alone, he dragged himself to his pickup and headed for town, stopping to open the ranch gate as he left, and getting out to close it again, thus losing, in his observance of rules, precious time and blood. Later, he commented, "How would it look, them having to come to the hospital to tell me their cows had gotten out?"

Accustomed to emergencies, my friends doctor each other from   34
the vet's bag with relish. When one old-timer suffered a heart attack
in hunting camp, his partner quickly stirred up a brew of red horse
liniment and hot water and made the half-conscious victim drink
it, then tied him onto a horse and led him twenty miles to town.
He regained consciousness and lived.

The roominess of the state has affected political attitudes as well.   35
Ranchers keep up with world politics and the convulsions of the
economy but are basically isolationists. Being used to running their
own small empires of land and livestock, they're suspicious of big
government. It's a "don't fence me in" holdover from a century ago.
They still want the elbow room their grandfathers had, so they're
strongly conservative, but with a populist twist.

Summer is the season when we get our "cowboy tans"—on the   36
lower parts of our faces and on three fourths of our arms. Excessive
heat, in the nineties and higher, sends us outside with the mosquitoes. In winter, we're tucked inside our houses, and the white
wasteland outside appears to be expanding, but in summer, all the
greenery abridges space. Summer is a go-ahead season. Every living thing is off the block and in the race: battalions of bugs in flight
and biting; bats swinging around my log cabin as if the bases were
loaded and someone had hit a home run. Some of summer's high-
speed growth is ominous: larkspur, death camas, and green grease-
wood can kill sheep—an ironic idea, dying in this desert from eating what is too verdant. With sixteen hours of daylight, farmers
and ranchers irrigate feverishly. There are first, second, and third
cuttings of hay, some crews averaging only four hours of sleep a
night for weeks. And, like the cowboys who in summer ride the
night rodeo circuit, nighthawks make daredevil dives at dusk with
an eerie whirring that sounds like a plane going down on the shim-
mering horizon.

In the town where I live, they've had to board up the dance-hall   37
windows because there have been so many fights. There's so little
to do except work that people wind up in a state of idle agitation
that becomes fatalistic, as if there were nothing to be done about
all this untapped energy. So the dark side to the grandeur of these
spaces is the small-mindedness that seals people in. Men become
hermits; women go mad. Cabin fever explodes into suicides, or
into grudges and lifelong family feuds. Two sisters in my area inherited a ranch but found they couldn't get along. They fenced the

place in half. When one's cows got out and mixed with the other's the women went at each other with shovels. They ended up in the same hospital room, but never spoke a word to each other for the rest of their lives.

Eccentricity ritualizes behavior. It's a shortcut through unmanageable emotions and strict social conventions. I knew a sheepherder named Fred who, at seventy-eight, still had a handsome face, which he kept smooth by plastering it each day with bag balm and Vaseline. He was curious, well-read, and had a fact-keeping mind to go along with his penchant for hoarding. His reliquary of gunnysacks, fence wire, wood, canned food, unopened Christmas presents, and magazines matched his odd collages of meals: sardines with maple syrup; vegetable soup garnished with Fig Newtons. His wagon was so overloaded that he had to sleep sitting up because there was no room on the bed. Despite his love of up-to-date information, Fred died from gangrene when an old-timer's remedy of fresh sheep manure, applied as a poultice to a bad cut, failed to save him.

After the brief lushness of summer, the sun moves south. The range grass is brown. Livestock has been trailed back down from the mountains. Waterholes begin to frost over at night. Last fall Martin asked me to accompany him on a pack trip. With five horses, we followed a river into the mountains behind the tiny Wyoming town of Meeteetse. Groves of aspen, red and orange, gave off a light that made us look toasted. Our hunting camp was so high that clouds skidded across our foreheads, then slowed to sail out across the warm valleys. Except for a bull moose who wandered into our camp and mistook our black gelding for a rival, we shot at nothing.

One of our evening entertainments was to watch the night sky. My dog, who also came on the trip, a dingo bred to herd sheep, is so used to the silence and empty skies that when an airplane flies over he always looks up and eyes the distant intruder quizzically. The sky, lately, seems to be much more crowded than it used to be. Satellites make their silent passes in the dark with great regularity. We counted eighteen in one hour's viewing. How odd to think that while they circumnavigated the planet, Martin and I had moved only six miles into our local wilderness, and had seen no other human for the two weeks we stayed there.

At night, by moonlight, the land is whittled to slivers—a ridge, a river, a strip of grassland stretching to the mountains, then the huge sky. One morning a full moon was setting in the west just as the sun was rising. I felt precariously balanced between the two as I loped across a meadow. For a moment, I could believe that the stars, which were still visible, work like cooper's bands, holding everything about Wyoming together. 41

Space has a spiritual equivalent, and can heal what is divided and burdensome in us. My grandchildren will probably use space shuttles for a honeymoon trip or to recover from heart attacks, but closer to home we might also learn how to carry space inside ourselves in the effortless way we carry our skins. Space represents sanity, not a life purified, dull or "spaced out" but one that might accommodate intelligently any idea or situation. 42

From the clayey soil of northern Wyoming is mined bentonite, which is used as a filler in candy, gum, and lipstick. We Americans are great on fillers, as if what we have, what we are, is not enough. We have a cultural tendency toward denial, but, being affluent, we strangle ourselves with what we can buy. We have only to look at the houses we build to see how we build *against* space, the way we drink against pain and loneliness. We fill up space as if it were a pie shell, with things whose opacity further obstructs our ability to see what is already there. 43

CONTENT

1. What are some of the influences of open space on the people of Wyoming?
2. How does Wyoming speech reflect the geography of the region?
3. Does enforced isolation affect the character of people negatively?

ORGANIZATION

4. Ehrlich's essay mixes narration and description by moving back and forth between descriptions of the landscape and its effect on people now and in the past. Given Ehrlich's purpose, is this an effective way to structure the essay?
5. Why does Ehrlich refer to the Indian history of the region and the coming of the pioneers? Is there anything in this historical narrative similar to Scott Momaday's "The Way to Rainy Mountain" (page179)?

TOPICS FOR WRITING

6. Read William Saroyan's "Places and People" (page 527). Write a narrative–descriptive essay demonstrating how an environment shaped the personality of someone you know.

7. Describe a place you are familiar with, and narrate something of its history.

PAUL THEROUX
The Bullet Train

*Paul Theroux's interest in travel dates back to his many years as an expatriate living in the Orient and in Africa. His books on train travel—*The Great Railway Bazaar *(1975) and* The Old Patagonian Express *(1979)—are classics of the genre. "The Bullet Train," an excerpt from* The Great Railway Bazaar, *records Theroux's impatience with the high-speed technology of Japanese society which Theroux experienced after riding on the slower but more humane Indian railroads.*

The bullet-nosed Hatsukari Limited Express (its name, "Early Bird," refers to its arrival in Aomori, not its departure from Tokyo) leaves Ueno Station every afternoon on the dot of four. Ueno is crowded with people wearing fur hats, carrying skis and heavy coats for the snow at the end of the line: these are the vacationers. But there are returning residents, too, smaller, darker, Eskimo-faced people, on their way back to Hokkaido. The Japanese expression *nobori-san* ("rustics") describes them: it literally means "the downers"; having taken the *nobori* "down-train," these visitors, country-cousins spending a holiday in Tokyo, are considered yokels. On the train they stay in their seats, kick their heavy shoes off, and sleep. They look relieved to be going home and carry with them souvenirs from Tokyo: cookies wrapped in cellophane, flowers in paper cones, dried fruit bound with ribbon, dolls in tissue, stuffed toys in boxes. The Japanese are marvelous packagers of merchandise. These souvenirs are crammed in the plastic shopping bags that form the basis of the Japanese traveler's luggage. And there are other parcels, for the *nobori-san*, not trusting the food on Japanese National Railways, brings his own lunch pail. When he wakes, he rummages at his feet and discovers a sealed tin of rice and fish that, without stretching or rising from his padded armchair, he eats, blowing and smacking. The train itself is silent; my memory of Japanese train noises was this sound of eating, which is also the sound of a grown man inflating a balloon.

An amplified music box, ten plunking notes, and a recorded   2 message preceded our stops. A warning is necessary because the stops are so brief: fifteen seconds at Minami–Urawa, a minute at Utsunomiya, and, two hours later, another one-minute halt at Fukushima. An unprepared passenger might be mangled by the door or might miss his stop altogether. Long before the music and the message, the experienced Japanese carry their shopping bags to the exit, and as soon as the train stops and a crack appears in the door, they begin pushing madly towards the platform. The platform, designed for laden, shoving people, is level with the threshold. The lights in the carriages are never off, making it impossible to sleep, but enabling a passenger to gather up his belongings at two in the morning when the train pulls in and pauses for fifteen seconds at his station.

Such efficiency! Such speed! But I longed for the sprawl of Indian   3 Railways, the wide berths in the wooden compartments that smelled of curry and cheroots; the laundry chits with "camisoles" and "collars" marked on them; over the sink a jug of water; and out in the hall a man with a bottle of beer on his tray: trains that chugged to the rhythm of "Alabammy Bound" or "Chattanooga Choo-Choo," embodying what was best in the railway bazaar. On such a slow train it was almost impossible to get duffilled.*

The odorless Japanese trains unnerved me and produced in me   4 a sweaty tension I had always associated with plane travel. They brought back the symptoms of encapsulated terror I had felt in southern Thailand's International Express—a kind of leaden suspense that had stolen upon me after several months of travel. Travel— even in ideal conditions—had begun to make me anxious, and I saw that in various places the constant movement had separated me so completely from my surroundings that I might have been anywhere strange, nagged by the seamless guilt an unemployed person feels moving from failure to failure. This baffled trance over-

*Left behind—Theroux's own coinage.

took me on the way to Aomori, and I think it had a great deal to do with the fact that I was traveling in a fast, dry bullet-train, among silent people who, even if they spoke, would be incomprehensible. I was trapped by the double-glazing. I couldn't even open the window! The train swished past the bright empty platforms of rural stations at night, and for long moments, experiencing a heightened form of the alienation I'd felt before, briefly, in secluded pockets of time, I could not imagine where I was or why I had come.

The book I was reading on that train upset me further. It was *Japanese Tales of Mystery and Imagination* by Edogawa Rampo. Rampo's real name is Hirai Taro, and like his namesake—his pen name is a Japanese version of Edgar Allan Poe—he specializes in tales of terror. His fictional inventions were ungainly, and his shin-barking prose style was an irritation; and yet I was held, fascinated by the very ineptitude of the stories, for it was as impossible to dismiss these horrors as it had been the grisly rigadoon the Nichigeki audience had considered an entertainment.* Here was another glimpse of the agonized Japanese spirit. But how to reconcile it with the silent figures in the overbright train, who moved as if at the command of transistors? Something was wrong; what I read contradicted the sight of these travelers. Here was the boy hero in "A Hell of Mirrors," with his "weird mania of optics," sealing himself in a globular mirror, masturbating at his monstrous reflection, and going mad with auto-voyeurism; and there, in the opposite seat in my train, was a boy the same age, peacefully transfixed by the head of the person in front of him. In another story, "The Human Chair," a lecherous chairmaker, "ugly beyond description," hides himself inside one of his own constructions, providing himself with food and water, and "for another of nature's needs I also inserted a large rubber bag." The chair in which he lies buried is sold to a lovely woman, who provides him with thrills each time she sits on him, not knowing she is sitting in the lap of a man who describes himself as "a worm . . . a loathsome creature." The human chair masturbates, then writes (somehow) the lovely woman a letter. A few seats up from me in the Hatsukari was a squat ugly man, whose fists were clenched on his knees: but he was smiling. Driven to distraction by Rampo, I finally decided to abandon him. I was sorry I

---

*A sadistic stage show Theroux had seen earlier at the Nichigeki Music Hall in Tokyo.

knew so little of the Japanese, but even sorrier that there was no refuge on this speeding train.

There was a young girl seated beside me. Very early in the trip I had established that she did not speak English, and for nearly the whole time since we had left Ueno Station she had been reading a thick comic book. When we arrived at the far north of Honshu, at Noheji Station (fifteen seconds) on Mutsu Bay, I looked out the window and saw snow—it lay between the tracks and on blue moonlit fields. The girl rose, put her comic down, and walked the length of the car to the toilet. A green TOILET OCCUPIED light went on, and while that light burned I read the comic. I was instructed and cautioned. The comic strips showed decapitations, cannibalism, people bristling with arrows like Saint Sebastian, people in flames, shrieking armies of marauders dismembering villagers, limbless people with dripping stumps, and, in general, mayhem. The drawings were not good, but they were clear. Between the bloody stories there were short comic ones and three of these depended for their effects on farting: a trapped man or woman bending over, exposing a great moon of buttock and emitting a jet of stink (gusts of soot drawn in wiggly lines and clouds) in the captors' faces. The green light went off. I dropped the comic. The girl returned to her seat and, so help me God, serenely returned to this distressing comic.

The loudspeakers blared at Aomori, the ferry landing, giving instructions, and when the train pulled into the station the passengers, who crowded into the aisle as soon as the first syllable of the message was heard, sprinted through the doors and down the platform. The chicken farmers with their souvenirs, the old ladies hobbling on wooden clogs, the youths with skis, the girl with her comic: through the lobby of the station, up the stairs, down several ramps, gathering speed and bumping each other, and tripping in the sandals that splay their feet into two broad toes—women shuffling, men running. Then to the row of turnstiles where tickets were punched, and six conductors waved people up the gangway and into their sections: First-Class Green Ticket Room, Ordinary Room, Berths, Second-Class Uncarpeted, Second-Class Carpeted (here passengers sat cross-legged on the floor). Within ten minutes the twelve hundred passengers had transferred themselves from the train to the ferry, and fifteen minutes after the Hatsukari had arrived at Aomori, the *Towada Maru* hooted and drew away from the dock to cross the Tsugaru Straits. At the Indian port of Rameswaram, a similar operation involving a train and a ship had taken almost seven hours.

I was in the Green Ticket Room with about 150 other people, who were, like me, trying to adjust the barber chairs that had been assigned to them. These sloping chairs were tilted back, and before the lights dimmed many people were snoring. The four-hour crossing was very rough; the snow at Aomori had been deep, and we were now sailing in a blizzard. The ship twisted sharply, its fittings made low ominous groans, spray flew onto the deck, and snowflakes sifted past the portholes. I went out to the windy deck, but couldn't stand the cold and the sight of so much black water and snow. I settled into my chair and tried to sleep. Because of the snowstorm, every forty-five seconds the ship's horn blew a moan into the straits.

At four o'clock there was birdsong—twittering and warbling—over the loudspeaker: another recording. But it was still very dark. A few words from the loudspeaker and everyone rose and rushed to the cabin doors. The ferry slipped sideways, the gangway was secured, the doors flew open, and everyone made for the waiting train through the dry snow on the ramps at Hakodate Station. Now I was running, too: I was going at Japanese speed. I had learned at Aomori that I had less than fifteen minutes to board the northbound train to Sapporo, and I had no wish to be duffilled in such a desolate place.

CONTENT

1. What essential contradiction does Theroux find in the Japanese? How does the "bullet train" itself underscore the contradiction?

2. Why does Theroux mention his own reading along with the comic book which the girl seated next to him is reading? Read Marie Winn's "Television and Violence" (page 483) to find some explanation for the content of the comic book. Do violent horror films fulfill the same function in our society?

ORGANIZATION

3. A train trip is an appropriate subject for combining narrative and descriptive writing. Isolate the narrative and descriptive

sections of Theroux's piece. Where is it most difficult to separate them? Why?

4. What function does the contrasting description of Indian Railways have on the description of Japanese Railways? What details produce what Theroux terms "encapsulated terror"?

TOPICS FOR WRITING

5. Narrate and describe a trip on an airplane or a train. Include something about the atmosphere created by the mode of travel and some description of your fellow passengers.

6. Describe an audience's reactions to a violent movie. Include in your description summaries of the plot, along with audience's reactions. Also, describe some members of the audience as they left the theater.

N. SCOTT MOMADAY
The Way to Rainy Mountain

N. Scott Momaday, one of America's foremost Native American writers, was born in Oklahoma in 1934, graduated from the University of New Mexico, and received a Ph.D. from Stanford University. His Kiowa ancestry is a significant feature of his fiction and his non-fiction. In 1969, he won the Pulitzer Prize for his novel House Made of Dawn. *In this excerpt from the autobiographical* The Way to Rainy Mountain *(1969), Momaday traces his roots to the migration of the Kiowas to Oklahoma and describes the last of the old people, his grandmother, who remembered the old ways.*

A single knoll rises out of the plain in Oklahoma, north and west   1
of the Wichita Range. For my people, the Kiowas, it is an old landmark, and they gave it the name Rainy Mountain. The hardest weather in the world is there. Winter brings blizzards, hot tornadic winds arise in the spring, and in summer the prairie is an anvil's edge. The grass turns brittle and brown, and it cracks beneath your feet. There are green belts along the rivers and creeks, linear groves of hickory and pecan, willow and witch hazel. At a distance in July or August the steaming foliage seems almost to writhe in fire. Great green-and-yellow grasshoppers are everywhere in the tall grass,

popping up like corn to sting the flesh, and tortoises crawl about on the red earth, going nowhere in the plenty of time. Loneliness is an aspect of the land. All things in the plain are isolate; there is no confusion of objects in the eye, but *one* hill or *one* tree or *one* man. To look upon that landscape in the early morning, with the sun at your back, is to lose the sense of proportion. Your imagination comes to life, and this, you think, is where Creation was begun.

I returned to Rainy Mountain in July. My grandmother had died   2
in the spring, and I wanted to be at her grave. She had lived to be very old and at last infirm. Her only living daughter was with her when she died, and I was told that in death her face was that of a child.

I like to think of her as a child. When she was born, the Kiowas   3
were living that last great moment of their history. For more than a hundred years they had controlled the open range from the Smoky Hill River to the Red, from the headwaters of the Canadian to the fork of the Arkansas and Cimarron. In alliance with the Comanches, they had ruled the whole of the southern Plains. War was their sacred business, and they were among the finest horsemen the world has ever known. But warfare for the Kiowas was preeminently a matter of disposition rather than of survival, and they never understood the grim, unrelenting advance of the U.S. Cavalry. When at last, divided and ill-provisioned, they were driven onto the Staked Plains in the cold rains of autumn, they fell into panic. In Palo Duro Canyon they abandoned their crucial stores to pillage and had nothing then but their lives. In order to save themselves, they surrendered to the soldiers at Fort Sill and were imprisoned in the old stone corral that now stands as a military museum. My grandmother was spared the humiliation of those high gray walls by eight or ten years, but she must have known from birth the affliction of defeat, the dark brooding of old warriors.

Her name was Aho, and she belonged to the last culture to evolve   4
in North America. Her forebears came down from the high country in western Montana nearly three centuries ago. They were a mountain people, a mysterious tribe of hunters whose language has never been positively classified in any major group. In the late seventeenth century they began a long migration to the south and east. It was a long journey toward the dawn, and it led to a golden age. Along the way the Kiowas were befriended by the Crows, who gave them the culture and religion of the Plains. They acquired horses,

and their ancient nomadic spirit was suddenly free of the ground. They acquired Tai-me, the sacred Sun Dance doll, from that moment the object and symbol of their worship, and so shared in the divinity of the sun. Not least, they acquired the sense of destiny, therefore courage and pride. When they entered upon the southern Plains, they had been transformed. No longer were they slaves to the simple necessity of survival; they were a lordly and dangerous society of fighters and thieves, hunters and priests of the sun. According to their origin myth, they entered the world through a hollow log. From one point of view, their migration was the fruit of an old prophecy, for indeed they emerged from a sunless world.

Although my grandmother lived out her long life in the shadow of Rainy Mountain, the immense landscape of the continental interior lay like memory in her blood. She could tell of the Crows, whom she had never seen, and of the Black Hills, where she had never been. I wanted to see in reality what she had seen more perfectly in the mind's eye, and traveled fifteen hundred miles to begin my pilgrimage.

Yellowstone, it seemed to me, was the top of the world, a region of deep lakes and dark timber, canyons and waterfalls. But, beautiful as it is, one might have the sense of confinement there. The skyline in all directions is close at hand, the high wall of the woods and deep cleavages of shade. There is a perfect freedom in the mountains, but it belongs to the eagle and the elk, the badger and the bear. The Kiowas reckoned their stature by the distance they could see, and they were bent and blind in the wilderness.

Descending eastward, the highland meadows are a stairway to the plain. In July the inland slope of the Rockies is luxuriant with flax and buckwheat, stonecrop and larkspur. The earth unfolds and the limit of the land recedes. Clusters of trees and animals grazing far in the distance cause the vision to reach away and wonder to build upon the mind. The sun follows a longer course in the day, and the sky is immense beyond all comparison. The great billowing clouds that sail upon it are shadows that move upon the grain like water, dividing light. Farther down, in the land of the Crows and Blackfeet, the plain is yellow. Sweet clover takes hold of the hills and bends upon itself to cover and seal the soil. There the Kiowas paused on their way; they had come to the place where they must change their lives. The sun is at home on the plains. Precisely there does it have the certain character of a god. When the Kiowas came to the land of the Crows, they could see the dark lees of the hills at dawn across the Bighorn River, the profusion of light on the grain shelves, the oldest deity ranging after the solstices. Not yet would they veer southward to the caldron of the land that lay below; they must wean their blood from the northern winter and hold the mountains a while longer in their view. They bore Tai-me in procession to the east.

A dark mist lay over the Black Hills, and the land was like iron. 8 At the top of a ridge I caught sight of Devil's Tower upthrust against the gray sky as if in the birth of time the core of the earth had broken through its crust and the motion of the world was begun. There are things in nature that engender an awful quiet in the heart of man; Devil's Tower is one of them. Two centuries ago, because they could not do otherwise, the Kiowas made a legend at the base of the rock. My grandmother said:

> "Eight children were there at play, seven sisters and their brother. Suddenly the boy was struck dumb; he trembled and began to run upon his hands and feet. His fingers became claws, and his body was covered with fur. Directly there was a bear where the boy had been. The sisters were terrified; they ran, and the bear after them. They came to the stump of a great tree, and the tree spoke to them. It bade them climb upon it, and as they did so, it began to rise into the air. The bear came to kill them, but they were just beyond its reach. It reared against the tree and scored the bark all around with its claws. The seven sisters were borne into the sky, and they became the stars of the Big Dipper."

From that moment, and so long as the legend lives, the Kiowas have kinsmen in the night sky. Whatever they were in the mountains, they could be no more. However tenuous their well-being, however much they had suffered and would suffer again, they had found a way out of the wilderness.

My grandmother had a reverence for the sun, a holy regard that 9 now is all but gone out of mankind. There was a wariness in her, and an ancient awe. She was a Christian in her later years, but she had come a long way about, and she never forgot her birthright. As a child she had been to the Sun Dances; she had taken part in those annual rites, and by them she had learned the restoration of her people in the presence of Tai-me. She was about seven when the last Kiowa Sun Dance was held in 1887 on the Washita River above Rainy Mountain Creek. The buffalo were gone. In order to consummate the ancient sacrifice—to impale the head of a buffalo bull upon the medicine tree—a delegation of old men journeyed into Texas, there to beg and barter for an animal from the Goodnight herd. She was ten when the Kiowas came together for the last time as a living Sun Dance culture. They could find no buffalo; they had to hang an old hide from the sacred tree. Before the dance could begin, a company of soldiers rode out from Fort Sill under orders to disperse the tribe. Forbidden without cause the essential act of their faith, having seen the wild herds slaughtered and left to rot upon the ground, the Kiowas backed away forever from the medicine tree. That was July 20, 1890, at the great bend of the Washita. My grandmother was there. Without bitterness, and for as long as she lived, she bore a vision of deicide.

Now that I can have her only in memory, I see my grandmother 10 in the several postures that were peculiar to her: standing at the wood stove on a winter morning and turning meat in a great iron skillet; sitting at the south window, bent above her beadwork, and afterwards, when her vision had failed, looking down for a long time into the fold of her hands; going out upon a cane, very slowly as she did when the weight of age came upon her; praying. I remember her most often at prayer. She made long, rambling prayers out of suffering and hope, having seen many things. I was never sure that I had the right to hear, so exclusive were they of all mere custom and company. The last time I saw her she prayed standing by the side of her bed at night, naked to the waist, the light of a kerosene lamp moving upon her dark skin. Her long, black hair, always drawn and braided in the day, lay upon her shoulders and against her breasts like a shawl. I do not speak Kiowa, and I never understood her prayers, but there was something inherently sad in the sound, some merest hesitation upon the syllables of sorrow. She began in a high and descending pitch, exhausting her breath to silence; then again and again—and always the same intensity of effort, of something that is, and is not, like urgency in the human voice. Transported so in the dancing light among the shadows of her room, she seemed beyond the reach of time. But that was illusion; I think I knew then that I should not see her again.

Houses are like sentinels in the plain, old keepers of the weather 11 watch. There, in a very little while, wood takes on the appearance of great age. All colors wear soon away in the wind and rain, and then the wood is burned gray and the grain appears and the nails turn red with rust. The windowpanes are black and opaque; you imagine there is nothing within, and indeed there are many ghosts, bones given up to the land. They stand here and there against the sky, and you approach them for a longer time than you expect. They belong in the distance; it is their domain.

Once there was a lot of sound in my grandmother's house, a lot of coming and going, feasting and talk. The summers there were full of excitement and reunion. The Kiowas are a summer people; they abide the cold and keep to themselves; but when the season turns and the land becomes warm and vital, they cannot hold still; an old love of going returns upon them. The aged visitors who came to my grandmother's house when I was a child were made of lean and leather, and they bore themselves upright. They wore great black hats and bright ample shirts that shook in the wind. They rubbed fat upon their hair and wound their braids with strips of colored cloth. Some of them painted their faces and carried the scars of old and cherished enmities. They were an old council of warlords, come to remind and be reminded of who they were. Their wives and daughters served them well. The women might indulge themselves; gossip was at once the mark and compensation of their servitude. They made loud and elaborate talk among themselves, full of jest and gesture, fright and false alarm. They went abroad in fringed and flowered shawls, bright beadwork and German silver. They were at home in the kitchen, and they prepared meals that were banquets.

There were frequent prayer meetings, and great nocturnal feasts. When I was a child, I played with my cousins outside, where the lamplight fell upon the ground and the singing of the old people rose up around us and carried away into the darkness. There were a lot of good things to eat, a lot of laughter and surprise. And afterwards, when the quiet returned, I lay down with my grandmother and could hear the frogs away by the river and feel the motion of the air.

Now there is a funeral silence in the rooms, the endless wake of some final word. The walls have closed in upon my grandmother's house. When I returned to it in mourning, I saw for the first time in my life how small it was. It was late at night, and there was a white moon, nearly full. I sat for a long time on the stone steps by the kitchen door. From there I could see out across the land; I could see the long row of trees by the creek, the low light upon the rolling plains, and the stars of the Big Dipper. Once I looked at the moon and caught sight of a strange thing. A cricket had perched upon the handrail, only a few inches away from me. My line of vision was such that the creature filled the moon like a fossil. It had gone there, I thought, to live and die, for there of all places, was its small definition made whole and eternal. A warm wind rose up and purled like the longing within me.

The next morning I awoke at dawn and went out on the dirt road   15
to Rainy Mountain. It was already hot, and the grasshoppers began to fill the air. Still, it was early in the morning, and the birds sang out of the shadows. The long yellow grass on the mountain shone in the bright light, and a scissortail hied above the land. There, where it ought to be, at the end of a long and legendary way, was my grandmother's grave. Here and there on the dark stones were ancestral names. Looking back once, I saw the mountain and came away.

CONTENT

1. Why does Rainy Mountain stir in Momaday memories of his grandmother and the great migration of the Kiowas from the northern mountains?
2. How does the adoption of the sun god define Kiowa life after the tribe reached the Great Plains? How does Momaday's opening description reflect this new emphasis in Kiowa life?
3. Examine the legends Momaday has embodied in his narrative. What does he mean when he says, in paragraph 8, "the Kiowas have kinsmen in the night sky"?

ORGANIZATION

4. Momaday has combined a description of his grandmother with a narrative of the Kiowa people. Where does one clearly break off and the other begin?
5. In paragraphs 14–15, when Momaday brings us back to the period after his grandmother's death, he resumes the descriptive mode with which he had begun the piece. Is there any difference in the mood and substance of the final descriptive paragraphs and those of the opening paragraphs?

TOPICS FOR WRITING

6. Read John Updike's "My Grandmother's Thimble" (page 138) and compare the religious details of the portrait of his Penn-

sylvania Dutch grandmother with those in Momaday's portrait
of his Kiowa grandmother.
7.   Write a description of a person who has influenced you. Include
in it a narrative section about an incident which illustrates that
influence.

TRACY KIDDER
The Soul of a New Machine

*A veteran of the war in Vietnam, Tracy Kidder received the 1982 Pulitzer Prize
for* The Soul Of a New Machine *(1981). His earlier book* The Road to Yuba
City *(1974) deals with the Juan Corona mass murder case. Kidder's special talent
for turning complicated material into an interesting story is revealed in the
following excerpt from* The Soul Of a New Machine.

In theory, a computer can mimic the behavior of anything. It can   1
do so accurately only if the thing being imitated is thoroughly defined.
So computers achieve only partial success, at best, when instructed
to simulate the behavior of a city or to foresee the future of a national
economy. Computers do well, however, when imitating other
machines, including other computers—unbuilt ones that exist only
on the paper of an architectural specification. You make the old
computer imitate the new by writing a program. This program—
the simulator—makes the existing computer respond to instructions just as the contemplated, unbuilt computer should. Essentially, your program translates instructions designed for the unbuilt
computer into instructions that the existing one obeys. You can
create a simulator that will make an old computer ape the fanciest
new computer you can imagine. People build new computers in
hardware and not in such a program because simulators are slow—
the Microteam's for instance, ran more slowly than Eagle* was supposed to run by a factor of about 100,000. A simulator makes a slow
computer but a fast tool.

---

*The supercomputer that Data General's Microteam (a team of computer engineers) was
recruited to build.

Alsing* wanted one. He had often wished he had a simulator,   2
for testing and correcting microcode.[†] On every other project, he
had been forced to debug the microcode by running it on the prototype hardware of the new machine. But the hardware of the new
machine was itself being debugged and indeed could not be fully
debugged without the microcode. This made for awkward situations and mysteries in the lab. If the machine failed, it was hard to
know what to blame first—the hardware, the microcode or the
diagnostic program. For several years now, before every project,
Alsing had held essentially the same conversation with West.[**]

"I want to build a simulator, Tom."   3

"It'll take too long, Alsing. The machine'll be debugged before   4
you get your simulator debugged."

This time, Alsing insisted. They could not build Eagle in any-   5
thing like a year if they had to debug all the microcode on prototypes. If they went that way, moreover, they'd need to have at least
one and probably two extra prototypes right from the start, and
that would mean a doubling of the boring, grueling work of updat-
ing boards. Alsing wanted a program that would behave like a
perfected Eagle, so that they could debug their microcode separately from the hardware.

West said: "Go ahead. But I betchya it'll all be over by the time   6
you get it done."

Simulators were at least ten years old. No great mysteries sur-   7
rounded them. After some calculation, however, Alsing realized
that a program to simulate Eagle would be huge. It might take a
seasoned programmer a year and a half to write such a thing, he
figured. But Alsing kept these calculations to himself.

Although his intentions were in the main unquestionably gentle,   8
Alsing seemed to have a constitutional aversion to the direct approach.
I was visiting him one evening that spring. We were sitting in his
living room, when the oldest of his three sons, a handsome, soft-
spoken and polite teenager, came to him complaining that all of the
TV sets were broken again.

"What did you want to watch?" Alsing asked him.   9

" 'Charlie's Angels,' Dad."   10

*Carl Alsing, second in charge of the Eagle project.
[†]The code that controls the actual circuits of the computer.
**Tom West, head of the Eagle Project.

"Gee, that's too bad about the TVs," said Alsing.

When his son had left the room, Alsing grimaced. "I'm terrible," he said.

He had grown worried that his boys were watching too much of the wrong sort of television—"evening violence and Saturday morning cartoons," he said. So one night he had gone around the house and had disabled all of the sets. On the theory that his sons would learn more from trying to repair a TV than from watching one, Alsing encouraged them to try to fix the things. He spent many pleasant Sunday mornings working on the sabotaged sets with his sons. His boys were learning more and more about TVs, but they hadn't yet gotten any of them to work. On occasion, however, when Alsing approved of a show that they wanted to watch, at least one set would, as if by magic, suddenly start working.

Who would Alsing get to write the simulator? Who could do it quickly enough for the thing to be useful? On the Microteam there was a veteran programmer, a jovial fellow named Dave Peck. Peck had a raucous laugh; it was his laugh preeminently that drove West to distraction. Data General employee number 257, Peck had performed his full share of round-the-clock programming. He had come over from Software to the Eclipse Group, because Alsing had promised him the chance to manage others for a change. Peck was a fast programmer. "The fastest I ever saw, the fastest in the East," said Ken Holberger.

Peck said he'd been told he was fast so often that he guessed he must be. "But programming's just obvious to me." The problem was that these days, it took him a long time to talk himself into writing a big program—longer, as a rule, than it took him to write the program. Peck could turn out a simulator quickly, if anybody could. (He would ultimately perform some crucial smaller programming projects for the group, about thirty-four in all.) Like Alsing, he had been thinking on his own about a simulator for debugging micro-code—just figuring out how he'd go about writing a simulator, in case he should get up the desire to do it. So far, however, the desire had not come.

The group also had another programmer. Among the first of the Microkids to arrive at Westborough* was a twenty-two-year-old phe-nomenon, a fellow with degrees in computer science and electrical

*Headquarters of Data General

engineering and a nearly perfect academic record in those areas. His name was Neal Firth. He liked to program computers. He said: "I may be a little vain. I took a course in college in machine code. It was supposed to be a flunk-out course. To me, it was extremely simple. It's always just seemed extremely logical to me, programming."

Alsing considered the situation. He had two confident programmers—one relatively inexperienced, the other reluctant. Somehow, out of the two of them, he should be able to get a simulator. He put Peck in charge of the effort, but only nominally. 17

Shortly after Firth arrived, Alsing sat down with him and discussed ideas for a simulator. "There are a number of things you have to do to write one," said Alsing, drawing a grossly oversimplified picture of the task. 18

"Yeah, I could do that," Firth replied. 19

They talked about simulators with growing enthusiasm, until Alsing felt they had "a nice little fire going." Then casually, Alsing popped the question: "How long do you think it would take to write this simulator?" 20

"Six weeks or two months?" said Firth. 21

"Oh, good," said Alsing. 22

When he was ten years old, Alsing remembered, he was given a book called *All You Need to Know about Radio and TV.* When he had read it from cover to cover, he really believed that he did know everything about radios and TVs. He didn't, of course, but thinking that he did had given him the confidence to take apart radios and TVs and in the process to learn what made them work. He had that experience in mind when he talked to Firth. "When Neal said he could do it in a couple of months, he was probably thinking back to how long term-projects in college took." Firth, Alsing reasoned, had not been performing make-work projects as many neophyte engineers do their first years out of school. He didn't know what he could not do. "I think that after our little talk, Neal had a picture in his mind that he knew all about simulators now. It was no problem. He could do it over the weekend." 23

Around this time, Alsing also sat down with Peck. Firth was Peck's responsibility, Alsing said. Peck should somehow lead Firth to complete a simulator in just a few months. So Peck explained to Firth his own ideas about simulators. He laid out the basic scheme for Firth, in greater detail than Alsing had. 24

Observing the two from a little distance, Alsing got the strong 25 impression that while Peck and Firth liked each other, neither was about to concede that the other was a better, faster programmer. A little friendly competition might work nicely here. Alsing went to Peck and said: "We really need some sort of simulator in six weeks. So, Dave, why don't you do a quick-and-dirty one, while Neal works on his bigger one?" Peck agreed. The contest began.

Every so often over the next month or so, Firth would visit Alsing 26 and tell him that *his* simulator was coming right along and was going to do many things that Peck's quick-and-dirty one would not.

"Oh, good," said Alsing. 27

Peck got his simulator written and running in about six weeks, 28 right on time. One member of the Microteam used it, but only for a while. Two and a half months after Peck finished, Firth's simulator became functional. Two months after that, Firth had refined it. He gave the Microteam a full-blown version of Eagle in a program—a wonderful machine, of paper, as it were.

If Firth had not built his paper Eagle, the lab might have looked 29 like a crowded car on a commuter train: Hardy Boys and Microkids bumping into each other, all tempers on edge. Everyone arguing about whose turn it is to update boards. West threatening to throw them all out of the lab and do it himself. The debugging proceeding ever so slowly. Microkids writing up sections of code, then waiting in line for a chance to test them on a prototype, and after getting a crack at the prototype and finding their code doesn't work, having to set up trace after trace with logic analyzers, trying to see what's going wrong. They will be lucky if they finish this computer in three years.

As it was in fact, the Microteam could test their code right at 30 their desks, via their own terminals. Firth's simulator was a program stored inside their computer, the Eclipse M/600—Trixie. They merely had to feed into Trixie the microcode they wanted to test, order up the simulator, and command it to run their code. They could order the simulator to stop working at any point in a microprogram. The simulator could not tell the microcoders all by itself what was wrong with their code, but it arranged for the storage of all the necessary information about what had taken place while the code was running, and would play all of it back upon demand. Thus, without having to invent ingenious approaches with logic analyzers, the team could examine each little step in their microprograms. They could find out what was going wrong in an instant, in many cases. In the Microteam's small corner of the world, Firth's was an heroic act.

When they first moved to Westborough, in the summer of 1978, Firth and his wife, Lynn, lived in an apartment not far from Building 14A/B. His working day began in the shower, and would continue as he walked to Westborough on those summer mornings. A lone figure walking along the side of the access road—a young man, stocky and graceful, with long black hair cut straight as a hedgerow in a line just above the shoulders, wearing glasses with large black frames and often a blue Windbreaker, and black shoes. At that hour, there would be a torrent of cars—grim faces behind the windshields—hurrying toward the plant. But Firth hardly noticed the traffic. He was building his simulator. It was not a trivial task.

Firth had to write a program for every microverb. Then he had to shuffle and reshuffle these programs. In the material Eagle, all the microverbs in a single microinstruction would be executed in parallel, at more or less the same time, between two ticks of the computer's clock. But the simulator was a program, in which events occur one step at a time; it could execute the various microverbs of a given microinstruction only serially, one after the other. And the order in which the microverbs of a given microinstruction were executed was often crucial; one verb could in effect cancel another.

UINST[+] also defined cases in which one microverb would alter the meaning of another one and cases in which one microverb would tweak two different pieces of hardware and mean two different things to each of them. From time to time, while he was building the simulator, features of the microcode and hardware of the material Eagle would be altered; Firth had to change his simulator accordingly. Moreover, he had to make his abstract machine useful to the Microkids. How would the people who were going to use the simulator extract information and give instructions? This is one of the most important and most often neglected issues that faces any programmer. Firth began his work pondering the question, and it showed. He made his paper machine completely "interactive."

[+]The micro instruction set, or rules preventing one microprogram from interfering with another.

"I guess nobody considered it a possible project in the time frame,"   3
Firth said, "but I didn't know that. To me, it seemed, well, chal-
lenging. It could be done. I was able to do it because I had no idea
of what was going on. Usually it was: 'We gotta have this feature
in the simulator by tommorow or poor old Jon Blau* won't be able
to do a thing.' That's usually how it was."

For two summers during college, Firth had worked as a manual   3
laborer for a company that produced computerized junk mail. He'd
often found himself in the back room with nothing to do, and he
would scout around for software documents that had been written
for the company's computers. One day he found a stack of programs
that a company engineer had created. Leafing through them, he
found a glaring error, one that would make it impossible for the
computers to address properly junk mail bound for California. Firth
had just begun to study programming, but the error was "just
obvious" to him. Remembering this incident years later, Firth said
that the engineer had probably been "programming by rote. He
wanted to make his program look like programs he'd seen before,
and that clearly wasn't gonna work." Firth always tried to avoid
such an approach. "I like to work around 'why,'" he told me. "I
prefer not to know the established limits and what other people
think, when I start a project."

Firth said he thought his interest in electronics began when he   3
was five years old. He was at a neighbor's house, playing with an
electrical toy. The neighbor's son, somewhat older than he was,
came in and warned him that he would get electrocuted if he did
certain things with that toy. But Firth had already done all those
things.

"I find myself very much of a loner," he said. "When I was younger,   3
I would sit and make model boats and planes endlessly." I saw him
at one of the team's parties, and he was very jolly, talking fast. He
often ate lunch with some of the other new recruits in the basement
and had, he felt, some fine conversations with them. He said he
liked technical discussions, but he also liked to talk about other
matters. "Like the ultimate meaning of life," he said, with a grin. "I
like to do strange things, go off and watch a tree for an hour. I can
do that. I've always found that I'm a little off the beaten track. It
doesn't bother me too much. I had a big interest in abstract music

*One of the Microkids.

in high school and no one else liked it. Maybe I'm right, maybe they are, but as far as I'm concerned they're entitled to their incorrect opinions."

Firth didn't often mingle with the rest of the group, after work. 38
He said that was because he was married and because he had moved some distance away from Westborough. I asked him, "Do you miss the society a bit?"

"I think I've always missed it, personally," he said. 39

Firth, who was born in Canada, went to high school in a suburb 40
of Chicago, "a neighborhood in which everyone was moving somewhere upward." His father was a regional sales manager for a company in the area. Firth excelled in high school, was placed in all accelerated courses, and had no trouble with any of them—and "no challenge," except the ones he found for himself in music and computers. He, too, met the machines in the form of "an ancient IBM." The high school kept its machine in a little room, which was left open for him during the summers. He would go in and program the computer all morning, and in the afternoons he'd practice with the band. It was one of those first-class midwestern high-school marching bands. Firth, in a big drum-major's hat, once led the band through a performance at Soldier Field in Chicago. He also played the contrabass clarinet, and twice performed with his high-school band under the directorship of Arthur Fiedler.* He earned his spending money playing the electric bass at dances.

When Firth got to college, he felt he had to choose between music 41
and computers. He had a flaw as a musician, he decided: he would always make a mistake. And he felt he would never be quite as good at music as he'd want to be. Programming came easily to him, although he found that he had to work extremely hard to do it very well. "I hate to say it, but in a way I feel that I can perfect it."

He was getting accolades now for his simulator. The team would 42
be nowhere without it; everyone said so. Firth said: "I can't say that in all cases I'm extremely pleased with it. I guess, finally, it is a pretty crafty little thing, but there's some real crud at the foundation."

We were sitting at a bar, one long quiet afternoon. I asked Firth 43
to explain his abstract machine to me. He tried. "Okay," he said, "I come to the simulator with the machine instructions to add two numbers. I also give you the microcode that tells the computer how

*Late conductor of the Boston Pops.

to do the ADD. Okay. I say, 'Simulator, execute the macroinstruction, ADD, at location so-and-so in simulated memory.' So I also had to simulate memory. But I also forgot to mention that when you wrote your microcode you also coded some decode information, which is information that the IP simulator will use." He said all this and more at such a clip, one digression leading to another, that I had to laugh. He laughed, too. He agreed he was a sucker for a digression.

"You kept it all in your head?" I asked.   44

"It was just obvious to me," he replied.   45

Firth had spent about three months getting all the concepts behind   46
his simulator straight, and he actually wrote the program in about a month. The rest of the time he spent on refinements. He could write two hundred to three hundred lines of code in his mind, but he had a hard time remembering his own phone number.

Luckily for him, somewhere in the bowels of Westborough existed   47
a computer, connected to the building's phone system. Through it you could program into your own office phone the numbers you called most often. Forever afterward, you could dial those numbers by punching out a three-digit code. Firth could remember the three-digit codes. He had completely forgotten his own phone number. It was a great relief to be able to do so. He did keep his number on a slip of paper in his desk drawer, though—just in case he should ever need to know it.

CONTENT

1. What is the function of the simulator in the development of the Eagle super-computer?
2. Why does Alsing set two programmers to the task of creating a simulator?
3. What is the point of the story about Alsing's having taken apart radios and TVs when he was ten years old?
4. What kind of person is Firth? Why does Kidder mention that his other love was music? Why did he abandon it in college?

ORGANIZATION

5. Why does Kidder interrupt the narrative of the creation of the simulator to tell us (in paragraphs 8–13 about Alsing's sons?

6. After narrating the story of how Firth created a simulator, Kidder creates an equally long portrait of Firth. Why doesn't the descriptive portrait precede the narration?

TOPICS FOR WRITING

7. Combine a descriptive portrait of someone with the story of their greatest accomplishment.
8. Narrate the story of how something complicated was solved. Within this narrative, weave several descriptive portraits of people involved in the solution.

PART 6
Exposition: Writing to Explain and Inform

O ther than works of literature, most of the material we read or write is expository writing. Exposition is simply the presentation of facts or ideas. In other words, expository writing is explanatory writing. Unsurprisingly, it appears in a multiplicity of forms:

1. Cookbooks, automobile repair manuals, directions for assembling a bicycle.

2. Newspaper reports, stock market and weather reports, many government documents.

3. Historical texts, explications of literature, science and mathematics textbooks.

4. Anthropological case studies, psychological reports, sociological studies.

5. Philosophical treatises, informal essays, some newspaper editorials.

These varied forms can be further classified into three basic kinds of exposition, grouped according to the degree of factuality, proof, or speculation, they set forth. For example, the response to an essay question on a history test would probably be purely informational; it might also contain speculations that would make the essay exploratory. A final examination essay in a chemistry class, on the other hand, would be more factual and involve more demonstration in the form of proof. We can, therefore, speak of three kinds of expository writing: scientific, informative, exploratory.*

*For this division I am indebted to James L. Kinneavy, *A Theory of Discourse* (Prentice Hall, 1979).

Scientific Writing   Most scientific writing is more objective (that is, more verifiable), uses more concrete language, and is more impersonal than other types of exposition. For example, here is a passage from Barry Commoner's *The Closing Circle* (Alfred A. Knopf, 1971):

> . . . strontium, a natural, harmless element, and its radioactive isotope, strontium 90, both move through the environment in concert with calcium, a chemically similar element. And calcium is avidly withdrawn from the soil by plants, becoming incorporated into food and then taken up in the human body. Once fallout appeared on earth, inevitably strontium 90 would accompany calcium as it moved through the food chain, ultimately becoming concentrated, along with calcium, in vegetables, in milk, in the bones of people.

Notice how the language and sentence structure do not call attention to themselves, but point dispassionately to Commoner's subject matter. The exposition is straightforward, factual, and makes no appeal to the emotions of the reader. The chain of reasoning here is based on specific, concrete, factual data. The passage begins with a statement describing the presence of the radioactive isotope, strontium 90; moves on to a description of its bonding with calcium; and ends with the logical conclusion that by moving up the food chain, the isotope is inevitably found in the bones of human beings. It does not betray Commoner's strong feelings about the radioactive poisoning of the atmosphere due to nuclear fallout, but relies on the reader to realize that radioactive materials are obviously harmful.

Informative Writing   Scientific writing is characterized by a high degree of verifiability—that is, given the facts and the chain of reasoning, the conclusions could be tested. Informative writing, on the other hand, presents information that is "news" in the sense that it is unforseen, unpredictable, and to some extent unexpected. Since most student writing is informative, this presents several problems. What seems to many students significant information is to many composition instructors trite and obvious. A student who offers the statement, "The Manhattan Telephone Directory is large," as an illustration of the size of New York City is apt to find "So?" written in the margin of the evaluated paper. But Gay Talese, working with the same material writes, "The Manhattan Telephone Directory has 776,300 names, of which 3,316 are Smith, 2,835 are Brown, 2,444 are Williams, 2,070 are Cohen—and one is Mike Krasilovsky." Talese's article "New York" is interesting as well as informative because the facts are so unusual. But how are you to judge whether a detail—or the entire piece of informative writing—is significant, unforeseen, or unusual? The significance of any piece of information depends on the sophistication of the intended audience. In most composition classes, it is a mistake to pitch the paper to the instructor; you would be wiser to assume your classmates are your audience and that their sophistication is at least equal to your own. Don't overestimate their familiarity with informative material, but don't condescend to them either.

Exploratory Writing Exploratory writing is speculation about the implications of the facts explained in informative writing. To put it another way, exploratory writing investigates significant questions, is less strictly objective or reportorial and perhaps more emotional than either scientific or informative writing. Exploratory writing dissects opinions, hypotheses, and stereotypes to see where they lead. Here is the opening paragraph of an exploratory essay by Joseph Wood Krutch:

> What is "nature"? One standard reference devotes five columns to fifteen different and legitimate definitions of the word. But for the purposes of this article the meaning is simple. Nature is that part of the world which man did not make and which has not been fundamentally changed by him. It is the mountains, the woods, the rivers, the trees, the plants, and the animals, which have continued to be very much what they would have been had he never existed. ["Man's Ancient, Powerful Link to Nature—A Source of Fear and Joy," *If You Don't Mind My Saying So. . .* (W. Sloan, 1969), 336.]

You might say, "This is obvious." Indeed, in one sense, it is. But Krutch's purpose is *not* to present startling new facts about nature, but to explore the philosophic and spiritual implications of man's being both part of and distinct from nature. The language is less concrete, the statements more tentative, more speculative, more open to a variety of explanations than it is in scientific or informative writing.

Even though you will seldom consciously set out to produce one of the three types of expository writing, you will always need to determine the level of factuality and objectivity appropriate for what you want to say. To do this, you must determine your primary purpose: Are you writing to prove a scientific hypothesis? Are you presenting "new" information to your audience? Or, are you speculating on a hypothesis to see what its implications are? A clear *purpose,* either stated or implied is essential to expository prose. A concise statement of your intent, usually in the form of a single sentence, is customarily called a *thesis statement.* The scope of the *topic* (frequently the grammatical subject of the thesis statement) should be sufficiently limited to be handled within the space allotted. Your particular focus is spelled out in what is called the *controlling idea* (often the predicate of the sentence). An example of the formulaic thesis statement is a sentence from the opening paragraph of an essay by George Orwell, "The English Class System":

Topic	Controlling Idea
The peculiarity of English class distinctions	is . . . that they are *anachronistic.*

With this thesis statement Orwell limits his discussion to the anachronistic nature of English class distinctions—not everything about them, not their injustice, but the peculiarity of the fact that they are relics of a bygone age.

A formula statement is clearly useful, but it is often difficult to include the topic and the focus in the same sentence without stretching the language or violating the rule of clarity. In the following two direct thesis statements taken from essays with radically different purposes, notice that the writers take several sentences to fully state their purposes, but use pronouns to link the sentences tightly together in series of connected ideas.

> Culture has another enemy, however, which did not exist to any alarming degree before this century and yet is here to stay. Its ways are so imperfectly understood that many people either do not see it as a threat or else underestimate it. This enemy, which I call pseudoculture, seems to me no less dangerous than the others. [George Elliott, "The Enemies of Intimacy," *Harper's* (July 1980), 50.]

> When I look through my own recipe for the perfect cup of tea, I find no fewer than eleven outstanding points. On perhaps two of them there would be pretty general agreement, but at least four others are acutely controversial. Here are my own eleven rules, every one of which I regard as golden. [George Orwell, "A Nice Cup of Tea," *As I Please* (Harcourt Brace Jovanovich, 1968), 41.]

Clearly, Elliott's topic is pseudoculture and his focus is its destructive effects, but he develops and further qualifies both topic and focus by adding details; he also leads into his topic gradually, taking his reader along with him. Like Elliott, Orwell gradually leads up to his topic (the perfect cup of tea) and focus (how to brew one); in this case, the gradual build up is almost dictated by the friendly, intimate tone of the piece. In both essays the organization and content are foreshadowed by the thesis.

Sometimes the thesis is called a *generative sentence* because, if properly written, it will generate the material to develop it as well as the pattern of organization to shape that material. Suppose, for example, you begin an essay with the sentence, "Most men live in harness." Not only would that sentence provoke a series of examples to substantiate the point—and, perhaps, some narratives to support the examples or even some cause–effect explanations of the example—but it would necessitate exemplification as a pattern of organization.

In fact many instructors insist on an explicit thesis statement at the beginning of an essay (at least at the outset of the term) to ensure that the essay does not stray from its announced topic, and to assure a minimal organization promised by the thesis. However, despite the generative value of a formal statement of purpose, not every piece of writing contains one. The purpose or main idea is frequently diffused throughout the essay in many of the statements that define the subtopics of the essay. Such essays have an implied thesis. (In analyzing these essays it is often good practice to frame a sentence which describes the writer's purpose.)

Just as an entire essay may have an explicit thesis, many supporting paragraphs contain an explicit *topic sentence*. A topic sentence tends to be more general, its language more abstract, and its content more a matter of opinion, inference, or judgment than the sentences which accompany it and develop it. In the following paragraph from Gay Talese's "New York" the first sentence is a judgment summing up a great many details, whereas the next sentences contain verifiable facts that illustrate and support the opening topic sentence.

New York is a city for eccentrics and a center for odd bits of information. New Yorkers blink twenty-eight times a minute, but forty when tense. Most popcorn chewers at Yankee Stadium stop chewing momentarily just before the pitch. Gum chewers on Macy's escalators stop chewing momentarily just before they get off—to concentrate on the last step. Coins, paper clips, ball-point pens, and little girls' pocketbooks are found by the workmen when they clean the sea lion's pool at the Bronx Zoo.

The topic sentence assembles what otherwise might seem stray bits of unrelated information. Without the topic sentence, each sentence would be random. With the topic sentence, the other sentences are assembled into a unified paragraph.

The characteristic "shape" of the *standard expository paragraph* is an inverted pyramid:

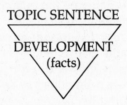

But some expository paragraphs build to a kind of climax, withholding the topic sentence until the end. For example, in "Here Is New York" (see pages 352–53), E. B. White gives specific examples first, then makes a judgment about them:

> At certain hours on certain days it is almost impossible to find an empty taxi and there is a great deal of chasing around after them. You grab a handle and open the door, and find that some other citizen is entering from the other side. Doormen grow rich blowing their whistles for cabs; and some doormen belong to no door at all—merely wander about through the streets, opening cabs for people as they happen to find them. By comparison with other less hectic days, the city is uncomfortable and inconvenient; but *New Yorkers temperamentally do not crave comfort and convenience—if they did they would live elsewhere.*

In this sort of paragraph, the most general part, the topic sentence, comes last, linking the details together, giving them a point, and imparting to the paragraph an upright pyramid shape:

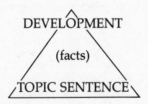

Bear in mind, however, that these shapes—the inverted triangle and the triangle—are only two of many a writer may employ; in fact, most paragraphs in an essay move back and forth between degrees of generalization and specificity. Notice that the degree of specificity of White's sentences varies: The first is less specific than the two which follow, but more specific than the topic sentence concluding the paragraph. Nonetheless, in a well-constructed essay, the topic sentences are always logical subdivisions of an overall thesis.

The content of the thesis statement dictates the kind of material appropriate for its development and the pattern of organization suitable to that development. In his *Rhetoric*, Aristotle suggested that one way to determine what to say about a subject is to proceed through a list of topics that would apply to any subject in general. Among the many such topics listed by Aristotle are definition, division, consequences, cause and effect, and comparison. If we frame (a few of) these topics in the form of a series of questions, their ability to generate material for the development of a thesis should become clear.

1. What is it?   (definition)

2. Are there examples of it?   (exemplification)

3. Can it be divided or classified under a larger category? (division/classification)

4. Is it similar to or different from something else?   (comparison/ contrast/analogy)

5. How is it made?   (process analysis)

By applying these questions to the subject, you can generate a significant amount of information. For example, if your topic involves the subject of inflation, you would, perhaps, begin by telling what constitutes inflation (definition), give some practical examples of items whose price has inflated dramatically over the last few years (exemplification), discuss various kinds of long- and short-term inflation (division), show the differences between inflation and depression (contrast), and trace the evolution of an inflationary spiral (process analysis). To see how such a heuristic method contributes to a finished essay, examine Sylvia Porter's essay on pages 383–85.

Each of these questions (and these, by the way are not the only ones we could ask), suggests material that will be arranged in a logical way; consequently, these labels—definition, exemplification, and so on—are often referred to as *patterns of organization*. We will use them in this sense to describe the predominant pattern of organization used in the selections which follow. You will notice, immediately, a single pattern rarely dominates an entire piece. An essay often incorporates material generated from answers to several questions about several topics. Therefore, such essays follow several patterns of organization. In this book, the essays are grouped under one pattern, in most cases because that is the *predominant* pattern of organization used, *not* the only pattern. Because most college writing is expository in nature, you will probably spend most of your time and energy learning to imitate and generate, on your own, the combinations of organizational patterns that appear in the following essays.

Definition

Definition is a pattern of organization which seeks to answer the question, "What is it?" Through definition a writer reveals the nature of a thing by describing its essential qualities, listing its characteristics, or giving examples of it.

Writers use definition when their subject has more than one acceptable meaning. Frequently, the subject is general, ambiguous, or vague. When the subject is indefinite, one of several meanings can be specified. For example, in an essay defining "nature," Joseph Wood Krutch points out that a standard dictionary lists fifteen meanings for the term, then specifies that "for the purposes of this article the meaning is simple. Nature is that part of the world which man did not make and which has not been fundamentally changed by him." In technical or scientific writing, terms often must be defined because the audience is unfamiliar with the language of the discipline. For example, through clear definition and example, John McPhee translates the technical term *d-limonene* into laymen's terms as he describes the process by which orange concentrate is made:

> Cutback is mainly fresh orange juice, but it contains additional flavor essences, peel oil and pulp. . . . The chief flavoring element in cutback is d-limonene, which is the main ingredient of peel oil. The oil cells in the skins of all citrus fruit are ninety per cent d-limonene. It is d-limonene that burns the lips of children sucking oranges. . . . D-limonene is what makes the leaves of all orange and grapefruit trees smell like lemons when crushed in the hand. [*Oranges* (Farrar, Straus and Giroux, 1967), 131.]

Definitions are of several types; we have just discussed *stipulative definition*, which in effect says, "Let us agree that for our purposes the word means. . ." In a *formal definition*, a word is placed in relation to a large category or class (genus), then differentiated from other members of that category according to its specific difference (species). A common dictionary definition of the word democracy follows the pattern of a formal definition: "Democracy is a form of government in which the supreme power is vested in the people and exercised directly by them or their elected agents under a free electoral system."

Word-to-be-defined	=	Classification	+	Differentiation
"democracy"		"a form of government"		1. "The supreme power is vested in the people and exercised directly by them" 2. "or by their elected agents under a free electoral system."

An *informal definition* merely lists the characteristics of a thing. Writing of the desert cactus, Edward Abbey lists the characteristics of one species and tells how it got its name:

> The chollas are the prickliest plants in the cactus family, and the prickliest of their kind is the small and shrubby teddy bear cholla. Paradoxically, the teddy bear's fierce armament accounts for its disarming nickname: its straw-colored spines and glochids are so numerous and close-set that the entire plant looks furry, especially when it glistens in a halo of bright sunlight. [*Cactus Country* (Time-Life, 1973), 88.]

Definition by contrast explains what a thing is by contrasting it with a different item of the same classification. Aldo Leopold opens his essay "Country" (see pages 216–18) by showing how country differs from "land":

> There is much confusion between land and country. Land is the place where corn, gullies and mortgages grow. Country is the personality of land, the collective harmony of its soil life and weather. Country knows no mortgages, no alphabetical agencies, no tobacco road; it is calmly aloof to these petty exigencies of its alleged owners.

An *etymological definition* (historical definition) reveals what a thing is by going back to the word's origins (its etymology) to show what is originally meant. For example, John McPhee (see pages 209–15) follows the botanical migration of oranges from the East to Europe by tracing the etymology of the word:

> The word "orange" evolved from Sanskrit. The Chinese word for orange, in ancient as well as modern Chinese, is *jyu*, but it did not migrate with the fruit. India was the first major stop in the westward travels of citrus. . . . The Hindus called an orange a *naranga*, the first syllable of which . . . was a prefix meaning fragrance. This became the Persian *naranj*, a word the Muslims carried through the Mediterranean. In Byzantium, an orange was a *nerantzion*. This, in Neo-Latin, became variously styled

as *arangium, arantium,* and *aurantium*—eventually producing *naranja,* in Spain, *laranja* in Portugal, *arancia* in Italy, and *orange* in France.

Whatever form of definition you use, remember that its purpose is to clarify and explain. A definition should never complicate or obscure a subject; it should add relevant information to the reader's knowledge of the subject.

SHORT EXAMPLE—DEFINITION

JOSEPH EPSTEIN

The Virtues of Ambition

Joseph Epstein was born in Chicago in 1937, and attended the University of Chicago. He has held a variety of editorial posts including those of associate editor of the New Leader, *senior editor of the* Encyclopedia Britannica, *and editor of the* American Scholar. *He is the author of* Divorced in America *(1974) and* Ambition *(1982), from which the present essay is excerpted. In it Epstein defines ambition and points out that the word has not always had a bad reputation.*

Ambition is one of those Rorschach words: define it and you instantly reveal a great deal about yourself. Even that most neutral of works, *Webster's,* in its Seventh New Collegiate Edition, gives itself away, defining ambition first and foremost as "an ardent desire for rank, fame, or power." Ardent immediately assumes a heat incommensurate with good sense and stability, and rank, fame, and power have come under heavy attack for at least a century. One can, after all, be ambitious for the public good, for the alleviation of suffering, for the enlightenment of mankind, though there are some who say that these are precisely the ambitious people most to be mistrusted.

Surely ambition is behind dreams of glory, of wealth, of love, of distinction, of accomplishment, of pleasure, of goodness. What life does with our dreams and expectations cannot, of course, be predicted. Some dreams, begun in selflessness, end in rancor; other dreams, begun in selfishness, end in large-heartedness. The unpredictability of the outcome of dreams is no reason to cease dreaming.

To be sure, ambition, the sheer thing unalloyed by some larger   3
purpose than merely clambering up, is never a pretty prospect to
ponder. The single-mindedly ambitious is an old human type—
"Cromwel, I charge thee, fling away Ambition," wrote Shakespeare
in *Henry VIII*. "By that sinne fell the Angles"—and scarcely a type
that has gone out of style, or soon figures to. As drunks have done
to alcohol, the single-minded have done to ambition—given it a
bad name. Like a taste for alcohol, too, ambition does not always
allow for easy satiation. Some people cannot handle it; it has brought
grief to others, and not merely the ambitious alone. Still, none of
this seems sufficient cause for driving ambition under the counter,
in an undeclared Volstead Act.*

By this I do not mean to say that ambition has gone or been   4
driven out of style. It hasn't. Or at least not completely. In our day
many people, goaded by ambition, go in for self-improvement programs of one kind or another: speed reading, assertiveness training, the study of books calling for looking out for number one and
other forms of aggressiveness. But such activities have always seemed
déclassé, and the sort of person who goes to est today thirty or
forty years ago might have enrolled in a Dale Carnegie course.† In
most respects, it appears that the more educated a person is, the
more hopeless life seems to him. This being so, ambition, to the
educated class, has come to seem pointless at best, vicious at worst.
Ambition connotes a certain Rotarian optimism, a thing unseemly,
in very poor taste, rather like a raging sexual appetite in some one
quite elderly. None of this, of course, has stopped the educated
classes from attempting to get their own out of the world—lots of
the best of everything, as a famous epicure once put it—which they
continue to do very effectively. To renunciation is thus added more
than a piquant touch of hypocrisy.

If the above assertions seem overstated, consider what seems to   5
me the unarguableness of the following assertions. If one feels the
stirrings of ambition, it is on the whole best to keep them hidden.
To say of a young man or woman that he or she is ambitious is no
longer, as it once was, a clear compliment. Rather the reverse. A
person called ambitious is likely to arouse anxiety, for in our day
anyone so called is thought to be threatening, possibly a trifle neu-

---

*The Eighteenth Amendment, prohibiting sale of alcoholic beverage.
†A self-help class based on the "power of positive thinking."

rotic. Energy is still valued, so too is competence, but ambition is in bad repute. And perhaps nowhere more than in America.

DISCUSSION

Epstein begins his definition of "ambition" with a disclaimer. The word defines a quality out of favor today, but Epstein asserts ambition is so protean that it contains many meanings. Epstein first uses a formal dictionary definition giving the denotation of the word, what it points to; then, he examines the connotations of ambition, all of them negative in today's society. In the second paragraph, Epstein shows, by contrast, that the qualities implied by ambition can be used for good as well as ill. The third paragraph combines the use of definition by example—the quotation from Shakespeare—with definition by analogy—the analogy of the alcoholic with the single-minded ambition for alcohol. Paragraphs four and five return to the connotations of the word: paragraph four, a historical definition showing the decline in value attached to ambition, and five, an informal definition. In these paragraphs of definition, Epstein lays the groundwork for an argument against society's negative appraisal of ambition. The piece demonstrates two important functions of definition: clarifying ambiguity and stipulating which definitions are apropos to the purpose of the essay.

JOHN McPHEE
Citrus Sinensis

John McPhee (born 1931) has written about everything from the New York Knicks (A Sense of Where You Are, 1969) to Alaska (Coming into the Country, 1977) to nuclear fission (The Curve of Binding Energy, 1974) to the Loch Ness monster (Pieces of the Frame, 1975). In the following exerpt from Oranges *(1967), McPhee's versatility is demonstrated as he clarifies his subject matter with an historical definition of "citrus sinensis," Florida's sweet orange.*

A tractor driver gave me a ride out to my car when I left the picking crew one day, and I've forgotten what I said to him when   1

I jumped up behind him, but whatever it was, he turned around with a look of recognition and said, "You come from apple country." In one sentence, he had defined the dimensions of his own world, the utterly parochial nature of it, its disciplined singleness, its weather, and its cycles of fruition. The appeal of that world and, to an even greater extent, the relief of it had increased in my mind with each day in the groves, among other reasons simply because gas stations, Burger Queens, and shopping centers so dominate the towns of central Florida that the over-all effect on a springtime visitor can be that he is in Trenton during an August heat wave. The groves, in absolute contrast, are both beautiful and quiet, at moments eerie. I retreated into them as often as I could. To someone who is alone in the groves, they can seem to be a vacant city, miles wide and miles long.

In late afternoons and early evenings, I sometimes stayed there to read, sitting on the sand against the trunk of a tree, thumbing through books that had been recommended to me by pomologists at the University of Florida's Citrus Experiment Station. They dealt with the history and botany of citrus, the physiology of the orange, citrus growing, citrus products, and citrus industries. The most absorbing was an encyclopedic treatise called *Hesperides: A History of the Culture and Use of Citrus Fruits*, written in the nineteen-thirties, in what was then Palestine, by a scholar named Samuel Tolkowsky and titled as a gesture of respect for the work of the Sienese priest, Giovanni Battista Ferrari, whose own *Hesperides* had appeared nearly three hundred years earlier. Tolkowsky's work included a kind of compendium of everything of importance—including its name-sake—that had been published on the subject in earlier centuries. Thomas Cardinal Wolsey, I found, had also warded off the unpleasant aspects of society by retreating into oranges. Going from place to place in sixteenth century London, he liked to carry in his hand an orange that had been capped and hollowed out. Inside it, he would put a bit of sponge, saturated with vinegar. With his nose resolutely pressed into the orange, he was insulated by the aroma of the peel and the vinegar against the noxious airs of London and his fellow men.

The evolution of citrus probably began in the Malay Archipelago at least twenty million years ago, when the islands of the South Pacific were still part of a body of land that included Asia and Australia. A bitter ancestral plant apparently made its way to what is now the Asian mainland, and from it developed the modern fruit. The evidence that this event occurred in the area of southern China is overwhelming, beginning with the fact that more citrus varieties and more citrus parasites can be found there than anywhere else. Spreading out to the rest of the world, Chinese citrus jumped the East China Sea and reached Japan by way of Formosa and intervening island groups. It moved eastward into the South Pacific, and the frequency of citrus in the islands today diminishes with distance from the mainland. In the junks of merchant seamen, seeds and trees were carried south to the shores of the Java Sea and into the Strait of Malacca, which was a kind of departure point for sometimes unexpected migrations to India and Africa on the strong westward currents of the Indian Ocean.

Among the first citrus varieties to make this journey—and then 4 to go on into the Mediterranean basin—was the citron, which acquired its name because of an early confusion with another tree. According to Tolkowsky, this confusion came about because the large, rough-skinned citron resembled the greenish-yellow cone of the cedars of Lebanon, and since citron trees and orange trees are nearly identical in shape and foliage, the confusion inevitably expanded. The Greeks called the citron a *kedromelon,* or "cedar apple." The Romans turned this into *malum citreum,* and applied the term— often shortened merely to *citreum*—to all the varied fruits of citrus trees. The second-century writer Apuleius, for one, objected. He had been born in Africa and knew a cedar cone from an orange. In the eighteenth century, the Swedish botanist Carolus Linnaeus nonetheless made the name "citrus" official for the genus. So lemons, limes, citrons, oranges, grapefruit, and tangerines are now grouped under a name that means cedar.

The word "orange" evolved from Sanskrit. The Chinese word 5 for orange, in ancient as well as modern Chinese, is *jyu,* but it did not migrate with the fruit. India was the first major stop in the westward travels of citrus, and the first mention of oranges in Sanskrit literature is found in a medical book called the *Charaka-Samhita,* which was compiled approximately two thousand years ago. The Hindus called an orange a *naranga,* the first syllable of which, according to Tolkowsky, was a prefix meaning fragrance. This became the Persian *naranj,* a word the Muslims carried through the Mediterranean. In Byzantium, an orange was a *nerantzion.* This, in Neo-Latin, became variously styled as *arangium, arantium* and *auran-*

tium—eventually producing *naranja* in Spain, *laranja* in Portugal, *arancia* in Italy, and *orange* in France.

Meanwhile, the Roman city of Arausio, in the South of France, had become, in the Provençal language, Aurenja—a name almost identical in sound and spelling to *auranja*, the Provençal word for orange. Gradually, the names of the city and the fruit evolved in the Provençal tongue to Orenge, and then to Orange. In the early sixteenth century, Philibert of Orange, prince of the city, was awarded a good part of the Netherlands for his political and military services to the Holy Roman Emperor, Charles V. The Prince had no immediate heir, and his possessions and titles eventually passed to a German nephew. This was William of Nassau, Prince of Orange, who founded the Dutch Republic and the House of Orange. In honor of William's descendants, Dutch explorers named the Orange River, in South Africa, and Cape Orange, in northern Brazil. Fort Orange was the name of a Dutch settlement that eventually developed into Albany, New York. After a Protestant prince of the House of Orange had served as King William III of England, a movement known as Orangeism was founded by Irish Protestants, who established the Orange Society, and even called their part of Ireland "The Orange." Commemorating their cause on the landscape of the New World, emigrant Orangemen gave the name "Orange" to towns, cities, and bodies of water, from Lake Orange, Maine, to Orangeburg, South Carolina. Orangemen changed the name of Newark Mountains, New Jersey, to Orange Dale, which eventually became simply Orange, New Jersey, with its satellite towns of West Orange, South Orange, and East Orange—all as the result of a similarity of sound between the name of a transalpine Roman city and the name of a citrus fruit.

Nominal confusion also resulted from a tendency among Romans and Greeks to call any kind of fruit an apple. When the Romans discovered the pomegranate in Punic Mauretania—now Morocco and Algeria—they called it the *malum punicum*. When they came upon the peach, in Persia, they called it the *malum persicum*. Centuries earlier, in Media and in Persia, botanists traveling with the conquering armies of Alexander the Great had found the citron and had named it, variously, the Median apple and the Persian apple. Working later with material left by Alexander's scientists in the archives of Babylon, Theophrastus, the greatest of Greek botanists, also described citrons as Persian and Median apples, and his work disseminated the terms throughout the ancient world. It was a "golden apple" that Paris gave to Aphrodite, thus opening his way to the heart of Helen. In Antiphanes' *The Boeotian Girl*, written in the fourth century B.C., a young man presents a citron to his mistress, and she says.

"I thought it came from the Hesperides,
For there they say the golden apples grow."

Other Greeks, it appears, thought that the golden apples were quinces. Tolkowsky points out that a frieze in the Temple of Zeus at Olympia shows Herakles holding a handful of quinces. In Rome, however, universal agreement seems to have been reached that the golden apples were citrus.

According to Father Ferrari, the Romans thought that citrons, oranges, lemons, and other citrus fruits came to Italy in the arms of the Hesperides—the daughters of Hesperis and Atlas—who crossed the Mediterranean from Africa in a giant shell. Oranges actually reached the Italian peninsula from India. In the first and second centuries A.D., it was only a seventy-day trip across the Indian Ocean from the Malabar Coast to the western shore of the Red Sea, twelve more days from Berenice by camel to the Nile, and another twelve down the river to waiting galleys at Alexandria. (Orange groves were established at Berenice and elsewhere on this route, which eventually branched into the Levant.) Toward the end of the Roman Empire, oranges were flourishing on the Italian Peninsula. After the fall of Rome, oranges played a part in the great Lombard invasion. A Byzantine governor of Rome, enraged at being summarily called back to Byzantium, sent an embassy with a selected display of Italian oranges to Alboin, King of the Lombards, inviting him to overrun Italy, which Alboin did.

In the sixth and seventh centuries, the forces of Islam conquered a wide corridor across the world from India to Spain, and orange, tangerine, and lemon trees today mark the track of the Muslim armies. After Moorish capitals had been established in Andalusia, desert artisans and architects, delirious in the presence of water, filled and surrounded their buildings with pools, cascades, and fountains, planting a small grove of oranges in the Great Mosque of Cordova and oranges and lemons in the interior courts of the Alhambra in Granada. One curious footnote to the rise of Islam developed in Italy in the eleventh century. A group of Norman pilgrims, on their way home from the Holy Land, came upon a band of warrior Muslims who were about to destroy the person and possessions of a Christian prince of Salerno. The Normans saved the prince and drove the Muslims away. Fearful of further attacks, the prince, like the Byzantine governor of Rome nearly five hundred years before him, sent an embassy with the pilgrims to the Duke of Normandy, accompanied by a mountainous gift of beautiful oranges, frankly tempting the Duke to conquer southern Italy—which he did, taking Sicily, too. The Norman conquest of Sicily turned into something of a scandal. Norman minds dissolved in the vapors of Muslim culture. Austere knights of Honfleur and Bayeux suddenly appeared in the streets of Palermo wearing flowing desert robes, and attracted to themselves harems of staggering diversity, while the Church raged. Norman pashas built their own alhambras. The Normans went Muslim with such remarkable style that even Muslim poets were soon praising the new Norman Xanadus. Of one such place, which included nine brooks and a small lake with an island covered with lemon and orange trees, the poet Abd ur-Rahman Ibn Mohammed Ibn Omar wrote:

> The oranges of the Island are like blazing fire
> Amongst the emerald boughs
> And the lemons are like the paleness of a lover
> Who has spent the night crying . . .

It is only in comparatively recent centuries that oranges, in Western countries, have actually been eaten as a food. Their earliest popularity in Europe seems to have been based on the ornamental appearance of the trees and the inspiring aroma of the peel and the blossoms. At the table, they were used as a seasoning for meat and fish and seldom consumed in any other way. Before 1500, European orange growers mainly grew Bitter Oranges, because they were more aromatic, better as seasoning, and hence more valuable. Dinner guests could measure their importance in the regard of their hosts by the number of oranges that came to the table. One fourteenth-century cookbook, describing a dinner given by an abbott of Langy for his superior, the Bishop of Paris, indicates how impressive a meal it was by noting that the roast fish was seasoned with powdered sugar and Sour Oranges. In 1529, the Archbishop of Milan gave a sixteen-course dinner that included caviar and oranges fried with sugar and cinnamon, brill and sardines with slices of orange and lemon, one thousand oysters with pepper and oranges, lobster salad with citrons, sturgeon in aspic covered with orange juice, fried sparrows with oranges, individual salads containing citrons into which the coat of arms of the diner had been carved, orange fritters, a soufflé full of raisins and pine nuts and covered with sugar and orange juice, five hundred fried oysters with lemon slices, and candied peels of citrons and oranges.

At about that time, Portuguese ships returned home from India   12 with sweet orange trees, and a new type spread through Europe. It became known as the Portugal Orange, and it quickly replaced the Bitter Orange in popularity throughout the continent. The word "Portugal" became synonymous with good sweet oranges in numerous countries, and, in fact, sweet oranges are still called Portugals in Greece, Albania, Rumania, parts of the Middle East, and some parts of Italy.

In most of Western Europe, the favor held by the Portugal Orange   13 was less enduring. Within a century after the first trees had come from India, Portuguese missionary monks sent word back from China that Chinese oranges were sweeter than sugar itself. One Portuguese Jesuit wrote that "the oranges of Canton might well be muscat grapes disguised." In 1635, a Chinese orange tree reached Lisbon, and before long the China Orange—a term still used in many countries to denote a fine sweet orange—was in demand all over Europe. The botanical name of the modern sweet orange, in fact, is *Citrus sinensis*.

CONTENT
1. McPhee defines what an orange is by telling some of its history. Where do oranges originally come from?
2. Why are so many places in America named "orange"?
3. Where does the English word "orange" come from?

ORGANIZATION
4. A potentially boring subject, this definition of the word "orange" is transformed into an interesting historical account. How does McPhee begin the account? What functions do the opening paragraphs serve?
5. How does McPhee enliven the broad historical definitions of "orange" and "citrus"?

TOPICS FOR WRITING

6. Look up the word "steward" in the *Oxford English Dictionary*. Write an historical definition of the word showing the changes in meaning the word has undergone.

7. Read H. L. Mencken's chapter on "Euphemisms" in *The American Language*, and write an essay explaining how the meanings of words from several professions have been changed in an attempt to upgrade the work.

ALDO LEOPOLD
Country

Aldo Leopold (1887–1948) is regarded by many conservationists as the father of American environmentalism. He worked for the U.S. Forest Service, helped found the Wilderness Society, and was instrumental in the establishment of Gila National Forest, the first Forest Wilderness Area in the United States. In the following selection from the posthumously published A Sand County Almanac *(1949), Leopold defines "country" by contrasting it with "land," a term with which it is often confused.*

There is much confusion between land and country. Land is the place where corn, gullies, and mortgages grow. Country is the personality of land, the collective harmony of its soil, life, and weather. Country knows no mortgages, no aphabetical agencies, no tobacco road; it is calmly aloof to these petty exigencies of its alleged owners. That the previous occupant of my farm was a bootlegger mattered not one whit to its grouse; they sailed as proudly over the thickets as if they were guests of a king.

Poor land may be rich country, and vice versa. Only economists mistake physical opulence for riches. Country may be rich despite a conspicuous poverty of physical endowment, and its quality may not be apparent at first glance, nor at all times.

I know, for example, a certain lakeshore, a cool austerity of pines and wave-washed sands. All day you see it only as something for the surf to pound, a dark ribbon that stretches farther than you can paddle, a monotony to mark the miles by. But toward sunset some vagrant breeze may waft a gull across a headland, behind which a sudden roistering of loons reveals the presence of a hidden bay. You are seized with an impulse to land, to set foot on bearberry carpets, to pluck a balsam bed, to pilfer beach plums or blueberries, or perhaps to poach a partridge from out those bosky quietudes that lie behind the dunes. A bay? Why not also a trout stream? Incisively the paddles clip little soughing swirls athwart the gunwale, the bow swings sharp shoreward and cleaves the greening depths for camp.

Later, a supper-smoke hangs lazily upon the bay; a fire flickers   4
under drooping boughs. It is a lean poor land, but rich country.

Some woods, perennially lush, are notably lacking in charm. Tall   5
clean-boled oaks and tulip poplars may be good to look at, from the road, but once inside one may find a coarseness of minor vegetation, a turbidity of waters, and a paucity of wildlife. I cannot explain why a red rivulet is not a brook. Neither can I, by logical deduction, prove that a thicket without the potential roar of a quail covey is only a thorny place. Yet every outdoorsman knows that this is true. That wildlife is merely something to shoot at or to look at is the grossest of fallacies. It often represents the difference between rich country and mere land.

There are woods that are plain to look at, but not to look into.   6
Nothing is plainer than a cornbelt woodlot; yet, if it be August, a crushed pennyroyal, or an over-ripe mayapple, tells you here is a place. October sun on a hickory nut is irrefutable evidence of good country; one senses not only hickory but a whole chain of further sequences: perhaps of oak coals in the dusk, a young squirrel browning, and a distant barred owl hilarious over his own joke.

The taste for country displays the same diversity in aesthetic   7
competence among individuals as the taste for opera, or oils. There are those who are willing to be herded in droves through "scenic" places; who find mountains grand if they be proper mountains with waterfalls, cliffs, and lakes. To such the Kansas plains are tedious. They see the endless corn, but not the heave and the grunt of the ox teams breaking the prairie. History, for them, grows on campuses. They look at the low horizon, but they cannot see it, as de Vaca did, under the bellies of the buffalo.

In country, as in people, a plain exterior often conceals hidden   8
riches, to perceive which requires much living in and with. Nothing is more monotonous than the juniper foothills, until some veteran

of a thousand summers, laden blue with berries, explodes in a blue burst of chattering jays. The drab sogginess of a March cornfield, saluted by one honker from the sky, is drab no more.

CONTENT

1. The informal contrasting definitions of "country" and "land" imply a value system that Leopold believes in. Describe that value system.
2. What does Leopold mean when he says, "Poor land may be rich country, and vice versa"?

ORGANIZATION

3. Leopold establishes his definitions before giving examples of what he means. What advantages are there in this strategy?
4. How does Leopold's comment, "a plain exterior often conceals hidden riches" reveal the organizational pattern of the essay?

TOPICS FOR WRITING

5. Select two terms that are often confused (for example, "nuclear superiority," and "nuclear parity"). Define each, citing examples to prove that there is a crucial difference between the terms.
6. Select a broad term ("family" for example), and define it informally by giving a series of specific examples.

GEORGE ORWELL
What Is Science?

George Orwell is well-known as a novelist, but he was also a prolific journalistic reporter and essayist, as attested by the four volumes of his Collected Essays, Journalism and Letters *(1971). In this brief commentary (written less than two months after the end of World War II), Orwell contends that the kind of education offered to students depends on how we define "science."*

In last week's *Tribune*, there was an intersting letter from Mr. J. Stewart Cook, in which he suggested that the best way of avoiding the danger of a "scientific hierarchy" wou.d be to see to it that every member of the general public was, as far as possible, scientifically educated. At the same time, scientists should be brought out of their isolation and encouraged to take a greater part in politics and administration.

As a general statement, I think most of us would agree with this, 2
but I notice that, as usual, Mr. Cook does not define science, and merely implies in passing that it means certain exact sciences whose experiments can be made under laboratory conditions. Thus, adult education tends "to neglect scientific studies in favour of literary, economic and social subjects," economics and sociology not being regarded as branches of science, apparently. This point is of great importance. For the word science is at present used in at least two meanings, and the whole question of scientific education is obscured by the current tendency to dodge from one meaning to the other.

Science is generally taken as meaning either (a) the exact sci- 3
ences, such as chemistry, physics, etc, or (b) a method of thought which obtains verifiable results by reasoning logically from observed fact.

If you ask any scientist, or indeed almost any educated person, 4
"What is science?" you are likely to get an answer approximating to (b). In everyday life, however, both in speaking and in writing, when people say "science" they mean (a). Science means something that happens in a laboratory: the very word calls up a picture of graphs, test-tubes, balances, Bunsen burners, microscopes. A biologist, an astronomer, perhaps a psychologist or a mathematician, is described as a "man of science": no one would think of applying this term to a statesman, a poet, a journalist, or even a philosopher. And those who tell us that the young must be scientifically educated mean, almost invariably, that they should be taught more about radioactivity, or the stars, or the physiology of their own bodies, rather than that they should be taught to think more exactly.

This confusion of meaning, which is partly deliberate, has in it 5
a great danger. Implied in the demand for more scientific education is the claim that if one has been scientifically trained one's approach to *all* subjects will be more intelligent than if one had had no such training. A scientist's political opinions, it is assumed, his opinions on sociological questions, on morals, on philosophy, perhaps even on the arts, will be more valuable than those of a layman. The world, in other words, would be a better place if the scientists were in control of it. But a "scientist," as we have just seen, means in

practice a specialist in one of the exact sciences. It follows that a chemist or a physicist, as such, is politically more intelligent than a poet or a lawyer, as such. And, in fact, there are already millions of people who do believe this.

But is it really true that a "scientist," in this narrower sense, is any likelier than other people to approach non-scientific problems in an objective way? There is not much reason for thinking so. Take one simple test—the ability to withstand nationalism. It is often loosely said that "Science is international," but in practice the scientific workers of all countries line up behind their own governments with fewer scruples than are felt by the writers and the artists. The German scientific community, as a whole, made no resistance to Hitler. Hitler may have ruined the long-term prospects of German science, but there were still plenty of gifted men to do the necessary research on such things as synthetic oil, jet planes, rocket projectiles and the atomic bomb. Without them the German war machine could never have been built up.

On the other hand, what happened to German literature when the Nazis came to power? I believe no exhaustive lists have been published, but I imagine that the number of German scientists— Jews apart—who voluntarily exiled themselves or were persecuted by the régime was much smaller than the number of writers and journalists. More sinister than this, a number of German scientists swallowed the monstrosity of "racial science." You can find some of the statements to which they set their names in Professor Brady's *The Spirit and Structure of German Fascism*.

But, in slightly different forms, it is the same picture everywhere. In England, a large proportion of our leading scientists accept the structure of capitalist society, as can be seen from the comparative freedom with which they are given knighthoods, baronetcies and ever peerages. Since Tennyson, no English writer worth reading—one might, perhaps, make an exception of Sir Max Beerbohm—has been given a title. And those English scientists who do not simply accept the *status quo* are frequently Communists, which means that, however intellectually scrupulous they may be in their own line of work, they are ready to be uncritical and even dishonest on certain subjects. The fact is that a mere training in one or more of the exact sciences, even combined with very high gifts, is no guarantee of a humane or sceptical outlook. The physicists of half a dozen great nations, all feverishly and secretly working away at the atomic bomb, are a demonstration of this.

But does all this mean that the general public should *not* be more 9
scientifically educated? On the contrary! All it means is that scientific education for the masses will do little good, and probably a lot
of harm, if it simply boils down to more physics, more chemistry,
more biology, etc to the detriment of literature and history. Its probable effect on the average human being would be to narrow the
range of his thoughts and make him more than ever contemptuous
of such knowledge as he did not possess: and his political reactions
would probably be somewhat less intelligent than those of an illiterate peasant who retained a few historical memories and a fairly
sound aesthetic sense.

Clearly, scientific education ought to mean the implanting of a 10
rational, sceptical, experimental habit of mind. It ought to mean
acquiring a *method*—a method that can be used on any problem that
one meets—and not simply piling up a lot of facts. Put it in those
words, and the apologist of scientific education will usually agree.
Press him further, ask him to particularise, and somehow it always
turns out that scientific education means more attention to the exact
sciences, in other words—more *facts*. The idea that science means
a way of looking at the world, and not simply a body of knowledge,
is in practice strongly resisted. I think sheer professional jealousy
is part of the reason for this. For if science is simply a method or
an attitude, so that anyone whose thought-processes are sufficiently rational can in some sense be described as a scientist—what
then becomes of the enormous prestige now enjoyed by the chemist, the physicist, etc and his claim to be somehow wiser than the
rest of us?

A hundred years ago, Charles Kingsley described science as 11
"making nasty smells in a laboratory." A year or two ago a young
industrial chemist informed me, smugly, that he "could not see
what was the use of poetry." So the pendulum swings to and fro,
but it does not seem to me that one attitude is any better than the
other. At the moment, science is on the up-grade, and so we hear,
quite rightly, the claim that the masses should be scientifically educated: we do not hear, as we ought, the counter-claim that the scientists themselves would benefit by a little education. Just before
writing this, I saw in an American magazine the statement that a
number of British and American physicists refused from the start
to do research on the atomic bomb, well knowing what use would
be made of it. Here you have a group of sane men in the middle of
a world of lunatics. And though no names were published, I think

it would be a safe guess that all of them were people with some kind of general cultural background, some acquaintance with history or literature or the arts—in short, people whose interests were not, in the current sense of the word, purely scientific.

CONTENT

1. What dangerous tendencies does Orwell see in the confusion between the two meanings popularly attributed to the word "science"?

2. Why is Orwell against too great an emphasis on teaching the exact sciences? What does such an education lack? What evidence does Orwell cite that indicates such an education is dangerous to the future of humanity?

3. What logical fallacies appear in paragraph 8? For example, what is the fallacy underlying Orwell's division of scientists into "those who accept titles" and those who are Communists? Why does he believe Communist scientists are either uncritical or dishonest? What are the implications of the last sentence in the paragraph? What does Orwell imply is the difference between physicists and writers?

ORGANIZATION

4. Orwell's definition of the two meanings of "science" employs contrast. How does Orwell organize the definitions so as to bring out the differences in meaning?

5. Why does Orwell begin his essay by replying to a letter to the *Tribune*? What misconception about the meaning of science does this allow him to answer?

TOPICS FOR WRITING

6. Choose a word whose meaning is steeped in controversy (for example: conservative, evolution, conservation). By contrasting two opposing definitions, show how one definition is more valid than the other.

7. Stipulate your own definitions of the word "science," and, disagreeing with Orwell's position, show how more education in the "exact sciences" is necessary for an intelligent citizenry at the end of the twentieth century.

Examples

When we want to explain what we mean, we naturally turn to *examples*. Yet we frequently write general statements that need supporting examples, and forget to supply them. Sometimes we make ambiguous statements that call for illustrations; sometimes we make statements that should be supported with facts; and sometimes our statements need further elaboration or expansion with more particulars and details. The requirements of *clarity, proof,* and *sufficient development,* therefore, frequently call for some kind of exemplification.

Clarity   The primary function of examples is to clarify. Perhaps the subject is complicated or tends to be abstract. In both cases, give one or more specific examples to illustrate the point and to bring it into contact with the concrete world. Ask yourself who the audience is, and whether it is as familiar with the subject as you are. What parts of the subject are likely to need the clarification of an example? As poet Robert Graves has suggested, you need to imagine the reader over your shoulder, looking at the page you've written, asking for explanations and clarifications of points that may not be immediately clear. For example (two words which should appear in nearly every expository essay), when E. B. White tells us that New York "insulates the individual," he follows that statement with several pages of examples of events going on in the city—from murders, accidental deaths, air shows, sporting events, to ocean liner departures, the arrival of the governor, and conventions—none of which White witnessed. The list of examples helps make his point: The events are so numerous and commonplace, they have no direct impact on him.

Proof   We make essentially three kinds of statements: reports, inferences, and judgments. "The current air temperature is 80° F" is a *report,* a fact we can verify by checking a thermometer. "It's going to rain" is an *inference,* a conclusion based on an observation of a dark, cloudy sky. "She is the worst governor the state has had in decades" is a *judgment,* simply an opinion regarding relative

223

goodness, badness, and so on. Reports rarely require examples for proof because they are either true or false; their reliability can be easily checked. Inferences and judgments, however, raise questions that demand documentation. "Why do you think it will rain?" "Why is she the worst governor?" Proper answers to these questions will necessarily be factual and closer to the level of actual experience than the initial statement. That is what writing well involves—making statements on a factual level where the reader can easily understand them. Examples help accomplish this aim.

Development Writers sometimes trap themselves in the belief that their subject involves such general knowledge that readers can fill in the details for themselves. This is almost always a mistake. A subject that is often ripe with opportunity for vivid detail yields a commonplace, stale, vague outline of the potentially perceptive essay. Even if the topic of the essay is generally understood and the thesis widely accepted, through careful development and thoughtful observation of details, the writer can produce a rich, interesting essay.

Expanding your writing through additional detail is not like blowing more hot air into a balloon, but rather fleshing out for the reader what otherwise is a skeletal sentence outline. For example, rural poor from the South find it difficult to adjust when they migrate to Northern industrial cities. That obvious statement presents the reader with an idea for an essay, but no details that will convince him that you know what you're talking about. But when Robert Coles provides detailed examples of multistoried houses with stairs, of door keys, mailboxes, and rooms with light switches, he has brought the idea of urban living down to a level of specificity that the reader can immediately apprehend and appreciate.

A final, and seemingly obvious, rule about using examples: They should truly exemplify. An atypical, uncharacteristic example will fail to illustrate, clarify, or prove your point. Coles' examples, on the other hand, look in two directions—toward the audience that understands them and toward the thesis that the examples support.

SHORT EXAMPLE—EXAMPLES

KEVIN STARR
Signs of the Times

Kevin Starr is a regular columnist for the San Francisco Examiner *and* Chronicle. *He has written a history of early California,* Americans and the California Dream 1850–1915 *(1973). In this brief piece from his column, Starr offers a series of short examples to illustrate his point about the value of instant visual recognition through trademarks.*

The bold lettering and bright red stripe of a package of Jell-o . . . the muscled arm, clenching an old-fashioned industrial hammer, gracing a box of Arm & Hammer baking soda . . . the near Jungian curve of the two capital C's in Coca-Cola . . . Sunkist, stamped on an orange or lemon . . . The SunMaid on a box of raisins, offering you the bounty of sun-drenched Fresno fields . . . William Penn beaming broadly from a cylindrical box of Quaker Oats . . . a turbaned Arab sipping a demitasse on a can of Hills Brothers coffee . . . the Morton salt girl, walking in the rain. 1

The list is endless of those trademarks, signs and symbols which specify a product but which also, because they have been with us so long, become interiorized reference points in our journey through America. . . . 2

Our industrial world signs and signifies itself through visual symbols, and of late this process of visual communication—in packaging trademarks, in interior design, in brochures, even in the way newspapers are graphically arranged—has become an even more important aspect of how we stabilize our identities, social and personal. 3

DISCUSSION

These paragraphs illustrate how a series of examples can clarify and amplify a single point. Note that the thesis sentence—"visual symbols . . . stabilize our identities, social and personal"—follows rather than preceeds the examples, a reverse of the usual strategy in such a series of short paragraphs. Starr seems to want the reader to visualize the symbols *before* he states their significance. He selects vivid, well-known, examples that are suitable for his purpose. His thesis about the reference points, the comfort we derive from familiar guidelines to help with our choices, is reinforced by repetition, but its chief force comes from the appropriateness of the examples.

GAY TALESE
New York

Gay Talese began his career as a reporter for the New York Times *in 1953; in 1966 he became a contributing editor to* Esquire *magazine. He has published a number of books many of which have biblical titles:* Honor Thy Father *(1971), about the mafia;* The Kingdom and the Power *(1969), about the rise of* The New York Times; *and* Thy Neighbor's Wife *(1980), about sexual freedom. Talese's power as a writer stems from his painstaking observations. "New York" is filled with detailed observations exemplifying New York's excitement and attraction.*

New York is a city of things unnoticed. It is a city with cats   1
sleeping under parked cars, two stone armadillos crawling up St. Patrick's Cathedral, and thousands of ants creeping on top of the Empire State Building. The ants probably were carried up there by wind or birds, but nobody is sure; nobody in New York knows any more about the ants than they do about the panhandler who takes taxis to the Bowery; or the dapper man who picks trash out of Sixth Avenue trash cans; or the medium in the West Seventies who claims, "I am clairvoyant, clairaudient and clairsensuous."

New York is a city for eccentrics and a center for odd bits of   2
information. New Yorkers blink twenty-eight times a minute, but forty when tense. Most popcorn chewers at Yankee Stadium stop chewing momentarily just before the pitch. Gumchewers on Macy's escalators stop chewing momentarily just before they get off—to concentrate on the last step. Coins, paper clips, ball-point pens,

and little girls' pocketbooks are found by workmen when they clean the sea lion's pool at the Bronx Zoo.

A Park Avenue doorman has parts of three bullets in his head —there since World War I. Several young gypsy daughters, influenced by television and literacy, are running away from home because they don't want to grow up and become fortune-tellers. Each month a hundred pounds of hair are delivered to Louis Feder on 545 Fifth Avenue, where blond hairpieces are made from German women's hair; brunette hairpieces from Italian women's hair; but no hairpieces from American women's hair which, says Mr. Feder, is weak from too frequent rinses and permanents.

Some of New York's best informed men are elevator operators, who rarely talk, but always listen—like doormen. Sardi's doormen listen to the comments made by Broadway's first-nighters walking by after the last act. They listen closely. They listen carefully. Within ten minutes they can tell you which shows will flop and which will be hits.

On Broadway each evening a big, dark, 1948 Rolls-Royce pulls into Forty-sixth Street—and out hop two little ladies armed with Bibles and signs reading, "The Damned Shall Perish." These ladies proceed to stand on the corner screaming at the multitudes of Broadway sinners, sometimes until three a.m., when their chauffeur in the Rolls picks them up and drives them back to Westchester.

By this time Fifth Avenue is deserted by all but a few strolling insomniacs, some cruising cabdrivers, and a group of sophisticated females who stand in store windows all night and day wearing cold, perfect smiles. Like sentries they line Fifth Avenue—these window mannequins who gaze onto the quiet street with tilted heads and pointed toes and long rubber fingers reaching for cigarettes that aren't there.

At five a.m. Manhattan is a town of tired trumpet players and homeward-bound bartenders. Pigeons control Park Avenue and strut unchallenged in the middle of the street. This is Manhattan's mellowest hour. Most *night* people are out of sight—but the *day* people have not yet appeared. Truck drivers and cabs are alert, yet they do not disturb the mood. They do not disturb the abandoned Rockefeller Center, or the motionless night watchmen in the Fulton Fish Market, or the gas-station attendant sleeping next to Sloppy Louie's with the radio on.

At five a.m. the Broadway regulars either have gone home or to   8
all-night coffee shops where, under the glaring light, you see their
whiskers and wear. And on Fifty-first Street a radio press car is
parked at the curb with a photographer who has nothing to do. So
he just sits there for a few nights, looks through the windshield
and soon becomes a keen observer of life after midnight.

"At one a.m.," he says, "Broadway is filled with wise guys and   9
with kids coming out of the Astor Hotel in white dinner jackets—
kids who drive to dances in their fathers' cars. You also see cleaning
ladies going home, always wearing kerchiefs. By two a.m. some of
the drinkers are getting out of hand, and this is the hour for bar
fights. At three a.m. the last show is over in the nightclubs, and
most of the tourists and out-of-town buyers are back in hotels. And
small-time comedians are criticizing big-time comedians in Han-
son's Drugstore. At four a.m., after the bars close, you see the
drunks come out—and also the pimps and prostitutes who take
advantage of drunks. At five a.m., though, it is mostly quiet. New
York is an entirely different city at five a.m."

At six a.m. the early workers begin to push up from the subways.   1
The traffic begins to move down Broadway like a river. And Mrs.
Mary Woody jumps out of bed, dashes to her office and phones
dozens of sleepy New Yorkers to say in a cheerful voice, rarely
appreciated: "Good morning. Time to get up." For twenty years, as
an operator of Western Union's Wake-Up Service, Mrs. Woody has
gotten millions out of bed.

By seven a.m. a floridly robust little man, looking very Parisian   1
in a blue beret and turtleneck sweater, moves in a hurried step along
Park Avenue visiting his wealthy lady friends—making certain that
each is given a brisk, before-breakfast rubdown. The uniformed
doormen greet him warmly and call him either "Biz" or "Mac"
because he is Biz Mackey, a ladies' masseur *extraordinaire*. He never
reveals the names of his customers, but most of them are middle-
aged and rich. He visits each of them in their apartments, and has
special keys to their bedrooms; he is often the first man they see in
the morning, and they lie in bed waiting for him.

The doormen that Biz passes each morning are generally an   1
obliging, endlessly articulate group of sidewalk diplomats who list
among their friends some of Manhattan's most powerful men, most
beautiful women and snootiest poodles. More often than not, the

doormen are big, slightly Gothic in design, and the possessors of eyes sharp enough to spot big tippers a block away in the year's thickest fog. Some East Side doormen are as proud as grandees, and their uniforms, heavily festooned, seem to come from the same tailor who outfitted Marshal Tito.*

Shortly after seven-thirty each morning hundreds of people are 13 lined along Forty-second Street waiting for the eight a.m. opening of the ten movie houses that stand almost shoulder-to-shoulder between Times Square and Eighth Avenue. Who are these people who go to the movies at eight a.m.? They are the city's insomniacs, night watchmen, and people who can't go home, do not want to go home, or have no home. They are derelicts, homosexuals, cops, hacks, truck drivers, cleaning ladies and restaurant men who have worked all night. They are also alcoholics who are waiting at eight a.m. to pay forty cents for a soft seat and to sleep in the dark smoky theatre. And yet, aside from being smoky, each of the Times Square's theatres has a special quality, or lack of quality, about it. At the Victory Theatre one finds horror films, while at the Times Square Theatre they feature only cowboy films. There are first-run films for forty cents at the Lyric, while at the Selwyn there are always second-run films for thirty cents. But if you go to the Apollo Theatre you will see, in addition to foreign films, people in the lobby talking with their hands. These are deaf-and-dumb movie fans who patronize the Apollo because they read the subtitles. The Apollo probably has the biggest deaf-and-dumb movie audience in the world.

New York is a city of 38,000 cabdrivers, 10,000 bus drivers, but 14 only one chauffeur who has a chauffeur. The wealthy chauffeur can be seen driving up Fifth Avenue each morning, and his name is Roosevelt Zanders. He earns $100,000 a year, is a gentleman of impeccable taste and, although he owns a $23,000 Rolls-Royce, does not scorn his friends who own Bentleys. For $150 a day, Mr. Zanders will drive anyone anywhere in his big, silver Rolls. Diplomats patronize him, models pose next to him, and each day he receives cables from around the world urging that he be waiting at Idlewild, on the docks, or outside the Plaza Hotel. Sometimes at night, however, he is too tired to drive anymore. So Bob Clarke, his chauffeur, takes over and Mr. Zanders relaxes in the back.

*Late President of Yugoslavia.

New York is a town of 3000 bootblacks whose brushes and rhythmic   1⁹
rag-snaps can be heard up and down Manhattan from midmorning
to midnight. They dodge cops, survive rainstorms, and thrive in
the Empire State Building as well as on the Staten Island Ferry. They
usually wear dirty shoes.

New York is a city of headless men who sit obscurely in subway   1⁶
booths all day and night selling tokens to people in a hurry. Each
weekday more than 4,500,000 riders pass these money changers
who seem to have neither heads, faces, nor personalities—only
fingers. Except when giving directions, their vocabulary consists
largely of three words: "How many, please?"

In New York there are 200 chestnut vendors, and they average   1⁵
$25 on a good day peddling soft, warm chestnuts. Like many ven-
dors, the chestnut men do not own their own rigs—they borrow
or rent them from pushcart makers such as David Amerman.

Mr. Amerman, with offices opposite a defunct public bathhouse   1.
on the Lower East Side, is New York's master builder of pushcarts.
His father and grandfather before him were pushcart makers, and
the family has long been a household word among the city's most
discriminating junkmen, fruit vendors and hot-dog peddlers.

In New York there are 500 mediums, ranging from semi-trance   1
to trance to deep-trance types. Most of them live in New York's
West Seventies and Eighties, and on Sundays some of these blocks
are comunicating with the dead, vibrating to trumpets, and solving
all problems.

The Manhattan Telephone Directory has 776,300 names, of which   2
3316 are Smith, 2835 are Brown, 2444 are Williams, 2070 are Cohen—
and one is Mike Krasilovsky. Anyone who doubts this last fact has
only to look at the top of page 876 where, in large black letters, is
this sign: "There is only one Mike Krasilovsky. Sterling 3-1990."

In New York the Fifth Avenue Lingerie shop is on Madison Ave-   2
nue; the Madison Pet Shop is on Lexington Avenue; the Park Avenue
Florist in on Madison Avenue, and the Lexington Hand Laundry is
on Third Avenue. New York is the home of 120 pawnbrokers and
it is where Bishop Sheen's brother, Dr. Sheen, shares an office with
one Dr. Bishop.

New York is a town of thirty tattooists where interest in mankind   2
is skin-deep, but whose impressions usually last a lifetime. Each
day the tattooists go pecking away over acres of anatomy. And in

downtown Manhattan, Stanley Moskowitz, a scion of a distinguished family of bowery skin-peckers, does a grand business.

When it rains in Manhattan, automobile traffic is slow, dates are 23 broken and, in hotel lobbies, people slump behind newspapers or walk aimlessly about with no place to sit, nobody to talk to, nothing to do. Taxis are harder to get; department stores do between fifteen and twenty-five percent less business, and the monkeys in the Bronx Zoo, having no audience, slouch grumpily in their cages looking more bored than the lobby-loungers.

While some New Yorkers become morose with rain, others prefer 24 it, like to walk in it, and say that on rainy days the city's buildings seem somehow cleaner—washed in an opalescence, like a Monet painting. There are fewer suicides in New York when it rains. But when the sun is shining, and New Yorkers seem happy, the depressed person sinks deeper into depression, and Bellevue Hospital gets more suicide calls.

New York is a town of 8485 telephone operators, 1364 Western 25 Union messenger boys, and 112 newspaper copyboys. An average baseball crowd at Yankee Stadium uses over ten gallons of liquid soap per game—an unofficial high mark for cleanliness in the major leagues; the stadium also has the league's top number of ushers (360), sweepers (72), and men's rooms (34).

New York is a town in which the brotherhood of Russian Bath 26 Rubbers, the only union advocating sweatshops, appears to be heading for its last rubdown. The union has been going in New York City for years, but now most of the rubbers are pushing seventy and are deaf—from all the water and the hot temperatures.

Each afternoon in New York a rather seedy saxophone player, 27 his cheeks blown out like a spinnaker, stands on the sidewalk playing *Danny Boy* in such a sad, sensitive way that he soon has half the neighborhood peeking out of windows tossing nickels, dimes and quarters at his feet. Some of the coins roll under parked cars, but most of them are caught in his outstretched hand. The saxophone player is a street musician named Joe Gabler; for the past thirty years he has serenaded every block in New York and has sometimes been tossed as much as $100 a day in coins. He is also hit with buckets of water, empty beer cans and eggs, and chased by wild dogs. He is believed to be the last of New York's ancient street musicians.

New York is a town of nineteen midget wrestlers. They all can
squeeze into the Hotel Holland's elevator, six can sleep in one bed,
eight can be comfortably transported to Madison Square Garden
in the chauffeur-driven Cadillac reserved for the midget wrestlers.

In New York from dawn to dusk to dawn, day after day, you can
hear the steady rumble of tires against the concrete span of George
Washington Bridge. The bridge is never completely still. It trembles
with traffic. It moves in the wind. Its great veins of steel swell when
hot and contract when cold; its span often is ten feet closer to the
Hudson River in summer than in winter. It is an almost restless
structure of graceful beauty which, like an irresistible seductress,
withholds secrets from the romantics who gaze upon it, the escapists who jump off it, the chubby girl who lumbers across its 3500-
foot span trying to reduce, and the 100,000 motorists who each day
cross it, smash into it, shortchange it, get jammed up on it.

When street traffic dwindles and most people are sleeping in
New York, some neighborhoods begin to crawl with cats. They move
quickly through the shadows of buildings; night watchmen, police-
men, garbage collectors and other nocturnal wanderers see them—
but never for long.

There are 200,000 stray cats in New York. A majority of them
hang around the fish market, or in Greenwich Village, and in the
East and West Side neighborhoods where garbage cans abound. No
part of the city is without its strays, however, and all-night garage
attendants in such busy neighborhoods as Fifty-fourth Street have
counted as many as twenty of them around the Ziegfeld Theatre
early in the morning. Troops of cats patrol the waterfront piers at
night searching for rats. Subway trackwalkers have discovered cats
living in the darkness. They seem never to get hit by trains, though
some are occasionally liquidated by the third rail. About twenty-
five cats live seventy-five feet below the west end of Grand Central
Terminal, are fed by the underground workers, and never wander
up into the daylight.

New York is a city in which large, cliff-dwelling hawks cling to
skyscrapers and occasionally zoom to snatch a pigeon over Central
Park, or Wall Street, or the Hudson River. Bird watchers have seen
these peregrine falcons circling lazily over the city. They have seen
them perched atop tall buildings, even around Times Square. About

twelve of these hawks patrol the city, sometimes with a wingspan of thirty-five inches. They have buzzed women on the roof of the St. Regis Hotel, have attacked repairmen on smokestacks, and, in August, 1947, two hawks jumped women residents in the recreation yard of the Home of the New York Guild for the Jewish Blind. Maintenance men at the Riverside Church have seen hawks dining on pigeons in the bell tower. The hawks remain there for only a little while. And then they fly out to the river, leaving pigeons' heads for the Riverside maintenance men to clean up. When the hawks return, they fly in quietly—*unnoticed*, like the cats ,the headless men, the ants, the ladies' masseur, the doorman with three bullets in his head, and most of the other offbeat wonders in this town without time.

CONTENT

1. What makes Talese's essay so interesting? Is there a special quality to the examples he has chosen? How does his statement in paragraph 2 that New York is, "a center for odd bits of information" define the kinds of examples he has chosen?
2. Are the statistics as interesting as the more developed examples? Are they as necessary to complete the intention of the essay?
3. In *Here Is New York*, E. B. White remarks that New Yorkers are often detached from the city because of its sheer size. How do Talese's examples convey New York's size?

ORGANIZATION

4. Talese employs several organizational devices to tie together what might otherwise be a loose catalogue of examples. Identify some of these devices. How does the conclusion give structure to the essay?
5. Talese ends his essay with the statement that New York is "a town without time." How does the major organizational device contradict this? Why isn't time used as an organizational device throughout the entire essay?

TOPICS FOR WRITING

6. Characterize your town or campus by organizing a series of examples around different activities that take place within a twelve-hour period.

7. Select a place that you feel is either traditional or unusual and give examples which support your view of that place.

ELLEN GOODMAN
The Maidenform Woman Administers Shock Treatment

Ellen Goodman's column has been syndicated in the nation's newspapers since 1976. Educated at Radcliffe, she became a reporter for Newsweek, *then a feature writer for the* Detroit Free Press, *and eventually joined the* Boston Globe *as a feature writer, and columnist. In 1980, she was awarded a Pulitzer Prize. Her writing has been collected in* Close to Home *(1979) and* At Large *(1980). "The Maidenform Woman Administers Shock Treatment" is characteristic of the concise yet penetrating insights Goodman delivers in her brief essays.*

It's not that I'd never seen her before.   1

Years ago, she was photographed outside of her apartment build-   2
ing, dressed in a fur coat and bra and panties. Since then she's been found in similar attire in theater and hotel lobbies. Usually, of course, you get used to this sort of thing if you live in a city long enough.

But it was a shock to see her in a hospital room. There she was,   3
hair tied back primly, medical chart in her left hand, pen in her right hand, long white jacket over her shoulders, exposing her lacy magenta bra and panties.

Was it possible? Why, yes! Stop the presses! The Maidenform   4
Woman Had Become a Doctor! According to the caption under this photograph, she was "making the rounds in her elegant Delectables."

At some point when I wasn't looking, everbody's favorite exhi-   5
bitionist must have actually gone to medical school. I suppose that I had underestimated her intelligence—this happens so often with attractive women. I always thought she was a candidate for a cold,

not a medical degree. I can only imagine the difficulties she had getting accepted, what with her portfolio and all.

But now any number of magazines are featuring her personal   6
success story. On their pages, the Maidenform woman is willingly displaying her new bedside manner in living color. Poised, concerned, even prim, young Dr. Maidenform is photographed looking down compassionately at her bedridden patient. We don't know exactly what the patient thinks of all this. Fortunately for her, his leg is in traction and he can't move. The other doctors in the ad seem quite unconcerned about her outfit. Dr. Maidenform seems to have made it in a world that is entirely non-sexist. They aren't even glancing in the direction of her non-air-brushed belly button!

Quite frankly, I must admit that the Maidenform Woman cured   7
me of a disease. She cured me of creeping complacency.

Until I saw her, I had become virtually numb to the advertising   8
image of that handy creature, "The New Woman." We are now out of the era of housewife-as-airhead. We've even come a long way from the year of coming a long way, baby.

We are plunging into the "successful woman as sex object" syn-   9
drome. The more real women break out of the mold, the more advertisers force them back in. We are now told that, for all the talk, the New Woman is just the Total Woman in updated gear.

Under the careful dress-for-success suit of an MBA is a woman   10
buying Office Legs for sex appeal. Around the briefcase of a lawyer is a hand shining with high-color nail gloss. Take away the lab coat, the stethoscope and syringe, and the doctor is just another set of "elegant delectables." The point in all this isn't especially subtle. As Jean Kilbourne, who has long studied media images of women, said, "It's out of the question that they would ever show a male doctor like that. She is aloof but available. Underneath she is still a sex object." Kilbourne's favorite entry in this category is a perfume ad that shows the successful woman mixing business with, uh, pleasure. In the first frame we see the busy executive at a business lunch with three men. In the second frame, we see her under the covers with one.

Advertisers have a big investment in this new-old image. I'm not   11
talking about the professional woman market. There are hardly enough women doctors to keep the magenta lace factory in business. But there are now an increasing number of women who see professionals as glamorous and want to identify with them.

The advertisers are betting that these women want, as the   12
Maidenform ad puts it, "just what the doctor ordered." So the doctor is ordered to strip, literally, her professional cover. She is revealed
in the flesh, to be—yes, indeed—just another woman insecure about
her femininity, just another woman in search of sex appeal, just
another women who needs "silky satin tricot with antique lace
scalloping."

Pretty soon, I suppose, she will need it in the Senate, in the   13
Supreme Court, even in the Oval Office. The Maidenform Woman.
You never know where she'll turn up.

CONTENT

1. Why does Goodman see the Maidenform ad as particularly
   offensive to women? In what ways is it worse than the ads
   featuring, what Goodman calls, the housewife-as-airhead?
2. How is the perfume ad, which Goodman cites similar to the
   Maidenform ad in its offensiveness?

ORGANIZATION

3. The first half of Goodman's essay focuses on the details of the
   Maidenform ad itself; the second half on the analysis of the ad
   and Goodman's reaction. Why does she employ this organization?
4. Goodman's essay follows an inductive pattern, beginning with
   a specific example, then moving toward general conclusions.
   Why does Goodman reserve the example of the perfume ad for
   the section of the essay that deals with general analysis?

TOPICS FOR WRITING

5. Select an ad aimed at the "New Woman" and analyze the image
   it presents.
6. Select an ad which presents an unflattering image of men and
   analyze its audience appeal.

GARRISON KEILLOR
How It Was in America
a Week Ago Tuesday

Garrison Keillor has recently become one of America's leading humorists. He is widely known as the founder (in 1974) and the master of ceremonies of "A Prairie Home Companion," a weekly program of live music and humor heard on 140 stations over National Public Radio. His offbeat humor often has a touching nostalgic quality to it, an element that captures the spirit and tone of the Midwest. "How It Was in America a Week Ago Tuesday," from Happy to Be Here *(1982), draws its humor from the many examples which poke fun at the you-are-there reporter who takes us on a tour of the minute details of daily life "in these United States."*

A couple of us were sitting around in the United States of America one night not long ago when we got this idea for a magazine article. We would call up housewives, farmers, doctors, white-collar workers, black people, students, town officials, teachers, urban planners, airline spokesmen, White House sources, leading economists, cabdrivers, newspaper editors, environmental experts, ministers, controversial writers, moderate Republicans, telephone operators, mediators, welfare recipients, observers, low-income families, grain brokers, country-and-western singers, skilled craftsmen, motorists, steelworkers, rural Americans, alternative life-stylists, bystanders, commuters, historians, gay persons, investors, and small children in California, Louisiana, Toledo, the Apostle Islands, San Jose, Syracuse, Cook County, the Great Plains, Poughkeepsie, New Jersey, North Dakota, Dallas, Duluth, Orlando, Knoxville, New York City, Wichita, Washington, D.C., Winnetka, Kennebunkport, Key Largo, Omaha, Amarillo, Ohio, Oklahoma, Amherst, Tallahassee, Tennessee, and East St. Louis, and ask "How's it going?" Then we would write the article.

All too often, we felt, the media are guilty of reporting the "big" stories and completely overlooking what it's all about—what people are up to and how it looks to them, the constant ebb and flow and pace and rhythm and ceaseless change of our lives, and more or less just what it's like to live in America today and have problems and hopes and fears and dreams and to go to work and come home and watch TV or go to a show or maybe just settle down with a good book or an in-depth magazine article.

Of course, we are all guilty of this to some extent. We tend to think of days as being rather similar to each other, except maybe Christmas, or New Year's or Saturday. However, as the editors of the *Life* Special Report on "One Day in the Life of America" wrote recently, "Days are like fingerprints, no one exactly like another in its whorls and ridges." Or, one might say, like magazine articles, each with its quite different paragraphs and neatly printed but various hundreds of words, many of them verbs.

Some people, in fact, may consider our project rather similar to the *Life* Special Report. But they are as different as two sunrises, or billfolds, or yesterday and tomorrow, or Oakland and Chicago Avenues in Minneapolis.

Hours before the sun, its rays racing westward at the speed of light, its estimated 267 tints dancing on the choppy, oil-streaked waters of the Atlantic, rose, Earth had turned the United States of America, time zone by time zone, into a Tuesday in midwinter. For most Americans, it came in their sleep in the middle of the night, marked by only a barely perceptible change in rapid eye movements, a slight shifting of position in bed. Their attitudes toward Tuesday were yet vague, uncomprehending. Awakened by telephone calls, they tended to feel it was something they could put off until morning.

Even as America slept, West Germany and the Soviet Union had forged ahead in Tuesday production, and Japan was going home to rest up for Wednesday. In a darkened Labor Department, at Fourteenth and Constitution in Washington, figures sheathed in Manila folders spelled out in eight-point type growing unemployment and spiraling inflation.

If there were fears or hopes among friends and foes that America might not get out of bed this morning, however, they were quickly dispelled. Already, the first of 125 million beds, 160 million cigarettes, and 40 million quarts of orange juice were creaking, smoking, and being poured. Four hundred million socks lay in sock drawers waiting to be worn, the holes in them totaling 700,000 square feet, almost as large as the White House grounds.

In the dim light of the Executive Bedroom, the 64-per-cent-approved President was assessing his own sock options. A few minutes before, in keeping with Presidential tradition, he had pulled on his pants one leg at a time, and now, donning a pair of wool sweat socks first worn by former President Eisenhower, he slipped into black hightop shoes from the Hoover Administration and made his way along a darkened corridor toward the Toaster Room.

As daylight spread over the populous, historic East to the fertile Midwest, far-flung Plains, scenic Mountain, and booming Pacific regions, lights came on in millions of homes, apartments, condominiums, town houses, duplexes, mobile homes, hospitals, halfway houses, and correctional institutions. Throats were cleared, toothpaste tubes squeezed, doors slammed, and long strips of bacon arrayed on pans to crackle over low-to-moderate heat. Women sighed, brushed their hair, scolded children, flipped pancakes, tied shoelaces. Men gulped coffee, scanned headlines, put on coats, started cars. Children whimpered, watched TV cartoons, kicked each other, left crusts, wheedled small change. Millions of dogs dozed in breakfast nooks or wandered aimlessly into living rooms. 9

In Eastport, Maine, the easternmost restaurant owner in the country, Buford Knapp, paused between orders of eggs and hashbrowns to raise his prices another nickel. Residents of the Gabriel Nursing Home in Minneapolis were wheeled to their windows for the flag-raising and pledge of allegiance. A bus rumbled along historic Market Street in San Francisco. A flock of bluebirds described graceful arcs over downtown Knoxville. 10

In the kitchen of a farm commune near Middlebury, Vermont, Norman Lefko slid a pan of blueberry muffins into the ancient wood stove and sat down at a plant table to read the Sunday *New York Times.* In New York, Craig Claiborne arose briefly for a glass of tomato juice. As he did so, Fargo housewife Eula Larpenteur prepared fried eggs, following Claiborne's own recipe ("Break the desired number of eggs into a saucer and slip them carefully into the pan. . . . If the eggs are to be cooked on both sides, turn with a pancake turner") and listening to "Don't Give Me a Drink," the new Carson Trucks hit. Meanwhile, Carson Trucks slept fitfully in the Cartesian Suite of the Mambo Motel in Shreveport, having played to an overflow crowd in the Memorial Auditorium the night before. At that moment, "Don't Give Me a Drink" was being heard in St. Louis, Orlando, Wichita, and Philadelphia (where baseballer Pete Rose had just nicked his cheek). It was not being heard in Chicago where 11

columnist Ann Landers was reading her first letter of the day. "Dear
Ann," it began. "The woman who said she was tired of her husband's snoring made me sick to my stomach. . . ."

And so the morning began. For several hours, time seemed to
pass quickly. Before Americans knew it, it was almost noon Eastern
Standard Time. They had worked hard, the more than 77 million
employed in mining, construction, manufacturing, transportation,
sales, finance, personal services, and government, and now it was
time for lunch. They had earned it. Although $1.75 billion of debt
had been incurred, 124 persons killed on highways, and $8 million
more spent on cigarettes than on education, $2 billion had been
added to the gross national product that Tuesday morning. Steel
had been rolled, buses driven, beds made, reports typed, tape
recorders assembled, Shakespeare taught, windows wiped, washing machines repaired, major policy changes announced. Now the
first of 4.6 million cans of soup were opened, the last of 2 million
plates of leftovers were brought out of refrigerators. Waxed paper
crackled in crowded lunchrooms, waitresses from Miami to Seattle
yelled, "One with, skip the pickle," and a gigantic tidal wave of egg
salad, tuna, and peanut butter was spread over 89 million slices of
bread. Among those who did not eat lunch were Baba Ram Dass,
Seiji Ozawa, Francis Tarkenton, and Selby Dale, a stockbroker in
San Diego. The Dow-Jones industrial average was down eight points
at noon, and his breakfast had come up at eleven.

As the nation slipped into afternoon, it seemed to lose stride and
falter. Clocks were watched, wheels spun. From the sequoia-shaded
Pacific Coast to the stubbled Kansas wheat fields to rockbound Maine,
the national mood shifted to one of boredom, then apathy and
resignation, with an occasional moment of outright despair. Many,
it is true, maintained momentum. The President, meeting with his
economic advisers, pledged continued efforts to curb inflation. The
Secretary of State, speaking at the National Press Club, called for
continued efforts to establish structures for peace. Hundreds of
other efforts continued, or were pledged or called for, as did numerous operations, campaigns, programs, and attempts. Talks on new
contracts continued. Searches for lost persons continued, and hopes
remained high. Wars against cancer, school dropouts, crime, unemployment, pollution, and discrimination went on, along with planning for the coming biennium, Middle East peace talks, "The Fan-

tasticks," and scores of investigations. Hearings resumed. Many ends, or the beginnnings of ends, were sighted.

Nonetheless, interest, for the most part, lagged. Polls showed a   14
twenty-five per cent jump in indecision after lunch: "Don't know" was up almost a third; "Don't care one way or the other" and "Both are just as bad" showed similar increases. In New Haven, sophomore Raymond Doswell took ten minutes to remember the composition of methane. In Albuquerque, New Mexico, Ernest Hollard, a thirty-two-year-old architect, lost the will to live. (Fortunately, nothing was wrong with him, and he soon felt cheerful enough to sharpen several pencils.) In Fargo, Eula Larpenteur called a local radio station and requested anything by the Chenilles. Henny Youngman spoke to a luncheon in Des Moines and made a joke about small businessmen. In hospitals around the country, thousands were treated for self-inflicted cuts suffered in moments of inattention. An estimated 40,000 lost faith in the political process, even though, as of midafternoon, it remained strong and viable. In Shreveport, Carson Trucks abused a bottle of cough syrup.

Many people knew it. Others wondered what it was. Some mis-   15
took it for something else. In New York, however, eating sautéed carrots boiled to extinction, Craig Claiborne knew it. John Simon knew it, and knew that he knew it. So did cabdriver Jack Poderhotz. ("People are sheer stark raving crazy nuts. Quote me.") In Colorado, author (*Fear and Loathing*) Hunter S. Thompson knew it. The big mudslide has started, he thought while writing. This is it. Giant hair balls roll westward, barbiturates float in the reservoirs. Merv smiles on television. The country bleeds from the gums, walks straight into trees.

Of the 6,554 luncheon audiences addressed today, most were told   16
not to sell short. Now, a scant two hours later, the country seemed less sure of itself and its destiny, values, strength, role in the free world, commitment to the arts, and the basic worth of its younger generation, most of whom were in school and, in turn, didn't care for it, if Janice Hoyt of Boise was typical. She thought it reeked.

In Washington, several high-ranking congressional sources felt   17
a sudden wave of intense personal disgust. Journalist Robert Sherrill wadded up a sheet of blank paper and threw it angrily at a potted culp. Eight news conferences were canceled for no reason, including one with a farm spokesman, who had planned to display a

hamburger bun and then reveal the few small crumbs of it that are the farmer's portion. Midway through his Chicago radio show, Studs Terkel—talking about the human spirit, the young, Joe Hill, Bach, Lady Day, the life urge, the "little man," Chaplin, the sea, and (his guest on the show) Phil Donahue—faltered, said "But of course that's only my opinion. Others may feel differently," and went to a commercial for patio furniture, causing several Evanston listeners to look out across Lake Michigan for a long time. Eagles were observed diving beak first into the frozen Mississippi north of Brainerd, Minnesota. Strange grinding noises over the horizon were heard by crews of oil tankers in the Gulf of Mexico.

As the sun swept westward toward the Far East, as long shadows fell, from the oyster beds of Maryland to Houston's Astrodome to Seattle's Puget Sound, few Americans took umbrage at the passing of the day, and regret was felt by few of the million who clogged freeways, jostled on trains and subways, jammed buses, piled into taxis, hopped on bicycles, or took off on foot for the 2.6-mile average trip home. At colleges around the country, suggested reading lists of books for further enrichment were stuffed in wastebaskets, and only 86 students remained after class for personal help. The Boston Bruins ended practice early. At the Purity Packing Plant, in Louisville, two workers scrawled obscenities on a hog carcass. In the Oval Office, the President looked at the last item on his schedule ("Call AFL–CIO—ask labor's coop in days, weeks ahead"), said, "The hell with it," and went upstairs to toss quoits. In the garden outside his window, a White House guard spat into a rosebush, chucked a rock at a sparrow. At the State Department, the search for lasting peace slowly wound down, ending officially at 7:40, when the Secretary was logged out of his office, trailed by his bodyguard, Knute. His mind, accustomed to penetrate far beyond the limits of normal men's endurance, had begun to lag shortly after 6. Left behind on his desk were four legal-size papers filled with doodled sketches of horses, slippers, obelisks, holsters, curtains, and peninsulas.

As his limousine sped away from the government curb, Mrs. Buford Knapp was putting on a Polynesian beach dress and coral accessories for a luau at the Eastport V.F.W.; Norman Lefko was carving a hand-made maple-syrup ladle; Eula Larpenteur was telling her husband, Stanley, to take it easy on their oldest son, Craig, sixteen, who was expected home momentarily from a brush with the law. Elsewhere, millions prepared for the evening. Tons of macaroni-and-cheese casseroles baked slowly in moderate heat, hundreds of square miles of tablecloth were smoothed out, and an estimated 45,000 women discovered, to their mild surprise, unsightly spots on glasses and dinnerware. Newspapers were opened, legs were crossed, and alcohol was consumed—enough to carry Bismarck, North Dakota, through the seven-month home-heating season.

At night, America becomes a study in contrasts between light 20 and darkness. This night was no exception. Street lights in cities, villages, townships twinkled in the cold winter air. Neon signs flashed their potpourri of messages. The lights in houses cast bright rectangular shapes onto snowy lawns and sidewalks. Car headlights made fascinating patterns, delicate traceries captured by hundreds of amateur photographers at slow shutter speeds. Traffic lights blinked red and green, as did the lights of aircraft, radio and television towers, police cars and other emergency vehicles, and hundreds of miles of unnoticed Christmas lights remaining on trees or outlining front porches.

At NBC master control in New York, technical difficulties pro- 21 duced a momentary blurring of John Chancellor, prompting 17.5 milion persons to lean forward and adjust their sets—an outlay of energy equivalent to 4,000 barrels of crude oil. A majority of Americans would spend at least part of the evening watching television, of which a small minority (28 per cent) would fall asleep while doing so. Others looked forward to movies, plays, ballets, concerts, or intimate dinner parties, for which women sat before mirrors making expressive faces and applying cosmetics, and spent an accumulated national total of almost 400 woman-years, or a lot longer than the Ming Dynasty. Meanwhile, men ran a Niagara of hot water into bathtubs and showers and shaved an area the size of the Pentagon.

Of the 3.5 million Americans who went "out" for the evening, 22 many had a good time, despite the dimly remembered uneasiness of the afternoon, while for countless others it was "O.K." or "not bad." Very few experienced real bummers. Those who did included Buford Knapp, who was publicly berated by his wife for not sending the clams back to the kitchen. She said there was dirt in them. Forty-five cultural events received poor reviews, including three Beethoven Sixth Symphonies ("An exercise in pointlessness," "A leaden sense of rhythm," and "If this is pastoral, then what is sheer tedium?," respectively), and roughly half of the evening's sporting events were lost by one team or the other.

Winning or losing, at home or away, shirts or skins, most Americans found some pleasure before midnight and retired at a reasonable hour to sleep for slightly less than eight hours (Tuesday night is the most restful night in the country—Saturday is the least, leading Sunday afternoon by only two hours—although urban sleepers do slightly better on Wednesday) and to dream, if a test group at U.C.L.A. was indicative, about familiar scenes and faces.

Not that there weren't disturbing signs to upset even the most complacent. In New York, hours after the market had closed, the Dow-Jones industrial average dropped three points unnoticed. In Dallas, a four-year-old child suddenly spoke in her sleep words of dire warning to her parents and to all Americans. And two women sitting in a back yard in Key West, Florida, observed a large, vacuum-cleaner-shaped object with flashing blue lights hover and then land fifty feet away, beside a garage. Two persons in yellow raincoats emerged, exposed themselves briefly, got back in the craft, and flew away. The craft emitted a low hum, like a dial tone. The persons appeared to be from another planet entirely.

If all was not well, it was nevertheless mostly pretty good, on balance. Despite its problems, the nation slipped into a fundamentally sound sleep. Many Americans tossed in their beds, got up to pace the floor, took aspirin, were troubled, pondered complex matters, stared at ceilings, but this was by no means common. And even the restless, for the most part, slept. From the vast bedroom suburbs of New Jersey to sleepy river towns in Minnesota to the long-slumbering natural resources in Alaska, America slept. It slept because it was tired. Soon it was midnight, and another day (and another magazine article) was over.

CONTENT

1. A parody makes fun of something by exaggerating its characteristics. Keillor's parody, as he tells us, is similar to *Life's* special report "One Day in the Life of America." It is also similar to Gay Talese's brand of reportage in "New York." What features of Keillor's parody are similar to Talese's essay?

2. How does Keillor make fun of the pretended all-encompassing you-are-there reportage? What other pretenses does he poke fun at? Why does he mix real people with fictional examples?

ORGANIZATION

3. Like Talese, Keillor makes use of the hours of the day to stack up his catalogue of examples. Why is this manner of organizing the examples funny in Keillor's hands?
4. Without the four-paragraph introduction, would the parody be evident? What other function does the introduction serve?

TOPICS FOR WRITING

5. Select a style of journalistic reportage, in magazines, newspapers, or TV (the style of interrogation used on "60 Minutes," for example) and, using several examples, write a parody of it.
6. Using examples, write a serious *Life Magazine* style hour-by-hour report of a day in the life of your home town.

ROBERT COLES
The Streets

Robert Coles (born 1929) is a child psychiatrist with Harvard University Health Services. His five-volume study, Children of Crisis *(1966–77), has been called the greatest social study ever undertaken by a single person in America. In the following exerpt from that study, Coles provides numerous telling examples to support his observations concerning the adjustment to urban life made by emigrants from the South and Appalachia.*

They come to the city streets. They come by car and by truck and by bus and by train. Rarely do they come by plane. They have said good-bye to a little town in the Delta, good-bye to Alabama's "Black Belt" or those towns in south Georgia just north of the Oke- fenokee Swamp or the lowlands of South Carolina or the eastern shore of North Carolina. Perhaps they have left one of Louisiana's parishes. Perhaps they once lived in Arkansas, near Little Rock or near Pine Bluff. Maybe they are not from the deep South. Maybe they are from Appalachia, from eastern Kentucky or western North Carolina or north central Tennessee or indeed just about all of West Virginia. Maybe they are from no single place; that is, maybe they have been migrant farm workers, who wander and wander, who may once have lived here or there, but now consider no town, no county, no state or even region their "home."

They come to the streets, all of them, from cabins and shacks, flat and rich farmlands or hills that somehow have been made to produce at least something. They come to the streets familiar with a way of life. They have, many of them (though by no means all of them), known the advantages of electricity, of a naked bulb to provide light, of an old refrigerator to keep food from rotting too fast. Good plumbing and heating are rather less familiar to those whom we call sharecroppers or tenant farmers from the rural South, whom we call migrant farm workers, whom we call mountaineers, Appalachia's yeomen from up the hollows. Other things are not familiar at all to such people: well-paid jobs, a sense of political power, a feeling of acceptance from schoolteachers or businessmen or sheriffs or county officials, and in addition, the experience of having a paved road near one's home, or sewer pipes leading to it, or good drinking water nearby.

They have said their good-byes, made their peace with their past, walked away, been driven away, slipped away, been picked up, been sent for. Some may have seen or been in a city before: Greenwood and Greenville in Mississippi, or Selma and Montgomery in Alabama, or Lexington in Kentucky or Charleston in West Virginia or Atlanta and New Orleans, those big, big cities. For many, though, the cities up North are the first cities they have looked at and lived in.

"Lord, I never knew there were so many buildings. Lord, I never knew what a street was, not really, not streets like we have up here, not miles and miles of them." In Tunica County, Mississippi, he had not been totally confined to a plantation, to a sharecropper's cabin and the land nearby that needed his care. He had gone into a town or two, walked down muddy paths along which one home after another stood. And he had even caught a glimpse of Memphis; on his way north he had seen the city he used to hear the Mister talk about, and the Missus, and those laughing, romping children not yet old enough to keep their distance—yes, he'd heard them, too, the little white boys and little white girls, talk on and on about

Memphis. But now he is in a city, up North in one. Now he lives there. Now, every single day, there are those streets. And now he is "used to things." What things, though? What up North has he day by day come to accept as the ordinary, the expected? "It started with the sidewalks and the sewers," he will say. He is trying to convey what took him by surprise when he "hit" Chicago, when he entered the city and saw one street and then another. They were beautifully paved. There were sewers. And black people lived all around. He had never before seen so many sewers. He had never before seen so many people, so many black people, and so many sidewalks and paved streets and sewers "that belong to them, the colored man." So it was that a "colored man" like him could at one point talk about "them." So it has been that mountaineers from eastern Kentucky and West Virginia can also feel a sense of detached surprise and wonder when they come to a city like Chicago and see those streets: "Who would ever believe it? Who would ever believe people live like this?" Then one asks what it is that he finds so unbelievable, and one hears again about sidewalks and sewers and firmly paved *roads*. It takes time for a man from a mountain hollow to talk about *streets*.

Yet, eventually they do; those former coal miners or subsistence farmers from Appalachia begin to say a lot about those streets. Friends or relatives come to visit or stay, and they must be shown things. There are lamps for instance, "outdoor lamps." Who would ever have thought that man could so firmly take command of night? A little girl from a place in Kentucky she is rapidly forgetting, but still just about remembers as "Winding Hollow," wants very much to remark upon that light, the light of streetlights: "I wonder how the moon feels? If I was the moon, I'd make a face at all the lamps on all the streets." She used to love the moon, her mother observes. The world seemed safer for the moon's night-light. But now the moon is almost unnecessary, one more faded miracle, one more outworn imperative. The city's streets conquer everything.

A black child in another city uses such military imagery, talks of conquests; he also hasn't been "up North" so long that he can't recall what it was like "back South," but he wants a visitor to know "there isn't any trouble around here you can't conquer, lick it and beat it flat, so long as you know the right person." He has heard that from others on the street, from others his age and older; "street talk" his mother calls the boy's statements—and those streets do indeed define one's sense of space, determine a good deal of how children speak and what they learn. Nor does the child's mother fail to comment on all that and more. The street she lives on is her backyard and front yard; it is the woods and the plantation and the county seat and the long road that leads to it. The street is flat, has no hills and no stream nearby, has no bank to sit on and lie down upon and use to "collect" one's strength. The street is lined with houses; it is "thick with them"—to the point that she and her neighbors sometimes take to wondering. Who in God's world ever had the gall to build so many houses? Where did they come from, all the people who live in those houses now and once lived in them over the years?

Other things inspire comment, too. As a matter of fact, these newcomers to our cities, these émigrés who have never left our own borders, these long-standing American citizens who have fled in desperation from the South to the North, from the quiet and isolated mountains to the crowded flatlands, be they white men or black men, young women or old women, they talk about flights of stairs or door locks or street numbers or mailboxes or light switches. For a while one thinks the problem is that of language; "they" have their words, their dialect, their way of putting things, and it is a matter of time before an outsider will be able to get the point, to understand why those simple, everyday words get mentioned so often—as if they are the keys to some mystery: "I've been here since the war, the Korean War. I came here from South Carolina. My husband was stationed up here, and he sent me a bus ticket. I never went back. I had my first baby inside me. The first surprise I had was the apartment building—I mean all the steps in it, the stairs and more stairs, until you think after climbing so many you'll be seeing the Lord himself." She goes on to remind her listener that in South Carolina there was exactly one step from the ground to the cabin in which she and her parents and her grandparents ("and the others before them") were born. That step was actually a stump of a tree half buried in the ground. The church she went to had "proper steps," two of them. And then suddenly she came to Boston, and encountered steps and steps and steps until she wondered in the beginning whether she could ever survive it all—lifting herself up and taking herself down again, and with no sunlight to help either. As for the hall lights in her "building," as she calls it, "they never have worked, not once."

More than steps get to her, though. The locks do, the endless 8
numbers of door locks. She was poor in South Carolina and she is
poor now. But back South one doesn't have to fasten down one's
poverty, defend it fearfully, worry about its vulnerability. Up North
it seems nothing can go unguarded, and indeed, "the nothing we
have is all locked up." She does, however, lose her keys sometimes—yes, the three keys, to the front door of their apartment and
the back door and the street door downstairs. Then she becomes
irritated and half amused. She also becomes nostalgic for a minute:
"I think to myself that before I came to the city I'd never seen a lock
in my life. That was the first thing I told my mother when I went
back to see her. I told her they're lock crazy up North. And it isn't
as if they're millionaires, our people up there."

She speaks about other matters to her mother. There are, again, 9
those flights of stairs that go round and round and lead from one
story to another. In one building she lived on the second story; in
another on the fifth, the *fifth*—which means she was so high up
she could imagine herself looking down on that small rural church
she recalls being so tall. She wonders to this day whether the water
tower she used to believe to be the tallest thing in the whole wide
world is as tall as her apartment house, which she now certainly
knows is far indeed from being the tallest building on the street,
let alone other streets. And since she tries to keep in touch with
her mother, even though neither of them is very good at writing,
there are those numbers to keep in mind. Whoever got *that* idea
anyway—of putting numbers on houses? Where do the numbers
on their street start? Where does the street start, for that matter? In
Dorchester County, South Carolina, so far as she knows, "there's
not a number there on any home." She never had a post office box
number, nor does her mother even today: "I write her name; I write
the town; I write South Carolina—and it gets there faster than
letters from her get to me."

Of course she gets her mail put into a mailbox, another one of 10
those newfangled devices that go with city living. Since letter boxes
in her building are private but commonly trespassed, she has to
have a "mail key," too. For a long while the boxes in her apartment
house were hopelessly inadequate—bent and punctured and covered with grime and scrawled words. Finally the postman complained, or higher officials in the post office did, or maybe it was
the welfare department, which mails out checks. Someone did, she

knows that, because the landlord was compelled to put in new boxes, and a policeman stood there watching while the job was done. It was a mixed blessing, needless to say: "I love the box, but the keys you need—just to stay alive up here in the city." She told her mother about her new mailbox. Her mother told the news to the lady who runs the grocery store and gasoline station and post office down in Dorchester County, South Carolina. She is a white woman, and her name is Mrs. Chalmers, and she had a laugh over that. She told her informant to write back to "the poor girl" in Boston and ask how the mailman ever makes sense of them all, the hundreds of boxes he must have to fill up every morning.

People manage to make their adjustments. There are spurts and lags, naturally. Some habits and customs are mastered more quickly than others. Some undreamed-of luxuries try the mind and soul more than others do. In Cleveland a man from "near Beekley," West Virginia, laughs about a few of his recent tribulations and compares them to what his ancestors had to go through—for they were also Americans who moved on (from the East Coast westward) when they had to: "I can't keep up with the light switches in this city. I think it's harder for me to figure out these lights than it was for my kin way back to cut a path through the hills and settle there. Everywhere you go here there's a switch. On and off, that's what you have to think about when you go into a room. Now who's supposed to know ever minute of his life where the switch is? I've been up in this place over a year and I forget, and I have my wife on my back, saying, "The switch is here, don't get dressed in darkness.' Well what's so damned wrong about darkness when it's early in the morning!"

In the cities late in the afternoon the lights appear, whether he or any other particular person likes it or not, and does or does not join in the act by turning a switch to ON. In the cities people seem to insist that darkness somehow be pushed into corners. There are plenty of those corners, especially in his neighborhood, but never in Ohio has he lived with the kind of darkness he everyday took for granted in West Virginia. He is the first one to point out that almost every street corner has lights, lights of all colors. There are streetlights—and the stores with their lights, and the gas stations with theirs, and the police cars with lights on their roofs, whirling around and around. And there are those signs, signs full of bulbs, signs that wait on the sun to leave so they can take over and say:

look over here, look and remember and buy, and if you do, we'll stay around and get called a success, catchy and clever and able to do our job, which is to light up your mind with desire.

He wants people to know he didn't live so far up a hollow that "this whole electric-light world up here in the city" is in and of itself strange to him. He had sockets with bulbs in them "back home" in his house, and he had television, also—so he really didn't expect to be as surprised as he was when he first came into Cleveland. He used to tighten the bulb in the evening, when he'd sit and smoke his pipe and get drowsy and half watch television. It was his children who often would pay full attention to it, "that picture box." And as a matter of fact, they were the ones who wanted him to loosen that bulb, so they could have the picture and nothing else all to themselves. But he liked to whittle, sometimes. And even if he didn't the evening is the right time to have a little light around. Mind, he says a *little* light, not so much light that one feels in China during the night—which is where he sometimes thinks he might be as he sits in his Cleveland apartment. China, he learned from a teacher a long time ago, is where the day goes when we have night.

In any event, now his children can't understand why he doesn't switch on all the lights, come dusk. Nor would they think of sitting and watching television in complete darkness. Why do his boys and girls require what they once would have abhorred, glowing lamps? He is quick to note the change and explain it: "It must be they used to want to have our cabin so pitch-black because that way they could lose themselves watching the programs and forget where they were. Now they're gone from there and up here. Now they're in the city, and the television programs are about the city. They don't have to imagine they're someplace else. They don't need it dark, so their minds can wander. *We've* wandered."

For people who come to the city from rural America, there is another irony awaiting them, in the form of cellars. How can it be that these city people—who live so curiously high up in the air, so removed from farms, so oblivious of all that goes into growing food and fetching water and hunting and fishing—how can it be that they have dug themselves so far into the ground? And anyway, what does go on in those cellars? They can be frightening places—dark as can be, low and dank and just plain underneath everything. Heat is made in them, in things called boilers. Pipes and wires go in and out of cellars, or basements, as some call them. And the rats, the rats that are so common, the rats that seem to a mother an inevitable part of her child's life, they also are supposed to come from those cellars: "I'd sooner die than go down into that cellar. I've heard about it. I've heard stories; I've heard there are so many rats down there you can't see anything but them, running all over, faster than squirrels and raccoons and rabbits, much faster. They tell me a city rat is like no other animal. They're in the biggest hurry. They're mean. They don't care about each other and they run and run, on the hunt for scraps of food. They don't know the sun. I do believe rats come into the cellars up from Hell. Hell can't be too far from here, anyway."

She has learned from her neighbor that down in the cellar of her building is a huge boiler, a furnace, "a hot, hot oven." Again she thinks of Hell—and expresses the mixed awe and astonishment and dread she feels, perhaps about a wider range of subjects than the one she mentions: "I never would have believed it until I saw for myself—the heat you can get in this building. You need no fireplaces and no stoves. All you do is turn them on and those radiators start click-clacking, knocking and knocking, *dancing*, my little girl says. Not always, of course; sometimes we don't get any heat—and then the city has to come and scare the landlord. But I still can't get too mad, because back home we'd sit around the stove, and if we went too far away, we'd just have to be cold. It was hard on the children; they didn't have the winter clothes they needed. In the city we get more heat than we ever dreamed we'd have, but my neighbor says they can explode, the boilers. I told her Hell will open up one day, and we'll all sink in—and maybe the boilers are owned by the devil. She thought I was fooling. I was—but maybe it's true. Maybe up here that can happen."

She believes that anything can happen "up here," in the noisy, crowded world of her building, her block, her street. In many northern cities a street contains thousands of people—as many, for instance, as everyone in a whole county of the rural South or Appalachia. And, of course, a street can be a center of commerce, a place where people buy and sell and eat and entertain and are entertained. I have walked a mile on her street with her two sons and seen the stores: the regular grocery stores; the Dignity Grocery, whose owners emphasize their Afro-American spirit; the large drugstore that sells just about anything; the hairdressers, some of whom sell wigs, straighten hair, have white women's faces and hairstyles in the store window, and some of whom say no, no, no—Afros, and nothing else. And there are the funeral parlors and insurance agencies, not unlike those one sees in southern towns. The two boys told me that when their mother came North she went to an undertaker to register with him. I asked them why she would do that, and one of them replied: "My grandma told her to do it, otherwise we could die, one of us, and there'd be no one to bury us, and no place to rest in." They worry about rest, such families do, worry a great deal about what will happen to them, finally, and where they will go next and, most of all, whether always and always they will be tired and unsatisfied and fearful—destined, that is, for "no place to rest in."

CONTENT

1. What urban phenomena must migrants from the rural South adjust to in northern cities?
2. Why does the wonder of newly arrived migrants center around electric lights? Why does abolishing darkness seem so strange to them? Is such progress, according to Coles, a mixed blessing?

ORGANIZATION

3. Coles presents his examples by citing a series of cases, and by using the interview method. Do you find this an effective way of organizing examples? Why or why not?
4. Aside from the buildings and the streets themselves, the most important examples occur in the body of Coles' piece—namely, keys, stairs, and light-switches. How does the earlier material on the streets and buildings help prepare for these examples?

TOPICS FOR WRITING

5. Select a street near where you live that has a distinctive character. Through a series of characteristic examples (people, objects, houses, and so on), explain what the street is like.
6. Interview someone who has just come to the United States from a foreign country (or someone who has just moved to your section of the country from elsewhere). What differences have they observed between their new surroundings and where they formerly lived? Write an essay on the subject using these examples.

Division/Classification

The pattern of *division* assumes that your subject matter can be broken up into parts. Virtually any subject can be subdivided into types—types of tourists, kinds of sports cars, and so on. An essay that uses this kind of organization is frequently called a "types of," or "kinds of" essay.

Classification, in contrast, assumes that the subject is already one smaller part of a larger entity. For instance, to be useful raw data must be organized around large categories to which specific pieces of data pertain. Such organization is regarded as classification because the movement is from the specific pieces of data to the larger categories (unlike division which begins with the large categories and proceeds to break them down). Notice that in his essay "Matters of Taste," Alexander Theroux groups specific candies into similar categories according to their primary property—"mumping" candies, trash candies, the coconut category, the peanut group, the licorice group, and so on. In this essay, classification is the organizing principle; Theroux begins with specific candies, then moves toward the more inclusive categories.

On the other hand, Freeman Dyson begins his essay with a logical division: " . . . civilizations in the universe should fall into three distinct types." In this instance, Dyson begins with a discussion of his subject as a category in itself, then proceeds to divide it into smaller, more manageable segments.

Remember, the difference between division and classification is largely in the direction you are moving: down into smaller units (division), or upward toward larger categories (classification). More than one layer of division is possible; the following piece, an interview at a game arcade, illustrates how some divisions can be like Chinese boxes, divisions within divisions:

> "There are three main groups," the first kid said. "There is the 'What-is-this-thing-supposed-to-be?'-they-ask-pointing-to-the-machine-group. Then, there's the average group. And there's the forever-playing group." The same kid, who falls into the would-be-forever-playing-if-he-had-enough-quarters group, proposed a subdivision of dedicated players. "Then, there are three main crowds. The Kong people—Donkey and

254

Crazy—and the Pac people, and the Defender people. The Kong people are the people who really just sit and live on the machine, sit and lie on the chairs—plus small people who sit on top of the machine and bug you. About eight people watching and lying and sitting on chairs around one machine. The Defender and Stargate people are sixteen-, seventeen-, eighteen-year-olds who come in two at a time to play doubles and score incredible scores to make the Immortals list. They smoke a lot and say 'damn' a lot—that's the only cuss they ever utter. . . . Ms. Pac-Man players in the Arcade room are mostly four or five minigirls with one older babysitter—an elder person, usually female—sitting on tabletops. . . . In the ice-cream place . . . the Ms. Pac-Man players are twelve-, thirteen-, fourteen-year-old boys, who pound the glass and swear furiously—mostly unmentionables," the first kid said. "I forgot another crowd, the Dig Dug crowd." The second kid disagreed. "That isn't a real crowd. Dig Dug hasn't gotten big enough for that yet." ["The Machines, *The New Yorker* (October 4, 1982), 34.]

Two rules should be followed in using *division* as a principle of organization. First, the subdivisions should be based on a single principle. Following a single principle of division, E. B. White divides New York City into three categories:

There are roughly three New Yorks. There is, first, the New York of the man or woman who was born here, who takes the city for granted and accepts its size and its turbulence as natural and inevitable.

Second, there is the New York of the commuter—the city that is devoured by locusts each day and spat out each night. Third, there is the New York of the person who was born somewhere else and came to New York in quest of something. [*Here Is New York* (Harper and Row, 1949), 17.]

The principle of division is not violated because the three New Yorks are considered from the perspective of the point of origin of the New Yorker, whether he is from New York itself, the suburbs, or a place out of town. It would not do to introduce, say, a fourth New York, that of the socialite or taxi driver because class or status is not the operating principle here. The second rule in division is that the classes should not overlap. In White's scheme, one is either a native resident, a resident by day only, or a resident from elsewhere. The categories are discrete. You couldn't have resident immigrants from the Caribbean as a category because it would overlap with the larger category, residents from elsewhere.

The pattern of organization called *division/classification* should help you to say something significant about your subject; it should not be merely a mechanical way of cutting up a larger topic into parts or classifying data into meaningless pigeon holes. There should be an operating principle, a purpose, behind the method you choose. This principle will help generate material for the essay and contribute to its organization.

SHORT EXAMPLE—DIVISION/CLASSIFICATION

EDWARD ABBEY
The Great American Desert

Edward Abbey is popularly known as a naturalist, chiefly because he has written extensively about the desert Southwest, but Abbey denies any special training as a naturalist, claiming he uses nature as a metaphor to express other things. The following short paragraph from The Journey Home *(1977) enumerates the conventional divisions of the Great American Desert.*

Geographers generally divide the North American desert—what was once termed "the Great American Desert"—into four distinct regions or subdeserts. These are the Sonoran Desert, which comprises southern Arizona, Baja California, and the state of Sonora in Mexico; the Chihuahuan Desert, which includes west Texas, southern New Mexico, and the states of Chihuahua and Coahuila in Mexico; the Mojave Desert, which includes southeastern California and small portions of Nevada, Utah, and Arizona; and the Great Basin Desert, which includes most of Utah and Nevada, northern Arizona, northwestern New Mexico, and much of Idaho and eastern Oregon.

DISCUSSION

This brief illustration of how division works begins with the subject to be divided (the North American desert), the number of divisions (four), and the basis for the division (geography). Abbey gives each of the regions of the Great American Desert a name to simplify the inclusion of the more specific examples which follow. Thus, the headings Sonoran, Chihuahuan, Mojave, and Great Basin include the specific areas which comprise "the Great American Desert."

Such use of division is a way of breaking down a larger more complicated subject into smaller, and therefore clearer, manageable parts.

SUSAN ALLEN TOTH
Cinematypes

Susan Allen Toth teaches English at Macalester College in St. Paul, Minnesota. She has published both scholarly articles in The New England Quarterly, Studies in Short Fiction, *and* The American Scholar, *as well as popular articles in* Harper's, Redbook *and* Ms. *Her first book,* Blooming, *was published in 1981. "Cinematypes" is a humorous look at how we choose our companions and our entertainment.*

Aaron takes me only to art films. That's what I call them, anyway: 1 strange movies with vague poetic images I don't always understand, long dreamy movies about a distant Technicolor past, even longer black-and-white movies about the general meaninglessness of life. We do not go unless at least one reputable critic has found the cinematography superb. We went to *The Devil's Eye*, and Aaron turned to me in the middle and said, "My God, this is *funny*." I do not think he was pleased.

When Aaron and I go to the movies, we drive our cars separately 2 and meet by the box office. Inside the theater he sits tentatively in his seat, ready to move if he can't see well, poised to leave if the film is disappointing. He leans away from me, careful not to touch the bare flesh of his arm against the bare flesh of mine. Sometimes he leans so far I am afraid he may be touching the woman on his other side. If the movie is very good, he leans forward, too, peering between the heads of the couple in front of us. The light from the screen bounces off his glasses; he gleams with intensity, sitting there on the edge of his seat, watching the screen. Once I tapped him on the arm so I could whisper a comment in his ear. He jumped.

After *Belle de Jour* Aaron said he wanted to ask me if he could 3 stay overnight. "But I can't," he shook his head mournfully before I had a chance to answer, "because I know I never sleep well in strange beds." Then he apologized for asking. "It's just that after a film like that," he said, "I feel the need to assert myself."

Pete takes me only to movies that he thinks have redeeming   4
social value. He doesn't call them "films." They tend to be about
poverty, war, injustice, political corruption, struggling unions in
the 1930s, and the military-industrial complex. Pete doesn't like
propaganda movies, though, and he doesn't like to be too depressed,
either. We stayed away from *The Sorrow and the Pity*; it would be, he
said, just too much. Besides, he assured me, things are never that
hopeless. So most of the movies we see are made in Hollywood.
Because they are always topical, these movies offer what Pete calls
"food for thought." When we saw *Coming Home*, Pete's jaw set so
firmly with the first half-hour that I knew we would end up at
Poppin' Fresh Pies afterward.

When Pete and I go to the movies, we take turns driving so no   5
one owes anyone else anything. We leave the car far from the theater
so we don't have to pay for a parking space. If it's raining or snow-
ing, Pete offers to let me off at the door, but I can tell he'll feel better
if I go with him while he finds a spot, so we share the walk too.
Inside the theater Pete will hold my hand firmly on his knee and
covers it completely with his own hand. His knee never twitches.
After a while, when the scarey part is past, he loosens his hand
slightly and I know that is a signal to take mine away. He sits companionably close, letting his jacket just touch my sweater, but he does
not infringe. He thinks I ought to know he is there if I need him.

One night, after *The China Syndrome*, I asked Pete if he wouldn't
like to stay for a second drink, even though it was past midnight.
He thought a while about that, considering my offer from all possible angles, but finally he said no. Relationships today, he said,
have a tendency to move too quickly.

Sam likes movies that are entertaining. By that he means movies
that Will Jones in the *Minneapolis Tribune* loved and either *Time* or
Newsweek rather liked; also movies that do not have sappy love
stories, are not musicals, do not have subtitles, and will not force
him to think. He does not go to movies to think. He liked *California
Suite* and *The Seduction of Joe Tynan*, though the plots, he said, could
have been zippier. He saw it all coming too far in advance, and that
took the fun out. He doesn't like to know what is going to happen.
"I just want my brain to be tickled," he says. It is very hard for me
to pick out movies for Sam.

When Sam takes me to the movies, he pays for everything. He

thinks that's what a man ought to do. But I buy my own popcorn, because he doesn't approve of it; the grease might smear his flannel slacks. Inside the theater, Sam makes himself comfortable. He takes off his jacket, puts one arm around me, and all during the movies he plays with my hand, stroking my palm, beating a small tattoo on my wrist. Although he watches the movie intently, his body operates on instinct. Once I inclined my head and kissed him lightly just behind his ear. He beat a faster tattoo on my wrist, quick and musical, but he didn't look away from the screen.

When Sam takes me home from the movies, he stands outside   9
my door and kisses me long and hard. He would like to come in, he says regretfully, but his steady girlfriend in Duluth wouldn't like it. When the *Tribune* gives a movie four stars, he has to save it to see with her. Otherwise her feelings might be hurt.

I go to some movies by myself. On rainy Sunday afternoons I   10
often sneak into a revival house or a college auditorium for old Technicolor musicals, *Kiss Me Kate, Seven Brides for Seven Brothers, Calamity Jane,* even, once, *The Sound of Music.* Wearing saggy jeans so I can prop my feet on the seat in front, I sit toward the rear where no one will see me. I eat large handfuls of popcorn with double butter. Once the movie starts, I feel completely at home. Howard Keel and I are old friends; I grin back at him on the screen. I know the sound tracks by heart. Sometimes when I get really carried away I hum along with Kathryn Grayson, remembering how I once thought I would fill out a formal like that. I am rather glad now I never did. Skirts whirl, feet tap, acrobatic young men perform impossible feats, and then the camera dissolves into a dream sequence I know I can comfortably follow. It is not, thank God, Bergman.

If I can't find an old musical, I settle for Hepburn and Tracy,   11
vintage Grant or Gable, on adventurous days Claudette Colbert or James Stewart. Before I buy my ticket I make sure it will all end happily. If necessary, I ask the girl at the box office. I have never seen *Stella Dallas* or *Intermezzo.* Over the years I have developed other pecadilloes: I will, for example, see anything that is redeemed by Thelma Ritter. At the end of *Daddy Long Legs* I wait happily for the scene when Fred Clark, no longer angry, at last pours Thelma a convivial drink. They smile at each other, I smile at them, I feel they are smiling at me. In the movies I go to by myself, the men and women always like each other.

CONTENT

1. What kind of person is each of Ms. Toth's companions? How do the movies they like and their behavior define them? What kind of person is she? How do you know?
2. What is the basis (or bases) of the division? Why does the recurrence of certain likes and dislikes in her companions make the piece funny?
3. How do Toth's descriptions help characterize each type? For example, Pete is described as sitting "companionably close," whereas Sam "plays with her hand."

ORGANIZATION

4. The essay is divided into three or four sections, depending on whether you regard Toth, herself, as a type. How well are the differences between the types revealed in each section?
5. Toth uses examples of movies to support each of her divisions. How well do her examples support her divisions? Are the examples necessary to make her point? Why?

TOPICS FOR WRITING

6. Divide any subject into types using a single basis for your division. Use examples to support the kinds of divisions you have created.
7. Following Toth's model, create your own "cinematypes." In setting up your own categories of moviegoers be sure to use examples familiar to the general reader.

ALEXANDER THEROUX
Matters of Taste

Alexander Theroux, the older brother of Paul Theroux (see page 174), is a former Trappist monk, novelist, author of children's books. His writing has appeared in Esquire *and the* National Review, *and he writes a column for* Boston *magazine. Theroux's style is eccentric and flamboyant, what one critic labelled a "Gothic garden." That style is one reason why his analysis of the various and sundry styles of candy is such fun to read.*

I believe there are few things that show as much variety—that 1
there is so much of—as American candy. The national profusion of
mints and munch, pops and drops, creamfills, cracknels, and chocolate crunch recapitulates the good and plenty of the Higher Who.

Candy has its connoisseurs and critics both. To some, for instance, 2
it's a subject of endlesss fascination—those for whom a root-beer
lozenge can taste like a glass of Shakespeare's "brown October" and
for whom little pilgrims made of maple sugar can look like Thracian
gold—and to others, of course, it's merely a wilderness of abomi-
nations. You can sample one piece with a glossoepiglottic gurgle of
joy or chew down another empty as shade, thin as fraud.

In a matter where tastes touch to such extremes one is compelled 3
to seek through survey what in the inquiry might yield, if not conclusions sociologically diagnostic, then at least a simple truth or
two. Which are the best candies? Which are the worst? And why?
A sense of fun can feed on queer candy, and there will be no end
of argument, needless to say. But, essentially, it's all in the *taste*.

The trash candies—a little lobby, all by itself, of the American 4
Dental Association—we can dismiss right away: candy cigarettes,
peanut brittle, peppermint lentils, Life Savers (white only), Necco
Wafers (black especially), Christmas candy in general, gumballs,
and above all that glaucous excuse for tuck called ribbon candy,
which little kids, for some reason, pounce on like a duck on a June
bug. I would put in this category all rock candy, general Woolwor-
thiana, and all those little nerks, cupcake sparkles, and decorative
sugars like silver buckshot that though inedible, are actually eaten
by the young and indiscriminate, whose teeth turn eerie almost on
contact.

In the category of the most abominable tasting, the winner—on 5
both an aesthetic and a gustatory level—must surely be the inscribed
Valentine candy heart ("Be Mine," "Hot Stuff," "Love Ya," et cetera).
In high competition, no doubt, are bubble-gum cigars, candy corn,
marshmallow chicks (bunnies, pumpkins, et cetera), Wacky Wafers
(eight absurd-tasting coins in as many flavors), Blow Pops—an owl's
pellet of gum inside a choco-pop!—Canada Mints, which taste like
petrified Egyptian lime, and, last but not least, those unmasticable
beige near-candy peanuts that, insipid as rubber erasers, not only
have no bite—the things just give up—but elicit an indescribable
antitaste that is best put somewhere between stale marshmallow

and dry wall. Every one of these candies, sweating right now in a glass case at your corner store, is to my mind proof positive of original sin. They can be available, I suggest, only for having become favorites of certain indiscriminate fatties at the Food and Drug Administraton who must buy them by the bag. But a bat could see they couldn't be a chum of ours if they chuckled.

Now, there are certain special geniuses who can distinguish can-   6 dies, like wine, by rare deduction: district, commune, vineyard, growth. They know all the wrappers, can tell twinkle from tartness in an instant, and often from sniffing nothing more than the empty cardboard sled of a good candy bar can summon up the scent of the far Moluccas. It is an art, or a skill at least *tending* to art. I won't boast the ability, but allow me, if you will, to be a professor of the fact of it. The connoisseur, let it be said, has no special advantage. Candy can be found everywhere: the airport lounge, the drugstore, the military PX, the student union, the movie house, the company vending machine—old slugs, staler than natron, bonking down into a tray—but the *locus classicus*, of course, is the corner store.

The old-fashioned candy store, located on a corner in the Amer-   7 ican consciousness, is almost obsolete. Its proprietor is always named Sam; for some reason he's always Jewish. Wearing a hat and an apron, he shuffles around on spongy shoes, still tweezers down products from the top shelf with one of those antique metal grapplers, and always keeps the lights off. He has the temperament of a black mamba and makes his best customers, little kids with faces like midway balloons, show him their nickels before they order. But he keeps the fullest glass case of penny candy in the city—spiced baby gums, malted milk balls, fruit slices, candy fish, aniseed balls, candy pebbles, jelly beans, raspberry stars, bull's-eyes, boiled sweets, the lot. The hit's pretty basic. You point, he scoops a dollop into a little white bag, weighs it, subtracts two, and then asks, "Wot else?"

A bright rack nearby holds the bars, brickbats, brand names.   8 Your habit's never fixed when you care about candy. You tend to look for new bars, recent mints, old issues. The log genre, you know, is relatively successful: Bolsters, Butterfingers, Clark Bars, Baby Ruths, O. Henrys, and the Zagnut with its sweet razor blades. Although they've dwindled in size, like the dollar that buys fewer and fewer of them, all have a lushness of weight and good nap and nacre, a chewiness, with tastes in suitable *contre coup* to the bite. You pity their distant cousins, the airy and unmemorable

Kit-Kats, Choco'lites, Caravels, and Paydays, johnny-come-latelies
with shallow souls and Rice Krispie hearts that taste like budgie
food. A submember of American candy, the peanut group, is strong—
crunch is often the kiss in a candy romance—and you might favor-
ably settle on several: Snickers, Go Aheads, Mr. Goodbars, Reese's
Peanut Butter Cups (of negligible crunch however), the Crispy, the
Crunch, the Munch—a nice trilogy of onomatopoeia—and even
the friendly little Creeper, a peanut-butter-filled tortoise great for
one-bite dispatch: Pleep!

Vices, naturally, coexist with virtues. The coconut category, for   9
instance—Mounds, Almond Joys, Waleecos, and their ilk—is
toothsome, but can often be tasted in flakes at the folds and rim
of your mouth days later. The licorice group, Nibs, Licorice Rolls,
Twizzlers, Switzer Twists, and various whips and shoelaces, often
smoky to congestion, usually leave a nice smack in the aftertaste.
The jawbreaker may last a long time, yes—but who wants it to?
Tootsie Pop Drops, Charms, Punch, Starburst Fruit Chews (sic!),
base-born products of base beds, are harder than affliction and
better used for checker pieces or musket flints or supports to justify
a listing bureau.

There are certain candies, however—counter, original, spare   10
strange—that are gems in both the bite and the taste, not the usual
grim marriage of magnesium stearate to lactic acid, but rare con-
fections at democratic prices. Like lesser breeds raising pluperfect
cain with the teeth, these are somehow always forgiven; any such
list must include: Mary Janes, Tootsie Rolls, Sky Bars, Squirrels,
Mint Juleps, the wondrous B-B Bats (a hobbit-sized banana taffy
pop still to be had for 3¢), and other unforgettable knops and knurls
like turtles, chocolate bark, peanut clusters, burnt peanuts, and
those genius-inspired pink pillows with the peanut-butter surprise
inside for which we're all so grateful. There's an *intelligence* here
that's difficult to explain, a sincerity at the essence of each, where
solid line plays against stipple and a truth function is solved always
to one's understanding and always—*O altitudo!*—to one's taste.

Candy is sold over the counter, won in raffles, awarded on quiz   11
shows, flogged door to door, shipped wholesale in boxes, thrown
out at ethnic festivals, and incessantly hawked on television commercials by magic merrymen—clownish pied-pipers in cap-and-
bells—who inspirit thousands of kids to come hopping and hurling
after them, singing all the way to Cavityville. Why do we eat it?

Who gets us started eating it? What sexual or social or semantic preferences are indicated by which pieces? The human palate— tempted perhaps by Nature *herself* in things like slippery elm, spruce gum, sassafras, and various berries—craves sweetness almost everywhere, so much so, in fact, that the flavor of candy commonly denominates American breath-fresheners, throat discs, mouth- wash, lipstick, fluoride treatments, toothpaste, cough syrup, break- fast cereals, and even dental floss, fruit salts, and glazes. It's with candy—whether boxed, bottled, or bowed that we say hello, good- bye, and I'm sorry. There are regional issues, candies that seem at home only in one place and weirdly forbidden in others (you don't eat it at the ballpark, for instance, but on the way there), and of course seasonal candies: Christmas tiffin, Valentine's Day assort- ments, Thanksgiving mixes, and the diverse quiddities of Easter: spongy chicks, milk-chocolate rabbits, and those monstrositous roc- like eggs twilled with piping on the outside and filled with a huge blob of neosaccharine galvaslab! Tastes change, develop, grow fixed. Your aunt likes mints. Old ladies prefer jars of crystallized ginger. Rednecks wolf Bolsters, trollops suck lollipops, college girls opt for berries-in-tins. Truck drivers love to click Gobstoppers around the teeth, pubescents crave sticky sweets, the viler the better, and of course great fat teenage boys, their complexions aflame with pim- ples and acne, aren't fussy and can gorge down a couple of dollars' worth of Milky Ways, $100,000 Bars, and forty-eleven liquid cher- ries at one go!

The novelty factor can't be discounted. The wrapper often mem- orizes a candy for you; so capitalism, with its Hollywood brain, has devised for us candies in a hundred shapes and shocks—no, I'm not thinking of the comparitively simple Bit-O-Honey, golden lugs on waxed paper, or Little Nips, wax tonic bottles filled with dis- gustingly sweet liquid, or even the Pez, those little units that, upon being thumbed, dispense one of the most evil-tasting cacochymicals on earth. Buttons-on-paper—a trash candy—is arguably redeemed by inventiveness of vehicle. But here I'm talking about packaging *curiosa*—the real hype! Flying Saucers, for example, a little plasti- cene capsule with candy twinkles inside! Big Fake Candy Pens, a goofy fountain pen cartridged with tiny pills that taste like canvatex! Razzles ("First It's a Candy, Then It's a Gum")! Bottle Caps ("The Soda Pop Candy")! Candy Rings, a rosary of cement-tasting beads strung to make up a fake watch, the dial of which can be eaten as a final emetic. Rock Candy on a String, blurbed on the box as effective for throat irritation: "Shakespeare in *Henry IV* mentions its therapeutic value." You believe it, right?

And then there's the pop group: Astro Pops, an umbrella-shaped sugar candy on a stick: Whistle Pops ("The Lollipop with the Built-in Whistle"); and Ring Pops, cherry- or watermelon-flavored gems on a plastic stick—you suck the jewel. So popular are the fizzing Zotz, the trifling Pixie Stix with its powdered sugar to be lapped out of a straw, the Lik-M-Aid Fun Dip, another do-it-yourself stick-licker, and the explosion candies like Space Dust, Volcano Rocks, and Pop Rocks that candy-store merchants have to keep behind the counter to prevent them from getting nobbled. Still, these pale next to the experience of eating just plain old jimmies (or sprinkles or chocolate shot, depending on where you live), which although generally reserved for, and ancillary to, ice cream, can be deliciously munched by the fistful for a real reward. With jimmies, we enter a new category all its own. M&M's for example: you don't eat them, you mump them.

Other mumping candies might be sugar babies, hostia almonds, bridge mixes, burnt peanuts, and pectin jelly beans. (Jelloids in general lend themselves well to the mump.) I don't think Goobers and Raisinets—dull separately—are worth anything unless both are poured into the pocket, commingled, and mumped by the handful at the movies. (The clicking sound they make is surely one of the few pleasures left in life.) This is a family that can also include Pom Poms, Junior Mints, Milk Duds, Boston Baked Beans, Sixlets ("Candy-coated chocolate-flavored candies"—a nice flourish, that), and the disappointingly banal Jujubes—which reminds me. There are certain candies, Jujubes for instance, that one is just too embarrassed to name out loud (forcing one to point through the candy case and simply grunt), and numbered among these must certainly be Nonpareils, Jujufruits, Horehound Drops, and Goldenberg's Peanut Chews. You know what I mean. "Give me a *mrmrglpxph* bar." And you point. Interesting, right?

Interesting. The very word is like a bell that tolls me back to more trenchant observations. Take the Sugar Daddy—it curls up like an elf-shoe after a manly bite and upon being sucked could actually be used for flypaper. (The same might be said for the gummier but more exquisite Bonomo's Turkish Taffy.) The Heath bar—interesting again—a knobby little placket that can be drawn down half-clenched teeth with a slucking sound for an instant chocolate rush, where-upon you're left with a lovely ingot of toffee as a sweet surprise. The flaccid Charleston Chew, warm, paradoxically becomes a proud phallus when cold. (Isn't there a metaphysics in the making here?) Who, until now, has ever given these candies the kind of credit they deserve?

I have my complaints, however, and many of them cross cate-gories. M&M's, for instance, click beautifully but never perspire—it's like eating bits of chrysoprase or sea shingle, you know? Tic Tacs, as well: brittle as gravel and brainless. And while Good 'n' Plenty's are worthy enough mumpers, that little worm of licorice inside somehow puts me off. There is, further, a tactile aspect in candy to be considered. Milk Duds are too nobby and ungeomet-rical, Junior Mints too relentlessly exact, whereas Reese's Peanut Butter Cups, with their deep-dish delicacy, fascinate me specifically for the strict ribbing around the sides. And then color. The inside of the vapid Three Musketeers bar is the color of wormwood. White bark? Leprosy. Penuche? Death. And then of Hot Tamales, Atom Bombs, cinnamon hearts, and red hots?—swift, slow, sweet, sour, a-dazzle, dim, okay, but personally I think it a matter of brev-iary that *heat* should have nothing at all to do with candy.

And then Chunkies—tragically, too big for one bite, too little for two. Tootsie Pops are always twiddling off the stick. The damnable tab never works on Hershey Kisses, and it takes a month and two days to open one; even the famous Hershey bar, maddeningly over-scored, can never be opened without breaking the bar, and prying is always required to open the ridiculously overglued outer wrap-per. (The one with almonds—why?—always slides right out!) And then there are those candies that always promise more than they ever give—the Marathon bar for length, cotton candy for beauty: neither tastes as good at it looks, as no kipper ever tastes as good as it smells; disappointment leads to resentment, and biases form. Jujyfruits—a viscous disaster that is harder than the magnificent British wine-gum (the single greatest candy on earth)—stick in the teeth like tar and have ruined more movies for me than Burt Rey-nolds, which is frankly going some. And finally Chuckles, father of those respectively descending little clones—spearmint leaves, orange slices, and gum drops—always taste better if dipped in ice water before eating, a want that otherwise keeps sending you to a water fountain for hausts that never seem to end.

You may reasonably charge me, in conclusion, with an insensi- 18
bility for mistreating a particular kind of candy that you, for one
reason or another, cherish, or bear me ill will for passing over another
without paying it due acknowledgment. But here it's clearly a question of taste, with reasoning generally subjective. Who, after all,
can really explain how tastes develop? Where preferences begin?
That they exist is sufficient, and fact, I suppose, becomes its own
significance. Which leads me to believe that what Dr. Johnson said
of Roman Catholics might less stupidly be said of candies: "In every
thing in which they differ from us, they are wrong."

CONTENT

1. Theroux's essay is nostalgic–comic. What makes it comic? Why
    is it nostalgic in places?
2. Does Theroux expect us to take his categories of candies and
    his judgments of them seriously? Why or why not?
3. How does the essay illustrate the dictum, "There is no quar-
    reling with taste"?

ORGANIZATION

4. Theroux classifies candies according to several categories: trash,
    the log genre, the peanut group, the coconut group, the licorice
    group, the pop groups, and mumping candies. Does he follow
    the rule for using a single criterion in setting up his categories?
    Why or why not?
5. Why does Theroux include the digression about the candy store
    proprietor (paragraph 7) in the middle of his discussion of types
    of candies?
6. Twice Theroux alludes to a poem by Gerard Manly Hopkins
    called "Pied Beauty." Look up the poem, find the lines he quotes,
    and see if it helps explain what otherwise might seem a hap-
    hazard, associative organization in Theroux's essay. Is there a
    method behind the mixed categories?

TOPICS FOR WRITING

7. Select a food or beverage (hamburgers, soft drinks) and using
    classification as your method of organization, write an essay
    following the "types of" pattern.

8. Write a classification or division essay on one of the following topics: types of tourists, small towns, teachers, coaches, friends, colleges, restaurants, or braggarts.

FREEMAN DYSON
Extraterrestrials

Freeman Dyson is well-known for his popular writing on physics in The New Yorker *and* Scientific American. *Born in Crowthorne, England in 1923, he came to the United States in 1947 as a Commonwealth Fellow, and joined the physics department at Cornell University in 1951. Since 1953, he has been a professor of physics at the Institute for Advanced Study in Princeton. Dyson has been a consultant to NASA, the Arms Control and Disarmament Agency, and the Defense Department. "Extraterrestrials," adapted from Dyson's autobiography* Disturbing the Universe *(1981), considers the types of extraterrestrial civilizations which might be contacted through infrared astronomy—and the odds against such contact.*

The Russian astronomer Kardashev has suggested that civiliza- 1 tions in the universe should fall into three distinct types. A type 1 civilization controls the resources of a planet. A type 2 civilization controls the resources of a star. A type 3 civilization controls the resources of a galaxy. We have not yet achieved type 1 status, but we shall probably do so within a few hundred years. The difference in size and power between types 1 and 2, or between types 2 and 3, is a factor of the order of ten billion, unimaginably large by human standards. But the process of exponential economic growth allows this immense gulf to be bridged remarkably rapidly. To grow by a factor of ten billion takes thirty-three doubling times. A society growing at a modest rate of one percent per year will make the transition from type 1 to type 2 in less than 2500 years. The transition from type 2 to type 3 will take longer than this, since it requires interstellar voyages. But the periods of transition are likely to be comparatively brief episodes in the history of any long-lived society. Hence Kardashev concludes that if we ever discover an extraterrestrial civilization, it will probably belong clearly to type 1, 2 or 3 rather than to one of the brief transitional phases.

In the long run, the only limits to the technological growth of a 2 society are internal. A society has always the option of limiting its growth, either by conscious decision or by stagnation or by disinterest. A society in which these internal limits are absent may continue its growth forever. A society which happens to possess a strong expansionist drive will expand its habitat from a single planet (type 1) to a biosphere exploiting an entire star (type 2) within a few thousand years, and from a single star to an entire galaxy (type 3) within a few thousand years. A species which has once passed beyond type 2 status is invulnerable to extinction by even the worst imaginable natural or artificial catastrophe. When we observe the universe, we have a better chance of discovering a society that has expanded into type 2 or 3 than one which has limited itself to type 1, even if the expansionist societies are as rare as one in a million.

Having defined the scale of technological actvities we may look for, I finally come to the questions which are of greatest interest to astronomers: What are the observable consequences of such activities? What kinds of observations will give us the best chance of recognizing them if they exist? It is convenient to discuss these questions separately for civilizations of type 1, 2, and 3. ₃

A type 1 civilization is undetectable at interstellar distances except by radio. The only chance of discovering a type 1 civilization is to follow the suggestion of Cocconi and Morrison and listen for radio messages. This is the method of search that our radio astronomers have followed for the last twenty years. ₄

A type 2 civilization may be a powerful radio source or it may not. So long as we are totally ignorant of the life style of its inhabitants, we cannot make any useful estimate of the volume or nature of their radio emissions. But there is one kind of emission which a type 2 civilization cannot avoid making. According to the second law of thermodynamics, a civilization which exploits the total energy output of a star must radiate away a large fraction of this energy in the form of waste heat. The waste heat is emitted into space as infrared radiation, which astronomers on earth can detect. Any type 2 civilization must be an infrared source with power comparable to the luminosity of a normal star. The infrared radiation will be mainly emitted from the warm outer surface of the biosphere in which the civilization lives. The biosphere will presumably be maintained at roughly terrestrial temperatures if creatures containing liquid water are living in it. The heat radiation from its surface then appears mainly in a band of wavelengths around ten microns (about ₅

twenty times the wavelength of visible light). The ten-micron band is fortunately a convenient one for infrared astronomers to work with, since our atmosphere is quite transparent to it.

After Cocconi and Morrison had started the scientific discussion of extraterrestrial intelligence, I made the suggestion that astronomers looking for artificial objects in the sky should begin by looking for strong sources of ten-micron infrared radiation. Of course it would be absurd to claim that evidence of intelligence has been found every time a new infrared source is discovered. The argument goes the other way. If an object in the sky is not an infrared source, then it cannot be the home of a type 2 civilization. So I suggested that astronomers should first make a survey of the sky to compile a catalog of infrared sources, and then look carefully at objects in the catalog with optical radio telescopes. Using these tactics, the search for radio messages would have greatly improved the chances of success. Instead of searching for radio messages over the whole sky, the radio astronomer could concentrate his listening upon a comparatively small number of accurately pinpointed directions. If one of the infrared sources turned out to be also a source of peculiar optical or radio signals, then one could begin to consider it a candidate for possible artificiality.

When I made this proposal twenty years ago, infrared astronomy had hardly begun. Only a few pioneers had started to look for infrared sources, using small telescopes and simple detecting equipment. Now the situation is quite different. Infrared astronomy is a major branch of astronomy. The sky has been surveyed and catalogs of sources exist. I do not claim any credit for this. The astronomers who surveyed the sky and compiled the catalogs were not looking for type 2 civilizations. They were just carrying one step further the traditional mission of astronomers, searching the sky to find out what is up there.

Up to now, the infrared astronomers have not found any objects that arouse suspicions of artificiality. Instead they have found a wonderful variety of natural objects, some of them within our galaxy and others outside it. Some of the objects are intelligible and others are not. A large number of them are dense clouds of dust, kept warm by hot stars which may or may not be visible. When the hot star is invisible such an object is called a "cocoon star," a star hidden in a cocoon of dust. Cocoon stars are often found in regions of space where brilliant newborn stars are also seen, for example in the great nebula in the constellation Orion. This fact makes it likely that the cocoon is a normal but short-lived phase in the process of birth of a star.

Superficially, there seems to be some similarity between a cocoon star and a type 2 civilization. In both cases we have an invisible star surrounded by a warm opaque shell which radiates strongly in the infrared. Why, then, does nobody believe that type 2 civilizations are living in the cocoon stars that have now been discovered? First, the cocoons are too luminous. Most of them are radiating hundreds or thousands of times as much energy as the sun. Stars with luminosity as high as this are necessarily short-lived by astronomical standards. A type 2 civilization would be much more likely to exist around a long-lived star like the sun. The infrared radiation which it emits would be hundreds of times fainter than the radiation which we detect from most of the cocoons. A second reason for not believing that cocoons are artificial is that their temperatures are too high to be appropriate for biospheres. Most of them have temperatures higher than 300 degrees centigrade, far above the range in which life as we know it can exist. A third reason is that there is direct visual evidence for dense dust clouds in the neighborhood of cocoons. We have no reason to expect that a type 2 civilization would find it necessary to surround itself with a smoke screen. The fourth and most conclusive reason for regarding cocoons as natural objects is the general context in which they occur. One sees in the same region of space new stars being born and large diffuse dust clouds condensing. The cocoons must be causally related to these other natural processes with which they are associated.

I have to admit that in the twenty years since I made my suggestion, infrared astronomy, with all its brilliant successes, has failed to produce evidence of type 2 civilizations. Should we then give up hope of its ever doing so? I do not believe we should. We can expect to find candidates for type 2 civilizations only when we explore infrared sources a hundred times fainter than the spectacular ones which the astronomers have observed so far. An astronomer prefers to spend his time at the telescope studying in detail one conspicuously interesting object, rather than cataloguing a long list of dim sources for future investigation. I do not blame the astonomers for skimming the cream off the bright sources before returning to the tedious work of surveying the faint ones. We will have to wait a few years before we have a complete survey of sources down to the luminosity of the sun. Only when we have a long list of faint sources can we hope that candidates for type 2 civilizations will appear among them. And we shall not know whether to take these candidates seriously until we have learned at least as much about the structure and distribution of the faint sources as we have now found out about the bright ones.

A type 3 civilization in a distant galaxy should produce emissions of radio, light and infrared radiation with an apparent brightness comparable with those of a type 2 civilization in our own galaxy. In particular, a type 3 civilization should be detectable as an extragalactic infrared source. However, a type 3 civilization would be harder than a type 2 to recognize, for two reasons. First, our ideas about the behavior of a type 3 civilization are even vaguer and more unreliable than our ideas about type 2. Second, we know much less about the structure and evolution of galaxies than we do about the birth and death of stars, and consequently we understand the naturally occurring extragalactic infrared sources even more poorly than we understand the natural sources in our galaxy. We understand the cocoon stars at least well enough to be confident that they are not type 2 civilizations. We do not understand the extragalactic infrared souces well enough to be confident of anything. We cannot expect to recognize a type 3 civilization for what it is until we have thoroughly explored the many strange and violent phenomena that we see occurring in the nuclei of distant galaxies.

Is it possible that a type 3 civilization could exist in our own galaxy? This is a question which deserves more serious thought than has been given to it. The answer is negative if we think of a type 3 civilization as overrunning the galaxy with ruthless efficiency and exploiting the light of every available star. However, other kinds of type 3 civilizations are conceivable. One attractive possibility is a civilization based on vegetation growing freely in space rather than on massive industrial hardware. A type 3 civilization might use comets rather than planets for its habitat, and trees rather than dynamos for its source of energy. If such a civilization does not already exist, perhaps we shall one day create it ourselves.

CONTENT

1. What is the basis for Dyson's categories of extraterrestrial civilizations? Does Dyson think such civilizations exist? Why?

2. What is infrared astronomy? Why haven't infrared astronomers found an extraterrestrial civilization?
3. How does Dyson explain the phenomena of cocoon stars (paragraph 8)? Why doesn't he think they host a type-2 civilization?

ORGANIZATION

4. After defining the differences between types 1, 2 and 3 civilizations, why does Dyson circle back to explain each one in more depth? Why didn't he combine his definitions and discussions?
5. Why is most of the development given to type 2 civilizations? Why least to type 1?

TOPICS FOR WRITING

6. Dyson's types of civilizations are based on inferences or guesses. Select a topic which you cannot know from firsthand experience, and discuss it by dividing it into types.
7. Write a "types of" essay in which you divide cultures within your own country into types.

Cause–Effect

familiar
famil

Many thesis statements written early in the term suffer from a lack of significance. The remedy for these trite and commonplace statements is often, simply, to add the word "because," or "since" and complete the sentence. Such an addition can transform an obvious thesis into a controversial and interesting one which will generate a *cause–effect* essay. If you begin an essay with a thesis that contends, "The Watts Riot was destructive," you have reached a virtual dead end, leaving you nothing to say except to document what is already obvious. But if you add "because" and complete the sentence—"the Watts Riot was destructive, not because of the physical damage done, although that was great, but because it destroyed much of the economic and community base, the leadership segment, on which that section of Los Angeles had formerly depended"—you have a thesis that is potentially informative and controversial. You are unlikely to find "trite" as an instructor's comment.

One way to view cause–effect productively in a composition class is to visualize it in terms of a temporal sequence. Consider your subject as an *effect* taking place now, or having taken place, and go back in time to trace the causes that produced it. Or, think first of your subject as a *cause*, then move ahead in time toward the present or future to account for, or predict, what effects will follow:

Past	Present	Future

CAUSE(S)◀——EFFECT(S)
                  CAUSE(S)——▶ EFFECT(S)

In our example, the Watts Riot, if you regard the subject as an effect, you would retrace the time line citing such causes that led up to the riot—high unemployment, police violence, a long hot summer, substandard housing, poor educational facilities, outside-owned businesses. If, on the other hand, you regard the Watts Riot as a cause, moving ahead on the time line would yield such potential effects as massive physical destruction to property, disruption of the community social structure, bitterness toward the establishment, community action programs, a police review board, local control of the school board, and locally owned businesses. Notice that some of the effects are past, and some are still happening, but the thrust of the cause-to-effect paper is toward the future, just as the thrust of the effect-to-cause paper is toward the past.

Quite often, especially in science and social science essays, causes and effects will be mixed in a chain in which one effect will, in turn, become a cause of a subsequent effect, and so on until the end of the chain is reached. Here is an example describing the chain of inter-related effects that would follow the explosion of a nuclear device over an American city.

Whereas most conventional bombs produce only one destructive effect—the shock wave—nuclear weapons produce many destructive effects. At the moment of explosion, when the temperature of the weapon material, instantly gasified, is at the superstellar level, the pressure is millions of times the normal atmospheric pressure. Immediately, radiation, consisting mainly of gamma rays, which are a very high energy form of electromagnetic radiation, begins to stream outward into the environment. This is called the "initial nuclear radiation," and is the first of the destructive effects of a nuclear explosion. In an air burst of a one-megaton bomb—a bomb with the explosive yield of a million tons of TNT, which is a medium-sized weapon in present-day nuclear arsenals—the initial nuclear radiation can kill unprotected human beings in an area of some six square miles. Virtually simultaneously with the initial nuclear radiation, in a second destructive effect of the explosion, an electromagnetic pulse is generated by the intense gamma radiation acting on the air. In a high-altitude detonation, the pulse can knock out electrical equipment over a wide area by inducing a powerful surge of voltage through various conductors, such as antennas, overhead power lines, pipes and railroad tracks. The Defense Department's Civil Preparedness Agency reported in 1977 that a single multi-kiloton nuclear weapon detonated one hundred and twenty-five miles over Omaha, Nebraska, could generate an electromagnetic pulse strong enough to damage solid-state electrical circuits throughout the entire continental United States and in parts of Canada and Mexico, and thus threaten to bring the economies of these countries to a halt. When the fusion and fission reactions have blown themselves out, a fireball takes shape. As it expands, energy is absorbed in the form of X-rays by the surrounding air, and then the air re-radiates a portion of that energy into the environment in the form of the thermal pulse—a wave of blinding light and intense heat—which is the third of the destructive effects of a nuclear explosion. [Jonathan Schell, "The Fate of the Earth," *The New Yorker* (Feb. 1, 1982), 55–56.]

In diagrammatic form, the chain of cause and effect looks something like this:

Principle Cause	*Chain of Effects* (numbered sequentially)
Detonation of a nuclear device	1. "initial nuclear radiation": (gamma rays)—cause 2

	2. electromagnetic pulse
	  surge of voltage
	  damage to solid state circuits
	  disruption of economy

	3. fireball
	  absorption of X rays
	  thermal pulse

In a chain of cause and effect such as the one used by Schell, the problem of organization is largely solved by the chronology of the chain, so effects are described in the time sequence in which they occur. In some essays, such as in the hypothetical paper on Watts, some further strategy is called for. In the Watts essay, the effects could be divided into favorable effects and unfavorable effects; which would come first would depend on the point you wanted to convey. It is good advice to end the paper with the effects which you feel are most important to making your point, and to bury in the middle of the paper the effect which is the weakest, the one you wish to deemphasize.

Of all the patterns of development which we have been discussing, cause and effect demands the highest kind of reasoned discourse between you and the reader. It demands not only that you prove the logic of the cause–effect relationship, but that you offer examples to support it. In no other patttern is the demand for logic so great or is its absence so clearly obvious to the reader. Despite these demands, cause–effect remains one of the most potent patterns for arousing high reader interest and ensuring that there is controversy and interest in your paper.

SHORT EXAMPLE—CAUSE-EFFECT

Milton Moskowitz, Michael Katz, and Robert Levering (editors)
Why Levi's Changed the 501

"Why Levi's Changed the 501" is taken from Everybody's Business: An Almanac. *True to the book's subtitle—*The Irreverent Guide to Corporate America—*this brief selection describes how the first change in the standard pair of button-front Levi's came about as a result of a strategically misplaced rivet.*

Picture a scene from the Old West, sometime in the 1870s. Weary cowboys in dusty Levi's gather around a blazing campfire, resting after a day of riding and roping on the open range. The lonely howl of a distant coyote counterpoints the notes of a guitar as the moon floats serenely overhead in an unpolluted sky afire with stars.

Suddenly a bellow of pain shatters the night, as a cowpoke leaps 2 away from the fire, dancing in agony. Hot Rivet Syndrome has claimed another victim.

In those days Levi's were made, as they had been from the first 3 days of Levi Strauss, with copper rivets at stress points to provide extra strength. On these original Levi's—model 501—there were rivets on the pockets, and there was a lone rivet at the crotch. The crotch rivet was the critical one: when cowboys crouched too long beside the campfire, the rivet grew uncomfortably hot.

For years the brave men of the West suffered from this curious 4 occupational hazard. But nothing was done about it until 1933, when Walter Haas, Sr., president of Levi Strauss, chanced to go camping in his Levi's 501s. Haas was crouched contentedly by a crackling campfire in the high Sierras, drinking in the pure mountain air, when he fell prey to Hot Rivet Syndrome. He consulted with professional wranglers in his party. Had they ever suffered the same mishap? An impassioned *yes* was the reply.

Haas vowed that the offending rivet must go, and the board of 5 directors voted it into extinction at their next meeting.

Except for eliminating the crotch rivet, the company has made 6 only one other stylistic change in its 501s since they were first marketed in 1873. Responding to schools' complaints that Levi's pocket rivets scratched school furniture, the company moved the rivets to the front pockets. Otherwise the Levi's 501 shrink-to-fit jeans on the market today are identical to the pants that won the West.

DISCUSSION

This brief account, explaining why Levi's removed the crotch rivet from the standard 501 jeans, makes its point effectively, not only because the opening cause–effect chain between the offending rivet and the uncomfortable cowboy is painfully established—heat (remote cause), hot crotch rivet (immediate cause), pained victim (effect)— but because the writer sets the scene in the opening two paragraphs, backtracks to explain the origins of the unforgiving rivet, and finally gets to his real point: how the president of the company, himself, had to fall prey to Hot Rivet Syndrome before it was removed. This final scene is all the more funny because the reader is already in on the cause–effect joke from the opening paragraphs. The final paragraph presents one last change in the rivets on Levi's and the reason for the change. Even though cause–effect writing is associated with explanations that begin with "since" or "because," as this short piece demonstrates, an interesting and clear cause–effect essay can be written within a narrative framework.

Aside from the essentially slapstick basic situation, much of the humor in this piece depends on the irreverence of the language. "Hot Rivet Syndrome," with its pseudo-psychological overtones, is merely a euphemism for what happened to the crouching cowboys. The stereotypical label "brave men of the West" seems to suggest that the cowboys' bravery was attributable only to their ability to withstand the pain of the "curious occupational hazard." The phrases "voted it into extinction" and "the pants that won the West" are both deliberate uses of overstatement for effect.

DON SHARP
Under the Hood

Don Sharp has written lovingly and knowingly about the giant threshing machines which he once used to operate during summer vacations, and about the elegance of the internal combustion engine. "Under the Hood" which originally appeared in the American Miscellany section of Harper's *won the Ken Purdy Award for Excellence in Automobile Journalism in 1981. Like Robert Pirsig's* Zen and the Art of Motorcycle Maintenance *(see pages 399–401), Sharp's essay suggests that there is more to repairing a vehicle than merely replacing parts.*

The owner of this 1966 Plymouth Valiant has made the rounds of car dealers. They will gladly sell him a new car—the latest model of government regulation and industrial enterprise—for $8,000, but they don't want his clattering, emphysemic old vehicle in trade. It isn't worth enough to justify the paperwork, a classified ad, and space on the used-car lot. "Sell it for junk," they tell him. "Scrap iron is high now, and they'll give you $25 for it."

The owner is hurt. He likes his car. It has served him well for 90,000-odd miles. It has a functional shape and he can get in and out of it easily. He can roll down his window in a light rain and not get his shoulder wet. The rear windows roll down, and he doesn't need an air conditioner. He can see out of it fore, aft, and abeam. He can hazard it on urban parking lots without fear of drastic, insurance-deductible casualty loss. His teenage children reject it as passé, so it is always available to him. It has no buzzers, and the only flashing lights are those he controls himself when signaling a turn. The owner, clearly one of the vanishing tribe, brings the car to a kindred spirit and asks me to rebuild it.

We do not discuss the cost. I do not advertise my services and 3 my sign is discreet. My shop is known by word of mouth, and those who spread the word emphasize my house rule: "A blank check and a free hand." That is, I do to your car what I think it needs and you pay for it; you trust me not to take advantage, I guarantee you good brakes, sound steering, and prompt starting, and you pay without quarrel. This kind of arrangement saves a lot of time haggling over the bill. It also imposes a tremendous burden of responsibility on me and on those who spread the word, and it puts a burden of trust on those who deliver their cars into my custody.

A relationship of that sort is about as profound as any that two 4 people can enjoy, even if it lasts no longer than the time required to reline a set of brakes. I think of hometown farmers who made sharecropping deals for the season on a handshake; then I go into a large garage and see the white-coated service writer noting the customer's every specification, calling attention to the fine print at the bottom of the work order, and requiring a contractual signature before even a brake-light bulb is replaced. I perceive in their transaction that ignorance of cause and effect breeds suspicion, and I wonder who is the smaller, the customer or the service writer, and how they came to be so small of spirit.

Under the hood of this ailing Valiant, I note a glistening line of 5 seeping oil where the oil pan meets the engine block. For thousands of miles, a piece of cork—a strip of bark from a Spanish tree—has stood firm between the pan and the block against churning oil heated to nearly 200 degrees, oil that sought vainly to escape its duty and was forced back to work by a stalwart gasket. But now, after years of perseverance, the gasket has lost its resilience and the craven oil escapes. Ecclesiastes allows a time for all things, and the time for this gasket has passed.

Higher up, between the block casting that forms the foundation 6 of the engine and cylinder-head casting that admits fresh air and exhausts oxidized air and fuel, is the head gasket, a piece of sheet metal as thin as a matchbook cover that has confined the multiple fires built within the engine to their proper domains. Now, a whitish-gray deposit betrays an eroded area from which blue flame spits every time the cylinder fires. The gasket is "blown."

Let us stop and think of large numbers. In the four-cycle engines that power all modern cars, a spark jumps a spark-plug gap and sets off a fire in a cylinder every time the crankshaft goes around twice. The crankshaft turns the transmission shaft, which turns the driveshaft, which turns the differential gears, which turn the rear axles, which turn the wheels (what could Aquinas* have done with something like that, had he addressed himself to the source of the spark or to the final destination of the wheels?). In 100,000 miles —a common life for modern engines—the engine will make some 260 million turns, and in half of those turns, 130 million of them, gasoline-fueled fire with a maximum temperature of 2,000 degrees (quickly falling to about 1,200 degrees) is built in each cylinder. The heat generated by the fire raises the pressure in the cylinder to about 700 pounds per square inch, if only for a brief instant before the piston moves and the pressure falls. A head gasket has to contend with heat and pressure like this all the time the engine is running, and, barring mishap, it will put up with it indefinitely.

This Plymouth has suffered mishap. I know it as soon as I raise the hood and see the telltale line of rust running across the underside of the hood: the mark of overheating. A water pump bearing or seal gave way, water leaked out, and was flung off the fan blades with enough force to embed particles of rust in the undercoating. Without cooling water, the engine grew too hot, and that's why the head gasket blew. In an engine, no cause exists without an effect. Unlike a court of law, wherein criminals are frequently absolved of wrongdoing, no engine component is without duty and responsibility, and failure cannot be mitigated by dubious explanations such as parental neglect or a crummy neighborhood.

Just as Sherlock Holmes would not be satisfied with one clue if he could find others, I study the oil filter. The block and oil pan are caked with seepings and drippings, but below the filter the caking is visibly less thick and somewhat soft. So: once upon a time, a careless service attendant must have ruined the gasket while install-

*St. Thomas Aquinas (1225–1274), Dominican philosopher and theologian, knows as "the subtle doctor."

ing a new oil filter. Oil en route to the bearings escaped and washed away the grime that had accumulated. Odds are that the oil level fell too low and the crankshaft bearings were starved for oil.

Bearings are flat strips of metal, formed into half-circles about as thick as a matchbook match and about an inch wide. The bearing surface itself—the surface that *bears* the crankshaft and that *bears* the load imposed by the fire-induced pressure above the pistons — is half as thick. Bearing metal is a drab, gray alloy, the principal component of which is *babbitt*, a low-friction metal porous enough to absorb oil but so soft that it must be allowed to withstand high pressures. (I like to think that Sinclair Lewis had metallurgy in mind when he named his protagonist George Babbit.) When the fire goes off above the piston and the pressure is transmitted to the crankshaft via the connecting rod, the babbitt-alloyed bearing pushes downward with a force of about 3,500 pounds per square inch. And it must not give way, must not be peened into foil and driven from its place in fragments.

Regard the fleshy end joint of your thumb and invite a 100-pound woman (or a pre-teen child, if no such woman be near to hand) to stand on it. Multiply the sensation by thirty-five and you get an idea of what the bearing is up against. Of course, the bearing enjoys a favorable handicap in the comparison because it works in a metal-to-metal environment heated to 180 degrees or so. The bearing is equal to its task so long as it is protected from direct metal-to-metal contact by a layer of lubricating oil, oil that must be forced into the space between the bearing and the crankshaft against that 3,500 pounds of force. True, the oil gets a lot of help from hydrodynamic action as the spinning of the crankshaft drags oil along with it, but lubrication depends primarily on a pump that forces oil through the engine at around 40 pounds of pressure.

If the oil level falls too low, the oil pump sucks in air. The oil gets as frothy as whipped cream and doesn't flow. In time, oil pressure will fall so low that the "idiot" light on the dashboard will flash, but long before then the bearing may have run "dry" and suffered considerable amounts of its metal to be peened away by those 3,500-pound hammer blows. "Considerable" may mean only .005 inches, or about the thickness of one sheet of 75-percent-cotton, 25-pound-per-ream dissertation bond—not much metal, but enough to allow oil to escape from the bearing even after the defective filter gasket is replaced and the oil supply replenished. From the time of oil starvation onward, the beaten bearing is a little disaster waiting to spoil a vacation or a commute to an important meeting.

Curious, that an unseen .005 inches of drab, gray metal worthy only to inspire the name of a poltroonish bourgeois should enjoy more consequence for human life than almost any equal thickness of a randomly chosen doctoral dissertation. Life is full of ironies.

The car I confront does not have an "idiot" light. It has an old-fashioned oil-pressure gauge. As the driver made his rounds from condominium to committee room, he could—if he cared or was ever so alert—monitor the health of his engine bearings by noting the oil pressure. Virtually all cars had gauges in the old days, but they began to disappear in the mid-'50s, and nowadays hardly any cars have them. In eliminating oil-pressure gauges, the car makers pleaded that, in their dismal experience, people didn't pay much attention to gauges. Accordingly, Detroit switched to the warning light, which was cheaper to manufacture anyway (and having saved a few bucks on the mechanicals, the manufacturer could afford to etch a design in the opera windows; this is called "progress"). Curious, in the midst of all this, that Chrysler Corporation, the maker of Plymouths and the victim of so much bad management over the past fifteen years, should have been the one car manufacturer to constantly assert, via a standard-equipment oil-pressure gauge, a faith in the awareness, judgment, and responsibility of drivers. That Chrysler did so may have something to do with its current problems.

The other car makers were probably right. Time was when most men knew how to replace their own distributor points, repair a flat tire, and install a battery. Women weren't assumed to know as much, but they were expected to know how to put a gear lever in neutral, set a choke and throttle, and crank a car by hand if the battery was dead. Now, odds are that 75 percent of men and a higher percentage of women don't even know how to work the jacks that come with their cars. To be sure, a bumper jack is an abominable contraption— the triumph of production economies over good sense—but it will do what it is supposed to do, and the fact that most drivers cannot make one work says much about the way motorists have changed over the past forty years.

About all that people will watch on the downslide of this century is the fuel gauge, for they don't like to be balked in their purpose. A lack of fuel will stop a car dead in its tracks and categorically prevent the driver from arriving at the meeting to consider tenure for a male associate professor with a black grandfather and a Chinese mother. Lack of fuel will stall a car in mid-intersection and leave dignity and image prey to the honks and curses of riffraff driving taxicabs and beer trucks, so people watch the fuel gauge as closely as they watch a pubescent daughter or a bearish stock.

But for the most part, once the key goes into the ignition, people 17 assign responsibility for the car's smooth running to someone else— to anybody but themselves. If the engine doesn't start, that's not because the driver has abused it, but because the manufacturer was remiss or the mechanic incompetent. (Both suspicions are reasonable, but they do not justify the driver's spineless passivity.) The driver considers himself merely a client of the vehicle. He proudly disclaims, at club and luncheon, any understanding of the dysfunctions of the machine. He must so disclaim, for to admit knowledge or to seek it actively would require an admission of responsibility and fault. To be wrong about inflation or the political aspirations of the Albanians doesn't cost anybody anything, but to claim to know why the car won't start and then to be proved wrong is both embarrassing and costly.

Few people would remove $500 from someone's pocket without 18 a qualm and put it in their own. Yet, the job-lot run of mechanics do it all the time. Mechanics and drivers alike: they gave up worrying long ago about the intricacies and demands of cause and effect. The mechanics do not attend closely to the behavior of the vehicle. Rather, they consult a book with flowcharts that says, "Try this, and if it doesn't work, try that." Or they hook the engine up to another machine and read gauges or cathode-ray-tube squiggles, but without realizing that gauges and squiggles are not reality but only tools used to aid perception of reality. A microscope is also a wonderful tool, but you still have to comprehend what you're looking for; else, like James Thurber, you get back the reflection of your own eye.

Mechanics, like academics and bureaucrats, have retreated too 19 far from the realities of their tasks. An engine runs badly. They consult the book. The book says to replace part A. They replace part A. The engine still runs badly, but the mechanic can deny the fact as handily as a socialist can deny that minimum-wage laws eventually lead to unemployment. Just as the driver doesn't care to know why his oil pressure drops from 40 to 30 to 20 pounds and then to zero, so the mechanic cares little for the casuistic distinctions

that suggest that part A is in good order but that some subtle con-
junction of wholesome part B with defective part C may be causing
the trouble. (I don't know about atheists in foxholes, but I doubt
that many Jesuits are found among incompetent mechanics.)

And why should the mechanic care? He gets paid in any event.   2
From the mechanic's point of view, he should get paid, for he sees
a federal judge hire academic consultants to advise about busing,
and after the whites have fled before the imperious column of yellow buses and left the schools blacker than ever, the judge hires
the consultants again to find out why the whites moved out. The
consultant gets paid in public money, whatever the effects his actions
have, even when he causes things he said would never happen.

Consider the garden-variety Herr Doktor who has spent a pleas-   2
ant series of warm fall weekends driving to a retreat in the Catskills;
his car has started with alacrity and run well despite a stuck choke.
Then, when the first blue norther of the season sends temperatures
toward zero, the faithful machine must be haggled into action and
proceeds haltingly down the road, gasping and backfiring. "Needs
a new carburetor," the mechanic says, and, to be sure, once a new
carburetor is installed, the car runs well again. Our Herr Doktor is
happy. His car did not run well; it got a new carburetor and ran
well again; ergo, the carburetor was at fault. Q.E.D.

Curious that in personal matters the classic *post hoc** fallacy should   2
be so readily accepted when it would be mocked by academic debate.
Our Herr Doktor should know, or at least suspect, that the carburetor that functioned so well for the past several months could
hardly have changed its nature overnight, and we might expect of
him a more diligent inquiry into its problems. But "I'm no mechanic,"
he chuckles to his colleagues, and they nod agreeably. Such skinned-
knuckle expertise would be unfitting in a man whose self-esteem
is equivalent to his uselessness with a wrench. Lillies of the postin-
dustrial field must concern themselves with weighty matters beyond
the ken of greasy laborers who drink beer at the end of a workday.

Another example will illustrate the point. A battery cable has an   2
end that is designed to connect to a terminal on the battery. Both
cable-end and battery-terminal surfaces look smooth, but aren't.
Those smooth surfaces are pitted and peaked, and only the peaks
touch each other. The pits collect water from the air, and the chemistry of electricity-carrying metals causes lead oxides to form in the

*"After this, therefore, because of this"

pits. The oxides progressively insulate the cable end and battery terminal from each other until the day that turning the key produces only a single, resounding *clunk* no more. The road service mechanic installs a new $75 battery and collects $25 for his trouble. Removing the cables from the old battery cleans their ends somewhat, so things work for a few days, and then the car again fails to start. The mechanic installs a $110 alternator, applies a $5 charge to the battery, and collects another $25; several days later he gives the battery another $5 charge, installs a $75 starter, and collects $25 more. In these instances, to charge the battery—to send current backwards from cable end to battery terminal—disturbs the oxides and temporarily improves their conductivity. Wriggling the charger clamps on the cable ends probably helps too. On the driver's last $25 visit, the mechanic sells another $5 battery charge and a pair of $25 battery cables. Total bill: $400, and all the car needed was to have its cable ends and battery terminal cleaned. The mechanic wasn't necessarily a thief. Perhaps, like academic education consultants, he just wasn't very smart—and his ilk abound; they are as plentiful as the drivers who will pay generously for the privilege of an aristocratic disdain of elementary cause and effect in a vehicular electrical system.

After a tolerably long practice as a mechanic, I firmly believe that 24 at least two-thirds of the batteries, starters, alternators, ignition coils, carburetors, and water pumps that are sold are not needed. Batteries, alternators, and starters are sold because battery-cable ends are dirty. A maladjusted or stuck automatic choke is cured by a new carburetor. Water pumps and alternators are sold to correct problems from loose fan belts. In the course of the replacement, the fan belt gets properly tightened, so the original problem disappears in the misguided cure, with mechanic and owner never the wiser.

I understand the venality (and laziness and ignorance) of 25 mechanics, and I understand the shop owner's need to pay a salary to someone to keep up with the IRS and OSHA forms. The shop marks up parts by 50 to 100 percent. When the car with the faulty choke comes in the door, the mechanic must make a choice: he can spend fifteen minutes fixing it and charge a half-hour's labor, or he can spend a half-hour replacing the carburetor (and charge for one hour) with one he buys for $80 and sells for $135. If the shop is a profit-making enterprise, the mechanic can hardly be blamed for selling the unneeded new carburetor, especially if the customer will stand still to be fleeced. Whether the mechanic acts from ignorance or larceny (the odds are about equal), the result is still a waste, one that arises from the driver's refusal to study the cause and effect of events that occur under the hood of his car.

The willingness of a people to accept responsibility for the machines   26
they depend on is a fair barometer of their sense of individual worth and of the moral strength of a culture. According to popular reports, the Russian working folk are a sorrowfully vodka-besotted lot; likewise, reports are that Russian drivers abuse their vehicles atrociously. In our unhappy country, as gauges for battery-changing (ammeters), cooling-water temperature, and oil pressure disappeared from dashboards, they were replaced by a big-brotherly series of cacophonous buzzers and flashing lights, buzzers and lights mandated by regulatory edict for the sole purpose of reminding the driver that the government considers him a hopeless fool. Concurrent with these developments has come social agitation and law known as "consumer protection," which is, in fact, an extension of the philosophy that people are morons for whom the government must provide outpatient care. People pay handsome taxes to be taught that they are not responsible and do not need to be. This is a long way from what the Puritans paid their tithes for, and, Salem witch trials aside, the Puritans got a better product for their money.

What is astounding and dismaying is how quickly people came   27
to believe in their own incompetence. In 1951, Eric Hoffer noted in *The True Believer* that a leader so disposed could make free people into slaves easier than he could turn slaves into free people (cf. Moses). Hoffer must be pained by the accuracy of his perception.

I do not claim that Everyman can be his own expert mechanic,   28
for I know that precious few can. I do claim that disdain for the beautiful series of cause-and-effect relationships ("beautiful" in the way that provoked Archimedes to proclaim "Eureka!") that move machines, and particularly the automobile, measures not only a man's wit but also a society's morals.

CONTENT

1. How does Sharp demonstrate that "in an engine no cause exists without an effect"? Are his examples easy to follow? Does he define any strange terms?

2. Is this essay merely about automobile repair? What other matters does Sharp address himself to? What does he mean by his final remark, " . . . disdain for the beautiful series of cause-and-effect relationships . . . that move machines, and particularly the automobile, measures not only a man's wit but also a society's morals"?
3. What reasons does Sharp give for people's ignorance of the cause-and-effect relationships in an auto's engine?

ORGANIZATION

4. How does Sharp's opening example bring home the cause–effect relationship with which the essay deals?
5. Is the material on oil pressure guages a digression, or does it relate in some way to the central cause–effect issue?
6. What is the function of the narrative concerning "Herr Doktor" (paragraph 21)? How do Sharp's remarks on consumer protection tie in with the narrative? With the concluding sentence of the opening narrative, "ignorance of cause and effect breeds suspicion"?

TOPICS FOR WRITING

7. Show how government regulations, other than the ones Sharp mentions, create a sense of irresponsibility among people.
8. Show how consumer protectionism has produced positive effects.

LESTER THUROW
An Economy That No Longer Performs

Lester C. Thurow has the ability to transform the complexities of economics into readable prose and economic theory into relevant contemporary history. "An Economy That No Longer Performs" is the opening chapter of Thurow's most popular book, The Zero-Sum Society *(1980). In this chapter, Thurow examines some of the reasons the United States' economy seems to be stagnating.*

After decades of believing in their economic invulnerability, Americans were jolted by the 1973-74 Arab oil embargo. The actions of a few desert sheiks could make *them* line up at the gas pump and substantially reduce *their* standard of living. Sudden economic vulnerability is disconcerting, just as that first small heart attack is disconcerting. It reminds us that our economy can be eclipsed.

When the shutdown of a major oil exporter for just a few months in 1979 once again resulted in the convulsions of gas lines, it was possible to ask whether that first mild heart attack was not the harbinger of something worse. Seemingly unsolvable problems were emerging everywhere—inflation, unemployment, slow growth, environmental decay, irreconcilable group demands, and complex, cumbersome regulations. Were the problems unsolvable or were our leaders incompetent? Had Americans lost the work ethic? Had we stopped inventing new processes and products? Should we invest more and consume less? Do we need to junk our social welfare, health, safety, and environmental protection systems in order to compete? Why were others doing better?

Where the U.S. economy had once generated the world's highest standard of living, it was now well down the list and slipping farther each year. Leaving the rich Middle East sheikdoms aside, we stood fifth among the nations of the world in per capital GNP in 1978, having been surpassed by Switzerland, Denmark, West Germany, and Sweden. Switzerland, which stood first, actually had a per capita GNP 45 percent larger than ours. And on the outside, the world's fastest economic runner, Japan, was advancing rapidly with a per capita GNP only 7 percent below ours. In our entire history we have never grown even half as rapidly as the Japanese.

While the slippage in our economic position was first noticed in the 1970s, our economic status was actually surpassed (after just half a century of delivering the world's highest standard of living) by Kuwait in the early 1950s. Kuwait was ignored, however, as a simple case of a country inheriting wealth (oil in the ground) rather than earning it. We failed to remember that our supremacy had also been based on a rich inheritance of vast mineral, energy, and climatic resources. No one inherited more wealth than we. We are not the little poor boy who worked his way to the top, but the little rich boy who inherited a vast fortune. Perhaps we had now squandered that inheritance. Perhaps we could not survive without it.

Of course, one can always argue that things are not really as bad as they seem. Since many goods are not traded in international markets and may be cheaper here than abroad, per capita GNP may paint too pessimistic a picture of our relative position. A group of American economists argued in 1975 that we still had the highest real standard of living among industrialized countries. What we lost in per capita GNP to the two or three countries that were then ahead of us, we more than made up in terms of lower living costs.

Whether this is still true today depends upon changes in the *terms of trade*—the amount of exports that you have to give up to get a given amount of imports. In Switzerland, for example, oil cost less in 1978 than it did in 1975. While the dollar price of oil is up, the value of the Swiss franc is up even more. Thus fewer domestic goods have to be given up to buy a given quantity of oil. The country's GNP simply buys more than it did. In countries like Switzerland, where imports are over one-third of the GNP, changes in the terms of trade can have a dramatic effect on the real standard of living.

While it is easy to calculate per capita GNPs, it is notoriously difficult to make precise standard-of-living comparisons among countries. In each country, individuals naturally shift their purchases toward those items that are relatively cheap in that country. Tastes, circumstances, traditions, and habits differ. Individuals do not buy the same basket of goods and services. What is a necessity in one country may be a luxury in another. Health care may be provided by government in one country and purchased privately in another. And how do you evaluate vast expenditures, such as those we make on health care, where we are spending more than the rest of the world by getting less if you look at life expectancy (U.S. males are now sixteenth in the world)?

But whatever our precise ranking at the moment, the rest of the world is catching up, and if they have not already surpassed us, they soon will. From many perspectives, this catching-up process is desirable. Most rich people find it more comfortable to live in a neighborhood with other rich people. The tensions are less and life is more enjoyable. What is not so comfortable is the prospect that our rich neighbors will continue to grow so rapidly that we slip into relative backwardness.

Up to now, we have comforted ourselves with the belief that the economic growth of others would slow down as soon as they had caught up with us. It was simply easier to adopt existing technologies than to develop new technologies—or so we told ourselves. But as other countries have approached our productivity levels, and as individual industries in these countries have begun to be more productive, the "catching-up" hypothesis becomes less and less persuasive.

In the period from 1972 to 1978, industrial productivity rose 1   10 percent per year in the United States, almost 4 percent in West Germany, and over 5 percent in Japan. These countries were introducing new products and improving the process of making old products faster than we were. Major American firms were reduced to marketing new consumer goods such as video recorders, which were made exclusively by the Japanese. In many industries, such as steel, we are now the ones with the "easy" task of adopting the technologies developed by others. But we don't. Instead of junking our old, obsolete open-hearth furnaces and shifting to the large oxygen furnaces and continuous casting of the Japanese, we retreat into protection against the "unfair" competition of Japanese steel companies. The result is a reduction in real incomes as we all pay more for steel than we should. As a result, our economy ends up with a weak steel industry that cannot compete and has no incentive to compete, given its protection in the U.S. market.

This relative economic decline has both economic and political   11 impacts. Economically, Americans face a relative decline in their standard of living. How will the average American react when it becomes obvious to the casual tourist (foreigners here, Americans there) that our economy is falling behind? Since we have never had that experience, no one knows; but if we are like human beings in the rest of the world, we won't like it. No one likes seeing others able to afford things that they cannot.

As gaps in living standards grow, so does dissatisfaction with   12 the performance of government and economy. The larger the income gap, the more revolutionary the demands for change. Today's poor countries are in turmoil, but it should be remembered that these countries are not poor compared with the poor centuries ago. They are only poor relative to what has been achieved in today's rich countries. If we become relatively poor, we are apt to be just as unhappy.

Politically a declining economy means that we have to be willing   1 to make greater sacrifices in our personal consumption to maintain any level of world influence. This can be done. The Russians have become our military and geopolitical equals despite a per capita GNP that is much lower than ours. They simply put a larger fraction of their GNP into defense. But the need to cut consumption creates strains in a democracy that do not exist in a dictatorship. Americans may gradually decide that they cannot afford to maintain a strategic military capability to defend countries that are richer than they are. They may decide that they cannot afford to lubricate peace settlements, such as that between Israel and Egypt, with large economic gifts. Some of the international economic burdens could be shifted to our wealthier allies, but this would inevitably mean letting them make more of the important international decisions. In many circumstances (Israel vs. Egypt?) the Germans and the Japanese may not make the same decisions that we would make.

The hard-core conservative solution is to "liberate free enterprise," reduce social expenditures, restructure taxes to encourage saving and investment (shift the tax burden from those who save, the rich, to those who consume, the poor), and eliminate government rules and regulations that do not help business. Specifically, the capital gains taxes that were reduced in 1978 should be reduced further; the "double" taxation of dividends should be ended; income transfer payments to the poor and the elderly should be frozen; environmentalism should be seen as an economic threat and rolled back. Laffer* curves sprout like weeds to show that taxes should be cut to restore personal initiative. Only by returning to the virtues of hard work and free enterprise can the economy be saved. 14

In thinking about this solution, it is well to remember that none of our competitors became successful by following this route. Government absorbs slightly over 30 percent of the GNP in the United States, but over 50 percent of the GNP in West Germany. Fifteen other countries collect a larger fraction of their GNP in taxes. 15

Other governments are not only larger; they are more pervasive. In West Germany, union leaders must by law sit on corporate boards. Sweden is famous for its comprehensive welfare state. Japan is marked by a degree of central investment planning and government control that would make any good capitalist cry. Other governments own or control major firms, such as Volkswagen or Renault. Ours is not the economy with the most rules and regulations; on the contrary, it is the one with the fewest rules and regulations. As many American firms have discovered to their horror, it simply 16

---

*Named for Arthur Laffer, Professor of Economics at U.C.L.A., who theorized that reduced taxes would stimulate investment.

isn't possible to fire workers abroad as it is here. It is a dubious achievement, but nowhere in the world is it easier to lay off workers.

Nor have our competitors unleashed work effort and savings by increasing income differentials. Indeed, they have done exactly the opposite. If you look at the earnings gap between the top and bottom 10 percent of the population, the West Germans work hard with 36 percent less inequality than we, and the Japanese work even harder with 50 percent less inequality. If income differentials encourage individual initiative, we should be full of initiative, since among industrialized countries, only the French surpass us in terms of inequality.

Moreover, our own history shows that our economic performance since the New Deal and the onset of government "interference" has been better than it was prior to the New Deal. Our best economic decades were the 1940s (real per capita GNP grew 36 percent), when the economy was run as a command (socialist) wartime economy, and the 1960s (real per capita GNP grew 30 percent), when we had all that growth in social welfare programs. Real per capita growth since the advent of government intervention has been more than twice as high as it was in the days when governments did not intervene or have social welfare programs.

The British are often held up as a horrible example of what will happen to us if we do not mend our ways and reverse the trend toward big government. But whatever is wrong with the British economy, it has little to do with the size of government. British growth fell behind that of the leading industrial countries in the nineteenth century and has remained behind ever since. Slow growth did not arrive with the Labour government in 1945. On the contrary, British growth since 1945 has actually been better than before. There is no doubt that the British economy is in sad shape, but as the West Germanys of the world demonstrate, its problems are not a simple function of government size.

As both our experience and foreign experience demonstrate, there is no conflict between social expenditures or government intervention and economic success. Indeed, the lack of investment planning, worker participation, and social spending may be a cause of our poor performance. As we, and others, have shown, social reforms can be productive, as well as just, if done in the right way. If done in the wrong way, they can, of course, be both disastrous and unjust. There may also be some merit in "liberating free enterprise" if it is done in the right way. There are certainly unnecessary rules and regulations that are now strangling our economy. The trick is not rules versus no rules, but finding the right rules.

The American problem is not returning to some golden age of economic growth (there was no such golden age) but in recognizing that we have an economic structure that has never in its entire history performed as well as Japan and West Germany have performed since World War II. We are now the ones who must copy and adapt the policies and innovations that have been successful elsewhere. To retreat into our mythical past is to guarantee that our days of economic glory are over.   21

CONTENT

1. What examples of our ailing economy does Thurow cite? How does our standard of living compare with that of other countries? Why is it difficult to make such comparisons?
2. To what does Thurow attribute our declining economy? Why does he reject what he calls the "hard-core conservative solution" to our economic problems? What evidence does he produce to support his claim that such solutions will not work?
3. Is Thurow's essay merely a criticism of those who would return to a "golden age of economic growth"? Or, does he offer some positive solutions to the economic problems of the '80s?

ORGANIZATION

4. What is the function of the opening paragraph in an essay tracing some of the causes of America's economic decline?
5. Why does Thurow devote the first part of his essay to a comparison of the GNP and standard of living of the United States with those of several other countries? Why does he place this comparison before his analysis of the causes of economic decline?
6. What are some of the effects of the American economic decline? Why are these effects described toward the end of the essay?

TOPICS FOR WRITING

7. Select some economic subject with which you have first-hand experience (for example, finding a part-time job, increased costs of texts or tuition, trying to buy a car with high interest rates) and account for the causes of the present situation.

8. Write an essay on the economic effects of a current technological advance such as solar energy or computers.

SALLY HELGESEN
The Man in the Movies

Sally Helgesen has been a regular contributor to many magazines including Harper's, Glamour, *and* Vogue. *She published* Wildcatters *(1981), and a new novel is scheduled for publication in 1984. "The Man in the Movies," which appeared in* Harpers, *argues that the disappearance from the movies of rugged he-man heroes like John Wayne, and their replacement by ineffectual boy heroes, is due to the influence of Marlon Brando.*

The elevation of the weak, confused, and childish male to the status of national culture hero and even sex object is one of the more remarkable legacies of the 1970s. Forgive me if I confess astonishment.

A simple example. By the end of the last decade, millions of women actually admitted to finding Woody Allen attractive. Contemplating such a phenomenon, generalized astonishment must give way to rage, to an intimation that there is something to be feared in all of this. Men will never be more than women expect them to be (the reverse of this is also true, of course), and to consider just how low expectations have fallen must give cause to real alarm.

In order to conceive of Woody Allen as a sex symbol, an ideal, a woman must repudiate respect for every manly virtue—courage, fortitude, a secure sense of self, magnanimity, diligence, adventurousness—and cultivate instead a taste for timidity, self-obsession, fussiness, pettiness, hysteria. She must abandon the idea that a good man is a loving father, a reliable provider, a self-confident lover, and, should it prove necessary, a brave soldier. She must instead approve a man who brags that he is incapable of being any of these things, a man who asks only to be babied, petted, and indulged, treated like an impossible but charming little boy.

Now I don't want to pick on Woody Allen (no, maybe I do—his cringing demeanor cries out for it, begs for mistreatment). But why restrict the scope of my scorn when so many are richly deserving? In recent years, social delinquents have been thrown up for general adulation in every field of endeavor. Among painters, the late Jackson Pollack leads the way, having in the last decade attained a reputation as a genius because of $2 million posthumous sales and a fine reputation for drunkenness, vandalism, and indulgent self-destruction. Among writers, we have as our elder statesmen eternal adolescents like Norman Mailer and Philip Roth; even Jack Kerouac is being resurrected for sentimental revival because of his disorderly hijinx. And pop idols of the music world, eagerly imitating the contrived poutings and posturing of Mick Jagger or the unfocused teenaged rage of the Bob Dylan of the Sixties, yield to none in their aggressive cultivation of childish attitudes.

The bad-boy mystique has gone well beyond the frontiers of art,   5
however. The underdog-as-hero mentality has brought to prominence politicians like Ted Kennedy and Jerry Brown, men admired for their weaknesses, their misconduct, their display of "human" frailties. The same mentality has inspired many an ailing conglomerate to cast its lot with some trumped-up boy genius rather than renouncing policies of economic shortsightedness. Examples abound. Around us we see the apotheosis of weakness.

But the movies have been America's most common cultural cur-   6
rency since the second world war, and it is in the movies that the image of man as a pouting child has been nurtured with particular consistency and exquisite nuance; it is in the movies that the mannerisms of ineffectuality have been perfected. The celluloid image has proven a powerful means of influencing human behavior and style; it is known, for example, that gangsters like the late Joey Gallo learned how to act like gangsters were *supposed* to act by watching John Garfield on screen. And so a look at how the image of men has changed in the movies offers a simple means by which the observer might trace the ascent of the childish man to his current curious status as hero. We've come a long way from John Wayne, from whom we expected everything, to Woody Allen, from whom we expect nothing, and an examination of the means and the method by which we have made the journey can tell us something about how we arrived here, and why we ever chose to come.

Before 1950, the image of the American male was defined in film   7
by the personae of actors like Gary Cooper, John Wayne, Jimmy Stewart, Humphrey Bogart, and Spencer Tracy. Cooper, Wayne,

and Stewart played brave, reliable, somewhat naive men, conscientious, solid idealists capable of settling vast frontiers. Bogart and
Tracy were more worldly, less conventional in their display of courage, but they played men who lived by a strict code of honor nonetheless. They were heroes. These men might be loners or they might
be leaders, but they were never, ever, childish. Courage and maturity were elements of their sexuality. When Mrs. Lopez, the local
whore with a heart of gold, told Gary Cooper's petulant young rival
in *High Noon* that it took more than broad shoulders to make a man,
everyone knew just what she meant. A man was a creature who
acted like a man.

The change from this clear definition of manhood began in the   8
1950s. It was signaled by the appearance, first on stage and then
very quickly on screen, of Marlon Brando. Brando brought something new into his performances. Along with the "thick tongue"
that outraged those who believed that the interests of clarity and
coherence were served by good enunciation, he brought an ability
to project confusion, vulnerability, pain, a touch of self-pity, and an
extreme defensiveness that made him seem startlingly real, a contrast to the clean-cut uncomplicated good guys who had been the
country's heroes until then. Opposite Brando, the straight guy's
strength seemed rigid, his good manners looked fussy. Brando's
presence was both a challenge to and a goof on the conventional
vision of maleness.

Brando's stage and screen presence was established by his por-   9
trayal of Stanley Kowalski in *A Streetcar Named Desire;* the role became
a prototype. Brando's Kowalski was a frustrated and angry loser
whom arbitrary fate had cast into a bad situation that he was too
confused and ignorant to control, and against which he reacted
with untempered rage. This rage, like that of the motorcycle bandit
Brando played in *The Wild One,* had no target: it was diffuse, emotional, inarticulate. But the means which Brando used to express
it—flinching glances, sardonic grumbles, and ironic grimaces that
hinted at vulnerability beneath the angry surface—were so well
suited to the display of emotion that they seemed to redefine the
possibilities of how a man could act.

Brando's early style was a powerful one, and it became important
to the subsequent history of acting for three reasons. First, it was
idiosyncratic; like Joyce's fiction, its "originality" led those who were
influenced by it into the *cul de sac* of imitation. Brando may have

expressed ambivalence to perfection, but ambivalence is a single emotion, a single attitude. The legions of actors who became obsessed with this one-note technique over the thirty years following Brando's debut found it difficult to develop any range or style not convoluted by a dynamic of ambivalence and irony.

Second, because Brando usually played men who acted one way   11
but who, the audience sensed, "really" were quite another way, he reversed the simple concept that a man can be judged by his actions and held responsible for them. His characters always seemed to be saying, look, I'm basically a good guy, or at least I'd *like* to be a good guy, but sometimes I do bad stuff and everything comes out wrong: don't judge me by what I do. This emphasis on intention rather than effects coincided in the early 1950s with America's fascination with psychotherapeutic principles, and the emphasis was indeed a consequence of the new "psychological" attitude. The oldstyle American hero had been a man of right action, but the new American antihero was a man of good intentions, most of which he was incapable of carrying out. In the wider world, he was impotent.

This brings us to the third reason for Brando's sustained influ-   12
ence, the most important one to the theme of this essay: his definition of masculine sexuality as something that proceeds from weakness rather than strength. Because the typical Brando hero of the early Fifties was ambivalent and emotionally confused, he could not summon the courage and maturity that had formerly been elements of a film hero's virility. Instead, he projected a kind of teenaged eroticism, intense and unfocused, which derived emotional power from an impossible passive yearning. Frustration was the bottom line of his sexuality, the frustration of a man who cannot control his fate.

Brando's Kowalski transmutes the child-parent dynamic into the   13
world of men and women. "Stel-lah!" he cries—"Mom-my!"— acknowledging the jealous dependence he has so transparently denied, and female hearts everywhere pound at evidence of such abject submission. Indeed, the early Brando's seductive charms are precisely those of the rebellious child who mocks parental worry over his carryings-on. Into the vacuum of his sulky passivity their frantic concern is drawn, and they begin to seem desperate by contrast. Such desperation, such control of one's attention by passive manipulation, feels like desire when unimpeded by the taboos that obtain between parent and child.

I have taken the space to dissect these elements of Brando's style   1
because, as they were the most obvious and startlingly "different,"
so also were they the most imitated and hence influential. Never
mind that Brando was often a genius in varying his style and giving
it resonance: his imitators were not. Montgomery Clift's wounded
fawn (or doe) vulnerability made him seem, like Brando, startlingly
"real" on screen. Recall the effectiveness of his mumbling opposite
the blustering John Wayne in *Red River;* such tender confusion only
accentuated Wayne's villainous rigidity and made him seem a parody of masculine power. But Clift, like Brando, was an original, and
even more than Brando, he established the passive child-man as
an object worthy of sexual interest. "Tell mamma! Tell mamma all!"
Elizabeth Taylor implored him in George Steven's *A Place in the Sun;*
the dialogue was improvised to exploit the strange off-screen dynamic
between the recalcitrant fearful actor and the most beautiful woman
in the world.

After Clift, things took a turn for the worse. James Dean, another   1
magnetic, almost emblematic figure in the American cinema, used
to phone both Clift and Brando so he could hear their voices and
imitate them. In his short, spectacular career, he managed to give
one single and continuous performance—that of a confused and
self-destructive delinquent with a heart of pure gold, whose negative conception of male adulthood (Jim Backus wearing an apron,
etc.) both rationalized his predicament and hinted that he would
never become an adult himself. By dying young, and in a manner
consonant with his own self-conscious myth, Dean became the Peter
Pan of American acting, flying off to Never-Never Land without
ever having to grow up.

Few successful actors since the late 1950s have escaped the influence of this trio. Men of talent and versatility like Robert DeNiro,
men with a strong screen presence like Al Pacino, men with a one-
note abashedness like Dustin Hoffman, men with nothing except
a tired bag of tricks and tics like John Savage, men with no more
than a blank coy visage like Richard Gere—such men have all inherited a common style that enables them to win important roles but
makes it difficult for them to portray responsible adults who are at
relative peace with society *or* doing something constructive about
it if they're not, and capable of maintaining a relationship with an
adult woman. As a result, the last decade has been notable for
having as its most memorable heroes a bizarre assortment of drug

abusers, mafia thugs, psychopathic neighborhood punks, rebellious cops, rootless troublemakers, and impotent, shell-shocked war veterans.

Alternatives to the angst-ridden heirs of Brando have usually   17
been boys-will-be-boys hi-jinx types like Paul Newman and Steve McQueen, men whose eternal adolescence is demonstrated not by pouting and brooding but by an undying fascination with driving at high speeds. And there is the comic celebration of perpetual childishness as exemplified by Woody Allen. But actors—even famous and financially successful ones—who fall outside the prevailing pale of hopeless immaturity find themselves plagued by unaccountable career difficulties: Burt Reynolds has trouble being taken seriously, while Jon Voight finds problems getting roles. The mere suggestion of emotional stability that clings to such men makes them ineligible to be film heroes.

The willful idiosyncracy of Brando's defining idiom, its psycho-   18
logical emphasis upon intent rather than effect, its eroticizing of frustration and powerlessness, all achieved an unpleasant apotheosis as the last decade closed with Brando's portrayal of Colonel Kurtz in *Apocalypse Now*. Kurtz personifies the aging adolescent, the man who, having avoided using power or assuming responsibility all his life, can only abuse it hideously when at last it is thrust upon him. The mishmash of this poorly realized character, who mutters fragments and keeps his head buried in his hands half the time, was perhaps intended as a metaphor for the darkness that lies at the heart of American imperialism or Western civilization or some such grand notion. But in this film it seemed more apt as a metaphor for the confusion of an over-wrought and over-used dramatic idiom that, grown old but not matured, could result in a half-digested parody like Kurtz.

* * *

Movies are only movies, of course, they are not real life. But film   19
stars are the country's popular heroes, and play roles that people act out in life. Their behavior and mannerisms on screen and their legends off screen define and mirror what is acceptable, what works, what wins the day, what wins the girl. And what embarrasses one.

Embarrassment is a powerful inhibitor, and while some might   20
argue that inhibition of any kind is an evil, it seems more sensible

to accept that, being human and thus imperfect, we would all do well to inhibit the display of those weaknesses and failings that do society no good. Embarrassment does this by setting standards, establishing taboos.

But with the current vaunting of vulnerability, nothing seems cause for shame. I recently read an interview with a famous authoress and her husband, who is a few years younger than she. Asked if this bothered him, he replied that it had once, but it didn't now because he'd realized that he and his wife were both "basically twelve-year-olds." Now perhaps this was intended to be cute; I am really not sure. It was enough for me to be astonished that a man in his thirties, the father of a child, would make such a coy and fatuous claim without embarrassment. In another time, I might have wondered, *What kind of man is this?* But in our world, where Woody Allen can win the hearts of millions by flaunting his childishness and lack of courage, such a question is redundant.

CONTENT

1.   What three reasons does Helgesen give for the importance of Marlon Brando's style of acting? How did it come to influence other actors?
2.   Helgesen says the theme of her essay is Brando's "redefinition of masculine sexuality as something that proceeds from weakness rather than strength." How does she illustrate this? What line of descent does she trace from Brando to Woody Allen? Is she merely concerned with actors and movies?
3.   How does Helgesen illustrate Brando's influence on contemporary actors? Are her examples convincing?

ORGANIZATION

4.   Helgesen uses examples of the bad-boy mystique from fields outside of the movies. Are these examples placed in strategic position? For example, does her point about social delinquents in paragraph 4 gain support from the examples she has chosen?
5.   How much of Helgesen's point depends on the contrast between the new style and old style heroes? Are the examples of the older man-of-action hero placed effectively in the essay?

6. Helgesen begins her essay with generalizations about society and closes in the same general style. Is this an effective organizational device?

TOPICS FOR WRITING

7. Write an essay arguing that Woody Allen as a hero is preferable to John Wayne as a hero. List the positive effects of Woody Allen's type of hero on contemporary male behavior.
8. Read the portrait of Marlon Brando by Truman Capote on pages 124–27. Combining this with your own experience of watching Brando in films, show a different set of effects from those Helgesen describes.

BARRY COMMONER
Nuclear Fire

Barry Commoner (born 1917), who ran for the Presidency of the United States in 1976 on an anti-nuclear platform, is a professor of plant physiology and director of the Center for the Biology of Natural Systems at Washington University in St. Louis. His writing has appeared in a number of national magazines. In "Nuclear Fire," an early chapter from The Closing Circle *(1971), Commoner explains how he initially became concerned with environmental issues when he discovered the cause–effect relationship between nuclear tests in the 1950s and the appearance of strontium 90 in the bones of young children.*

I learned about the environment from the United States Atomic Energy Commission in 1953. Until then, like most people, I had taken the air, water, soil, and our natural surroundings more or less for granted. Although I was a scientist working on the fundamental properties of living things, I had received hardly any training in the special branch of biology that deals with environmental relations—ecology. However, like most of the scientists who had worked for the U.S. war program during World War II, I was overwhelmingly concerned with the new, enormously destructive force of nuclear energy born during the war.

In 1946 the Atomic Energy Commission (AEC) was created, to take charge of a massive U.S. program to develop the military, scientific, and industrial potential of atomic and nuclear energy. By 1951 the United States had exploded sixteen test bombs and the Soviet Union, thirteen, and the following year Great Britain joined in with its first test.

These explosions took place in remote, uninhabited areas of the world and their results were blanketed in military secrecy. The AEC normally issued only a terse announcement that a test had taken place, that a bomb's radiation had been confined to a local area, and in any case was "harmless" to the public. Public discussion of the nuclear arms race was muzzled by Cold War hysteria and McCarthyism.* But nature broke through these barriers.

On April 26, 1953, the city of Troy, New York, was drenched with a sudden cloudburst. As the rain fell, physicists in nearby university laboratories who were experimenting with radioactivity noticed a sudden surge in their "background" radiation counts. They soon discovered that the rain was highly radioactive and surmised that radioactive debris—fallout—from nuclear tests in Nevada had been carried by winds across the country and brought to earth by the heavy rain. Some of the physicists warned their wives to bring the children inside; but they made no public report, for that would violate the secrecy rules. However, scientists have a strong tendency to communicate among themselves, and soon physicists in laboratories throughout the United States were privately testing the radioactivity in rainfall and in dust wiped off their cars. It was everywhere: air, rain, soil, food, and water were contaminated by the radioactivity from nuclear explosions. Despite official secrecy, atomic energy had made its environmental debut.

All atomic radiation is destructive to living things, and many biologists regarded fallout as a potential hazard to everything alive. But, as the AEC was quick to point out, the fallout radiation reaching a person from the air, dust, or soil was low—not much higher than the intensity of radiation naturally emanated in the external environment from radium in rocks and by cosmic rays from outer space. And much of it was incapable of penetrating very deeply

---

*A period in the 1950s noted for its reactionary anti-communism, and named for the late Senator Joe McCarthy of Wisconsin.

into the body. The hazard of such radiation, from outside the body, was slight—or so it seemed.

Then a new fallout term turned up in private conversations among scientists—strontium 90. My own experience is probably typical of most nonphysicists who had no professional interest in environmental radioactivity. I recall several cryptic remarks by physicist friends that radioactive strontium—strontium 90—had been detected in fallout. More meaningful was the worried look that accompanied the information; for some reason, which was never stated, strontium 90 appeared to be a particularly dangerous form of radioactivity.

As it happens, strontium, a natural, harmless element, and its radioactive isotope, strontium 90, both move through the environment in concert with calcium, a chemically similar element. And calcium is avidly withdrawn from the soil by plants, becoming incorporated into food and then taken up in the human body. Once fallout appeared on the earth, inevitably strontium 90 would accompany calcium as it moved through the food chain, ultimately becoming concentrated, along with calcium, in vegetables, in milk, in the bones of people.

Radiation from strontium 90 cannot penetrate through more than a small fraction of an inch of living tissue. However, once it is incorporated into the body, the isotope becomes closely packed around the living cells of the bone. These cells then lie within easy reach of strontium 90 radiation, and the risk to them—for example, from cancer—becomes enormously more severe than the risk from the same amount of strontium 90 outside the body. Suddenly, many of us in the scientific community began to worry about the fallout, and by the end of 1953 this concern broke through the screen of secrecy, and the fallout problem became public. Then a serious accident during an AEC test in the Pacific Ocean in March 1954 helped to dramatize the fallout problem—the unexpected exposure to fallout of the crew of the Japanese fishing boat *The Lucky Dragon*. A number of sailors suffered serious radiation sickness; several later died of it.

In 1953 the AEC had claimed that the hazard of strontium 90 was limited to "the ingestion of bone splinters which might be intermingled with muscle tissue during the butchering and cutting of meat." By 1954 open scientific discussion of the biology of strontium 90 absorption had reminded the AEC that most people ingest far more calcium—and with it, strontium 90—from milk than from splinters of bone in their hamburgers. In that year the AEC initiated an urgent project to find ways of removing strontium 90 from contaminated milk.

Before long, strontium 90 data from all parts of the world began to appear in scientific journals, and it became clear that tests of nuclear weapons had unwittingly set off the first global environmental experiment in human history. Fallout had spread strontium 90—and several other radioactive elements—into the huge planetary network of living things; man-made radioactivity had accumulated in every plant, animal, and microorganism on the earth.

For many of us, the meaning of the environment and its importance to human life was suddenly brought to light. With elaborate skill and enormous resources, the AEC—and its Soviet and British counterparts—had accomplished what they thought to be a specific, technological feat for the single purpose of producing huge, destructive explosions. No one had *intended* to poison the earth with radioactivity or to threaten the health of human beings. But now, for the first time in the history of man, children grew up with strontium 90 built into their bones and iodine 131 embedded in their thyroid glands.

What linked the secret, supposedly isolated, nuclear explosions to the children was the environment. Winds carried fallout debris from the test site across the face of the globe; rain and snow brought it to earth; the growth of grass and food crops drew it from the soil; foods carried fallout radioactivity into the children's bodies; natural biological processes in their bones and glands intensely concentrated the radioactive elements and amplified the risk to the children's health. Each nuclear explosion thrust radioactivity into the environment, the elaborate communication network in which every living thing is enmeshed. Unwittingly, the military technicians had tied their bombs into the network, with results that no one wanted—or could have predicted.

The nuclear tests revealed how little we knew about the environmental network. When the test program began, it was assumed that fallout driven into the stratosphere by the force of a nuclear explosion would remain there for years, allowing time for much of the initial radioactivity to decay harmlessly. Only later was it learned that there are currents in the stratosphere that carry fallout to the earth in a matter of months and which, rather than allowing it to spread evenly over the globe, dump most of it in the North Temperate Zone. About 80 per cent of the world's people live there. Contrary to AEC expectations, Arctic Eskimos and Laplanders had much more fallout radioactivity in their bodies than did people in the temperate zones of the world, although the amount of fallout reaching the ground in the Arctic was less than a tenth of that in the North Temperate Zone. The reason: the distinctive biological chain of the Arctic, where lichens, unlike grass, take up fallout directly from the air rather than through the soil, which can dilute it. Thus, lichens introduce intense radioactivity into the caribou and reindeer which eat them, and into the Eskimos and Laplanders who live on caribou and reindeer. We are still unable to explain large variations in fallout uptake in local regions of the North Temperate Zone—why milk in Mandan, North Dakota, or New Orleans, Louisiana, has exceeded all other United States milk supplies in strontium 90 level, or why the world's record for strontium 90 in milk is held by the area of Milan, Italy.

We also learned, from fallout, how little was known about the risks incurred by large populations exposed to radiation or toxic substances. Before the advent of nuclear energy, medical experience with the internal effects of radiation was very limited, based largely on the fate of several hundred unfortunate women who in the 1920s had used their lips to point up brushes for applying radium-containing luminous paint on watch dials. Standards of radiation exposure were set on the assumption that, at some minimal level, the body would experience no harm at all from radiation, and the AEC used these standards in order to support their claim that fallout was "harmless" to the population as a whole. Later, when it was realized that unlike industrial workers, the general population is unable to escape exposure (for example, by quitting a job) and includes especially susceptible individuals such as children and the aged, the "acceptable" limits were reduced to about 3 per cent of their original value. Finally, experiments showed that *every* exposure to radiation, however small, carries with it *some* risk, in the form of genetic damage or cancer; that there is no absolutely "harmless" exposure to radiation. So that in the end, despite its complex scientific features, the problem of exposure to radiation becomes not a scientific matter, but one of public morality. For no one can say, on scientific grounds, how many children ought to risk thyroid cancer or genetic defects from fallout for the sake of developing a

14

new nuclear weapon, which itself is only a step toward world catastrophe. This becomes not a matter for "expert" decision, but for public judgment—a political question, and a moral one.

Fallout made its political debut in the 1956 U.S. presidential contest between Adlai E. Stevenson and Dwight D. Eisenhower. During the campaign, Dr. Evarts Graham of Washington University, a pioneer in lung surgery and the effects of smoking on lung cancer, asked several of us in the university's science faculty to prepare factual material on fallout, which Dr. Graham incorporated into a letter to Mr. Stevenson. When the letter was read in the course of a campaign speech by Mr. Stevenson, a central issue of the campaign was joined.

Mr. Stevenson lost the election, but his defeat convinced many scientists of the vital need to get the facts about nuclear weapons to the public.

In 1958 some of us at Washington University in St. Louis, together with a group of civic leaders, organized the St. Louis Committee for Nuclear Information, which through its magazine and speakers' bureau pioneered the development of what has since become the scientists' information movement, now largely devoted to public education about all environmental problems. Many of us went out into the community, to PTA meetings, to church and civic groups and tried to explain what the fallout hassle was about. We talked about the origin of strontium 90 and iodine 131 in nuclear explosions and their movement through the environment into human bodies. We discussed the potential human cost of the supposed benefits of new nuclear weapons. We emphasized that the balancing of social judgment against cost should be made by every citizen and not left to the experts. And similar efforts were being made in many parts of the country.

In 1963, much to the surprise of political observers, the United States Senate overwhelmingly confirmed the United States-USSR Limited Nuclear Test Ban Treaty ending the testing of nuclear weapons in the atmosphere by the two great nuclear powers. This unexpected event was a tribute to the political effectiveness of the scientists' campaign to inform the public about fallout.

The Nuclear Test Ban Treaty should be regarded, I believe, as the first victorious battle in the campaign to save the environment—and its human inhabitants—from the blind assaults of modern technology. It was only a small victory, for U.S. and Soviet nuclear tests continue in underground vaults, and China and France, which are not bound by the Treaty, continue atmospheric testing. But although the Nuclear Test Ban Treaty has failed to stop the nuclear arms race, it has had two important results. The first is that it has saved lives.

The human cost of fallout is not exactly known. What is known, and widely acknowledged, is that a number of serious hazards to human health—cancer, genetic defects, general life-shortening— are instigated by radiation. A good part of the natural incidence of cancer and genetic defects must be due to the "natural" (i.e., pre-fallout) level of radiation from radioactive rocks and cosmic rays. From a comparison of the natural rate of radiation-induced genetic defects with the rate of defects following the extra radiation due to fallout, it can be estimated that fallout had probably caused about 5,000 defective births in the U.S. population and about 86,000 in the world population up to 1963. The United Nations Scientific Committee on the Effects of Atomic Radiation has made a similar estimate: between 2,500 and 100,000 serious genetic defects, world-wide, due to tests up to 1958. On the other hand, Dr. Ernest Stern-glass estimates that fallout may be responsible for 400,000 infant and fetal deaths in the United States alone. Dr. Arthur R. Tamplin of the AEC's Livermore (California) Laboratory believes that a better estimate of the number of such deaths due to fallout is 4,000. Obviously the exact estimate of the human cost of fallout radiation is a matter of dispute. But the crucial scientific fact, which none of the contending parties now denies, is that fallout has exacted *some* cost in human disease and death. And the effect of the Nuclear Test Ban Treaty on that cost is equally clear. Had nuclear testing contin-ued until 1970 at the 1962 rate, the fallout radiation burden borne by human beings would now be much greater than it is—in the case of strontium 90, about eight to ten times greater.

The second important result of the treaty is that it established that nuclear weaponry is a *scientific* failure. We now know that nuclear weapons are, in fact, incapable of defending the nation: regardless of the outcome of a nuclear war between the two major powers, neither society would survive the holocaust. In this sense, the nuclear bomb is a useless weapon—a fact of which the government was apparently unaware when the decision to "go nuclear" was made sometime after 1945. No elaborate proof is needed for this assertion. It is now widely recognized that the failure of nuclear "defense"

20

21

lies in the ecological disasters that it would surely set off. To show that the United States military were unaware of this fatal fault of nuclear weapons, it is sufficient to quote the following from a 1961 report of the Rand Corporation to the United States Air Force on the ecological consequences of nuclear war:

> It is a point of view which has been strangely neglected (although many have been vaguely concerned), and detailed research is conspicuously absent. . . . Many of the ecological principles underlying the problems involved are not part of the intellectual equipment of people ordinarily concerned with Civil Defense and postwar recovery.

Like the nuclear test program, the entire system of nuclear weaponry, when subjected to an environmental test, fails.

That the AEC failed to learn a lesson in environmental science from its experience with nuclear weapons is also evident in its later efforts to develop the peaceful uses of nuclear energy. Here, for example, are samples of the efforts of Dr. Gerald W. Johnson, associate director of the Plowshare program (an AEC program to use nuclear explosions for peacetime purposes): April 1964, Columbus, Mississippi—proposal to use nuclear explosives in the construction of a 253-mile canal from the Tennessee River to the Gulf of Mexico. February 1965, St. Louis, Missouri—proposal to use nuclear explosives "inexpensively to blast navigational obstructions" in the Mississippi River. September 1965, Seattle, Washington—proposal to use nuclear explosives to dig a canal from the Columbia River to Puget Sound.

In making these proposals, AEC officials always warned the public that the promised project would have to be preceded by extensive research, designed to work out a few remaining wrinkles in the technology of nuclear excavations. These included minimizing the radiation hazard and finding some way around a provision of the Nuclear Test Ban Treaty against dissemination of radioactive material outside the nation's borders.

The needed research has now been completed in connection with a proposal to blast a new sea-level canal across the Isthmus of Panama. This was so monumental a scheme as to require a six-year study by a presidential commission. The commission's report, issued in December 1970, is illuminating. After spending $17 million studying the possibility of constructing the canal with nuclear explosives, the commission recommended that the canal be constructed by *conventional* methods. The reasons given for rejecting the nuclear approach included "unanswered questions about the safety of nuclear devices" and "possible conflicts with the Nuclear Test Ban Treaty."

In April 1964, Dr. Johnson, speaking at Columbus, Mississippi, was asked by a member of the audience: "Has Project Plowshare ever done anything of practical benefit to us?"   26

His reply: "The answer is no."   27

Today the answer is still no. Since it began in 1957, the Plowshare program has produced stacks of reports, dozens of scientific symposia, numerous press releases—and two wells that yield gas which is probably too radioactive for commercial use. The total cost is about $138 million. In 1970 federal funds were withdrawn from Plowshare, and there is little prospect that they will be restored. Plowshare has been a $138 million exercise in futility. It has foundered in the environment.   28

The only peacetime use of nuclear energy which is now *operational* is the generation of electric power. Like every other nuclear activity in the United States, this is under the aegis of the AEC. In its enabling legislation, the AEC is charged with promoting the domestic use of nuclear energy. It also sets the safety standards for the construction and operation of nuclear plants, grants the necessary licenses, and checks for violations. With this unprecedented range of administrative powers concentrated in a single agency, along with the AEC's overriding importance in the national military program and its essentially unhindered access to funds, the nuclear power industry has grown rapidly.   29

The first full-scale nuclear power plant in the United States went into operation in 1957. By 1965 there were eleven operating plants. In 1970 fourteen plants were in operation, and seventy-eight more were under construction or in preparation. By 1975 eighty-four plants are expected to be in operation. Although nuclear plants now account for only about one per cent of the nation's total electric output, this figure is expected to rise to 37 per cent by 1980 and to more than 50 per cent by 2000.   30

In the light of these statistics, the nuclear power industry in the United States would appear to be a spectacular success story. However, anyone attending the industry's annual meeting, the Atomic Industrial Forum, in 1970, would have received a very different impression. In past years such meetings were devoted to speeches   31 extolling the undiluted virtues of nuclear power and to more technical expositions on the engineering of nuclear reactors. That year a new subject dominated the talks: ecology. For the first time, the industry had been forced publicly to face the environmental consequences of its operation. And the outlook was not very bright.

Unlike fossil-fuel power plants, nuclear power plants do not produce chemical pollutants such as sulfur dioxide or dust. However, they do produce radioactive pollutants. The AEC claims that this is no cause for public concern because nuclear plants release radioactive materials into the environment in amounts which are well below AEC safety standards. Nevertheless, in recent years public concern has been sufficiently intense to delay, and in some cases block, the construction of several projected power plants. In the words of the then chairman of the AEC, Dr. Glenn T. Seaborg, "The public is up-tight about the environment."

But the AEC has been harassed by more than public complaints. In Minnesota the State Water Pollution Control Agency adopted environmental requirements for a proposed nuclear reactor which are appreciably more stringent than those of the AEC. The AEC disputed the state's right to impose these standards, and the power company attacked the action in the courts. Then a new concern about the environmental effects of radiation arose within the AEC's own Livermore Laboratory. There, in 1963—the year of the limited Nuclear Test Ban Treaty—the AEC decided to establish a research group to "plan and conduct studies of environmental contamination due to release of radioactivity from nuclear detonations for peaceful or military purposes." Dr. John W. Gofman, professor of medical physics at the University of California (which operates the Livermore Laboratory for the AEC), was chosen to direct the program. Since 1963 Dr. Gofman, in collaboration with Dr. Tamplin, has produced a long series of reports on radioactive contamination of the environment. A chief outcome of this work is their proposal that the AEC radiation standards be reduced to 1/10 their present level —a proposal which was then intensely opposed by the AEC and the nuclear power industry.

Some sense of the scope of this controversy can be gained from the following: Drs. Gofman and Tamplin concluded that if the radiation dosage "acceptable" under AEC standards were in fact received by the total United States population, the result would be 32,000 extra deaths each year, from cancer and leukemia. In rebuttal, the late Dr. Theos J. Thompson, an AEC commissioner, asserted that radiation exposure to the general population due to the actual operation of the nuclear power industry is less than 1/17,000 of the exposure permitted by the AEC standard. On the other hand, Dr. K.Z. Morgan of the AEC's Oak Ridge National Laboratory has calculated that extra deaths annually due to all types of radiation-induced disease resulting from present nuclear industry operations are about one-half per cent of the deaths expected from exposure at the acceptable standard. This would leave little room for complacency, for the expected expansion of the nuclear power industry might well take radiation exposures beyond even the present "acceptable" standard by the year 2000, which itself might be reduced as well.

In 1971, after strongly resisting proposals for more stringent reactor emission standards, the AEC gave in to a degree by proposing an appreciable reduction in permissible radioactive release. However, in taking this action, the AEC gave no explanation for its earlier opposition to more rigorous standards or for its continued opposition to the Gofman-Tamplin proposal. Until these discrepancies are cleared up, the controversy over the environmental effects of nuclear power plants will continue. Yet on the outcome of this controversy hangs the entire future of the nuclear power industry. Radioactive emissions from nuclear plants may arise from the development of tiny leaks in the metal sheaths around the reactor's fuel elements. The fabrication of these sheaths is an exacting task; long stretches of thin metal tubing must be made to withstand not only mechanical strains, but also the deteriorating effects of intense radiation. Reducing the present amounts of radioactive emissions will require either the improvement of this already highly advanced and difficult technology or the addition of devices which remove, much more effectively than at present, radioactive materials in liquid and gaseous reactor effluents. Either of these developments would be sufficiently expensive to reduce the present economic position that nuclear power holds, tenuously, against competition from more conventional generators. If the power industry is required to adjust to this change through its own private enterprise, it will be forced, by economic considerations, to choose conventional generators over nuclear ones. On the other hand, if the difference is to be made up by government subsidy, the industry faces the prospect of admitting deeper government penetration into its economic operations.

35

At the same time, the power industry is confronted by a growing   36
national shortage of electricity. Blackouts and brownouts have become
increasingly commonplace in certain areas of the United States.
Thus, on one hand, the industry is pressed to construct new power
plants as soon as possible; on the other, it faces the need to choose
between nuclear generators and conventional ones. The hope that
the bonanza of nuclear power would enable the nation to expand
power generation without restraint has suddenly been shattered
against the same barrier which nuclear technology has, at every
turn, confronted—the environment.

When the world learned, on that fateful day in 1945, of the suc-   37
cessful construction of an atomic bomb, it was clear that a new
period in human history had begun. Those who have marked the
day by remembering the Hiroshima dead foresaw an era of deadly
peril for humanity and feared an inexorable march toward the holocaust of a Third, and final, World War. Those who sensed, instead,
in the brilliant flash of the bomb that man had at last "harnessed
the power of the stars," dreamed of an era in which, with unlimited
power, mankind—or some lesser portion of it—could achieve all
the goals that power commands.

As the atomic era has unfolded since 1945, the contrast between   38
these two visions has sharpened and the gulf between those who
follow them has grown wider. On one side are those who fear that
humanity will be crushed beneath the ungovernable power of nuclear
technology; many of them are the young, who were born with the
bomb and have lived a life in which, because of it, doomsday may
come tomorrow. On the other side are some of the elders, who
possess or hope to possess some of the new power, if need be at
the cost of human lives.

Despite this confrontation, there is a widespread conviction that   39
the new knowledge is sound, that the new technology is therefore
competent, and that the new power is thereby irresistible. The first
25 years of the atomic age tell us that this belief is deeply, tragically,
wrong. Isolated on a Pacific island or confined to the grounds of a
power plant, nuclear energy is a success. It works: it vaporizes the
island; it sends electricity surging out of the power plant. But neither the island nor the power plant—nor anything else on the earth's
surface—exists apart from the thin, dynamic fabric that envelopes
the planet: its environment, the ecosphere. And once power from
the split atom impinges on the environment, as it must, we discover

that our knowledge is incomplete, that the new technology is therefore incompetent and that the new power is thereby something that *must* be governed if we are to survive.

This, it seems to me, is the meaning of the first environmental   40 encounter of the new age of technology. Our experience with nuclear power tells us that modern technology has achieved a scale and intensity that begin to match that of the global system in which we live. It reminds us that we cannot wield this power without deeply intruding on the delicate environmental fabric that supports us. It warns us that our capability to intrude on the environment far outstrips our knowledge of the consequences. It tells us that every environmental incursion, whatever its benefits, has a cost—which, from the still silent testimony of the world's nuclear weapons, may be survival.

Yet this same experience with the first 25 years of the nuclear age   41 has a more hopeful message: seen in its true, environmental context, the power of nuclear technology is subject less to the control of the technologist than to the governance of the public will.

CONTENT

1. Commoner has covered a wide range of nuclear issues in this piece, from nuclear fallout of atmospheric testing to nuclear power plants. Does any single concern link these diverse topics?
2. Do you agree with Commoner's final statement? Why or why not?
3. How well does Commoner explain the connection between strontium 90 and health hazards? Is his argument convincing?

ORGANIZATION

4. Why does Commoner begin with his personal recollections of the connection between nuclear energy and human health?
5. Compare Commoner's position on nuclear weapons and a potential holocaust with those of Hans Bethe and Jonathan Schell (quoted on page 275). Who presents the most convincing cause–effect argument for the danger posed by nuclear armaments? Why?
6. What were the effects of the Nuclear Test Ban Treaty? How is this cause–effect sequence linked with the cause–effect sequence dealing with strontium 90? Is this organization effective?

TOPICS FOR WRITING

7. Select a controversial subject (such as air bags being required in autos), and using cause–effect, argue in favor of, or against the proposal.

8. Write an essay on the positive or negative effects of playing video games.

Comparison/Contrast

Next to giving examples, *comparison and contrast* are two of the most common ways of developing and clarifying a subject. *Comparison* shows the similarities between two or more items belonging to the same class or category. For example, you might wish to show the similarities between two cars, two books, two teachers, two resorts, two border towns—the list is endless. *Contrast* reveals the differences between any of the above pairs. In both cases, the point of showing the similarities or differences is illumination, the desire to explain something about the subject by showing how it resembles or differs from something else. For example, you might wish to compare the foreign policies of two Democratic Presidents—Harry S. Truman and Jimmy Carter—or two Republican Presidents—Gerry Ford, and Ronald Reagan. It would make little sense, however, to compare the skill of Reggie Jackson with that of Ronald Reagan, unless you placed them in a larger category—"public figures" or "celebrities"—and wished to make a point that would link the two men—for example, how public figures handle threats on their lives.

Remember, the purpose of comparison and contrast is to clarify, to illuminate the subject; so both obvious and far-fetched similarities and differences should be avoided unless they clarify or illuminate. For example, if you wish to make the point that compared with that of doctors, nurses' pay is inequitable, it would serve no purpose to compare the pay of interns with that of experienced nurses. But, if you compare the pay of RNs with that of experienced physicans, and if you compare their work hours and the expense of their education, then your comparison would both clarify and illuminate your point. This is what David Osborne does in his essay "Rich Doctors, Poor Nurses."

Once you have your examples in hand, how do you organize a comparison or contrast? Let's return to the earlier hypothetical comparison of two Democratic Presidents—Harry S. Truman and Jimmy Carter—to illustrate some alternate ways to organize a comparison of their foreign policies. Suppose you wish to point out three similarities: (1) Both were confronted with Russian aggression overseas; (2) both contended with a Congress reluctant to assist in implementing their foreign policy; and (3) both were compelled to take unpopular stands on foreign policy issues. No doubt you would want to produce examples to support these similarities, but how should you group this material? The usual methods are called the *unit method* and the *parts method*. In the unit method, each item—Truman and Carter—is thought of as a single unit, and all three similarities are discussed in succession. Graphically, it would look like this:

	Truman	*Carter*
Unit Method	Characteristic 1	Characteristic 1
	Characteristic 2	Characteristic 2
	Characteristic 3	Characteristic 3

But the *parts method* breaks up the items into parts and treats each characteristic together. A parts comparison would look like this:

	Truman *Carter*	*Truman* *Carter*	*Truman* *Carter*
Parts Method			
	Characteristic 1	Characteristic 2	Characteristic 3

Neither method is more correct than the other, but each has distinct advantages and disadvantages that make it more or less appropriate, depending on your intention. The parts method gives a sharper comparison or contrast, but the totality of the items may be lost in this fragmentary approach; the unit method gives the reader a sense of the complete item in each case, but the comparable or contrasting details may be forgotten by the time you get to the second item unless you add summary reminders, here and there, of what went before.

The following selection, which contrasts two different theories about the effectiveness of government monetary and fiscal policies on economic activities, uses the unit method of organizing. Notice how the contrasting characteristics of the Keynesians and the Monetarists are treated in two separate units.

It's not quite the Montagues and the Capulets, even the Hatfields and the McCoys, again, but a long-time feud has been raging between two prominent "families" of economists.

One clan—the Keynesians, self-styled followers (or disciples) of John Maynard Keynes—argues that money and monetary policy have little or no impact on income and employment, particularly during severe economic downturns; and that government taxation and spending are the most effective remedies for inflation and unemployment, especially the latter.

The other group—the Monetarists, largely rallying around Milton Friedman of the University of Chicago—emphasizes money's role in the economic process. Spurning the notion that fiscal policy is paramount, they argue that a rule which requires the monetary authorities to cause the stock of money to increase at some constant rate, say 3 percent annually, would effectively reduce fluctuations in prices, output, and employment. [J. H. Wood, "Money and Output: Keynes and Friedman in Historical Perspective," *Business Review* (September 1974), 3–4.]

Many writers mix the two patterns. A writer can present some of the characteristics in unit form and finish up by switching to the parts method. We can only suggest, in the short space of this introduction, how these two patterns can be mixed, but here is a transitional passage from Bruce Catton's essay contrasting the characters of Civil War generals Lee and Grant, the first paragraph of which sums up the contrasting unit pattern showing the differences between Grant and Lee; the second paragraph begins the parts pattern which compares the two men.

So Grant and Lee were in complete contrast, representing two diametrically opposed elements in American life. Grant was the modern man emerging, beyond him, ready to come on the stage, was the great age of steel and machinery, of crowded cities and a restless burgeoning vitality. Lee might have ridden down from the old age of chivalry, lance in hand, silken banner fluttering over his head. Each man the perfect champion of his cause, drawing both his strengths and his weaknesses from the people he led.

Yet it was not all contrast, after all. Different as they were—in background, in personality, in underlying aspiration—these two great soldiers had much in common. Under everything else, they were marvelous fighters. Furthermore, their fighting qualities were really very much alike. ["Grant and Lee: A Study in Contrasts," *The American Story,* ed. Earl Schenck Miers (Channel Press, 1956), 222.]

Like Catton's subjects, many things have *both* similarities and differences; consequently, if it is within your purposes, you can mix comparison with contrast or units with parts.

Successful comparisons and contrasts, then, follow from a clear purpose and a logical plan of organization. Wendell Berry's essay "The Road and the Wheel" opens with a clear statement of the purpose and the items of his contrast: "There are, I believe, two fundamentally opposed views of the nature of human life and experience in the world: one holds that though natural processes may be cyclic, there is within a human domain the processes of which are linear; the other, much older, holds that human life is subject to the same cyclic patterns as all other life." Berry later summarized the contrasting characteristics of his two views with a schematic outline in the middle of his essay indicating the plan he has been following. Even this bare outline demonstrates that Berry's careful organization is a result of planning, not happenstance.

The opposing characteristics of the linear and cyclic visions might be graphed something like this:

Linear	*Cyclic*
Progress—The conquest of nature	Atonement with creation*
The Promised Land Motif in the Westward Movement	Black Elk's sacred hoop, the community of creation
Heavenly aspiration without earthy reconciliation or stewardship. The creation as commodity.	Reconciliation of heaven and earth in aspiration toward responsible life. The creation as source *and end.*
Training—Programming	Education—Culture Process
Possession	Usufruct, relinquishment
Quantity	Quality
Newness—The unique and "original"	Renewal—the recurring
Life	Life and death

The strategy employed here—an explicit statement of purpose and a logical outline—is a good one to follow if you wish to ensure that your essay is clear and logical.

*See "The Likenesses of Atonement (At-one-ment)" (pages 358–62) in the section on Analogy.

SHORT EXAMPLE—COMPARISON/CONTRAST

CARSON McCULLERS
The Lover and the Beloved

Carson McCullers (1917–1967) published her first novel The Heart Is a Lonely
Hunter *(1940) at age 23. Reflections in a Golden Eye (1941), A Member of
the Wedding (1946) (adapted by McCullers in 1950 for the stage), and* Clock
Without Hands *(1961), all have the common subjects of the power of love and
the persistence of pain and loneliness. In the following selection from* The Ballad
of the Sad Cafe *(1951), McCullers explains how even a grotesque person can
become a love object, and that there is a profound difference between being a lover
and being the beloved.*

First of all, love is a joint experience between two persons—but 1
the fact that it is a joint experience does not mean that it is a similar
experience to the two people involved. There are the lover and the
beloved, but these two come from different countries. Often the
beloved is only a stimulus for all the stored-up love which has lain
quiet within the lover for a long time hitherto. And somehow every
lover knows this. He feels in his soul that his love is a solitary thing.
He comes to know a new, strange loneliness and it is this knowledge
which makes him suffer. So there is only one thing for the lover to
do. He must house his love within himself as best he can; he must
create for himself a whole new inward world—a world intense and
strange, complete in himself. Let it be added here that this lover
about whom we speak need not necessarily be a young man saving
for a wedding ring—this lover can be man, woman, child, or indeed
any human creature on this earth.

Now, the beloved can also be of any description. The most out- 2
landish people can be the stimulus for love. A man may be a dod-
dering great-grandfather and still love only a strange girl he saw in
the streets of Cheehaw one afternoon two decades past. The preacher
may love a fallen woman. The beloved may be treacherous, greasy-
headed, and given to evil habits. Yes, and the lover may see this as
clearly as anyone else—but that does not affect the evolution of his
love one whit. A most mediocre person can be the object of a love
which is wild, extravagant, and beautiful as the poison lilies of the
swamp. A good man may be the stimulus for a love both violent

and debased, or a jabbering madman may bring about in the soul of someone a tender and simple idyll. Therefore, the value and quality of any love is determined solely by the lover himself.

It is for this reason that most of us would rather love than be   3 loved. Almost everyone wants to be the lover. And the curt truth is that, in a deep secret way, the state of being beloved is intolerable to many. The beloved fears and hates the lover, and with the best of reasons. For the lover is forever trying to strip bare his beloved. The lover craves any possible relation with the beloved, even if this experience can cause him only pain.

DISCUSSION

McCullers, by contrasting the qualities of the lover with the beloved, is demonstrating the power of love to change or inflict suffering on the lover, and, paradoxically, the resentment that the beloved feels over this intrusion into what has hitherto been the private domain of the beloved. The passage uses the unit method to discuss the qualities of the lover in the first paragraph and the contrasting characteristics of the beloved in the second paragraph. The contrast is signalled in the first paragraph by the clause, "these two come from different countries." The third paragraph, using the parts method, juxtaposes these qualities more closely, swinging back and forth in alternate sentences between the lover and the beloved. The pathetic picture of the lover-as-fool and the portrait of the beloved-as-ingrate dominate the contrast. McCullers claims that lovers are possessed of a divine madness which transforms even a dull, average person into something "wild, extravagant, and beautiful as the poison lilies of the swamp." Notice how the generalizations and abstractions of the first paragraph become much more vivid and concrete when McCullers describes the beloved. The overall purpose is to focus on the pain and loneliness that often accompany love.

JOAN DIDION
Many Mansions

*Joan Didion was educated at the University of California, Berkeley. She has
written three novels—*Run, River *(1963),* Play It As It Lays *(1970) and*
A Book of Common Prayer *(1976)—several screenplays—*A Star Is Born
(1976), and most recently True Confessions *(1981) with her husband, novelist
John Gregory Dunne. Her essays—collected in two volumes:* Slouching Toward
Bethlehem *(1979), and* The White Album *(1979)—are known for their sharp
social observations and her penetrating wit.* "Many Mansions" *goes well beyond
the absurd California situation which produced two unliveable Governor's
mansions to comment on contemporary values.*

The new official residence for governors of California, unland-   1
scaped, unfurnished, and unoccupied since the day construction
stopped in 1975, stands on eleven acres of oaks and olives on a
bluff overlooking the American River outside Sacramento. This is
the twelve-thousand-square-foot house that Ronald and Nancy
Reagan built. This is the sixteen-room house in which Jerry Brown
declined to live. This is the vacant house which cost the State of
California one-million-four, not including the property, which was
purchased in 1969 and donated to the state by such friends of the
Reagans as Leonard K. Firestone of Firestone Tire and Rubber and
Taft Schreiber of the Music Corporation of America and Holmes
Tuttle, the Los Angeles Ford dealer. All day at this empty house
three maintenance men try to keep the bulletproof windows clean
and the cobwebs swept and the wild grass green and the rattle-
snakes down by the river and away from the thirty-five exterior wood
and glass doors. All night at this empty house the lights stay on
behind the eight-foot chainlink fence and the guard dogs lie at bay
and the telephone, when it rings, startles by the fact that it works.
"Governor's Residence," the guards answer, their voices laconic,
matter-of-fact, quite as if there were some phantom governor to
connect. Wild grass grows where the tennis court was to have been.
Wild grass grows where the pool and sauna were to have been. The
American is the river in which gold was discovered in 1848, and it
once ran fast and full past here, but lately there have been upstream
dams and dry years. Much of the bed is exposed. The far bank has
been dredged and graded. That the river is running low is of no

real account, however, since one of the many peculiarities of the new Governor's Residence is that it is so situated as to have no clear view of the river.

It is an altogether curious structure, this one-story one-million-four dream house of Ronald and Nancy Reagan's. Were the house on the market (which it will probably not be, since, at the time it was costing a million-four, local real estate agents seemed to agree on $300,000 as the top price ever paid for a house in Sacramento County), the words used to describe it would be "open" and "contemporary," although technically it is neither. "Flow" is a word that crops up quite a bit when one is walking through the place, and so is "resemble." The walls "resemble" local adobe, but they are not: they are the same concrete blocks, plastered and painted a rather stale yellowed cream, used in so many supermarkets and housing projects and Coca-Cola bottling plants. The door frames and the exposed beams "resemble" native redwood, but they are not: they are construction-grade lumber of indeterminate quality, stained brown. If anyone ever moves in, the concrete floors will be carpeted, wall to wall. If anyone ever moves in, the thirty-five exterior wood and glass doors, possibly the single distinctive feature in the house, will be, according to plan, "draped." The bathrooms are small and standard. The family bedrooms open directly onto the nonexistent swimming pool, with all its potential for noise and distraction. To one side of the fireplace in the formal living room there is what is known in the trade as a "wet bar," a cabinet for bottles and glasses with a sink and a long vinyl-topped counter. (This vinyl "resembles" slate.) In the entire house there are only enough bookshelves for a set of the World Book and some Books of the Month, plus maybe three Royal Doulton figurines and a back file of *Connoisseur*, but there is $90,000 worth of other teak cabinetry, including the "refreshment center" in the "recreation room." There is that most ubiquitous of all "luxury features," a bidet in the master bathroom. There is one of those kitchens which seem designed exclusively for defrosting by microwave and compacting trash. It is a house built for a family of snackers.

And yet, appliances notwithstanding, it is hard to see where the million-four went. The place has been called, by Jerry Brown, a "Taj Mahal." It has been called a "white elephant," a "resort," a "monument to the colossal ego of our former governor." It is not exactly any of these things. It is simply and rather astonishingly an enlarged version of a very common kind of California tract house, a monument not to colossal ego but to a weird absence of ego, a case study in the architecture of limited possibilities, insistently and malevolently "democratic," flattened out, mediocre and "open" and as devoid of privacy or personal eccentricity as the lobby area in a Ramada Inn. It is the architecture of "background music," decorators, "good taste." I recall once interviewing Nancy Reagan, at a time when her husband was governor and the construction on this house had not yet begun. We drove down to the State Capitol Building that day, and Mrs. Reagan showed me how she had lightened and brightened offices there by replacing the old burnished leather on the walls with the kind of beige burlap then favored in new office buildings. I mention this because it was on my mind as I walked through the empty house on the American River outside Sacramento.

From 1903 until Ronald Reagan, who lived in a rented house in 4 Sacramento while he was governor ($1,200 a month, payable by the state to a group of Reagan's friends), the governors of California lived in a large white Victorian Gothic House at 16th and H Streets in Sacramento. This extremely individual house, three stories and a cupola and the face of Columbia the Gem of the Ocean worked into the molding over every door, was built in 1877 by a Sacramento hardware merchant named Albert Gallatin. The state paid $32,500 for it in 1903 and my father was born in a house a block away in 1908. This part of town has since run to seed and small business, the kind of place where both Squeaky Fromme and Patricia Hearst could and probably did go about their business unnoticed, but the Governor's Mansion, unoccupied and open to the public as State Historical Landmark Number 823, remains Sacramento's premier example of eccentric domestic architecture.

As it happens I used to go there once in a while, when Earl 5 Warren was governor and his daughter Nina was a year ahead of me at C.K. McClatchy Senior High School. Nina was always called "Honey Bear" in the papers and in *Life* magazine but she was called "Nina" at C. K. McClatchy Senior High School and she was called "Nina" (or sometimes "Warren") at weekly meetings of the Mañana Club, a local institution to which we both belonged. I recall being initiated into the Mañana Club one night at the old Governor's Mansion, in a ceremony which involved being blindfolded and standing around Nina's bedroom in a state of high apprehension about secret rites which never materialized. It was the custom for the members to hurl mild insults at the initiates, and I remember being dumbfounded to hear Nina, by my fourteen-year-old lights the most glamorous and unapproachable fifteen-year-old in America, characterize me as "stuck on herself." There in the Governor's Mansion that night I learned for the first time that my face to the world was not necessarily the face in my mirror. "No smoking on the third floor," everyone kept saying. "Mrs. Warren *said*. No smoking on the third floor *or else*."

Firetrap or not, the old Governor's Mansion was at that time my favorite house in the world, and probably still is. The morning after I was shown the new "Residence" I visited the old "Mansion," took the public tour with a group of perhaps twenty people, none of whom seemed to find it as ideal as I did. "All those stairs," they murmured, as if stairs could no longer be tolerated by human physiology. "All those stairs," and "all that waste space." The old Governor's Mansion does have stairs and waste space, which is precisely why it remains the kind of house in which sixty adolescent girls might gather and never interrupt the real life of the household. The bedrooms are big and private and high- ceilinged and they do not open on the swimming pool and one can imagine reading in one of them, or writing a book, or closing the door and crying until dinner. The bathrooms are big and airy and they do not have bidets but they do have room for hampers, and dressing tables, and chairs on which to sit and read a story to a child in the bathtub. There are hallways wide and narrow, stairs front and back, sewing rooms, ironing rooms, secret rooms. On the gilt mirror in the library there is worked a bust of Shakespeare, a pretty fancy for a hardware merchant in a California farm town in 1877. In the kitchen there is no trash compactor and there is no "island" with the appliances built in but there are two pantries, and a nice old table with a marble top for rolling out pastry and making divinity fudge and chocolate leaves. The morning I took the tour our guide asked if anyone could think why the old table had a marble top. There were a dozen or so other women in the group, each of an age to have cooked unnumbered meals, but not one of them could think of a single use for a slab of marble in the kitchen. It occurred to me that we had finally evolved a society in which knowledge of pastry marble, like a taste for stairs and closed doors, could be construed as "elitist," and as I left the Governor's Mansion I felt very like the heroine of Mary McCarthy's *Birds of America*, the one who located America's moral decline in the disappearance of the first course.

A guard sleeps at night in the old mansion, which has been   7
condemned as a dwelling by the state fire marshal. It costs about
$85,000 a year to keep guards at the new official residence. Mean-
while the current governor of California, Edmund G. Brown, Jr.,
sleeps on a mattress on the floor in the famous apartment for which
he pays $275 a month out of his own $49,100 annual salary. This
has considerable and potent symbolic value, as do the two empty
houses themselves, most particularly the house the Reagans built
on the river. It is a great point around the Capitol these days to
have "never seen" the house on the river. The governor himself
has "never seen" it. The governor's press secretary, Elisabeth Cole-
man, has "never seen" it. The governor's chief of staff, Gary Davis,
admits to having seen it, but only once, when "Mary McGrory
wanted to see it." This unseen house on the river is, Jerry Brown
has said, "not my style."

As a matter of fact this is precisely the point about the house on   8
the river—the house is not Jerry Brown's style, not Mary McGrory's
style, *not our style*—and it is a point which presents a certain problem, since the house so clearly *is* the style not only of Jerry Brown's
predecessor but of millions of Jerry Brown's constituents. Words
are chosen carefully. Reasonable objections are framed. One hears
about how the house is too far from the Capitol, too far from the
Legislature. One hears about the folly of running such a lavish
establishment for an unmarried governor and one hears about the
governor's temperamental austerity. One hears every possible reason for not living in the house except the one that counts: it is the
kind of house that has a wet bar in the living room. It is the kind
of house that has a refreshment center. It is the kind of house in
which one does not live, but there is no way to say this without
getting into touchy evanescent and finally inadmissable questions
of taste, and ultimately of class. I have seldom seen a house so
evocative of the unspeakable.

CONTENT

1. What does Didion mean when she says in the conclusion of her
   essay that the new governor's mansion is "evocative of the
   unspeakable"? Does she just mean that people don't like to talk
   about it?

2.   What details does Didion single out in each mansion? From her presentation, which mansion do you think she prefers? Why? How does the narrative about the pastry marble (paragraph 6) bring home her point about the mansions?

ORGANIZATION

3.   Didion has chosen to organize her contrasting descriptions of the two mansions using the unit method. What is the advantage of this?

4.   Why does Didion include the narrative section (paragraph 5) about her initiation into a secret society in high school? Does it interrupt the contrast? How does it contrast with the last line of paragraph 2 describing the new mansion as "a house built for a family of snackers"?

5.   Why does Didion include the final two paragraphs after the description of the old mansion?

TOPICS FOR WRITING

6.   Poet Philip Larkin has written, "How we live measures our own natures." Contrast two residences, or two rooms occupied by different people, to illustrate Larkin's point.

7.   Describe an old house and a new house in your neighborhood, drawing a contrast between them and explaining which you prefer.

DAVID OSBORNE
Rich Doctors, Poor Nurses

David Osborne (born 1951) has written for the New Republic, Harper's, The Atlantic, The New York Times Magazine, *and* Mother Jones. *A specialist in political and economic affairs, he occasionally writes about medicine, an interest he shares with his wife who is a resident in obstetrics and gynecology at Yale New Haven Hospital. In "Rich Doctors, Poor Nurses," Osborne takes a hard look at the economic disparity between the earnings of doctors and nurses, compares the required education and responsibilities of each profession, and concludes that doctors are "cashing in" in an unprecedented way in our society, while nurses are exploited for performing what is traditionally regarded as "women's work."*

Equality of material reward is not our nation's strong suit. To pick 1
a nice, clean statistic, the top 10 percent of all American workers
take home some twenty times what their counterparts on the bottom rung earn. West Germany, Japan, and Sweden sport ratios
closer to ten to one.

Until recently, many defenders of the American Way tended to 2
be vaguely embarrassed by such comparisons. But in the current
ideological climate, American inequality tends to be quite readily
and bluntly justified as the product of a free economy, unencum-
bered by social-democratic meddling. Do executives at large corporations average over $500,000 a year while the average American
worker falls short of $15,000? Well (our president might reassure
us), that is simply the market working its magic—allocating scarce
resources, rewarding merit, providing incentives for the players in
our economic game to develop skills, assume responsibility, take
risks, or endure unpleasant travail.

The economic justification for our material inequality is not just 3
an appealing theory: it purports to reflect how things actually work.
Does it? Certainly a good deal of casual evidence suggests that it
does not. American executive salaries, for example, have kept on
rising in recent years even as the economic performance of American firms has deteriorated. "Any similarity between rewards received
and performances demonstrated often seems almost coincidental,"
concluded a recent *Fortune* magazine survey of 140 companies.

But top corporate executives are a tiny minority, a relatively small 4
number of well-born, well-positioned, or even unscrupulous individuals. To better test the connection between individual prosperity
and productivity, we might look at our third largest industry,
accounting for a tenth of our GNP: the health care business.

Average earnings in health care are similar to those in other 5
industries, but, as health economist Victor Fuchs puts it, "the coef-
ficient of variation, which measures the relative variance or inequality in earnings, is higher for health than for any other industry." In
other words: doctors make lots of money, while nurses make little.
And the question is, does this vast disparity between doctors' and
nurses' earnings reflect the free market at work, rewarding risk,
skill, and effort, or is it the result of less easily justifiable causes?

As of 1980, there were approximately 450,000 physicians active 6
in the United States, as compared with about 1.2 million registered
nurses (RNs), 400,000 licensed practical nurses (LPNs), and almost

a million nurses' aides, orderlies, and assistants. To get these terms straight, the aides and orderlies do the most menial work, while LPNs generally also do physical labor, such as changing sheets and helping patients out of bed. The RNs are in charge, with responsibility for executing doctors' orders, giving medications, and keeping track of patients' conditions. LPNs normally have only a year of training, while RNs average three years (many have bachelor's and master's degrees). The word "nurse" in the industry is used almost synonymously with RN—a custom I will follow.

According to the American Nurses Association, registered nurses earned an average of $19,381 per annum in January 1982. The figures varied from $27,865 for administrators down to $12,872 for RNs in physicians' offices (an interesting comment on doctor-nurse relationships). The most typical RNs—staff nurses in hospitals—averaged $18,331.

According to *Medical Economics*, a trade publication that publishes annual surveys of doctors' earnings, the median net income for a private, office-based physician in 1980 was $83,700. The one in eleven doctors who worked full time on the staff of a hospital made less—$61,590 in 1980—but he or she also garnered more benefits, such as retirement plans, malpractice insurance, and sometimes free offices in which to see private patients. Since physicians' earnings have recently been rising by about $5,000 a year, the office-based median is undoubtably over $90,000 by now, and even that may be low. *Medical Economic's* figures are provided by physicians themselves who are considered notorious underreporters by the IRS.

Comparing doctors' and nurses' incomes is tricky, however. It is often said, on the basis of figures like those just cited, that doctors earn more than five times as much as nurses. But to generate a fair comparison one must make quite a few adjustments, all allowing room for bias. First, we are comparing an average for nurses with a median for physicians, the median being the point at which 50 percent make more and 50 percent less. According to *Medical Economics*, averages tend to run 20 percent higher than medians when it comes to physicians—placing the current average at around $110,000—because a minority of superrich doctors (heart surgeons and the like) skew the figures upward. The median may be more representative, as *Medical Economics* argues. Still, over a third of all office-based physicians made over $100,000 even in 1980, and by 1982 the typical doctor could expect many good years at well over the magic hundred grand. Splitting the difference, let us take $100,000 as a fair average for office-based physicians in 1982.

Doctors, however, work longer hours than nurses. *Medical Eco-* 10 *nomics* says the median is sixty-one hours, a figure that could well be inflated, since part-time physicians are probably less likely to return the survey form than those with full practices (and other sources give lower figures). Full-time RNs work an average of forty-one hours a week, according to the Bureau of Labor Statistics. But in the nurses' case the figure should probably be adjusted upward, since many nurses routinely put in unpaid overtime to complete their paperwork and make sure the next shift has adequate information on its patients.

Again using strictly seat-of-the-pants methodology, let us say 11 doctors work sixty hours a week and nurses forty-five. So, for a fair comparison of earnings, we must knock 25 percent off the figure for physicians. Comparing $75,000 with $19,381—or $18,331, the most representative figure—we find physicians making roughly four times as much as nurses.

If the free market were working, the income differential between 12 doctors and nurses would be just enough to assure a sufficient supply of the two professions. Reality, however, appears to conform with theory in neither case, for our nation faces not only a looming glut of doctors but an acute shortage of nurses.

Nursing publications estimate that 100,000 budgeted RN posi- 13 tions are going begging every year. The shortage is nationwide, affecting 88 percent of all medical institutions. The more desperate among them are paying bounty hunters, offering free cars and Hawaiian vacations, or providing housing, day care, and the like to lure nurses.

Poor pay is not the only reason for this shortage, apparently, and 14 may not be even the primary reason. In most surveys nurses complain bitterly about their lack of authority and power within the medical hierarchy. Traditionally they have been treated as doctors' handmaidens, even being required to stand when a white-frocked physician entered the room. There are also problems of stress, overwork, irregular hours (the most acute shortages are normally on the night shift), and—perhaps equally important—an absence of significant channels for advancement.

If staff RNs want to advance in their profession, they cannot 15 gradually be promoted to new levels within nursing. They must go into teaching or administration, fields with inherently limited job openings, neither of which has much to do with patient care, or go back to school and train for a year or two to become nurse-midwives, nurse-practitioners, or nurse-anesthetists. These specialties are still very small, their combined membership reaching only about 30,000 in 1980. For the average RN, there is little option but to tolerate the frustration and boredom of an essentially deadended job.

Such non-wage-related complaints don't explain away the nurse shortage. On the contrary; in a free market one of the functions of income differences is to compensate for such complaints by luring workers into unpleasant jobs with greater amounts of cash. Nurses' salaries have begun to rise in response to the shortage (50 percent in the last five years, from a 1977 average of only $13,000), but that has barely been enough to stay ahead of inflation and—more to the point—not enough to eliminate the shortage. In fact, according to the American Hospital Association, there are nearly 400,000 qualified registered nurses who have chosen not to work as nurses.

At the more affluent end of the health-care pay scale, the situation is exactly reversed. Doctors have gone from being too few in the 1960s to too many today. Thanks to an intense federal effort to finance an expansion of medical schools, the number of medical students more than doubled between 1960 and 1980. The total number of physicians rose from 259,000 to 447,000 with government predictions of 643,000 by the year 2000. According to the Graduate Medical Education National Advisory Committee (GMENAC), a high-level body set up under HEW to study the problem, the nation will have a surplus of 70,000 doctors by 1990 and 145,000 by the turn of the century.

Already there is a glut in some areas and specialties, with doctors beginning to recruit patients away from their colleagues and many areas recommending that new physicians go elsewhere. The surplus exists primarily in the highest-paid specialties, such as surgery—not surprising, perhaps, until you realize that in the theoretical market (and in other professions like engineering), high pay is a response to labor *shortage*, while oversupply of a given type of specialist is supposed to bring pay scales down until the surplus disappears. By 1990, GMENAC predicts, serious physician shortages will remain only in three of the lowest-paid branches of the profession—child psychiatry, general psychiatry, and preventive medicine—plus emergency medicine, a new field with a high rate of "burnout."

Doctors' incomes are losing pace in areas of oversupply, such as   19
New England and the Middle Atlantic states, because patient visits per doctor are declining. But doctors' *fees* have not slowed or fallen, as they are supposed to during a glut. And the doctor glut like the nurse shortage, shows no sign of disappearing.

Why is it that doctors can make so much, and nurses so little,   20
despite the supply imbalance? As anyone unlucky enough to have stayed in the hospital knows, nurses do valuable work, just like doctors. They too are professionals, investing an average of three years in their education and training. They often compare them- selves to teachers, physical therapists, and pharmacists, yet they are paid far less.

On the nurses' end of the inequality, some of the answers are   21
obvious. Nursing has always been considered women's work—tra- ditionally poorly paid and, until recently, associated with a captive labor market. Women simply did not have hundreds of other career options, and once they became nurses they could not easily switch to other industries. Others who work in hospitals—computer tech- nicians, managers, electricians, accountants, even pharmacists and physical therapists—can easily find work outside hospitals. Most nurses cannot. In small and medium-sized communities there are often only one or two hospitals, and again, traditionally the average woman has not been able to move from city to city or state to state quite as easily as the average man. Unions in nursing have been weak, in sharp contrast to the immense power of the doctors' union, the American Medical Association.

After a brief period when Medicare and Medicaid money set   22
hospitals awash in federal funds, nurses' wages were depressed during the 1970s as pressure mounted on hospitals to contain soar- ing costs. Nurses' salaries account for at least 25 percent of hospital costs. Unable to control other expenses, such as energy, supplies, and salaries of physicians, hospitals tried assiduously to keep the lid on in the only place they could: nurses' wages.

Trying to explain doctors' incomes is a bit more puzzling. There   23
are three common justifications for incomes in the doctors' range. First, they might be necessary to entice people into taking socially necessary risks. But this argument, while it may apply to oil drilling

or starting silicon-chip factories, will not wash for medicine. It is not easy to get into medical school, but once there, a budding young doctor has as close to a sure thing as our society offers. Few people flunk out of med school these days, and even if one despises patients or faints at the sight of blood, one can always go into radiology or pathology and pull down an easy $100,000 a year. Risk is all but eliminated from the picture.

High salaries are also justified as compensation for bearing heavy responsibilities. This argument clearly has some validity when applied to physicians. Doctors do make life-and-death decisions, and surely that calls for some incentive. But nurses also bear a burden of responsibility. Does the difference really justify a four-to-one income ratio? The argument seems to fall flat when one realizes that two of the hightest-paid medical specialties are those with the least responsibility for patients. They are radiology (in which one makes diagnoses for other doctors' patients with X rays, ultrasound, CAT scanners, and the like) and pathology (in which one examines cell specimens in a laboratory). Both specialties have median incomes well above those of even surgeons and obstetricians.

Finally, there is the justification you will most often hear from doctors themselves: the long and expensive period of education and training necessary to enter medicine. Most American doctors have put in eight hard years of higher education, followed by three to five years of residency. In recent years most have racked up $20,000, $30,000, or even $50,000 in debts, depending on family finances and tuition levels. For most aspiring doctors, deferred gratification has become a way of life, often well into their thirties.

Having witnessed my own wife going through this process, I can testify that it has tremendous impact. Students decide on medical school, in my experience, with little thought of financial reward. At age twenty there are many quicker, easier paths to wealth, including law school and business school. The medical initiation process—twelve years of grueling eighty-hour weeks, in which one grubs around in everything from cankers to cadavers—is simply too long to embark on for mercenary reasons. The motives of premeds certainly run the gamut—from longing for security and status to true fascination with medicine—but big money is rarely among them.

By the end of medical school, however, the picture has changed. Exhausted, deeply in debt, approaching their thirties, the new M.D.s have had it with deferred gratification. Visions of BMWs and Caribbean vacations dance in their heads. They want it bad, and most believe they deserve it. Unfortunately, they know the worst is yet to come. Depending on their specialty, they face three, four, or five years of sheer exhaustion, working 100 hours per week, doing without sleep every third night, and giving up any hope of a social life—all for four or five dollars an hour.

Looked at subjectively, then, and given the typical doctor's famine-feast cycle of reward, the problem may be understandable. By objective economic standards, however, it appears that doctors cash in to an extent hardly justified by any economic calculation. Doctors' debts seem staggering, until one realizes that nurses have debts left over from training, too, and that the typical medical student's debts average out to less than $1,000 a year more than a typical nurse's, over an entire career. In fact, if you view medical school as an investment (of tuition and forgone earnings) by doctors in themselves, with the payoff being the difference between an M.D.'s and an ordinary college graduate's income, then the rate of return on that investment (judged by one 1970 study to be 22 percent) is roughly double the return on funds spent for a college education. In other words, even taking into account all the debts and deferred gratification, the doctors' implicit bargain turns out to be a very lucrative deal.

28

CONTENT

1. What are some of the differences between nurses' rewards and those of medical doctors? Are the rewards merely financial?
2. What similarities between the professions of nurse and doctor argue against the present disparity of income?
3. Why does Osborne attack the notion that supply and demand, as well as reward for hard work, are the primary factors that determine economic rewards? What evidence does he produce to the contrary?

ORGANIZATION

4. Why does Osborne give so much space to the calculations involved in determining the relative salaries of doctors and nurses?
5. The sixth paragraph defines terms such as LPNs and RNs. Why?

6. After salaries, Osborne extends the comparison to education and relative numbers of doctors and nurses. Why do these comparisons follow salaries? Would it be more effective to lead up to the salaries?
7. What parts of this essay might be called cause–effect?

TOPICS FOR WRITING

8. Osborne begins his essay with the statement, "Equality of material reward is not our nation's strong suit." In "An Economy That No Longer Performs," Lester Thurow observes, "If income differentials encourage individual initiative, we should be full of initiative." Compare two professions, other than nurse and physician, and show how these statements are true.
9. Osborne claims that one reason why nurses are so poorly paid is because nursing has been traditionally regarded as women's work. Draw a comparison between two related professions, one traditionally male, the other traditionally female, and show how the same situation of inequality exists.

MARGARET MEAD
To Both Their Own

Margaret Mead (1901–1978) has gained a world-wide reputation as the author of over twenty books in the field of anthropology. With her classic study, Coming of Age in Samoa *(1928), she began a life-long commitment to the study of the peoples of the South Pacific. In her later years, Mead was especially instrumental in applying her anthropological research to the problems of contemporary society. "To Both Their Own" from* Male and Female *(1949) is an example of the application of Margaret Mead's accumulated wisdom and good sense to the volatile issue of male and female roles.*

Each sex may be distorted by the presence of the other sex, or it may be given a fuller sense of sex membership. Either solution is possible, neither is inevitable. If parents define one child as less complete, less potentially gifted, with less right to be free, less claim to love and protection, or less a source of pride to themselves than the other, the child of that sex will, in many cases, feel envy. If society defines each sex as having inalienable and valuable qualities of its own but does not relate those qualities to the reproductive differences between the sexes, then each sex may be proud and strong, but some of the values that come from sex contrast will be lacking. If women are defined without reference to their maternity, men may find their own masculinity seems inadequate, because its continuance into paternity will also lose definition. And if men are defined in terms of paternity rather than as lovers, women will find that their own capacities of wifehood have been muted in favour of their capacities for motherhood.

Externally at some given period of history and in some set of social arrangements it may often look as if one sex gained and the other lost, but such gains and losses must in the end be temporary. To the extent that women are denied the right to use their minds, their sons suffer as well as their daughters. An over-emphasis on the importance of virility will in the end make the lives of men as instrumental as an over-emphasis on their merely reproductive functions makes the lives of women. If our analysis is deep enough and our time-perspective long enough, if we hold in mind all the various possibilities that other cultures hint at or fully embody, it is possible to say that to the extent that either sex is disadvantaged, the whole culture is poorer, and the sex that, superficially, inherits the earth, inherits only a very partial legacy. The more whole the culture, the more whole each member, each man, each woman, each child will be. Each sex is shaped from birth by the presence and the behaviour of both sexes, and each sex is dependent upon both. The myths that conjure up islands of women who live all alone without men always contain, and rightly, some flaw in the picture. A one-sex world would be an imperfect world, for it would be a world without a future. Only a denial of life itself makes it possible to deny the interdependence of the sexes. Once that interdependence is recognized and traced in minute detail to the infant's first experience of the contrast between the extra roughness of a shaven cheek and a deeper voice and his mother's softer skin and higher voice, any program which claims that the wholeness of one sex can be advanced without considering the other is automatically disallowed. Isolated consideration of the position of women becomes as essentially one-sided as the isolated consideration of the position of men. We must think instead of how to live in a two-sex world so that each sex will benefit at every point from each expression of the presence of two sexes.

To insist on building a world in which both sexes benefit does not mean that we gloss over or deny the differential vulnerability of either sex, the learnings that are harder for boys, the learnings that are harder for girls, the periods of greater physical vulnerability for one sex than the other. This does not mean that we deny that when both sexes are cared for more by the mother than by the father, the learnings will be different as the boy accepts a first-beloved person who is unlike himself and the girl one who is like herself, as each lives out its first warm contacts with the world with eager little mouths that for one will remain a prototype of adult relationships, but for the other will be reversed. Nor does it mean that we fail to recognize the period when the little girl's sex membership is so much less explicit than the little boy's that while he is proudly, exhibitionistically sure of his masculinity, she has to ignore what seems like a deficiency in herself in favour of a promised future maternity. It means recognizing that training to control elimination, to plan, to respond, to inhibit, appropriately, in terms of time and place, has a different impact on the boy and on the girl. It does mean that we also recognize that as both children seize on the behaviour of grown men and women to give them clues as to what their future rôles will be, the conspicuousness of pregnancy to which the girl can look forward overshadows the paternal rôle that is so much harder for a small boy's imagination to follow through. As the girl is left vulnerable to any cultural arrangements that seem to deny her some freedom—the right to use her mind or her body in some way that is permitted to a boy—so the boy is left vulnerable to cultural arrangements that spur him on to efforts that may be beyond his strength, if achievement is defined as necessary to validate an otherwise imperfect maleness.

Giving each sex its due, a full recognition of its special vulnerabilities and needs for protection, means looking beyond the superficial resemblances during the period of later childhood when both boys and girls, each having laid many of the problems of sex adjustment aside, seem so eager to learn, and so able to learn the same things. Paced too closely together, with a school system that closes its eyes to the speed with which the girls are outdistancing the boys in height, and the greater ease that girls have in learning certain kinds of lessons, both boys and girls may be injured during this period, the boy given a fear of the superiority of the girl, the girl given a fear of being superior to the boy. Each fear is deeply detrimental to the full development of each sex later, but it operates differently, making the boy angry and grudging about achievement in women, making the girl frightened and deprecatory about her own gifts. At puberty, there is again a difference. The girl's attainment of puberty is definite and clear. Only cultural arrangements which insist that chronological age is more important than maturity, or which fail to recognize that late maturation is as normal as early, can make the girl as doubtful of herself and of her full sex membership as is the boy as he responds to the less sure, less definite signs of his own puberty.

As young adults ready for a full sex relationship, both boy and   5 girl are limited by the irrevocability of a full sex experience for a woman as compared with that of a man. This irrevocability of the severed hymen often stays the man's spontaneity as greatly as it does the girl's. Then in the full sex relationship there is again a shift. The man may live over again phantasies of re-entering his mother's body, but the woman must accept her obligation to herself, the willingness to become a body in which new life is sheltered. However, once she has borne a child, her full sex membership, her ability to conceive and carry and bear another human being, is assured and can never be taken away from her. The male who has impregnated a female is given no such full assurance; his paternity remains to the end inferential, his full sex membership has to be referred again and again to continual potency rather than to past paternity. And with advancing years, the woman faces a moment when giving up her productive maternity will occur as irrevocably and unmistakably as the beginning was once signalled at menarche. But the male's loss of his potential paternity, like the diminution of his potency, is gradual, indefinite, reversible. It has neither the quality of a single devastating event which is the way women often experience the menopause, nor the possibility of a peaceful acceptance of a consummated step in life, which is also possible to women. He keeps the rewards and the psychological hazards that go with a less punctuated ageing process.

Our tendency at present is to minimize all these differences in   6 learning, in rhythm, in type and timing of rewards, and at most to try to obliterate particular differences that are seen as handicaps on one sex. If boys are harder to train, train them harder; if girls grow faster than boys, separate them, so the boys won't be damaged; if women have a little less strength than men, invent machines so that they can still do the same work. But every adjustment that minimizes a difference, a vulnerability, in one sex, a differential strength in the other, diminishes their possibility of complementing each other, and corresponds—symbolically—to sealing off the constructive receptivity of the female and the vigorous outgoing constructive activity of the male, muting them both in the end to a duller version of human life, in which each is denied the fullness of humanity that each might have had. Guard each sex in its vulnerable moments we must, protect and cherish them through the crises that at some times are so much harder for one sex than for the other. But as we guard, we may also keep the differences. Simply compensating for differences is in the end a form of denial.

But if each sex is to realize sex membership fully, each boy and each girl must also feel as a whole human being. We are human beings first, and while sex membership very quickly overrides race feeling, so that boys of a race that assumes itself superior will express themselves as more willing to be males of the "inferior" race than to be females in their own, people do not similarly choose not to be human. The most boldly swaggering male would be staggered by the choice of keeping his masculinity at the price of becoming a lion, or a stag, the most deeply maternal female would not elect to be turned into a ewe or a doe rather than lose her femininity. Humanity at any price, but please God, a human being of my own sex, fully, sums up the approach that men and women make in every culture in the world. We may bring them up to wish they had been born a member of the other sex, and so impair forever their full and happy functioning, but even so they would not barter away their humanity. Yet we have seen how damaging to full sex membership can be some of the conventions by which each society has differentiated the sexes. Every known society creates and maintains artificial occupational divisions and personality expectations for each sex that limit the humanity of the other sex. One form that these distinctions take is to deny the range of difference among the members of one sex, and so insist that all men should be taller than all women, so that any man who is shorter than any woman is less a man. This is the simplest form of a damaging conventionalization. But there are a thousand others, rooted in our failure to recognize the great variety of human beings who are now mingled and mated in one great mélange that includes temperamental contrasts as great as if the rabbit mated with the lion and sheep with leopards. Characteristic after characteristic in which the differences within a sex are so great that there is enormous overlapping are artificially assigned as masculine or feminine. Hairiness may be repudiated by both sexes and men forced to shave their beards and women to shave their legs and armpits; hairiness may be a proof of maleness, so that women shave their heads and men wear false curls. Shaving takes time, the male who has no beard feels unmanned, the woman who has three hairs between her breasts may be taken for a witch, and even so adjustment to such stereotypes does relatively much less harm than when personality differences are assigned in the same way. If initiative is limited to one sex, especially in sex relationships themselves, a great number of marriages will be distorted and often destroyed, to the extent that the one to whose sex initiative is forbidden is the one of that particular pair who is able to initiate, and so either refrains from the relationship or conceals and manipulates and falsifies it. As with initiative, so with responsiveness. Each sex is capable of taking certain kinds and certain types of initiative, and some individuals in each sex in relation to some individuals of the other sex, at certain times, in certain places, should, if they are to act as whole individuals, be initiating regardless of their sex, or be responsive regardless of their sex. If the stereotypes forbid this, it is hazardous for each to do so. We may go up the scale from simple physical differences through complementary definitions that overstress the rôle of sex difference and extend it inappropriately to other aspects of life, to stereotypes of such complex activities as those involved in the formal use of the intellect, in the arts, in government, and in religion.

In all these complex achievements of civilization, those activities which are mankind's glory, and upon which depends our hope of survival in this world that we have built, there has been this tendency to make artificial distinctions that limit an activity to one sex, and by denying the actual potentialities of human beings limit not only both men and women, but also equally the development of the activity itself. Singing may be taken as a very simple example. There are societies in which nobody sings in anything but a flat, rhythmic, dull chant. Significantly enough, Manus, which is built on the duller similarities of men and women, is such a society. There are societies in which women sing, and men sing falsetto. There have probably been societies in which men sang and only women who could sing alto were allowed to sing. There are societies that wished to achieve the full beauty of a chorus which spanned the possibilities of the human voice, but in linking religion and music together also wished to ban women, as unsuited for an active rôle in the church, from the choir. Boys' voices provide an apparently good substitute. So also do eunuchs, and so in the end we may have music modelled on a perfect orchestration of men and women's voices, but at the price of the exclusion of women and the castration of men.

Throughout history, the more complex activities have been defined and re-defined, now as male, now as female, now as neither, sometimes as drawing equally on the gifts of both sexes, sometimes as drawing differentially on both sexes. When an activity to which each could have contributed—and probably all complex activities belong in this class—is limited to one sex, a rich differentiated quality is lost from the activity itself. Once a complex activity is defined as belonging to one sex, the entrance of the other sex into it is made difficult and compromising. There is no heavy taboo in Bali against a woman if she wishes, or a man if he wishes, practising the special arts of the other sex. But painting in Bali has been a male art. When a gifted little adolescent girl in the village of Batoean, where there were already some sixty young men experimenting with the modern innovation of painting on paper, tried a new way of painting— by setting down what she saw rather than painting conventionalized stylized representations of the world—the boy artists derided and discouraged her until she gave up and made poor imitations of their style. The very difference in sex that made it possible for her to see a little differently, and so make an innovation, also made her so vulnerable that her innovation could be destroyed. Conversely, the entrance of one sex into the activities of the other if the other has less prestige may be simply destructive. In ancient Samoa, the women made lovely bark-cloth, pressing out the fluctuating, beautifully soft lines against mats on which the pattern was sewed in coconut-leaf riblets. When iron tools were introduced, the men, because men were defined as the carvers, learned to carve wooden pattern-boards that were stronger and easier to work with than the old fragile mats. But the designs, made for an art for which they had no feeling, suffered, became stiff and dull, and even the women's attempt to get some freedon back into the designs by painting imitations rather than using the boards failed.

In religion we find the same gamut. Religious experience and religious leadership may be permitted to one sex alone, and the periodic outbreak of vision in the wrong sex may be penalized. A woman may be branded as a witch, a man as an invert. The whole picture may become so confused between real gift and social definition of sex rôle that we get the final institutionalized patterns that confuse sex inversion, transvestitism, and religious functions, as among some Siberian tribes. It is always possible for society to deny to one sex that which both sexes are able to do; no human gift is strong enough to flower fully in a person who is threatened with loss of sex membership. The insistence on limiting a two-sex potentiality to one sex results in the terrible tragedies of wrong definition of one's own sex in the man who becomes a homosexual because of the way in which society defines his desire to paint or to dance, or in the woman who becomes a homosexual because she likes to ride horses, or use a slide-rule. If the interest the other sex takes in one-sex activity is strong enough, then the intruders may win, as men have been largely driven from teaching in the schools of the United States. Or even more peculiar things may happen. In some particular place and time a developing medical practice may include obstetrics within the proper sphere of the doctor. Those male physicians who have had the strongest interest in the reproductive capacities of women may gravitate initially towards obstetrics and pediatrics. So also may females whose interest in medicine has been defined as male. There may come to be a group of practitioners that includes males who have been very strongly influenced by their conceptions of what a female rôle is, and females who are strongly repelled by their conceptions of the limitations of the female rôle. Together they may shape medical practice into strange forms in which the women who might make a contribution from a first-hand knowledge of femininity are silent, and the men are left freer to follow their phantasies than they would have been had there been no women among them. Such a development may sometimes finally include a determination to indoctrinate women in "natural childbirth," in fact to return to them the simple power of bearing their own children, which in the course of a most devoted but one-sided development of medicine has practically been taken away from them.

I have elaborated this particular example in some detail, because no matter with what goodwill we may embark on a program of actually rearing both men and women to make their full and special contributions in all the complex processes of civilization—medicine and law, education and religion, the arts and sciences—the task will be very difficult. Where an occupation or an art is defined as feminine, the males who are attracted to it are either already in some way injured or may be injured if they try to practise it. If simple social definition does not set them to doubting their manhood, the very feminine rules and procedures of the occupation itself may so befuddle and exasperate them that they inevitably do not do different and good work, but similar and worse work, than the women who are already there. When an occupation is defined as masculine the women who first enter it will be similarly handicapped. They may have entered it out of a simple drive to act like a male, to compete with males, to prove that they are as good as males. Such a drive, compensatory and derivative rather than primary, will blur their vision and make clumsy fingers that should be deft as they try to act out the behaviour of the other sex, deemed so desirable. Or if they enter the occupation not out of any desire to compete with men, but out of simple primary motivations, of curiosity or a desire to create or to participate in some activity that is fascinating in itself, they too, like the men who enter occupations in which women have set the style, will find themselves handicapped at every turn by a style that has been completely set by the other sex. As the member of another culture fumbles and stumbles in a different land, with hand stretched out for a door-knob that is not there, a foot raised for a step that is missing, an appetite that rises insistently at an hour when there is no food, and an ear trained to wake to sounds that are never heard in these strange streets, so the immigrant coming into an occupation that has been the sole preserve of the other sex will stumble and fumble and do less than is in him or her to do. How can such an immigrant compete with those whose upbringing fits them to find their way, effortlessly, gracefully, with never a false step or a wasted motion? Whether it be the arts or the sciences, the whole pattern of thought, the whole symbolic system within which the novice must work, facilitates every step taken by the expected sex, obstructs every step taken by the unexpected sex. These same one-sex patterns also restrict the sex that practises them the longer they are practised by one sex alone, and not made new by the interwoven imaginations of both. It may even be that one of the explanations which lie behind the decline of great periods of civilized activity, when philosophies fail, arts decline, and religions lose their vigour, may be found to be a too rigid adherence to the insights and the gifts of one sex. The higher the development of some faculty of creativeness that has been defined as rigidly male or rigidly female, the more the personality of the practitioner is split, and the deeper the danger that the personal life of mating and parenthood, which must be keyed to the presence of the other sex, may be divorced from the creative life of thought and action. This may in turn result in a secondary solution, such as the split in Greek society between the uneducated wife and the sophisticated mistress; it may push a large part of society towards celibacy or homosexuality, simply because a heterosexual relationship involves unbearable complications. The deeper the commitment to a creative activity becomes, be it government or science, industry or the arts, religion or exploration, the more the participating individuals will seek wholeness in it, and the more they will be vulnerable if the activity itself is one that only partially expresses our full two-sexed humanity.

There is likewise the very simple consideration that when we have no indication that intelligence is limited to one sex, any occupational restriction that prevents gifted women from exercising their gifts leaves them, and also the world that is sorely in need of every gift, the poorer. I have not put this consideration first, because there is still the possibility that the world might lose more by sacrificing sex differentiation than it would lose by limiting the exercise of that intelligence to certain ways of life. It is of very doubtful value to enlist the gifts of women if bringing women into fields that have been defined as male frightens the men, unsexes the women, muffles and distorts the contribution the women could make, either because their presence excludes men from the occupation or because it changes the quality of the men who enter it. There is slight gain if the struggle the intruders have to go through limits any primary feminine contribution they could make. It can be cogently argued that the profession of education—which should be by both sexes for both sexes—has lost as much if not more than it has gained as men departed not only from the primary grades, where the special gifts of women were badly needed, but from the higher grades, where boys have suffered because taught only by women. Men teachers took refuge in the universities, where they jealously guard their departments against the entrance of any woman into fields

12

where women's insights are needed. Such sequence can well make one pause, and suggest that the cure is often worse than the disease.

This is more likely to be so whenever women's abilities are seen [13] quantitatively in relation to men's. The phrasing is then that there are many women who are as bright or brighter, as strong or stronger, as good or better organizers, than men. Crusades based on the rights of women to enter any field are likely to recoil upon themselves. The entrance of women is defined as competitive, and this is dangerous, whether the competition be expressed in the Soviet woman railroad engineer's plaint that women are allowed to run only engines on freight trains, or in the devastating antagonisms that are likely to occur in America, where it is so hard to forgive any person who wins in the same race, although so easy to acclaim success in races one has not entered. Almost every excursion of American women into fields that women had never, or at least not for many epochs, entered has been phrased in just these competitive terms.

* * *

It is folly to ignore the signs which warn us that the present [14] terms on which women are lured by their own curiosities and drives developed under the same educational system as boys, or forced by social conditions that deny homes and children to many women— a fourth of American women reach the menopause having borne no children—are bad for both men and women. We have to count very carefully what gains there are, what possibilities there are of drawing rapidly enough upon the sensitivities of both men and women to right the balance and still go on.

There will be very great temptations in America to right the bal- [15] ance rudely, to tighten the lines against the continued entrance of women into these new fields, rather than to change the nature of that entrance. To the extent that we do go backwards we lose an opportunity to make the social inventions that will make it possible for women to contribute as much to civilization as they now contribute to the continuance of the race. As matters now stand and have stood through history, we have drawn on the gifts of men in both ways, and on the gifts of women almost entirely in one way. From each sex, society has asked that they so live that others may be born, that they cherish their masculinity and femininity, discipline it to the demands of parenthood, and leave new lives behind them when they die. This has meant that men had to be willing to choose, win, and keep women as lovers, protect and provide for them as husbands, and protect and provide for their children as fathers. It has meant that women have had to be willing to accept men as lovers, live with them as wives, and conceive, bear, feed, and cherish their children. Any society disappears which fails to make these demands on its members and to receive this much from them.

But from men, society has also asked and received something more than this. For thousands of generations men have been asked to do something more than be good lovers and husbands and fathers, even with all that that involved of husbandry and organization and protection against attack. They have been asked to develop and elaborate, each in terms of his own ability, the structure within which the children are reared, to build higher towers, or wider roads, to dream new dreams and see new visions, to penetrate ever farther into the secrets of nature, to learn new ways of making life more human and more rewarding. And within the whole adventure there has been a silent subtle division of labour, which had its roots perhaps in a period of history when the creativeness of bearing children outweighted in splendour every act that men performed, however they danced and pantomimed the pretence that the novices were really their children after all. In this division of labour, there was the assumption that bearing children is enough for the women, and in the rest of the task all the elaborations belong to men. This assumption becomes the less tenable the more men succeed in those elaborations which they have taken on themselves. As a civilization becomes complex, human life is defined in individual terms as well as in the service of the race, and the great structures of law and government, religion and art and science, become something highly valued for themselves. Practised by men, they become indicators of masculine humanity, and men take great pride in these achievements. To the extent that women are barred from them, women become less human. An illiterate woman is no less human than an illiterate man. As long as few men write and most men cannot, a woman may suffer no loss in her sense of herself. But when writing becomes almost universal—access to books, increased precision of thought, possibilities of communication— then if women cannot learn to write because they are women, they

16

lose stature, and the whole subtle process begins by which the wholeness of both sexes is undermined. When the women's sense of loss of participation is compensated for by other forms of power, by the iron will of the mother-in-law who has been the docile, home-bound wife—as in China and Japan—then the equilibrating pattern may take the form of covert distortions of human relationships that may persist over centuries. When women's sense of impaired participation in society is expressed directly, in rebellion against restrictions that it has placed on her, we may find instead the sort of freedom for women that occurred just before the breakdown of the Roman Empire, or in the goals of the women's movement of the last century. But whatever the compensatory adjustment within society, women's belief in their own power to contribute directly to human culture will be subtly and deeply impaired, and men's isolation, either covertly threatened or openly attacked, in a world that they have built alone will increase.

If we once accept the premise that we can build a better world   17 by using the different gifts of each sex, we shall have two kinds of freedom, freedom to use untapped gifts of each sex, and freedom to admit freely and cultivate in each sex their special superiorities. We may well find that there are certain fields, such as physical sciences, mathematics, and instrumental music, in which men by virtue of their sex, as well as by virtue of their qualities as special gifted human beings, will always have that razor-edge of extra gift which makes all the difference, and that while women may easily follow where men lead, men will always make the new discoveries. We may equally well find that women, through the learning involved in maternity, which once experienced can be taught more easily to all women, even childless women, than to men, have a special superiority in those human sciences which involve that type of understanding which until it is analyzed is called intuition. If intuition is based, as it seems to be, upon an ability to recognize difference from the self rather than upon one to project the self in building a construct or a hypothesis, it may well be that the greatest intuitive gifts will be found among women. Just as for endless ages men's mathematical gifts were neglected and people counted one, two, two and one, and a dog, or were limited to counting on the fingers of their hands, so women's intuitive gifts have lain fallow, uncultivated, uncivilized.

Once it is possible to say it is as important to take women's gifts 18
and make them available to both men and women, in transmittable
form, as it was to take men's gifts and make the civilization built
upon them available to both men and women, we shall have enriched
our society. And we shall be ready to synthesize both kinds of gifts
in the sciences, which are now sadly lop-sided with their far greater
knowledge of how to destroy than of how to construct, far better
equipped to analyze the world of matter into which man can project
his intelligence than the world of human relations, which requires
the socialized use of intuition. The mother who must learn that the
infant who was but an hour ago a part of her body is now a different
individual, with its own hungers and its own needs, and that if she
listens to her own body to interpret the child, the child will die, is
schooled in an irreplaceable school. As she learns to attend to that
different individual, she develops a special way of thinking and
feeling about human beings. We can leave these special learnings
at the present level, or convert them into a more elaborate part of
our civilization. Already the men and women who are working
together in the human sciences are finding the greatly increased
understanding that comes from the way in which their insights
complement each other. We are learning that we pay different prices
for our insights: for instance, to understand the way a culture social-
izes children a man must return in imagination to childhood, but a
woman has also another and different path, to learn to understand
the mothers of these children. Yet both are necessary, and the skill
of one sex gives only a partial answer. We can build a whole society
only by using the gifts special to each sex and those shared by both
sexes—by using the gifts of the whole of humanity.

Every step away from a tangled situation, in which moves and 19
counter-moves have been made over centuries, is a painful step,
itself inevitably imperfect. Here is a vicious circle to which it is not
possible to assign either a beginning or an end, in which men's
over-estimation of women's rôles, or women's over-estimation of
men's rôles, leads one sex or the other to arrogate, to neglect, or
even to relinquish part of our so dearly won humanity. Those who
would break the circle are themselves a product of it, express some
of its defects in their every gesture, may be only strong enough to
challenge it, not able actually to break it. Yet once identified, once
analyzed, it should be possible to create a climate of opinion in

which others, a little less the product of the dark past because they have been reared with a light in their hand that can shine backwards as well as forwards, may in turn take the next step. Only by recognizing that each change in human society must be made by those who carry in every cell of their bodies the very reason why the change is necessary can we school our hearts to the patience to build truly and well, recognizing that it is not only the price, but also the glory, of our humanity that civilization must be built by human beings.

CONTENT

1. What different talents does Mead see in the sexes? Is she against sex differentiation in occupation? Why or why not? What criteria would she use in determining the fitness of one sex or another to perform a certain occupation?

2. In paragraph 2 Mead says, "Only a denial of life makes it possible to deny the interdependence of the sexes. . . . Simply compensating for differences is in the end a form of denial." What kinds of compensation is she referring to? What does she mean by interdependence? Is she merely referring to biology?

3. In paragraph 18 Mead says, "We can build a whole society only by using both the gifts special to each sex and those shared by both sexes—by using the gifts of the whole of humanity." What examples can you think of where removing the occupational assignments to one sex would improve the quality of the work and benefit humanity?

ORGANIZATION

4. Which paragraphs emphasize similarities and differences between the two sexes? Why doesn't Mead group these together in one section of the essay?

5. Why does the first paragraph have a series of statements beginning with "if"? Do any subsequent paragraphs explore the "if" hypothesis of the first paragraph? What parts of the essay are cause–effect? What parts are exemplification?

6. Why does Mead organize her material placing primary emphasis on biological and cultural differences between the sexes in the first part of the essay, then switching emphasis to the occu-

pational opportunities for both sexes in the second half of her essay?

TOPICS FOR WRITING

7. Make a list of the special talents of men and women. Write an essay showing that women or men perform better in some occupations than their opposite sex.

8. Write an essay showing how the special contributions of *both* sexes would help improve the quality of a particular profession. Reread Mead's remarks about the sciences and medicine before you select your particular topic.

Analogy

We use *analogy* to compare two things that belong to different classes or categories. An analogy stipulates limited likenesses between two things which are essentially dissimilar. For example, if you wished to explain how the heart works, you might decide to compare it to a pump. Like a pump, the heart circulates material in a closed system by keeping it at a constant pressure. Like a pump, the heart has valves that open and close; and like a pump, its operation can be interrupted if one of the tubes leading to it becomes blocked. Of course, the introduction of a mechanical heart may have made this analogy seem more like a comparison, but the living heart and the mechanical pump still belong to different orders of being; consequently, they form an analogy. Often, an analogy involves a familiar term and an unfamiliar one, the objective being to explain the unfamiliar term by comparing it with the familiar one. In the previous example, you would be assuming your audience was familiar with how a pump works, but less familiar with how the heart works.

Analogy is meant as a demonstration, not as a logical proof that such similarities do, in fact, exist. Analogy differs from direct comparison in that in comparison the two items *do* belong to the same class; moreover, to point out similarities in a comparison is to insist that they are, in fact, alike. Analogy serves to clarify the unfamiliar, whereas comparison specifies the actual features that two things have in common. To compare Protestantism and Catholicism—two forms of Christianity—for instance would be a straightforward comparison because the items obviously belong to the same class, and the purpose would be to illuminate both. But to compare government with religion is to draw an analogy, since the two are essentially unlike. In the following analogy by Richard Reeves, notice how government and religion are brought together to comment on Americans' attitudes toward government; notice, too, that the items are juxtaposed only temporarily to clarify a point. Reeves actually does not believe that government and religion are similar institutions, except in the limited ways he points out in the analogy.

The government, trusted and feared, obeyed and avoided, revered and disdained, had become very much like a religion. Its role was to confront

evil for the rest of us. Somehow, it had to make us better than we knew
we were, because the ideas that were being enforced, the ideas of America, were bigger and better than Americans. Most Americans supported
the reinforcement of the national rhetoric, even while protesting the
growth of the secular church to meet evils old or new, growing or being
redefined. The support, the basic trust in the public solution, existed
even as the American congregation sought out private solutions—and
new ways to evade the multiplying laws and the bureaus, rules, and
enforcers. It was, of course, the way people have always believed in and
dealt with religions. No one can play by all those rules, all those com-
mandments. But they can say they do, and they can try—and trying
makes them, often, hypocrites and fools. And often decent. And dem-
ocrats. Americans. ["Along Tocqueville's Path," *The New Yorker* (April 12,
1982), 104–106.]

In framing an analogy to clarify a difficult subject, it is often
useful to put it in the form of a question. For example: "How is
Congress like a circus?" "How is inflation like a parasite?" "How is
getting a college education like running a race (or participating in
any sport)?" "How is writing a paper like cooking a meal?" "How
is travelling in a foreign country like being blindfolded?" Because
creating analogies is like creating figures of speech (see pages 120–
21), everyone has his or her own ideas about where to find similarities; however, audience receptivity must be kept in mind if the
analogy is to succeed in clarifying the subject.

Finally, because an analogy is a partial comparison of two things,
it is clear that the differences will outweigh the similarities. Should
you explore the differences as well? The only answer to the question
is equivocal: "It depends." It depends on whether pointing out the
differences would undermine the similarities the analogy has already
constructed or would further clarify the unfamiliar item you are
attempting to explain. Notice in the following quotation from an
article by Jonathan Schell ["The Fate of the Earth—Part I," *The New
Yorker* (Feb. 1, 1982), 100], how Schell begins by rejecting someone
else's analogy of the earth as a biological cell before going ahead to
offer his own analogy of the earth as an individual person:

Dr. [Lewis] Thomas, for one, has likened the earth to a cell. The analogy
is compelling, but in one noteworthy respect, at least, there is a difference between the earth and a cell: whereas each cell is one among
billions struck from the same genetic mold, the earth, as the mother of
all life, has no living parent. If the behavior of the cells is often predictable, it is because they exist en masse, and what a billion of them,
programmed by their genetic material, a billion times the billion and

first is likely to do again. But the earth is a member of no class as yet open to our observation which would permit the drawing of such inferences by generalization. When it comes to predict its tolerance to perturbances, we are in the position of someone asked to deduce the whole of medicine by observing one human being. With respect to its individuality, then, the earth is not so much like a cell as like an individual person. Like a person, the earth is unique; like a person, it is sacred; and like a person, it is unpredictable by the generalizing laws of science.

When extended too far, analogies lapse into absurdity. Walker Percy's analogy between the segregated South and a man with a toothache does not extend the analogy absurdly to suggest that the Justice Department is like a dentist. Furthermore, analogies are not logical evidence; they are merely useful ways of clarifying an unfamiliar topic. Like the other patterns of development, analogy is a useful device for elaborating on a subject—if you can keep these limitations in mind when using it.

SHORT EXAMPLE–ANALOGY

E. B. WHITE
Here Is New York

New York, E.B. White suggests, is like a poem: Its beauty lies in its compressing many things into a small space. (For a biographical note on White, see page 97.)

A poem compresses much in a small space and adds music, thus   1
heightening its meaning. The city is like poetry: it compresses all life, all races and breeds, into a small island and adds music and the accompaniment of internal engines. The island of Manhattan is without any doubt the greatest human concentrate on earth, the poem whose magic is comprehensible to millions of permanent residents but whose full meaning will alway remain illusive. At the feet of the tallest and plushiest offices lie the crummiest slums. The genteel mysteries housed in the Riverside Church are only a few blocks from the voodoo charms of Harlem. The merchant princes, riding to Wall Street in their limousines down the East River Drive,

pass within a few hundred yards of the gypsy kings; but the princes do not know they are passing the kings, and the kings are not up yet anyway—they live a more leisurely life than the princes and get drunk more consistently.

DISCUSSION

White's analogy opens with a sentence that sounds like a definition: "A poem compresses much in a small space and adds music, thus heightening its meaning," and proceeds to show how the analogy— "the city is like poetry" fits the requirements of the definition. White follows these statements with a series of improbable paradoxes that show how much compression there really is in the city: skyscrapers and slums, genteel Christianity and exotic vodooism, millionaires and bums. All this compression, along with the music of the city's traffic, like a poem creates an incomprehensible kind of "magic." White's analogy explains the incomprehensibility of the city in terms of the illusiveness of the poem. Both halves of the analogy have the added common quality of compression. White elaborates on this quality in his series of examples. The analogy is successful because the compression of the city is clarified by the developed analogy.

WALKER PERCY
Southern Comfort

Walker Percy (born 1916) is one of America's foremost novelists. His first novel The Moviegoer *(1961) won the National Book Award for fiction. The Second* Coming *(1981), received the Pulitzer Prize. In "Southern Comfort," Percy compares the South's loss of racial bigotry to a man rid of a troubling toothache, but the analogy of loss ends there.*

The South in its present state might be compared to a man who 1
has had a bad toothache for as long as he can remember and has all of a sudden gotten over it. So constant and nagging has been

the pain that he long ago came to accept it as the normal unpleasant condition of his existence. In fact, it never occurred to him to imagine life without it. How does such a man spend his time, energies, talents and mental capacities? In seeking relief from the pain, by drugs, anesthesia, distraction, games, war, whatever—or, failing that, by actually enjoying the pain, the way one probes an aching tooth with one's tongue.

Then one fine morning he wakes to find the pain is gone. At first he doesn't know what has happened except that things are somehow different. Then he realizes what has happened and for a while takes pleasure in it. He can't believe his good fortune. But, as time goes on, he discovers that he is faced with a new and somewhat unsettling problem. The problem is, What is he going to do with himself now that he no longer has the pain to worry about, the tooth to tongue?

What has happened, of course, is that for the first time in 150 years the South and southerners, and I mean both white and black southerners, no longer suffer the unique onus, the peculiar burden of race that came to be part of the very connotation of the word *South.* I am not going to argue about what was good and what was bad about the South's racial experience. We're interested here in what was uniquely oppressive for both white and black and which has now vanished. And to say that it has vanished is not of course to suggest that there do not remain serious, even critical, areas of race relations in all of American society, the South included.

Let me give an instance or two of what I mean by the siphoning off of southern talent, by the obsessive tonguing of this particular tooth. The figure of 150 years I got from the history books. But from my own experience, say the past fifty years, I can give a simple example of what I have in mind. During my lifetime and up until a few years ago, I can recall not a single southern politician—and only the rare writer—who was not obsessed with the problem of the relation of white people and black people. It was, in fact, for better or worse, the very condition of being southern.

The obsession almost invariably took polemical form. One either defended the South or attacked the South. What one did not do, did not have the time to do, was take a good look at the South.

Thus Sen. Richard Russell of Georgia, an extraordinarily able and talented man, a man of great character and rectitude. I am sure he accomplished many and varied legislative goals. Yet the only thing

I remember about him was his great skill in devising parliamentary tactics to defeat or delay this or that voting-rights bill.

I think next of my own kinsman, William Alexander Percy, who 7 devoted a large part of his autobiography to defending the South against "northern liberals." He wrote a whole chapter in defense of sharecropping. Again, I am not interested in arguing the issue, beyond admitting that in his place and time I'd have felt the same defensiveness and would probably have written similar polemics.

Then, I think of the novelist Richard Wright, who never really 8 came to terms with his own southernness, his Americanness, or for that matter his blackness.

The point of course is that the South does not now need defend- 9 ing. Even George Wallace has trouble working himself up to take on "northern liberals." The astounding dimension of the change is that the virtues and faults of the South are the virtues and faults of the nation, no more and no less. The old enemy is no longer there, or if he is, he is too busy with his own troubles. There is no one throwing punches and no one to counterpunch. At least as far as writers are concerned, it does not now occur to a serious writer in the North to "attack" the South or to a serious southern writer to "defend" the South. Perhaps it is not an unhealthy thing for a satirical writer like me to feel free to take on North and South. And for the first time in my experience a black writer, Toni Morrison, has written a novel that is not about White and Black as such, Black *vs.* White, North and South as such, but about people.

I cannot speak for the politician, but to me as a writer it appears 10 that what needs not so much defending as understanding, recon- ciling, rejoicing in, ridiculing, cracking jokes about, healing, affirm- ing, is not the southern experience but the American experience. And since every writer must write of his own experience—or else not write at all—the southern writer necessarily writes of the South, but he writes of it in terms that are immediately translatable to the American experience and, if he is good enough, to the human experience.

Consider, for example, two southern writers who lived during 11 this period of the long Southern Obsession and who were great enough to transcend it: William Faulkner and Flannery O'Connor. They had their problems. O'Connor succeeded, I think, largely by steering clear of race—with a couple of notable exceptions. Mainly she stuck to whites—figuring, I guess, that whites had enough trouble with themselves without dragging in white-black troubles. Faulkner wobbled. He was at his best in *The Sound and the Fury* with Dilsey and her relationship with the Compsons. No one will ever surpass him on these grounds. But he could also drift into sentimental paternalism and even at times sound like a Mississippi secessionist.

How, into what channels, will southern energies be directed now that the obsession is behind us? Will southerners have a distinctive contribution to make, say in politics or literature? Or will they simply meld into the great American flux?

One possible future is fairly obvious, is indeed already upon us: the ongoing shift in population and economic power to the so-called Sunbelt. To many this is the future that not only goes without saying but is also desirable. One can simply extrapolate the future from what is happening here and now in the southern United States, from Hilton Head to Dallas and indeed—and this is what worries me—on to Phoenix and Los Angeles. The likeliest and, to me, the not wholly desirable future of the region is an ever more prosperous Southern Rim stretching from coast to coast, an L.A.-Dallas-Atlanta axis (the Atlanta of the Omni and the Peachtree Plaza), an agribusiness-sports-vacation-retirement-show-biz culture with its spiritual center perhaps at Oral Roberts University, its media center in Atlanta, its entertainment industry shared by Disney World, the Superdome, and Hollywood. In this scenario the coastal plain of the old Southeast will be preserved as a kind of museum, much like Williamsburg.

One doesn't have to be a prophet to predict with considerable confidence that sooner or later the failing northern cities must either be abandoned or be bailed out by some kind of domestic Marshall Plan—and why not, after all? Everyone else has benefited: Germany, Italy, Japan, Guatemala—everyone except, of course, the defeated Confederacy after the Civil War. The great cities must be saved, and they will be, and guess who will be paying the freight for the next thirty or forty years, that is, guess who will be paying more than their share of federal taxes while Detroiters, New Yorkers, Bostonians pay less? The taxpayers of the Southern Rim. And perhaps this is only as it should be. It gives a certain satisfaction, the South having to save the Union. After all, it is our turn.

* * *

I have no idea whether in the year 2000 we of the Southeast, the 15
old Confederacy, will simply have become a quaint corner of the
teeming Southern Rim, some 100 million souls with their populaton
center and spiritual heartland somewhere between Dallas and L.A.;
whether our best writers will be doing soap opera in Atlanta or
writing up restored houses in *Southern Living*, our best composers
turning out country-and-western in Nashville, our best film directors making sequels to *Walking Tall* and *Smokey and the Bandit*; whether
our supreme cultural achievement will be the year Alabama ranked
number one, the Atlanta Falcons won the Super Bowl, and Bobby
Jones III made it a grand slam at Augusta.

There is nothing wrong with any of these achievements. The 16
name of the game has always been excellence—excellence in business, politics, literature, sports, whatever. The difference is that the
peculiar isolation and disabilities under which the South labored
for so long and which served some southern writers so well and
preoccupied all southern politicians are now things of the past.
Now the South appears to have won after all, and both the southern
writer and politician are somewhat at a loss.

Of course something else could happen in the old Southeast, 17
something besides the building of more Hyatts and Hiltons and the
preserving of old buildings, perhaps even something comparable
to the astonishing burst of creative energy in Virginia 200 years ago.

At least we have gotten past the point Mr. Dabbs spoke of when 18
he said that the trouble with the South was that it could not quarrel
with itself. Not only do I feel free to quarrel with the South, or the
North, or the U.S., I feel obliged to. A nice lady in my home town
said to me the other day: You're just like certain other southern
writers—no sooner do you get published in New York than you
turn on the South and criticize it. At the time I didn't have the
nerve, but I felt like saying: You're damn right, lady, I sure do.

Whichever way it goes, Sunbelt or southeastern renascence, one 19
thing seems reasonably certain: the southerner will be, is already,
much more like his ancestor in 1820 than his ancestor in 1920. That
is, he is both southern and American, but much more like other
Americans than he is different. If he is black, he may discover to
his amazement that he is more like his white countrymen, for better
or worse, than he is like Ugandans. Like most of us, he is out to
make a life for himself, make money, build a house, raise a family,
buy a Winnebago or a Sony Trinitron, go skiing at Aspen.

Yet maybe the southerner will retain a soupçon of difference. And who knows? It might even leaven the lump.

CONTENT

1. What similarities does Percy find in the analogy between a man with a toothache and the South's preoccupation with race?
2. What illustrations does Percy offer of the siphoning off of southern talent because of this preoccupation? Why has the obsession ended?
3. What further developments does Percy envision in the South? Does he think the shift of capital and culture to the Sunbelt will be an unmixed blessing? Why or why not?

ORGANIZATION

4. Percy begins with a clever analogy. Does he continue to develop the analogy throughout the essay?
5. Which paragraphs are developed by using examples? Which paragraphs follow a cause–effect pattern?

TOPICS FOR WRITING

6. Write an essay on the subject of prejudice (religious, racial, sexual, cultural, age), developing part of the essay using an analogy.
7. Discuss some recent change in society by using an analogy.

WENDELL BERRY
The Likenesses of Atonement (At-one-ment)

Wendell Berry combines the best worlds of teaching, writing, and farming. He has written three novels, five volumes of poetry, and is best known for his collections of essays: The Long-Legged House *(1969),* A Continuous Harmony *(1972), and* Essays Cultural and Agricultural *(1982). He teaches English at the University of Kentucky, and lives with his family on a farm on the*

Kentucky River outside Port Royal, Kentucky. In "The Likenesses of Atonement (At-one-ment)," Berry presents in a simple analogy the essential tenets of the creed he lives by, a creed based on the harmony, or at-one-ness, of all things.

Living in our speech, though no longer in our consciousness, is 1 an ancient system of analogies that clarifies a series of mutually defining and sustaining unities: of farmer and field, of husband and wife, of the world and God. The language both of our literature and of our everyday speech is full of references and allusions to this expansive metaphor of farming and marriage and worship. A man planting a crop is like a man making love to his wife, and vice versa: he is a husband or a husbandman. A man praying is like a lover, or he is like a plant in a field waiting for rain. As husbandman, a man is both the steward and the likeness of God, the greater husbandman. God is the lover of the world and its faithful husband. Jesus is a bridegroom. And he is a planter; his words are seeds. God is a shepherd and we are his sheep. And so on.

All the essential relationships are comprehended in this meta- 2 phor. A farmer's relation to his land is the basic and central connection in the relation of humanity to the creation; the agricultural relation *stands for* the larger relation. Similarly, marriage is the basic and central community tie; it begins and stands for the relation we have to family and to the larger circles of human association. And these relationships to the creation and to the human community are in turn basic to, and may stand for, our relationship to God— or to the sustaining mysteries and powers of the creation.

(These three relationships are dependent—and even intent— 3 upon renewals of various sorts: of season, of fertility, of sexual energy, of love, of faith. And these concepts of renewal are always accompanied by concepts of loss or death; in order for the renewal to take place, the old must be not forgotten but relinquished; in order to become what we may be, we must cease to be as we are; in order to leave life we must lose it. Our language bears abundant testimony to these deaths: the year's death that precedes spring; the burial of the seed before germination; sexual death, as in the Elizabethan metaphor; death as the definitive term of marriage; the spiritual death that must precede rebirth; the death of the body that must precede resurrection.)

As the metaphor comprehends all the essential relationships, so too it comprehends all the essential moralities. The moralities are ultimately emulative. For the metaphor does not merely perceive the likeness of these relationships. It perceives also that they are understandable only in terms of each other. They are the closed system of our experience; no instructions come from outside. A man finally cannot act upon the basis of absolute law, for the law is more fragmentary than his own experience; finally, he must emulate in one relationship what he knows of another. Thus, if the metaphor of atonement is alive in his consciousness, he will see that he should love and care for his land as for his wife, that his relation to his place in the world is as solemn and demanding, and as blessed, as marriage; and he will see that he should respect his marriage as he respects the mysteries and transcendent powers— that is, as a sacrament. Or—to move in the opposite direction through the changes of the metaphor—in order to care properly for his land he will see that he must emulate the Creator: to learn to use and preserve the open fields, as Sir Albert Howard said, he must look into the woods; he must study and follow natural process; he must understand the *husbanding* that, in nature, always accompanies providing.

Like any interlinking system, this one fails in the failure of any one of its parts. When we obscure or corrupt our understanding of any one of the basic unities, we begin to misunderstand all of them. The vital knowledge dies out of our consciousness and becomes fossilized in our speech and our culture. This is our condition now. We have severed the vital links of the atonement metaphor, and we did this initially, I think, by degrading and obscuring our connection to the land, by looking upon the land as merchandise and ourselves as its traveling salesmen.

I do not know how exact a case might be made, but it seems to me that there is a historical parallel, in white American history, between the treatment of the land and the treatment of women. The frontier, for instance, was notoriously exploitive of both, and I believe for largely the same reasons. Many of the early farmers seem to have worn out farms and wives with equal regardlessness, interested in both mainly for what they would produce, crops and dollars, labor and sons; they clambered upon their fields and upon their wives, struggling for an economic foothold, the having and holding that cannot come until both fields and wives are properly cherished. And today there seems to me a distinct connection between our nomadism (our "social mobility") and the nearly universal disintegration of our marriages and families.

The prevalent assumption appears to be that marriage problems are problems strictly of "human relations": if the husband and wife will only assent to a number of truisms about "respect for the other person," "giving and taking," et cetera, and if they will only "understand" each other, then it is believed that their problems will be solved. The difficulty is that marriage is only partly a matter of "human relations," and only partly a circumstance of the emotions. It is also, and as much as anything, a practical circumstance. It is very much under the influence of things and people outside itself; that is, it must make a household, it must make a place for itself in the world and in the community. But with us, getting someplace always involves going somewhere. Every professional advance leads to a new place, a new house, a new neighborhood. Our marriages are always being cut off from what they have made; their substance is always disappearing into the thin air of human relations. 7

I think there is a limit to the portability of human relationships. Tribal nomads, when they moved, moved as a tribe; their personal and cultural identity—their household and community—accompanied them as they went. But our modern urban nomads are always moving away from the particulars by which they know themselves, and moving into abstraction (*a* house, *a* neighborhood, *a* job) in which they can only feel threatened by new particulars. The marriage becomes a sort of assembly-line product, made partly here and partly there, the whole of it never quite coming into view. Provided they stay married (which is unlikely) until the children leave (which is usually soon), the nomadic husband and wife who look to see what their marriage has been—that is to say, what it *is*—are apt to see only the lines in each other's face. 8

The carelessness of place that must accompany our sort of nomadism makes a vagueness in marriage that is its antithesis. And vagueness in marriage, the most sacred human bond and perhaps the basic metaphor of our moral and religious tradition, cannot help but produce a diminishment of reverence, and of the care for the earth that must accompany reverence. 9

When the metaphor of atonement ceases to be a live function of 10 our consciousness, we lose the means of relationship. We become isolated in ourselves, and our behavior becomes the erratic destructive behavior of people who have no bonds and no limits.

CONTENT

1. What is the central analogy of Berry's essay? Is there one analogy or are there three?
2. What is the meaning of the pun in the title "At-one-ment"? What should be "at one"?
3. What historical example does Berry cite to illustrate how the unity of reverence for the land and one's wife was shattered?
4. Why does Berry feel that today's "nomadism" is destructive to marriage?

ORGANIZATION

5. Berry's essay is divided into two parts: the first emphasizing the positive aspects of the analogy; the second, the negative aspects of violating what Berry calls the "basic metaphor of our moral and religious tradition." Where is the break between the two halves of the essay? Why does Berry work from the positive to the negative? What is his basic purpose?
6. Show how the opening sentence of this essay is a thesis announcing the organization of the entire essay.

TOPICS FOR WRITING

7. Find an analogy which expresses the relationship between: good friends, members of a class, parents and children, doctors and patients, brothers and sisters.
8. Find a hidden metaphor in our language that expresses social or moral relationships; use it as the basis of an essay. (Use the *Oxford English Dictionary* or Eric Partridge's *Origins* as your source.)

Process Analysis

Process analysis, like narration, involves telling a story—in this case the story of how something is made, how it works, how it is done, or even, how it came into being. A process analysis essay is often called a "how to" paper, and it includes such diverse types of writing as recipes in a cookbook, an account of how a bill becomes a law in a political science text, an explanation of how to change a tire in an automobile owner's manual, directions in a chemistry lab manual about how to make hydrogen sulfide, a description of how a baleen whale feeds. All of these different kinds of writing have one thing in common—they explain "how."

The best examples of a process essay's pattern of organization are cookbook recipes; they have all four of the essential elements of a process. The following recipe for a scrambled omelette is a step-by-step process containing all four essential elements of any process analysis:

Scrambled Omelette

This is best in a French omelette pan, but a skillet can be used. For 1 omelette, 1 to 2 servings. Time: Less than 30 seconds of cooking.

> 2 or 3 eggs
> Big pinch of salt
> Pinch of pepper
> A mixing bowl
> A table fork
> 1 Tablespoon butter
> An omelette pan 7 inches in diameter at the bottom

Step 1
Beat the eggs and seasonings in the mixing bowl for 20 to 30 seconds until the white and yolks are just blended.

Step 2
Place the butter in the pan and set over very high heat. If you have an electric heat element, it should be red hot. As the butter melts, tilt the pan in all directions to film the sides. When you see that the foam has almost subsided in the pan and the butter is on the point of coloring, it is an indication that it is hot enough to pour in the eggs.

Step 3
Hold the panhandle with your left hand, thumb on top, and immediately start sliding the pan back and forth rapidly over the heat. At the same time, fork in right hand, its flat side against the bottom of the pan, stir the eggs quickly to spread them continuously all over the bottom of the pan as they thicken. In 3 or 4 seconds they will become a light, broken custard. (A filling would go in at this point.)

Step 4
Then lift the handle of the pan to tilt it at a 45-degree angle over the heat, and rapidly gather the eggs at the far lip of the pan with the back of your fork. Still holding the pan tilted over the heat, run your fork around the lip of the pan under the far edge of the omelette to be sure it has not adhered to the pan.

Step 5
Give 4 or 5 short, sharp blows on the handle of the pan with your right fist to loosen the omelette and make the far edge curl over onto itself.

Hold the pan tilted over the heat for 1 or 2 seconds, very lightly, but not too long or the egg will overcook. The center of the omelette should remain soft and creamy.

Turn the omelette onto the plate . . . , rub the top with a bit of butter, and serve as soon as possible. [Julia Child, Louisette Bertholle, Simone Beck, *Mastering the Art of French Cooking* (Alfred A. Knopf, 1971), Vol. 1, 129–31.]

The four elements of a process are:

1. *What's needed* Most processes—the mechanical ones and scientific ones, anyway—involve some raw materials or ingredients that are about to undergo some kind of change. There is often some sort of machinery needed to cause the change. The cookbook recipe begins with the list of ingredients—eggs, butter, spices—and any equipment necessary to make the recipe: a 7" pan, a blender.

2. *The element of time* A cookbook recipe indicates how long each stage should take, and the stages themselves are presented in a chronological order: "Beat the eggs and seasonings . . . for 20 to 30 seconds. . ."

3. *The process itself* The process involves a narration of the step-by-step procedure in the order that makes the most logical sense. The steps are numbered or are signalled by words like "next," "then," or "when," which mark the transitions between the steps. The changes brought about in the product are indicated as it goes through tem-

porary transformations; in our omelette recipe, for example, "when you see that the foam has almost subsided in the pan . . ."

4. *The end product* The cookbook recipe tells you at the outset what process you are up to, whether it's making brownies or a soup. The quantity or physical appearance of the final product is also indicated at the conclusion of the process; thus a cookbook indicates how many the recipe serves, and perhaps something of the dish's color, shape or texture.

As we mentioned before, there are several types of processes. It is wise to determine which type you are dealing with: Some emphasize change more than others; some involve tools, machinery, or apparatus, while others do not; and some involve as much description as narration and explanation.

Mechanical Process   This is the type of process that we encounter every day when we read instructions about how to put something together. The many do-it-yourself books, which teach everything from how to build your own patio to how to change the sparkplugs in your car, are all examples of mechanical processes.

The following is a simple mechanical process explaining how to replace spark plugs in three easy steps:

1. Unfasten the spark plug cables by pulling on the boot, not on the cable itself.

2. Unscrew and remove the old spark plugs with their metal gaskets.

3. Set the gap on the new plugs to the correct clearance, and install them. Reconnect the spark plug cables in the correct order.

Notice that the process simply involves performing the necessary steps; the writer is unconcerned with the scientific principles which lie behind the functioning of the spark plug.

Scientific Process   Any process that involves the demonstration of scientific principles—or an explanation of a natural process that is not purely mechanical—is a scientific process. There may seem little difference between the mechanical process (which explains how to replace spark plugs) and the following paragraph (which explains how an accumulator battery works), but this second example is a scientific process because it emphasizes the scientific principles, the chemistry involved in the process:

> By far the most common batteries are accumulators of the lead acid type. These have interleaved lead grids, alternately connected to the positive and negative terminal posts, immersed in dilute sulphuric acid. The positive plate of a charged accumulator has its grids filled with lead peroxide and the negative plate with spongy lead.
>
> As the battery discharges, the peroxide changes to lead sulphate, having taken some of the sulphur from the acid, and the same change affects the spongy lead plate. When both plates are the same and all the sulphur has gone from the acid, leaving only water, the battery cannot produce any more current. By applying a charging current across the terminals the chemical action can be reversed. [John Day, *The Bosch Book of the Motor Car* (St. Martin's Press, 1976), 207.]

Scientific process is distinct from cause–effect analysis since the writer's primary purpose is to tell the story of the process, not to explore in any detailed way the causal features of the sequence.

Historical Process   All processes involve time and change of some kind, but when you chronicle the stages of change, you are involved in documenting historical process. (This activity differs from the historian's search for the meaning of historic events, an activity involving causal analysis). The chronological account of how the Federal Constitution was adopted, state by state or the many historical accounts of how the frontier was settled are accounts of historical processes. Peter Matthiessen's book *Wildlife in America* (1959) contains many historical accounts of how a number of once plentiful species became extict or endangered. His account of the destruction of the passenger pigeon, an historial process, doesn't dwell so much on the biology of the species (or on the causal factors of its extinction), but on the historical stages which, in Matthiessen's words, "whirled into the vortex of extinction . . . the most numerous bird ever to exist on earth."

Process analysis may not seem the most elegant or intellectual pattern of organization. However, in an increasingly specialized world where one person's knowledge of a process is another person's ignorance, process analysis becomes increasingly necessary to both readers and writers. Without process analysis to provide explanations in fields outside our own range of expertise, it would be virtually impossible to follow or give many explanations intended for a non-specialized audience.

SHORT EXAMPLE—PROCESS ANALYSIS

TRACY KIDDER
The Future of the Photovoltaic Cell

Tracy Kidder (see page 186), although he has also written prize-winning fiction, is most well known for his lucid approach to complicated technical subjects. For example, when Kidder explains it, the transformation of sunlight to electrical energy in a silicon wafer seems a simple process.

In solid-state physics lies a fundamental surprise, like the rabbit inside a magician's top hat. This is the recognition that the apparently quiescent, lumpish things of nature may be veritable carnivals of change and motion on the inside. Most solar cells on the market today are made of silicon, which along with oxygen is found in ordinary sand and is the second most abundant element on earth. A few complex, expensive processes tear the silicon away from the oxygen and convert it into a very thin wafer of crystal. Sunlight penetrating such a crystalline wafer will transfer some of its energy to some of the atomic particles inside—specifically, to the little bits of matter called electrons. (As high school courses in physics teach, electrons are what make electricity; a flow of electrons *is* an electrical current.) In effect, the light that enters the wafer of silicon will knock some electrons away from their atoms and set them free.

But to manage this small internal ferment, to make the electrons move in an orderly, useful fashion, the manufacturer must turn the silicon wafer into a sandwich. Imagine two slightly different slices of material fused together face to face. In a sense, a very rough and incomplete one, this sandwich is a battery, one slice representing the positive pole, the other the negative; an external wire connects the two open faces. Put this contraption out in the sun. The light passes through one slice of the sandwich and, reaching the area where the two slices meet, breaks chemical bonds, releasing electrons. If the wafer were not a sandwich but all of a piece, the freed electrons would quickly return where they came from, and that would be the end of it. But by giving the wafer two sides, imbued with opposite electrical properties, the manufacturer has created an internal pressure which forces the loosened electrons to one side of the sandwich and the broken bonds to the other. The broken bonds and electrons are of opposite charges. They are attracted to each other. But they cannot flow back the way they came: the pressure is one-way. So the electrons take the path of least resistance, and flow outward to the open face on their side of the wafer and into the external wire. Attach to this wire a small bulb and it should light up.

DISCUSSION

Because the function of this process analysis is to explain how a photovoltaic cell works, Kidder chooses to discuss the scientific principles behind the operation in his first paragraph. This preliminary explanation makes it easier to concentrate on the process itself in the second paragraph. Kidder, therefore, explains the elementary physics involved when a crystalline wafer of silicon is exposed to sunlight. With the fundamentals out of the way, Kidder then uses an analogy to help the reader visualize a single photovoltaic silicone cell. He compares the silicon wafer first to a sandwich (to give the reader some idea of its shape), then to a battery to make its electrical operation comprehensible. All the parts of a process are here: the material involved, the stages of the process, and finally, the end product—in this case usable electrical energy. The entire process is simplified by Kidder's first explaining the purpose of the wafer sandwich, and then his showing what would happen if such a shape were not used. The final product, lighting a small bulb, clearly illustrates the applicability of the process. Like any good explanation of a scientific process, Kidder's is clear and comphrensible to a layman with no prior knowledge of the process itself or the principles behind it.

MICHAEL LENEHAN
The Quality of the Instrument

Michael Lenehan (born 1949) graduated from the University of Notre Dame in 1971, and since 1972 has been a writer and editor with a weekly, The Chicago Reader. *He writes on "whatever strikes my fancy," and in 1978 won the*

Westinghouse Science Writing Award for an article on bees and beekeeping. Since 1981, he has been a contributor to Atlantic where "The Quality of the Instrument" first appeared. In this selection, adapted from the longer essay, Lenehan explains how a Steinway grand piano emerges "from a pile of dusty, weather-beaten wood."

When I first visited the Steinway & Sons plant, on a hot, sticky morning last summer, Peter Perez, then the president of the company, took me on a hurried tour of the premises. I recall very little of the tour's middle parts, but I was struck dumb by its beginning and end—the lumberyard and the loading dock, where I saw essentially the same things I would have seen a hundred years before. The lumberyard, just outside the south wall of the factory complex, was a most unimpressive sight. Perez told me that I was looking at more than a million dollars' worth of wood from many faraway places, but all I saw was stack after stack of boards discolored by the elements; to my unschooled eye, they looked unfit for a little boy's treehouse. Seconds later, however—or so it seemed—I stood on the loading dock, at the north end of the factory, and there I beheld a Steinway model D, the eight-foot, eleven-and-three-quarter-inch, $28,000 concert grand piano on which the company's coveted reputation rests. It seemed to me a sculpture. This was the model played by Josef Hofmann, Vladimir Horowitz, and countless other great artists. The pianist and historian Arthur Loesser, a man not given to syrupy enthusiasms, had once described its sound as "a tone that craved to stream out of itself, to blend with all other tone, to merge ecstatically into a universal ocean of tone." According to a much-repeated estimate made years ago, it comprised some 12,000 parts, from inch-long bits of maple to a 340-pound plate of cast iron. It had taken nearly a year to build and had passed through the hands of more than 200 workers. None of these facts, however, impressed me as much as the look of the thing: the sinuous curves of its open top, the bold diagonals of its bass strings; its satiny black lacquer, vivid red felt and cloth, brilliant white keys, and lustrous brass-colored metal. It reeked of quality. I marveled that it had been made from a pile of dusty, weather-beaten wood, and I returned the next day to see how it had been done.

On August 21, 1981, I went to the fourth floor of the plant to meet a few parts: a rim that had been constructed in early February; a soundboard that had been finished in June; a cast-iron plate that had been delivered from a foundry in Ohio at about the same time. A model D—its name would be K 2571—was about to be constructed from these parts and thousands of others, and I planned to attend the creation. A supervisor on the floor heard of my intention and amused himself with it. He made a few quick mental calculations and announced, grinning, "You'll be with us for Christmas!" I was.

The wood that is transformed into a Steinway model D is of several different kinds, each with its own characteristics and purposes. Yellow poplar, which is soft and relatively cheap, is used as the "core wood" of such flat, tablelike parts as the piano's top; it is veneered with mahogany to give an attractive appearance. Maple is used where extreme hardness is necessary—for example, in the pin block, also called the wrest plank, which must hold the tuning pins tight against the tension of the strings, and in the action, whose hundreds of tiny moving parts must be machined to precise tolerances. Sitka spruce, light in weight and high in strength, is used for structural cross braces; also, because it has long, parallel fibers that vibrate freely, it is used in the soundboard, the thin panel inside the case that amplifies the vibrations of the strings and projects their sound into the air.

Before these woods can begin their year-long journey through the factory, they must wait outside, drying and curing, for nine months or more. Warren Albrecht, Steinway's lumber buyer and wood technologist, told me that some of the lumber arriving in the yard is actually up to 80 percent water. The water has to go. Wood expands and contracts as it takes on and loses moisture; before being fashioned into parts that will fit together, it must be dried to a water content of about 6 percent, to minimize the possible changes in dimension. Breathing the New York air for several months is the first of two drying steps; despite rain and snow, this reduces the wood's water content to about 25 percent. Wringing out the remainder usually requires several weeks of kiln drying, in cavernous rooms where temperatures of up to 160 degrees Fahrenheit shrink the lumber to about nine-tenths of its original volume. I asked Albrecht to take me into one of the kilns, but found standing for a few seconds at the open door of one quite sufficient to satisfy my curiosity.

After drying, the wood goes to the crosscut department, on the first floor of the factory, to be prepared for the woodworkers. Here the discolored surfaces are planed away—the wood looks new again. Boards are cut to convenient lengths according to their destinies, and all sections containing knots and other intolerable imperfections are thrown on the scrap heap. Another third of the lumber's original volume is lost in this way. Along with the cuttings, shavings, and sawdust produced elsewhere in the factory, the scrap goes into a wood-burning boiler that supplements the plant's conventional oil furnace. All told, as much as 60 percent of the lumber Steinway buys either evaporates or goes up in smoke. The rest goes into pianos.

In various departments on the first and second floors of the factory, the wood is transformed from boards into rough approximations of piano parts. A naif in the ways of woodworking, I found in these departments the answers to questions I had never thought of asking. For example: Given that maple trees grow up and down, as a rule, how does one obtain the curvaceous contours of a grand piano's rim? If the top of a piano measures roughly sixty inches at its widest point, does one need a five-foot-thick poplar tree to make it? If birch, the wood from which piano legs are carved, is generally available in the form of boards no more than three inches thick, whence come the blocky chunks of wood with which the carvers start?

In a word, the answer to these questions is glue. The block from which a model-D leg is carved is made of two pieces of birch glued together. The large sheet of poplar that becomes a top is simply fifteen to twenty boards glued together along their lengths. Much of the gluing is done on gangly "glue wheels," which look vaguely like giant metal Rolodexes; their "cards," a dozen or so per wheel, are clamp assemblies that hold the pieces of wood in place while the glue sets. The blocks and panels that result are slapdash—irregularly shaped, and patterned with streams of hardened excess glue—but when they have been planed and sanded the seams virtually disappear, and the pieces look almost as if they had been cut whole from oversize trees.

Having heard comments around the factory about the difficulty of obtaining wood in convenient sizes, I asked Warren Albrecht if this gluing of blocks and panels was a traditional woodworking practice or a new one made necessary by the limited sizes in which lumber is available today. He answered that it was a little bit of both. "We don't have the selection of trees we used to have, because trees of the quality we need take, let's say, a hundred years to grow to full size; they don't grow them to full size anymore. So the boards are getting narrower, and we probably have to put more boards in a panel than we used to. But woodworkers have pretty much always glued up panels. The concept itself, I guess, has been around for the entire history of the piano. You have to do it, for certain items."

Albrecht went on to correct the mistaken assumption implied in my question: that a built-up block or panel is weaker, less stable, or somehow inferior to a piece of wood cut solid from a log. "The glue is stronger than the wood," he said. "If you do a proper job of gluing a panel and then try to break that panel, you'll find the wood is going to break rather than the glue joint. Gluing also helps because any one board might have a tendency to, say, shrink or swell more than another board. By putting boards of varying characteristics together, you can compensate. You'll get an overall average stability."

The most difficult gluing job in the creation of a Steinway—and the most spectacular, a favorite on the factory visitors' tour—is the construction of the rim. Actually there are two rims: the outer rim, the piano's exterior wall; and the inner rim, a shallower interior wall that forms a ledge to which the cast-iron plate and soundboard are attached. Most piano makers build the two rims separately: they make the inner rim first, build the piano's works onto it, and then glue the outer rim around it. Steinway builds the inner and outer rims together, as a single piece, which makes for stronger, more integral construction, perhaps a better sound, and certainly a lot more work.

The rim begins as quarter-inch-thick slats of maple, which arrive at the lumberyard in various lengths and widths, none of them appropriate to the task. Some of the slats must be "paneled," or glued along their lengths, to a width of about twelve and one-half inches—the approximate depth of the model D's outer rim. Others must be "ripped," or sawed along their lengths, to about half that width—the inner rim. Boards of like width are glued and tongue-jointed to a length of twenty-two feet, which is roughly the measure of the piano's perimeter from the bass side around to the treble. (There is no left and right in a piano factory, only bass and treble.) Typically, a "book" of boards—one rim's worth—consists of nine narrow maple boards, five wider ones, and four layers of other types added for strength and decoration. At this point the rim wood is about 10 percent water instead of the usual 6. The extra moisture is needed for pliability, because the eighteen layers of wood, some three and one-half inches thick in all, are about to be coerced—bent, shoved, and grunted over—into the impossible curves that make up the shape of a grand piano. Not one at a time, but all at once.

This happens in a large basement room where eight massive piano-shaped forms of steel, their perimeters fitted with gargantuan screws and clamps, stand along two walls almost like instruments in a showroom. These are rimbending presses, the tools of the maple's fate. The model-D press goes into service most mornings at 9:45, when the rim-department crew returns from its coffee break. As a special precaution—one of many taken throughout the factory for the model D—one man stays behind at break time to mix a new batch of urea-resin glue, which is most effective when it is fresh. This is done because the D rim is the largest Steinway makes—and therefore the most susceptible to failure—and because the model D is the flagship of the Steinway line. Not that it happens, but if the rim of a baby grand model S were to spring apart at the seams one day, it would most likely be in the living room of a kindly old music teacher somewhere in the Midwest; if a model D were to come unglued it might be on the stage of a Carnegie Hall. 12

The crew of six, some with glue buckets, rags, and brushes in hand, line up in single file along a narrow bench about two feet high. At one end of this bench is an automatic glue applicator, a wringer-like machine through which the department's foreman, Ralph D'Alleva, feeds the wooden layers one at a time. The long boards have been scored on both sides to give the best possible gluing surface. They have also been arranged so that the "inside" of one board—the side that grew closest to the center of the tree—faces the "outside" of the next; each layer will thus counteract the warping tendency of its neighbor. As each board emerges from the gluing machine, the workers line it up on the bench. Some spread glue over spots the machine has missed, and one cleans excess glue with a wet rag. D'Alleva yells "Glue!" and a man appears at his side with a bucket, emptying it into the machine. The work is hurried. Once the glue is applied, the crew has twenty minutes to get the wood clamped into the press. In the old days, when they used hot glue made from animal matter, they had even less time. 13

Within a few minutes, the "book" has been assembled and aligned on the bench, the wider layers of the outer rim on top. Now the 14 crewmen, protecting their hands with thick sheets of sandpaper, lift the heavy mass of wood and struggle hurriedly with it to the press. Starting at the front, or keyboard end, of the piano, they lay and clamp the book first along the straight bass side of the press— the easy part. Next, however, comes an extremely difficult part, the virtual ninety-degree bend at the back. D'Alleva says, "All right, start movin'," and there follows a flurry of heaving, shoving, and pulling against the wood's desire to remain straight. A few men apply clamps and tighten screws with T-bars bigger than tire irons. Another evens the layers with a block of wood, setting it against their edges and pounding it from above with a large hammer. The block he uses is itself a section cut from an old laminated rim—a reminder, perhaps, that this crazy process will really work, that the wood will stay in place once the glue dries.

The wood's resistance increases as the men wrap it around to the treble side of the press. One of the crew takes up a wooden lever about five feet tall, shaped roughly like a lowercase letter *b*, and, as a couple of others pull the last section of rim into place with a block and tackle, he and a few mates apply the bulbous end of the lever against the wood and press it into the graceful curve near the front of the piano. They look remarkably like the Marines who raised the flag over Iwo Jima. "Push!" "Get it!" "Once more!" . . .

"Okay!" Suddenly, the frenzy subsides. The rebellious wood is locked safely in the press. A couple of crewmen casually tighten clamps, and the rest walk off to their next task.

The rim of K 2571 was bent in this fashion on February 6, 1981. The next workday, it was removed from the press, upended, and placed in a brace that kept its ends from flying out. It spent ten weeks in the humidity-controlled rim-bending room, during which time the maple's water content was slowly reduced to about 6 percent. By then, the wood had "forgotten" its original shape. In April, it was taken to the frazing department, where workers sawed, planed, and sanded it to specifications, and from there it went to the case-making department, where cross braces, a key bed, and a pin block were installed. Now a "case" instead of a "rim," it went in June to the lacquer department, where, except for very rare special orders, each model D receives five coats of functional, basic black.

At about the same time the lacquering began on the fourth floor of the factory, a soundboard and a cast-iron plate were taking shape on the first and second floors. The soundboard's function is to amplify the sound of a slender string into a sound capable of filling a concert hall, and every detail of its construction is aimed at maximizing its ability to vibrate. The wood is an expensive grade of Sitka spruce, with no fewer than ten grains, or growth rings, per inch. It is sawed from the log so that its grain lines—and thus its vibrating fibers—run straight along the length of each board. The soundboard panel, made of about twenty boards glued together along their lengths, is thinned in places, like the face of a fine violin, to encourage movement. Finally, and most important, the board is made to bow out slightly in the center: the bridge, the long, snaky strip of laminated maple on which the strings will rest, is affixed to the top of the panel, and ribs are affixed to the underside, such that the board is distorted into a slight crown, increasing its ability to project sound waves into the air.

The cast-iron plate, made by the Wickham Piano Plate Company, of Springfield, Ohio, arrived at the factory an intricately shaped but roughly finished hunk of dull gray metal. Workers in the plate department, on the first floor of the factory, ground down its rough edges, smoothed its surface, painted it gold, and buffed it to a soft, brassy luster. Also, with the guidance of templates prepared and maintained by the engineering department—"patterns," they are called—they installed the pieces that would later determine the crucial placement of the strings: the agraffes, the guideposts through which the strings emerge at the front of the piano; and the hitch pins, around which they loop in the back. 19

The cast-iron plate embodies the two major design elements that propelled Steinway & Sons to the top of the piano business in the mid-1800s. One of these elements was the use of the plate itself, which permitted much higher string tension than could be borne by pianos made entirely of wood or of wood fortified with metal bars. The added strength allowed the use of bigger—and thus louder—strings. The second design element was the piano's "scale," which is essentially the arrangement of its strings—their vibrating lengths, their placement on the bridge, and the point at which they are struck by the hammers. 20

The most important feature of the new Steinway scale was the "overstringing" technique, in which the bass strings, instead of running parallel to the others, are fanned over them diagonally in a second tier of strings; this permitted longer bass strings and, again, more volume. Neither of these design elements was radical: 21 overstringing had been used in square pianos since the 1830s; the metal plate had been developed by the Boston piano maker Alpheus Babcock in the 1820s, and Jonas Chickering, also of Boston—the foremost American piano maker before the Steinways came along— had been using it in his grand pianos since the 1840s. The Steinways' masterstroke was to combine the two ideas in a new design, which also included heavier hammers to excite the heavier strings, a subtly improved action to permit control of the heavier hammers, and a repositioning of the bridge from the rear of the soundboard toward the middle.

The result was an instrument unlike any heard before. Hector Berlioz, encountering the Steinway at the international exposition of Paris in 1867, remarked not only on its "splendid and noble sonority" but on the ingenuity of its scaling, which subdued the "terrible resonance of the minor seventh," an undesirable overtone occasionally heard from other pianos of the time. The exposition's jurors were likewise impressed: even though none of them was an American (patriotism was often an important factor in these international trade shows), they awarded the Steinway their gold medal. Within a few years, the prestigious old piano houses of Europe were fading into obscurity, and the rest of the industry was quickly adopting what had come to be called the "American system" or "Steinway system" of piano design. Those terms are not used much today, because today there is no other system.

CONTENT

1. Why does Lenehan begin his process by describing the final product: a $28,000 concert grand piano? Why does the first paragraph also include a description of the Steinway lumberyard?

2. Why is so much space given over to the process of constructing the rim? What surprises Lenehan about the material that goes into its construction?

3. Lenehan gives considerable space to the cast-iron plate and the soundboard. What is unique about this feature of the Steinway piano?

ORGANIZATION

4. How many of the ingredients of the typical process analysis are present in Lenehan's essay? What kind of process is it?

5. One of the problems in organizing this particular process is that different parts of the process are going on simultaneously. How does Lenehan get around this?
6. How much attention does Lenehan give to materials, tools, and the final product? Does he explain any technical terms to the uninitiated? Is the process interesting and clear?

TOPICS FOR WRITING
7. Explain a mechanical process that involves assembling a number of separate parts.
8. Explain how to make an item with which most people are unfamiliar.

LEWIS THOMAS
How We Process Information

Lewis Thomas, physician, teacher administrator, writer, began in 1971 to write a monthly column in the New England Journal of Medicine *under the title "Notes of a Biology Watcher." When these were published in book form in 1974 under the title* The Lives of a Cell: Notes of a Biology Watcher, *Thomas won a National Book Award. A second collection appeared in 1979 under the title* The Medusa and the Snail. *In the following essay Thomas contends that without ambiguity in language we might engage in small talk, but we would not be capable of communicating new information.*

According to the linguistic school currently on top, human beings are all born with a genetic endowment for recognizing and formulating language. This must mean that we possess genes for all kinds of information, with strands of special, peculiarly human DNA for the discernment of meaning in syntax. We must imagine the morphogenesis of deep structures*, built into our minds, for coding out, like proteins, the parts of speech. Correct grammar (correct in the logical, not fashionable, sense) is as much a biologic characteristic of our species as feathers on birds.

If this is true, it would mean that the human mind is preset, in some primary sense, to generate more than just the parts of speech. Since everything else that we recognize as human behavior derives

*That is, the origin of the grammatical formulae.

from the central mechanism of language, the same sets of genes are at least indirectly responsible for governing such astonishing behavior as in the concert hall, where hundreds of people crowd together, silent, head-tilted, meditating, listening to music as though receiving instructions, or in a gallery, moving along slowly, peering, never looking at each other, concentrating as though reading directions.

This view of things is compatible with the very old notion that a framework for meaning is somehow built into our minds at birth. We start our lives with templates, and attach to them, as we go along, various things that fit. There are neural centers for generating, spontaneously, numberless hypotheses about the facts of life. We store up information the way cells store energy. When we are lucky enough to find a direct match between a receptor and a fact, there is a deep explosion in the mind; the idea suddenly enlarges, rounds up, bursts with new energy, and begins to replicate. At times there are chains of reverberating explosions, shaking everything: the imagination, as we say, is staggered.

This system seems to be restricted to human beings, since we are the only beings with language, although chimpanzees may have the capability of manipulating symbols with a certain syntax. The great difference between us and the other animals may be the qualitative difference made by speech. We live by making transformations of energy into words, storing it up, and releasing it in controlled explosions.

Speechless animals cannot do this sort of thing, and they are limited to single-stage transactions. They wander, as we do, searching for facts to fit their sparser stock of hypotheses, but when the receptor meets its match, there is only a single thud. Without language, the energy that is encoiled, springlike, inside information can only be used once. The solitary wasp, Sphex, nearing her time of eggs, travels aloft with a single theory about caterpillars. She is, in fact, a winged receptor for caterpillars. Finding one to match the hypothesis, she swoops, pins it, paralyzes it, carries it off, and descends to deposit it precisely in front of the door of the round burrow (which, obsessed by a different version of the same theory, she had prepared beforehand). She drops the beast, enters the burrow, inspects the interior for last-minute irregularities, then comes out to pull it in for the egg-laying. It has the orderly, stepwise look of a well-thought-out business. But if, while she is inside inspecting, you move the caterpillar a short distance, she has a less sensible second thought about the matter. She emerges, searches for a moment, finds it, drags it back to the original spot, drops it again and runs inside to check the burrow again. If you move the caterpillar again, she will repeat the program, and you can keep her totally preoccupied for as long as you have the patience and the heart for it. It is a compulsive, essentially neurotic kind of behavior, as mindless as an Ionesco character, but the wasp cannot imagine any other way of doing the thing.

Lymphocytes, like wasps, are genetically programmed for exploration, but each of them seems to be permitted a different, solitary idea. They roam through the tissues, sensing and monitoring. Since there are so many of them, they can make collective guesses at almost anything antigenic on the surface of the earth, but they must do their work one notion at a time. They carry specific information in their surface receptors, presented in the form of a question: is there, anywhere out there, my particular molecular configuration? It seems to be in the nature of biologic information that it not only stores itself up as energy but also instigates a search for more. It is an insatiable mechanism. 6

Lymphocytes are apparently informed about everything foreign around them, and some of them come equipped for fitting with polymers that do not exist until organic chemists synthesize them in their laboratories. The cells can do more than predict reality; they are evidently programmed with wild guesses as well. 7

Not all animals have lymphocytes with the same range of information, as you might expect. As with language, the system is governed by genes, and there are genetic differences between species and between inbred animals of the same species. There are polymers that will fit the receptors of one line of guinea pigs or mice but not others; there are responders and non-responders. 8

When the connection is made, and a particular lymphocyte with a particular receptor is brought into the presence of the particular antigen, one of the greatest small spectacles in nature occurs. The cell enlarges, begins making new DNA at a great rate, and turns into what is termed, appropriately, a blast. It then begins dividing, replicating itself into a new colony of identical cells, all labeled with the same receptor, primed with the same question. The new cluster is a memory, nothing less. 9

For this kind of mechanism to be useful, the cells are required to stick precisely to the point. Any ambiguity, any tendency to wander from the matter at hand, will introduce grave hazards for the cells, and even more for the host in which they live. Minor inaccuracies may cause reactions in which neighboring cells are recognized as foreign, and done in. There is a theory that the process of aging may be due to the cumulative effect of imprecision, a gradual degrading of information. It is not a system that allows for deviating.

Perhaps it is in this respect that language differs most sharply from other biologic systems for communication. Ambiguity seems to be an essential, indispensable element for the transfer of information from one place to another by words, where matters of real importance are concerned. It is often necessary, for meaning to come through, that there be an almost vague sense of strangeness and askewness. Speechless animals and cells cannot do this. The specifically locked-on antigen at the surface of a lymphocyte does not send the cell off in search of something totally different; when a bee is tracking sugar by polarized light, observing the sun as though consulting his watch, he does not veer away to discover an unimaginable marvel of a flower. Only the human mind is designed to work in this way, programmed to drift away in the presence of locked-on information, straying from each point in a hunt for a better, different point.

If it were not for the capacity of ambiguity, for the sensing of strangeness, that words in all languages provide, we would have no way of recognizing the layers of counterpoint in meaning, and we might be spending all our time sitting on stone fences, staring into the sun. To be sure, we would always have had some everyday use to make of the alphabet, and we might have reached the same capacity for small talk, but it is unlikely that we would have been able to evolve from words to Bach. The great thing about human language is that it prevents us from sticking to the matter at hand.

CONTENT

1. Why does Thomas believe that for all human beings the ability to use language is a "genetic endowment"? How is information stored as energy?

2. How does the human endowment of language differ from the information stored as energy in speechless animals?

3. What does Thomas mean when he says that without ambiguity in language, "it is unlikely that we would have been able to evolve from words to Bach"?

ORGANIZATION

4. Thomas opens his essay with a consideration of how language is a genetic endowment. Next, he considers the case of two organisms: a wasp and lymphocytes. Why does he return to language at the end of his essay?

5. How effective are the explanations of the three processes for drawing upon stored information? Why did Thomas choose the examples of the wasp and lymphocytes?

6. How does Thomas organize the contrast between the way humans and other organisms process information? Could he have organized the essay differently—say, around the progression from simpler to more complex organisms? Would it be as effective?

TOPICS FOR WRITING

7. Explain a complicated process by comparing it to a simpler but comparable one.

8. Write a process analysis in which you incorporate an analogy to clarify the process.

PART 7
Mixed Patterns of Exposition

Y ou have already learned that patterns of organizing expository writing—definition, examples, division, and so on—are actually derived from ways of finding ideas, a procedure that dates back to Aristotle. So, if like Norman Cousins you wished to write about "placebos," you might logically begin with the question, "What is a placebo?" The answer to this question would lead you inevitably to use definition as your pattern of organization. Or if, like Edward Abbey, you were writing about the Great American Desert, you might begin with the question, "What kinds of desert are there?" You would then be using division as your method of organizing the answer. Or if, again like Cousins, you wanted to know what were the effects of placebos on patients, you would organize your material in one of the patterns appropriate to cause–effect.

You have also seen at the end of the sections on narrative and descriptive writing that it is rare for a piece of writing to be exclusively of one kind or another; in fact, it is more common for a writer to employ several techniques of organization within the same piece. Carefully examine the following selection. Notice that each section is addressed to a different question about the subject, and that each section *of the same essay* has a different pattern of organization.

Definition   Inflation, in the simplest of words, is an unhealthily rapid
What is it?   rise in prices over a relatively short span of time.

Its results, expressed in one way: a sharp erosion in the buying power of the currency you use to conduct all your transactions at home and in your business or profession; plus a dwindling in the future buying power of the funds you put away in cash savings or the equivalent (life insurance, U.S. savings bonds, and the like); an undermining in the value of most other investments.

Its results, expressed in another way: an upsurge in your living costs, which few can offset successfully and which, therefore, puts you in a budget squeeze, reduces your standard of living despite pay hikes you may win, all but destroys your confidence and peace of mind.

Division
What kinds
are there?

But that's not the whole tale, for there are two types of inflation—drastically different from each other.

The first type is called "demand-pull," which means that demands for goods and services during a specified period are exceeding the available supplies of those goods and services and this excess of demand (fueled by more than adequate cash or credit in the hands of buyers) is "pulling up" prices.

A classic illustration of demand-pull inflation occurred in food prices—especially meat prices—during the early post-World War II period. Millions of newly properous U.S. workers and their families sharply hiked their demands for meat, more millions steadily increased their purchases of higher quality meats, shoppers the nation over loaded their supermarket carts with roasts, steaks, lamb, veal.

The continued buying of a limited supply of meats rapidly pulled up meat prices, until the spiral culminated in the blowoff in meat prices in the wild inflation of 1974—and (at least temporarily) interrupted the long-term upsurge in our consumption of meats.

The second type is called "cost-push," which means that mounting costs of producing goods and services during a specified period are "pushing up" prices. For many, many years—possibly the longest span in modern times—we have been in the clutch of this cost-push inflation in the United States. And no end to this form of inflation is yet in sight. The leapfrogging of prices over wages, then wages over prices, then prices over wages, and on and on continues.

Cause-effect
What are its
effects?

Perhaps the most insidious evil in the overall evil of pernicious inflation is the spreading expectation that inflation will become permanent—a "psychology of inflation" that is dangerously self-fulfilling.

As millions of Americans become resigned to the prospect that the price spiral is a fact of life to be accepted for the indefinite future, these unhealthy developments follow:

More and more workers demand wage hikes to keep up with past price increases and to get a jump ahead of future price increases—thereby adding to the current inflation rate.

More and more union leaders insist on cost of living adjustment clauses in their union contracts to give them automatic pay raises as the Consumer Price Index climbs. As the 1980s approached, an estimated half of our total population—Social Security and welfare recipients as well as workers—already were converted by "COLAs."

More and more businesses boost prices in anticipation of the wage demands and of the eventual imposition of mandatory wage-price controls.

More and more consumers try to buy big-and small-ticket items "ahead" to beat the price increases they are sure will come.

The whole sick pyramid collapses into a business slump, which leads to "reflation" policies and a new round of inflation. [Sylvia Porter, *Sylvia Porter's New Money Book for the 80's* (Avon, 1980), 4–6.]

This example—and the other examples which follow this introduction—show that real writing grows out of the writer's search for material about the subject, and that the appropriate pattern of organization follows this search. This is no less true of utilitarian writing explaining how something works than of more profound writing about social and economic issues. Most professional writing is the end product of a complicated series of choices, many of which led to the pattern of organization the essay would finally take.

But how does this process of choices work in practice? How conscious are writers about the choices they will make when they select certain patterns to organize their material? Do they think of these forms as they write or do these emerge spontaneously? In one of his letters, E. B. White wrote, "I always write a thing first and think about it afterward, which is not a bad procedure, because the easiest way to have consecutive thoughts is to start putting them down." Edward Hoagland has written about the dissolving of forms in contemporary prose, where all types of writing mix: "Prose has no partitions now. . . . No forms exist anymore, except that to work as a single observer, using the resources of only one mind, and to work with words—this is being a writer." If these remarks seem to indicate that forms are ignored by writers, let's listen to descriptions of how two writers work: John McPhee (a deliberate writer searching for the underlying organic form hidden somewhere in the voluminous notes he has transcribed) and Tom Wolfe (also wondering what shape in which to cast several month's worth of research, but more impatient than McPhee to get it down on paper).

McPhee's painstaking analysis of his material, his search for the right form or pattern of organization, typifies the logical approach favored by most instructors. The plan grows out of the material; the form which emerges serves both to eliminate material and to shape the remaining contents. Here is how McPhee works:

> These are his topics, the formal segments of narrative, which he then writes on a series of index cards. After assembling the stack, he fans them out and begins to play a sort of writer's solitaire, studying the possibilities of order. Decisions don't come easily; a story has many potential sequences, and each chain produces a calculus of desired and undesired effects, depending on factors like character and theme. When he has the cards in a satisfactory arrangement, he thumbtacks them to a large bulletin board.
>
> . . . he next codes the duplicate set of notes and then scissors its sheets apart, cutting large blocks of paragraphs and two or three line ribbons. In a few hours he has reduced the sheets to thousands of scraps, which he sorts into file folders, one folder for each topical index card on the bulletin board. These folders are precompositional skeletons of the narrative segments he will refine when writing a first draft. With the folders squared away in a vertical file, he is ready to write. A large steel dart on the bulletin board marks his progress. He stabs the dart under an index card, opens a folder, further sorts scraps and ribbons until this segment also has a "logical" structure. Then, without invoking the muse, he begins to type his first draft, picking up where the lead ends. When he finishes a folder, he moves the dart, gets the next folder, sorts it out, and continues to type. [*The John McPhee Reader,* ed. and introduction by William L. Howarth (Farrar, Straus & Giroux, 1976), *xv.*]

If this seems too deliberate, too mechanical a procedure, compare McPhee's approach with this account by Tom Wolfe which explains that he has just about given up trying to find any form that will fit his miscellaneous rough notes, so he simply begins to type out those notes in a narrative explaining where he got his information.

> At first I couldn't even write the story. . . . I had a lot of trouble analyzing exactly what I had on my hands. . . . I started typing the notes

out in the form of a memorandum that began, "Dear Byron." I started typing away, starting right with the first time I saw any custom cars in California. I started recording it all, and inside of a couple of hours, typing along like a madman, I could tell that something was beginning to happen. . . . I wrapped up the memorandum about 6:15 a.m., and by this time it was 49 pages long. I took it over to *Esquire* as soon as they opened up, about 9:30 a.m. About 4 p.m. I got a call from Byron Dobell [the managing editor at *Esquire*]. He told me they were striking out the "Dear Byron" at the top of the memorandum and running the rest of it in the magazine. That was the story, "The Kandy-Kolored Tangerine-Flake Streamline Baby." [*The Kandy-Kolored Tangerine-Flake Streamline Baby* (Farrar, Straus & Giroux, 1965), *xii–xiii*.]

What these two accounts say, finally, is that really good writing reduces itself not only to the search for interesting and original ideas and an effective style, but also to the right organizational pattern or form—what Aristotle called "disposition." To find the right order of ideas, you must first know the patterns available to you and then use them—all of them—not mechanically, but with discretion, searching for that effective combination of patterns that will most completely develop your ideas and express the connections between them. Rarely will one of these patterns alone sufficiently contain all your ideas; more likely, as in the selections which follow, your essays will employ several patterns. As essayist/novelist Herb Gold has observed, "Not all organizing and structuring are rational." It may help to know that a famous sports writer, A. J. Liebling, once called one of his essays which used a variety of patterns, "a mixed pickles story." The essential criterion is: "Does it work?" Regardless of which patterns, or how many of them, you use to communicate your thoughts, if the form and content match, then your essay is at least well organized. If good organization is coupled with effective style and interesting ideas you may, like the writers who follow, produce a memorable piece of prose writing.

SHORT EXAMPLE

LOREN EISELEY

How Flowers Changed the World

Loren Eiseley (1907–1977) had the uncanny ability to translate the complexities of science and anthropology to everyday life in a clear, poetic style. His essays and histories of science include The Immense Journey *(1957),* The Mind as Nature *(1962),* The Unexpected Universe *(1969),* The Invisible Universe *(1972), and* The Star-Thrower *(1979). "How the Flowers Changed the World" examines the evolution of flowers and shows how our very existence depends on simple things we take for granted, like the miracle of flowers.*

When the first simple flower bloomed on some raw upland late in the Dinosaur Age, it was wind pollinated, just like its early pine-cone relatives. It was a very inconspicuous flower because it had not yet evolved the idea of using the surer attraction of birds and insects to achieve the transportation of pollen. It sowed its own pollen and received the pollen of other flowers by the simple vagaries of the wind. Many plants in regions where insect life is scant still follow this principle today. Nevertheless, the true flower—and the seed that it produced—was a profound innovation in the world of life.

In a way, this event parallels, in the plant world, what happened among animals. Consider the relative chance for survival of the exteriorly deposited egg of a fish in contrast with the fertilized egg of a mammal, carefully retained for months in the mother's body until the young animal (or human being) is developed to a point where it may survive. The biological wastage is less—and so it is with the flowering plants. The primitive spore, a single cell fertilized in the beginning by a swimming sperm, did not promote rapid distribution, and the young plant, moreover, had to struggle up from nothing. No one had left it any food except what it could get by its own unaided efforts.

By contrast, the true flowering plants (angiosperm itself means "encased seed") grew a seed in the heart of a flower, a seed whose development was initiated by a fertilizing pollen grain independent of outside moisture. But the seed, unlike the developing spore, is already a fully equipped *embryonic plant* packed in a little enclosed box stuffed full of nutritious food. Moreover, by featherdown attachments, as in dandelion or milkweed seed, it can be wafted upward on gusts and ride the wind for miles; or with hooks it can cling to a bear's or a rabbit's hide; or like some of the berries, it can be covered with a juicy, attractive fruit to lure birds, pass undigested through their intestinal tracts and be voided miles away.

The ramifications of this biological invention were endless. Plants 4 traveled as they had never traveled before. They got into strange environments heretofore never entered by the old spore plants or stiff pine-cone-seed plants. The well-fed, carefully cherished little embryos raised their heads everywhere. Many of the older plants with more primitive reproductive mechanisms began to fade away under this unequal contest. They contracted their range into secluded environments. Some like the giant redwoods, lingered on as relics; many vanished entirely.

The world of the giants was a dying world. These fantastic little 5 seeds skipping and hopping and flying about the woods and valleys brought with them an amazing adaptability. If our whole lives had not been spent in the midst of it, it would astound us. The old, stiff, sky-reaching wooden world had changed into something that glowed here and there with strange colors, put out queer, unheard-of fruits and little intricately carved seed cases, and, most important of all, produced concentrated foods in a way that the land had never seen before, or dreamed of back in the fish-eating, leaf-crunching days of the dinosaurs.

That food came from three sources, all produced by the repro- 6 ductive system of the flowering plants. There were the tantalizing nectars and pollens intended to draw insects for pollenizing purposes, and which are responsible also for that wonderful jeweled creation, the hummingbird. There were the juicy and enticing fruits to attract larger animals, and in which tough-coated seeds were concealed, as in the tomato, for example. Then, as if this were not enough, there was the food in the actual seed itself, the food intended to nourish the embryo. All over the world, like hot corn in a popper, these incredible elaborations of the flowering plants kept exploding. In a movement that was almost instantaneous, geologically speaking, the angiosperms had taken over the world. Grass was beginning to cover the bare earth until, today, there are over six thousand species. All kinds of vines and bushes squirmed and writhed under new trees and flying seeds.

The explosion was having its effect on animal life also. Specialized groups of insects were arising to feed on the new sources of food and, incidentally and unknowingly, to pollinate the plant. The flowers bloomed and bloomed in ever larger and more spectacular varieties. Some were pale unearthly night flowers intended to lure moths in the evening twilight, some among the orchids even took the shape of female spiders in order to attract wandering males, some flamed redly in the light of noon or twinkled modestly in the meadow grasses. Intricate mechanisms splashed pollen on the breasts of hummingbirds, or stamped it on the bellies of black, grumbling bees droning assiduously from blossom to blossom. Honey ran, insects multiplied, and even the descendants of that toothed and ancient lizard-bird had become strangely altered. Equipped with prodding beaks instead of biting teeth they pecked the seeds and gobbled the insects that were really converted nectar.

DISCUSSION

This selection illustrates most of the patterns of organization found in exposition. The first paragraph, while describing the characteristics of the earliest simple flowers, also explains how they propagated. The second paragraph compares the chances for survival of those early simple plants to survival of similar species in the animal kingdom. Once Eiseley has established the superiority of those species that carry their own food supply, he contrasts the earlier simple flowers with later angiosperms. Paragraph 3 is not just a contrasting paragraph; it also contains a definition and explains the process by which flowering plants propagate. The remaining four paragraphs all contain some form of cause–effect organization. Paragraph 4 lists the first effect: the replacement of the older spore plants or stiff pinecone-seed plants by the more easily propagated seed plants. The next paragraph presents a contrasting description of the newer brightly colored plants and the older towering wooden plants. The food encasing the seeds in the newer plants is divided into several types: nectars and pollens, fruits, and seeds themselves. In paragraph 6, other examples of angiosperms conclude the paragraph. Finally, paragraph 7 is a chain of effects stretching from the plant into the animal kingdom. Simply listing these paragraph patterns may make Eiseley's essay seem dull, but in fact, Eiseley's account of a world no one has ever seen is as lively and vivid as a good story.

Each of the patterns is used appropriately; together they form a chain of reasoning from one paragraph to the next. For example, the paragraph that classifies the food of the newer plants precedes the paragraph that describes the effect of such food on the animal kingdom. The example of the hummingbird appears in both paragraphs to illustrate the evolving dependence of animals and plants. The patterns of organization employed by Eiseley act both as heuristic devices, aiding in the search for ideas, and as ready-made forms for enclosing those ideas.

CALVIN TRILLIN
Hong Kong Dream

Calvin Trillin (born 1935) has entertained readers of The New Yorker *with his accounts of out of the way places and culinary delights since 1963. His essays are collected in* U.S. Journal *(1971),* American Fried: Adventures of a Happy Eater *(1974), and* Alice, Let's Eat: Further Adventures of a Happy Eater *(1978). Trillin has also written several volumes of fiction. "Hong Kong Dream" from* Third Helpings *(1983) illustrates Trillin's unending search for honest food in a world increasingly given to the dishonesties of haughty cuisine or styrofoam packaging.*

I can't count the number of hours I have spent in Chinatown   1
dreaming of Hong Kong. The spell usually comes over me after dinner, as I stroll with fellow-eaters down Mott Street, ostensibly engaged in what passes for after-dinner conversation on those outings—a sort of post-game analysis of the stuffed bean curd, maybe, or some mild disagreement over whether the pan-fried flounder was really as good as the last time. We are usually walking toward the amusement arcade on Mott Street near Bowery, where it is possible to finish off an evening in Chinatown by playing ticktacktoe with a live chicken. A bag of fortune cookies awaits anyone who beats the chicken, but, as far as I know, nobody ever has. The chicken gets to go first—a sign on the outside of the cage lights up "Bird's Turn" as soon as the coins are dropped—and that advantage seems to be enough to carry the day. Some people believe the chicken always wins because it is being coached by a computer that tells it

where to peck by means of light bulbs that can't quite be seen from the outside of the cage. Some people think the chicken always wins because it happens to be one smart chicken. Sometimes during that after-dinner stroll—when we are discussing the pan-fried flounder or when our best ticktacktoe player is being wiped out by a chicken or when my wife and I are negotiating with our children over whether it would be appropriate to compensate for our failure to win the fortune cookies by asking the Häagen-Dazs store and the David's Cookies store next to it to join forces for a chocolate-chocolate-chip-ice-cream sandwich on chocolate-chunk cookies or when I drop in to the supermarket across from the arcade to replenish my supply of fried dried peas—I am often heard to murmur, "I'd really like to go to Hong Kong."

"Don't you mean China?" one of my companions has sometimes said.

No, not China. I'll admit that the coverage of those banquets thrown during Richard Nixon's first visit briefly stirred in me some Presidential ambitions that had been dormant ever since I discovered, at the age of fourteen, that the President was responsible for making a budget. For those of us who spend a lot of our evenings on Mott Street discussing stuffed bean curd, it was difficult to look at pictures of Nixon sitting at the banquet table—sitting there with a look that suggested he was longing for a simple dish of cottage cheese at his desk or for dinner at one of those Southern California restaurants where salad with Green Goddess dressing is set before you with the menu—and restrain ourselves from thinking, Why him? The opening of China to tourists did present a temptation. In New York, there are people—some of them in my own family—who find it odd to eat four or five Chinese meals in a row; in China, I often remind them, there are a billion or so people who find nothing odd about it at all. Soon, though, reports began to drift back from Chinatown denizens who had visited the People's Republic, enduring tours of primary schools and irrigation projects just to get a crack at the restaurants: the non-Presidential food was disappointing. The Chinese, I was given to believe, had other priorities—getting on with the revolution and that sort of thing. Fine. I'd wait. Meanwhile, I dreamed of Hong Kong.

For years, while China watchers gathered in Hong Kong to interpret and reinterpret every bit of news from Peking, I remained in New York—a Hong Kong-watcher. From thousands of miles away,

I analyzed news from the colony in terms of how it might affect my vision. When there were reports that another few hundred thousand people had been permitted to leave China for Hong Kong, I could see gifted chefs from Shanghai and Peking and Chiu Chow and Hunan—people who had chafed for years at having to read "The Little Red Book" when they wanted to be reading recipes— rushing over the border, ready to knock themselves out for the running dogs of Yankee imperialism. In Hong Kong, I figured, people who felt the need to skip from one cuisine to another at every meal, like some fickle débutante who can't permit herself to dance with the same boy twice in a row, could simply say something like "We just had Cantonese last night—why don't we go to a Peking place for lunch?" When I read several years ago that the Chinese businessmen of Hong Kong had far outstripped the English bankers who once dominated the economy of the colony—partly because real estate, traditionally controlled by the Chinese, grew to be much more valuable than whatever business was conducted on it—I could envision managers of the most expensive dining spots gratefully crossing Yorkshire pudding off their menus and beginning to compete ferociously for the hottest refugee chef. (But would rising real estate values force rents too high for the sort of restaurants that concentrated on food rather than on flashy surroundings? We Hong Kong-watchers had a seminar on that one, over salt-baked chicken and dried Chinese mushrooms with bean curd.) When I read of Hong Kong's importance to the People's Republic of China as a source of foreign exchange, I could envision the political détente of my dreams—ingredients from the heartland of Communist China flowing into a place where capitalist Chinese eaters were only too happy to pay for them. When the turmoil of the Cultural Revolution spilled over into Hong Kong, reviving talk of how easily China could take over the colony, some Hong Kong-watchers thought the dream had been shattered, but I was not among them. "Can't you see?" I would say. "Now they'll be eating like there's no tomorrow."

My dream of Hong Kong was not a criticism of Chinatown. I 5 love Chinatown. I love the outdoor market that has grown up along Canal Street, and I love the food stores where I can't ever seem to get anyone to tell me what anything is in English. I'm even fond of the chicken who plays ticktacktoe; I've never been a sore loser. I count myself fortunate to live a bike ride away from a neighborhood that is always mentioned—along with Hong Kong and Taiwan and

Tokyo—whenever serious eaters of Chinese food talk of the world's great concentrations of Chinese restaurants. Still, Hong Kong is always mentioned first. There are weekend mountain climbers who take great joy in hauling themselves around the Adirondacks, but they dream of Nepal. Eventually, if they're lucky, they get to Nepal. Eventually, I got to Hong Kong.

We were sitting in a restaurant called Orchid Garden, in the Wanchai district, beginning our first meal in Hong Kong, and I had just sampled something called fish-brain soup. I was about to comment. My wife was looking a bit anxious. She was concerned, I think, that over the years I might have created a vision of Hong Kong in my mind that could not be matched by the reality—like some harried businessman who finally arrives in what he has pictured as the remote, otherworldly peace of a Tahiti beach only to be hustled by a couple of hip beach-umbrella salesmen wearing "Souvenir of Fort Lauderdale" T-shirts. Even before we had a meal, she must have noticed my surprise at discovering that most of the other visitors in Hong Kong seemed to be there for purposes other than eating. That's the sort of thing that can put a visionary off his stride. How would the obsessed mountain climber feel if he arrived in Nepal after years of fantasizing about a clamber up the Himalayas and found that most of the other tourists had come to observe the jute harvest? It appeared that just about everyone else had come to Hong Kong to shop. Hong Kong has dozens of vast shopping malls—floor after floor of shops run by cheerfully competitive merchants who knock off ten per cent at the hint of a frown and have never heard of sales tax. There are restaurants in some of the shopping malls, but most of the visitors seemed too busy shopping to eat. It was obvious that they would have come to Hong Kong even if it had been one of those British colonies where the natives have been taught to observe the Queen's birthday by boiling Brussels sprouts for a full month and a half. That very morning, in the lobby of a hotel, my wife had noticed a couple in late middle age suddenly drawing close to share some whispered intimacy, in what she took to be a scene of enduring affection until one of the softly spoken phrases reached her ears—"customs declaration."

The sight of all those shoppers racing around, their shopping bags bulging and their minds feverish with schemes for flimflamming the customs man, had not really disturbed me. Hong Kong is the sort of place that can provide more than one vision. There must be people, for instance, who see it as a symbol of flat-out free enterprise prospering next to the world's largest Communist society, and there must be people who see it as a hideous example of capitalist materialism next to an inspiring land of collective sacrifice—although either vision would be blurred by a visit to the People's Republic department stores in Hong Kong, which accept American Express, Diners Club, Visa, and MasterCard. What can the struggle of two great forces for domination of the world mean if the Reds are on Diners? My own vision could be similarly blurred, my wife knew, if the fish-brain soup turned out to be only marginally superior to the bird's-nest soup or hot-and-sour soup routinely ladled out in Chinatown—the sort of first course that would be mentioned briefly on the after-dinner stroll as a lead-in to the subject of whether we should try the fried dumplings next time. I had another spoonful. "To quote Brigham Young, a man who never ate a shrimp," I said, " 'This is the place!' "

I'm tempted to say that I never doubted for a moment that it 8 would be, but, of course, I had my doubts. Even before our first meal, though, my confidence was being shored up. Like so many other visitors, I had rushed out on my first morning to make a purchase—in my case, a guide to Hong Kong restaurants—and I was rewarded by learning that the discussions in Hong Kong about what the colony's future will be after the British lease on the New Territories expires in 1997 are rivalled in intensity by the discussions about which restaurant serves the best Peking duck. My vision of Hong Kong was built on the belief that it would be not simply a place where the fish-brain soup dazzled but also a place where people took it for granted that a normal response to hearing a visitor ask "What's Macao like?" would be to offer an opinion on which Macanese restaurant offers the most succulent prawns—a place, in other words, where priorities had been established. Within a couple of days, I felt like a China-watcher who, after having spent years spinning out generalizations about China based on the flimsiest perusal of monitored radio broadcasts and fanciful refugee accounts, is finally permitted to make an extended visit to the mainland and finds, to his astonishment, that he was right all along.

At the precise moment that this feeling came over me we had 9 just finished dinner at a businessmen's club called the Shanghai Fraternity Association. We had eaten smoked fish and drunken chicken and something resembling bok choy and shark's-fin soup and mixed vegetables and fried pork and river shrimp and Shanghai dumplings and a sort of sesame fritter. What I had to keep reminding myself was that we were consuming the Hong Kong version of club food. One of our dining companions, an ore trader of Shanghainese background, had spent part of his afternoon consulting with the club management about precisely what should be served. That, I was told, is routine among Hong Kong businessmen who entertain. I tried to imagine an English or an American businessman giving over part of his afternoon to planning a meal at his club. Even if it occurred to him to do it, what would he say? "Let's be sure to have some of those overcooked canned vegetables, Emile. And what sort of spongy gray meat is good this time of year? And a dinner salad of iceberg lettuce would be nice, I think. With Green Goddess dressing."

It was the rain that drove me into the Central Market of Hong Kong. I stayed only a couple of minutes. I have a weakness for markets, but when it comes to Chinese food I have always operated under the policy that the less known about the preparation the better. Even in Chinatown, it seems to me, a wise diner who is invited to visit the kitchen replies by saying, as politely as possible, that he has a pressing engagement elsewhere. That policy of selective ignorance should obviously be followed in Hong Kong, where old hands are often heard to mutter, "The Cantonese will eat anything." What astounded me about the Central Market—in the short time I had for observation before I decided that I preferred the rain—was not simply that it was a place where a moderately energetic public-health inspector could write his year's quota of citations in fifteen or twenty minutes. I was even more amazed by the fact that although the same purveyors presumably operated out of the market routinely day after day there was something impromptu about it. People squatted on the floor here and there, between a basket of squid and a couple of discarded cattle heads, as if they had merely wandered by to say hello to a fishmonger friend who said, "Listen, Joe, as long as you're here, why don't you just sit yourself down on the floor over there and peel this pile of shrimp?"

Even after I started giving the Central Market a wide berth, I found unwelcome knowledge creeping through my defenses. In Chinatown, for instance, I had always taken it for granted that the "bird's nest" in bird's-nest soup is a direct translation of some evocative Chinese phrase describing some sort of vegetable that grows only in certain districts of certain provinces. It wasn't until I wandered into some Hong Kong shops that specialize in selling them that I realized that a bird's nest is—well, a bird's nest. A swallow's nest, to be exact, usually imported from Thailand. What did that say about fish-brain soup?

Whatever it was, I resolved not to listen to it. "It's all a matter of   12
mind-set," I informed my wife. "What we're talking about here is a vision, a ceremony. A person taking Communion doesn't need to know where the wafers came from." Fortunately, the rain got worse; even strolling along Hong Kong streets became difficult. I suppose there were visitors to Hong Kong who fretted about being prevented from taking in the countryside of the New Territories and observing the culture of the inhabitants. The shoppers must have been irritated, considering how easily a sodden shopping bag can break through at the bottom. I remained cheerful. Between meals, I sat in the hotel room going over lists of restaurants, protected from markets and shops—from everything except the final results.

Duck better than any duck I had tasted in Chinatown. Fried   13
seaweed better than the fried seaweed we used to eat in Peking restaurants in London. Shad brought to the table sizzling on an iron plate. Yak fondue. Dim sum. More dim sum. Duck tongues (undoubtedly, I told myself, some colorful Chinese phrase for a particularly conventional cut of beef). Minced abalone and pork wrapped in lettuce leaves. I was reeling. I wondered what happened to some of those mountain climbers when they finally got to Nepal. Did they get up there on one Himalaya or another, in that thin air, and decide that they could never return to a place where mountain climbing meant schlepping to foothills on the weekend? Did they just stay in Nepal, eking out a living as consultants to the jute marketing board?

The question was in my mind one evening when we were having   14
dinner in what appeared to be a rather ordinary Hong Kong restaurant—it was a last-minute substitution after a place my research dredged up turned out to be closed—and noticed on the menu some of the same dishes served by one of our favorite restaurants in Chinatown. We ordered two of them—roast pigeon and fried fresh milk with crabmeat. The pigeon was a lot better than the Chinatown version. The fried fresh milk with crabmeat was so much better that it tasted like a different dish.

"We haven't tried the pepper-and-salty shrimp," my wife said.   15

We had both noticed it on the menu. As it happens, the China-town restaurant's finest dish—even better than the pigeon or the fried fresh milk with crabmeat—is by far the best version of pepper-and-salty shrimp I have eaten in New York.

I thought about ordering it. I suspected it would be superior to the Chinatown version, but I wasn't sure I wanted to find out. Something about finding out seemed almost disloyal. I live only a bike ride away from Chinatown. I miss it when I'm out of the city—even when I'm in Hong Kong. I miss the stroll down Mott Street. I almost miss the chicken.

"I think I'm kind of full," I said. "Maybe we should save it for next time."

CONTENT

1. How does Trillin convey the single-mindedness of his purpose in visiting Hong Kong? Does he help us to identify with his obsession through tone and distance? How?
2. What humor is involved in his behind-the-scene glimpses of Chinese cuisine? How does his discovery of the literalness of the Chinese menu temporarily disturb his pleasure?
3. In the final restaurant scene, why doesn't Trillin order the pep-per-and-salty-shrimp? Is it really because he's full?

ORGANIZATION

4. How does Trillin's opening description of New York City's Chi-natown help set the scene for his "Hong Kong Dream"? How does Trillin's first person narration bring us directly into the restaurant scene when he arrives in Hong Kong?
5. If the restaurants match his "Hong Kong Dream," what motive is he dismayed to find among other visitors to the colony? Why does he follow the restaurant scene with descriptions of other tourists less interested in food? Why does he follow that description with a narrative of the men's club luncheon? How is this also another kind of contrast?
6. What is the tone of the market scene and the passages about the names of menu items? How is this consistent with the tone of the entire essay? Do you identify with Trillin?

TOPICS FOR WRITING

7. Write an informal essay narrating your first experience eating an exotic foreign food.

8. Write an informal essay about a trip somewhere where you found yourself attracted to things different from what the place was noted for or what attracted other tourists.

ROBERT M. PIRSIG
Zen and the Art of Motorcycle Maintenance

Robert M. Pirsig was born in Minneapolis, Minnesota in 1928. In the summer of 1968, accompanied by his 11-year-old son, Chris, Pirsig took a motorcycle trip from Minnesota to California. The trip forms the basis for his book Zen and the Art of Motorcycle Maintenance *(1974), an odyssey in time and space, in which the narrator tries to find his lost self (whom he calls Phaedrus) and re-establish a relationship with his son. In this passage, he relates the art of maintaining a motorcycle to the dilemma of viewing the world from the classic or romantic perspective.*

On this machine I've done the tuning so many times it's become   1
a ritual. I don't have to think much about how to do it anymore.
Just mainly look for anything unusual. The engine has picked up
a noise that sounds like a loose tappet but could be something
worse, so I'm going to tune it now and see if it goes away. Tappet
adjustment has to be done with the engine cold, which means
wherever you park it for the night is where you work on it the next
morning, which is why I'm on a shady curbstone back of a hotel
in Miles City, Montana. Right now the air is cool in the shade and
will be for an hour or so until the sun gets around the tree branches,
which is good for working on cycles. It's important not to tune these
machines in the direct sun or late in the day when your brain gets
muddy because even if you've been through it a hundred times you
should be alert and looking for things.

Not everyone undertands what a completely rational process this is, this maintenance of a motorcycle. They think it's some kind of "knack" or some kind of "affinity for machines" in operation. They are right, but the knack is almost purely a process of reason, and most of the troubles are caused by what old time radio men called a "short between the earphones," failures to use the head properly. A motorcycle functions entirely in accordance with the laws of reason, and a study of the art of motorcycle maintenance is really a miniature study of the art of rationality itself. I said yesterday that the ghost of rationality was what Phaedrus pursued and what led to his insanity, but to get into that it's vital to stay with down-to-earth examples of rationality, so as not to get lost in generalities no one else can understand. Talk about rationality can get very confusing unless the things with which rationality deals are also included.

We are at the classic-romantic barrier now, where on one side we see a cycle as it appears immediately—and this is an important way of seeing it—and where on the other side we can begin to see it as a mechanic does in terms of underlying form—and this is an important way of seeing things too. These tools for example—this wrench— has a certain romantic beauty to it, but its purpose is always purely classical. It's designed to change the underlying form of the machine.

The porcelain inside this first plug is very dark. That is classically as well as romantically ugly because it means the cylinder is getting too much gas and not enough air. The carbon molecules in the gasoline aren't finding enough oxygen to combine with and they're just sitting here loading up the plug. Coming into town yesterday the idle was loping a little, which is a symptom of the same thing.

Just to see if it's just the one cylinder that's rich I check the other one. They're both the same. I get out a pocket knife, grab a stick lying in the gutter and whittle down the end to clean out the plugs, wondering what could be the cause of the richness. That wouldn't have anything to do with rods or valves. And carbs rarely go out of adjustment. The main jets are oversized, which causes richness at high speeds but the plugs were a lot cleaner than this before with the *same* jets. Mystery. You're always surrounded by them. But if you tried to solve them all, you'd never get the machine fixed. There's no immediate answer so I just leave it as a hanging question.

The first tappet is right on, no adjustment required, so I move on to the next. Still plenty of time before the sun gets past those trees . . . I always feel like I'm in church when I do this . . . The gage is some kind of religious icon and I'm performing a holy rite with it. It is a member of a set called "precision measuring instruments" which in a classic sense has a profound meaning.

In a motorcycle this precision isn't maintained for any romantic 7 or perfectionist reasons. It's simply that the enormous forces of heat and explosive pressure inside this engine can only be controlled through the kind of precision these instruments give. When each explosion takes place it drives a connecting rod onto the crankshaft with a surface pressure of many tons per square inch. If the fit of the rod to the crankshaft is precise the explosion force will be transferred smoothly and the metal will be able to stand it. But if the fit is loose by a distance of only a few thousandths of an inch the force will be delivered suddenly, like a hammer blow, and the rod, bearing and crankshaft surface will soon be pounded flat, creating a noise which at first sounds a lot like loose tappets. That's the reason I'm checking it now. If it *is* a loose rod and I try to make it to the mountains without an overhaul, it will soon get louder and louder until the rod tears itself free, slams into the spinning crankshaft and destroys the engine. Sometimes broken rods will pile right down through the crankcase and dump all the oil onto the road. All you can do then is start walking.

But all this can be prevented by a few thousandths of an inch fit 8 which precision measuring instruments give, and this is their classical beauty—not what you see, but what they mean—what they are capable of in terms of control of underlying form.

The second tappet's fine. I swing over to the street side of the 9 machine and start on the other cylinder.

CONTENT

1. What examples does Pirsig give to support his statement, "A motorcycle functions entirely in accordance with the laws of reason"?

2. From the examples that he gives, can you establish a definition of what Pirsig means by "classic" and "romantic"? How can the same object be both classic and romantic according to this definition?

3. How does Pirsig carry through the passage his opening notion that tuning a motorcycle is a "ritual"? Does he just mean something repeatedly done? Is there any other language employed to suggest he means more?

ORGANIZATION

4. Although this passage seems primarily a process analysis—"How to Tune a Motorcycle"—it is actually much more and employs a number of different organizational patterns. Where is exemplification used? In paragraph 2, Pirsig says, "Talk about rationality can get very confusing unless the things with which rationality deals are also included." How does this statement explain his extreme emphasis on minute details?

5. Which paragraphs are given over to a contrast between classic and romantic? Why doesn't Pirsig define the terms in this passage?

6. Where is cause–effect used as a pattern of organization? Is it effectively used? Why does Pirsig place it after his discovery of carbon on the plugs and his discussion of rationality? What would happen if the discussion of the broken rod were placed in the first paragraph where the loose tappet is mentioned? What would be lost?

TOPICS FOR WRITING

7. Describe some ritual you have performed repeatedly—either a mechanical repair, a chore, a form of exercise—analyze its steps, and explain why you derive satisfaction from repeatedly performing it.

8. Describe an object—a machine, a building, a tool—in which the external form perfectly matches its underlying function. Show how the details of the form make the function efficient. Or, choose some common object in which form is ill-matched to function. Suggest how you might improve it.

NORMAN COUSINS
The Mysterious Placebo

Norman Cousins (born 1912) has been associated with The Saturday Review *for over 30 years. His columns have been collected in* Writing for Love or Money *(1949), but since his recovery from a near fatal illness, Cousins has devoted considerable energy to teaching the value of positive thought in helping patients to recover.* Anatomy of an Illness as Perceived by the Patient: Reflections on Healing and Regeneration *(1979) was a national best seller. "The Mysterious Placebo" typifies Cousins' belief that healing takes place not always as a result of an effective drug, but as a result of the patient's belief in his own power to get well.*

Over long centuries, doctors have been educated by their patients 1 to observe the prescription ritual. Most people seem to feel their complaints are not taken seriously unless they are in possession of a little slip of paper with indecipherable but magic markings. To the patient, a prescription is a certificate of assured recovery. It is the doctor's IOU that promises good health. It is the psychological umbilical cord that provides a nourishing and continuing connection between physician and patient.

The doctor knows that it is the prescription slip itself, even more 2 than what is written on it, that is often the vital ingredient for enabling a patient to get rid of whatever is ailing him. Drugs are not always necessary. Belief in recovery always is. And so the doctor may prescribe a placebo in cases where reassurance for the patient is far more useful than a famous-name pill three times a day.

This strange-sounding word, placebo, is pointing medical sci- 3 ence straight in the direction of something akin to a revolution in the theory and practice of medicine. The study of the placebo is opening up vast areas of knowledge about the way the human body heals itself and about the mysterious ability of the brain to order biochemical changes that are essential for combating disease.

The word placebo comes from the Latin verb meaning "I shall 4 please." A placebo in the classical sense, then, is an imitation med-icine—generally an innocuous milk-sugar tablet dressed up like an authentic pill—given more for the purpose of placating a patient than for meeting a clearly diagnosed organic need. The placebo's most frequent use in recent years, however, has been in the testing of new drugs. Effects achieved by the preparation being tested are measured against those that follow the administration of a "dummy drug" or placebo.

For a long time, placebos were in general disrepute with a large part of the medical profession. The term, for many doctors, had connotations of quack remedies or "pseudomedicaments." There was also a feeling that placebos were largely a shortcut for some practitioners who were unable to take the time and trouble to get at the real source of a patient's malaise.

Today, however, the once lowly placebo is receiving serious attention from medical scholars. Medical investigators such as Dr. Arthur K. Shapiro, the late Dr. Henry K. Beecher, Dr. Stewart Wolf, and Dr. Louis Lasagna have found substantial evidence that the placebo not only can be made to look like a powerful medication but can actually act like a medication. They regard it not just as a physician's psychological prop in the treatment of certain patients but as an authentic therapeutic agent for altering body chemistry and for helping to mobilize the body's defenses in combating disorder or disease.

While the way the placebo works inside the body is still not completely understood, some placebo researchers theorize that it activates the cerebral cortex, which in turn switches on the endocrine system in general and the adrenal glands in particular. Whatever the precise pathways through the mind and body, enough evidence aleady exists to indicate that placebos can be as potent as—and sometimes more potent than—the active drugs they replace.

"Placebos," Dr. Shapiro has written in the *American Journal of Psychotherapy,* "can have profound effects on organic illness, including incurable malignancies." One wonders whether this fact may be the key to the puzzle of those cancer sufferers who, according to documented accounts, have recovered after taking Laetril, even though many of the nation's leading cancer research centers have been unable to find any medicinal value in this particular substance.

It is obviously absurd to say that doctors should never prescribe pharmacologically active drugs. There are times when medication is absolutely essential. But the good doctor is always mindful of its power. No greater popular fallacy exists about medicine than that a drug is like an arrow that can be shot at a particularized target. Its actual effect is more like a shower of porcupine quills. Any drug— or food, for that matter—goes through a process in which the human system breaks it down for use by the whole.

There is almost no drug, therefore, that does not have some side- 10
effects. And the more vaunted the prescription—antibiotics,
cortisone, tranquilizers, antihypertensive compounds, antiinflam-
matory agents, muscle relaxers—the greater the problem of
adverse side-effects. Drugs can alter or rearrange the balances in
the bloodstream. They can cause the blood to clot faster or slower.
They can reduce the level of oxygen in the blood. They can prod
the endocrine system, increase the flow of hydrochloric acid to the
stomach, slow down or speed up the passage of blood through the
heart, impair the blood-making function of the body by depressing
the bone marrow, reduce or increase blood pressure, or affect the
sodium-potassium exchange, which has a vital part in the body's
chemical balance.

The problem posed by many drugs is that they do these things 11
apart from the purpose intended by the physician. There is always
the need, therefore, for the doctor to balance off the particularized
therapy against the generalized dangers. The more powerful the
drug, the more precarious his balancing act.

Complicating the doctor's dilemma about drugs is the fact that 12
many people tend to regard drugs as though they were automobiles. Each year has to have its new models, and the more powerful
the better. Too many patients feel the doctor is lacking unless a
prescription calls for a new antibiotic or other miracle drug that the
patient has heard about from a friend or read about in the press.

Because of the very real dangers associated with powerful new 13
drugs, the prudent modern physician takes full advantage of his
freedom of choice, specifying potent drugs when he feels they are
absolutely necessary, but disregarding them, prescribing placebos
or nothing at all, when they are not.

A hypothetical illustration of how a placebo works is the case of 14
a young businessman who visits his doctor and complains of severe
headaches and abdominal pains. After listening carefully to the
patient describe not only his pains but his problems, the physician
decides that the businessman is suffering from a common disease
of the twentieth century: stress. The fact that stress doesn't come
from germs or viruses doesn't make its effects any the less serious.
Apart from severe illness, it can lead to alcoholism, drug addiction,
suicide, family breakdown, joblessness. In extreme form, stress can
cause symptoms of conversion hysteria—a malaise described by
Jean Charcot, Freud's teacher. The patient's worry and fears are

converted into genuine physical symptoms that can be terribly painful or even crippling.

In sympathetic questioning, the doctor learns that the business-man is worried about the ill health of his pregnant wife and about newly hired young people in his office who seem to him to be angling for his job. The doctor recognizes that his first need is to reassure the patient that nothing is fundamentally wrong with his health. But he is careful not to suggest in any way that the man's pains are unreal or not to be taken seriously. Patients tend to think they have been accused of having imagined their symptoms, of malingering, if their complaint is diagnosed as being pyschogenic in origin.

The doctor knows that his patient, in accordance with conven-tion, would probably be uncomfortable without a prescription. But the doctor also knows the limitations of medication. He is reluctant to prescribe tranquilizers because of what he believes would be adverse effects in this particular case. He knows that aspirin would relieve the headaches but would also complicate the gastro-intes-tinal problem, since even a single aspirin tablet can cause internal bleeding. He rules out digestive aids because he knows that the stomach pains are induced by emotional problems. So the doctor writes a prescription that, first of all, cannot possibly harm the patient and, secondly, might clear up his symptoms. The doctor tells the businessman that the particular prescription will do a great deal of good and that he will recover completely. Then he takes time to discuss with his patient the possible ways of meeting the prob-lems at home and at the office.

A week later the businessman telephones the doctor to report that the prescription has worked wonders. The headaches have disappeared and the abdominal pains have lessened. He is less apprehensive about his wife's condition following her visit to the obstetrician, and he seems to be getting along better at the office. How much longer should he take the medicine?

The doctor says that the prescription will probably not have to be refilled but to be sure to telephone if the symptoms recur.

The "wonder" pills, of course, were nothing more than placebos. They had no pharmacological properties. But they worked as well as they did for the businessman because they triggered his body's own ability to right itself, given reasonable conditions of freedom from stress and his complete confidence that the doctor knew what he was doing.

Studies show that up to 90 percent of patients who reach out for medical help are suffering from self-limiting disorders well within the range of the body's own healing powers. The most valuable physician—to a patient and to society—knows how to distinguish effectively between the large number of patients who can get well without heroic intervention and the much smaller number who can't. Such a physician loses no time in mobilizing all the scientific resources and facilities available, but he is careful not to slow up the natural recovery process of those who need his expert reassurance even more than they need his drugs. He may, for such people, prescribe a placebo—both because the patient feels more comfortable with a prescription in his hand and because the doctor knows that the placebo can actually serve a therapeutic purpose.

The placebo, then, is not so much a pill as a process. The process begins with the patient's confidence in the doctor and extends through to the full functioning of his own immunological and healing system. The process works not because of any magic in the tablet but because the human body is its own best apothecary and because the most successful prescriptions are those filled by the body itself.

Berton Roueché, one of America's most talented medical reporters, wrote an article for the *New Yorker* magazine in 1960 in which he said that the placebo derives its power from the "infinite capacity of the human mind for self-deception." This interpretation is not held by placebo scholars. They believe that the placebo is powerful not because it "fools" the body but because it translates the will to live into a physical reality. And they have been able to document the fact that the placebo triggers specific biochemical changes in the body. The fact that a placebo will have no physiological effect if the patient knows it is a placebo only confirms something about the capacity of the human body to transform hope into tangible and essential biochemical change.

The placebo is proof that there is no real separation between mind and body. Illness is always an interaction between both. It can begin in the mind and affect the body, or it can begin in the body and affect the mind, both of which are served by the same bloodstream. Attempts to treat most mental diseases as though they were completely free of physical causes and attempts to treat most bodily diseases as though the mind were in no way involved must be considered archaic in the light of new evidence about the way the human body functions.

* * *

It is doubtful whether the placebo—or any drug, for that matter—would get very far without a patient's robust will to live. For the will to live is a window on the future. It opens the individual to such help as the outside world has to offer, and it connects that help to the body's own capability for fighting disease. It enables the human body to make the most of itself. The placebo has a role to play in transforming the will to live from a poetical conception to a physical reality and a governing force.

In the end, the greatest value of the placebo is what it can tell us about life. Like a celestial chaperon, the placebo leads us through the uncharted passageways of mind and gives us a greater sense of infinity than if we were to spend all our days with our eyes hypnotically glued to the giant telescope at Mt. Palomar. What we see ultimately is that the placebo isn't really necessary and that the mind can carry out its difficult and wondrous missions unprompted by little pills. The placebo is only a tangible object made essential in an age that feels uncomfortable with intangibles, an age that prefers to think that every inner effect must have an outer cause. Since it has size and shape and can be hand-held, the placebo satisfies the contemporary craving for visible mechanisms and visible answers. But the placebo dissolves on scrutiny, telling us that it cannot relieve us of the need to think deeply about ourselves.

The placebo, then, is an emissary between the will to live and the body. But the emissary is expendable. If we can liberate ourselves from tangibles, we can connect hope and the will to live directly to the ability of the body to meet great threats and challenges. The mind can carry out its ultimate functions and powers over the body without the illusion of material intervention. "The mind," said John Milton, "is its own place, and in itself can make a heaven of hell, and a hell of heaven."

Science is concocting exotic terms like biofeedback to describe the control by the mind over the autonomic nervous system. But labels are unimportant; what is important is the knowledge that human beings are not locked into fixed limitations. The quest for perfectibility is not a presumption or a blasphemy but the highest manifestation of a great design.

Some years ago, I had an opportunity to observe African witch-doctor medicine at first hand in the Gabon jungle country. At the dinner table of the Schweitzer Hospital at Lambarene, I had ventured the remark that the local people were lucky to have access to the Schweitzer clinic instead of having to depend on witch-doctor supernaturalism. Dr. Schweitzer asked how much I knew about witch doctors. I was trapped by my ignorance—and we both knew it. The next day *le grand docteur* took me to a nearby jungle clearing, where he introduced me to *un de mes collègues**, an elderly witch doctor. After a respectful exchange of greetings, Dr. Schweitzer suggested that his American friend be allowed to observe African medicine.

For the next two hours, we stood off to one side and watched the witch doctor at work. With some patients, the witch doctor merely put herbs in a brown paper bag and instructed the ill person in their use. With other patients, he gave no herbs but filled the air with incantations. A third category of patients he merely spoke to in a subdued voice and pointed to Dr. Schweitzer.

On our way back to the clinic, Dr. Schweitzer explained what had happened. The people who had assorted complaints that the witch doctor was able to diagnose readily were given special herbs to make into brews. Dr. Schweitzer guessed that most of those patients would improve very rapidly since they had only functional, rather than organic, disturbances. Therefore, the "medications" were not really a major factor. The second group had psychogenic ailments that were treated with African psychotherapy. The third group had more substantial physical problems, such as massive hernias or extrauterine pregnancies or dislocated shoulders or tumorous conditions. Many of these problems required surgery, and the witch doctor was redirecting the patients to Dr. Schweitzer himself.

"Some of my steadiest customers are referred to me by witch doctors," Dr. Schweitzer said with only the slightest trace of a smile. "Don't expect me to be too critical of them."

When I asked Dr. Schweitzer how he accounted for the fact that anyone could possibly expect to become well after having been treated by a witch doctor, he said that I was asking him to divulge

28

29

30

31

32

*One of my colleagues.

a secret that doctors carried around inside them ever since Hippocrates.

"But I'll tell you anyway," he said, his face still illuminated by that half-smile. "The witch doctor succeeds for the same reason all the rest of us succeed. Each patient carries his own doctor inside him. They come to us not knowing that truth. We are at our best when we give the doctor who resides within each patient a chance to go to work."

The placebo is the doctor who resides within.

CONTENT

1. What does "placebo" mean, and why does Cousins call it "the doctor within"?
2. What evidence is there for the belief that placebos do more than "fool the body"?
3. How are the effects of a placebo proof of Cousin's belief that since the mind and body are one the treatment of illnesses needs to take both into account?

ORGANIZATION

4. What kind of definition does Cousins use in defining "placebo"? Why does he use definition in the beginning of his essay?
5. What is the point of the hypothetical example of the young businessman who is given a placebo by his doctor (paragraph 14)? What other examples does Cousins use?
6. How does the narrative about Dr. Schweitzer provide a fitting conclusion for Cousins' essay? How does the witchdoctor's division of patients support Cousins' view about competence in doctors?

TOPICS FOR WRITING

7. Write an essay elaborating on Dr. Schweitzer's point that, "Each patient carries his own doctor inside him."
8. Write an essay on our culture's tendency to want instant drug cures for major and minor ailments. You might use TV ads to support your point.

GEORGE V. HIGGINS
Clumsy Oafs, Unlettered Louts

George V. Higgins (born 1939) was a lawyer in the Massachusetts Attorney General's office in the Organized Crime Section and the Criminal Division, an Assistant U.S. Attorney for the District of Massachusetts, and since 1973 has been in private practice. In addition to his legal writing, Higgins has published short stories, essays, and three novels: The Friends of Eddie Coyle *(1972),* The Digger's Game *(1973), and* Cogan's Trade *(1974). In "Clumsy Oafs, Unlettered Louts," a law professor laments the sad state to which students have fallen in the last decade, and he blames the school system for not being more honest about the special abilities and limitations of each student.*

"It's television," the law school professor in Boston explained. 1
"Television and some other things. You've been away from teaching, how long now?"

"Five years." 2

"Five years," he said. "Well, that was just long enough. See in 3
'73, '74—was that the last time you taught until now?" It was. "They weren't in the graduate schools then. They hadn't got there yet. They were being handed along through college, after they'd been handed along through high school, which they got to when they were shipped along from junior high after the elementary-school teachers gave up hope on them. This is the 'Sesame Street' Generation. They didn't have to read for Big Bird. When they got older, they didn't have to read for Fred Flintstone. They didn't read for Mister Rogers, but he didn't throw them out of his neighborhood."

"When they went to school," he said, "nobody made them read. 4
Oh, some teachers did, because it filled out the time that was left after they got through cutting up construction paper and visiting the zoos where you can touch the lambs and pet the snakes. Just before the bus left for the trolley museum where you can ring the bell. Ding Dong. But the teachers who made them read were dull, and they could be avoided by a determined kid who didn't want to read and was the president of the camera club and treasurer of the magic society and the hope of the tennis team. Some kids read, but they were the wimps. Nobody imitated them. They only read because they had acne and they couldn't break a tackle or hit the curve ball."

"That isn't new."

"No," he said, "of course it isn't new. It was the same thirty years ago. The kids who went out for sports and played the games and were the cheeleaders: they were the role models. The wimps read books and wore glasses and went home in the afternoon where their mummies gave them milk and cookies and encouraged them to read because they were realistic enough to know that they had given birth to wimps who couldn't catch a forward pass, let alone throw one, and the kid might as well read Emily Dickinson instead of getting his brains beat out trying to do something that he didn't have the build for.

"The difference," he said, "the difference is that thirty years ago, the wimps went on to college. They got 725s on the College Boards because they really had the book learning. That was all they had, but they had it. The halfback that could run through the first floor of an apartment building without opening a door or breaking stride went to college and trampled linemen for four years before he graduated in phys. ed. or didn't graduate at all, and then he got a pro contract. The wimp went on to graduate from school and associated with his kind.

"It was a nice, neat system," the law professor said. "Everybody knew where he stood. Oh, there were some people who made everybody feel uncomfortable—the Pete Dawkins type who went to West Point, starred in football, and also got a Rhodes Scholarship before going off to Nam to win a Silver Star for combat heroism— but it was otherwise pretty much a sort of ad hoc feudal system reinvented: you had your clerisy, your class clowns, and your athletic heroes. They were separate. Nobody expected Mickey Rooney to make the crucial block that led to victory over old Siwash—he was off planning the Victory Dance. Nobody expected the class genius to be pretty—she was the new Madame Curie. And why the hell would any self-respecting male want to get her pants off?

"It was easier," he said. "It was a lot easier. It was painful and there were a lot of hurt feelings, because Madame Curie really did want to get felt up and the class clown would have liked to make a B-minus at least once in a while. The halfback had a glimmer of his future, which was wearing a uniform of polished cotton and humping refrigerators on a padded two-wheeler out of a freight truck and up an elevator to the appliance floor, and he did not like the prospect. But it was easier, just the same. Nobody had to be a Renaissance man. Nobody was expected to be.

"Now," he said, "it's different. Now everyone is expected to be 10 well-rounded—Renaissance men, no matter what the genital realities. But that, of course, is impossible, because people like that don't appear in large numbers. That means that most people will not be able to meet the standards. Which, in turn, means that most people will feel inadequate—as, of course, they are, in one respect or another. I know a guy who climbed Mount Washington in the winter and skied the north face, which is about the most dangerous thing you can do in New England in the winter, and he's in perfect shape. The guy couldn't add a column of figures or read *The Sun Also Rises* without assistance, and I would certainly be killed if I tried what he did, going up or going down. Who's better?

"Neither of us. People do different things. But the educational 11 structure is set up to deny that. Everybody is equal in everything. I don't mean the system says I should ski the north face and not get killed. I don't mean the system says he should be able to try a case intelligently in a court of law, which I could do because I am a wimp with impeccable credentials. What I mean is that the system decrees that I *can* ski the north face without injuring myself, and he *can* try a case intelligently, even though it is patently obvious to any fool that neither of us can do the same things. That way, he is not disappointed that he is not very smart, and I am not saddened because I am a clumsy fool.

"The trouble is that this is not true," the professor said. "I am, 12 as a matter of fact, a clumsy oaf. He is, as a matter of fact, an unlettered lout. He is stupid and I am uncoordinated. It doesn't do any good to convince either of us of the contrary, and it can end up doing a lot of harm. I may end up killing myself on the north face, and he can waste his life attempting intellectual tasks utterly beyond his capacities. Our feelings have been spared, but the truth has not been served.

"That is the trouble with education now," he said. "We are always 13 calculating from the lowest common denominator, because we don't want anyone to get upset. It starts in the first grade, earlier if there is a kindergarten. Sarah's mud pie is just as laudable an accomplishment as Scotty's house of blocks and Tommy's comprehension of the collected works of Dick and Jane. Teddy plays the flute and he does Mozart, while Julie kicks the soccer ball like a rocket and Ellen knows what Tolstoy had in mind when he wrote *War and Peace.* 'Aren't *all* the children doing so *well*?'

"Sure they are. But they are not doing equally well at all things. Ellen is likely to do better at higher levels of education than Tommy. But Tommy will probably do a lot better than Sarah when they get into high school, and Teddy really ought to concentrate on music because he'll never make a decent mud pie, and besides, it'll get dirt in his flute.

"Every single one of those kids," the professor said, "will come out of that initial experience in education with an evaluation of academic promise. The black kid is capable of breathtaking accomplishments because he knows all about dashikis. Teddy needs to spend more time with a second-baseman's glove and less with the flute, and it would help if he learned to read *Dick and Jane*. Scotty has a fine sense of spatial relationships, and should do well in math.

"As a result," he said, "they *all* do well. You look at the grade records that they get all the way through school, and they are magnificent. The black kid knows *Roots* and *Manchild in the Promised Land* by heart before he's twelve. Ellen couldn't play 'Tea for Two' on the piano if you held a gun to her head, but she has a definite point of view on the validity of Jesse Weston's disquisition on the legend of Parsifal, and she is only twelve. Tommy got a harpsichord for Christmas, and plays it to the delight of all visitors, but Tommy passed English with flying colors even though he never grasped *Silas Marner*. Scotty is a mathematical genius and should probably go to architectural school, but he gets an *A* in English even though he's still not sure what Dickens had in mind in *A Christmas Carol*.

"And every day," the professor said, "they go home after school and watch television. Now you think about what that means. To them. You cannot lie to a kid successfully. This cannot be done. If you lie to a kid and tell him that he can do something when he knows very well that he cannot do it, he will try it. And of course he will fail. When you tell him that he has succeeded, he knows you are lying. He will never trust you again. He will be right.

"After you have lied to him in the fifth grade, he will be promoted to the sixth grade. There somebody else will lie to him. He will recognize it instantly. The same thing will happen in the seventh grade, all the way to high-school graduation. He will get the impression that people lie to him in order to get rid of him. This may be

good training for the adult world, but it is poor training for performance in that world.

"He knows, in his bones, that there are a good many things that   19
he cannot possibly do. He knows, in addition, that he has not done
them. And he knows, simultaneously, that people have made
allowances for the fact that he cannot do those things. He expects
that they will continue to do so. He knows they are condescending
to him, a realization he does not like, but one he will take. Because
he has grown cynical. He knows that some Ellen will become the
teacher's pet in English, because she reads all the time, but he also
knows that he will get a creditable grade in English even though
he does not read at all, because nobody wants to hurt his feelings.
So he doesn't read. What he does learn to do is take tests, fake it,
and wait for the next falsehood. He is never disappointed. Never.

"In time," the professor said, "he arrives at graduate school. By   20
now he has been conditioned. Badly conditioned, but conditioned
nonetheless. He has a little knowledge—very little—and that is
dangerous. It is dangerous because what little knowledge he has is
true.

"He knows, however dimly, that people have condescended to   21
him, all the way along the line. He knows that they have lied to
him. He knows damned well that he doesn't know very much. But
he is pretty confident that people will continue to make allowances
for him, as they always have—and he knows why.

"Once the kid discovers the reason that people are letting him   22
slide by," the professor said, "he becomes an academic version of
the welfare recipient. The welfare official needs welfare clients, more
and more of them, to keep up the caseload and justify the bureaucracy that employs him. He is a welfare recipient just the same as
the welfare recipient is a welfare recipient: he needs welfare recipients to account for his own employment. So he goes out and recruits
them.

"University faculties," the professor said, "need students. Uni-   23
versity faculties get students from the same sources used by the
faculties of kindergartens, elementary schools, junior highs, and
high schools: wombs. 'You breed 'em, we teach 'em.'

"Wombs haven't been delivering on schedule, not for several   24
years. We're running short of students. Haven't got enough students, don't need as many faculty. Not as much administration. Not
as much in grants from the government and the foundations.

Remember when the market for Beaujolais all of a sudden skyrocketed, and a whole bunch of French vintners started shipping *vin ordinaire* to the states, with Beaujolais labels on it? Big scandal. Same thing is happening now on the campuses. Confounded women started using birth control. Shortage of kids. Can't just take the cream of the crop anymore. Whole crop isn't big enough. Therefore, got to take the culls now. Don't take the culls, won't have enough kids sitting down to listen to the learned professors. Classes get too small, courses get dropped. Courses get dropped, professors get dropped. Easy as that.

"Now," he said, "you keep in mind what I said: those kids are cynical, and they don't know anything, but they are not stupid. By the time they get to college, let alone graduate from school, they understand what is going on. You have the hangover of the Sixties, when the kids got a say in running the universities. You have the hangover of the Seventies when the kids coming into the universities were the kids coming out of the secondary schools where they never learned to read and expected every class to be like watching Johnny Carson. That is two hangovers, two hangovers at a time. If you can imagine that. You now have kids who don't read, demanding half-assed courses where they don't have to read, from people who are supposed to be teachers but are afraid to stand up to the kids because *they need those kids.*

"So," he said, "on the undergraduate level we teach them macramé and call it comparative literature. We inflate the grades, as their teachers did in the other schools, and for the same reason—because we have to. We give B.A.'s to a bunch of clods who think Dante Alighieri was a tight end of the Green Bay Packers when Vince Lombardi was coaching. Because we need them and we are scared of them.

"Let me tell you something," he said. "I was at a dinner party and I got started on third-year law students who don't know the rules of evidence. This professor of journalism, graduate level, tells me he's got M.A. candidates who won't read newspapers. And then this medical-school prof chimes in and says: 'You ought to see what we're turning out—don't get sick.' "

"This isn't funny," I said.

"Funny?" he said. "It's pitiable. If they're strong and tall, we bring them in to play basketball, and we pass them. If they're short and rich, we bring them in to get the tuition, and we pass them. If they're members of some minority group, any minority group, we admit them and we get up new courses on the literature of the veld. Which they do not read. And we pass them. We turn out slobs every June, *magna cum laude.* And we know it.

"The sad part of it is," he said, "they know it too. They wait for   30
Johnny Carson to do the monologue, and he always does. They hate him for it, and he gives them top grades. That costs a minimum of seven grand a year per student, and it's a joke. Not a very good joke, either."

"I'm not laughing," I said.   31

"Neither am I," he said, getting up. "I've got a class."   32

CONTENT

1. Explain the meaning of the title of Higgins' essay. What changes does Higgins claim have taken place in higher education since 1974?
2. What has caused the decline in student preparation according to Higgins?
3. To what extent is the end of the baby boom responsible for grade inflation? Is TV responsible for lower skills?
4. What does Higgins claim used to be the system for admission into graduate or professional studies?

ORGANIZATION

5. Higgins uses a dialogue format to explain his position. Why does the law professor have as his audience someone who has been out of teaching for five years?
6. What contrast does the essay establish to support the idea that standards have slipped? How does the description of the hypothetical class going through the educational system lead into Higgins' point that such unprepared students are like welfare recipients?
7. Higgins ends his essay claiming that there is a cause–effect relationship between the end of the baby boom and grade inflation. Why has he saved this until the end of the essay? How effective is the analogy comparing the student who has been lied to and a welfare recipient?

TOPICS FOR WRITING

8. Disagree with Higgins' assessment of the educational standards by citing recent evidence to indicate that test scores are up and grade inflation is down.
9. Write an essay for or against the idea that watching TV leads to lower reading ability.

JOHN McPHEE
Pieces of the Frame

John McPhee (see page 209) often uses a spell-binding narrative to join different kinds of material. "Pieces of the Frame" starts out with the story of a family picnic in Scotland, weaves in material about Scotland's geology, and works its way toward considering the mystery of the Loch Ness Monster.

On the edge of Invermoriston Forest, I was trying to explain raised beaches, the fifty-foot beaches of Scotland, so called because they are about that far above the sea. Waves never touch them. Tides don't come near reaching them. Shell and shingle, whitened like bones, they are aftereffects of the ice, two miles thick, that once rested on Scotland and actually shoved Scotland down into the earth. When the ice melted, the sea slowly came up, but so did the land, sluggishly recovering its buoyancy over the molten center of things. After the sea had increased as much as it was going to, the land kept rising, and beaches were lifted into the air, some as much as fifty feet.

That was how I understood the story, and I was doing what I could to say it in a way that would make it intelligible to an audience of four children (mine—all girls, and all quite young), but the distractions were so numerous that I never really had a chance. My family and I were having a lakeside lunch—milk, potato sticks, lambs' tongues, shortbread, white chocolate, Mini-Dunlop cheese— beside a stream in a grove of birches that was backed by dense reforested pines. The pines covered steep slopes toward summits two thousand feet above us. It was late spring, but there were snowfields up there nonetheless, and the water we drank had been snow in the mountains that morning.

Near us, another family, also with small children, was having what was evidently a birthday picnic. They had arrived after we were already settled, and they had chosen—I don't know why, with acre upon acre of unpeopled and essentially similar terrain to move about in—to unpack all their special effects (a glistening white cake, noisemakers, conical cardboard orange hats) only forty or fifty yards away. I tried to ignore them and go on with my ruminations on the raised beaches. There were no raised beaches in that place, at least not in the usual form, but the children had seen them and had played on them elsewhere in the Highlands, and I thought that if they could understand how such phenomena had come to be, they might in turn be able to imagine the great, long lake now before them—Loch Ness—as the sea lock, the arm of the Atlantic, that it once was, and how marine creatures in exceptional variety had once freely moved in and out of it, some inevitably remaining.

Losing interest in the birthday party, my youngest daughter said, "I want to see the monster."

This had already become another distraction. In much the way that, in the United States, NO HUNTING signs are posted every other tree along blacktop country roads, cardboard signs of about the same size had been tacked to trees and poles along the lake. There were several in the birch grove. Printed in royal blue on a white background, they said "Any members of the general public who genuinely believe they have seen an unusual creature or object in or on the shores of Loch Ness are requested to report the occurrence to Expedition Headquarters at Achnahannet, two miles south of Urquhart Castle. If unable to report in person, they may telephone the Expedition (No. Drumnadrochit 358). Reports will only be of interest from people willing to give their full name and address and fill in a Sighting Report Form, which will be sent on request. Thank you for your cooperation. Published by the Lock Ness Phenomena Investigation Bureau, 23 Ashley Place, London, S.W. 1, and printed at the Courier Office, Inverness."

"What makes you think the monster wants to see *you?*" I said to my youngest one. "There won't be any sightings today, anyway. There's too much wind out there."

The wind on the lake was quite strong. It was blowing from the north. There were whitecaps, and the ranks of the waves were

3

4

5

6

7

uniform in our perspective, which was high. Watching the waves, I remembered canoe trips when I was ten or eleven years old, trying to achieve some sort of momentum against white-capping headwinds between Rogers Rock and Sabbath Day Point on Lake George. Lake George was for beginners who could learn in its unwild basin the essentials they would need to know on longer trips in later years in wildernesses they would seek out. But now, watching the north wind go down the lake in Scotland, I could not remember headwinds anywhere as powerful and savage as they had been in that so-styled lake for beginners, and I could feel again the skin rubbed off my hands. The likeness was in more than the wind, however. It was in appearance, the shape, and the scale—about a mile from side to side—of Loch Ness, which, like the American lake, is at least twenty times longer than it is wide, a long deep cleft, positioned like some great geophysical ax-cut between its lateral hills. I remember being told, around the fire at night, stories of the first white man who saw Lake George. He was a travelling French priest, intent on converting the Mohawks and other nations of the Iroquois. He had come from Orléans. He said that the lake was the most beautiful he had ever seen, and he named it the Lake of the Blessed Sacrament. The Indians, observing that the priest blessed them with his right hand, held him down and chewed away his fingers until the fingers were stumps and the hand was pulp. Later, when the priest did not stop his work, the Indians axed the top of his skull, and then cut off his head.

Lake George is so clear that objects far below the surface, such as white stones or hovering bass, can be seen in total definition. The water of Loch Ness is so dark with the tints of peat that on a flat-calm day it looks like black glass. Three or four feet below the surface is an obscurity so complete that experienced divers have retreated from it in frustration, and in some cases in fear. A swimmer looking up toward a bright sky from a distance of inches beneath the surface has the impression that he is afloat in very dark tea. Lake George is nearly two hundred feet deep in places, has numerous islands, and with its bays and points, is prototypal of beautiful mountain lakes of grand dimension in every part of the world. Loch Ness is like almost no other lake anywhere. Its shores are formidably and somewhat unnaturally parallel. It has no islands. Its riparian walls go straight down. It's bottom is flat, and in most places is seven hundred feet deep, a mean depth far greater than the mean depth of the North Sea. Loch Ness holds a fantastic volume of water, the entire runoff of any number of northern glens—Glen Affric, Glen Cannich, Glen Moriston, Glen Farrar, Glen Urquhart. All these valleys, impressive in themselves, are petals to Glen More, the Great Glen. Loch Ness is the principal basin of the Great Glen, and the Great Glen is the epicenter of the Highlands. A few miles of silt, carried into the lake by rivers, long ago dammed the seaward end, changing the original sea loch into a freshwater lake, but so slowly that marine creatures trapped within it had a chance to adapt themselves. Meanwhile the land kept rising, and with it the new lake. The surface of Loch Ness is fifty-two feet above sea level.

My wife listened with some interest when, repeating all this, I 9 made an expanded attempt to enrich everyone's experience, but nothing was going through to the children. "I want to see the monster," the youngest one said again, speaking for all. They didn't want to know how or why the so-called monster might have come into that particular lake. They just wanted to see it. But the wind was not slowing up out there on the lake.

All of us looked now at the family that was having the birthday 10 picnic, for the father had stood up shouting and had flung a large piece of the birthday cake at his wife. It missed her and spattered in bits in the branches of a tree. She shouted back at him something to the effect that he was depraved and cruel, and he in turn bellowed that she was a carbon of her bloody mother and that he was fed up. She said she had had all she could ever take, and was going home—to England, apparently. With that, she ran up the hillside and soon was out of sight in the pines. At first, he did not follow, but he suddenly was on his feet and shouting serial threats as he too went out of range in the pines. Meanwhile, their children, all but one, were crying. The one that wasn't crying was the girl whose birthday it was, and she just sat without moving, under a conical orange hat, staring emptily in the direction of the lake.

We went to our car and sat in it for some time, trying not to be 11 keeping too obvious an eye on the children in the birch grove, who eventually began to play at being bailiffs of the birthday picnic and made such a mess that finally the girl whose birthday it was began to cry, and she was still crying when her father came out of the pines. I then drove north.

The road—the A-82—stayed close to the lake, often on ledges that had been blasted into the mountainsides. The steep forests continued, broken now and again, on one shore or the other, by fields of fern, clumps of bright-yellow whin, and isolated stands of cedar. Along the far shore were widely separated houses and farms, which to the eyes of a traveller appeared almost unbelievably luxuriant after the spare desolation of some higher glens. We came to the top of the rise and suddenly saw, on the right-hand side of the road, on the edge of a high meadow that sloped sharply a considerable distance to the lake, a cluster of caravans and other vehicles, arranged in the shape of a C, with an opening toward the road— much like a circle of prairie schooners, formed for protection against savage attack. All but one or two of the vehicles were painted bright lily-pad green. The compound, in its compact half acre, was surrounded by a fence, to keep out, among other things, sheep, which were grazing all over the slope in deep-green turf among buttercups, daisies, and thistles. Gulls above beat hard into the wind, then turned and planed toward the south. Gulls are inland birds in Scotland, there being so little distance from anywhere to the sea. A big fireplace had been made from rocks of the sort that were scattered all over the meadow. And on the lakeward side a platform had been built, its level eminence emphasizing the declivity of the hill, which dropped away below it. Mounted on the platform was a thirty-five millimeter motion-picture camera with an enormous telephoto lens. From its point of view, two hundred feet above the lake and protruding like a gargoyle, the camera could take in a bedazzling panorama that covered thousands of acres of water.

This was Expedition Headquarters, the principal field station of the Lock Ness Phenomena Investigation Bureau—dues five pounds per annum, life membership one hundred pounds, tax on donations recoverable under covenant. Those who join the bureau receive newsletters and annual reports, and are eligible to participate in the fieldwork if they so desire. I turned into the compound and parked between two bright-green reconditioned old London taxis. The central area had long since been worn grassless, and was covered at this moment with fine-grain dust. People were coming and going. The place seemed rather public, as if it were a depot. No one even halfway interested in the natural history of the Great Glen would think of driving up the A-82 without stopping in there. Since the A-82 is the principal route between Glasgow and Inverness, it is not surprising that the apparently amphibious creature 'as yet unnamed, the so-called Loch Ness Monster, has been seen not only from the highway but on it.

The atmosphere around the headquarters suggested a scientific 14 frontier and also a boom town, much as Cape Canaveral and Cocoa Beach do. There were, as well, cirrus wisps of show business and fine arts. Probably the one word that might have been applied to everyone present was adventurer. There was, at any rate, nothing emphatically laboratorial about the place, although the prevailing mood seemed to be one not of holiday but of matter-of-fact application and patient dedication. A telephone call came in that day, to the caravan that served as an office, from a woman who owned an inn south of Inverarigaig, on the other side of the lake. She said that she had seen the creature that morning just forty yards off-shore—three humps, nothing else to report, and being very busy just now, thank you very much, good day. This was recorded, with no particular display of excitement, by an extremely attractive young woman who appeared to be in her late twenties, an artist from London who had missed but one summer at Loch Ness in seven years. She wore sandals, dungarees, a firmly stretched black pullover, and gold earrings. Her name was Mary Piercy, and her toes were painted pink. The bulletin board where she recorded the sighting resembled the kind used in railway stations for the listing of incoming trains.

The office walls were decorated with photographs of the monster 15 in various postures—basking, cruising, diving, splashing, looking up inquisitively. A counter was covered with some of the essential bibliography: the bureau's annual report (twenty-nine sightings the previous year), J. A. Carruth's *Loch Ness and Its Monster* (The Abbey Press, Fort Augustus), Tim Dinsdale's *Loch Ness Monster* (Routledge and Kegan Paul, London), and a report by the Joint Air Reconnaissance Center of the Royal Air Force on a motion picture of the monster swimming about half a mile on the lake's surface. These books and documents could, in turn, lead the interested reader to less available but nonetheless highly relevant works such as R. T. Gould's *Loch Ness Monster and Others* and Constance Whytes's *More Than a Legend*.

My children looked over the photographs with absorption but 16 not a great deal of awe, and they bought about a dozen postcards with glossy prints of a picture of the monster—three humps showing, much the same sight that the innkeeper had described—that had been taken by a man named Stuart, directly across the lake from Urquhat Castle. The three younger girls then ran out into the meadow and began to pick daisies and buttercups. Their mother and sister sat down in the sun to read about the creature in the lake, and to write postcards. We were on our way to Inverness, but with no need to hurry. "Dear Grammy, we came to see the monster today."

From the office to the camera-observation platform to the caravan that served as a pocket mess hall, I wandered around among the crew, was offered and accepted tea, and squinted with imaginary experience up and down the lake, where the whitecaps had, if anything, increased. Among the crew at the time were two Canadians, a Swede, an Australian, three Americans, two Englishmen, a Welshman, and one Scot. Two were women. When I asked one of the crew members if he knew what some of the others did, vocationally, when they were not at Loch Ness, he said, "I'm not sure what they are. We don't go into that." This was obviously a place where now was all that mattered, and in such a milieu it is distinctly pleasant to accept that approach to things. Nonetheless, I found that I couldn't adhere completely to this principle, and I did find out that one man was a medical doctor, another a farmer, another a retired naval officer, and that several, inevitably, were students. The daily watch begins at four in the morning and goes on, as one fellow put it, "as long as we can stand up." It has been the pattern among the hundred of sightings reported that the early-morning hours are the most promising ones. Camera stations are manned until ten at night, dawn and sunset being so close to midnight at that latitude in summer, but the sentries tend to thin out with the lengthening of the day. During the autumn, the size of the crew reduces precipitously toward one.

One man lives at the headquarters all year long. His name is Clem Lister Skelton. "I've been staring at that bloody piece of water since five o'clock," he said, while he drank tea in the mess caravan.

"Is there a technique?" I asked him.

"Just look," he said. "Look. Run your eye over the water in one quick skim. What we're looking for is not hard to see. You just sit and sort of gaze at the loch, that's all. Mutter a few incantations. That's all there is to do. In wintertime, very often, it's just myself.

And of course one keeps a very much more perfunctory watch in the winter. I saw it once in a snowstorm, though, and that was the only time I've had a clear view of the head and neck. The neck is obviously very mobile. The creature was quite big, but it wasn't as big as a seventy-foot MFV. Motor fishing vessel. I'd been closer to it, but I hadn't seen as much of it before. I've seen it eight times. The last time was in September. Only the back. Just the sort of upturned boat, which is the classic view of it."

Skelton drank some more tea, and refilled a cup he had given   21
me. "I must know what it is," he went on. "I shall never rest peacefully until I know what it is. Some of the largest creatures in the world are out there, and we can't name them. It may take ten years, but we're going to identify the genus. Most people are not as fanatical as I, but I would like to see this through to the end, if I don't get too broke first."

Skelton is a tall, offhand man, English, with reddish hair that is   22
disheveled in long strings from the thinning crown of his head. In outline, Skelton's life there in the caravan on the edge of the high meadow over the lake, in a place that must be uncorrectably gloomy during the wet rains of winter, seemed cagelike and hopeless to me—unacceptably lonely. The impression he gave was of a man who had drawn a circle around himself many hundreds of miles from the rest of his life. But how could I know? He was saying that he had flown Super-marine Spitfires for the R.A.F. during the Second World War. His father had been a soldier, and when Skelton was a boy, he lived, as he put it, "all over the place." As an adult, he became first an actor, later a writer and director of films. He acted in London in plays like *March Hare* and *Saraband for Dead Lovers.* One film he directed was, in his words, "a dreadful thing called *Saul and David.*" These appearances on the surface apparently did not occur so frequently that he needed to do nothing else for a livelihood. He also directed, in the course of many years, several hundred educational films. The publisher who distributed some of these films was David James, a friend of Skelton's, and at that time a Member of Parliament. James happened to be, as well, the founder of the Loch Ness Phenomena Investigation Bureau—phenomena, because, for breeding purposes, there would have to be at least two monsters living in the lake at any one time, probably more, and in fact two had on occasion been sighted simultaneously. James asked Skelton if he would go up to the lake and give the bureau

the benefit of his technical knowledge of movie cameras. "Anything for a laugh," Skelton had said to James. This was in the early nineteen-sixties. "I came for a fortnight," Skelton said now, in the caravan. "And I saw it. I wanted to know what it was, and I've wanted to know what it was ever since. I thought I'd have time to write up here, but I haven't. I don't do anything now except hunt this beast."

Skelton talked on about what the monster might be—a magnified newt, a long-necked variety of giant seal, an unextinct *Elasmosaurus*. Visitors wandered by in groups outside the caravan, and unexplained strangers kept coming in for tea. In the air was a feeling, utterly belied by the relative permanence of the place, of a country carnival on a two-night stand. The caravans themselves, in their alignment, suggested a section of a midway. I remembered a woman shouting to attract people to a big caravan on a carnival midway one night in May in New Jersey. That was some time ago. I must have been nineteen. The woman, who was standing on a small platform, was fifty or sixty, and she was trying to get people to go into the caravan to see big jungle cats, I suppose, and brown bears—"Ferocious Beasts," at any rate, according to block lettering on the side of the caravan. A steel cage containing a small black bear had been set up on two sawhorses outside the caravan—a fragment to imply what might be found on a larger scale inside.

So young that it was no more than two feet from nose to tail, the bear was engaged in desperate motion, racing along one side of the cage from corner to corner, striking the steel bars bluntly with its nose. Whirling then, tossing its head over its shoulder like a racing swimmer, it turned and bolted crazily for the opposite end. Its eyes were deep red, and shining in a kind of full-sighted blindness. It had gone mad there in the cage, and its motion, rhythmic and tortured, never ceased, back and forth, back and forth, the head tossing with each jarring turn. The animal abraded its flanks on the steel bars as it ran. Hair and skin had scraped from its sides so that pink flesh showed in the downpour of the carnival arc lights. Blood drained freely through the thinned hair of its belly and dropped onto the floor of the cage. What had a paralyzing effect on me was the animal's almost perfect and now involuntary rhythm—the wild toss of the head after the crash into the corner, the turn, the scraping run, the crash again at the other end, never stopping, metronomic—the exposed interior of some brutal and organic timepiece.

Beside the cage, the plump, impervious woman, red-faced, red-nosed, kept shouting to the crowds, but she said to me, leaning down, her own eyes bloodshot, "Why don't you move on, sonny, if you ain't going to buy a ticket? Beat it. Come on, now. Move on."

"We argue about what it is," Skelton said. "I'm inclined to think 26 it's a giant slug, but there is an amazingly impressive theory for its being a worm. You can't rule out that it's one of the big dinosaurs, but I think this is more wishful thinking than anything else." In the late nineteen-thirties, a large and exotic footprint was found along the shore of Loch Ness. It was meticulously studied by various people and was assumed, for a time, to be an impression from a foot or flipper of the monster. Eventually, the print was identified. Someone who owned the preserved foot of a hippopotamus had successfully brought off a hoax that put layers of mockery and incredibility over the creature in the lake for many years. The Second World War further diverted any serious interest that amateurs or naturalists might have taken. Sightings continued, however, in a consistent pattern, and finally, in the early nineteen-sixties, the Loch Ness Phenomena Investigation Bureau was established. "I have no plans whatever for leaving," Skelton said. "I am prepared to stay here ad infinitum. All my worldly goods are here."

A dark-haired young woman had stepped into the caravan and 27 poured herself a cup of tea. Skelton, introducing her to me, said, "If the beast has done nothing else, it has brought me a wife. She was studying Gaelic and Scottish history at Edinburgh University, and she walked into the glen one day, and I said, 'That is the girl I am going to marry.'" He gestured toward a window of the caravan, which framed a view of the hills and the lake. "The Great Glen is one of the most beautiful places in the world," he continued. "It is peaceful here. I'd be happy here all my life, even if there were nothing in the loch. I've even committed the unforgivable sin of going to sleep in the sun during a flat calm. With enough time, we could shoot the beast with a crossbow and a line, and get a bit of skin. We could also shoot a small transmitter into its hide and learn more than we know now about its habits and characteristics."

The creature swims with remarkable speed, as much as ten or 28 fifteen knots when it is really moving. It makes no noise other than seismic splashes, but it is apparently responsive in a highly sensitive way to sound. A shout, an approaching engine, any loud report, will send it into an immediate dive, and this shyness is in large part the cause of its inaccessibility, and therefore of its mystery. Curiously, though, reverberate sound was what apparently brought the creature widespread attention, for the first sequence of frequent sightings occurred in 1933, when the A-82 was blasted into the cliffsides of the western shore of the lake. Immense boulders kept falling into the depths, and shock waves from dynamite repeatedly ran through the water, causing the creature to lose confidence in its environment and to alter, at least temporarily, its shy and preferentially nocturnal life. In that year it was first observed on land, perhaps attempting to seek a way out forever from the detonations that had alarmed it. A couple named Spicer saw it, near Inverarigaig, and later described its long, serpentine neck, followed by an ungainly hulk of body, lurching toward the lake and disappearing into high undergrowth as they approached.

With the exception of one report recorded in the sixth century, which said that a monster (fitting the description of the contemporary creatures of the lake) had killed a man with a single bite, there have been no other examples of savagery on its part. To the contrary, its sensitivity to people seems to be acute, and it keeps a wide margin between itself and mankind. In all likelihood, it feeds on fish and particularly on eels, of which there are millions in the lake. Loch Ness is unparalleled in eel-fishing circles, and has drawn commercial eel fishermen from all over the United Kingdom. The monster has been observed with its neck bent down in the water, like a swan feeding. When the creatures die, they apparently settle into the seven-hundred-foot floor of the lake, where the temperature is always forty-two degrees Fahrenheit—so cold that the lake is known for never giving up its dead. Loch Ness never freezes, despite its high latitude, so if the creature breathes air, as has seemed apparent from the reports of observers who have watched its mouth rhythmically opening and closing, it does not lose access to the surface in winter. It clearly prefers the smooth, unbaked waterscapes of summer, however, for it seems to love to bask in the sun, like an upturned boat, slowly rolling, plunging, squirming around with what can only be taken as pleasure. By observers' reports, the creature has two pairs of lateral flippers, and when it swims off, tail thrashing, it leaves behind it a wake as impressive as the wake of a small warship. When it dives from a still position, it inexplicably goes down without leaving a bubble. When it dives as it swims, it leaves on the surface a churning signature of foam.

Skelton leaned back against the wall of the caravan in a slouched and nonchalant posture. He was wearing a dark blue tie that was monogrammed in small block letters sewn with white thread— L.N.I. (Loch Ness Investigation). Above the monogram and embroidered also in white thread was a small depiction of the monster—humps undulant, head high, tail extending astern. Skelton gave the tie a flick with one hand. "You get this with a five-pound membership," he said.

The sea-serpent effect given by the white thread on the tie was less a stylization than an attempt toward a naturalistic sketch. As I studied it there, framed on Skelton's chest, the thought occurred to me that there was something inconvenient about the monster's actual appearance. In every sense except possibly the sense that involves cruelty, the creature in Loch Ness is indeed a monster. An average taken from many films and sightings gives its mature length at about forty feet. Its general appearance is repulsive, in the instant and radical sense in which reptiles are repulsive to many human beings, and any number of people might find difficulty in accepting a creature that looks like the one that was slain by St. George. Its neck, about six feet long, columnar, powerfully muscled, is the neck of a serpent. Its head, scarcely broader than the neck, is a serpent's head, with uncompromising, lenticular eyes. Sometimes as it swims it holds its head and neck erect. The creature's mouth is at least a foot wide. Its body undulates. Its skin glistens when wet and appears coarse, mottled, gray, and elephantine when exposed to the air long enough to become dry. The tail, long and columnar, stretches back to something of a point. It seemed to me, sitting there at Headquarters, that the classical, mythical, dragon likeness of this animate thing—the modified dinosaur, the fantastically exaggerated newt—was an impediment to the work of the investigation bureau, which has no pertinent interest in what the monster resembles or calls to mind but a great deal in what it actually is, the goal being a final and positive identification of the genus.

"What we need is a good, lengthy, basking sighting," Skelton said. "We've had one long surfacing—twenty-five minutes. I saw it. Opposite Urquhart Castle. We only had a twelve-inch lens then, at four and a half miles. We have thirty-six inch lenses now. We need a long, clear, close-up—in color."

My children had watched, some months earlier, the killing of a small snake on a lawn in Maryland. About eighteen inches long, it came out from a basement-window well, through a covering lattice of redwood, and was noticed with shouts and shrieks by the children and a young retriever that barked at the snake and leaped about it in a circle. We were the weekend guests of another family, and eight children in all crowded around the snake, which had been gliding slowly across the lawn during the moments after it had been seen, but had now stopped and was turning its head from side to side in apparent indecision. Our host hurried into his garage and came running back to the lawn with a long shovel. Before he killed the snake, his wife urged him not to. She said the snake could not possibly be poisonous. He said, "How do you know?" The children, mine and theirs, looked back and forth from him to her. The dog began to bark more rapidly and at a higher pitch.

"It has none of the markings. There is nothing triangular about its head," she told him.

"That may very well be," he said. "But you can't be sure."

"It is *not* poisonous. Leave it alone. Look at all these children."

"I can't help that."

"It is *not* poisonous."

"How do you know?"

"I know."

He hit the snake with the flat of the shovel, and it writhed. He hit it again. It kept moving. He hit it a third time, and it stopped. Its underside, whitish green, segmental, turned up. The children moved in for a closer look.

CONTENT

1. The Loch Ness Monster has fascinated people because of its connection with ancient legends of sea monsters. What seems to be McPhee's attitude toward the desire to solve the mystery of the monster? Would he rather live in a world with or without mysteries? How do you know?

2. What is the conflict in McPhee's narrative? Explain how the following quotations illustrate the two forces in conflict: "I must know what it is. I shall never rest peacefully until I know what it is." "Its general appearance is repulsive, in the instant and radical sense in which reptiles are repulsive to many human beings."

3. Characterize Clem Lister Skelton. Is he a character type? In what ways? In what ways is he not?

ORGANIZATION

4. McPhee's essays are notable for their unusual organization. Frequently, he interrupts the flow of a story with what seems extraneous material. Examine several of these "digressions" to see how they function to build the conflict or resolve it.
5. What is the function of the description of Scotland's fifty foot high beaches? Why does McPhee open his narrative with the violent ending of a picnicking family's birthday outing and close with another violent act?
6. Why does McPhee include a comparison between Loch Ness and Lake George (paragraphs 7–8) in his narrative? What is the funcion of the flashback to McPhee's childhood recollection of a carnival and caged bear (paragraphs 23–25)? Why is the snake killing incident (paragraphs 33–41) placed as a resolution?

TOPICS FOR WRITING

7. Write a narrative centering on a irrational human fear; explain how the fear was either mastered or succumbed to.
8. Write a narrative which includes a comparison and a description.
9. Narrate an incident from your childhood, the significance of which you later came to realize. Use cause/effect and examples.
10. Narrate a trip to a place which held unusual interest for you.

PETER MARIN
Coming to Terms With Vietnam

Peter Marin, a native of Brooklyn, New York, is a writer and poet whose special province is ethics and morality. He is co-author of The Limits of Schooling *(1975), and* Understanding Drug Use *(1971), and author of* In a Man's Time *(1974). He received a grant from the Guggenheim Foundation for work on a book entitled* Conscience and the Common Good. *"Coming to Terms with Vietnam," a part of that study, argues that until Americans face the problems of the Vietnam veterans, there will be no peace in America's conscience over the war.*

The fevers of war are once again upon us. They do not yet rage openly, but beneath the surface of recent American events can be felt the gathering strength of attitudes and emotions that permit us to think about war in ways that were impossible even a year ago. We hear almost daily the militant pronouncements of our political candidates and news of escalating appropriations for arms. We seem to be witnessing the remilitarization of America, a process that has not yet brought us to the brink of war, but has already established in many minds the groundwork for war: a revitalized sense of our moral superiority, a heightened fear of the malevolent forces surrounding us, and a belief in our capacity to temper our use of violence.

Whether it be the Nicaraguan revolution, the hostage crisis, the rise in OPEC prices, the Russian invasion of Afghanistan, or the fighting in Iraq and Iran, our inability to control events and our inept response to them have demanded from us a rethinking of our political and moral relation to the world. But we neglect this crucial task. Instead, we have lapsed happily into the familiar attitudes that marked the Cold War in the Fifties and the Asian debacle of the Sixties: we clench our fists and mutter comforting platitudes to ourselves, cheerfully lost among the same illusions that proved so disastrous a decade ago.

It is fashionable now, in some circles, to see this renewed military hubris as both inevitable and necessary. We are told that we are merely leaving behind, as we must, guilt that paralyzed us for a decade after the war in Vietnam. But that, I think, misstates the case. What paralyzed us was not simply the guilt felt about Vietnam, but our inability to confront and comprehend that guilt: our refusal to face squarely what happened and why, and our unwillingness to determine, in the light of the past, our moral obligations for the future. In short, we spent a decade denying and evading guilt rather than using it to our advantage.

Yet the moral quandaries remain. Vietnam is with us still, laden with meaning, constraining some of us, eating at others, pushed out of sight but present in the various shames we feel as we look at the flag, in our naive dreams of easy peace or our violent fantasies of virtue and power. Sometimes, for a moment, one gets glimpses of the barely hidden anger and guilt. When, for instance, California's Gov. Jerry Brown appointed Jane Fonda to the state's arts council and the state senate refused the ratify the appointment, the air was filled suddenly with violent response. To the senators, Ms. Fonda was "a traitor"; to her, they were fascists. One could feel the sudden, brutal, and still unresolved memory of the war.

The same volatility appears in private conversations. Mention Vietnam, the veterans, guilt, or responsibility, and the air becomes rife with accusations, defenses, justifications, and confusions. A split is revealed not only among us but also within each one of us: each of us lives with the sense of having left undone a series of tasks we can neither name nor understand, but which we know with a terrible intensity constitute the war's legacy.

None of us has faced the specter of his *own* culpability—not Nixon's, not Kissinger's—but the way in which each one of us, actively or passively, contributed to the killing, the taxes we paid, officials we elected, lessons we taught in the classroom, obedience we taught, the endless round of incipient and explicit influences that made countless young men willing to kill for the worst of causes in the worst of ways. We have skirted the sort of passionate and open self-investigation that members of a democratic society must conduct to protect others from themselves, a rethinking of values and allegiances that have had brutal effects. In setting the war aside we have failed to push ourselves far enough, failed to raise the crucial questions about ourselves that we ought to confront. We have failed to indicate that we will be much different from what we have been in the past.

We have had our texts, that is true. Book after book about the war has come off the presses, placing blame, analyzing causes, condemning Nixon, Kissinger, and Westmoreland and their abuses of power. But most of these seem to have missed the point, ascribing to the war political errors or the excess of a few men, as if all of us in America had somehow been fooled into fighting.

That was not the case at all, of course. Though resisted from the start, the war was a popular one; we reelected Nixon in the middle of it, and we were led further into it not so much by lies as by our nationalistic sense of unsullied virtue and by the difficulty we have in seeing the reality of events, the justice of other's causes, or the suffering we inflict upon them. Few of the books on Vietnam raise the questions we should have faced: the full extent of the atrocities committed and the participation in those atrocities of ordinary soldiers, ordinary citizens, and ordinary children.

* * *

There are, too, the veterans among us, enigmatic and for the
most part silent, harboring the truths the rest of us do not want to
hear. We have statistics on their suicide rate and the extent of their
drug addiction, but nobody bothers much with the reality behind
those figures, with what the vets saw and did, or were *asked* to do,
and how the permutations of guilt (the guilt they feel, the guilt we
deny) are at work within them. Here, too, silence reigns, perhaps
in large part because we discourage the vets from speaking by refus-
ing to listen. Even when the vets protest or speak out, they have
little to say about the war itself. They almost always voice their own
grievances: how they were treated, the paucity of their benefits, the
refusal of their countrymen to pay attention to them. Their protests
against Agent Orange are solely personal; they never remind us
(nor do we care to remember) what the poison must also have done
and be doing to generations of Vietnamese. What they avoid, as do
we all, is the immense task of coming to terms with what went on
in Vietnam—the killing and the attendant guilt— and the fact that
neither they nor we know how to respond to those realities.

* * *

I remember, for instance, one veteran's story about his return to
the States. He had been a part of what he called an "assassination
squad," spending long periods of time on his own, out of touch
with both his superiors and comrades, apparently working independently on his assigned tasks. He described coming home in a
series of almost surrealistic vignettes: being lectured in the airport
by an officer for playing cards with his buddies and "giving the
service a bad name"; being asked by the first civilian he had met in
months about "them niggers in the army, the ones too chicken-shit
to fight"; falling asleep in his seat and then waking from a nightmare of war, shaking and sweating, to find that everyone close to
him had moved several seats away; and, finally, meeting his parents
at the airport and finding it impossible to speak. They drove home
in silence and then sat together in the kitchen, and his mother, in
passing, apologized for there being "nothing in the house to eat."
That did it; he broke. Raging, he went from cupboard to cupboard,
shelf to shelf, flinging doors open, pulling down cans and boxes
and bags, piling them higher and higher on the table until they
spilled over onto the floor and everything edible in the house was
spread out in front of them.

"I couldn't believe it," he said, shaking his head as he told me "I'd been over there for years, killing those bastards who were living in their tunnels like rats and had nothing to eat but mud and a few goddamn moldy grains of rice, and who watched their kids starve to death or go up in smoke, and she said *nothing to eat*, and I ended up in the kitchen crying and shouting: *Nothing to eat, nothing to eat!*"

The story is not particularly special; I might have recounted a dozen others like it, some about the war itself, and more dramatic. But the point would be the same. No image, no technical effect, no posed theatrical scene, comes even close to the power and meaning of one man speaking quietly, telling the truth of his experience.

The Guilt-bearers Among Us

It is inevitable, then, that we come to the veterans themselves. If two of the keys to the comprehension of the past and the creation of the future are memory and speech, it is in their memories, and in the possibilities of their speech, that the antidotes to our silence and fantasy lie. It is their voices—real voices, grounded in the real—that may have the power to call us back from our illusions to the discomforting concreteness of our acts. The questions of silence and speech, which remain for the rest of us theoretical questions, are for our veterans personal quandaries, sources of personal pain; at least some of them are forced by the circumstances of their lives to struggle inwardly, and apparently endlessly, with the problems all of us should but do not confront.

The real issue, to put it bluntly, is *guilt*: how, as a nation and as individuals, we perceive our culpability and determine what it requires of us. We must concern ourselves with the discovery of fact, the location of responsibility, the discussion of causes, the acknowledgment of moral debt and how it might be repaid—not in terms of who supposedly led us astray, but in terms of how each one of us may have contributed to the war or to its underlying causes. The "horror" of war is really very easy to confront; it demands nothing of us save the capacity not to flinch. But guilt and responsibility, if one takes them seriously, are something else altogether. For they imply a debt, something to be done, changed lives—and that is much harder on both individuals and a nation, for it implies a moral labor as strenuous and demanding as the war that preceded it.

Decades ago Karl Jaspers, the German philosopher who fled his country during the second world war, returned to Germany once the war was over and gave several lectures under the title "The

Question of German Guilt." His purpose was neither to castigate his people nor to find particular men to blame, but simply to establish the realms of discourse and thought in which, collectively and individually, they were responsible for reviewing their past acts and determining their future behavior. There are obvious differences between the Germans' situation and our own, but Jasper's work is relevant to us, especially because we have spent so little time thinking about guilt productively.

We, like the Germans, fought a war marked by racism, atrocities, and what many called genocide; we too, as a people, actively supported or tolerated the annihilation of a civilian population; we too watched our neighbors, brothers, and children devastate a nation in our name; we too elected our leaders knowingly, welcomed their small reassuring lies, applauded the suppression of dissent at home, and were more concerned with our power than the suffering it caused; and, finally, we too, in the war's aftermath, have denied responsibility for what occurred, have pleaded ignorance, have blamed everyone but ourselves.

But all of us, according to Jaspers, are responsible for the acts of war, accountable for the personal and social acts that contribute to war long before it has begun: the distractions, evasions, failures of nerve and resistance, mindless enthusiasms and neutralities with which we replace our responsibilities as citizens, as moral agents. In this regard each of us is guilty or, at least, guilty enough to share the burden of guilt that we happily assign, after the war, to those leaders and soldiers we ourselves produced.

Jaspers distinguished among four kinds of guilt: criminal, political, moral, and metaphysical. The first two types are essentially simple. Criminal law involves civil law; judgment is made by a judge or jury. Political guilt involves the collective crimes of a state, its leaders or its citizens; these are judged—as at Nuremberg—by the war's victors in accordance with international conventions. But the second two kinds of guilt—moral and metaphysical—are far more complicated, for they involve the judgments men make about themselves according to conscience, and it is these judgments, made privately and communally, that determine a nation's moral nature. It is quite possible, in Jasper's eyes, and sometimes necessary, for men who might be innocent in criminal and political terms to find themselves morally and metaphysically guilty, and to struggle to restore to themselves and to their community what they find missing from their moral lives.

Moral guilt, for Jaspers, involves the responsibility of all persons   19
for all of their acts and the consequences of their acts—even under
orders, even in the midst of war. "It is never true," he writes, "that
'orders are orders.' Every deed remains subject to moral judgment."
He means *every* deed: not only the acts of those who gave or took
orders but even the apparently innocuous acts of those who in
civilian life contributed in any way to the institutions and social
attitudes that made such violence possible. Even those not directly
responsible for the war, even those who stood against it have in its
wake an obligation to both their country's victims and their fellow-
citizens; to create a moral climate in which *all* individuals can examine the complexities of guilt and the nature of their moral obligations. "Moral guilt," Jaspers writes, "can only truthfully be discussed in a loving struggle between men who maintain solidarity
among themselves."

Metaphysical guilt, for Jaspers, has to do with the relation of   20
man to God and the ways in which men have somehow betrayed
their given covenant with Him. It refers to our fundamental failure,
at work not only in war but ubiquitously, to extend our own sense
of human reciprocity or responsibility past the ordinary limits of
family or nation to include those unlike ourselves. With metaphysical guilt, as with moral guilt, the power of judgment belongs to
each man in relation to himself; he is answerable to both his own
conscience and to God, and he remains responsible—at the heart
of his own privacy—for setting right what he himself perceives as
wrong.

One might argue with these categories, of course. For many of   21
us the line between moral and metaphysical guilt is not as easily
drawn as it is for Jaspers. But such arguments are not important.
What *is* important is the fact that Jaspers takes guilt seriously and
understands it as a natural and inevitable consequence of all human
activity. Guilt has, for him, little to do with breast-beating and weeping, sackcloth and ashes. He does not see it, as we do in America,
as a condition to be escaped or denied; it has nothing to do with
punishment. It is, rather, a kind of awareness, a form of acknowledgment, a way of so clearly seeing one's relation to the past, and
one's past actions, that one is moved by reason and conscience to
rethink and remake the nature of one's moral life. It is a practical
matter, a kind of perceived debt requiring and impelling further
action. It is, in a sense, a question men pose to themselves and
which they answer with what they do with their lives.

The purpose of such an answer has little to do with absolution   2
or atonement. The dead, after all, remain dead. The maimed remain
maimed. It is no more possible to "absolve" oneself of guilt than it
is to bring the dead back to life or erase the suffering one has caused.
But it *is* possible to live in the future in a way that makes sense of
the past, and to restore to one's life the moral legitimacy that has
been lost. No man can determine for another precisely what it is
that the other, in his own privacy, may find he must do; but one
can say that the legitimacy of all moral life depends on the willingness of men to struggle with such questions before they decide
what to do. All men, like all nations, are tested twice in the moral
realm: first by what they do, then by what they make of what they
do. A condition of guilt, a sense of one's own guilt, denotes a kind
of second chance; men are, as if by a kind of grace, given a chance
to repay to the living what it is they find themselves owing the
dead.

Conscience Endangered

It is obvious that these notions—taken seriously—would require   2
from us much more, as individuals, than we have so far been willing
to accept as part of the debt conferred upon us by the war. We
would have to consider, above all else, the institutions, attitudes,
and systems of authority that made possible both our actions in
Vietnam and the willingness of our young men to partake in them.
We would have to ask ourselves about the extent to which we were
responsible not only for the war but for the schooling we give our
young and the ways we encourage obedience and the suspension
of moral judgment—the violence and incipient racism at work in
our streets and minds; the myths and distractions of media that
wrap us endlessly in dreams and fantasies; the caste and class blind-
nesses that teach us, continuously, an indifference to all those unlike
ourselves; the tendency at work everywhere among us, on both
the Left and Right, to presume virtue and moral superiority for
oneself, while casting one's opponents as knaves; and the failure
of both our artists and thinkers to place at the heart of their concerns
a passion for conscience or justice. Finally, in terms of "metaphysical" guilt, we would have to consider precisely what we believe
one person owes another, or what he owes to *which* others, and
how responsible each of us must be in relation to moral choice,
especially in the face of what our country asks us to do.

But these questions, which hung in the air for the war's duration   24
and ought now to inform the heart of every private existence, have
ceased for most of us to have any power. The notion of conscience
itself has become almost exotic; genuinely moral concerns, genuinely moral lives, have become so rare among us that they seem
eccentric.

I remember once talking to a psychologist who worked for the   25
Veterans' Administration. I asked him how he and his colleagues
dealt with the problem of guilt.

"We *don't* deal with it," he said. "It does not exist for us. For us,   26
everything is a problem in *adjustment.*"

How different would it be anywhere else in our culture? What   27
has changed radically in the last several decades is not so much our
behavior, but how we *think* about it: the ways we measure action
and its consequences, and how we hold ourselves or one another
responsible for things. One can search in vain these days—not only
in therapeutic texts, but in those dealing with morality or politics—
for the word *conscience.* Our philosophers long ago reduced ethical
questions to problems in epistemology, and even our religions have
ceased to offer us much in this realm, concerned as they are with
the problems of salvation rather than the complexities of concrete
moral life in the real world.

The Veterans' Private Wars

This, in part, is what makes our veterans so important. The vets   28
know conscience exists; they are immersed in it. They face daily, as
a part of their private and personal lives, the questions that at best
remain abstract for the rest of us. In a sense, they are still walking
point for us, confronting a landscape as alien as anything they faced
in Vietnam, still doing for the rest of us the dangerous tasks that
we pretend do not exist.

Guilt, I know, is not the only possible explanation for the pain   29
and rage they feel. Obviously, they suffer not only the alienation
experienced by the participants of any war but also problems unique
to the war in Vietnam: their disappointment at their treatment at
home; their anger at the absence of gratitude, attention, respect, or
aid; their resentment at having risked their lives and seen men die
in a war now regretted or forgotten. But behind all of that, and
mixed inextricably with it, is something more, something perhaps
not even privately admitted: the anger of the veterans at them-

selves, their grief at having fought and killed in the wrong war, for the wrong reasons, in the wrong way.

One cannot know precisely how many veterans are thus troubled. Despite everything written about it, the war remains, still, a mystery for most of us. We cannot know precisely what went on, how frequently atrocities occurred, how many men and women were wantonly slaughtered or raped, how many villages were carelessly destroyed—or how many of our soldiers were directly involved. But certainly all of that plays a part in what many of our veterans now suffer. I am thinking not only of the outspoken and angry veterans such as the Vietnam Veterans Against the War but also about all those others in whom shame and guilt may take a disguised and unrecognizable form: the suicides reported and unreported; the cases of addiction, criminality, depression, schizophrenia, and all those other conditions that may be in part maladies of conscience; the drifters and drinkers and compulsive talkers and weepers one can find in the cheap hotels and taverns of any American city; the armed and angry vets one finds in southern and mountain states awaiting Armageddon and hating both their government and those who criticize it; and even (or perhaps especially) the "well-adjusted" who go about their daily business without apparent doubt or dread or drama, who never speak about the war but who wake alone in the dark dreaming of war, caught in its terrors still.

No doubt complex forces are at work in all of these instances, but who can doubt that in all of them conscious or unconscious guilt plays a part? Even in the cases in which vets deny feeling guilty, how can one tell how much of that is true, and how much they may be hiding from themselves? The past, after all, has not held still; it has pursued us these last several years even as we have tried to leave it behind. Almost every bit of information we have had about the war since its end has called its legitimacy into question and revealed the cupidity of those who oversaw it. Devastating as this information ought to have been to all Americans, it has certainly disturbed many of our vets even more; and those among them who have consciously tried—as many have—to discover retrospectively the truths of the war find themselves in the predicament of Oedipus; every step they take toward the truth brings them closer to their own guilt.

The real issue, for each of the veterans, is not whether it was a   32
just war, or if he belonged there in the first place; it is, rather, the
way the war was fought: the wholesale slaughter of innocents, the
devastation of the countryside, and the extent and nature of our
atrocities which have never been and may never be fully known.

I think, as I write, of several conversations I have had with vets   33
in recent months. There is no way, really, in a few words, to describe
the range of feelings and reactions that come into play in their voices
and faces as they speak. Often what passes across their faces is at
odds with the words; one feels as if one is listening to two voices
at once, or as if they desperately want to tell you what they are busy
keeping you from finding out. I recall, in particular, the way vets
describe their reception in America after the war. They were shocked,
they explain, to find themselves treated by their countrymen as if
they were at fault. This was especially true on college campuses,
where they were spat upon, ostracized, and called babykillers or
murderers. Something more than injury or confusion creeps into
their voices: something plaintive, yearning. The words *babykiller*
and *murderer* become in their mouths a kind of self accusation, as
if the savagery they ascribe to their critics is a part of their own
inner life for which they seek absolution.

At such times one finds oneself wanting to reach out to smooth   34
away their pain. But how is one to do that? Many vets, actually, find
themselves *more* guilty than they appear to other members of society; they judge themselves more harshly than they are judged by
others. Yet their feelings about themselves, as painful as they are,
may well be morally accurate. The guilt they feel is—dare one say
it?—appropriate. True, many killed out of ignorance; but though
others may forgive them, many men, as they grow older and learn
more about the past, cannot forgive themselves.

Here one hesitates, of course. There are areas in which no man   35
can adequately judge another; even though some sort of general
guilt exists, who can say of any particular man, *this* is how much
he must feel or suffer? Every vet had his own situation, his own
war. Some, of course, killed gladly, arbitrarily. But others killed
reluctantly, or in a hallucinatory fog, distanced from their actions
by music or drugs. Still others killed against their will, lacking the
courage or foolishness to resist; and others killed because they had
been trained to do it, or for the reasons at work in almost any of

us: because they were there, or were told to kill, or because others were trying to kill them. There are so many different stories, so many different motives, that one wants, perpetually, to shade every statement with explanations, provisos, disclaimers. Three such forms of extenuation come to mind, which ought to enter into every judgment—about ourselves or others—that we make about guilt.

First, there is the complexity of guilt, the difficulty in separating out individual responsibility in the midst of war from the more general responsibility of a people or a nation. "Sheeit," a vet said to me once, "I come from Dallas, man. What in hell did I know back then? Even in '68, everyone I knew was for the war: teachers, parents, clergymen even. Dissenters? They were just dirty northern hippies to us. I was just *doin' right.*"

Behind the shared guilt for the war lies a deeper and more general guilt, one that includes all the other forms of obvious or incipient violence at home or abroad that prepare the way for war. Daily, even in supposed "peace," we are complicitous in distant places with brutality and murder, in political partnership with thugs and knaves. And the same thing goes on here at home in those quarters of our cities we carefully avoid. If our boys in Vietnam were not trained to kill throughout their lives, they were at least readied for it through the mix of national pride, obedience, superiority, and racism we teach in our schools and encourage in our communities. In a way, few of the men who fought in Vietnam were ever really there, ever really saw the place and their enemies. They were locked, still, in our classrooms, in our national dreams, in our old Hollywood films, living out, almost like robots, the pervasive national myths of virtue, prowess, and power.

Second, there is the nature of the war itself. It was, after all, a civil war, a guerrilla war. Though Coppola* is partly right in seeing it in terms of advanced technology pitted against native innocence and faith, down on the ground, in hand-to-hand combat, our young troops were often out of their league, confronted not only by sophisticated and dedicated soldiers, but also by an entire civilian population that saw them as intruders, invaders—a situation for which nothing had prepared them. For many of our troops the war was like a perpetual Halloween Night grown brutally real. A sense of trespass and illegitimacy shrouded every moment; they were like

---

*Francis Ford Coppola, director of the film about the Vietnamese War, *Apocalypse Now.*

grown children in the wrong place, always in someone else's garden, ready to fire or flee in an instant. Even innocuous objects took on a malevolent life of their own. Viet Cong tripwires made each twig and stone a threat. Our soldiers carried bits of wire to fit over the mouths of softdrink bottles to protect themselves from the glass shards planted by the Viet Cong; they held the bottles up to the light to make sure they were not half-filled with gasoline. Vets have told me about whores in Saigon who lined their vaginas with razor blades to mutilate GIs. And I remember a vet who said to me (not without awe):

"It was the Viet Cong women scared me the most. If you were   39
wounded in battle, the men would use the chance to escape. But
the women! They'd come out to where you were and cut off your
head or your balls."

Are such stories true? It almost does not matter. What does mat-   40
ter is that Americans believed them and that they reveal to us a bit
of the nightmare landscape Vietnam became for our vets.

"It was like the goddamn West," a vet once said to me. "I was   41
more frightened of other Americans than of the Viet Cong. Guns
everywhere, everyone armed. I got so used to it I carried a piece
for months back in America, and I was ready to use it—not on the
enemy but on Americans."

At times supplies were so short that vets traded the scavenged   42
parts of enemy bodies in the Saigon markets for the very same
supplies intended for them in the first place: weapons, boots, or
rain gear. Others became so disgusted with the perpetual theft of
their food that they wrote to American corporations, asking in vain
for their food to be sent directly to them.

"I was from the city streets," a young man said to me, "and so I   43
was used to it all—the graft, the theft, the crooked authority. I knew
all about American corruption. But the farm kids! Christ, when
they saw all that, it damn near blew them away. It was worse than
combat, to see their own country's shabbiness."

No doubt this was intensified by the effects upon our troops of   44
what they saw in the midst of their own army: the stupidity and
dishonesty of their leaders and the cupidity and corruption pandemic behind the lines. Every vet I know has stories to tell about
vanishing supplies, open theft, drug trafficking, black marketeering, and gangsterlike confrontations that extended into Vietnam the
normal life of American city streets.

And there is, finally, human nature itself, the apparent need and even the right of men to forget after a war what they have done or seen in it. The forgetfulness that no society can afford is undeniably a blessing for individual men, a kind of soothing boon that allows them to recover from the past. There are certain acts so terrible that only their victims can afford to remember them; those who have committed them must forget, if only to stay sane.

I remember reading about a German ex-officer discovered years after the end of the second world war hundreds of miles deep in the African bush in a house on stilts at a river's edge, where he lived with his native wife and five children. When his captors asked him whether he was the man they were seeking, he said: "I am another."

And perhaps he was. Nature has its own forms of absolution, and they have little to do with justice. Memory's power is countered by another power, perhaps as strong: the capacity to sunder the present from the past. One thinks of Lt. William Calley under house arrest, so typically American: baby-faced, soft-toned, with his southern-belle sweetie beside him, his evenings of television and TV dinners and ice cream for dessert. His banality was equal in its small way to Adolf Eichmann's: no sorrow, no shame, not even the visible signs of memory or a sense of what it might be that was so disturbing to those condemning him.

Horrible, one thinks at first. But is it? If it is horrible, it is also fully human, almost universal—and understandable. We have already seen the effects of the past on those of our veterans who can neither forget nor stand its memory. For every man who succeeds in making something of the past, several—who knows how many?—come to grief. Without the community of loving others about whom Jaspers spoke, those others whose burdens ease one's own, forgetfulness may be nature's kindest gift, and something that all men must be allowed, for perhaps nothing else will heal their wounds.

A Collective Confession

And yet despite the universality of guilt and the extenuations of war, it seems just that the war belongs to our vets, that they are its keepers. I do not mean of its statistics, or of the analysis of its causes or the particulars of blame; these will be pursued by others, scholars who come later, dissecting the war, laying out its details at a safe distance. But the nature of the war, and the fact and feel of it—the conflicts and private struggles of conscience, the horrors that exist simultaneously outside and inside a man—all of these belong to the vets, for who else has it in their power to keep us straight, and who else has the knowledge required to do it?

I remember, a few years ago in Michigan, accompanying a woman   50
to a graduate seminar in psychology given by a friend of hers. The students were supposed to be discussing conscience and ethics, but they were not up to it. They were young, inexperienced, over-schooled. All value, they kept insisting, was relative, arbitrary; truth was what anyone believed it was; who were we, asked one or two, to say the Germans ought not to have killed the Jews? It must have seemed right at the time.

Only one man among them was different. Black, older than the   51
rest, he had been in Vietnam. Reluctantly, only because I asked, he described his experiences there: how he had awakened one morning, after months of combat, weeping and shivering, unable to continue, frightened and ashamed of the killing he had done, full of self-hatred. Those in the room fell silent suddenly; reality had intruded upon them. But they were not up to it; they had to evade it. "Just shell shock," the army doctors had told the vet, and now the students had a similar explanation. "Conditioning," they said—that was all. First taught not to kill, then asked to kill, he had been caught between two arbitrary orders.

I still remember the look on the vet's face. He smiled at me and   52
shook his head, as if to say: *You see it man, who needs this shit?* And what could I respond? That what he had said needed saying, whether they heard it or not? That it was precisely *because* the others did not understand that it needed saying? That he must keep faith with the dead even if the living kept no faith with him?

The vets must speak—both for our good and their own. They   53
know firsthand—as most of us should but do not—that guilt is real, and that men cannot be fully human or whole without coming to terms with their relation to suffering others.

Will the vets speak? Some of them, I suppose, have no choice.   54
They are unable either to forget the past or come to terms with it without speaking. Every war, whatever its nature, is followed by a sort of lag time, a period of assimilation and silence during which, as most men forget the past, a few mine from the past what they later speak into the world.

* * *

And it has taken European film makers nearly forty years to confront the complex moral issues of the holocaust. Perhaps something similar will happen with Vietnam. Our great texts, and a period of rich understanding, may yet be ahead of us; new books still working in the minds of silent men and new films may, a decade from now, confront us with the truth of the past in a way we have not yet learned to manage.

The problem with that, of course, is that it may come too late to do much good. Even our young seem, at the moment, affected by our appetite for war. A few days ago a veteran I know who teaches a highschool class told me about an experiment he conducted:

"I like to set up mock elections in historical contexts," he said. "Last week I chose the later stages of the Vietnam war, just about the time we mined Haiphong harbor. One of the student-candidates was a dove who promised to end the war. The other was a hawk who wanted not only to mine the harbor but also to use nuclear weapons."

"And who won?" I asked.

"The hawk," he said, "in a landslide."

I have little doubt we will come fully round, as nations usually do, to where we were before, perhaps a bit wiser, but not much, and subject continuously each one of us and each of our children to the pressures, influences, and conditioning that lead men everywhere to war. We are not much worse in America than people anywhere, but we are not much better either, and our shared national moral life (and therefore the destinies of countless others affected by our choices) hangs perpetually in a kind of uneasy balance, slanted toward violence but checked by decency. All that protects us from the worst aspects of our nature is simply a humility grounded in the consciousness of our past fallibility and the memory of what we have done to others.

I am not arguing here for a pure pacifism—though given the human capacity for error there is an argument to be made on that count. What I *am* arguing for here is simply the minimal moral ground for any just society: the willingness of all men and women to accept absolute responsibility for the nature of their acts and their consequences, especially in those matters involving others and life and death. It is individual judgment, choice, and responsibility that leaven and define the nature of shared moral life. Nations and national leaders must be constrained and circumscribed by ethical standards passionately maintained by every private citizen: the capacity to see others clearly, to understand the relationship of one's life to theirs, and to judge the demands of the state and resist its power and propaganda in accordance with one's best and private sense of justice.

It has fallen to the vets to remind us of this, and what we owe   62
them in return is everything we can do to make that task easier. This includes not only a willingness to consider the war itself and our own culpability, but also a willingness to begin the reexamination and recreation of the debauched moral landscape in which their struggles occur.

As it now stands, those veterans who take guilt seriously are set   63
apart from others, isolated by their seriousness. But it is, ironically, their guilt that joins them to others, thrusts them violently into the human world. They must understand not only that they may be guilty but that they are guilty *too*, in the same way that other men are guilty—not necessarily in a special way but simply in a more obvious way. Their guilt derived from the war is not so different, really, from the guilt of the man who has two coats while another has none, or the guilt of the overfed in a hungry world, or the guilt of those who remain oblivious and protected by privilege in a world of impermissible pain. Only when all of us take seriously the possibility of our own culpability will the vets understand that *their* guilt, as terrible and demanding as it may seem, makes them human rather than monstrous.

Yet, having said all that, I must add that it is not likely to occur.   64
For the most part the vets will be left to confront their guilt on their own. The only other Americans to confront their own guilt may well be those who stumble accidentally—and almost unwillingly— into its acknowledgment.

I am thinking, as I write, of something that happened later that   65
night in Michigan. After the seminar my friend and I sat in the kitchen with the wife of her professor-friend, as she told us what he had neglected to explain himself—that he had become a member of a Charismatic Catholic sect, now spoke in tongues, and was convinced that all human evil could be traced to possession by the devil, and had little to do with choice. Later, we went down the street to a neighborhood bar. It was the night of the first Ford-Carter election debate, the one in which the equipment failed. As we sat at our tables, silently watching the bar's patrons watching in silence

the two figures voiceless at their lecterns, a young man came over and talked to us. He was a veteran—hair in a ponytail, wearing an army jacket, carrying a guitar case. He set it down and introduced himself and launched into a soliloquy—the kind one sometimes hears from disturbed veterans: brilliant, schizzy, disjointed, heartbreaking, shifting from his childhood to the war to America to God to Carter to Ford to his parents to the army doctors to the powers who ran the country to the CIA's plot to cheat him of sleep and drive him insane. He proceeded lucidly for a while, and then suddenly his language came apart. Flashes of madness appeared; one could hear, behind the words, bomb blasts and rifle fire and the dead falling around him, and when he had finished he put one hand on my friend's arm and one on mine. "I don't know you," he said, "but you're all right. I'd like to have had parents like you, or maybe even kids."

Outside on the street, my friend, remembering the seminar and the professor's wife and the vet, put her head on my shoulder and wept. "I did not think," she said, "that it had come to this." ⁶⁶

Yet it *had* come to "this," though my friend, like the rest of us, had trouble grasping the pain and death incumbent upon us, or the cost to others of our careless posturing, arrogance, and rage. Weeping, I know, solves nothing; morality is an activity, not a sentiment; and yet there was something in my friend's weeping, as there was in the black veteran's tears in the midst of the war, that seems to me to hold the key to the recreation of ethical life. ⁶⁷

It was as if, in relief, she had set free the stirring of memory, the raw beginnings of speech: the angers and sympathies and griefs and regrets that form the human center of the moral world. ⁶⁸

That, perhaps, was what her weeping meant. And if it did, God grant her, as well as the rest of us, the courage and tenacity to see through to its end the ethical journey such weeping begins. ⁶⁹

CONTENT

1. Is Marin right in suggesting there is a new wave of militarism in the United States? Has the country come to terms with Vietnam?
2. Why does Marin contend that our salvation lies in listening to the Vietnam veterans, and thus coming to terms with our own

guilt? Why does he think Americans should continue to feel guilt about Vietnam?
3. How do the veterans' stories that Marin relates help clarify what he means by our moral and metaphysical guilt? What is the function of the two classroom anecdotes (paragraphs 50–52 and 57–59) involving students with either no memory or no experience of Vietnam?

ORGANIZATION

4. What is the function of Karl Jaspers' categories of guilt (paragraph 18) in helping explain Marin's thesis?
5. Locate narrative examples in Marin's essay. Show how they help make the abstract ethical discussion clear and relevant.
6. Where do comparisons occur? What is their function? Is definition used in the essay? Where? To what effect?
7. Does Marin document the effects of the war on veterans? On the American public? How does this material relate to his thesis?

TOPICS FOR WRITING

8. Show how the popular media (movies, songs, television) have kept the memory of Vietnam alive and thus have restored America's conscience.
9. Write an essay developing Marin's opening summation of America's present mood as one of "a revitalized sense of moral superiority, a heightened sense of the malevolent forces surrounding us, and a belief in our capacity to temper our use of violence."

PART 8
Persuasion: Writing to Convince

One of the most forceful public demonstrations of the power of persuasion occurred on August 28, 1963 when Dr. Martin Luther King delivered his famous "I Have a Dream" speech which left a crowd of 250,000 gathered for the March on Washington in stunned silence. Here are the final words of that speech.

I say to you today even though we face the difficulties of today and tomorrow, I still have a dream. It is a dream that is deeply rooted in the American dream. I have a dream that one day this nation will rise up, live out the true meaning of its creed: We hold these truths to be self-evident, that all men are created equal.

I have a dream that one day on the red hills of Georgia the sons of former slaves and the sons of former slaveowners will be able to sit down together at the table of brotherhood. I have a dream that one day even the state of Mississippi, a state sweltering with the heat of oppression, will be transformed into an oasis of freedom and justice.

I have a dream that my four little children one day will live in a nation where they will not be judged by the color of their skin, but by the content of their character.

I have a dream that one day every valley shall be exalted, every hill and mountain shall be made low. The rough places will be made plain and the crooked places will be made straight. This is the faith that I go back to the South with. With this faith we will be able to hew out of the mountains of despair the stone of hope. With this faith we will be able to work together, to pray together, to struggle together, to go to jail together, to stand up for freedom together, knowing we will be free one day.

This will be the day when all of God's children will be able to sing with new meaning, 'Let freedom ring.' So let freedom ring from the prodigious hilltops of New Hampshire; let freedom ring from the mighty mountains of New York. But not only that. Let freedom ring from Stone Mountain of Georgia. Let freedom ring from every hill and molehill of Mississippi, from every mountainside.

When we allow freedom to ring from every town and every hamlet, from every state and every city, we will be able to speed up that day when all of God's children, black men and white men, Jews and Gentiles, Protestants and Catholics, will be able to join hands and sing in the words of the old Negro spiritual, "Free at last! Free at last! Great God A-mighty, we are free at last!" [Coretta Scott King, *My Life with Martin Luther King, Jr.* (Holt, Rinehart and Winston, 1969), 239–40.]

What makes this speech so powerful is the sweep of emotion which carried the audience along on the tide of the repeated refrains: "I have a dream . . . ," "With this faith . . . ," "Let freedom ring. . . ." The audience was also moved by the echoes from the Declaration of Independence ("We hold these truths to be self-evident . . .") and the Bible ("Every valley shall be exalted . . ."), and by the figurative language ("an oasis of freedom and justice," "hew out of the mountain of despair the stone of hope"). What finally makes the speech so persuasive is Dr. King's obvious sincerity.

All three of these things—the emotions and ideas, the style and the character of the speaker—comprise what we call rhetoric. Aristotle defined rhetoric as "the faculty of discovering . . . what are the available means of persuasion." In fact, until well into the nineteenth century, rhetoric and persuasion were synonymous. Originally rhetoric involved the means by which speakers could move people to action, stir their emotions, or gain their conviction. As such, rhetoric dealt with three things: first, the character of the speaker (since we are concerned with writing, we will use the term "writer"); second, the seeming or plausible proofs for the writer's position—that is, finding the arguments that would emotionally or intellectually persuade the audience; third, the verbal act or message—that is, the rhetorical style which would accomplish the first two ends.

In persuasion, the primary focus is on what works with the audience—that is, how convincing the writer is personally, intellectually, and stylistically in gaining the audience's confidence, agreement, and admiration. Persuasion is not concerned with whether the speech or essay is true—whether or not it mirrors reality—but with whether or not it will effectively move the audience. The *rhetor* is in search of those arguments which are already "in" the audience, those convictions, positions, ideas which they already accept as true. As a result of this pragmatic approach, today the word "rhetoric" is sometimes used to refer to an insincere statement, something with more form than substance. Perhaps some of our distrust of rhetoric stems from our fear of being manipulated. Often the word is preceded by an adjective such as "empty" or "political," but you need not take this cynical viewpoint to justify the use of persuasion for a desirable social or personal end. Some of the persuasive essays which follow, for example, argue for greater safety laws in logging (Hager), for preserving real wilderness in some of our national parks (Abbey), and for more significant issues to be raised by the women's movement (Didion). After reading any of these persuasive essays, it would be difficult to take a cynical view of the art of persuasion. So rhetoric can be used for society's benefit or its detriment, depending on how the audience and the persuader interact. The means of persuasion are available to everyone—not only to Tom Paines, Abraham Lincolns, and John Kennedys, but to Stalins and Hitlers as well. Effective rhetoric consists of four kinds of arguments: ethical, pathetic, logical, and rhetorical.

Ethical argument deals with the character of the writer—that is, in the modern sense, his "image." According to Aristotle, the writer should have *good sense, good will,* and a *good character.* By good sense, Aristotle meant that the writer should have practical knowledge of his subject; by good will that he should not appear to represent special interests, but have the welfare of the audience at heart; by good character that he appear as one unlikely to deceive the audience. Some of these qualities are conveyed by the style of the writer, which reflects his or her personality and potential objectivity or bias; some are a result of the material: the facts and the author's familiarity with them. For example, Stan Hager, as is obvious from the content of his essay, has been a logger for thirteen years and, therefore certainly has an expert's knowledge of logging operations (good sense). His objectivity (good will) and honesty (good character) can be inferred from statements such as the following:

> Clearly, large companies could *save* money by employing one full-time safety inspector for every fifty workers. The inspector might issue warnings on the first offense, a one-day layoff on the second, and dismissal on the third—or whatever other penalties seemed appropriate. . . Since, on an average, every accident costs the employer five times its apparent dollar amount (compensation plus paid medical expenses), such a safety program properly administered would save money as well as lives.

Hager's statement is only one of many conclusions he reaches in his essay. Even taken out of context, it shows an honest awareness of the needs of the public and the employer; it clearly seems to be motivated *not* by self interest, but by what is best for the logger, the public, and the employer. Although we know Hager is a logger, he seems both sincere and objective; we believe he has an ethical character.

The Greek word for emotions is "pathos." *Pathetic argument* consists of appeals to those emotions which are likely to sway the particular audience. For example, President Kennedy's "Inaugural Address" appealed to Americans' sense of patriotism, their generosity to poorer nations, their desire for peace, their determination to remain militarily strong, their sense of excitement at the wonders of science and space exploration:

> To those people in the huts and villages of half the globe struggling to break the bonds of mass misery, we pledge our best efforts to help them help themselves, for whatever period is required—not because the communists may be doing it, not because we seek their votes, but because it is right. If a free society cannot help the many who are poor, it cannot save the few who are rich. . .
>
> Finally, to those nations who would make themselves our adversary, we offer not a pledge but a request: that both sides begin anew the quest for peace, before the dark powers of destruction unleashed by science engulf all humanity in planned or accidental self-destruction.
>
> We dare not tempt them with weakness. For only when our arms are sufficient beyond doubt can we be certain beyond doubt that they will never be employed.
>
> But neither can two great and powerful groups of nations take comfort from our present course—both sides overburdened by the cost of modern weapons, both rightly alarmed by the steady spread of the deadly atom, yet both racing to alter that uncertain balance of terror that stays the hand of mankind's final war. . .
>
> Let both sides seek to invoke the wonders of science instead of its terrors. Together let us explore the stars, conquer the deserts, eradicate disease, tap the ocean depths and encourage the arts and commerce.
>
> Let both sides unite to heed in all corners of the earth the command of Isaiah—to "undo the heavy burdens . . . (and) let the oppressed go free."
>
> And if a beach-head of cooperation may push back the jungle of suspicion, let both sides join in creating a new endeavor, not a new balance of power, but a new world of law, where the strong are just and the weak secure and the peace preserved.

A study of the emotional appeals of even this brief excerpt from the speech will reveal that it maintains a balance between appealing to the conflicting fear of change and the desire for change under the leadership of the New Frontier, thereby meeting the various emotional needs of its audience. Notice, for example, that Kennedy speaks of "the dark powers of destruction unleashed by science," of "the deadly atom," and of "the uncertain balance of terror" before he "invokes the wonders of science." Clearly, Kennedy has manipulated his audience's fears before appealing to their idealism.

Logical argument consists in finding the most effective arguments to support the writer's thesis. Aristotle presents several lists of *topoi*—literally "places" where one can go to find an appropriate argument. One of the exercises in the schools of rhetoric was to take a subject through each of the topics to see what information it would yield. For example, under the *topoi* of "definition" you might place the subject of mercy killing, thereby asking, "What is mercy killing?" The possible answers would then lead to several distinctions such as between pulling the plug on life-support systems, discontinuing medication, or terminating the life of a patient by more direct means. By placing the subject or any of the answers under other *topoi*—such as induction, time, division, consequences—you then systematically examine what you, or more importantly (since it is the audience that needs to be convinced), what the audience already knows. Not surprisingly, some of the *topoi* later become methods of paragraph development.

Aristotle also advocated the use of *enthymemes*, shortened deductive syllogisms in which one or more of the steps have been omitted because it has already been accepted as true by the audience. For example, here is a deductive syllogism:

MAJOR PREMISE   Mercy killing is a direct act.
MINOR PREMISE   Withholding drugs is not a direct act.
CONCLUSION   Therefore, withholding drugs is not mercy killing.

Were it to appear as an enthymeme, it might take this form:

MAJOR PREMISE   Mercy killing is a direct act.
CONCLUSION   Therefore, withholding drugs is not mercy killing.
(The MINOR PREMISE, "Withholding drugs is not a direct act," is understood and accepted as true.)

or:

MINOR PREMISE   Witholding drugs is not a direct act.
CONCLUSION   Therefore, withholding drugs is not mercy killing.
(The MAJOR PREMISE, "Mercy killing is a direct act," is understood and accepted as true.)

Persuasive writing rarely contains a complete syllogism. Instead, one of the premises or the conclusion itself will be left unstated, largely because that is the part the writer has determined the audience has already accepted.

Before we leave logical proof, let's examine the distinction between the previously introduced terms "deduction," and "induction." As we have seen, *deductive reasoning* follows the formal pattern of reasoning (syllogism) from already established premises (major and minor) to a conclusion. The premises must be true if the conclusion which follows them is to be true. *Inductive reasoning* is often identified with the scientific method. Induction reasons from a series of specific, verifiable observations to a general conclusion which incorporates the observations. For example, if for three successive years you saw cherry trees blooming in April in Washington, D.C., you would arrive at the inductive conclusion, "Cherry trees bloom in April in Washington, D.C." Your inductive conclusion would, however, be only as strong as your evidence (an early spring might force you to change the generalization). These forms of reasoning, plus facts and examples to support them make up what is called logical argument.

Rhetorical argument is strictly speaking not an argument in the same sense as the others, but is the style of a persuasive essay which lends support to the other arguments. Aristotle describes effective rhetorical style as having the following characteristics:

1. Clarity—the subject matter is presented in a manner which the audience can follow.

2. Dignity—the style leaves a good impression on the audience.

3. Propriety—the style has been adapted to the audience's levels of sophistication and knowledge.

4. Correctness—the style follows the rules of the language.

Although many rhetoricians disagree about how many parts a persuasive essay should have, the ancient rhetorical tradition listed seven. It is interesting to analyze modern practice to see how many of these parts are still to be found in a work, and in what order they occur. The traditional parts of a persuasive speech (essay) are:

1. Entrance—in which the speaker/writer introduces the topic.

2. Exposition—in which the speaker/writer gives the background or circumstances necessary to understand the points at issue.

3. Proposition—in which the speaker/writer explicitly states his position.

4. Division—in which the speaker/writer outlines the points he is going to prove.

5. Confirmation—in which the writer gives the body of the proofs.

6. Confutation—in which the writer refutes the opposition's arguments.

7. Conclusion—in which the writer summarizes key points, reviews the issues, and finally appeals to the emotions of the audience.

Although a writer who adhered rigidly to this outline would produce a highly artificial essay, the outline does provide a useful working model that anyone can use to structure the parts of a persuasive essay.

SHORT EXAMPLE

HANS BETHE
The Nuclear Freeze

Hans Bethe (born 1906) was awarded the Nobel Prize in Physics in 1967. During 1943–46, Bethe headed the theoretical physics division at Los Alamos. He headed a Presidential study on disarmament in 1958, and was a member of the President's Science Advisory Committee from 1956 until 1960. His publications in physics include Elementary Nuclear Theory *(1957),* Quantum Mechanics of One and Two Electron Atoms *(1957) and* Intermediate Quantum Mechanics *(1964). In this excerpt from a contrasting set of arguments on the subject of a nuclear freeze—the other was by Edward Teller, the father of the hydrogen bomb—Bethe explains why he favors an immediate verifiable freeze on building more nuclear armaments.*

I was one of the scientists at the Los Alamos National Laboratory,   1
which developed the atomic bomb during World War II. We thought
at the time that the United States might deploy a few dozen nuclear
weapons. Not in our worst nightmares did we imagine that someday there would be about 10,000 strategic nuclear weapons in the
United States and a similar number in the Soviet Union. These large
numbers make no sense, even if we wished to destroy *all* military
and industrial targets in the Soviet Union. At this level of arma-
ment, as Henry Kissinger said many years ago, it is meaningless
to ask who is ahead and who is behind.

* * *

The number of warheads in our strategic forces increased from   2
about 4,000 in 1970 to 10,000 in 1980, while the Soviet Union's
increased from about 1,800 to 6,000 by 1980 and 8,000 by 1982. The
Soviet buildup followed ours by about five years. The best way to
stop further buildup is a freeze, followed by negotiated, substantial
arms reductions.

The arms race must stop. At every step, we have taken the lead.   3
We were the first to deploy ICBMs by the hundreds. We invented
MIRV, the multiple independently targeted re-entry vehicle, by which
one missile can send many, in some cases 10, warheads to different
places in enemy territory. Despite a warning from our Arms Control
and Disarmament Agency that MIRV would benefit the Soviets,
with their heavier ICBMs, more than us, we refused to include it
in the SALT I agreement. We deployed MIRV; the Soviet Union
followed a few years later, with the result that these are the Soviet
missiles our Defense Department now fears the most. If we engage
in another arms buildup, it will again cause a Soviet countermove.

* * *

One of the worst features of the arms race is that nationalistic   4
passions are excited in order to make Congress and the taxpayers
willing to finance the arms race. These passions in turn make war
more likely. Instead, the goals for Washington and Moscow ought
to be some measure of political reconciliation, based on a mutual
understanding that neither party benefits from the current costly
and dangerous confrontations.

DISCUSSION

Arguing on the affirmative side of the controversial issue of a nuclear freeze, physicist Hans Bethe uses three forms of argument in his persuasive essay. He begins with an ethical argument, citing his expertise with nuclear weapons. In the first paragraph, he states the essential logical reason for his opposition to a further nuclear buildup—that 10,000 strategic nuclear weapons on each side are already far too many for defensive purposes. His logical argument is presented in the second and third paragraphs in which he cites the number and kinds of missiles held by each of the major nuclear powers and describes the stages of the buildup. In the third paragraph, he uses past experience to suggest the consequences of each stage of a nuclear buildup, as well as to predict the consequences of a new escalation on our part. The last argument, the appeal to emotion, appears in the final paragraph: Bethe contends that a resurgence of nationalistic passions inevitably follows an arms race and that only through reconciliation can the Soviet Union and the United States prevent the disastrous consequences of succumbing to those passions. Bethe's persuasive essay is a cameo version of the three kinds of argument. His argument is logical, emotional, and authoritative.

STAN HAGER
In the Logging Woods

Stan Hager, like his father, is a logger who began working in the woods at age 15 and, in his own words has "continued to earn my beans killing trees ever since." After a logging accident in 1966, Hager wrote this essay—the first he ever wrote for publication—about which he says: "The blue-collar world is not a more primitive version of academia or the white-collar world. There are differences in kind—more, I would say, in perceptions than in values." Currently, Hager is a freelance writer who operates a firewood business in Northern California.

In the predawn chill of an early October morning, two oddly dressed men leave their pickup parked by a dirt road in the Sierra Nevada and begin trudging up a steep, brush-covered hillside.

They are dressed in heavy black pants, gray "hickory" shirts, massive boots studded with inch-long caulks, and battered hard hats. Each carries a chain saw over his shoulder, a gallon of oil, two and a half gallons of gas, his lunch, water bag, ax, fifty-foot tape for measuring logs, fire extinguisher, shovel, and assorted tools. The older man, Martin, separates from his son about halfway up the slope and walks sidehill for a hundred yards or so in the blue-gray dimness to the place where he had stopped felling timber the day before. He is breathing heavily and already perspiring beneath the accustomed weight of his gear.

The autumn push is on, with mills driving their crews to get in every possible stick of timber before winter slaps ten feet of snow over the forests. Martin, his two brothers, and his son have worked eleven days straight in an effort to stay ahead of the tractors, which are hauling logs out of the woods as quickly as the men can cut them. As the sky lightens, a north wind rises and rattles the frost-laden branches through which the man moves. The going is easier when Martin reaches the area of downed timber. Here the forest is wheat-field dense, and he is able to walk the giant stalks—felled side by side and neatly limbed and bucked (cut into logs)—the rest of the way up to the dark wall of standing trees. Working his way uphill, he hears his son's saw start, falter, start again, and settle into a varying, rhythmic whine that tells Martin the boy is limbing and bucking a tree he felled the day before. It is still too dark to see the trees clearly enough for felling, and, really, it is too dark for limbing and bucking, but Wes is a hard worker, and he hopes to get enough lead on the tractors to take a day off for hunting before the season ends.

Martin's hands, circulation impaired by thirty years of heat, cold, and numbing vibration, are almost devoid of feeling as he sets his saw and fuel by the base of the yellow pine he has chosen as his first tree of the day. He ignores his hands and the insistent ache in the leg that was crushed by a rolling log years before. He remembers a yellow-jacket nest near the base of the tree. He'd intended to douse the nest with gas the previous afternoon so that the wasps would leave by morning. It has been excavated during the night, as neatly as with a shovel, and Martin grins as he sees it and makes a mental note to tell his boy at lunchtime that he has found a bear for him to hunt on their first day off.

The pine leans heavily uphill into the standing timber, its top a 4
twenty-foot spike of dead wood where lightning had struck it. Martin first makes an undercut, chopping out a pie-shaped wedge of wood in the direction in which he wants the tree to fall. He then matches the undercut on the opposite side of the trunk with a single back- cut that will sever the tree from its stump. Finishing the final inch of his back cut, Martin runs quickly sidehill as the tree shudders and begins its plunge to earth. The yellow pine slaps the other trees in its fall, stripping branches and bowing their trunks like giant catapults. As the brushed trees straighten, the air fills with a green death of needles and heavy limbs, and the snag top comes floating down to stick into the ground by the fresh stump. Martin, safely behind a neighboring bole, hears and feels a "whump" as his son, a quarter-mile away, fells a tree.

"Big one," he thinks, "to be felt at this distance." 5

The rhythm, the working monotony of the day, takes over as he 6 fells, limbs, and bucks tree after tree. Anything done long enough becomes routine, even the destruction of 200-foot-tall trees, and he works automatically, gauging the lean of trees, checking for signs of rot in their stumps, driving plastic wedges with his ax, dodging limbs and tops as they fly back toward him.

At nine o'clock Martin, stopping for his third tank of gas, cocks 7 an ear in the direction of his son. There is no sound of the boy's saw.

"Gassing up," the man thinks as he returns to work. 8

There is still no sound of saw at his next filling, and he begins 9 to worry. He mounts a stump and shouts in the direction of his son, but the gathering wind tears the sound from his mouth and shreds it almost as it leaves his lips. He begins walking toward his son, worried but unsure if he could hear the boy's saw in the rising wind.

Wesley is still alive. His skull is crushed like a hard-boiled egg 10 dropped on a counter, and one leg is a mass of raw flesh where a broken limb gouged almost through it. His hands make twitching, crablike movements in the pine needles and red dirt where he lies. As nearly as could be determined, Wesley had undercut a small, rotten white fir and was preparing to fell it when he noticed a small pine that had been pushed over by a previously felled tree. Not wanting to cover the unbucked tree with the fir, he had taken the chance of working beneath the undercut tree. Weak wood and a north wind drove the tree directly over him as Wesley, back turned and chain saw screaming, limbed the little pine. He died in his father's arms without regaining consciousness. Martin and his two brothers were back at work three days later.

That is timber felling. With a death rate of 12.5 per 1,000 workers per year and a basic compensation rate of $20 paid in for every $100 in wages, it is one of the most perilous occupations on earth. If professional football were as lethal, a fan could expect to see a tackle bleeding to death or a linebacker crushed to jelly about once every other Sunday. If you worked in an office with 500 people, and if your work were as hazardous, hardly a day would pass without one of your fellows being carried past your cubicle on a stretcher. Six or seven times a year you could anticipate stepping over the lifeless body of a co-worker on your way to the water cooler. I have never worked in an office, but I find it difficult to believe that carnage on this scale would be tolerated for long. As for football, since one player paralyzed during the course of the season provokes tsunamis of shock and concern among the fans and elicits grave opinions from sportswriters all over the country, it seems probable that if six or seven men were killed on the field in a year, enough angry voices would rise to abolish or change the sport.

In the logging woods a worse carnage is accepted as a matter of course. When I went back to work for Martin the spring following his son's death, we talked for twenty minutes before I said, "Sure too bad about Wes, Martin."

"Yes," he said, "sometimes it happens that way."

Almost two years have elapsed since the last time I lay on the white sheets of an emergency-room bed undergoing the ritual cleansing, debridement, and stitching required to treat a serious chain-saw wound—my third in fifteen years. One stares at the ceiling or walls or the bland face of the nurse or any place but the damaged area where the doctor is probing and snipping, removing wood chips and tattered flesh. Occasionally, one glances at the doctor's face as if to judge from his expression the extent of one's ruin. Is the doctor skilled? Did he have enough sleep last night? Are any nerves cut? How long will I be off work? These thoughts skitter through the mind and are crowded out by the image of the saw, engine roaring, rebounding toward an unprotected leg.

Thirteen months ago I heard of the death of Wes Hedrick—the   15
latest of my friends and acquaintances to be killed while felling
timber. We had worked together the year before, and one noontime
he kidded me about being fat. The next morning I put a handful of
red ants into his lunchpail.

These two violent incidents, Wes's death and my arm injury,   16
intrude upon my thoughts with a starkness that overshadows the
canoe trips, book chats, and other quiet good times that have
intervened.

I wonder: are the deaths and manglings—my crippled left arm,   17
Bob Sari's limp, John Cort's widow—inevitable, part of the sad but
unavoidable tax levied by an industrial civilization? The answer is
only a qualified yes. Timber felling is a fearsome business in which
antlike workers manipulate giant vegetables, thirty or forty times
their own height and weighing as much as half a million pounds,
on treacherous ground and in all weather. The timber faller's chief
tool, a chain saw, bears little resemblance to the toy one sees adver-
tised on television, and is arguably the most dangerous appliance
on earth to the man using it. My felling saw (a Stihl 090) has a
fifteen-horsepower engine driving its heavy steel chain around a
four-foot bar at the speed of 6,000 feet per minute. It will cut through
a thirty-inch log in less than a minute and through an arm or leg
in a split second.

When, in felling a tree or bucking a log, the tip of the bar strikes   18
an unseen limb or a sapling, the machine kicks back with appalling
speed and violence, directly at the operator. Perhaps an Olympic
weight lifter could control a big saw kicking back; I can't, and I
know men much stronger than I who can't either.

In addition to the saw and the menace of falling trees, there are   19
a host of other hazards to threaten the timber faller, ranging from
wasps to rattlesnakes, from rolling logs to heavy tractors operating
on steep ground. It is obvious that timber felling can never be as
safe as, say, big-city police work, or high-rise construction. It could,
however, be a great deal less dangerous than it is now.

There are two government organizations in California whose   20
domains most frequently intersect those of the logger: the State
Labor Commission and the office of Cal OSHA (California Occupational Safety and Health Administration). The State Labor Commission settles most disputes arising between employer and worker,

and is granted the authority to determine the amount of compensation awarded to an injured worker. Nicholas von Hoffman suggests, in *Make-Believe Presidents*, that workmen's-compensation laws were drafted primarily on behalf of industry, in response to judicial decisions that established the right of workers to sue for accidents resulting from unsafe working conditions. That is, they had their genesis in a perceived need for industry to indemnify itself against the claims of workers. This origin is perhaps reflected in the fact that benefits paid out, however welcome they may be to the disabled worker, are still rather paltry compared with awards from private sources for similarly severe injuries of non-industrial origin. For example, my own worst injury to date was a twelve-inch-long, bone-deep gash that severed the biceps, tendons, and median nerves of my left arm, leaving me with a rated 47 percent permanent disability in this limb and necessitating a three-and-a-half-year layoff while the nerves regenerated and the biceps stretched back into usable shape. The injury netted me a total of $12,615 in disability payments and $7,000 or $8,000 in medical, surgical, and rehabilitation payments. A compensation for death now pays about $50,000, not a great deal these days. My several dealings with the state authority show it to be fair and moderately efficient—but certainly not generous.

Cal OSHA has a mandate fully as large as its title suggests. It is responsible for the safety of all but a relative handful of California workers. At present, this prodigous task seems a bit too much for the staff. Cal OSHA has, since its inception in 1973, suffered persistent criticism from both industry, and journalists. Some of the opprobrium is deserved, some is unfair, and much of it seems motivated by the industry's calculated wish to discredit the organization. For a number of reasons it is difficult to assess accurately whether OSHA has had any salutary effect on logging. Recent data are almost impossible to obtain—at least from Cal OSHA itself. In fact, the statistics cited here are derived from published insurance rates, and from a variety of publications issued by the California Division of Labor Statistics, in particular one grisly but informative pamphlet entitled *Work Injuries in Logging, California 1970*. Apparently OSHA must rely on these sources as well. One difficulty with such figures is that many are derived from data submitted by the woodworking industry. Another is that they are so long out of date.

As in most cases where the bulk of hard information is issued by the industry itself, there are some discrepancies and elisions in logging-injury statistics that reflect either sloppy bookkeeping or a deliberate attempt to disguise embarrassing data. For example, none of the civil servants at the Division of Labor Statistics seems to know the organization of the woodworking industry, and clearly the industry is not eager to enlighten them. I will quote a few sentences from the introduction to *Work Injuries in Logging, California:*

> Very diverse activities are included within the lumber and wood products industry, ranging from work in the woods to the fabrication of wooden ladders . . . . It is obvious that some activities are more hazardous than others . . . . as the bulk of the logging operations in California are [sic] carried on by companies that operate sawmills as well, a work injury rate is not available for logging activities separately from sawmill operation.

To a person with any background in lumbering at all, this disclaimer is patently absurd. The two activities in woodworking— logging and milling—are as separate and distinct as, say, iron-ore mining and steel production when these take place on opposite sides of Lake Superior. There is virtually *no* crossover. A worker does not operate a planer in the mill one day and the next drive a hundred miles into the woods to fell trees. My best guess is that the California lumber industry is well aware of the appallingly hazardous nature of West Coast logging, and is at some pains to bury this information by averaging it with statistics from other, safer activities. One must wonder at OSHA's credulity and lack of curiosity, however, since logging is one of five industries first targeted for special attention. [23]

Whatever its origin, this confusion in the state's data for 1970 and the absence of any more recent and precise figures for injuries and deaths send one back to the insurance companies to discover whether logging casualties have declined as a result of OSHA's accident-prevention programs. As nearly as I can tell, the insurance rates on timber felling, after climbing for several years, have leveled off at around $20 and have stayed there for the most part since 1975. At least as far as the actuaries are concerned, circumstances have not improved measurably since the arrival of OSHA. Two fundamental weaknesses in the OSHA program must account for its failure: enforcement, which I shall discuss later, and the standards—the specific safety rules governing logging. [24]

A chronic, often-cited problem with the directiveness of Cal OSHA is a class of regulations that are usually referred to by OSHA workers themselves as "the cracked toilet seat syndrome," after a rule (largely ignored now) that proscribed the use of cracked toilet seats by workers, for hygienic reasons. The effect of the multitude of similarly stupid or unenforceable regulations imposed by OSHA is to vitiate and obscure the rather small number that do make sense and should be implemented.

A single example of an unenforceable order will serve: "6286 (a) Undercuts shall be of a size to safely guide the trees and minimize the possibility of splitting."

This is a very useful rule but absolutely impossible to observe, except after the fact. After an improperly undercut tree has toppled sideways and crushed a cat skinner on his tractor or barberchaired (split because of a heavy lean and insufficient undercut) and wiped out the man felling it, a trained OSHA employee arriving on the spot *might* be able to make a case for violation of this rule. But I seriously doubt that a court would go on to convict the logger or the company under most circumstances. A rule like this is virtually useless, since the only one capable of judging the efficacy of his undercut is the man felling the tree. Either he knows his business or he doesn't. If he doesn't, it is likely that either he or someone within a tree-length will pay some heavy dues.

At least the undercutting regulation is reasonable. The following regulation is not: "6292 (1) (4) Fuel saw only in conditions not conducive to fire hazards."

Briefly: there *are* no such conditions in a logging area, unless one were to carry his saw half a mile or so to the nearest road eight or ten times a day for fueling. Timber fallers are paid by what they cut. Since few loggers take any breaks at all, or more than twenty minutes for lunch, they simply rebel at the loss of time and energy these trips would involve.

Finally, there are regulations that should exist and do not. For three years, the large California logging concerns and their spokesmen, such as Associated California Loggers, have blocked an attempt to force all men handling a saw in the woods to wear fiber-glass chaps. These leggings have been required for all state and federal workers who handle chain saws for at least ten years. *Work Injuries in Logging, California* states that in 1970, 103 injuries sustained by fallers—38 percent of the total—involved the lower extremities.

The vast majority of these were saw cuts from kickbacks, and most of *these* would have been prevented by this one piece of safety apparel. The logging concerns fear that outfitting their men with these chaps will reduce productivity. Gary Robeson, a dedicated and conscientious enforcement officer for OSHA in Redding, California, has persuaded a couple of large lumber firms to try them on a voluntary basis. The effect has been a striking reduction in leg injuries and no apparent decline in productivity.

An even more glaring regulatory omission affects the manufacturers of chain saws. Saw cuts resulting from kickbacks accounted for one-eighth of *all logging* (not just felling) injuries in 1970. In addition, saw kickbacks nationwide, including logging, farming, woodcutting, and weekend use—produced an astounding 52,000 injuries and deaths. The highly publicized accidents that resulted from the faulty Pinto automobile and the Firestone 500 tire pale when compared with this figure. Most kickback injuries would have been less serious or prevented with addition to the saw of a simple, lightweight, inexpensive device that has been on the market for years. The automatic chainbrake stops the chain immediately when the operator's left hand slips or is dislodged from the handle of the saw. This feature is available on some saws that weigh less than ten pounds and cost less than $150. It should be required on every chain saw sold in the country. If one large state mandated this device as a requirement for marketing chain saws within its borders, it would soon be impossible to buy a saw anywhere in the country without it.

Attending to the public complaints of U.S. business, one might think that commerce is so hampered by regulations and by the rulebook automatons enforcing them that it is virtually impossible to pull a toaster off the assembly line without bumping into five government employees on hand to inspect it. But at Cal OSHA, at least, there is a severe shortage of employees to enforce the rules. Two men at the Redding office are responsible for an area larger than New York State, a region comprising five counties, all with substantial logging activity and high accident rates.

The logging itself takes place at hundreds of scattered and inaccessible sites—most of them several hours' drive from the main office. Unless two companies happen to be working near each other, it is usually an all-day job for an inspector to visit just one logging site (unannounced). Even then, he will probably be unable to inspect the whole sprawling operation. This is one reason why OSHA has had so little impact on logging. Another reason is simple ignorance. I could find no one in the Sacramento regional office who knew anything about logging at all. When I first appeared at the OSHA consultation office, in the guise of a felling contractor soliciting help in forming a safety program for my men, the consultant assigned to me did not understand the term *buck* as applied to cutting a tree into logs. This, in spite of the fact that the words *buck, bucker,* and *bucking* appear five times in the page and a half of orders specifically covering timber fallers.

OSHA faces an additional difficulty that relates directly to the character of lumberjacks themselves. Two OSHA workers I talked with have characterized the nature of timber fallers as "macho." I think "proud fatalism" would be a more apt term for the attitudes these men bring to their work. They are rugged, skilled men, most of them itinerant and non-union, receiving large wages of $150 to $200 a day in exchange for work that is fully understood by fewer than 1,000 men in the state of California. Many of the men working in logging can do any job in the woods—except felling.

An apprenticeship of at least three to five years is requisite background for timber felling, and most men who attempt it find that they are physically or temperamentally unsuited to the task; in addition to being dangerous, log cutting is extremely hard work. A man felling a large tree can (and should) peremptorily order the removal of any individual or machine from the affected area. When he does so, no one argues with or second-guesses him. Such a worker reacts poorly to an upbraiding from a fuzzy-cheeked safety inspector with limited knowledge of the forest.

Unfortunately, the logger's resistance to the rules is usually rewarded by the boss, who is worried less about the expense of an accident to the company than about turning out the lumber. A number of OSHA's regulations that would reduce logging injuries significantly and immediately can be enforced only by the logging companies, which must first see that it is in their interest to do so. One simply states that, "While felling, fallers shall be so located that they will not endanger other employees." The importance of this order is apparent if one considers the thirty-six fatalities occasioned by falling trees or snags during the period 1966-72. Nine of these deaths are listed as having been caused by a tree being felled on someone other than the timber faller himself: someone working too close to the man felling.

The act of felling is dependent on such variables as the lean of   37
the tree, the presence of rot in the stump (rot weakens the hinge
of wood that is the only means of aiming and controlling the descent
of the tree), sudden winds that can blow a tree back against the
lean, the presence of weak, dead wood in the trunk, which cause
the tree to break into pieces as it falls, and above all, the skill, greed,
and weariness of the man doing the job.

In spite of these hazards, and in spite of the rule, it has been the   38
practice on *every* job I have ever worked in California to employ
men within a tree-length of trees being felled. For example, four
years ago I was a felling boss for Robinson Timber of Grass Valley.
The trees were very large. The felling area was in a poorly drained
valley between two high ridges. The same moist, rich soil that promoted tree growth caused the trees to be so shallow-rooted that
several times a day a large tree would topple one or more of its
companions in the course of its fall.

On a typical day I might have, a hundred feet away from me,   39
two of my own buckers cutting up trees I had felled, a choker-setter
putting cables on the logs—often as soon as they were bucked—
and a cat skinner driving back and forth, hauling the logs close to
or even across the direction in which I was felling. In addition, a
public-access road ran almost through the center of one brushy
stand of timber no greater than forty or fifty acres in total area. (I
can report, somewhat wryly, that my only felling casualty there was
my own pickup, which I had parked on the access road and promptly
totaled with a tree pushed over by another tree.)

These are insane conditions. When I finally tired of working in   40
constant fear of killing one of my own men (my father and a close
friend were among those with me) or one of the rigging crew, and
complained to the company foreman, he laughed. "Hell, if we don't
stay on your ass, you bastards won't get anything done," he said,
or words very much to that effect. I was making good money, so I
did not complain further. It is interesting that this same company,
cutting in the same place the year before, had had a bucker cut
squarely in half when a tree fell across the man's back and the log
he was leaning over. The timber faller had apparently lost track of
his worker's location in the thick undergrowth.

That such negligence continues to be tolerated and even encour-   41
aged was demonstrated to me early last July. On a job near Donner
Summit, I found myself felling trees within killing distance of a
landing crew (two or three "knot bumpers" trimming logs and pass-

ing them on to a loader operator), various trucks and drivers, and two tractors running back and forth unpredictably. It is chilling to contemplate the fact that it was my third day on the job, and none of the men trusting their lives to my skill and judgment had any knowledge of my competence.

Safety standards at present are the awkward child of an uneasy union between OSHA workers, who would like to eliminate every last pinched finger and stubbed toe, and "industry leaders" who want to be left alone to make money. The best way to derive standards would be to examine past injuries, heavily weighting the factors of cause, severity, and specific task at the time of injury, in order to predict future accidents. In timber felling, these would comprise, chiefly, such contingencies as men working too close to timber fallers, men working alone (a common though illegal procedure that may have helped to kill Wes Hedrick), and the absence of a chainbrake on chain saws. Once the *major* causes of death and injury are isolated, appropriate rules governing these hazards should be drafted and rigorously enforced. Since OSHA workers cannot be ubiquitous, they should be selective and severe. In spite of carping by industry, "serious" violations (those requiring a heavy fine or, upon recurrence, imprisonment) are rarely cited; instead, the OSHA office usually issues a "general" citation, which is no more than a warning.

Workers generally, and loggers especially, should be better acquainted with OSHA and should come to view it in the same light as they now do the State Compensation Board and the Labor Commission: a forum where their complaints will be heard fairly and impartially. Workers would be friendlier to OSHA if the regulations were revised and simplified, since, as things stand, virtually everything a timber faller does violates some regulation.

Finally, the industries involved should be made to see that safety is in their own economic interest. Insurance rates are based on an "experience rating," which is derived from the actual occurrence of injuries per work force for a given company. The fewer injuries per man-hour worked, the lower the insurance rate. At $200 a day, I was costing my last employer $40 in compensation for every eight hours I worked. A good experience rating could have lowered this by as much as 40 percent—saving $16 a day for myself alone. Clearly, larger companies could *save* money by employing one full-time safety inspector for every fifty workers. The inspector might issue warnings on the first offense, a one-day layoff on the second, and dismissal on the third—or whatever other penalties seemed appropriate. No doubt some loggers would sue if thus penalized, but Georgia Pacific, Fibreboard, et alia surely command the legal talent to overrule their employees.

At present, for example, men can and do get the pink slip for   45
smoking a cigarette in an area of presumed fire danger. Since, on an average, every accident costs the employer five times its apparent dollar amount (compensation paid plus medical expenses), such a program properly administered would save money as well as lives.

Given the astounding range of valid apprehensions available to   46
the modern worrier—nuclear leakage, omnipresent carcinogens, fuel shortages—no one, I suppose, is going to be unduly concerned about the deaths and maimings of a relative handful of lumberjacks each year. On an absolute scale, about as many people die annually in this country from insect stings as are killed while felling timber.

Still, timber felling presents in exaggerated form lapses in worker   47
safety, government regulation, and the practices and attitudes of industry—both willful and unintended—that are common to all occupations. If a safety program can be devised that works for loggers, it can probably be modified to work almost anywhere.

CONTENT

1. What is Hager's proposition? What is he trying to get his audience to agree to? Is he successful? Why or why not?
2. What kinds of logical proof does Hager offer? Are the statistics convincing? How is the opening narrative part of Hager's essay a pathetic argument?
3. In paragraph 11, is the analogy of injuries among loggers compared with injuries among football players or office workers effective? Why does Hager use it?
4. Locate places in the essay where Hager is appealing to ethical argument. How effective is this proof?

ORGANIZATION

5. Hager postpones stating his proposition until after the opening narrative. Why? Why does Hager mix his personal experiences with statistical data about the accident rate?

6. Why does Hager describe some of the OSHA regulations before presenting some further regulations of his own? How is this tactical organization more effective than merely presenting a series of suggested new regulations? What objections does Hager anticipate to the regulations?
7. Do Hager's narrative examples of his own working conditions offer substantial enough proof of the need for the regulations he has proposed?

TOPICS FOR WRITING

8. Find an unsafe condition on your campus or in your home town. Offer a persuasive argument for regulations to eliminate or mitigate the danger.
9. Write a persuasive essay arguing for or against stronger environmental protection laws to regulate land fills and toxic waste disposal sites.

EDWARD ABBEY
Polemic: Industrial Tourism and the National Parks

Edward Abbey (see page 256) denies any special training as a naturalist, claiming he uses nature as a metaphor for other things. Nonetheless, between 1956 and 1971, Abbey worked seasonally for the National Park Service as a park ranger and fire lookout. In this essay, he proposes to ban automobiles from the National Parks. Aside from citing the historic precedents, he argues that "a man on foot, on horseback or on a bicycle will see more, feel more, enjoy more in one mile than the motorized tourists can in a hundred miles."

The Park Service, established by Congress in 1916, was directed not only to administer the parks but also to "provide for the enjoyment of same in such manner and by such means as will leave them unimpaired for the enjoyment of future generations." This appropriately ambiguous language, employed long before the onslaught of the automobile, has been understood in various and often opposing ways ever since. The Park Service, like any other big organization, includes factions and factions. The Developers, the dominant faction, place their emphasis on the words *"provide for the enjoyment."* The Preservers, a minority but also strong, emphasize the words *"leave them unimpaired."* It is apparent, then, that we cannot decide the question of development versus preservation by a simple referral to holy writ or an attempt to guess the intention of the founding fathers; we must make up our own minds and decide for ourselves what the national parks should be and what purpose they should serve.

The first issue that appears when we get into this matter, the   2
most important issue and perhaps the only issue, is the one called *accessibility.* The Developers insist that the parks must be made fully accessible not only to people but also to their machines, that is, to automobiles, motorboats, etc. The Preservers argue, in principle at least, that wilderness and motors are incompatible and that the former can best be experienced, understood, and enjoyed when the machines are left behind where they belong—on the superhighways and in the parking lots, on the reservoirs and in the marinas.

What does accessibility mean? Is there any spot on earth that   3
men have not proved accessible by the simplest means—feet and legs and heart? Even Mt. McKinley, even Everest, have been surmounted by men on foot. Some of them, incidentally, rank amateurs, to the horror and indignation of the professional mountaineers.) The interior of the Grand Canyon, a fiercely hot and hostile abyss, is visited each summer by thousands and thousands of tourists of the most banal and unadventurous type, many of them on foot—self-propelled, so to speak—and the others on the back of mules. Thousands climb each summer to the summit of Mt. Whitney, highest point in the forty-eight United States, while multitudes of others wander on foot or on horseback through the ranges of the Sierras, the Rockies, the Big Smokies, the Cascades and the mountains of New England. Still more hundreds and thousands float or paddle each year down the currents of the Salmon, the Snake, the Allagash, the Yampa, the Green, The Rio Grande, the Ozark, the St. Croix and those portions of the Colorado which have not yet been destroyed by the dam builders. And most significant, these hordes of nonmotorized tourists, hungry for a taste of the difficult, the original, the real, do not consist solely of people young and athletic but also of old folks, fat folks, pale-faced office clerks who don't know a rucksack from a haversack, and even children. The

one thing they all have in common is the refusal to live always like sardines in a can—they are determined to get outside of their motorcars for at least a few weeks each year.

This being the case, why is the Park Service generally so anxious to accommodate that other crowd, the indolent millions born on wheels and suckled on gasoline, who expect and demand paved highways to lead them in comfort, ease and safety into every nook and corner of the national parks? For the answer to that we must consider the character of what I call Industrial Tourism and the quality of the mechanized tourists—the Wheelchair Explorers— who are at once the consumers, the raw material and the victims of Industrial Tourism.

Industrial Tourism is a big business. It means money. It includes the motel and restaurant owners, the gasoline retailers, the oil corporations, the road-building contractors, the heavy equipment manufacturers, the state and federal engineering agencies and the sovereign, all-powerful automotive industry. These various interests are well organized, command more wealth than most modern nations, and are represented in Congress with a strength far greater than is justified in any constitutional or democratic sense. (Modern politics is expensive—power follows money.) Through Congress the tourism industry can bring enormous pressure to bear upon such a slender reed in the executive branch as the poor old Park Service, a pressure which is also exerted on every other possible level—local, state, regional—and through advertising and the well-established habits of a wasteful nation.

When a new national park, national monument, national seashore, or whatever it may be called is set up, the various forces of Industrial Tourism, on all levels, immediately expect action—meaning specifically a road-building program. Where trails or primitive dirt roads already exist, the Industry expects—it hardly needs to ask—that these be developed into modern paved highways. On the local level, for example, the first thing that the superintendent of a new park can anticipate being asked, when he attends his first meeting of the area's Chamber of Commerce, is not "Will roads be built?" but rather "When does construction begin?" and "Why the delay?"

(The Natural Money-Mint. With supersensitive antennae these operatives from the C. of C. look into red canyons and see only green, stand among flowers snorting out the smell of money, and hear, while thunderstorms rumble over mountains, the fall of a dollar bill on motel carpeting.)

Accustomed to this sort of relentless pressure since its founding, it is little wonder that the Park Service, through a process of natural selection, has tended to evolve a type of administration which, far from resisting such pressure, has usually been more than willing to accommodate it, even to encourage it. Not from any peculiar moral weakness but simply because such well-adapted administrators are themselves believers in a policy of economic development. "Resource management" is the current term. Old foot trails may be neglected, back-country ranger stations left unmanned, and interpretive and protective services inadequately staffed, but the administrators know from long experience that millions for asphalt can always be found; Congress is always willing to appropriate money for more and bigger paved roads, anywhere—particularly if they form loops. Loop drives are extremely popular with the petroleum industry—they bring the motorist right back to the same gas station from which he started.   8

Great though it is, however, the power of the tourist business would not in itself be sufficient to shape Park Service policy. To all accusations of excessive development the administrators can reply, as they will if pressed hard enough, that they are giving the public what it wants, that their primary duty is to serve the public not preserve the wilds. "Parks are for people" is the public-relations slogan, which decoded means that the parks are for people-in-automobiles. Behind the slogan is the assumption that the majority of Americans, exactly like the managers of the tourist industry, expect and demand to see their national parks from the comfort, security, and convenience of their automobiles.   9

Is this assuumption correct? Perhaps. Does that justify the continued and increasing erosion of the parks? It does not. Which brings me to the final aspect of the problem of Industrial Tourism: the Industrial Tourists themselves.   10

They work hard, these people. They roll up incredible mileages on their odometers, rack up state after state in two-week transcontinental motor marathons, knock off one national park after another, take millions of square yards of photographs, and endure patiently the most prolonged discomforts: the tedious traffic jams, the awful food of park cafeterias and roadside eateries, the nocturnal search for a place to sleep or camp, the dreary routine of One-Stop Service,   11 the endless lines of creeping traffic, the smell of exhaust fumes, the ever-proliferating Rules & Regulations, the fees and the bills and the service charges, the boiling radiator and the flat tire and the vapor lock, the surly retorts of room clerks and traffic cops, the incessant jostling of the anxious crowds, the irritation and restlessness of their children, the worry of their wives, and the long drive home at night in a stream of racing cars against the lights of another stream racing in the opposite direction, passing now and then the obscure tangle, the shattered glass, the patrolman's lurid blinker light, of one more wreck.

Hard work. And risky. Too much for some, who have given up the struggle on the highways in exchange for an entirely different kind of vacation—out in the open, on their own feet, following the quiet trail through forest and mountains, bedding down at evening under the stars, when and where they feel like it, at a time when the Industrial Tourists are still hunting for a place to park their automobiles.

Industrial Tourism is a threat to the national parks. But the chief victims of the system are the motorized tourists. They are being robbed and robbing themselves. So long as they are unwilling to crawl out of their cars they will not discover the treasures of the national parks and will never escape the stress and turmoil of those urban-suburban complexes which they had hoped, presumably, to leave behind for a while.

How to pry the tourists out of their automobiles, out of their back-breaking upholstered mechanized wheelchairs and onto their feet, onto the strange warmth and solidity of Mother Earth again? This is the problem which the Park Service should confront directly, not evasively, and which it cannot resolve by simply submitting and conforming to the automobile habit. The automobile, which began as a transportation convenience, has become a bloody tyrant (50,000 lives a year), and it is the responsibility of the Park Service, as well as that of everyone else concerned with preserving both wilderness and civilization, to begin a campaign of resistance. The automotive combine has almost succeeded in strangling our cities; we need not let it also destroy our national parks.

It will be objected that a constantly increasing population makes resistance and conservation a hopeless battle. This is true. Unless a way is found to stabilize the nation's population, the parks cannot be saved. Or anything else worth a damn. Wilderness preservation, like a hundred other good causes, will be forgotten under the overwhelming pressure of a struggle for mere survival and sanity in a completely urbanized, completely industrialized, ever more crowded environment. For my own part I would rather take my chances in a thermonuclear war than live in such a world.

Assuming, however, that population growth will be halted at a 16 tolerable level before catastrophe does it for us, it remains permissible to talk about such things as the national parks. Having indulged myself in a number of harsh judgments upon the Park Service, the tourist industry, and the motoring public, I now feel entitled to make some constructive, practical, sensible proposals for the salvation of both parks and people.

(1) No more cars in national parks. Let the people walk. Or ride 17 horses, bicycles, mules, wild pigs—anything—but keep the automobiles and the motorcycles and all their motorized relatives out. We have agreed not to drive our automobiles into cathedrals, concert halls, art museums, legislative assemblies, private bedrooms and other sanctums of our culture; we should treat our national parks with the same deference, for they, too, are holy places. An increasingly pagan and hedonistic people (thank God!), we are learning finally that the forests and mountains and desert canyons are holier than our churches. Therefore let us behave accordingly.

Consider a concrete example and what could be done with it: 18 Yosemite Valley in Yosemite National Park. At present a dusty milling confusion of motor vehicles and ponderous camping machinery, it could be returned to relative beauty and order by the simple expedient of requiring all visitors, at the park entrance, to lock up their automobiles and continue their tour on the seats of good workable bicycles supplied free of charge by the United States Government.

Let our people travel light and free on their bicycles—nothing 19 on the back but a shirt, nothing tied to the bike but a slicker, in case of rain. Their bedrolls, their backpacks, their tents, their food and cooking kits will be trucked in for them, free of charge, to the campground of their choice in the Valley, by the Park Service. (Why not? The roads will still be there.) Once in the Valley they will find the concessioners waiting, ready to supply whatever needs might have been overlooked, or to furnish rooms and meals for those who don't want to camp out.

The same thing could be done at Grand Canyon or at Yellowstone 20 or at any of our other shrines to the out-of-doors. There is no compelling reason, for example, why tourists need to drive their automobiles to the very brink of the Grand Canyon's south rim. They could *walk* that last mile. Better yet, the Park Service should build an enormous parking lot about ten miles south of Grand Canyon Village and another east of Desert View. At those points, as at Yosemite, our people could emerge from their steaming shells of steel and glass and climb upon horses or bicycles for the final leg of the journey. On the rim, as at present, the hotels and restaurants will remain to serve the physical needs of the park visitors. Trips along the rim would also be made on foot, on horseback, or— utilizing the paved road which already exists—on bicycles. For those willing to go all the way from one parking lot to the other, a distance of some sixty or seventy miles, we might provide bus service back to their cars, a service which would at the same time effect a convenient exchange of bicycles and/or horses between the two terminals.

What about children? What about the aged and infirm? Frankly, we need waste little sympathy on these two pressure groups. Children too small to ride bicycles and too heavy to be borne on their parents' backs need only wait a few years—if they are not run over by automobiles they will grow into a lifetime of joyous adventure, if we save the parks and *leave them unimpaired for the enjoyment of future generations.* The aged merit even less sympathy: after all they had the opportunity to see the country when it was still relatively unspoiled. However, we'll stretch a point for those too old or too sickly to mount a bicycle and let them ride the shuttle buses.

I can foresee complaints. The motorized tourists, reluctant to give up the old ways, will complain that they can't see enough without their automobiles to bear them swiftly (traffic permitting) through the parks. But this is nonsense. A man on foot, on horseback or on a bicycle will see more, feel more, enjoy more in one mile then the motorized tourists can in a hundred miles. Better to idle through one park in two weeks than try to race through a dozen in the same amount of time. Those who are familiar with both modes of travel know from experience that this is true; the rest have only to make the experiment to discover the same truth for themselves.

They will complain of physical hardship, these sons of the pioneers. Not for long; once they rediscover the pleasures of actually operating their own limbs and senses in a varied, spontaneous, voluntary style, they will complain instead of crawling back into a car; they may even object to returning to desk and office and that dry wall box on Mossy Brook Circle. The fires of revolt may be kindled—which means hope for us all.

(2) No more new roads in national parks. After banning private 24 automobiles the second step should be easy. Where paved roads are already in existence they will be reserved for the bicycles and essential in-park services, such as shuttle buses, the trucking of camping gear and concessioners' supplies. Where dirt roads already exist they too will be reserved for nonmotorized traffic. Plans for new roads can be discarded and in their place a program of trail-building begun, badly needed in some of the parks and in many of the national monuments. In mountainous areas it may be desirable to build emergency shelters along the trails and bike roads; in desert regions a water supply might have to be provided at certain points—wells drilled and handpumps installed if feasible.

Once people are liberated from the confines of automobiles there 25 will be a greatly increased interest in hiking, exploring, and back-country packtrips. Fortunately the parks, by the mere elimination of motor traffic, will come to seem far bigger than they are now—there will be more room for more persons, an astonishing expansion of space. This follows from the interesting fact that a motorized vehicle, when not at rest, requires the volume of space far out of proportion to its size. To illustrate: imagine a lake approximately ten miles long and on the average one mile wide. A single motor-boat could easily circumnavigate the lake in an hour; ten motorboats would begin to crowd it; twenty or thirty, all in operation, would dominate the lake to the exclusion of any other form of activity; and fifty would create the hazards, confusion, and turmoil that makes pleasure impossible. Suppose we banned motorboats and allowed only canoes and rowboats; we would see at once the lake seemed ten or perhaps a hundred times bigger. The same things holds true, to an even greater degree, for the automobile. Distance and space are functions of speed and time. Without expending a single dollar from the United States Treasury we could, if we wanted to, multiply the area of our national parks tenfold or a hundredfold—simply by banning the private automobile. The next generation, all 250 million of them, would be grateful to us.

(3) Put the park rangers to work. Lazy scheming loafers, they've 26 wasted too many years selling tickets at toll booths and sitting behind desks filling out charts and tables in the vain effort to appease the mania for statistics which torments the Washington office. Put them

to work. They're supposed to be rangers—make the bums range; kick them out of those overheated air-conditioned offices, yank them out of those overstuffed patrol cars, and drive them out on the trails where they should be, leading the dudes over hill and dale, safely into and back out of the wilderness. It won't hurt them to work off a little office fat; it'll do them good, help take their minds off each other's wives, and give them a chance to get out of reach of the boss—a blessing for all concerned.

They will be needed on the trail. Once we outlaw the motors and stop the road-building and force the multitudes back on their feet, the people will need leaders. A venturesome minority will always be eager to set off on their own, and no obstacles should be placed in their path; let them take risks, for Godsake, let them get lost, sunburnt, stranded, drowned, eaten by bears, buried alive under avalanches—that is the right and privilege of any free American. But the rest, the majority, most of them new to the out-of-doors, will need and welcome assistance, instruction and guidance. Many will not know how to saddle a horse, read a topographical map, follow a trail over slickrock, memorize landmarks, build a fire in rain, treat snakebite, rappel down a cliff, glissade down a glacier, read a compass, find water under sand, load a burro, splint a broken bone, bury a body, patch a rubber boat, portage a waterfall, survive a blizzard, avoid lightning, cook a porcupine, comfort a girl during a thunderstorm, predict the weather, dodge falling rock, climb out of a box canyon, or pour piss out of a boot. Park rangers know these things, or should know them, or used to know them and can relearn; they will be needed. In addition to this sort of practical guide service the ranger will also be a bit of a naturalist, able to edify the party in his charge with the natural and human history of the area, in detail and in broad outline.

Critics of my program will argue that it is too late for such a radical reformation of a people's approach to the out-of-doors, that the pattern is too deeply set, and that the majority of Americans would not be willing to emerge from the familiar luxury of their automobiles, even briefly, to try the little-known and problematic advantages of the bicycle, the saddle horse, and the footpath. This might be so; but how can we be sure unless we dare the experiment? I, for one, suspect that millions of our citizens, especially the young, are yearning for adventure, difficulty, challenge—they will respond with enthusiasm. What we must do, prodding the Park Service into the forefront of the demonstration, is provide these young people with the opportunity, the assistance, and the necessary encouragement.

How could this most easily be done? By following the steps I have proposed, plus reducing the expenses of wilderness recreation to the minimal level. Guide service by rangers should, of course, be free to the public. Money saved by *not* constructing more paved highways into the parks should be sufficient to finance the cost of bicycles and horses for the entire park system. Elimination of automobile traffic would allow the Park Service to save more millions now spent on road maintenance, police work and paper work. Whatever the cost, however financed, the benefits for park visitors in health and happiness—virtues unknown to the statisticians— would be immeasurable. 29

Excluding the automobile from the heart of the great cities has been seriously advocated by thoughtful observers of our urban problems. It seems to me an equally proper solution to the problems besetting our national parks. Of course it would be a serious blow to Industrial Tourism and would be bitterly resisted by those who profit from that industry. Exclusion of automobiles would also require a revolution in the thinking of Park Service officialdom and in the assumptions of most American tourists. But such a revolution, like it or not, is precisely what is needed. The only foreseeable alternative, given the current trend of things, is the gradual destruction of our national park system. 30

Let us therefore steal a slogan from the Development Fever Faction in the Park Service. The parks, they say, are for people. Very well. At the main entrance to each national park and national monument we shall erect a billboard one hundred feet high, two hundred feet wide, gorgeously filigreed in brilliant neon and outlined with blinker lights, exploding stars, flashing prayer wheels and great Byzantine phallic symbols that gush like geysers every thirty seconds. (You could set your watch by them.) Behind the fireworks will loom the figure of Smokey the Bear, taller than a pine tree, with eyes in his head that swivel back and forth, watching YOU, and ears that actually twitch. Push a button and Smokey will recite, for the benefit of children and government officials who might otherwise have trouble with some of the big words, in a voice ursine, 31 loud and clear, the message spelled out on the face of the billboard. To wit:

> HOWDY FOLKS, WELCOME. THIS IS YOUR NATIONAL PARK, ESTABLISHED FOR THE PLEASURE OF YOU AND ALL PEOPLE EVERYWHERE. PARK YOUR CAR, JEEP, TRUCK, TANK, MOTORBIKE, MOTORBOAT, JETBOAT, AIRBOAT, SUBMARINE, AIRPLANE, JETPLANE, HELICOPTER, HOVERCRAFT, WINGED MOTORCYCLE, ROCKETSHIP, OR ANY OTHER CONCEIVABLE TYPE OF MOTORIZED VEHICLE IN THE WORLD'S BIGGEST PARKINGLOT BEHIND THE COMFORT STATION IMMEDIATELY TO YOUR REAR. GET OUT OF YOUR MOTORIZED VEHICLE, GET ON YOUR HORSE, MULE, BICYCLE OR FEET AND COME IN.
> ENJOY YOURSELVES. THIS HERE PARK IS FOR *people*.

CONTENT

1. Why is Abbey against the continued dominance of our national parks by the automobile? What reasons does he give? Are they convincing? What objections does he foresee? Does he answer them? Does he overlook any objections?

2. Is Abbey justified in his attack on what he calls "industrial tourism"? In your experience, is his description of the average American's vacation in the park system accurate?

ORGANIZATION

3. How well does Abbey's "polemic" fit the traditional outline of the parts of a persuasive essay? Are any parts missing?

4. Why has Abbey opened the essay with an attack on "industrial tourism"? Why doesn't he present his proposition first?

5. Are Abbey's logical reasons presented in the most effective order? Why does he present his refutation immediately after each point of his proposal instead of at the end of his complete proposal? Is this the most effective way to organize this particular argument?

TOPICS FOR WRITING

6. Write a persuasive essay in which you disagree with Abbey and contend that more roads should be built opening up some of our less accessible national parks.

7. Write an essay in which you argue for an expansion of existing national parks (particularly in urban areas) or for selling off some of the land because the parks are underutilized.

MARIE WINN
Television and Violence:
A New Approach

Marie Winn is widely known for her books about children. The Plug-In Drug
*(1977), her most controversial book, is a study of the television viewing habits of
middle-class families in Denver and New York. "Television and Violence"
examines the often-expressed assumption that the increase in violence among
adolescents is caused by excessive television viewing.*

Searching for a Link

The subject of television violence and its potential effect on chil-   1
dren has long been a source of controversy. Congressional studies
were carried out in 1954, 1961, 1964, and 1970. When the Surgeon
General's *Report on Television and Social Behavior* was published in
1972, four of the five volumes were devoted to studies dealing with
the effects of viewing violent television programs. Indeed, most
seminars, articles, and studies considering the effect of television
on children focus on this single issue.

The intense interest in the effect of television violence upon chil-   2
dren is understandable: the number of juveniles arrested for serious
and violent crimes increased 1600 *percent* between the years 1952
and 1972, according to FBI figures.[1] Since this is the very period in
which television became ascendant in the lives of American children, and since the programs children watch are saturated with
crime and destruction, it has long seemed reasonable to search for
a link between the two.

And yet this link continues to elude social scientists and research-   3
ers, in spite of their great efforts to demonstate its existence. The
truly repugnant, sadistic, amazingly various violence appearing on
home screens must surely have subtle effects upon children's
behavior, but it clearly does not cause them to behave in seriously
antisocial ways. After all, the majority of American children are
regularly exposed to those violent programs that have been proposed as a causative factor in the increase of juvenile violence, and
yet the children involved in the FBI statistics are but a small pro-

---

[1]"Skyrocketing Juvenile Crime," *The New York Times,* February 21, 1975.

portion of the viewing population. And while a number of research studies *do* indicate a relationship between viewing violence on television and subsequent aggressive behavior, that behavior as seen in the research laboratory obviously does not involve rape or murder, the serious crimes included in the FBI report, but rather ordinary childish aggression—pushing, shoving, hitting, and so on.

Common sense balks at the idea that television violence will lead normal children to become juvenile delinquents. Indeed, it is the intuitive certainty that watching violent programs will not turn their children into rapists and murderers that permits parents to be lax about their children's indulgence in their favorite, invariably violent, programs in spite of the earnest advice of psychologists and educators.

It is particularly hard for parents to buy the idea that television instigates aggressive behavior when its function in the home is so different. There, television keeps children quiet and passive, cuts down loud and boisterous play, prevents outbursts between brothers and sisters, and eliminates a number of potentially destructive household "experiments" children might be indulging in were they not occupied by "Kung Fu" or "Batman."

Selma Fraiberg gives a sensible reason for rejecting a direct connection between normal children's viewing of violent programs and an epidemic of violence:

> I do not mean . . . that the vulgar fiction of television is capable of turning our children into delinquents. The influence of such fiction on children's attitudes and conduct is really more subtle. We need to remember that it is the parents who are the progenitors of conscience and that a child who has strong ties to his parents will not overthrow their teachings more easily than he could abandon his parents themselves. I do not think that any of us here needs to fear this kind of corruption of our children.[2]

A further flaw in the argument that violence on television might cause children to behave more violently has been stated by a television critic who points out that if this were true, there would be a concomitant effect produced by the inevitable moralistic and "good" aspects of those same violent programs:

> If indeed the cumulative watching is turning us all, gradually, into depraved beings, then the cumulative watching of good must be turning

[2]Quoted from address to Child Study Association of America, 1961.

us all, gradually into saints! You cannot have one without the other. That is, unless you are prepared to demonstrate that evil is something like cholesterol—something that slowly accumulates and clogs the system, while good is something like spinach, easily digested and quickly excreted.[3]

But if it is not the violent content of television programs that leads to violent behavior, is it merely a coincidence that the entry of television into the American home brought in its wake one of the worst epidemics of juvenile violence in the nation's history? As a professor of law and sociology stated in response to the suggestion that television is a contributing factor to juvenile violence: "I'm not suggesting a direct connection [with television] but it's inconceivable that there is no effect.[4] 8

There are indeed reasons to believe that television is deeply implicated in the new upsurge of juvenile aggression, particulary in the development of a new and frightening breed of juvenile offender, but those searching for a direct link between violent programs and violent actions are on a wrong tack. The *experience* of television itself (regardless of content) and its effects upon a child's perception of reality may be a more profitable line of inquiry. 9

Why So Much Violence?

In trying to understand the relationship between television viewing and violent behavior, one must first confront the curious fact that television today is dominated by violent programs. This was not always the case. It is noteworthy that between 1951 and 1953 there was a 15 percent increase in violent incidents on the television screen. And between 1954 and 1961 the percentage of primetime programming devoted to action adventures featuring violence went from an average of 17 percent to about 60 percent of all programs. By 1964, according to the National Association for Better Radio and Television, almost 200 hours a week were devoted to crime scenes, with over 500 killings committed on the home screen! This reflects a 20 percent increase of violence on television over 1958 programming, and a 90 percent increase since 1952.[5] 10

[3]Edith Efron, "Does Television Violence Really Affect TV Viewers?" *TV Guide*, June 14, 1975.
[4]Enid Nemy, "Violent Crime by Young People: No Easy Answers," *The New York Times*, March 17, 1975.
[5]*Crime on Television: A Survey Report* (Los Angeles: National Association for Better Radio and Television, 1964).

Why did television, relatively nonviolent at its start, gradually   11
become the hotbed of crime and mayhem it now is? Are people
more fond of violence today than they were in 1950?

The answer to the first question is simple: people *want* violence   12
on television. The rating system that effectively controls what appears
on national television indicates that the public regularly chooses
violent programs over more peaceful alternatives. Clearly there exists
no evil conspiracy of wicked advertisers and network executives to
destroy American morals and values by feeding citizens a steady
diet of death and destruction. To the contrary, the advertisers meekly
protest they would gladly give the public "Pollyanna" round the
clock if that's what people would watch. (And they probably would.)
But the rating system shows that people won't watch "Pollyanna"
when they can watch "Dragnet." Advertisers want to make sure
that the greatest number of people will watch *their* program, and
they have learned that their chances are better if their program is
action-packed.

The answer to *why* people choose to view violence on television,   13
and why there has been an increase in violent programming in spite
of periodic outcries from government investigating commissions,
educators, and parents' coalitions, lies, as do all the answers to basic
questions about television viewing, in the very nature of the television experience—in its essential passivity.

In viewing television the grown-up, as well as the child, is taking   14
advantage of an easily available opportunity to withdraw from the
world of activity into the realm of nondoing, nonthinking, indeed,
temporary nonexisting. But the viewer does not choose to watch
soothing, relaxing programs on his television set, though his main
purpose in watching is often to be soothed and relaxed. Instead he
opts for frantic programs filled with the most violent activities imaginable—deaths, tortures, car crashes, all to the accompaniment of
frenzied music. The screen is a madhouse of activity as the viewer
sits back in a paradoxical state of perfect repose.

By choosing the most active programs possible, the viewer is   15
able to approximate a *feeling* of activity, with all the sensations of
involvement, while enjoying the safety and security of total passivity. He is enjoying a *simulation* of activity in the hope that it will
compensate for the actuality that he is involved in a passive, one-
way experience.

Once the attraction of television violence is recognized as a com- 16
pensation for the viewer's enforced passivity, the gradual increase
of violence on television within the last two decades becomes
understandable. For during that period not only did television ownership increase enormously, but people began to spend more of
their time watching television. Between 1950 and 1975, for instance,
television household use increased from 4 hours and 25 minutes
per day to 6 hours and 8 minutes per day.[6] Apparently, as television
viewing increases in proportion to more active experiences in people's lives, their need for the pseudo- satisfactions of simulated activity
on their television screens increases as well. A quiet, contemplative,
slow-paced program might only underscore the uncomfortable fact
that they are not really having experiences at all while they are
watching television.

Reality and Unreality

The idea that television experiences can lead to a feeling of activ- 17
ity, that a person can somehow be deceived into feeling that he is
actually experiencing those television happenings, raises a most
important question about the television experience: what effect does
the constant intake of simulated reality have upon the viewer's perceptions of actual reality?

Two professors at the Annenberg School of Communications at 18
the University of Pennsylvania, Larry Gross and George Gerbner,
have studied some of the effects of television "reality" upon people's ideas and beliefs pertaining to the real world. The results of
their investigations suggest that the television experience impinges
significantly upon viewers' perceptions of reality.

Gerbner and Gross asked heavy television viewers and light tele- 19
vision viewers certain questions about the real world. The multi-
ple-choice quiz offered accurate answers together with answers that
reflected a bias characteristic of the television world. The researchers discovered that heavy viewers of television chose the television-
biased answers far more often than they chose the accurate answers,
while light viewers were more likely to choose the correct answers.

For example, the subjects were asked to guess their own chances 20
of encountering violence in any given week. They were given the

[6]*Nielsen Television Index* (A.C. Nielsen Co., Hackensack, N.J.).

possible answers of 50—50, 10—1, and 100—1. The statistical chances that the average person will encounter personal violence in the course of a week are about 100—1, but heavy television viewers consistently chose the answers 50—50 or 10—1, reflecting the "reality" of television programs where violence prevails. The light viewers chose the right answer far more consistently.

The heavy viewers answered many other questions in a way revealing that what they saw on television had altered their perceptions of the world and society. They were more likely than light viewers to overestimate the U.S. proportion of the world population, for instance. They also overestimated the percentages of people employed as professionals, as athletes, and as entertainers in the "real world," just as television overemphasizes the importance of these groups.

Education played no significant role in ameliorating the distortions of reality produced by heavy television watching. In most cases college-educated subjects were just as likely as those with only a grade-school education to choose the television-biased answers.[7]

The viewers' incorrect notions about the real world do not come from misleading newscasts or factual programs. The mistaken notions arise from repeated viewing of *fictional* programs performed in a realistic style within a realistic framework. These programs, it appears, begin to take on a confusing reality for the viewer, just as a very powerful dream may sometimes create confusion about whether a subsequent event was a dream or whether it actually happened. After seeing violence dealt out day after day on television programs, the viewer incorporates it into his reality, in spite of the fact that while he watches he *knows* that the programs are fictional. The violent television world distorts the viewer's perceptions of the real world, and his expectations of violence in life reflect his exposure to violence on television.

But once television fantasy becomes incorporated into the viewer's reality, the real world takes on a tinge of fantasy—or dullness because it fails to confirm the expectations created by televised "life." The separation between the real and the unreal becomes blurred; all of life becomes more dreamlike as the boundaries between the real and the unreal merge. The consequences of this merger appear in our daily papers and on the news.

[7]Larry Gross, "The 'Real' World of Television," *Today's Education*, January-February, 1974.

People attending a real parade find it dull and say, "We should   25
have stayed home and watched it on television. It would have been
more exciting."[8]

A woman passes a burning building and says to her friend, "Don't   26
worry, they're probably making a TV movie."[9]

Members of a real California family live out their lives in weekly   27
installments as part of a television series, with infidelity, discovered
homosexuality, and divorce happening before the viewers' eyes,
happening "for real" on TV.[10]

Thirty-seven people see a young woman murdered in their   28
courtyard and look on passively without coming to her aid as if it
were a television drama.[11]

A seventeen-year-old boy who lived through a devastating tor-   29
nado says, "Man, it was just like something on TV."[12]

Dulling Sensitivity

A disturbing possibility exists that the television experience has   30
not merely blurred the distinctions between the real and the unreal
for steady viewers, but that by doing so it has dulled their sensitivities to real events. For when the reality of a situation is diminished,
people are able to react to it less emotionally, more as spectators.

An experiment devised by Dr. Victor Cline at the University of   31
Utah Laboratories compared the emotional responses of two groups
of boys between the ages of 5 and 14 to a graphically violent television program.[13] One group had seen little or no television in the
previous two years. The other group had watched a great deal of
television, an average of 42 hours a week for at least two years.

As the two groups of boys watched an eight-minute sequence   32
from the Kirk Douglas movie about boxing, *Champion*, their emotional responses were recorded on a physiograph, an instrument
not unlike an elaborate lie detector that measures heart action, res-
piration, perspiration, and other body responses.

[8]Kurt Lang and Gladys Engel Lang, "The Unique Perspective of Television and Its
Effects—A Pilot Study," *American Sociological Review*, February, 1953.

[9]*Mainliner Magazine*, July, 1974.

[10]See Roger Rosenblatt's "Residuals on an American Family," *New Republic*, November 23,
1974; for a discussion of the Loud family and their appearance on "An American Family."

[11]See *The New York Times*, April 12, 1964, for an account of the Kitty Genovese murder.

[12]Quoted by Edmund Carpenter in *Oh What a Blow That Phantom Gave Me* (New York: Holt,
Rinehard, Winston, 1972).

[13]Victor Cline, *The Desensitization of Children to Television Violence* (Bethesda, Md.: National
Institutes of Health, 1972).

According to their reactions as measured on the physiograph, the boys with a history of heavy television viewing were significantly less aroused by what they saw. They had, the researchers concluded, become so habituated to emotion-arousing events on television that their sensitivities had become blunted. Since they had inevitably watched many violent television programs in the course of their 42 hours of viewing a week, the researchers assumed their desensitization was an effect of constant exposure to violent content. The brunt of the author's subsequent writings has been against violence on television. In an article entitled "Television Violence: How It Damages Your Children," Cline concludes his warnings about the dangers of television violence with a plea for better programming, and even includes a few words of praise for programs like "The Waltons."[14]

And yet the children upon whose diminished emotional reactions he based his conclusions watched 42 hours of televison a week or more, while the children whose reactions were undulled watched almost no televison at all. Common sense suggests that 42 hours a week of *any* televison program might tip the balance from reality to unreality in a child's life sufficiently to lower his arousal level. Six hours daily of "The Waltons" seems just as likely to affect a child's ability to respond normally to human realities as an equal amount of "Mod Squad" or "Adam-12" or any of the other programs that Cline and others are exercised about.

A New Kind of Criminal

Dr. Cline's experiment requires a sensitive instrument to measure the emotional responses, or lack of them, in his young subjects. The effects of television viewing upon normal children's perceptions of and responses to real-life situations are surely subtle and measurable only with a finely calibrated machine, if at all. A different situation obtains with disturbed children, or children from pathological backgrounds. Watching television may affect such children far more profoundly.

A child therapist notes:

"I find that watching television is most destructive for psychotic children. The very thing I want to help them to understand is the real world, to increase their awareness of reality, of cause and effect.

[14]Victor Cline, "Televsion Violence—How it Damages Your Children," *Ladies' Home Journal*, February, 1975.

This is very much shattered by the illogic of cartoon characters being able to fly through the air, for instance, or the other fantastic things that seem so real on television. Some of these children have omnipotent fantasies. They think they can fly, too. They see someone going *zap* with his hand and making another person disappear and their omnipotent fantasy is only reinforced. Of course, the concept of one person making another disappear is also terrifying to a psychotic child, because that's what he deeply believes anyhow."

The observation that television distorts reality far more for a disturbed child than for a normal child may bear a relation to the epidemic of juvenile crime in the last two decades. For there is no doubt that the children involved in serious crimes today are not normal. Their histories reveal without exception a background of poverty, degradation, neglect, scholastic failure, frustration, family pathology . . . and heavy television viewing. But while poverty and family pathology did not appear for the first time in American society in the decades between 1952 and 1972, a frightening new breed of juvenile offender did. "It is as though our society had bred a new genetic strain," writes a reporter in *The New York Times*, "the child-murderer who feels no remorse and is scarcely conscious of his acts."[15]

Almost daily the newspapers report juvenile crimes that fill the hearts of normal readers with horror and disbelief: ten- and twelve-year-old muggers preying on the elderly, casually torturing and murdering their helpless victims, often for small gains; youths assailing a bicyclist in the park and beating him to death with a chain before escaping with his bike; kids breaking into an apartment and stomping an elderly man or drowning a woman in her bathtub.[16]

Law officers and authorities frequently blame lenient laws for the incidence of these crimes. Since in most states lawbreakers under the age of 16 are handled by a family court whose guiding philosophy is rehabilitation rather than punishment or detention for the protection of society, these young criminals need not be deterred by the fear of severe punishment: the harshest action facing a youth under 16 who commits murder in many states is confinement for

38

39

40

[15]Ted Morgan, "They Think 'I Can Kill Because I'm 14,'" *The New York Times Magazine,* January 19, 1975.
[16]See "Youthful Violence Grows," *The New York Times,* November 4, 1974; and "Tale of a Young Mugger," *The New York Times,* April 11, 1976.

up to 18 months in a public or private institution. But there is something new about these chidren, something that cannot be explained away as an arrogant belief that the law will be lenient toward them, that they can literally get away with murder.

"The law says a child should be treated differently because he can be rehabilitated," says a Brooklyn police officer, "but kids weren't committing the types of crimes you see now . . . kids have changed."[17]

The common factor characterizing these "changed" kids who kill, torture, and rape seems to be a form of emotional detachment that allows them to commit unspeakable crimes with a complete absence of normal feelings such as guilt or remorse. It is as if they were dealing with inanimate objects, not with human beings at all. "It's almost as though they looked at the person who got killed as a window they were going to jimmie, as an obstacle, something that got in their way," says Charles King, director in charge of rehabilitation of New York State's Division for Youth.[18]

Today certain courts are even beginning to place juveniles in secure facilities in response to "the new type of child who is coming into the system." A psychiatrist connected with the Brooklyn Family Court describes these children as showing "a total lack of guilt and lack of respect for life. To them another person is a thing—they are wild organisms who cannot allow anyone to stand in their way."[19]

If, indeed, a new breed of juvenile offender has appeared in the last two decades, can this be accounted for by the great new element that has been introduced into children's lives within that time span—television? Poverty, family pathology leading to severe personality disorders, neglect, inadequate schools, all these, alas, are old and familiar afflictions for certain portions of American society.

But the five, six, seven hours a day that troubled children spend watching television, more hours than they spend at any other real-life activity, is a distinctly new phenomenon. Is it possible that all these hours disturbed chidren spend involved in an experience that dulls the boundaries between the real and the unreal, that projects human images and the *illusion* of human feelings, while requiring

---

[17]Quoted by Morgan, *op. cit.*

[18]Quoted in "Youthful Violence Grows," *The New York Times*, November 4, 1974.

[19]Dr. Denise Shine, head of the Rapid Intervention psychiatrists' office in Brooklyn Family Court, quoted in Morgan, *op. cit.*

no human responses from the viewer, encourages them to detach themselves from their antisocial acts in a new and horrible way?

If it is, then the total banishment of violence from the television 46 screen will not mitigate the dehumanizing effects of long periods of televison viewing upon disturbed children. For the problem is not that they learn *how* to commit violence from watching violence on television (although perhaps they sometimes do), but that television conditions them to deal with real people as if they were on a television screen. Thus they are able to "turn them off," quite simply, with a knife or a gun or a chain, with as little remorse as if they were turning off a television set.

CONTENT

1. According to Winn, does TV watching cause violence? Why or why not? Why do people prefer to watch violent TV programs?
2. What is the effect of excessive TV watching on children's sense of reality? What connection does Winn see between dulled sensitivity and violence?
3. How does Winn define the "new criminal"? To what does she attribute the actions of these criminals?

ORGANIZATION

4. Winn makes her argument in stages: first, she begins with the search for a connection between TV and criminal violence. Why does she argue against such a connection as the first step in constructing her own argument?
5. As the second step in her argument, Winn presents empirical evidence to the effect that excessive TV watching distorts one's perception of reality. Why does Winn conclude this part of her argument with several examples?
6. How does Winn link the dulling of sensitivity caused by watching TV an average of 42 hours a week and the behavior of the new breed of adolescent criminal? How do her examples illustrate the dehumanized behavior linked to TV watching?

TOPICS FOR WRITING

7. Write your own persuasive essay on the primary causes of violence.

8. In *Computer Power and Human Reason,* Joseph Weizenbaum contends that computer programmers who work long and intensively on computers begin to see everything in the real world in terms of the computer. Write a persuasive essay arguing that this "tunnel vision," which occurs in many jobs, needs compensations other than watching TV.

JOAN DIDION
The Women's Movement

In 1982, Joan Didion visited El Salvador; her most recent book Salvador *(1983), is a journalistic account of that war-shattered third world nation. In this piece from* The White Album *(1979), Didion argues that the women's movement has fallen on evil times. What was once a revolutionary movement that threatened to remake our society has fallen into triviality and childishness.*

To make an omelette you need not only those broken eggs but someone "oppressed" to break them: every revolutionist is presumed to understand that, and also every woman, which either does or does not make fifty-one per cent of the population of the United States a potentially revolutionary class. The creation of this revolutionary "class" was from the virtual beginning the "idea" of the women's movement, and the tendency for popular discussion of the movement to center for so long around day-care centers is yet another instance of that studied resistance to political ideas which characterizes our national life.

"The new feminism is not just the revival of a serious political movement for social equality," the feminist theorist Shulamith Firestone announced flatly in 1970. "It is the second wave of the most important revolution in history." This was scarcely a statement of purpose anyone could find cryptic, and it was scarcely the only statement of its kind in the literature of the movement. Nonetheless, in 1972, in a "special issue" on women, *Time* was still musing genially that the movement might well succeed in bringing about "fewer diapers and more Dante."

That was a very pretty image, the idle ladies sitting in the gazebo 3
and murmuring *lasciate ogni speranza*,* but it depended entirely
upon the popular view of the movement as some kind of collective
inchoate yearning for "fulfillment," or "self-expression," a yearning
absolutely devoid of ideas and capable of engendering only the
most *pro forma* benevolent interest. In fact there was an idea, and
the idea was Marxist, and it was precisely to the extent that there
was this Marxist idea that the curious historical anomaly known as
the women's movement would have seemed to have any interest
at all. Marxism in this country had ever been an eccentric and quix-
otic passion. One oppressed class after another had seemed finally
to miss the point. The have-nots, it turned out, aspired mainly to
having. The minorities seemed to promise more, but finally disappointed: it developed that they actually cared about the issues,
that they tended to see the integration of the luncheonette and the
seat in the front of the bus as real goals, and only rarely as ploys,
counters in a larger game. They resisted that essential inductive
leap from the immediate reform to the social ideal, and, just as
disappointingly, they failed to perceive their common cause with
other minorities, continued to exhibit a self-interest disconcerting
in the extreme to organizers steeped in the rhetoric of "brotherhood."

And then, at that exact dispirited moment when there seemed 4
no one at all willing to play the proletariat, along came the women's
movement, and the invention of women as a "class." One could
not help admiring the radical simplicity of this instant transfigu-
ration. The notion that, in the absence of a cooperative proletariat,
a revolutionary class might simply be invented, made up, "named"
and so brought into existence, seemed at once so pragmatic and so
visionary, so precisely Emersonian, that it took the breath away,
exactly confirmed one's idea of where nineteenth-century transcen-
dental instincts, crossed with a late reading of Engels and Marx,
might lead. To read the theorists of the women's movement was to
think not of Mary Wollstonecraft but of Margaret Fuller at her most
high-minded, of rushing position papers off to mimeo and drinking
tea from paper cups in lieu of eating lunch; of thin raincoats on
bitter nights. If the family was the last fortress of capitalism, then

*From Dante's *Inferno*, Canto 3, the inscription over the gates of hell: "Leave every hope
behind . . ."

let us abolish the family. If the necessity for conventional reproduction of the species seemed unfair to women, then let us transcend via technology, "the very organization of nature," the oppression, as Shulamith Firestone saw it, "that goes back through recorded
history to the animal kingdom itself." *I accept the universe,* Margaret
Fuller had finally allowed: Shulamith Firestone did not.

It seemed very New England, this febrile and cerebral passion.
The solemn *a priori* idealism in the guise of radical materialism
somehow bespoke old-fashioned self-reliance and prudent sacrifice. The clumsy torrent of words became a principle, a renunciation
of style as unserious. The rhetorical willingness to break eggs became,
in practice, only a thrifty capacity for finding the sermon in every
stone. Burn the literature, Ti-Grace Atkinson said in effect when it
was suggested that, even come the revolution, there would still
remain the whole body of "sexist" Western literature. But of course
no books would be burned: the women of this movement were
perfectly capable of crafting didactic revisions of whatever apparently intractable material came to hand. "As a parent you should
become an interpreter of myths," advised Letty Cottin Pogrebin in
the preview issue of *Ms.* "Portions of any fairy tale or children's
story can be salvaged during a critique session with your child."
Other literary analysts devised ways to salvage other books: Isabel
Archer in *The Portrait of a Lady* need no longer be the victim of her
own idealism. She could be, instead, the victim of a sexist society,
a woman who had "internalized the conventional definition of wife."
The narrator of Mary McCarthy's *The Company She Keeps* could be
seen as "enslaved because she persists in looking for her identity
in a man." Similarly, Miss McCarthy's *The Group* could serve to illustrate "what happens to women who have been educated at first-
rate women's colleges—taught philosophy and history—and then
are consigned to breast-feeding and gourmet cooking."

The idea that fiction has certain irreducible ambiguities seemed
never to occur to these women, nor should it have, for fiction is in
most ways hostile to ideology. They had invented a class; now they
had only to make that class conscious. They seized as a political
technique a kind of shared testimony at first called a "rap session,"
then called "consciousness-raising," and in any case a therapeuti-
cally oriented American reinterpretation, according to the British
feminist Juliet Mitchell, of a Chinese revolutionary practice known

as "speaking bitterness." They purged and regrouped and purged again, worried out one another's errors and deviations, the "elitism" here, the "careerism" there. It would have been merely sententious to call some of their thinking Stalinist: of course it was. It would have been pointless even to speak of whether one considered these women "right" or "wrong," meaningless to dwell upon the obvious, upon the coarsening of moral imagination to which such social idealism so often leads. To believe in the "greater good" is to operate, necessarily, in a certain ethical suspension. Ask anyone committed to Marxist analysis how many angels can dance on the head of a pin, and you will be asked in return to never mind the angels, tell me who controls the production of pins.

To those of us who remain committed mainly to the exploration of moral distinctions and ambiguities, the feminist analysis may have seemed a particularly narrow and cracked determinism. Nonetheless it was serious, and for these high-strung idealists to find themselves out of the mimeo room and onto the Cavett show must have been in certain ways more unsettling to them than it ever was to the viewers. They were being heard, and yet not really. Attention was finally being paid, and yet that attention was mired in the trivial. Even the brightest movement women found themselves engaged in sullen public colloquies about the inequities of dishwashing and the intolerable humiliations of being observed by construction workers on Sixth Avenue. (This grievance was not atypic in that discussion of it seemed always to take on unexplored Ms. Scarlett overtones, suggestions of fragile cultivated flowers being "spoken to," and therefore violated, by uppity proles.) They totted up the pans scoured, the towels picked off the bathroom floor, the loads of laundry done in a lifetime. Cooking a meal could only be "dogwork," and to claim any pleasure from it was evidence of craven acquiescence in one's own forced labor. Small children could only be odious mechanisms for the spilling and digesting of food, for robbing women of their "freedom." It was a long way from Simone de Beauvoir's grave and awesome recognition of woman's role as "the Other" to the notion that the first step in changing that role was Alix Kates Shulman's marriage contract ("wife strips beds, husband remakes them"), a document reproduced in *Ms.*, but it was toward just such trivialization that the women's movement seemed to be heading.

Of course this litany of trivia was crucial to the movement in the beginning, a key technique in the politicizing of women who had perhaps been conditioned to obscure their resentments even from themselves. Mrs. Shulman's discovery that she had less time than her husband seemed to have was precisely the kind of chord the movement had hoped to strike in all women (the "click! of recognition," as Jane O'Reilly described it), but such discoveries could be of no use at all if one refused to perceive the larger point, failed to make that inductive leap from the personal to the political. Splitting up the week into hours during which the children were directed to address their "personal questions" to either one parent or another might or might not have improved the quality of Mr. and Mrs. Shulman's marriage, but the improvement of marriages would not a revolution make. It could be very useful to call housework, as Lenin did, "the most unproductive, the most barbarous and the most arduous work a woman can do," but it could be useful only as the first step in a political process, only in the "awakening" of a class to its position, useful only as a metaphor: to believe, during the late Sixties and early Seventies in the United States of America, that the words had literal meaning was not only to stall the movement in the personal but to seriously delude oneself.

More and more, as the literature of the movement began to reflect the thinking of women who did not really understand the movement's ideological base, one had the sense of this stall, this delusion, the sense that the drilling of the theorists had struck only some psychic hardpan dense with superstitions and little sophistries, wish fulfillment, self-loathing and bitter fancies. To read even desultorily in this literature was to recognize instantly a certain dolorous phantasm, an imagined Everywoman with whom the authors seemed to identify all too entirely. This ubiquitous construct was everyone's victim but her own. She was persecuted even by her gynecologist, who made her beg in vain for contraceptives. She particularly needed contraceptives because she was raped on every date, raped by her husband, and raped finally on the abortionist's table. During the fashion for shoes with pointed toes, she, like "many women," had her toes amputated. She was so intimidated by cosmetics advertising that she would sleep "huge portions" of her day in order to forestall wrinkling, and when awake she was enslaved by detergent commercials on television. She sent her child to a nursery school where the little girls huddled in a "doll corner," and were forcibly restrained from playing with building blocks. Should she work she was paid "three to ten times less" than an (always) unqualified man holding the same job, was prevented from attending business lunches because she would be "embarrassed" to appear in public with a man not her husband, and, when she traveled alone, faced a choice between humiliation in a restaurant and "eating a doughnut" in her hotel room.

The half-truths, repeated, authenticated themselves. The bitter fancies assumed their own logic. To ask the obvious—why she did not get herself another gynecologist, another job, why she did not get out of bed and turn off the television set, or why, the most eccentric detail, she stayed in hotels where only doughnuts could be obtained from room service—was to join this argument at its own spooky level, a level which had only the most tenuous and unfortunate relationship to the actual condition of being a woman. That many women are victims of condescension and exploitation and sex-role stereotyping was scarcely news, but neither was it news that other women are not: nobody forces women to buy the package.

But of course something other than an objection to being "discriminated against" was at work here, something other than an aversion to being "stereotyped" in one's sex role. Increasingly it seemed that the aversion was to adult sexual life itself: how much cleaner to stay forever children. One is constantly struck, in the accounts of lesbian relationships which appear from time to time in movement literature, by the emphasis on the superior "tenderness" of the relationship, the "gentleness" of the sexual connection, as if the participants were wounded birds. The derogation of assertiveness as "machismo" has achieved such currency that one imagines several million women too delicate to deal at any level with an overtly heterosexual man. Just as one had gotten the unintended but inescapable suggestion, when told about the "terror and revulsion" experienced by women in the vicinity of construction sites, of creatures too "tender" for the abrasiveness of daily life, too fragile for the streets, so now one was getting, in the later literature of the movement, the impression of women too "sensitive" for the difficulties of adult life, women unequipped for reality and grasping at the movement as a rationale for denying that reality. The transient stab of dread and loss which accompanies menstruation simply never happens: we only thought it happened, because a male-chauvinist psychiatrist told us so. No woman need have bad dreams after an abortion: she has only been told she should. The power of sex is just an oppressive myth, no longer to be feared, because what the sexual connection really amounts to, we learn in one woman's account of a postmarital affair presented as liberated and liberating, is "wisecracking and laughing" and "lying together and then leaping up to play and sing the entire *Sesame Street Songbook.*" All one's actual apprehension of what it is like to be a woman, the irreconcilable difference of it—that sense of living one's deepest life underwater, that dark involvement with blood and birth and death—could now be declared invalid, unnecessary, *one never felt it at all.*

One was only told it, and now one is to be reprogrammed, fixed up, rendered again as inviolate and unstained as the "modern" little girls in the Tampax advertisements. More and more we have been hearing the wishful voices of just such perpetual adolescents, the voices of women scarred not by their class position as women but by the failure of their childhood expectations and misapprehensions. "Nobody ever so much as mentioned" to Susan Edmiston "that when you say 'I do,' what you are doing is not, as you thought, vowing your eternal love, but rather subscribing to a whole system of rights, obligations and responsibilities that may well be anathema to your most cherished beliefs." To Ellen Peck, "the birth of children too often means the dissolution of romance, the loss of freedom, the abandonment of ideals to economics." A young woman described on the cover of *New York* as "The Suburban Housewife Who Bought the Promises of Women's Lib and Came to the City to Live Them" tells us what promises she bought: "The chance to respond to the bright lights and civilization of the Big Apple, yes. The chance to compete, yes. But most of all, the chance to have some fun. Fun is what's been missing."

Eternal love, romance, fun. The Big Apple. These are relatively rare expectations in the arrangements of consenting adults, although not in those of children, and it wrenches the heart to read about these women in their brave new lives. An ex-wife and mother of three speaks of her plan to "play out my college girl's dream. I am going to New York to become this famous writer. Or this working writer. Failing that, I will get a job in publishing." She mentions a friend, another young woman who "had never had any other life than as a daughter or wife or mother" but who is "just discovering herself to be a gifted potter." The childlike resourcefulness—to get a job in publishing, to become a gifted potter!—bewilders the imagination. The astral discontent with actual lives, actual men, the denial of the real generative possibilities of adult sexual life, somehow touches beyond words. "It is the right of the oppressed to organize around their oppression *as they see and define it*," the movement theorists insist doggedly in an effort to solve the question of these women, to convince themselves that what is going on is still a political process, but the handwriting is already on the wall. These are converts who want not a revolution but "romance," who believe not in the oppression of women but in their own chances for a new life in exactly the mold of their old life. In certain ways they tell us sadder things about what the culture has done to them than the theorists ever did, and they also tell us, I suspect, that the movement is no longer a cause but a symptom.

CONTENT

1. Why does Didion conclude that "the [women's] movement is no longer a cause but a symptom"? Why has it changed?
2. To bring more women into the movement, feminists began to politicise women by exposing their hidden resentments; then (paragraph 9) "the movement began to reflect the thinking of women who did not really understand the movement's ideological base." How did trivia begin to replace ideology?
3. Why, in its final stage, did the movement attract women who wished to "stay forever children"? Is Didion fair in her judgment about the unrealistic expectations of such women? Do the TV and magazine ads directed at the "new woman" contribute to these unrealistic expectations?

ORGANIZATION

4. Didion's argument follows a cause–effect organization. By first tracing the early history of the movement, how does she persuade the reader that the movement has been "trivialized"?
5. How effective are her examples from feminist literature in establishing the revolutionary ideology of the early stages of the movement? How do her later examples illustrate its trivialization?

TOPICS FOR WRITING

6. Read Margaret Mead's "To Both Their Own" (pages 334–49) and write a persuasive essay arguing for or against a revolutionary approach to the solution of the division of labor between men and women.

7. Read Ellen Goodman's "The Maidenform Woman Administers Shock Treatment" (pages 234–36) and write an essay showing how advertising trivializes by oversimplifying the complexity of male and female roles.

JAMES FALLOWS
The Draft: Why the Country Needs It

James Fallows, born in Philadelphia in 1949, received his B.A. from Harvard University in 1970. In 1972, he became the editor of Washington Monthly; *since 1979, he has been the Washington editor of the* Atlantic Monthly. *In the following essay, Fallows takes a dispassionate look at a controversial issue and presents arguments in favor of a widely unpopular position.*

I am more than angry. I did not give birth to my one and only son to have him snatched away from me 18 years later. My child has been loved and cared for and taught right from wrong and *will not* be fed into any egomaniac's war machine.

Our 18- to 25-year-olds have not brought this world to its present sorry state. Men over the age of 35, down through the centuries, have brought us here, and we women have been in silent accord.

Well, this is one woman, one mother, who says *no*. I did not go through the magnificent agony of childbirth to have that glorious young life snuffed out.

Until the presidents, premiers, supreme rulers, politburos, senators and congressmen of the world are ready to physically, as opposed to verbally, lead the world into combat, they can bloody well forget my child.

Unite mothers! Don't throw your sons and daughters away. Sometime, somewhere, women have just got to say *no*.

No. No. No. No. No. Never my child.

—Louise M. Saylor

(Letter published in the Washington *Post*, January 28, 1980.)

Nor my child, Mrs. Saylor. Nor either of my mother's sons when, 1
ten years ago, both were classified I-A. But *whose*, then? As our
statesmen talk again of resisting aggression and demonstrating our
will—as they talk, that is, of sending someone's sons (or daughters)
to bear arms overseas—the only fair and decent answer to that
question lies in a return to the draft.

I am speaking here not of the health of the military but of the 2
character of the society the military defends. The circumstances in
which that society will choose to go to war, the way its wars will be
fought, and its success in absorbing the consequent suffering depend
on its answer to the question Whose sons will go?

History rarely offers itself in lessons clear enough to be deci- 3
phered at a time when their message still applies. But of all the
hackneyed "lessons" of Vietnam, one still applies with no reser-
vations: that we wound ourselves gravely if we flinch from honest
answers about who will serve. During the five or six years of the
heaviest draft calls for Vietnam, there was the starkest class division
in American military service since the days of purchased draft
deferments in the Civil War. Good intentions lay at the root of many
of these inequities. The college-student deferment, the various
"hardship" exemptions, Robert McNamara's plan to give "disadvantaged" youngsters a chance to better themselves in the military,
even General Hershey's intelligence test to determine who could
remain in school—all were designed to allot American talent in the
most productive way. The intent was to distinguish those who could
best serve the nation with their minds from those who should offer
their stout hearts and strong backs. The effect was to place the poor
and the black in the trenches (and later in the coffins and the rehabilitation wards), and their "betters" in colleges or elsewhere far
from the sounds of war. I speak as one who took full advantage of
the college-student deferment and later exploited the loopholes in
the physical qualification standards that, for college students armed
with a doctor's letter and advice from the campus draft counseling
center, could so easily be parlayed into the "unfit for service" des-
ignation known as a I-Y. Ask anyone who went to college in those
days how many of his classmates saw combat in Vietnam. Of my
1200 classmates at Harvard, I know of only two, one of them a
veteran who joined the class late. The records show another fifty-
five in the reserves, the stateside Army, or military service of some

other kind. There may be more; the alumni lists are not complete. See how this compares with the Memorial Roll from a public high school in a big city or a West Virginia hill town.

For all the talk about conflict between "young" and "old" that the war caused, the lasting breach was among the young. In the protest marches on the Pentagon and the Capitol, students felt either scorn for or estrangement from the young soldiers who stood guard. What must the soldiers have felt about these, their privileged contemporaries, who taunted them so? To those who opposed the war, the ones who served were, first, animals and killers; then "suckers" who were trapped by the system, deserving pity but no respect; and finally invisible men. Their courage, discipline, and sacrifice counted for less than their collective taint for being associated with a losing war. A returned veteran might win limited redemption if he publicly recanted, like a lapsed Communist fingering his former associates before the HUAC. Otherwise, he was expected to keep his experiences to himself. Most veterans knew the honor they had earned, even as they knew better than anyone else the horror of the war. They came to resent being made to suppress those feelings by students who chose not to join them and who, having escaped the war without pain, now prefer to put the whole episode in the past. Perhaps no one traversed that era without pain, but pain of the psychic variety left arms, legs, life intact and did not impede progress in one's career. For people of my generation—I speak in the narrow sense of males between the ages of twenty-eight and thirty-six or thirty-seven—this wound will never fully heal. If you doubt that, sit two thirty-two-year-olds down together, one who served in Vietnam and one who did not, and ask them to talk about those years.

At least there was theoretical consistency between what the students of those days recommended for others and what they did themselves. Their point was that no one should go to war, starting with them. It should also be said that their objection to the war, at least in my view, was important and right. And while they—we—may have proven more effective and determined in acts of individual salvation than in anything else, they at least paid lip service to the idea of the "categorical imperative," that they should not expect others to bear a burden they considered unacceptable for themselves.

* * *

The Vietnam draft was unfair racially, economically, education-   6
ally. By every one of those measures, the volunteer Army is less
representative still. Libertarians argue that military service should
be a matter of choice, but the plain fact is that service in the volunteer force is too frequently dictated by economics. Army enlisted
ranks E1 through E4—the privates and corporals, the cannon fod-
der, the ones who will fight and die—are 36 percent black now. By
the Army's own projections, they will be 42 percent black in three
years. When other "minorities" are taken into account, we will have,
for the first time, an army whose fighting members are mainly
"non-majority," or more bluntly, a black and brown army defending
a mainly white nation. The military has been an avenue of opportunity of many young blacks. They may well be first-class fighting
men. They do not represent the nation.

Such a selective bearing of the burden has destructive spiritual   7
effects in a nation based on the democratic creed. But its practical
implications can be quite as grave. The effect of a fair, representative
draft is to hold the public hostage to the consequences of its decisions, much as children's presence in the public schools focuses
parents' attention on the quality of the schools. If citizens are willing
to countenance a decision that means that *someone's* child may die,
they may contemplate more deeply if there is the possibility that
the child will be theirs. Indeed, I would like to extend this principle
even further. Young men of nineteen are rightly suspicious of the
congressmen and columnists who urge them to the fore. I wish
there were a practical way to resurrect the provisions of the amended
Selective Service Act of 1940, which raised the draft age to forty-
four. Such a gesture might symbolize the desire to offset the historic
injustice of the Vietnam draft, as well as suggest the possibility that,
when a bellicose columnist recommends dispatching American forces
to Pakistan, he might also realize that he could end up as a gunner
in a tank.

Perhaps the absence of a World War II-scale peril makes such a   8
proposal unrealistic; still, the columnist or congressman should have
to contemplate the possibility that his son would be there, in trench
or tank. Under the volunteer Army that possibility will not arise,
and the lack of such a prospect can affect behavior deeply. Recall
how, during Vietnam, protest grew more broad-based and respect-
able when the graduate school deferment was eliminated in 1968.

For many families in positions of influence the war was no longer a question of someone else's son. How much earlier would the war have ended had college students been vulnerable from the start?

Those newly concerned families were no better and no worse ⁹ than other people at other times; they were responding to a normal human instinct, of the sort our political system is designed to channel toward constructive ends. It was an instinct that Richard Nixon and Henry Kissinger understood very well, as they deliberately shifted the burden of the war off draftees and finally off Americans, to free their hands to pursue their chosen course. Recall how fast protest ebbed with the coming of the volunteer Army and "Vietnamization" in the early 1970s. For this reason, the likes of Nixon and Kissinger might regard a return to the draft as a step in the wrong direction, for it would sap the resolve necessary for a strong foreign policy and introduce the weakening element of domestic dissent. At times leaders must take actions that seem heartless and unfair, and that an informed public would probably not approve. Winston Churchill let Coventry be bombed, because to sound the air-raid sirens and save its citizens would have tipped off the Germans that Britain had broken their code. But in the long run, a nation cannot sustain a policy whose consequences the public is not willing to bear. If it decides not to pay the price to defend itself, it will be defenseless. That is the risk of democracy.

What kind of draft? More than anything else, a *fair* one, with as ¹⁰ few holes as possible to wriggle through. The 1971 Selective Service Act, passed when the heavy draft calls had already ended, theoretically closed most of the loopholes. But if real trouble should begin, those nine-year-old patches* might give way before political pressures unless we concentrate again on the mechanics of an equitable draft. "Fairness" does not mean that everyone need serve. This year 4.3 million people will turn eighteen, 2.2 million women and 2.1 million men. For the last few years, the military has been taking 400,000 people annually into the Volunteer Army—or, in raw figures, only one in ten of the total available pool. Using today's mental and physical standards, the military knocks off 30 percent of the manpower pool as unqualified, and it excludes women from combat positions. When these calculations are combined with the diminishing number of young men—only 1.6 million men will turn

---

*As of 1980

eighteen in 1993—the military projects that it will need to attract one of every three "qualified and available men" by the end of the 1980s.

Read another way, this means that a draft need affect *no more* than one in three—and probably far fewer. To make the draft seem— and be—fair, the pool of potential draftees should be as large as possible, even if only a few will eventually be picked. Those who are "disabled" in the common meaning of the term—the blind, paraplegics—should be excluded, but not the asthmatics and trick-back cases who are perfectly capable of performing non-combat military jobs. The military's physical requirements now assume that nearly all men must theoretically be fit for combat, even though only 14 percent of all male soldiers hold combat jobs. The proportion of draftees destined for combat would probably be higher, since those are the positions now most understrength; if actual fighting should begin it would be higher still. But combat will never represent the preponderance of military positions, and its requirements should not blindly dictate who is eligible for the draft. Instead, everyone without serious handicap should be eligible for selection by lottery—men and women, students and non-students. Once the lottery had determined *who* would serve, assignments based on physical classifications could determine where and how.

The question of women's service is the most emotionally troubling aspect of this generally emotional issue, but the progress of domestic politics over the last ten years suggests that the answer is clear. If any sexual distinctions that would deny a woman her place as a construction worker or a telephone pole climber have been forbidden by legislators and courts, what possible distinction can spare women the obligation to perform similar functions in military construction units or the Signal Corps? President Carter recognized this reality in deciding to include women in his initial draft registration order. If women are drafted, they have an ironclad case for passage of the Equal Rights Amendment. If they are not, their claim for equal treatment elsewhere becomes less compelling. At the same time, it is troubling to think of women in combat, or of mothers being drafted, and a sensible draft law would have to recognize such exceptions.

There should be no educational deferments except for students still in high school, and possibly in two other cases. One would be for college students who enroll in ROTC; like their counterparts in the service academies, they would be exchanging four years of protected education for a longer tour of duty as an officer after graduation. The other exception might be for doctors, possessors of a skill the military needs but cannot sensibly produce on its own. If potential doctors wanted to be spared all eligibility for the draft, they could enter a program like the Navy's V-12 during World War II, in which they could take a speeded-up college course and receive a publicly subsidized medical education, after which they would owe several years' service as military doctors. Except in the most far-fetched situations, "hardship" cases should be taken care of by compensation rather than by exemption. If these are permitted, they become an invitation to abuse: who can forget George Hamilton pleading hardship as his mother's sole supporting son? Instead, the government should offset hardship with support payments to the needy dependents.

One resists the idea of lottery, because it adds to the system the very element of caprice and unfairness it is so important to remove. But since only a fraction of those eligible to serve are actually required, there seems no other equitable way to distribute the burden. With a well-established lottery, every male and female might know at age eighteen whether he or she was near the top of the list and very likely to be called, or near the bottom and almost certainly protected. How far the draft calls went down the list would depend on how many people volunteered and how many more were needed.

None of these concerns and prescriptions would matter if the volunteer Army were what it so often seemed in the last few years—a stand-in, a symbol, designed to keep the machinery running and the troops in place, not to be sent into action for any cause less urgent than absolute survival. But now we hear from every quarter that the next decade will be a time of testing, that our will and our strategy and our manpower will be on the line. The nature of this challenge, and the style of our response, are what we should be thinking and talking about now. Our discussions will never be honest, nor our decisions just, as long as we count on "suckers" to do the job.

CONTENT

1. Why does Fallows cite the experience of the Vietnam War to support his argument for reinstituting the draft? Why does he feel the volunteer army is unfair and dangerous?

2. How does Fallows disarm the opponents of a fair draft law? Why does he frequently cite the draft law operating during WWII? What provisions of that draft law would he like to see enacted?
3. What is Fallows' position on drafting women? On what does he base his position? What limitations would be placed on physical exemptions and hardship cases?

ORGANIZATION

4. This is almost a classic example of the traditional organization of a persuasive essay, except for the "Confutation" which is combined with the "Confirmation" or proof. Why does Fallows combine his reasons for his position with answers to objections from his opponents? Is this an effective organization?
5. How does Fallows use the background of Vietnam and the negative experience with the draft as an additional logical reason to support a new draft?
6. How is Fallows' summation both a new argument and an emotional appeal taken from the earlier part of the essay?

TOPICS FOR WRITING

7. Write a persuasive essay in rebuttal of Fallows' argument.
8. Write a persuasive essay agreeing or disagreeing with Fallows' position on drafting women.
9. Read Peter Marin's "Coming to Terms with Vietnam" (pages 431–48). Write a persuasive essay arguing for greater recognition of the veterans of the Vietnam War.

TOM BETHELL
Against Bilingual Education

Tom Bethell was born in London, England in 1940 and, after receiving his M.A. from Trinity College, Oxford University in 1962, came to the United States. In 1975 he became editor of Washington Monthly, *and in 1976, Washington editor of* Harper's. *"The Case Against Bilingual Education" is an incisive argument against what Bethell, a political conservative, sees as an unnecessary and ineffective government program.*

This year the United States government, which I am beginning to think is afflicted with a death wish, is spending $150 million on "bilingual education" programs in American classrooms. There is nothing "bi" about it, however. The languages in which instruction is conducted now include: Central Yup'ik, Aleut, Yup'ik, Gwich'in, Athabascan (the foregoing in Alaska), Navajo, Tagalog, Pima, Plaute (I promise I'm not making this up), Ilocano, Cambodian, Yiddish, Chinese, Vietnamese, Punjabi, Greek, Italian, Korean, Polish, French, Haitian, Haitian-French, Portuguese, Arabic, Crow (yes, Virginia. . .), Cree, Keresian, Tewa, Apache, Mohawk, Japanese, Lakota, Choctaw, Samoan, Chamorro, Carolinian, Creek-Seminole, and Russian.

And there are more, such as Trukese, Palauna, Ulithian, Woleian, Marshallese, Kusaian, Ponapean, and, not least, Yapese. And Spanish—how could I have so nearly forgotten it? The bilingual education program is more or less the Hispanic equivalent of affirmative action, creating jobs for thousands of Spanish teachers; by which I mean teachers who speak Spanish, although not necessarily English, it has turned out. One observer has described the HEW-sponsored program as "affirmative ethnicity." Although Spanish is only one of seventy languages in which instruction is carried on (I seem to have missed a good many of them), it accounts for 80 percent of the program.

Bilingual education is an idea that appeals to teachers of Spanish and other tongues, but also to those who never did think that another idea, the United States of America, was a particularly good one to begin with, and that the sooner it is restored to its component "ethnic" parts the better off we shall all be. Such people have been welcomed with open arms into the upper reaches of the federal government in recent years, giving rise to the suspicion of a death wish.

The bilingual education program began in a small way (the way such programs always begin) in 1968, when the Elementary and Secondary Education Act of 1965 was amended (by what is always referred to as "Title VII") to permit the development of "pilot projects" to help *poor* children who were "educationally disadvantaged because of their inability to speak English," and whose parents were either on welfare or earing less than $3,000 a year. At this germinal stage the program cost a mere $7.5 million, and as its sponsors (among them Sen. Alan Cranston of California) later boasted, it was enacted without any public challenge whatever.

"With practically no one paying heed," Stephen Rosenfeld wrote 5
in the *Washington Post* in 1974 (i.e., six years after the program began),

> Congress has radically altered the traditional way by which immigrants
> become Americanized. No longer will the public schools be expected to
> serve largely as a "melting pot," assimilating foreigners to a common
> culture. Rather, under a substantial new program for "bilingual educa-
> tion, the schools—in addition to teaching English—are to teach "home"
> language and culture to children who speak English poorly.

Rosenfeld raised the important point that "it is not clear how 6
educating children in the language and culture of their ancestral
homeland will better equip them for the rigors of contemporary life
in the United States." But in response, a withering blast of disap-
proval was directed at the *Post's* "Letters" column. Hadn't he heard?
The melting pot had been removed from the stove.

Bureaucratic imperative (and, I would argue, a surreptitious death 7
wish) dictated that the $7.5 million "pilot program" of 1968 grow
into something more luxuriant and permanent. As it happened,
the U.S. Supreme Court decision *Lau v. Nichols*, handed down in
1974, provided the stimulus.

In this case, Legal Services attorneys in Chinatown sued a San 8
Francisco school district on behalf of 1,800 Chinese-speaking students, claiming that they had been denied special instruction in
English. The contention that these pupils had a *constitutional* right
to such instruction (as was implied by filing the suit in federal court)
was denied both by the federal district court and the appeals court.
The Justice Department entered the case when it was heard before
the Supreme Court, arguing that the school district was in violation
of a 1970 memorandum issued by HEW's Office for Civil Rights.
This memorandum in turn was based on the 1964 Civil Rights Act,
which decreed (among other things) that the recipients of federal
funds cannot be discriminated against on the basis of national origin. The 1970 memorandum defined language as basic to national
origin and required schools to take "affirmative steps" to correct
English-language deficiencies.

Evidently intimidated by this rhetorical flourishing of "rights," 9
the Supreme Court unanimously affirmed that federally funded
schools must "rectify the language deficiency in order to open
instruction to students who had "linguistic deficiencies." In effect,
the Office for Civil Rights had taken the position that the immigrant's tongue was to be regarded as a right, not an impediment,
and the Supreme Court had meekly gone along with the argument.

Armed now with this judicial mandate, HEW's civil-rights militants went on the offensive, threatening widespread funding cutoffs. No longer would the old method of teaching immigrants be countenanced (throwing them into the English language and allowing them to sink or swim). No longer! Now the righteous activists within government had exactly what they are forever searching for: a huddled mass of yearning . . .victims! Discriminated against the moment they arrive at *these* teeming, wretched, racist, ethnocentric shores!

America the Bad . . . One Nation, Full of Victims . . . Divisible. (I have in my hands an odious document, the "Third Annual Report of the National Council on Bilingual Education," which remarks that "Cubans admitted after Castro; and more recently Vietnamese refugees . . . became citizens unintentionally." No doubt they are yearning to be free to return to Ho Chi Minh City and Havana.) That's about the size of it in the 1970s, and so it came to pass that the Office for Civil Rights "targeted" 334 school districts, which would have to start "bilingual-bicultural" classes promptly or risk having their federal funds cut off.

"The OCR [Office for Civil Rights] policy is difficult to explain," Noel Epstein remarked in a thoughtful survey of bilingual education titled "Language, Ethnicity and the Schools" and published recently by the Institute for Educational Leadership. "There is no federal legal requirement for schools to provide bilingual or bicultural education." The Supreme Court had merely said that *some* remedy was needed—not necessarily bilingual education. For example, the Chinese children in the *Lau* case could have been given extra instruction in English, to bring them up to par. But the Office for Civil Rights took the position that they would have to be taught school subjects—mathematics, geography, history, et cetera—in Chinese. And the Court's ruling had said nothing at all about bi*cultural* instruction. (This turns out to mean teaching that in any transaction with the "home" country, America tends to be in the wrong.)

In any event, the bilingual education program was duly expanded by Congress in 1974. It would no longer be just for poor children; all limited-English speakers would qualify; the experimental nature of the program was played down, and there was the important addition of biculturalism, which is summarized in a revealing paragraph in Epstein's booklet:

> Bicultural instruction was elevated to a required component of Title VII programs. The definition of "bilingual" education now meant such instruction had

*to be given "with appreciation for the cultural heritage of such children. . . ."
This underlined the fact that language and culture were not merely being used
as vehicles for the transmission of information but as the central sources of ethnic
identity. The U.S. Civil Rights Commission had in fact urged the name of the
law be changed to "The Bilingual Bicultural Education Act," but key Senate staff
members blocked this idea. They feared it would "flag a potentially dangerous
issue that might defeat the overall measure," Dr. Susan Gilbert Schneider reports
in a valuable dissertation on the making of the 1974 act. Some lobby groups had
expressed discomfort about federally sponsored biculturalism. The National
Association of School Boards suggested that the legislation could be read as
promoting a divisive, Canadian-style biculturalism.*

It certainly could. Notice, however, the strong suggestion here 14
that the objection was not so much to the possibility of cutting up
the country, as to being *seen* to promote this possibility, which of
course might defeat it. As I say, these things are best kept surreptitious—at the level of anonymous "Senate staff members."

At this stage the bilingual seed had indeed taken root. Congres- 15
sional appropriations had increased from the beggarly $7.5 million
to $85 million in fiscal year 1975. The Office for Civil Rights was on
the alert. A potential 3.6 million "victimized" children of "limited
English-speaking ability" had been identified, and they would furnish the raw material for an almost endless number of bureaucratic
experiments. Militant Chicanos, suddenly sought out to fill ethnic
teaching quotas, stood on the sidelines, ready to pour a bucket of
guilt over any old-fashioned, demurring Yankee who might raise a
voice in protest.

Even so, there was a cloud on the horizon—perhaps only a con- 16
ceptual cloud, but nevertheless an important one, as follows: the
idea behind bilingual education was that children would begin to
learn school subjects in their native tongue while they were learning
English elsewhere—in special English classes, on the playground,
through exposure to American society generally. But while they
were in this "stage of transition"—learning English—instruction
in the home tongue would ensure that they were not needlessly
held back academically. Then, when they had a sufficient grasp of
English, they could be removed from the bilingual classes and
instructed in the normal way. That, at least, was the idea behind
bilingual education originally.

But you see the problem, no doubt. At bottom, this is the same 17
old imperialism. It is a "melting pot" solution. The children learn
English after all—perhaps fairly rapidly. And at that point there is

no reason to keep them in bilingual programs. Moreover, from the point of view of HEW's civil-rights militants, there is rapid improvement by the "victims"—another unfortunate outcome.

The riposte has been predictable—namely, to keep the children in programs of bilingual instruction long after they know English. This has been justified by redefining the problem in the schools as one of "maintenance" of the home tongue, rather than "transition" to the English tongue. You will hear a lot of talk in and around HEW's numerous office buildings in Washington about the relative merits of maintenance versus transition. Of course, Congress originally had "transition" in mind, but "maintenance" is slowly but steadily winning the day.

The issue was debated this year in Congress when Title VII came up for renewal. Some Congressmen, alerted to the fact that children were still being instructed in Spanish, Aleut, or Yapese in the twelfth grade, tried to argue that bilingual instruction should not last for more than two years. But this proposal was roundly criticized by Messrs. Edward Roybal of California, Baltasar Corrada of Puerto Rico, Phillip Burton of California, Paul Simon of Illinois, and others. In the end the language was left vague, giving school boards the discretion to continue "bilingual maintenance" as long as they desired. Currently, fewer than one-third of the 290,000 students enrolled in various bilingual programs are significantly limited in their English-speaking ability.

Then a new cloud appeared on the horizon. If you put a group of children, let's say children from China, in a classroom together in order to teach them English, that's segregation, right? Watch out, then. Here come the civil-rights militants on the rampage once again, ready to demolish the very program they had done so much to encourage. But there was a simple remedy that would send them trotting tamely homeward. As follows: Put the "Anglos" in with the ethnics. In case you hadn't heard, "Anglo" is the name given these days to Americans who haven't got a drop of ethnicity to their names—the ones who have already been melted down, so to speak.

Putting Anglos into the bilingual program killed two birds with one stone. It circumvented the "segregation" difficulty, and—far more to the point—it meant that the Anglos (just the ones who needed it!) would be exposed to the kind of cultural revisionism that is the covert purpose behind so much of the bilingual program. Put more simply, Mary Beth and Sue Anne would at last learn the new truth: the Indians, not the cowboys, were the good guys, Texas was an ill-gotten gain, and so on.

As Congressman Simon of Illinois put it so delicately, so *surreptitiously*: "I hope that in the conference committee we can get this thing modified as we had it in subcommittee, to make clear that we ought to encourage our English-language students to be in those classes so that you can have the interplay." 22

As things worked out, up to 40 percent of the classes may permissibly be "Anglo," Congress decreed. And this year there has been another important change: an expanded definition of students who will be eligible for bilingual instruction. No longer will it be confined to those with limited English-*speaking* ability. Now the program will be open to those with "limited English proficiency in understanding, speaking, reading, and writing." This, of course, could be construed as applying to almost anyone in elementary or high school these days. 23

To accommodate this expansion, future Congressional appropriations for bilingual education will increase in leaps and bounds: $200 million next year, $250 million the year after, and so on in $50 million jumps, until $400 million is spent in 1983, when the program will once again be reviewed by Congress. 24

Meanwhile, HEW's Office of Education (that is, the *E* of HEW) appears to be getting alarmed at this runaway program. It commissioned a study by the American Institutes for Research in Palo Alto, and this study turned out to be highly critical of bilingual education. The Office of Education then drew attention to this by announcing the findings at a press conference. ("They've got it in for us," someone at the Bilingual Office told me. "Whenever there's an unfavorable study, they call a press conference. Whenever there's a favorable study, they keep quiet about it.") 25

In any event, the Palo Alto study claimed that children in bilingual classes were doing no better academically, and perhaps were doing slightly worse, than children from similar backgrounds in regular English classes. The study also reported that 85 percent of the students were being kept in bilingual classes after they were capable of learning in English. 26

There has been very little Congressional opposition to the bilingual programs, thus bearing out what the Washington writer Fred Reed has called the Guppy Law: "When outrageous expenditures are divided finely enough, the public will not have enough stake 27 in any one expenditure to squelch it." (Reed adds, in a brilliant analysis of the problem: "A tactic of the politically crafty is to pose questions in terms of rightful virtue. 'What? You oppose a mere $40 million subsidy of codpiece manufacture by the Nez Percé? So! You are against Indians . . . .' The thudding opprobrium of anti-Indianism outweighs the $40 million guppy bite in the legislators' eyes.")

Risking that opprobrium, John Ashbrook of Ohio tried to cut out the bilingual program altogether. Referring to the evidence that the program wasn't working, but the budget for it was increasing annually, Ashbrook said that "when one rewards failure, one buys failure." On the House floor he added: "The program is actually preventing children from learning English. Someday somebody is going to have to teach those young people to speak English or else they are going to become public charges. Our educational system is finding it increasingly difficult today to teach English-speaking children to read their own language. When children come out of the Spanish-language schools or Choctaw-language schools which call themselves bilingual, how is our educational system going to make them literate in what will still be a completely alien tongue . . .?"

The answer, of course, is that there will be demands not for literacy in English but for public signs in Spanish (or Choctaw, et cetera), laws promulgated in Spanish, courtroom proceedings in Spanish, and so on. These demands are already being felt—and met, in part. As so often happens, the ill effects of one government program result in the demand for another government program, rather than the abolition of the original one.

This was borne out by what happened next. When the amendment abolishing bilingual education was proposed by Ashbrook (who is usually regarded in Washington as one of those curmudgeons who can be safely ignored), *not one* Congressman rose to support it, which says something of the efficacy of the Guppy Law. Instead, the House was treated to some pusillanimous remarks by Congressman Claude Pepper of Florida—a state in which it is, of course, politically unwise to resist the expenditure of federal money "targeted" for Hispanics. Pepper said: "Now there is something like parity between the population of the United States and Latin America. My information is that by the year 2000 there probably will be 600 million people living in Latin America, and about 300 million people living in the United States."

Perhaps, then, it would be in order for the "Anglos" to retreat even further, before they are entirely overwhelmed. This brings to mind a most interesting remark made by Dr. Josue Gonzalez, the director-designate of the Office of Bilingual Education (the head of the program, in other words), in the course of an interview that he granted me. Actually, Dr. Gonzalez said many interesting things. He suggested a possible cause of the rift with the Office of Education. "Bilingual education was hatched in Congress, not in the bureaucracy," he said. "The constituents [i.e., Hispanics, mostly] talked directly to Congress. Most government programs are generated by so-called administrative proposal—that is, from within the bureaucracies themselves."

He said of regular public education in America: "I've plotted it   32
on a graph: by the year 2010, most college graduates will be mutes!" (No *wonder* the Office of Education isn't too wildly enthusiastic.) And he said that, contrary to what one might imagine, many "Anglo" parents are in fact only too anxious for their children to enroll in a bilingual course. (If Johnny doesn't learn anything else, at least he might as well learn Spanish—that at least is my interpretation.)

The melting-pot idea is dead, Dr. Gonzalez kept reassuring me.   33
Why? I asked him. What was his proof of this? He then made what I felt was a revealing observation, and one that is not normally raised at all, although it exists at the subliminal level. "We must allow for diversity . . . ," he began, then, suddenly veering off: "The counterculture of the 1960s showed that. Even the WASP middle-American showed that the monolithic culture doesn't exist. Within the group, even, they were rejecting their own values."

I imagine that Attila or Alaric, in an expansive and explanatory   34
mood, might have said much the same thing to some sodden Roman senators who were trying to figure out how it was that Rome fell, exactly.

Dr. Gonzalez had me there and he knew it, so he promptly   35
resumed the offensive. "There are those who say that to speak whatever language you speak is a human right," he went on. "The Helsinki Agreements and the President's Commission on Foreign Language Study commit us to the study of foreign languages. Why not our own—domestic—languages?"

Later on I decided to repeat this last comment to George Weber,   36
the associate director of the Council for Basic Education, a somewhat lonely group in Washington. The grandson of German immigrants, Mr. Weber speaks perfect English. "Only in America," he

said. "Only in America would someone say a stupid thing like that. Can you imagine a Turk arriving in France and complaining that he was being denied his human rights because he was taught at school in French, not Turkish? What do you think the French would say to that?"

CONTENT

1. What evidence does Bethell provide that the real issue behind bilingual education is the clash between the melting-pot idea of ethnic assimilation and the concept of ethnic diversity?
2. By what stages were the original intentions of the bilingual program subverted? What evidence does Bethell produce to prove that the intention of teaching English to disadvantaged students has not been fulfilled?
3. How has what Bethell calls the Guppy Law prevented Congress from cutting appropriations for a program that has failed?

ORGANIZATION

4. Bethell tips his hand about his position on bilingual education even before he states his proposition. How do his opening three paragraphs imply his position?
5. Why does Bethell give a detailed history of the evolution of the program? How does this serve as part of his logical proof?
6. How does the juxtaposition of Ashbrook and Pepper in Congress, and then Gonzales and Weber as educators from opposing camps, help provide emotional support for Bethell's position? To which of his audience's feelings does Bethell appeal?

TOPICS FOR WRITING

7. Write a rebuttal to Bethell's position, arguing the preservation of ethnic diversity is both desirable and necessary.
8. Write an essay arguing that the specific demands of economic survival necessitate literacy in English.

PART 9
Style

If you were to ask most people what they meant by prose style, they would probably reply, "the *way* something is written." This isn't a bad definition, but it implies that there is a real distinction between *what* is written (the *contents* of a piece) and *how* it is written (the *manner*, or style of a piece). In fact, when an author has something to say and has taken some care to say it clearly and gracefully, there is little distinction between the words chosen and the ideas they express.

All style is a product of two things: *audience* and *purpose*. How you view these ulterior features of a piece of writing (both of which have to do with content) will determine what combination of the five elements of style you choose. These five elements of style—words (diction), sentence structure, voice, tone, and distance—can be combined in a variety of ways. The possible combinations allow writers to adjust their prose styles to the prospective audience, to the purpose of the writing, and the expression of the writer's personality. Analogous to these choices is the almost automatic way in which each of us talks to different audiences (friends, parents, teachers, acquaintances), varying our vocabulary, our voice, our tone—in short, our appearance—for each different audience. Much the same thing is true of prose style, although there are certain unvarying features of writing style which, like personality, remain constant reminders of our individuality.

You need, therefore, to identify your audience at the outset. A professional author writing for a periodical has none of the problems of a student writer; the author is writing for what is in most cases a clearly defined readership. Other professionals—doctors, lawyers, professors—write for an audience of peers or, at times, for a popular audience unfamiliar with the subject matter and special language of the discipline. Student writing is another matter. In most writing classes, your classmates are your audience. In some classes, the instructor is the only audience; in such cases, however, if you write only to satisfy the instructor, you may develop too narrow a range of styles.

Defining your purpose also helps determine your choices among the varying elements of style. For example, you should determine whether your purpose is expressive, recreational, exploratory, explanatory, or persuasive. Looking at examples of each element of style will help clarify how audience and purpose determine the appropriate combination of stylistic elements.

Diction (Word Choice)   Because English offers so many synonyms, one of the choices open to you is to select from among words of approximately the same meaning, the one that is most appropriate. Remember that words differ not only in denotation, but also in connotation (see descriptive writing). For example, both Gay Talese and Loren Eiseley have described Manhattan's pigeons in the early morning light. Talese writes, "Pigeons control Park Avenue and *strut* unchallenged in the middle of the street." In the same morning light, Eiseley's pigeons "were beginning to *float* outward upon the city. . . They were *pouring* upward in a light that was not yet perceptible to human eyes." The verb "strut" not only has a different denotation from Eiseley's verbs, "float" and "pour," it also connotes a certain cockiness on the part of the pigeons who, for the moment at least, control the most prestigious street in New York. Eiseley's verbs, on the other hand, are much more intangible, more ethereal; the pigeons have little to do with the human world and seem to dominate a detached, unreal, and mystical realm. All this is implied in the connotation of the verbs. The word choice in these examples is determined by the different purposes of each piece of writing; Talese's reportorial writing is more concrete, and metaphoric; Eiseley's exploratory writing more abstract and philosophical. (See the discussion of concrete words in Part 3.)

Sentence Structure   Jonathan Swift defined effective style as "the proper words in the proper place." The first of these elements, diction, we have already considered; the second, sentence structure, has two variables. Obviously, the first of these variables we'll call sentence construction; the other variable is sentence length. Sentences can be short, as in most reportorial writing; of moderate length, as in most explanatory writing; or long, as in most exploratory philosophical writing. For example, notice how the short sentences of William Saroyan's reportorial writing seem like a direct conversation with the reader. Such a style is called *colloquial* because it resembles speech.

> The minute we met, that was it. We belonged to each other. Forever. It was a fact. I was born there. I wasn't born in Bitlis, Marseilles, London, New York, or anywhere else. I was born in Fresno. It was my place. I loved it. I hated it. But had I been born in Paris, I would have loved Paris, and I would have hated it.

Contrast Saroyan's style with the *formal style* of John Fowles. Not only is the diction more abstract, less like speech, but the sentences are considerably longer, more consciously structured for reading than for speaking.

> I began this wander through the trees—we shall come to them literally, by the end—in search of that much looser use of the word *art* to describe a way of knowing and experiencing and enjoying outside the major modes of science and art proper, a way not concerned with scientific discovery and artifacts, a way that is internally and externally creative, that leaves very little public trace, and yet that, for those very reasons, is almost wholly concentrated in its own creative process.

Fowles' thought is not completed until you have read the final "that" clause which ends the sentence, and which contains the most important concept in the sentence. To follow the interrelationship between the parts of this long sentence, it is necessary to see the sentence constructed out of a series of parallel clauses: first, clauses which begin with the words "a way"—"a way of knowing and experiencing . . . ," "a way not concerned . . . ," and "a way that is internally and externally . . ."; then, clauses which begin with "that"— "that is internally . . . ," "that leaves very little . . . ," and "and yet that . . ." Such long sentences employing parallel constructions and abstract diction are characteristic of a *formal style*.

An *informal style* uses moderately long sentences mixed with shorter sentences, and uses a mixture of concrete and abstract diction. Consider these two sentences from Edward Hoagland's essay, "Howling Back at the Wolves":

> Wolves have marvellous legs. The first thing one notices about them is how high they are set on their skinny legs, and the instant, blurred gait these can switch into, bicycling away, carrying them as much as forty miles in a day. [*Red Wolves and Black Bears* (Random House, 1976), 8.]

Hoagland's second longer sentence—with its concrete diction and parallel construction—clarifies the first short sentence, especially the abstract adjective "marvellous," and this mixture is characteristic of *informal style*.

Voice, Tone, and Distance   The final three elements of style should be considered together because they all have to do with the personality of the writer—that is, how you present yourself to your audience. Just as you form impressions of people from talking to them over the telephone (even before you have met them), you also form impressions about the writer from the *voice* which seems to speak to you from the pages of an essay. Margaret Mead seems a very different woman from either Joan Didion or Annie Dillard; certainly you would have no trouble distinguishing the voice of S. J. Perelman from that of Edward Abbey.

Tone is an aspect of voice. The tone in a speaking voice reveals the intention of the speaker and the attitude of the speaker toward the audience. "You've done it again," could be uttered triumphantly by an excited teammate who is congratulating a place kicker who has just kicked her second field goal of a game or disgustedly by a father who is surveying the second dented fender in the family car. The *tone* of a piece of writing reveals whether it is to be taken seriously, humorously, ironically; whether the essay is exploring ideas, affirming them, or explaining them. Here are two pieces about baseball. In the first, the tone is one of serious reminiscence, recalling a memory from the past to illustrate the vividness of baseball's great moments.

> The presiding memory of that late summer is of Yastrzemski approaching the plate, once again in a situation, where all hope rests on him, and settling himself in the batter's box—touching his helmet, tugging at his belt, and just touching the tip of the bat to the ground, in precisely the same set of features—and then, in a storm of noise and pleading, swinging violently and perfectly. [Roger Angell, "The Interior Stadium," *The Summer Game* (Viking Press, 1972), 298–99.]

Contrast the tone of that paragraph with the following example, where the tone is one of mock seriousness, of humorous imitation of what the writer calls "The Bigs," the players in the major leagues. The slow-pitch softball player is asked to, at least, *look* like a big leaguer.

When going up to bat, don't step right into the batter's box as if it were an elevator. The box is your turf, your stage. Take possession of it slowly and deliberately, starting with a lot of back-bending, knee-stretching, and torso-revolving in the on-deck circle. Then, approaching the box, step outside it and tap the dirt off your spikes with your bat. You don't have spikes, you have sneakers, of course, but the significance of the tapping is the same. Then, upon entering the box, spit on the ground. It is a way of saying, "This here is mine. This is where I get my hits." Spit frequently. Spit at all crucial moments. Spit correctly. Spit should be blown, not ptuied weakly with the lips, which often results in a dribble. Spitting should convey forcefulness of purpose, concentration, pride. Spit down, not in the direction of others. [Garrison Keillor, "Attitude," *Happy to be Here* (Atheneum, 1982), 77–78.]

Finally, *distance* refers to the figurative proximity of the audience to the writer. If, for example, the essay has serious, intimate tone, the distance between the writer and the audience will be small. If, on the other hand, the tone of the essay is impersonal and aloof, then the distance will be great. In most formal writing, the distance between author and audience is greater than in informal or colloquial writing.

In the following two paragraphs, the differences in tone and distance are shaped by the different intentions of each writer. In the first, Edward Abbey is showing that the scarcity of water is the desert's unique characteristic and warning those who believe they can make the arid Southwest bloom that there is a price to pay. The tone is one of serious warning, of irritation with those who fail to see the obvious. There is some distance between the writer and the audience because Abbey assumes the role of a knowing instructor for the audience.

Water, water, water . . . . There is no shortage of water in the desert but exactly the right amount, a perfect ratio of water to rock, of water to sand, insuring that wide, free, open, generous spacing among plants and animals, homes and towns and cities, which makes the arid West so different from any other part of the nation. There is no lack of water here, unless you try to establish a city where no city should be. ["Water," *Desert Solitaire* (McGraw-Hill, 1968), 126.]

In contrast, Loren Eiseley's tone of quiet, wondering speculation includes the reader. Consequently, there is little distance separating the inquisitive writer from the equally admiring reader.

If there is magic on this planet, it is contained in water. Its least stir even, as now in a rain pond on a flat roof opposite my office, is enough to bring me searching to the window. A wind ripple may translate itself into life. I have a constant feeling that some time I may witness that momentous miracle on a city roof, see life veritably and suddenly boiling out of a heap of rusted pipes and old television aerials. ["The Flow of the River," *The Immense Journey* (Random House, 1957), 15.]

Style, then, cannot be reduced to a simple formula: words + sentences + voice + tone + distance = style. Effective style is a result of a series of complex interrelationships which, in turn, grow out of the choices a writer has made. It is also, finally, a product of that indefinable element—the personality of the writer. Just as you develop aspects of your personality by imitating people whose traits you admire, you can develop an admirable prose style by imitating those writers whose work you admire.

JIMMY BRESLIN
A Beautiful Custom

Jimmy Breslin, although he still calls himself a reporter, is known to readers across the nation as a newspaper columnist. His facility for capturing the essential flavor of the city for the ordinary citizens, the people who ride the subway, made him an instant success. Breslin's books include Can't Anybody Here Play This Game *(1963),* The World of Jimmy Breslin *(1967), and* The Gang Who Couldn't Shoot Straight *(1960). "A Beautiful Custom" is characteristic of Breslin's simple, direct, straightforward style.*

Yesterday afternoon, under a glaring sky which held only the   1
suggestion of clouds, Louis Tomback walked slowly up the concrete ramp from the Brooklyn end of the Williamsburg Bridge and, as he has on every Rosh Hashana for thirty years, he kept going until he reached the middle of the bridge.

When he got there, Tomback turned the empty pockets of his   2
blue suit inside out. Then he looked down at the East River and, with BMT trains drowning out his words, he recited the *tashlikh*, the prayer of purification. Nearly three hundred others, who had come from Brooklyn and downtown New York, were on the bridge doing the same thing.

This is one of the oldest, and easily one of the most beautiful,   3
customs you see in New York. Earlier, Tomback, an Orthodox Jew,
had said prayers in the synagogue to ask his God to forgive him
for all the sins he had committed in the last year. Now, symbolic of
this, he was standing high above the East River and, as he prayed,
he was throwing his sins onto the water, which was moving swiftly
under this old bridge.

You had a cigarette while the man prayed, and all you could think   4
of was what it would be like if you could throw away everything
you'd ever done wrong, and the memories of it too, and throw it
onto that river and let it go out with the current.

People have been standing on the Williamsburg Bridge on Rosh   5
Hashana and thinking like this for years. Once, the bridge was
crowded with thousands of people over the day. All of them came
from the downtown East Side and Williamsburg. But both these
parts of this town are changing, just like nearly every other part of
the city, and yesterday the people who came onto the bridge were
only in the hundreds.

"I've done this all my life," Tomback said when he was through   6
with his prayer. "But only the old ones are here now. The young
ones, they are all gone. I'm a retired man. I worked at dresses. I
still live on Bedford Avenue. But my children, I can't speak for what
my children are doing today. They're gone. They're out on Long
Island."

"Everything is changing," Tomback was told.   7

"Changing? Who ever heard of Long Island? Now Long Island   8
is a place where your children go away to when they leave."

Then Tomback started to walk back down the ramp to Williams-   9
burg and a group of others turned and headed toward the downtown East Side. Next year, if they make this trip, there will be even
fewer people because the old Jewish people are becoming fewer in
these areas.

You could see that any place you went yesterday afternoon. On   10
the Manhattan end of the bridge, Delancey Street was Saturday-
empty and gratings were drawn in front of the doors of all the shops
because of the holiday.

But off this main street it was different. This was, in recent times,   11
the nation's great Jewish ghetto, these ugly five- and six-story tenements which run for block after block. Originally Germans settled
in them; then the Irish came and, after them, the Jews. Today the

Puerto Ricans have moved heavily into the area and the Jews, as did the Irish before them, are moving out, and yesterday, on the downtown East Side, Rosh Hashana simply was not that big a holiday.

Stores were open on every block. The tin soft-drink signs all said "Bodega" under them and there were Spanish-American dry-goods stores, and Latin tunes came out of the loudspeakers in the music stores. At one time any Christian kid living at a place like Fourth and Avenue C could do pretty well for himself by running up and down tenement stairs and lighting stoves for the Jewish women who could not so much as turn a gas jet on Rosh Hashana.

Yesterday it was all gone. On Sixth Street, between Avenues B and C, for example, there is an old four-story red brick synagogue, Congregation Ahawath Yeshurin Shara Torah. Attached to it is an identical building, the bricks painted gray, which houses the Iglesia de Dios (Lunes . . . Oración, 8 p.m.).

And when the few old men walked out of the synagogue late in the afternoon, the stoop of the tenement next door was crowded with Puerto Rican kids who spoke in this clipped, high-pitched language which must have sounded as strange to the Jewish men as their Yiddish did to the Irish.

The move now, as Tomback noted sadly on the Williamsburg Bridge yesterday, is to places like Long Island, and the young ones who go there all have a valid reason.

"You can't live in the city any more," this fellow Manny Goldberg, who lives in Scarsdale, was saying one night. "You got kids, you got to give them a chance to live. How can you raise a kid in the city? It's impossible."

He comes off Avenue C and slept three in a bed until he was eighteen.

CONTENT

1. Rosh Hashana, or the Day of Atonement, is an important Jewish holy day. What custom does Breslin describe? Why is it rare to observe this custom in New York today?
2. Where has New York City's Jewish population gone? Is this confirmed by other observations Breslin makes? Why have the Jews left? What is Breslin's attitude?

3. What kind of language is used in Breslin's essay? What kinds of sentences? What is the tone of the piece? Is the distance between the writer and his audience great or small?

ORGANIZATION

4. Like a good journalist, Breslin gives the time, setting and the main character in the first paragraph. Before he interviews Louis Tomback, what does Breslin add? Why?
5. What device does Breslin use to organize the information about the changes that have taken place in the neighborhood in recent years?

TOPICS FOR WRITING

6. Describe a tradition that has passed. Write for an audience unfamiliar with the tradition, and choose a colloquial style.
7. Write a short essay describing changes that have taken place in your neighborhood. Perhaps use Breslin's technique of interviewing an older resident who has lived through the changes.

WILLIAM SAROYAN
Places and People

William Saroyan (1908–1981) once estimated that between 1934 and 1940 he wrote over 500 stories. Without benefit of formal education—he left school at age 15—he produced short stories, novels, and plays that were critical as well as popular successes. The Daring Young Man on the Flying Trapeze *(1934), a collection of short stories, led him to New York where his plays* My Heart's in the Highlands *(1939) and* The Time of Your Life *(1940) were produced, the latter winning both the Drama Critics Circle Award and the Pulitzer Prize. Saroyan's direct, unpremeditated style reflects his optimistic belief in the essential goodness of human beings.*

Where you are dropped, as the saying is, is who you are, at least   1
in a certain limited sense. If you are dropped in Bitlis but are soon taken to New York, Bitlis is less who you are than New York is. But

the place you knew first is at least a large part of who you are. Places make people. They very definitely do, almost physically. Places procreate. They are part of the human procreation process. There are many men and women who wouldn't think of engaging in the procreative act in certain places of the world, and there are other places in which nothing seems more right and pleasant. There are places that are all business, and places that are all fun and frolic, and still other places that are all light and song and the senses and love.

After the World, after being Anywhere at all, my place was Fresno, and as far as I am concerned it was the very best possible place for me to be—and for this reason: that's where I was dropped. The minute we met, that was it. We belonged to each other. Forever. It was a fact. I was born there. I wasn't born in Bitlis, Marseilles, London, New York, or anywhere else. I was born in Fresno. It was my place. I loved it. I hated it. But had I been born in Paris, I would have loved Paris, and I would have hated it. Fresno had great early appeal for me. It had a fine smell of dust, of the desert, of rocks baking in the sun, of sand with cactus growing out of it, of water flowing in rivers and ditches, of orchards and vineyards set out in great geometric patterns, of leaf and blossom and fruit. It also had all of the smells of rot, decay, and ferment: the great heaps of grape pulp and skin at the wineries sent a smell all through the town if there was a little wind stirring. There were also the magnificent smells in the house in which one did one's early time: the very walls themselves, the people who lived in the house, and the things they cooked or baked: Armenian bread, for instance, in the three popular forms prepared by the Saroyan family: the round, wafer-thin flat bread, the oval loaf bread only an inch or two thick, and the diamond-shaped little loaves of butter bread. There was also always the smell of various green things, or growing things—parsley, mint, basil, onions, bell peppers, tomatoes, cucumbers, and so on and so forth. All of these things were a part of the place, and very quickly a part of me. For instance, after I got out of the National Guard in Los Angeles in August of 1926 I was still half-sick from the sickness I had fought in the furnished room behind the brand-new Public Library. Something was wrong. I wasn't myself. Things were assaulting me from all sides, breaking me up. I wasn't in one piece.

2

As I was standing on a corner waiting for a cop to wave the 3
pedestrians across the street, a car drew up and stopped, and at
the wheel was my father's kid brother Mihran. I couldn't believe
my eyes. I was just eighteen, he was about thirty-two, at the wheel
of his old Buick, with the top down.

That evening he took me to a Greek restaurant where the food 4
was like the food at home. I ate vegetables with lamb, and that was
it—the good food with the good smell brought me back together
again. And so did running unexpectedly into a member of my family. Fresno was my place, and my family was my place.

How lucky every man is in being where he is, and from the 5
millions of years of his people, whoever they are. Well, he can be
sure of one thing, if they are here at all, they've been everywhere,
they've been everybody—he is himself the King of Kings.

CONTENT

1. What does Saroyan mean when he says, in the first paragraph,
   "Places make people"?
2. How well does Saroyan convey the feeling of growing up in an
   Armenian household in Fresno?
3. Why was he feeling sick in Los Angeles, and how did his young
   uncle cure his illness? What is the meaning of the last sentence?

ORGANIZATION

4. The first paragraph uses abstractions and has few sense impressions. The second paragraph has very concrete diction and many
   sense impressions. Why has Saroyan organized these two paragraphs to contrast with each other?
5. Paragraphs 3 and 4 are narrating an incident that happened
   away from Fresno. Why has Saroyan ended with this brief
   narrative?

TOPICS FOR WRITING

6. Write a familiar essay in an intimate tone in which you explain
   that where you grew up made you the person you are today.
7. Write a familiar autobiographical essay explaining that for you,
   family and a sense of place are intimately connected.

ANNIE DILLARD
Teaching a Stone to Talk

Annie Dillard won the Pulitzer Prize for her first book, Pilgrim at Tinker Creek *(1974), a collection of familiar essays, personal observations, and natural history. Similar in tone and content, but different in setting, is* Teaching a Stone to Talk *(1982), from which the following selection is taken. It contains the essentials of Dillard's style—a perceptive description of a situation or place which is then used as a departure point for examining one of life's mysteries and wonders. In this case, the mute testimony of the palo santo trees of the Galapagos Islands offers what Dillard considers an appropriate image for humanity.*

The island where I live is peopled with cranks like myself. In a cedar-shake shack on a cliff is a man in his thirties who lives alone with a stone he is trying to teach to talk.

Wisecracks on this topic abound, as you might expect, but they are made, as it were, perfunctorily, and mostly by the young. For in fact, almost everyone here respects what Larry is doing, as do I, which is why I am protecting his (or her) privacy, and confusing for you the details. It could be, for instance, a pinch of sand he is teaching to talk, or a prolonged northerly, or any one of a number of waves. But it is, I assure you, a stone. It is—for I have seen it— a palm-sized, oval beach cobble whose dark gray is cut by a band of white which runs around and, presumably, through it; such stones we call "wishing stones," for reasons obscure but not, I think, unimaginable.

He keeps it on a shelf. Usually the stone lies protected by a square of untanned leather, like a canary asleep under its cloth. Larry removes the cover for the stone's lessons, or, more accurately, I should say for the ritual or rituals they perform together several times a day.

No one knows what goes on at these sessions, least of all myself, for I know Larry but slightly, and that owing only to a mix-up in our mail. I assume that, like any other meaningful effort, the ritual involves sacrifice, the suppression of self-consciousness, and a certain precise tilt of the will, so that the will becomes transparent and hollow, a channel for the work. I wish him well. It is a noble work, and beats, from any angle, selling shoes.

Reports differ on precisely what he expects or wants the stone to say. I do not think he expects the stone to speak as we do, and describe for us its long life and many, or few, sensations. I think instead that he is trying to teach it to say a single word, such as "cup," or"uncle." For this purpose he has not, as some have seriously suggested, carved the stone a little mouth, or furnished it in any way with a pocket of air which it might then expel. Rather— and I think he is wise in this—he plans to initiate his son, who is now an infant living with Larry's estranged wife, into the work, so that it may continue and bear fruit after his death.

Nature's silence is its one remark, and every flake of world is a   6 chip off that old mute and immutable block. The Chinese say that we live in the world of the ten thousand things. Each of the ten thousand cries out to us precisely nothing.

God used to rage at the Israelites for frequenting sacred groves.   7 I wish I could find one. Martin Buber says, "The crisis of all primitive mankind comes with the discovery of that which is fundamentally not-holy, the a-sacramental, which withstands the methods, and which has no 'hour,' a province which steadily enlarges itself." Now we are no longer primitive; now the whole world seems not-holy. We have drained the light from the boughs in the sacred grove and snuffed it in the high places and along the banks of sacred streams. We as a people have moved from pantheism to panatheism. Silence is not our heritage but our destiny; we live where we want to live.

The soul may ask God for anything, and never fail. You may ask   8 God for his presence, or for wisdom, and receive each at his hands. Or you may ask God, in the words of the shopkeeper's little gag sign, that he not go away mad, but just go away. Once, in Israel, an extended family of nomads did that. They heard God's speech and found it too loud. The wilderness generation was at Sinai; it witnessed there the thick darkness where God was: "And all the people saw the thunderings, and the lightnings, and the noise of the trumpet, and the mountain smoking." It scared them witless. Then they asked Moses to beg God, please, never to speak to them directly again. "Let not God speak with us, lest we die." Moses took the message. And God, pitying their fear, agreed. And he added to Moses, "Go say to them, *Get into your tents again.*"

It is difficult to undo our own damage, and to recall to our pres-   9 ence that which we have asked to leave. It is hard to desecrate a grove and change your mind. The very holy mountains are keeping mum. We doused the burning bush and cannot rekindle it; we are lighting matches in vain under every green tree. Did the wind once cry, and the hills shout forth praise? Now speech has perished from among the lifeless things of earth, and living things say very little to very few. Birds may crank out sweet gibberish and monkeys howl; horses neigh and pigs say, as you recall, oink oink. But so do cobbles rumble when a wave recedes, and thunders break the air in lightning storms. I call these noises silence. It could be that wherever there is motion there is noise, as when a whale breeches and smacks the water—and wherever there is stillness there is the still small voice, God's speaking from the whirlwind, nature's old song and dance, the show we drove from town. At any rate, now it is all we can do, and among our best efforts, to try to teach a given human language, English, to chimpanzees.

In the forties an American psychologist and his wife tried to teach a chimp actually to speak. At the end of three years the creature could pronounce, in a hoarse whisper, the words "mama," "papa," and "cup." After another three years of training she could whisper, with difficulty, still only "mama," "papa," and "cup." The more recent successes at teaching chimpanzees American Sign Language are well known. Just the other day a chimp told us, if we can believe that we truly share a vocabulary, that she had been sad in the morning. I'm sorry we asked.

What have we been doing all these centuries but trying to call God back to the mountain, or, failing that, raise a peep out of anything that isn't us? What is the difference between a cathedral and a physics lab? Are they not both saying Hello? We spy on whales and on interstellar radio objects; we starve ourselves and pray till we're blue.

I have been reading comparative cosmology. At this time most cosmologists favor the picture of the evolving universe described by Lemaître and Gamow. But I prefer a suggestion made years ago by Paul Valéry. He set forth the notion that the universe might be "head-shaped." To what is the head listening, what does it see, of what does it think? Or is the universe and all it contains a snippet of mind?

The mountains are great stone bells; they clang together like nuns. Who shushed the stars? A thousand million galaxies are easily seen in the Palomar reflector; collisions between and among them do, of course, occur. But these collisions are very long and silent slides. Billions of stars sift among each other untouched, too distant even to be moved, heedless as always, hushed. The sea pronounces something, over and over, in a hoarse whisper; I can't quite make it out. But God knows I've tried.

At a certain point you say to the woods, to the sea, to the mountains, the world, Now I am ready. Now I will stop and be wholly attentive. You empty yourself and wait, listening. After a time you hear it: there is nothing there. There is nothing but those things only, those created objects, discrete, growing or holding, or swaying, being rained on or raining, held, flooding or ebbing, standing, or spread. You feel the world's word as a tension, a hum, a single chorused note everywhere the same. This is it: this hum is the silence. Nature does utter a peep—just this one. The birds and insects, the meadows and swamps and rivers and stones and mountains and clouds: they all do it; they all don't do it. There is a vibrancy to the silence, a suppression, as if someone were gagging the world. But you wait, you give your life's length to listening, and nothing happens. The ice rolls up, the ice rolls back, and still that single note obtains. The tension, or lack of it, is intolerable. The silence is not actually suppression; instead, it is all there is.

We are here to witness. There is nothing else to do with those mute materials we do not need. Until Larry teaches his stone to talk, until God changes his mind, or until the pagan gods slip back to their hilltop groves, all we can do with the whole inhuman array is watch it. We can stage our own act on the planet—build our cities on its plains, dam its rivers, plant its topsoils—but our meaningful activity scarcely covers the terrain. We don't use the songbirds, for instance. We don't eat many of them; we can't befriend them; we can't persuade them to eat more mosquitoes or plant fewer weed seeds. We can only witness them—whoever they are. If we weren't here, they would be songbirds falling in the forest. If we weren't here, material events such as the passage of seasons would lack even the meager meanings we are able to muster for them. The show would play to an empty house, as do all those stars that fall in the daytime. That is why I take walks: to keep an eye on things. And that is why I went to the Galapagos Islands.

All of this becomes especially clear on the Galapagos Islands. The Galapagos Islands blew up out of the ocean, some plants blew in on them, some animals drifted aboard and evolved weird forms— and there they all are. The Galapagos are a kind of metaphysics laboratory, almost wholly uncluttered by human culture or history. Whatever happens on those bare volcanic rocks happens in full view, whether anyone is watching or not.

What happens there is this, and precious little it is: clouds come and go as well as the round of similar seasons; a pig eats a tortoise or doesn't eat a tortoise; Pacific waves fall up and slide back; a lichen expands; night follows day; an albatross dies and dries on a cliff; a cool current upwells from the ocean floor; fishes multiply, flies swarm, stars rise and fall, and diving birds dive. The news, in other words, breaks on the beaches. And taking it all in are the trees. The palo santo trees crowd the hillsides like any outdoor audience; they face the lagoons, the lava lowlands, and the shores.

I have some experience of these palo santo trees. They interest me as emblems of the muteness of the human stance in relation to all that is not human. I see us all as palo santo trees, holy sticks, together watching everything that we watch, and growing in silence.

In the Galapagos, I didn't notice the palo santo trees for a long time. Like everyone else, I specialized in sea lions. My shipmates and I liked the sea lions, envied their lives. Their joy seemed conscious. They were engaged in full-time play. They were all either fat or dead. By day they played in the shallows, alone or together, greeting each other and us with great noises of joy, or they took a turn offshore and body-surfed in the breakers, exultant. By night on the sand they lay in each other's flippers and slept. My shipmates joked, often, that when they "came back," they would just as soon do it all over again as sea lions. I concurred. The sea lion game looked unbeatable.

But, a year and a half later, I returned to those unpeopled islands. In the interval my attachment to them had shifted, and my memories of them had altered, the way memories do, like particolored pebbles rolled back and forth over a grating, so that after a time those hard bright ones, the ones you thought you would never lose, have vanished, passed through the grating, and only a few big, unexpected ones remain, no longer unnoticed but now selected out for some meaning, large and unknown.

Such were the palo santo trees. Before, I had never given them   21
a thought. They were just miles of half-dead trees on the red lava
sea cliffs of some deserted islands. They were only a name in a
notebook: "Palo santo—those strange white trees." Look at the sea
lions! Look at the flightless cormorants, the penguins, the iguanas,
the sunset! But after eighteen months the wonderful cormorants,
penguins, iguanas, sunsets, and even the sea lions had dropped
from my holey heart. I returned to the Galapagos to see the palo
santo trees.

They are thin, pale, wispy trees. You walk among them on the   22
lowland deserts, where they grow beside the prickly pear. You see
them from the water on the steeps that face the sea, hundreds
together small and thin and spread, and so much more pale than
their red soils that any black-and-white print of them looks like a
negative. Their stands look like blasted orchards. At every season
they all seem newly dead, pale and bare as birches drowned in a
beaver pond—for at every season they look leafless, paralyzed, and
mute. But, in fact, you can see during the rainy months a few meager deciduous leaves here and there on their brittle twigs. And
hundreds of lichens always grow on their bark in overlapping
explosions which barely enlarge in the course of the decade, lichens
pink and orange, lavender, yellow, and green. The palo santo trees
bear the lichens effortlessly, unconsciously, the way they bear
everything. Their multitudes, transparent as line drawings, crowd
the cliffsides like whirling dancers, like empty groves, and look out
over cliff-wrecked breakers toward more unpeopled islands, with
their freakish lizards and birds, toward the grieving lagoons and
the bays where the sea lions wander, and beyond to the clamoring
seas.

Now I no longer concurred with my shipmates' joke; I no longer   23
wanted to "come back" as a sea lion. For I thought, and I still think,
that if I came back to life in the sunlight where everything changes,
I would like to come back as a palo santo tree, one of thousands on
a cliffside on those godforsaken islands, where a million events
occur among the witless, where a splash of rain may drop on a
yellow iguana the size of a dachshund, and ten minutes later the
iguana may blink. I would like to come back as a palo santo tree on
the weather side of an island, so that I could be, myself, a perfect
witness, and look, mute, and wave my arms.

The silence is all there is. It is the alpha and the omega. It is God's brooding over the face of the waters; it is the blended note of the ten thousand things, the whine of wings. You take a step in the right direction to pray to this silence, and even to address the prayer to "World." Distinctions blur. Quit your tents. Pray without ceasing.

CONTENT

1. What does Dillard mean by "Nature's silence is its one remark" (paragraph 6)? Does she mean that there are not noises in nature or that none of the noises mean anything?

2. In paragraph 15 Dillard says, "We are here to witness." What does she mean by witness? Does the term have religious connotations? Why does she allude to the power of God's voice in the Old Testament? Why to pantheism?

3. Why does the silence of nature become especially clear on the Galapagos Islands? If she were to be reincarnated, why does Dillard wish to return as a palo santo tree?

ORGANIZATION

4. Sandwiched between the opening narrative of the man who was teaching a stone to talk and the closing narrative of the trip to the Galapagos Islands is a philosophical examination of the silence of the universe. Are these three parts written in the same style? Does the diction, sentence structure, tone, or distance change?

5. Dillard writes in a cryptic style, sometimes hinting at things rather than explicitly stating them. For example, in paragraph 14 she speaks of the tension of the world arising from the suppression of a vibrancy, a hum, "as if someone were gagging the world." Can you find other such suggestive statements? What do you think each means?

TOPICS FOR WRITING

6. Disagreeing with Dillard, write an informal essay describing some natural phenomenon in which you did find meaning.

7. Read John Fowles' "Seeing Nature Whole" (page 549). Write an informal essay comparing Fowles' approach to nature with Dillard's.

ROGER ANGELL
The Interior Stadium

*Roger Angell, best known for his baseball writings, was born in New York City
in 1920. Angell joined the staff of* The New Yorker *in 1956 and has been a
fiction editor and regular contributor ever since. He is the author of several books:*
The Stone Arbor *(1961),* A Day in the Life of Roger Angell *(1971), and*
The Summer Game *(1972) of which "The Interior Stadium" is the final essay.
Angell's description of the book is an apt summary of "The Interior Stadium":
"My main job, as I conceived it, was to continue to try to give the feel of
things—to explain baseball as it happened to me, at a distance and in retrospect."*

Sports are too much with us. Late and soon, sitting and watch-   1
ing—mostly watching on television—we lay waste our powers of
identification and enthusiasm and, in time, attention as more and
more closing rallies and crucial putts and late field goals and final
playoffs and sudden deaths and world records and world champi-
onships unreel themselves ceaselessly before our half-lidded eyes.
Professional leagues expand like bubble gum, ever larger and thinner, and the extended sporting seasons, now bunching and overlapping at the ends, conclude in exhaustion and the wrong weather.
So, too, goes the secondary business of sports—the news or non-
news off the field. Sports announcers (ex-halfbacks in Mod hair-
dos) bring us another live, exclusive interview in depth with the
twitchy coach of some as yet undefeated basketball team, or with a
weeping (for joy) fourteen-year-old champion female backstroker,
and the sports pages, now almost the largest single part of the
newspaper, brim with salary disputes, medical bulletins, franchise
maneuverings, all-star ballots, drug scandals, close-up biogs, after-
dinner tributes, union tactics, weekend wrapups, wire-service polls,
draft-choice trades, clubhouse gossip, and the latest odds. The
American obsession with sports in not a new phenomenon, of course,
except in its current dimensions, its excessive excessiveness. What
is new, and what must at times unsettle even the most devout and
unselective fan, is a curious sense of loss. In the midst of all these
successive spectacles and instant replays and endless reportings
and recapitulations, we seem to have forgotten what we came for.
More and more, each sport resembles all sports; the flavor, the

special joys of place and season, the unique displays of courage and strength and style that once isolated each game and fixed it in our affections have disappeared somewhere in the noise and crush.

Of all sports, none has been so buffeted about by this unselective proliferation, so maligned by contemporary cant, or so indifferently defended as baseball. Yet the game somehow remains the same, obdurately unaltered and comparable only with itself. Baseball has one saving grace that distinguishes it—for me, at any rate— from every other sport. Because of its pace, and thus the perfectly observed balance, both physical and psychological, between opposing forces, its clean lines can be restored in retrospect. This inner game— baseball in the mind—has no season, but it is best played in the winter, without the distraction of other baseball news. At first, it is a game of recollections, recapturings, and visions. Figures and occasions return, enormous sounds rise and swell, and the interior stadium fills with light and yields up the sight of a young ballplayer—some hero perfectly memorized—just completing his own unique swing and now racing toward first. See the way he runs? Yes, that's him! Unmistakable, he leans in, still following the distant flight of the ball with his eyes, and takes his big turn at the base. Yet this is only the beginning, for baseball in the mind is not a mere returning. In time, this easy summoning up of restored players, winning hits, and famous rallies gives way to reconsiderations and reflections about the sport itself. By thinking about baseball like this—by playing it over, keeping it warm in a cold season—we begin to make discoveries. With luck, we may even penetrate some of its mysteries. One of those mysteries is its vividness—the absolutely distinct inner vision we retain of that hitter, that eager baserunner, of however long ago.

* * *

Baseball, I must conclude, is intensely remembered because only baseball is so intensely watched. The game forces intensity upon us. In the ballpark, scattered across an immense green, each player is isolated in our attention, utterly visible. Watch that fielder just below us. Little seems to be expected of him. He waits in easy composure, his hands on his knees; when the ball at last soars or bounces out to him, he seizes it and dispatches it with swift, haughty ease. It all looks easy, slow, and, above all, safe. Yet we know better, for what is certain in baseball is that someone, perhaps several people, will fail. They will be searched out, caught in the open, and defeated, and there will be no confusion about it or sharing of the blame. This is sure to happen, because what baseball requires of its athletes, of course, is nothing less than perfection, and perfection cannot be eased or divided. Every movement of every game, from first pitch to last out, is measured and recorded against an absolute standard, and thus each success is also a failure. Credit that strikeout to the pitcher, but also count it against the batter's average; mark this run unearned, because the left fielder bobbled the ball for an instant and a runner moved up. Yet, faced with this sudden and repeated presence of danger, the big-league player defends himself with such courage and skill that the illusion of safety is sustained. Tension is screwed tighter and tighter as the certain downfall is postponed again and again, so that when disaster does come—a half-topped infield hit, a walk on a close three-and-two call, a low drive up the middle that just eludes the diving shortstop—we rise and cry out. It is a spontaneous, inevitable, irresistible reaction.

Televised baseball, I must add, does not seem capable of trans- 4 mitting this emotion. Most baseball is seen on the tube now, and it is presented faithfully and with great technical skill. But the medium is irrevocably two-dimensional; even with several cameras, television cannot bring us the essential distances of the game—the simultaneous flight of a batted ball and its pursuit by the racing, straining outfielders, the swift convergence of runner and ball at a base. Foreshortened on our screen, the players on the field appear to be squashed together, almost touching each other, and, watching them, we lose the sense of their separateness and lonesome waiting.

* * *

Always, it seems, there is something more to be discovered about 5 this game. Sit quietly in the upper stand and look at the field. Half close your eyes against the sun, so that the players recede a little, and watch the movements of baseball. The pitcher, immobile on the mound, holds the inert white ball, his little lump of physics. Now, with abrupt gestures, he gives it enormous speed and direction, converting it suddenly into a line, a moving line. The batter, wielding a plane, attempts to intercept the line and acutely alter it, but he fails; the ball, a line again, is redrawn to the pitcher, in the center of this square, the diamond. Again the pitcher studies his task—the projection of his next line through the smallest possible segment of an invisible seven-sided solid (the strike zone has depth as well as height and width) sixty feet and six inches away; again the batter considers his even more difficult proposition, which is to reverse this imminent white speck, to redirect its energy not in a soft parabola or a series of diminishing squiggles but into a beautiful and dangerous new force, of perfect straightness and immense distance. In time, these and other lines are drawn on the field; the batter and the fielders are also transformed into fluidity, moving and converging, and we see now that all movement in baseball is a convergence toward fixed points—the pitched ball toward the plate, the thrown ball toward the right angles of the bases, the batted ball toward the as yet undrawn but already visible point of congruence with either the ground or a glove. Simultaneously, the fielders hasten toward that same point of meeting with the ball, and both the base-runner and the ball, now redirected, toward their encounter at the base. From our perch, we can sometimes see three or four or more such geometries appearing at the same instant on the green board below us, and, mathematicians that we are, can sense their solution even before they are fully drawn. It is neat, it is pretty, it is satisfying. Scientists speak of the profoundly moving aesthetic beauty of mathematics, and perhaps the baseball field is one of the few places where the rest of us can glimpse this mystery.

The last dimension is time. Within the ballpark, time moves differently, marked by no clock except the events of the game. This is the unique, unchangeable feature of baseball, and perhaps explains why this sport, for all the enormous changes it has undergone in the past decade or two, remains somehow rustic, unviolent, and introspective. Baseball's time is seamless and invisible, a bubble within which players move at exactly the same pace and rhythms as all their predecessors. This is the way the game was played in our youth and in our fathers' youth, and even back then—back in the country days—there must have been the same feeling that time could be stopped. Since baseball time is measured only in outs, all you have to do is succeed utterly; keep hitting, keep the rally alive, and you have defeated time. You remain forever young. Sitting in the stands, we sense this, if only dimly. The players below us— Mays, DiMaggio, Ruth, Snodgrass—swim and blur in memory, the ball floats over to Terry Turner, and the end of this game may never come.

CONTENT

1. According to Angell, what are some of baseball's unique qualities?
2. How does televised baseball interfere with several of these qualities?
3. Loosely paraphrasing William Wordsworth, Angell begins his essay, "Sports are too much with us." What examples does he give of this? How does Angell's game of "interior baseball" provide a saving grace from this obsession with sports?
4. What is the tone of paragraphs 1 and 2? How is the opening parody of Wordsworth appropriate to a "memory piece"?
5. Study the sentence structure and length in paragraph 5. What is the effect of long sentences with parallel main clauses ("the pitcher holds . . . he gives . . . the batter attempts . . . he fails . . . the pitcher studies . . . etc.)? Does it give us any sense of the action?

ORGANIZATION

6. At the end of his essay Angell draws an analogy between baseball, physics, geometry, and mathematics. How does he elaborate each part of the analogy?
7. Why does Angell introduce the analogy at the *end* of the essay? How does his earlier statement that baseball is a game of "clean lines" prepare the reader for the final analogy?

TOPICS FOR WRITING

8. Select a sport such as basketball, football, track, etc., and analyze it by isolating some of its unique qualities through an analogy.
9. Draw a comparison between the geometry of baseball and that of football or basketball. Which is "cleaner"? Which is more complex?

LOREN EISELEY
Man the Firemaker

Loren Eiseley, in addition to his anthropological writings, produced two volumes of poetry—Another Kind of Autumn (1977) and The Innocent Assassins (1978). In this essay from The Star Thrower (1979), Eiseley announces that his intention is to trace the "part that fire has played in the human journey across the planet." The style of that tracing is at once scientific and poetic.

Man, it is well to remember, is the discoverer but not the inventor of fire. Long before this meddling little Prometheus took to experimenting with flints, then matches, and finally (we hope not too finally) hydrogen bombs, fires had burned on this planet. Volcanoes had belched molten lava, lightning had struck in dry grass, winds had rubbed dead branches against each other until they burst into flame. There are evidences of fire in ancient fossil beds that lie deep below the time of man.

Man did not invent fire but he did make it one of the giant powers on the earth. He began this experiment long ago in the red morning of the human mind. Today he continues it in the midst of coruscating heat that is capable of rending the very fabric of his universe. Man's long adventure with knowledge has, to a very marked degree, been a climb up the heat ladder, for heat alone enables man to mold metals and glassware, to create his great chemical industries, to drive his swift machines. It is my intention here to trace man's manipulation of this force far back into its ice-age beginnings and to observe the part that fire has played in the human journey across the planet. The torch has been carried smoking through the ages of glacial advance. As we follow man on this journey, we shall learn another aspect of his nature: that he is himself a consuming fire.

At just what level in his intellectual development man mastered the art of making fire is still unknown. Neanderthal man of 50,000 years ago certainly knew the art. Traces of the use of fire have turned up in a cave of Peking man, the primitive human being of at least 250,000 years ago who had a brain only about two-thirds the size of modern man's. And in 1947 Raymond Dart of Witwatersrand University announced the discovery in South Africa of *Australopithecus prometheus*, a man-ape cranium recovered from deposits which he believed showed traces of burned bone.

This startling announcement of the possible use of fire by a sub- 4
human creature raised a considerable storm in anthropological circles. The chemical identifications purporting to indicate evidence
of fire are now considered highly questionable. It has also been
intimated that the evidence may represent only traces of a natural
brush fire. Certainly, so long as the South African man-apes have
not been clearly shown to be tool users, wide doubts about their
use of fire will remain. There are later sites of tool-using human
beings which do not show traces of fire.

Until there is proof to the contrary, it would seem wise to date 5
the earliest use of fire to Peking man—*Sinanthropus*. Other human
sites of the same antiquity have not yielded evidence of ash, but
this is not surprising, for as a new discovery the use of fire would
have taken time to diffuse from one group to another. Whether it
was discovered once or several times we have no way of knowing.
The fact that fire was in worldwide use at the beginning of man's
civilized history enables us to infer that it is an old human culture
trait—doubtless one of the earliest. Furthermore, it is likely that
man used fire long before he became sophisticated enough to produce it himself.

In 1865 Sir John Lubbock, a British banker who made a hobby of 6
popular writing on science, observed: "There can be no doubt that
man originally crept over the earth's surface, little by little, year by
year, just, for instance, as the weeds of Europe are now gradually
but surely creeping over the surface of Australia." This remark was,
in its time, a very shrewd and sensible observation. We know today,
however, that there have been times when man suddenly made
great strides across the face of the earth. I want to review one of
those startling expansions—a lost episode in which fire played a
tremendous part. To make its outlines clear we shall have to review
the human drama in three acts.

The earliest humanlike animals we can discern are the man-apes 7
of South Africa. Perhaps walking upright on two feet, this creature
seems to have been roaming the East African grasslands about one
million years ago. Our ancestor, proto-man, probably emerged from
the tropics and diffused over the region of warm climate in Eurasia
and North Africa. He must have been dependent upon small game,
insects, wild seeds, and fruits. His life was hard, his search for food
incessant, his numbers were small.

The second stage in human history is represented by the first
true men. Paleoanthropic man is clearly a tool user, a worker in
stone and bone, but there is still something of the isolated tinkerer
and fumbler about him. His numbers are still sparse, judging from
the paucity of skeletal remains. Short, stocky, and powerful, he
spread over the most temperate portions of the Afro-Eurasiatic land
mass but never attempted the passage through the high Arctic to
America. Through scores of millennia he drifted with the seasons,
seemingly content with his troglodyte existence, making little serious change in his array of flint tools. It is quite clear that some of
these men knew the use of fire, but many may not have.

The third act begins some 15,000 or 20,000 years ago. The last
great ice sheet still lies across northern Europe and North America.
Roving on the open tundra and grasslands below those ice sheets
is the best-fed and most varied assemblage of grass-eating animals
the world has ever seen. Giant long-horned bison, the huge wild
cattle of the Pleistocene, graze on both continents. Mammoth and
mastodon wander about in such numbers that their bones are later
to astonish the first American colonists. Suddenly, into this late
paradise of game, there erupts our own species of man—*Homo
sapiens*. Just where he came from we do not know. Tall, lithe, long-
limbed, he is destined to overrun the continents in the blink of a
geological eye. He has an excellent projectile weapon in the shape
of the spear thrower. His flint work is meticulous and sharp. And
the most aggressive carnivore the world has ever seen comes at a
time made for his success: the grasslands are alive with seemingly
inexhaustible herds of game.

Yet fire as much as flesh was the magic that opened the way for
the supremacy of *Homo sapiens*. We know that he was already the
master of fire, for the track of it runs from camp to buried camp:
the blackened bones of the animals he killed, mute testimony to the
relentless step of man across the continents, lie in hundreds of sites
in the Old and the New Worlds. Meat, more precious than the gold
for which men later struggled, supplied the energy that carried man
across the world. Had it not been for fire, however, all that enormous source of life would have been denied to him: he would have
gone on drinking the blood from small kills, chewing wearily at
uncooked bone ends or masticating the crackling bodies of
grasshoppers.

Fire shortens the digestive process. It breaks down tough masses 11
of flesh into food that the human stomach can easily assimilate. Fire
made the difference that enabled man to expand his numbers rapidly and to press on from hunting to more advanced cultures. Yet
we take fire so much for granted that this first great upswing in
human numbers, this first real gain in the seizure of vast quantities
of free energy, has to a remarkable degree eluded our attention.

With fire primitive man did more than cook his meat. He extended 12
the pasture for grazing herds. A considerable school of thought,
represented by such men as the geographer Carl Sauer and the
anthropologist Omer Stewart, believes that the early use of fire by
the aborigines of the New World greatly expanded the grassland
areas. Stewart says: "The number of tribes reported using fire leads
one to the conclusion that burning of vegetation was a universal
culture pattern among the Indians of the U.S. Furthermore, the
amount of burning leads to the deduction that nearly all vegetation
in America at the time of discovery and exploration was what ecol-
ogists would call fire vegetation. That is to say, fire was a major
factor, along with soil, moisture, temperature, wind, animals, and
so forth, in determining the types of plants occurring in any region.
It follows then, that the vegetation of the Great Plains was a fire
vegetation." In short, the so-called primeval wilderness which awed
our forefathers had already felt the fire of the Indian hunter. Here,
as in many other regions, man's fire altered the ecology of the earth.

It had its effect not only on the flora but also on the fauna. Of 13
the great herds of grazing animals that flourished in America in the
last Ice Age, not a single trace remains—the American elephants,
camels, long-horned bison are all gone. Not all of them were struck
down by the hunters' weapons. Sauer argues that a major explanation of the extinction of the great American mammals may be
fire. He says that the aborigines used fire drives to stampede game,
and he contends that this weapon would have worked with peculiar
effectiveness to exterminate such lumbering creatures as the mammoth. I have stood in a gully in western Kansas and seen outlined
in the earth the fragmented black bones of scores of bison who had
perished in what was probably a man-made conflagration. If, at the
end of Pleistocene times, vast ecological changes occurred, if cli-
mates shifted, if lakes dried and in other places forests sprang up,
and if, in this uncertain and unsteady time, man came with flint

and fire upon the animal world about him, he may well have triggered a catastrophic decline and extinction. Five thousand years of man and his smoking weapon rolling down the wind may have finished the story for many a slow-witted animal species. In the great scale of geological time this act of destruction amounts to but one brief hunt.

Man, as I have said, is himself a flame. He has burned through 14 the animal world and appropriated its vast stores of protein for his own. When the great herds failed over many areas, he had to devise new ways to feed his increase or drop back himself into a precarious balance with nature. Here and there on the world's margins there have survived into modern times men who were forced into just such local adjustments. Simple hunters and collectors of small game in impoverished areas, they maintain themselves with difficulty. Their numbers remain the same through generations. Their economy permits no bursts of energy beyond what is necessary for the simple age-old struggle with nature. Perhaps, as we view the looming shadow of atomic disaster, this way of life takes on a certain dignity today.

Nevertheless there is no road back; the primitive way is no longer 15 our way. We are the inheritors of an aggressive culture which, when the great herds disappeared, turned to agriculture. Here again the magic of fire fed the great human wave and built up man's numbers and civilization.

Man's first chemical experiment involving the use of heat was to 16 make foods digestible. He had cooked his meat; now he used fire to crack his grain. In the process of adopting the agricultural way of life he made his second chemical experiment with heat: baking pottery. Ceramics may have sprung in part from the need for storage vessels to protect harvested grain from the incursions of rats and mice and moisture. At any rate, the potter's art spread with the revolutionary shift in food production in early Neolithic times.

People who have only played with mud pies or made little sun- 1 dried vessels of clay are apt to think of ceramics as a simple art. Actually it is not. The sundried vessels of our childhood experiments would melt in the first rain that struck them. To produce true pottery one must destroy the elasticity of clay through a chemical process which can be induced only by subjecting the clay to an intense baking at a temperature of at least 400 to 500 degrees centigrade. The baking drives out the so-called water of constitution from the aluminum silicate in the clay. Thereafter the clay will no longer dissolve in water; a truly fired vessel will survive in the ground for centuries. This is why pottery is so important to the archaeologist. It is impervious to the decay that overtakes many other substances, and, since it was manufactured in quantity, it may tell tales of the past when other clues fail us.

Pottery can be hardened in an open campfire, but the results can never be so excellent as those achieved in a kiln. At some point the early potter must have learned that he could concentrate and conserve heat by covering his fire—perhaps making it in a hole or trench. From this it was a step to the true closed kiln, in which there was a lower chamber for the fire and an upper one for the pottery. Most of the earthenware of simple cultures was fired at temperatures around 500 degrees centigrade, but really thorough firing demands temperatures in the neighborhood of 900 degrees.

After man had learned to change the chemical nature of clay, he began to use fire to transform other raw materials—ores into metals, for instance. One measure of civilization is the number of materials manipulated. The savage contents himself with a few raw materials which can be shaped without the application of high temperatures. Civilized man uses fire to extract, alter, or synthesize a multitude of substances.

By the time metals came into extended use, the precious flame no longer burned in the open campfire, radiating its heat away into the dark or flickering on the bronzed faces of the hunters. Instead it roared in confined furnaces and was fed oxygen through crude bellows. One of the by-products of more intensified experiments with heat was glass—the strange, impassive substance which, in the form of the chemist's flask, the astronomer's telescope, the biologist's microscope, and the mirror, has contributed so vastly to our knowledge of ourselves and the universe.

We hear a good deal about the Iron Age, or age of metals, as a great jump forward in man's history; actually the metals themselves played a comparatively small part in the rise of the first great civilizations. While men learned to use bronze, which demands little more heat than is necessary to produce good ceramics, and later iron, for tools and ornaments, the use of metal did not make a really massive change in civilization for well over 1,500 years. It was what Leslie White of the University of Michigan calls the "Fuel Revolution" that brought the metals into their own. Coal, oil, and gas, new sources of energy, combined with the invention of the steam and combustion engines, ushered in the new age. It was not metals as tools, but metals combined with heat in new furnaces and power machinery that took human society off its thousand-year plateau and made possible another enormous upswing in human numbers, with all the social repercussions.

Today the flames grow hotter in the furnaces. Man has come far up the heat ladder. The creature that crept furred through the glitter of blue glacial nights lives surrounded by the hiss of steam, the roar of engines, and the bubbling of vats. Like a long-armed crab, he manipulates the tongs in dangerous atomic furnaces. In asbestos suits he plunges into the flaming debris of hideous accidents. With intricate heat-measuring instruments he investigates the secrets of the stars, and he has already found heat-resistant alloys that have enabled him to hurl himself into space.

How far will he go? Three hundred years of the scientific method have built the great sky-touching buildings and nourished the incalculable fertility of the human species. But man is also *Homo duplex*, as they knew in the darker ages. He partakes of evil and of good, of god and of man. Both struggle in him perpetually. And he is himself a flame—a great, roaring, wasteful furnace devouring irreplaceable substances of the earth. Before this century is out, either *Homo duplex* must learn that knowledge without greatness of spirit is not enough for man, or there will remain only his calcined cities and the little charcoal of his bones.

CONTENT

1. Unlike the informal and colloquial styles, the style of Eiseley's formal essay reveals less of the writer, and more of the substance of the essay. Where is the formal thesis statement?
2. Why does Eiseley survey man's use of fire from prehistoric times to the present? Is the information obvious or does Eiseley reveal purposes in man's use of fire that you had not thought of before?
3. Why does Eiseley repeat several times that man is, himself, a flame, "a great, roaring, wasteful furnace devouring irreplacable substances of the earth"?

ORGANIZATION

4. In form, Eiseley's essay is a process analysis. What type of process? How great is the distance between reader and writer?

How does the use of first person pronouns "I" and "we" bring the reader somewhat closer than is usual in formal writing? What would be the effect of substituting the more impersonal "one"?

5. Show how the cause–effect consequences of fire crop up throughout the essay, giving the essay its primary theme.

TOPICS FOR WRITING

6. Show how man's conquest of another element, air, for example, has led to unforeseen consequences.

7. Examine one aspect of man's use of fire which Eiseley has surveyed—for example, man's use of fire in agriculture or making pottery—and write a formal essay on its effects upon one cultural group.

JOHN FOWLES
Seeing Nature Whole

John Fowles (born 1926) is one of those rarities of contemporary literature: a best-selling novelist with a genuine philosophy of life. Fowles has said, "Writing is part of my existentialist view of life . . . . I don't see that you can write seriously without having a philosophy of both life and literature to back you." He has written poetry, fiction and essays: several of his novels have been made into movies. Among his books are The Collector *(1963),* The Aristos: A Self Portrait in Ideas *(1964),* The Magus *(1966),* The French Lieutenant's Woman *(1969), and* Daniel Martin *(1977). Fowles' erudition is impressive and his style is richly complex. "Seeing Nature Whole" is from* The Tree *(1980); in it, Fowles traces the origin of modern man's faulty way of viewing nature and contends that we should adopt a pre-Linnaean way of looking at nature, one that neither classifies nor looks for purposefulness.*

A few years ago I stood in a historic place. It was not a great battlefield, a house, a square, the site of one famous event; but the site only of countless small ones—a neat little eighteenth-century garden, formally divided by gravel walks into parterres, with a small wooden house in one corner, where the garden's owner had once lived. There is only one other garden to compare with it in human history, and that is the one in the Book of Genesis, which never existed outside words. The one in which I stood is very real and it lies in the old Swedish university town of Uppsala. Its owner was the great warehouse clerk and indexer of nature, Carl von Linné, better known as Linnaeus, who between 1730 and 1760 docketed, or attempted to docket, most of animate being. Perhaps nothing is more moving at Uppsala than the actual smallness and ordered simplicity of that garden and the immense consequences that sprung from it in terms of the way we see and think about the external world. It is something more than another famous shrine for lovers of nature, like Selborne* or Coate Farm° or Walden Pond. In fact, for all its air of gentle peace, it is closer to a nuclear explosion, whose radiations and mutations inside the human brain were incalculable and continue to be so: the place where an intellectual seed landed, and is now grown to a tree that shadows the entire globe.

I am a heretic about Linnaeus, and find nothing less strange, or   2
more poetically just, than that he should have gone mad at the end of his life. I do not dispute the value of the tool he gave to natural science—which was in itself no more than a shrewd extension of the Aristotelian system and which someone else would soon have elaborated, if he had not—but I have doubts about the lasting change it has effected in ordinary human consciousness.

Evolution has turned man into a sharply isolating creature, seeing   3
the world not only anthropocentrically but singly, mirroring the way we like to think of our private selves. Almost all our art before the Impressionists—or their St. John the Baptist, William Turner—betrays our love of clearly defined boundaries, unique identities, of the individual thing released from the confusion of background. This power of detaching an object from its surroundings and making us concentrate on it is an implicit criterion in all our judgments on the more realistic side of visual art, and very similar, if not identical, to what we require of optical instruments like microscopes and telescopes—which is to magnify, to focus sharper, to distinguish better, to single out. A great deal of science is devoted to this same end: to providing specific labels, explaining specific mecha-

*An English village where the naturalist Gilbert White wrote his classic *Natural History and Antiquities* (1789).
°Home of naturalist-novelist Richard Jeffries who wrote several famous books about the farm: *Round about a Great Estate* (1880), *The Old House at Coate* (1948). Jeffries also set a novel there—*Bevis* (1882).

nisms and ecologies—in short, to sorting and tidying what seem in the mass indistinguishable one from the other. Even the simplest knowledge of the names and habits of flowers or trees starts this distinguishing or individuating process, and removes us a step from total reality toward anthropocentrism; that is, it acts mentally as an equivalent of the camera's viewfinder. Already it destroys or curtails certain possibilities of seeing, apprehending, and experiencing. And that is the bitter fruit from the tree of Uppsalan knowledge.

It also begs considerable questions as to the realities of the boundaries we impose on what we see. In a wood, the actual visual "frontier" of any one tree is usually impossible to distinguish, at least in summer. We feel, or think we feel, nearest to a tree's "essence" (or that of its species) when it chances to stand, like us, in isolation; but evolution did not intend trees to grow singly. Far more than ourselves they are social creatures, and no more natural as isolated specimens than man is a marooned sailor or a hermit. Their society in turn creates or supports other societies of plants, insects, birds, mammals, microorganisms, all of which we may choose to isolate and section off, but which remain no less the ideal entity, or whole experience, of the wood—and indeed are still so seen by most of primitive mankind.

Scientists restrict the word *symbiotic* to those relationships between species that bring some detectable mutual benefit; but the true wood, the true place of any kind, is the sum of all its phenomena. They are all in some sense symbiotic, being together in a togetherness of beings. It is only because such a vast sum of interactions and coincidences in time and place is beyond science's calculation (a scientist might say beyond useful function, even if calculable) that we so habitually ignore it, and treat the flight of the bird and the branch it flies from, the leaf in the wind and its shadow on the ground, as separate events, or riddles. What bird? Which branch? What leaf? Which shadow? These question-boundaries (where do I file that?) are ours, not of reality. We are led to them, caged by them not only culturally and intellectually, but quite physically, by the restlessness of our eyes and their limited field and acuity of vision. Long before the glass lens and the movie camera were invented, they existed in our eyes and minds, both in our mode of perception and in our mode of analyzing the perceived: endless short sequence and jumpcut, endless need to edit and arrange this raw material.

The Cost of Understanding

I spent all my younger life as a more or less orthodox amateur 6
naturalist; as a pseudoscientist, treating nature as some sort of intellectual puzzle, or game, in which being able to name names and explain behaviorisms—to identify and to understand machinery—constituted all the pleasures and the prizes. I became slowly aware of the inadequacy of this approach: that it insidiously cast nature as a kind of opponent, an opposite team to be outwitted and beaten: that in a number of very important ways it distracted from the total experience and the total meaning of nature—and not only of what I personally needed from nature, not only as I had long, if largely unconsciously, begun to feel it (which was neither scientifically nor sentimentally, but in a way for which I had, and still have, no word). I came to believe that this approach represented a major human alienation, affecting all of us, both personally and socially; moreover, that such alienation had much more ancient roots behind the historical accident of its present scientific, or pseudoscientific, form.

Naming things is always implicitly categorizing and therefore 7
collecting them, attempting to own them; and because man is a highly acquisitive creature, brainwashed by most modern societies into believing that the act of acquisition is more enjoyable than the fact of having acquired, that getting beats having got, mere names and the objects they are tied to soon become stale. There is a constant need, or compulsion, to seek new objects and names—in the context of nature, new species and experiences. Everyday ones grow mute with familiarity, so known they become unknown; and not only in nonhuman nature. Only fools think our attitude to our fellow men is a thing distinct from our attitude to "lesser" life on this planet.

All this is an unhappy legacy of Victorian science, which was so 8
characteristically obsessed with both the machine and exact taxonomy. Only the other day I came upon a letter in a forgotten drawer of the little museum of which I am curator. It was from a well-known Victorian fern expert and about some twenty or so specimens he had been sent from Dorset—all reducible, to a modern botanist, to three species. But this worthy gentleman felt obliged, in a welter of Latin polysyllables, to grant each specimen some new subspecific or varietal rank, as if they were unbaptized children and might all go to hell if they were not given individual names. It would be absurd to deny the Victorians their enormous achievements in

saner scientific fields, and I am not engaging in some sort of Luddite fantasy, wishing the machine they invented had been different, or even not at all. But we are far better at seeing the immediate advantages of such gains in knowledge of the exterior world than at assessing the costs of them. The particular cost of understanding the mechanism of nature, of having so successfully itemized and pigeonholed it, lies most of all in the ordinary person's perception of it, in his ability to live with and care for it—and not to see it as enemy, challenge, defiance. Selection from total reality is no less necessary in science than it is in art; but outside those domains (in both of which the final test of selection is utility, or yield, to our own species) it seriously distorts and limits any worthwhile relationship.

I caused my hosts at Uppsala, where I went to lecture on the   9
novel, some puzzlement by demanding (the literary business once over) to see Linnaeus's garden rather than the treasures of one of the most famous libraries in Europe. The feeling that I was not behaving as a decent writer should was familiar. Again and again in recent years I have told visiting literary academics that the key to my fiction, for what it is worth, lies in my relationship with nature—I might almost have said, for reasons I will explain, in trees. And again and again I have seen, under varying degrees of politeness, this assertion treated as some sort of irrelevant quirk, eccentricity, devious evasion of what must be the real truth: literary influences and theories of fiction, and all the rest of that purely intellectual midden that faculty hens and cocks so like scratching over. Of course such matters are a part of the truth, but they are no more the whole truth than that the tree we see above ground is the whole tree. Even if we do discuss nature, I soon sense that we are talking about two different things: on their side some abstract intellectual concept, and on mine an experience whose deepest value lies in the fact that it cannot be directly described by any art . . . including that of words.

One interrogator even accused me of bad faith: that if I sincerely   10
felt so deeply on the matter, I should write more about it. But what I gain most from nature is beyond words. To try to capture it verbally immediately places me in the same boat as the namers and would-be owners of nature—that is, it exiles me from what I most need to learn. It is a little as it is in atomic physics, where the very

act of observation changes what is observed; though here the catch lies in trying to describe the observation. To enter upon such a description is like trying to capture the uncapturable. Its only purpose can be to flatter the vanity of the describer—a function painfully obvious in many of the more sentimental natural-history writers.

But I think the most harmful change brought about by Victorian science in our attitude toward nature lies in the demand that our relation with it must be purposive, industrious, always seeking greater knowledge. This dreadfully serious and puritanical approach (nowhere better exhibited in the nineteenth century than in the countless penny magazines aimed at young people) has had two very harmful effects. One is that it turned the vast majority of contemporary Western mankind away from what had become altogether too much like a duty, or a school lesson; the second is that the far saner eighteenth-century attitude, which viewed nature as a mirror for philosophers, as an evoker of emotion, as a pleasure, a poem, was forgotten. There are intellectual reasons as well for this. Darwin made sentimental innocence, nature as mainly personal or aesthetic experience, vaguely wicked. Not only did he propose a mechanism seemingly as iron as the steam engine, but his very method of discovery, and its success in solving a great conundrum, offered an equally iron or one-sided model for the amateur naturalist himself, and made the older and more humanist approach seem childish. A "good" amateur naturalist today merely means one whose work is valued by the professional scientists in his field.

An additional element of alienation has come with motion pictures and television, which are selective in another way. They present natural reality not only through other eyes, but in a version of it in which the novelty or rarity of the subject plays a preponderant part in choice and treatment. Of course the nature film or program has an entertainment value; of course there are some social goods in the now-ubiquitous availability of copies of other people's images and opinions of actual things and events; but, as with the Linnaean system, there is a cost. Being taken by camera into the deepest African jungle, across the Arctic wastes, thirty fathoms deep in the sea, may seem a "miracle of modern technology"; but it will no more bring the viewer nearer the reality of nature, or to a proper human relationship with the actual nature around him, than merely reading novels is likely to teach the writing of them. The most one can say is that it may help; a much more common result is to be persuaded of the futility of even trying.

Increasingly, we live (and not only in terms of nature and novels) by the old tag, *Aut Caesar, aut nullus*—"If I can't be Caesar, I'll be no one." If I can't have the knowledge of a scientist, I'll know nothing. If I can't have superb close-ups and rare creatures in the nature around me, to hell with it. Perhaps any representation of nature is better, to those remote from it in their daily lives, than none. Yet a great deal of such representation seems to me to descend straight from the concept of the menagerie, another sadly alienating selection, or reduction, from reality. Poking umbrellas through iron bars did not cease with the transition from the zoo to the screen.

The Myth of the Green Man

Much of seventeenth- and eighteenth-century science and erudition is obsolete nonsense in modern scientific terms: in its personal interpolations, its diffuse reasoning, its misinterpreted evidence, its frequent blend of the humanities with science proper—its quotations from Horace and Virgil in the middle of a treatise on forestry. But one general, if unconscious, assumption lying behind almost all pre-Victorian science—that it is being presented by an entire human being, with all his complexities, to an audience of other entire human beings—has been much too soon dismissed as a mere historical phenomenon, at best exhibiting an engaging amateurishness, at worst sheer stupidity, from neither of which we have anything to learn. It is not, of course, the fault of modern scientists that most of their formal discourse is now of so abstruse a nature that only their fellow specialists can hope to understand it, that the discourse itself is increasingly mechanical, with words reduced to cogs and treated as poor substitutes for some more purely scientific formulation; nor is it directly their fault that their vision of empirical knowledge, the all-important value they put on proved or demonstrable fact, has seeped down to dominate the popular view of nature—and our education about it. Our fallacy lies in supposing that the limiting nature of scientific method corresponds to the nature of ordinary experience.

Ordinary experience, from waking second to second, is in fact highly synthetic (in the sense of combinative or constructive), and made of a complexity of strands, past memories and present perceptions, times and places, private and public history, hopelessly beyond science's powers to analyze. It is quintessentially "wild," one might say unphilosophical, irrational, uncontrollable, incalculable. In fact, it corresponds very closely—despite our endless efforts to "garden," to invent disciplining social and intellectual systems—to wild nature. Almost all the richness of our personal existence derives from this synthetic and eternally present "confused" consciousness of both internal and external reality, and not least because we know it is beyond the analytical, or destructive, capacity of science.

Half by its principles, half by its inventions, science now largely   16
dictates and forms our common, or public, perception of and attitudes toward external reality. One can speak of an attitude that is generally held by society; but society itself is an abstraction, a Linnaeus-like label we apply to a group of individuals seen in a certain context and for a certain purpose; and before the attitude can be generally held, it must pass through the filter of the individual consciousness, where this irreducible "wild" component lies—the one that may agree with science and society but can never be wholly plumbed or commanded by them. One of the oldest and most diffused bodies of myth and folklore has accreted around the idea of the man in the trees. In all his manifestations, as dryad, as stag-headed Herne, as outlaw, he possesses the characteristic of elusiveness, a power of "melting" into the trees, and I am certain the attraction of the myth is so profound and universal because it is constantly "played" inside every consciousness.

This notion of the green man—or green woman, as novelist and   17
naturalist W. H. Hudson* made her—seen as emblem of the close connection between the actuality of present consciousness (not least in its habitual flight into a mental greenwood) and what seems to me lost by science in man's attitude toward nature—that is, the "wild" side of his own, his inner feeling as opposed to the outer, factbound, conforming face imposed by fashion—helped me question my old psuedoscientist self. But it also misled me for a time. In the 1950s I grew interested in the Zen theories of "seeing" and of aesthetics: of learning to look beyond names at things-in- them-

---

*An allusion to Rima the birdgirl, who lives in the forests of Orinoco in Hudson's exotic novel *Green Mansions* (1916).

selves. I stopped bothering to identify species new to me; I concentrated more and more on the familiar, daily nature around me, where I then lived. But living without names is impossible, if not downright idiocy, in a writer; and living without explanation or speculation as to causality, little better—for Western man, at least. I discovered, too, that there was less conflict than I had imagined between nature as external assembly of names and facts and nature as internal feeling; that the two modes of seeing or knowing could in fact marry and take place almost simultaneously, and enrich each other.

Nature's Ultrahumanity

Achieving a relationship with nature is both a science and an art, beyond mere knowledge or mere feeling alone; and, I now think, beyond Oriental mysticism, transcendentalism, "meditation techniques," and the rest—or at least as we in the West have converted them to our use, which seems increasingly in a narcissistic way: to make ourselves feel more positive, more meaningful, more dynamic. I do not believe nature is to be reached that way either, by turning it into a therapy, a free clinic for admirers of their own sensitivity. The subtlest of our alienations from it, the most difficult to comprehend, is our eternal need to use it in some way, to derive some personal yield. We shall never fully understand nature (or ourselves), and certainly never respect it, until we dissociate the wild from the notion of usability—however innocent and harmless the use. For it is the general uselessness of so much of nature that lies at the root of our ancient hostility and indifference to it.   18

There is a kind of coldness—I would rather say a stillness, an empty space—at the heart of our forced coexistence with all the other species of the planet. The naturalist Richard Jeffries coined a word for it: the *ultrahumanity* of all this is not man . . . not with us or against us, but outside and beyond us, truly alien. It may sound paradoxical, but we shall not cease to be alienated—by our knowledge, by our greed, by our vanity—from nature until we grant it its unconscious alienation from us.   19

I am not one of those supreme optimists who think all the world's ills, and especially this growing rift between man and nature, can be cured by a return to a quasi-agricultural, ecologically "caring" society. It is not that I doubt it might theoretically be so cured; but   20 the possibility of the return defeats my powers of imagination. The majority of Western man are now urban, and the whole world will soon follow suit. A significant tilt of balance in human history is expected by the end of the coming decade: more than half of all mankind will by then have moved inside towns and cities. Any hope of reversing that trend, short of some universal catastrophe, is as tiny and precarious as the monarch butterflies I watched, an autumn or two ago, migrating among the Fifth Avenue skyscrapers in central Manhattan. All chance of a close acquaintance with nature, be it through intellect and education, be it in the simplest way of all, by having it near at hand, recedes from the many, who already effectively live in a support system in outer space, a creation of science, and without means to escape it, culturally or economically.

But the problem is not, or only minimally, that nature itself is in   21 imminent danger or that we shall lose touch with it simply because we have less access to it. A number of species, environments, unusual ecologies are in danger. There are major pollution problems. But even in our most densely populated countries the ordinary wild remains far from the brink of extinction. We may not exaggerate the future threats and dangers, but we do exaggerate the present and actual state of this global nation—underestimate the degree to which it is still surviving and accessible to those who want to experience it. It is far less nature itself that is yet in true danger than our attitude toward it. Already we behave as if we live in a world that holds only a remnant of what there actually is—in a world that may come, but remains a black hypothesis, not a present reality.

I believe the major cause of this more mental than physical rift   22 lies less in the folly or one-sidedness of our societies and educational systems, or in the historical evolution of man into a predominantly urban and industrial creature, a thinking termite, than in the way we have, during these past 150 years, devalued the kind of experience or knowledge we loosely define as art, and especially in the way we have failed to grasp its deepest difference from science. No art is truly teachable in its essence. All the knowledge in the world of its techniques can provide in itself no more than imitations or replicas of previous art. What is irreplaceable in any object of art is never, in the final analysis, its techinique or craft, but the personality of the artist, the expression of his or her unique and individual feeling. All major advances in technique have come about to serve this need. Techniques in themselves are always reducible to sciences—that is, to learnability. Once Joyce has written, Picasso painted, Webern composed, it requires only a minimal gift, besides patience and practice, to copy their techniques exactly. Yet we all know why this kind of technique-copy, even when it is so painstakingly done—for instance, in painting—that it deceives museum and auction-house experts, is counted worthless beside the work of the original artist. It is not *of* him or her; it is not art, but imitation.

As it is with the true "making" arts, so it is with the other aspects   23 of human life of which we say that full knowledge or experience also requires an art—some inwardly creative or purely personal factor beyond the power of external teaching to instill or science to predict. Attempts to impart recipes or set formulas as to practice and enjoyment are always two-edged, since the question is not so much whether they may or may not enrich the normal experience of that abstract thing, the normal man or woman, but the certainty that they must in some way damage that other essential component of the process, the contribution of the artist in this sense—the individual experiencer, the "green man" hidden in the leaves of his unique and once-only being.

Telling people why, how, and when they ought to feel this or   24 that—whether it be with regard to the enjoyment of nature, of food, of sex, or anything else—may, undoubtedly sometimes does, have a useful function in dispelling various kinds of socially harmful ignorance. But what this instruction cannot give is the deepest benefit of any art, be it of making or of knowing or of experiencing: which is self-expression and self-discovery. The last thing a sex manual can be is an *Ars amoris*—a science of coupling, perhaps, but never an art of love. Exactly the same is true of so many nature manuals. They may teach you how and what to look for, what to question in external nature, but never in your own nature.

In science greater knowledge is always and indisputably good;   25 it is by no means so throughout all human existence. We know it from art proper, where achievement and great factual knowledge, or taste, or intelligence, are in no way essential companions; if they were, our best artists would also be our most learned academics. We can know it by reducing the matter to the absurd, and imagining that God, or some protean visitor from outer space, were at one fell swoop to grant us all of knowable knowledge. Such omniscience would be worse than the worst natural catastrophe for our species as a whole; it would extinguish its soul, lose it all pleasure and reason for living.

This is not the only area in which, like the rogue computer of science fiction, some socially or culturally consecrated proposition—which may be true or good in its social or cultural context—extends itself to the individual; but it is one of the most devitalizing. Most mature artists know that great general knowledge is more a hindrance than a help. It is only innately mechanical, salami-factory novelists who set such great store by research: in nine cases out of ten what natural knowledge and imagination cannot supply is in any case precisely what needs to be left out. The green man in all of us is well aware of this. In practice we spend far more time rejecting knowledge than trying to gain it, and wisely so. But it is in the nature of all society, let alone one deeply imbued with a scientific and technological ethos, to bombard us with ever more knowledge—and to consider any questioning or rejection of it unpatriotic and immoral.

Art and nature are siblings, branches of the one tree, and nowhere more than in the continuing inexplicability of many of their processes—and above all those of creation and of effect on their respective audiences. Our approach to art, as to nature, has become increasingly scientized (and dreadfully serious) during this past century. It sometimes seems now as if it is principally there not for itself but to provide material for labeling, classifying, analyzing—specimens for "setting," as I used to set moths and butterflies. This is, of course, especially true of—and pernicious in—our schools and universities. I think the first sign that I might one day become a novelist (though I did not then realize it) was the passionate detestation I developed at my own school for all those editions of examination books that began with a long introduction: an anatomy lesson that always reduced the original text to a corpse by the time one got to it, a lifeless demonstration of a preestablished proposition. It took me years to realize that even geniuses, the Shakespeares, the Racines, the Austens, have human faults.

Random Personal Creativity

Obscurity, the opportunity a work of art gives for professional explainers to show their skills, has become almost an aesthetic virtue; at another extreme, the notion of art as vocation (that is, something to which one is genetically suited) is dismissed as nonscientific and inegalitarian. It is not a gift beyond personal choice, but one that can be acquired, like knowledge of science, by rote, recipe, and hard work. Elsewhere we become so patterned and persuaded by the tone of the more serious reviewing of art in our magazines and newspapers that we no longer notice their overwhelmingly scientific tone, or the paradox of this knowing-naming technique being applied to a nonscientific object—one whose production the artist himself cannot fully explain, and one whose effect the vast majority of the nonreviewing audience do not attempt to explain.

The professional critic or academic would no doubt say this is   29
mere ignorance, that both artists and audiences have been taught to understand themselves and the object that links them, to make the relationship articulate and fully conscious—defoliate the wicked green man, hunt him out of his trees. Of course there is a place for the scientific, or quasi-scientific, analysis of art, as there is (and far greater) for that of nature. But the danger, in both art and nature, is that all emphasis is placed on the created, not the creation.

All artifacts, all bits of scientific knowledge, have one thing in   30
common: that is, they come to us from the past, they are relics of something already observed, deduced, formulated, created, and as such qualify to go through the Linnaean, and every other, scientific mill. Yet we cannot say that the "green" or creating process does not happen or has no importance just because it is largely private and beyond lucid description and rational analysis. We might as well argue that the young wheatplant is irrelevant because it can yield nothing to the miller and his stones. We know that in any sane reality the green blade is as much the ripe grain as the child is father to the man. Nor of course does the simile apply to art alone, since we are all in a way creating our future out of our present, our "published" outward behavior out of our inner green being. One main reason we may seldom feel this happening is that society does not want us to. Such random personal creativity is offensive to all machines.

I began this wander through the trees—we shall come to them   31
literally, by the end—in search of that much looser use of the word *art* to describe a way of knowing and experiencing and enjoying outside the major modes of science and art proper, a way not concerned with scientific discovery and artifacts, a way that is inter-

nally rather than externally creative, that leaves very little public trace, and yet that, for those very reasons, is almost wholly concentrated in its own creative process. It is really only the qualified scientist or artist who can escape from the interiority and constant now-ness, the green chaos of this experience, by making some aspect of it exterior and so fixing it in the past time, or known knowledge. Thereby they create new, essentially parasitical, orders and categories of phenomena that in turn require both a science and an art of experiencing.

But nature is unlike art in terms of its product—what we in general know it by. The difference is that it is not only created, an external object with a history, and so belonging to a past, but also creating in the present, as we experience it. As we watch, it is, so to speak, rewriting, reformulating, repainting, rephotographing itself. It refuses to stay fixed and fossilized in the past, as both the scientist and the artist feel it somehow ought to; and both will generally try to impose this fossilization on it. Verb tenses can be very misleading here: we stick adamantly in speech to the strict protocol of actual time. Of and in the present we speak in the present, of the past in the past. But our psychological tenses can be very different. Perhaps because I am a writer (and nothing is more fictitious than the past in which the first, intensely alive and present, draft of a novel goes down on the page), I long ago noticed this in my naturalist self: that is, a disproportionately backward element in any present experience of nature, a retreat or running-back to past knowledge and experience, whether it was the definite past of personal memory or the indefinite, the imperfect, or stored "-ological" knowledge and proper scientific behavior. This seemed to me often to cast a mysterious veil of deadness, of having already happened, over the actual and present event or phenomenon.

I had a vivid example of it only a few years ago in France, long after I thought I had grown wise to this self-imposed brainwashing. I came on my first Military orchid, a species I had long wanted to encounter but hitherto had never seen outside a book. I fell on my knees before it in a way that all botanists will know. I identified, to be quite certain, with Professors Clapham, Tutin, and Warburg in hand (the standard British *Flora*), I measured, I photographed, I worked out where I was on the map, for future reference. I was excited, very happy, one always remembers one's "firsts" of the rarer species. Yet five minutes after my wife had finally (other women are not the only form of adultery) torn me away, I suffered a strange feeling. I realized I had not actually *seen* the three plants in the little colony we had found. Despite all the identifying, measuring, photographing, I had managed to set the experience in a kind of present past, a having-looked, even as I was temporarily and physically still looking. If I had had the courage, and my wife the patience, I would have asked her to turn and drive back, because I knew I had just fallen, in the stupidest possible way, into an ancient trap. It is not necessarily too little knowledge that causes ignorance; possessing too much, or wanting to gain too much, can produce the same result.

There is something in the nature of nature, in its presentness, 34 its seeming transience, its creative ferment and hidden potential, that corresponds very closely with the wild, or green-man, part of our own psyches; and it is a something that disappears as soon as it is relegated to an automatic pastness, a status of merely classifiable *thing*, image taken *then*. "Thing" and "then" attract each other. If it is thing, it was then; if it was then, it is thing. We lack trust in the present, this moment, this actual seeing, because our culture tells us to trust only the reported back, the publicly framed, the edited, the thing set in the clearly artistic or the clearly scientific angle of perspective. One of the deepest lessons we have to learn is that nature, of its nature, resists this. It waits to be seen otherwise, in its individual presentness and from our individual presentness.

I come now near the heart of what seems to me to be the single 35 greatest danger in the rich legacy left us by Linnaeus and the other founding fathers of all our sciences and scientific mores and methods—or more fairly, left us by our leaping evolutionary ingenuity in the invention of tools. All tools, from the simplest word to the most advanced space probe, are disturbers and rearrangers of primordial nature and reality—are, in the dictionary definition, "mechanical implements for working upon something." What they have done, and I suspect in direct proportion to our ever-increasing dependence on them, is to addict us to purpose, both to looking for purpose in everything external to us and to looking internally for purpose in everything we do—to seek explanation of the outside world by purpose, to justify our seeking by purpose. This addiction to finding a reason, a function, a quantifiable yield, has now infiltrated all aspects of our lives—and become effectively synonymous with pleasure. The modern version of hell is purposelessness.

Nature suffers particularly in this, and our indifference and hostility to it is closely connected with the fact that its only purpose appears to be being and surviving. We may think that this comprehends all animate existence, including our own, and so it must, finally; but we have long ceased to be content with so abstract a motive. A scientist would rightly say that all form and behavior in nature is highly purposive, or strictly designed for the end of survival—specific or genetic, according to theory. But most of this functional purpose is hidden to the nonscientist, indecipherable; and the immense variety of nature appears to hide nothing, nothing but a green chaos at the core—which we brilliantly purposive apes can use and exploit as we please, with a free conscience.

A green chaos. Or a wood.

* * *

Science is centrally, almost metaphysically, obsessed by general truths, by classifications that stop at the species, by functional laws whose worth is valued by their universality; by statistics, where a Bach or a da Vinci is no more than a quotom, a hole in a computer tape. The scientist has even to generalize himself, to subtract all personal feeling from the conduct of experiment and observation and from the enunciation of its results. He may study individuals, but only to help establish more widely applicable laws and facts. Science has little time for minor exceptions. But all nature, like all humanity, is made of minor exceptions, of entities that in some way, however scientifically disregardable, do not conform to the general rule. A belief in this kind of exception is as central to art as a belief in the utility of generalization is to science; indeed one might almost call art that branch of science that present science is prevented, by its own constricting tenets and philosophies (that old *hortus conclusus* again), from reaching.

I see little hope of any recognition of this until we accept three things about nature. One is that knowing it fully is an art as well as a science. The second is that the heart of this art lies in our own personal nature and its relationship to other nature—never in nature as a collection of "things" outside us. The last is that this kind of

knowledge, or relationship, is not reproducible by any other means—
by painting, by photography, by words, by science itself. They may
encourage, foster, and help induce the art of the relationship; but
they cannot reproduce it, any more than a painting can reproduce
a symphony, or the reverse. In the end they can serve only as an
inferior substitute, especially if we use them as some people use
sexual relationships, merely to flatter and justify ourselves.

There is a deeper wickedness still in Voltaire's unregenerate ani-   40
mal. It won't be owned, or more precisely, it will not be disani-
mated, unsouled, by the manner in which we try to own it. When
it is owned, it disappears. Perhaps nowhere is our human mania
for possessing, our delusion that what is owned cannot have a soul
of its own, more harmful to us. This disanimation justified all the
horrors of the African slave trade. If the black man is so stupid that
he can be enslaved, he cannot have the soul of a white man, he
must be mere animal. We have yet to cross the threshold of eman-
cipating mere animals; but we should not forget what began the
emancipation of the slaves in Britain and America. It was not science
or scientific reason, but religious conscience and fellow-feeling.

Unlike white sharks, trees do not even possess the ability to   41
defend themselves when attacked; what arms they sometimes have,
like thorns, are static; and their size and immobility means they
cannot hide. They are the most defenseless of creation in regard to
man, universally placed by him below the level of animate feeling,
and so the most prone to destruction. Their main evolutionary
defense, as with many social animals, birds, and fishes, lies in their
innumerability, that is, in their capacity to reproduce—in which,
for trees, longevity plays a major part. Perhaps it is this passive,
patient nature of their system of self-preservation that has allowed
man, despite his ancient fears of what they may harbor in terms of
other nature (and supernature), to forgive them in one aspect, to
see something that is also protective, maternal, even womblike in
their silent depths.

All through history trees have provided sanctuary and refuge   42
for both the justly and the unjustly persecuted and hunted. In the
wood I know best there is a dell, among beeches, at the foot of a
chalk cliff. Not a person a month goes there now, since it is well
away from any path. But three centuries ago it was crowded every
Sunday, for it is where the Independents came, from miles around
along the border of Devon and Dorset, to hold their forbidden

services. There are freedoms in woods that our ancestors perhaps realized more fully than we do. I used this wood, and even this one particular dell, in *The French Lieutenant's Woman*, for scenes that it seemed to me, in a story about self-liberation, could have no other setting.

This is the main reason I see trees, the wood, as the best analogue of prose fiction. All novels are also, in some way, exercises in attaining freedom—even when, at an extreme, they deny the possibility of its existence. Some such process of retreat from the normal world— however much the theme and surface is to be of the normal world— is inherent in any act of artistic creation, let alone that specific kind of writing that deals in imaginary situations and characters. And a part of that retreat must always be into a "wild," or ordinarily repressed and socially hidden, self: into a place always a complexity beyond daily (or artistic) reality, never fully comprehensible, mappable, explicable, eternally more potential than realized, yet where no one will ever penetrate as far as we have. It is our passage, our mystery alone, however miserable the account that is brought out for the world to see or hear or read second-hand.

The aritst's experience here is only a special—unusually prolonged and self-conscious—case of the universal individual one. The return to the green chaos, the deep forest and refuge of the unconscious, is a nightly phenomenon, and one that psychiatrists—and torturers—tell us is essential to the human mind. Without it, it disintegrates and goes mad. If I cherish trees beyond all personal (and perhaps rather peculiar) need and liking of them, it is because of this, their natural correspondence with the greener, more mysterious processes of mind—and because they also seem to me the best, most revealing messengers to us from all nature, the nearest its heart.

No religion is the only religion, no church the true church; and natural religion, rooted in love of nature, is no exception. But in all the long-cultivated and economically exploited lands of the world our woodlands are the last fragments of comparatively unadulterated nature, and so the most accessible outward correlatives and providers of the relationship, the feeling, the knowledge that we are in danger of losing: the last green churches and chapels outside the walled civilization and culture we have made with our tools. And this is so however far we may have fled, or evolved away from knowledge of, attachment to, interest in the wild—or use of its imagery to describe our more hidden selves and mental quirks

To see woods and forests merely scientifically, economically, top- 46 ographically, or aesthetically—not to understand that their greatest utility lies not in the facts derivable from them, or in their timber and fruit, or their landscape charm, or their utility as subject matter for the artist—proves the gathering speed with which we are retreating into outer space from all other life on this planet.

Of course there are scientists who are aware of this profoundest 47 and most dangerous of all alienation, and warn us of it; or who see hope in a rational remedy, in more education and knowledge, in committee and legislation. I wish them well in all of that, but I am a pessimist; what science and "reason" caused, they cannot cure. As long as nature is seen as in some way outside us, frontiered and foreign, *separate*, it is lost both to us and in us. The two natures, private and public, human and nonhuman, cannot be divorced; any more than nature, or life itself, can ever be truly understood vicariously, solely through other people's eyes and knowledge. Neither art nor science, however great, however profound, can finally help.

I pray my pessimism is exaggerated, and that we shall recover 48 from this folly resenting the fact that we are, for all practical purposes, caged on our planet, of pretending that our life on it is a temporary inconvenience in a place we have outgrown, a boardinghouse we shall soon be leaving, and for whose other inhabitants and whose contents we need have neither respect nor concern. Scientists speak of biological processes re-created in the laboratory as being done *in vitro*—in glass, not in nature. The evolution of human mentality has put us all *in vitro* now, behind the glass wall of our own ingenuity.

There is a spiritual corollary to the way we are currently defo- 49 resting and denaturing our planet. In the end what we must most defoliate and deprive is ourselves. We might as soon start collecting up the world's poetry, every line and every copy, to burn it in a final pyre—and think we should lead richer and happier lives thereafter.

CONTENT

1. What does Fowles mean by "the green man in the tree"? Why are trees and woods so important to him?

2. Would Fowles agree with Orwell's position in "What is Science?" (pages 218–22) that too much fact gathering does not lead to greater intelligence or insight?

3. Why is Fowles opposed to the purposeful approach of science? Why does he find it "poetically just" (paragraph 2) that Linnaeus "should have gone mad at the end of his life"? Why is he opposed to the systematizing that Linnaeus introduced?

4. Would Fowles agree with Annie Dillard ("Teaching a Stone to Talk") that there is a stillness at the heart of nature, and that humans will always be alienated from nature?

ORGANIZATION

5. What characteristics of formal style do you find in Fowles' essay? Does the essay depart from formal style in any way? Is its organization logical and strictly formal? Why or why not?

6. Why does Fowles begin with his experiences in Uppsala? How is this narrative an appropriate lead-in to his thesis?

7. Fowles introduces the image of the tree into the essay early, and returns to it in key places. Note the references to trees and woods, and explain how each reference contributes to the part of the discussion in which it is found.

8. Why does Fowles pause at one point (paragraphs 22–26) to discuss the difference between original art and imitation? How does he tie this into his previous discussion of the green man in all of us?

TOPICS FOR WRITING

9. Read Annie Dillard's "Teaching a Stone to Talk," and write a formal essay comparing her ideas with Fowles' on the topic of mankind's alienation from nature.

10. Fowles claims that man sees nature as an opponent. Write a formal essay illustrating the validity of Fowles' assertion.

11. Develop an essay around Fowles' idea that, " . . . it is in the nature of all society, to bombard us with ever more knowledge–and to consider any questioning or rejection of it unpatriotic and immoral."